Beria, My Father

Beria, My Father

Inside Stalin's Kremlin

SERGO BERIA

Edited by Françoise Thom

English translation by Brian Pearce

Duckworth

First published in 2001 by
Gerald Duckworth & Co. Ltd.
61 Frith Street, London W1D 3JL
Tel: 020 7434 4242
Fax: 020 7434 4420
Email: enquiries@duckworth-publishers.co.uk
www.ducknet.co.uk

A catalogue record for this book is available
from the British Library

ISBN 0 7156 3062 8

Typeset by
Derek Doyle and Associates, Liverpool
Printed in Great Britain by
Bookcraft (Bath) Ltd, Midsomer Norton, Avon

Contents

Editor's Preface

After the collapse of Communism and the partial opening of the Soviet archives, historians of the USSR and of Communism enjoyed a period of euphoria. At last we were going to learn what had gone on in the entrails of the sphinx, the jealously-guarded secrets of the Kremlin were to be exposed to the gaze of outsiders ... These expectations were fulfilled only in part. The Soviet archives made available were, in fact, far more eloquent concerning the peripheral mechanisms of the regime and on the working of the bureaucracies that flourished around the dark nucleus of the Central Committee than they were on the actual heart of the totalitarian machine, especially from the time when it reached perfection towards the end of the 1930s. On the whole it has remained as mysterious a creature as ever, an oyster which refuses to be prised open. We know very little about the Politburo in the 1940s and 1950s, either through the caprices of Russia's policy on the declassification of archives, or, more probably, owing to the desire of the Soviet leaders themselves to hide from posterity the innermost springs of their conduct, or else because of the successive purges carried out in the archives by Stalin's heirs, anxious to wipe away all traces of their crimes.

This is the context in which we must judge the value of a testimony such as Sergo Beria's. The story told by the son of the man whom people called Stalin's butcher takes us, over many years, right inside the narrow circle within which everything in the USSR and a large part of the world was decided. As Stalin's right-hand man for a long time, Beria holds the keys to many secrets of the Politburo. Like Eichmann and Mengele for the Nazis, he symbolises the worst of the Communist excesses within his own country and beyond. His name still evokes a vitriolic hatred in the hearts of many in the West and in Eastern Europe, and his popular image is that of a sinister, sadistic spymaster with whips in his office and the habit of driving down the windswept avenues of Moscow on the prowl for women. It is this combination of an insatiable libido matched by ruthless ambition, unspeakable cruelty and an explosive temper that set Beria truly apart from other Politburo. Having – some say – poisoned Stalin when he became infirm on 5 March 1953, Beria combined the internal and external security services under his command the next day, in a move that made him seem destined to take Stalin's chair. Had his colleagues not struck him down a hundred days later by arresting, trying and executing him on charges of being among other things a British spy, it would have appeared at the time that the man considered Stalin's evil genius was well on his way to replacing his former master and surpassing him in cruelty.

To be sure, Stalin had had no need of instigation from Beria in order to launch collectivisation, deport the kulaks (peasants), starve the Ukrainians to death, set up the trials and organise the 'great terror' of 1937. But Beria was no mean helper in implementing those horrors at a local level when he was still a Party chief in Georgia. He had organised and directed the terror in his own fiefdom, where the period 1937-1938 has left a frightful memory. Torture was practised on a large scale and there are several testimonies to torture sessions presided over by Beria in person in Tbilisi and, later, in Moscow. When Beria replaced the Russian Yezhov at the head of the NKVD at the end of 1938, he put an end to the 'great terror' (evidently at Stalin's behest) and released a large number of prisoners, but without ceasing to practise repression and torture. He organised the massacre of the Polish officers at Katyn in the spring of 1940, the assassination of Trotsky, the deportation of the peoples and the repressive measures taken during the war. He remained at the head of the NKVD until January 1946, when perhaps even Stalin had started to fear the man he had created and ordered him to devote himself to building the atomic bomb and administering some vital sectors of the Soviet economy. The testimonies also confirm the kidnapping of women and what people in Tbilisi called Beria's 'Sultan's habits'.

But what constitutes the excitement of these memoirs is also why we should exercise care while reading them. Sergo Beria grew up in a world of lies and of half-truths, lies that were all the more inextricable because the truth was unbearable. Like all of his generation, he was exposed to surreal ideological beliefs. Added to this was the position of his father, whose activities were barely mentioned in the family but echoes of which must have reached his son's ears. Above all there was the ambiguity of Lavrenti Beria himself: outwardly an efficient servant of the Soviet regime, but one whose dominant passion seems to have been a deep hatred of his fellow Georgian, Stalin. Plunged since his earliest years into a world of pretences, young Sergo himself took refuge in the certainties of the heart. Between his mother, who still idolised Stalin, and tried to protect Sergo from cruel reality and his father, who succeeded less and less in hiding from him his execration of the dictator, this model son was torn in two, and this ambivalence still marks the work that we have before us. The trial and execution of his father at the hands of Khrushchev, in 1953, months after Stalin's death, and the subsequent blackening of his father's name, was a body blow from which Sergo Beria never truly recovered. In this book he speaks as before an imaginary jury, poised to pass judgment. Throughout his life he has sought to act the witness for the defence – first by becoming an exemplary Soviet citizen who made Red Army missiles for the man who had caused his father's downfall, then, after the *perestroika*, by publishing his own version, sometimes a very subjective one, of the facts, and particularly of those things of which his father was accused. It is one reason why an integral part of this book is the extensive apparatus of notes corroborating Sergo Beria's testimony, or contradicting it, as the case may be.

Sergo Beria's testimony is also part of those endless, bickering feuds of Communists – or for that matter participants of any failed totalitarian regime – apportioning blame on one another by revealing choice sections of the truth. Both Stalin's daughter Svetlana Allilueva and Khrushchev wrote their memoirs. Sergo's is the third (and probably last) to appear from someone within Stalin's circle. Beria is today perceived in accordance with history as written by Khrushchev. It was Khrushchev who, for obvious reasons, first styled the chief of Stalin's police a cold-blooded monster, a primitive brute, a sadistic torturer, a diabolical intriguer, a sex maniac crouched on the lookout in his black limousine as he drove about Moscow, grabbing women off the streets. To the end of his life Khrushchev remained very proud of having liquidated Beria. After all, it was thanks to the coup d'état that he organised against Beria that Khrushchev took power and managed to establish, to some degree, the legitimacy of his position within the Party's ruling élite. In order that his exploit might be properly appreciated, Beria's image had to be painted as black as possible.

This was one of the reasons for the trial of Beria and his accomplices being held in camera in 1953, ending in their death sentences in December of that year. Another reason for that trial was acknowledged later by Khrushchev – it was a first attempt at taking account of Stalin's crimes without accusing Stalin himself, putting responsibility for them on to 'the Beria gang' and presenting Beria as 'Stalin's evil genius'. This version was taken up by Svetlana Allilueva, for understandable reasons. She had already been encouraged to take this line by Stalin himself. In its most brilliant passages this book shows that Stalin knew the art of making out his wicked actions to be initiatives forced on him by those around him, and he loved making Beria play the role of 'the bad man' (for example, when he presented him to Roosevelt as 'our Himmler', a joke which greatly embarrassed the American president). At Stalin's court Khrushchev survived by playing the buffoon, Beria by playing the executioner. Each had the right physique for the job.

It is on the mentality of the Soviet leaders that this book offers the most interesting revelations. The deep-seated hatred of Russia and the far-reaching importance of nationality in the power balance comes as a surprise (see more about this in the Editor's Note). As we read, we find that they are all aware that they are participating in a criminal regime and committing infamous deeds. Some of them, at least, know that they will have accounts to render to posterity. Every apparatchik of a certain rank begins to compile dossiers that compromise his rivals and potential opponents. These dossiers concern crimes committed by order of higher authority. Like a Mafia 'godfather', Stalin takes care to compromise his confederates in systematic fashion, and any attempt to get out of this duty to murder, collectively or individually, brings down his suspicion and his vengeance. The Soviet regime emerges as a regime of blackmailers, a supremely hypocritical regime in which vice never stops paying homage to virtue and in which baseness disguises itself as duty, cowardice as altruism, treason as charity, sadism as efficiency, stupidity as patriotism.

Yet the great historical interest of this book extends far beyond Kremlin gossip. This is most of all a document about daily life at the Kremlin. Khrushchev's memoirs are full of gaps, self-justifications and even just plain lies, yet they constitute, in spite of that, a fascinating and irreplaceable document for the historian. This book, too, adds to our knowledge, in particular to the role of anti-Russian sentiment and Beria's surprising part in this. To be sure, Beria confided little to his son regarding his activities and plans. But the young man had the gift of observation, a delicate sensibility and the sharp memory characteristic of all who live in the midst of what is left unspoken. He frequented the company of his father's helpers, high-ranking military men, some members of the Politburo and their wives. He looked on Stalin with the adoring eyes of a teenager, then observed him through his father's implacable gaze. Time has stood still for him. Moreover, Sergo Beria significantly chose a career that was very different from his father, an unassuming job as an engineer. However much he may fail, his struggle to come to terms with a horrendous and painful past is a serious one, as serious as the system and the family he grew up in allowed.

Françoise Thom

Editor's Note

Sergo Beria's book can be approached in two distinct ways. The first consists of 'neutral' parts, those in which his father was not directly involved and where the author's will to construct an apologia does not entail the risk of Sergo distorting the truth. Even with this restricted approach the reader will find a wealth of material about the Stalin period and the causes of the Terror. His opening chapters reveal everything from the mentality of the leaders of the republics of the USSR, their relations with Moscow, the extent and limits of their power within their respective fiefs, to their ways of life, the way in which local intrigues were interwoven with the struggle for power at the top, Moscow's instruments of control and the role played by the republics in the aims of the foreign policy worked out in Moscow. After Beria's arrival in the capital we find á vivid picture of Stalin's immediate entourage, of groups tearing each other apart and of the byzantine forms assumed by this perpetual fight to the death, including an analysis of Stalin's policy on the eve of the war.

But Sergo Beria's story is also a unique testimony of the war as experienced by a son of the nomenklatura and of how he saw relations with the Western allies. There are colourful portraits of the members of the Politburo and their wives after the war, a breathtaking description of Stalin's strategy for controlling his world and calling the country to heel after the relatively 'liberal' period of the war, and his insistence on the priority to be given to the nuclear project in a USSR in ruins. Sergo Beria vividly captures the exacerbation of the struggle for the succession at the time when Stalin's physical decline became obvious. Finally, we can follow him in his evocative description of the madness of Stalin's last months, which is fully corroborated by the accounts left by other witnesses and by what the archives have revealed. Moreover, Sergo's narrative must be read throughout against the salient fact that Stalin and Beria were two Georgians ruling the vast Russian empire and its dominions, and that Stalin's death must have upset the delicate balance that existed.

The second approach concerns itself directly with the question of what we are to believe in the testimony of a son about a father whom he clearly worshipped. Should we reject everything because of the evident partiality of the writer and of what we know of Beria from other sources? To what extent do these descriptions of Beria by Stalin and Khrushchev correspond to reality?

What this enquiry amounts to is granting Sergo Beria his wish of allowing history to pass judgement on his father. There is obviously no question here of rehabilitating Beria – even his son is not attempting that – but of putting together all the evidence in his case. Beria committed many crimes, but the same can be said of his colleagues in the Politburo who sent thousands to their deaths. Khrushchev, for example, distinguished himself by his zeal in the purges carried out in Moscow and then in the Ukraine, and certainly had no less blood on his conscience than Beria. But he beat Beria in the fight for the succession to Stalin and therefore was able to put his hands on the archives, destroying documents that incriminated him, concocting for posterity his own version of the past, and showing more concern to put himself in a good light and 'compromise' his rivals than to serve the cause of truth. But the indisputable truth is that they both took an active part in a deeply criminal regime.

Khrushchev's version remained almost intact until the declassification in 1991 of the minutes of the July 1953 Plenum, which was devoted to condemning Beria after his arrest on 26 June 1953 and until statements were made by some pioneers of perestroika such as the Russian A. Yakovlev, who did not hesitate to name Beria as the only real reformer among Stalin's successors. It was the minutes of the July 1953 Plenum which led the author of these lines to take an interest in Beria as an individual and to record the testimony offered by his son.

Research in newly declassified archives has led to remarkable discoveries. They have raised rather than answered questions about this character who was the most powerful man in the USSR for such a short period of time.

As said before, Beria did not resume direction of the police and state security services (now also including the precursor of the KGB) until 6 March 1953, the day after Stalin's death. Yet, instead of consolidating his mammoth power and deploying his newly regained control over the security files on his colleagues, Beria started bombarding them with an array of initiatives to de-Stalinise the USSR.

To be sure, there was a widely shared consensus about the need for de-Stalinisation. But this did not extend to all the matters Beria put forward in rapid succession. From 6 March he reduced the economic jurisdiction of the police and announced that he wanted to pass responsibility for the Gulag on to the Ministry of Justice. On 13 March he charged four NKVD committees with re-examining some notorious show trials, including the trial of the Jewish Antifascist Committee, and persecution of the Jews ended forthwith. On 14 March, the State and Party apparatus were separated, with Malenkov becoming President and Khrushchev Leader of a weakened Communist Party. On 15 March, Beria gained control over censorship, the Glavlit, and expunged Stalin's name from the press in a very short time, while anti-Western propaganda became muted. On 21 March, Beria attacked the Stalinised central state and proposed ending the giant Socialist construction sites (which would in turn end the need for the Gulag). Three days later he addressed a paper to the Presidium in which he detailed that there were 2,526,402 people in the Gulag, of whom 221,435 were 'State criminals'. On 27 March, 1,178,422 prisoners were freed and their numbers continued to swell under his stewardship until his fall from power (from July the Gulag complement went up again). In a secret memorandum circulated to the NKVD on 4 April, Beria forbade torture in prisons and detention centres. On the same day, *Pravda* carried an NKVD announcement which cleared Jewish doctors (accused by Stalin in the previous year of wanting to poison Politburo members). It was the first public attack against Stalin, it left the country reeling, and Beria had imposed it on his reluctant colleagues. In order to soften their resistance he had them listen to tapes of Stalin, in which he demanded the torture of people accused of certain things and revealed the extent of his paranoia. Famous writers like K. Simonov attended these sessions.

Curiously, many of the charges brought against Beria at his show trial departed from the usual allegations formulated in this sort of Communist ceremony. True, Beria was described as a British agent and was said to have wished to organise a coup d'état and to have put the security organs above control by the Party. Alongside these ritual litanies (which included the accusation that he had tried to undermine collective cattle breeding and vegetable production programmes), however, there were other precise accusations of an unfamiliar kind, the addition of which outlined a political project that was coherent and far-reaching. They implied overturning Soviet foreign policy (Beria wanted to hand over the GDR to the German Federal Republic), setting aside the Communist Party (Beria wanted to deprive it of control over the economy), a reform of the empire (Beria wanted to release the republics from Russian domination) and introducing glasnost (Beria wanted to end the jamming of Western broadcasts).

The speakers at the Plenum took turns in declaring that 'Beria was no Communist'. Strange as it may seem, a charge of that sort was not routine in such circumstances. One would have expected to find that he was accused of 'right deviationism' or 'Trotskyism'. It is enough to compare the July 1953 Plenum with those of February 1955 and June 1957, when Malenkov and the 'anti-Party group' were condemned, in order to appreciate the degree to which the Soviet leaders felt threatened by Beria.

Nothing came near the hatred that broke over their fallen Georgian colleague. And this hatred is certainly not explained just by Beria's past crimes. (In his memoirs Khrushchev writes a eulogy on the Russian Yezhov, Beria's predecessor at the NKVD and the organiser of the 'great terror'.) Looking at the archives, Beria launched his national policy in April. He started by sending NKVD officers to the republics of the USSR, charging them to find out what was happening there and, most of all, to find compromising facts on Party dignitaries. Based on these reports of the flagrant collapse of Party policies, Beria addressed a number of recommendations to his colleagues. They all pointed in the same direction: ending the Russian tutelage of the republics. Beria, for example, proposed to recall the Russian Party functionaries from the Baltic States, to cease the practice of flanking the Party leader of the republics with a supervisory Russian Secretary. He went so far as to recommend 'forbidding the customary imposition of Eastern Ukrainians as leaders on Western Ukraine.' Secretly he started negotiating with the Primate of the Russian Orthodox Church, Yosyf Slipyi, an ex-Gulag prisoner, in order to normalise relationships with the Vatican and legalising the Uniate Church.

Beria approached East Germany in exactly the same way as the republics. On 20 April, a committee of enquiry despatched by him delivered a crushing report on its leader, Ulbricht, and his clan. On 27 May the famous meeting of the Council of Ministers regarding the situation of the GDR took place. Beria could barely disguise his disdain. 'The GDR? What of the GDR? It isn't even a real state. It only manages to stay together because of Soviet troops, no matter that it calls itself German Democratic Republic.' This imprudent frankness did little but augment the fears that his colleagues increasingly felt. 'It is the discussion of the German issue which unmasked Beria most as a provocateur and an imperialist agent,' confided Khrushchev to the Plenum of July 1953.

For a time, however, Beria was able to pursue his German policies. On 10 June, with a heavy heart, the East German Politburo announced its 'new direction', inspired by Beria: 'reinforcement of the rule of law, re-establishment of small and medium industry and small and medium commerce, annulment of farm expropriations, restitution of property confiscated from people who had fled the country but had returned, amnesty, facilities for the movement of people between East and West, an end to the fight against the Protestant church.'

In parallel, Beria continued to dismantle the Soviet penitentiary system and the vast network of camps and colonies of exiles. On 2 May he presented a memorandum on the Politburo decision of 21 February 1948 which laid down exile in perpetuity for people condemned of counter-revolutionary crimes who had served their sentence: 'Soviet penal legislation does not consider punishment as a means of protecting society, rather as the measure of a circumscribed crime ... It determines a system of penalties with a strictly prescribed duration ... Soviet law forbids imposition of a new penalty for the same crime.' It recommended repealing the decision and releasing the people in exile under it. On 16 June, restrictions placed by the regime on passports were lifted and 3,900,000 people previously condemned to exile, mostly Kulaks, could reclaim their freedom of movement: their passports would be renewed without mention of their previous status.

Small wonder then that Beria's fellow Politburo members had reason to take fright. Beria's policies would have led very quickly to the collapse of the soviet empire in Europe and the destabilisation of the entire USSR. The Berlin insurrection of 17 June and the rising of the Gulag in the summer of 1953 were the first warning shots of what was about to happen. As Kaganovitch said in the July Plenum: 'We must in all fairness realise that if the Presidium had delayed action by even a few days, we might today have had to deal with an entirely different situation.' (So, when did Beria's colleagues start to plot against him? Was it when the German issue arose? Or was it, as some testimonies seem to suggest, already happening when Stalin was alive?)

There are a number of things Sergo Beria's documents show with a sufficient degree of certainty. Few sources illustrate in such telling detail and with such precision the techniques of Stalin's regime at its maturity, the breakup of the ruling oligarchy into rival groups which Stalin adroitly set one against another, and the way in which he transformed the struggle for his succession into an instrument of his own power. Sergo Beria also shows how deep ran the animosity between the government apparatus and that of the Party. He often returns to the hatred of the Party shown by his father, and we can follow him now that we know that, during the 'hundred days' after Stalin's death, Beria tried to implement a programme of reforms which provided for the Communist Party to be set aside and replaced by the state machine.

Sergo Beria's account confirms the importance of the role played by the national factor among the Soviet élite. He shows that there was a real, even if hidden, solidarity between the non-Russian citizens of the empire, both those who came from the union republics and those from the republics belonging to the Russian Federation, such as Tatarstan, and that the 'Russophiles' were aware of these affinities and were afraid of them. Stalin knew, too, how to play masterfully on the secret war being waged between the group of non-Russians dominated by Beria and the 'Russophile' group led by Zhdanov, outwardly giving preference to the 'Russian chauvinists' but without allowing the non-Russian faction to be completely crushed.

Beria is presented by his son as a constant adversary of the most fundamental tendencies of Bolshevism – its predilection for force, slavery, messianism and aggression against foreign countries. Some of his accounts may give a deceptive impression of the 'democracy' prevailing in the Politburo's debates. In actual fact, however, Stalin did not tolerate any contradiction and, according to the historian D. Volkogonov, who had access to his most private notebooks, he never took notice of any opinion expressed by one of his circle. Let us not forget that the members of the Politburo, Beria included, were utterly terrorised by Stalin. As against that, it is perfectly believable that, in the family, Beria boasted of his initiatives and even of his plain speaking before Stalin (notwithstanding the fact that the homes of Politburo members were bugged).

Beria was therefore not the proclaimed oppositionist that we might infer from some of his son's descriptions. Nevertheless, like other members of the Politburo, he did try to influence the tyrant. Like all great manipulators, Stalin was himself open to manipulation. It is not certain in what direction Beria's influence was exerted. Was he really in favour of 'Finlandising', i.e. turning the countries of central and Eastern Europe into neutral territories, rather than communising them? Study of the policy pursued after the war in those countries does indeed reveal that there were contradictions and hesitations among the Soviet leaders. The measures taken by Beria after Stalin's death do show clearly his desire to lighten the control exercised by Moscow over its satellites and even over the republics of the USSR, and to abandon the GDR by shaking off the Ulbricht clique.

In fact it is in this short period which separates the death of Stalin from the fall of Beria (5 March-26 June 1953) that we have to seek the true political physiognomy of this strange person. The main thrust has been given above. In three months, the Gulag lost almost half of its inmates, the great construction works of socialism were closed down, the collective farm system was subjected to criticism in the republics, the Party apparatus was put on the sidelines, and Beria began to attack the countersiege regime on the frontiers of the USSR. What was Beria after? Did he aim to achieve absolute power through this strategy of de-Stalinisation, as his enemies claimed? Was it a miscalculation of the force of revolution, such as Gorbachev's, or was it merely a calculating but failed move to sideline the Russophiles in the Politburo? Did he want to paper over his own reputation as a cold-blooded torturer and sexual maniac, as has often been said? When Stalin died, Beria laid down rules for the struggle for power which survived him and ended by bringing about the fall of the system. He wanted to use the crimes of the past to neutralise his rivals. But did he really intend to go back as far as Lenin and expose publicly the defects of Bolshevism, as his son declares? No document has proved that, up till now.

These questions provoke others about the man Beria. What was the basis for the hatred of Stalin which he gradually ceased concealing from his son? Must we seek its causes solely in the thirst for power felt by someone whose imperious temperament made it hard for him to bend to the will of another? And, above all, how far did that hatred take Lavrenti Beria? Why did Stalin keep beside him for so long a man whom he had very soon begun to distrust – Stalin who had not hesitated to get rid of the high command of the Red Army on the eve of the war? Had Stalin begun to fear Beria, as Khrushchev claims?

Sergo Beria depicts a Stalin suffering from megalomania, one who had lost all sense of reality and was dreaming of conquering the world. Khrushchev shows him, on the contrary, as trembling before the Americans, convinced that war was imminent, yet terrified by this prospect. What was true? Whom was Stalin deceiving? Hatred of Stalin is at the origin of both of these pictures, that of Beria when he portrays a megalomaniac Stalin and that of Khrushchev when he describes a Stalin in abject fear. The state of our knowledge enables us to say one thing only, that the USSR was actually preparing for war. And, during the last months of Stalin's life, a collective hysteria seemed to take hold of the country. Stalin had indeed become a public danger, whether because he was intoxicated by an illusory sense of invincibility or because paranoia had deprived him of the power to reason.

Without doubt, Sergo Beria's testimony has the merit that it depicts the hideous world, made up of petty intrigues and great crimes, in which the Soviet leaders evolved, and the psychological mechanisms by which they sought to protect themselves from it. He sheds some light on Beria's ambivalent stature. Even in democratic post-glasnost Russia, the Beria affair remains enshrouded in mystery. On 29 May 2000, the Military Division of the Russian Supreme Court decided not to revise the judgment against Beria demanded by the families of his co-conspirators under new legislation. Assessing the evidence afresh, it did not drop the previous charges according to which, up to his arrest, Beria 'entertained and developed relations with foreign intelligence services, camouflaging them carefully ... After Stalin's death, Beria decided to accelerate his anti-Soviet plans, which led to his unmasking a short while later.' Who Beria was needs further research, but it is clear that he was a far more enigmatic figure than Khrushchev's sex-crazed maniac.

Françoise Thom 2001

In Stalin's Shadow

My Origins

Our family came from an ancient principality in Western Georgia called Mingrelia. As my mother emphasised when she introduced me to Georgian history, our country had undergone many vicissitudes.[1] While the Georgians generally were restless under Russian domination, the Mingrelians were the most rebellious of them all to the Tsar's rule. This people, more mobile and almost opportunistic, with a temperament more fiery than the other Georgian nations, always remained fiercely attached to its freedom. My father used to say of the Mingrelians that they were sailors in their souls, a race of traders who liked to knock about the world.

My grandfather was a well-to-do peasant who lived by cattle rearing. One day he was obliged to flee because he had killed one of the Tsar's officials. The whole village bore witness that the man had died as the result of a fall, but the authorities remained sceptical. Having sold all his property and greased the palm of the police so as to stay out of custody, he took refuge in the heights of Abkhazia, in the village of Merkheuli. There it was that he married my grandmother, in 1898. She was of the lineage of the Princes Dzhakeli, a family distinguished since the ninth century. When my grandfather met her she was a widow bringing up the two children from her first marriage on her own. My grandfather was seven years younger than she was, he was educated and very handsome. Many years later my grandmother saw fit to tell me: 'I realised quite well that he had not married me for love. But I was mad about him and promised myself that I would do everything to make him happy.' This grandfather of mine was irascible in the extreme. Three children were born of their union – a son who died in infancy, a daughter who became deaf at the age of three months from the consequences of chicken pox, and my father, the eldest, born in 1899. It was in this mountain village that he took his first steps. My grandfather taught him to weed the fields of maize. He took the boy with him when he went to look after his flocks in the mountains and taught him the names of the stars. 'He wrapped me in a woollen cloak,' my father recalled with emotion, 'and made me lie down by his side. I was happy to be with him.'

My father went to school at the age of seven. Georgian schools being forbidden – the Russification policy was in full swing – he was sent to a Russian establishment at Sukhumi, a port on the Black Sea. My grandfather had to sell some land in order to pay for his education, despite the efforts made by my grandmother, who earned a little money from dress-making. She rented a room from a Georgian merchant, Erkomashvili, and lived there with my father, who was an excellent pupil. This merchant had grown rich by setting fire to his storehouses, which he had previously insured. My grandmother sewed dresses for him. His daughter, Lena Erkomashvili, had studied at the Smolny Institute in Petersburg. Having become friendly with my father, a boy of eight or nine at the time, she introduced him to Georgian history and literature. After the Bolsheviks came to power the Erkomashvilis' property was confiscated and I don't know what the family's fate was.[2] My father had also a teacher of litera-ture who became fond of him. Later, whenever his business took him to Sukhumi, my father would visit this teacher, as a pilgrimage of gratitude. He even took me to visit the lady one day, but the recalling of his childhood memories made me yawn in boredom and this greatly annoyed him.

At fifteen, having decided to become an architect, he went to Baku, a very cosmopolitan town at that time, in order to study at the Polytechnic Institute, which specialised in architecture, geology and petrochemistry. It was not financed by the state but by Russian and Azeri industrialists. My father was, from those days, deeply interested in the oil industry.

He retained some memories from that period of his life. In particular, he told me how he had suffered from the snubs of a mathematics teacher, an arrogant Russian who despised the Georgians. When my father succeeded in solving a difficult problem, this teacher said to him: 'Eh! And where do *you* come from?'

'From Sukhumi,' he replied.

'Ah!' said the teacher. 'And there was I thinking that only monkeys lived there!' Touched to the quick, my father set himself to work as hard as he could, so that this teacher was eventually obliged to admit that 'he would never have believed he could find anyone so gifted among the Georgians.' My father also gave French lessons to the children of rich Armenian merchants. Though he spoke not a word of French, he managed to keep up the illusion for nearly six months! His ability to get out of awkward situations became legendary.

The Georgians sought each other's company. Most of them were older than my father and spent most of their time having fun. Neglecting their studies, they got my father to produce their draft plans for them. 'The day came,' he told me, 'when I could stand this no longer and kicked over the traces. They wanted to beat me but it was I who beat them.' Some of his fellow students had given up their studies in order to engage in the trade in pure spirit from Tsaritsyn. As the customs officials proved rather too zealous, they had the idea of bringing in their contraband in a coffin accompanied by a little old woman who made the whole journey intoning 'Spiritus, spiritus!'

During this period my father nearly died from an attack of dysentery, and his mother had to come to Baku for a couple of months to look after him. Having heard that raw eggs would help him to recover, he swallowed fifteen of them every day. He was terrifyingly skeletal when he returned to his studies.

In 1916 those students at the Institute who were well up in geodesy were sent to the Romanian front, my father among them. He recalled with some nostalgia his fellow students who had managed to continue their studies in Petersburg and find work in their speciality. He, ever active, joined in 1915 the Social-Democratic group which existed within the Institute's Georgian Association.[3] According to my mother it was his sociable nature rather than ideological conviction that led him to join. All those around him were Social Democrats and, as he did not want to keep apart, he copied his compatriots in the task of distributing leaflets (which they got printed by a state printing house). This group was linked with a Bolshevik Party cell, one of whose members was Mikoyan.

First struggles

In April 1918 a Bolshevik Commune was established in Baku, a Bolshevik islet in independent Transcaucasia.[4] Industry was paralysed, shops looted, wages left unpaid, and famine was not long in coming. The romanticism of the revolutionary ideas was soon subjected to a harsh test. When the Communists had to flee, the Bolshevik A. Dzhaparidze, one of the members of the Commune, asked my father to stay behind in the town. He agreed because his mother and his deaf-mute sister were also in Baku, which was occupied by the Turks, and later by the British, and they might die of hunger.[5] He wanted to be with them so as to help them. His comrades obtained a bag of rice for him: for six months this rice, cooked with cheese, was the only food for himself and his family. His first mission and that of his group was directed against the Musavat.[6] His experience in intelligence work goes back to that time: 'I was thrown into the water without knowing how to swim', he said. He retained a taste for intelligence work, whereas he never liked engaging in counter-espionage. He told me that the Turks had installed a substantial and powerful network of spies in Baku. Mikoyan gave him the task of combating this network, though he denied this later.

When the British established themselves in Baku, they put the oil industry in working order again. The famine which had been raging before they arrived now came to an end. My father explained to me that the British had carefully prepared for their occupation of Azerbaijan. They had defined their objectives, provided for the material base that would make possible the realising of these objectives, and sought out the people on the spot who might put their policy into effect. Their rich colonial experience was apparent in every way. 'The British never improvise,' he would often repeat to me. He contrasted them in this respect with the Americans, who entered the war in 1941 unprepared and even had to have recourse to the British in organising their own intelligence service.[7]

The Eleventh Army, destined to sovietise Transcaucasia, was formed at Astrakhan at the beginning of 1919 by Kirov, Ordzhonikidze and others. They began to recruit youngsters for underground activity. On 8 April 1920 Ordzhonikidze was given the task of co-ordinating Bolshevik policy in Transcaucasia, at the head of the Kavburo, the Bolshevik general staff responsible for communising the Caucasus. Kirov was his deputy. When the Bolshevik regime had been installed in Baku, on 27 April 1920, Kirov sent my father on a secret mission to Georgia. Kirov himself, as ambassador in Tbilisi, directed the Bolsheviks' underground networks in Georgia.[8] My father was in prison in Tbilisi in May and June 1920, being released in July thanks to intervention by Kirov with the Menshevik government of Georgia.

My Mother

My mother came from a milieu very different from my father's. Her mother belonged to a great Mingrelian family, the Chikovanis. A believer without being a fanatic, she had a passion for music and loved to sing while playing the guitar. Her husband was a Gegechkori, one of whose ancestors had been ennobled for his exploits during the war with the Turks. My grandmother was his second wife and my mother was their only child. My grandfather adored her. The excellent education she received in Russian schools did not turn her against Georgia. Her parents taught her first of all to read and write her mother tongue. They sent her to Kutaisi to carry on her secondary studies in a grammar school for the nobility. My grandfather visited her every week. My mother was still a child when he unfortunately fell victim to a tragic event. When, at the age of 70, he was accompanying a peasant delegation which came to lay its grievances before the Russian authorities, a gendarme, for some unknown reason – my grandfather was anything but a revolutionary – fired on him and hit him in the legs. The old man died of his wounds. My mother was much affected by this. As she saw it, the Tsarist regime had murdered her father. After my grandfather's death, my mother went, accordingly, to Tbilisi to live with her uncle Sasha, a Bolshevik. It was another uncle, Evgeni, however, who supported her materially. He was a Menshevik. That may seem odd today but one has to remember that in those days betrayal was not commonplace. Sasha and Evgeni could meet, even during the period when Evgeni was Minister of Foreign Affairs in the Menshevik government of Georgia while Sasha continued his underground activity.

My mother was beautiful, and kind in a way that one felt at one's first contact with her. Good-humoured and straightforward, there was something radiant about her that never failed to affect people. One day, when she was visiting her uncle Sasha in prison, her eyes met those of my father, who was locked up with him. She was 15 at the time and he noticed her. 'It was as though a shining cherub had entered the prison. I said to myself: that's the woman I must have,' he told me one day. My mother felt pity for this small, puny young man and urged Sasha to share with him the food she had brought, so that he could put on weight again. In their prison fellowship Uncle Sasha undertook to introduce my father to the ancient history of Georgia. The irony of fate willed that, later, he who, during their lively discussions in the cell, accused my father of being 'a spy for the Russian army', contributed to the Sovietisation of his country with the help of a troop of Ingushes[9] while my father, who defended himself by appealing to the unity of the Social-Democratic movement, was unable to conceal his sympathy for some aspects of Menshevik policy.[10] It was thus my great-uncle Sasha who began to open my father's eyes. The influence of my mother and of her friends subsequently completed this work. At the time of their first meetings, however, my father's ignorance of Georgia's history was stunning. 'He was an internationalist to the very marrow of his bones,' my mother once said to me when recalling that period.

Chekist

In July 1920, after his release from prison, my father had to quit Georgia for Baku, leaving my mother behind him. It was in Azerbaijan, Sovietised since April, that, thanks to Bagirov, he joined the Cheka.[11] His work in the Cheka was not, for him, a definitively chosen career. He hoped indeed to resume his studies and become an engineer. My father did not see my mother again till February 1921, after Ordzhonikidze had entered Georgia at the head of the Red Army.[12] He returned to Tbilisi to ask for her hand.

She was not yet 17 while he was 22. 'He was thin as a rake, very shy, and one noticed only his eyes. But he was a charmer. And he pleased me because he treated me as an equal when he spoke to me,' my mother told me. She had golden auburn hair, eyes the colour of dark honey and a face that was a perfect oval, with delicate features. My father courted her by inventing every imaginable pretext to call and see her at Sasha's. My mother adored music and he eventually noticed this. Not being himself a musician, he pestered a friend, who was, to teach him to play a waltz by Chopin. After a few months he was able to sit down at the piano and perform before my fascinated mother the waltz that he had so laboriously learnt. One day he took her aside and said, right out: 'Listen, you're leading a boring life here. Marry me. I work in the Cheka but I have big plans. I want to become a specialist in the oil industry ...' And my mother agreed. My great-uncle Sasha opposed the marriage, considering that she was too young for it. So, without saying anything, but with the complicity of one of her cousins who helped her pack, my mother eloped along with my father, merely leaving a letter behind her. At that time, Sasha Gegechkori was Minister of Internal Affairs in the Bolshevik government that had been established in Tbilisi. He looked for the couple in vain and telephoned to Bagirov: 'Wretch! You send me bandits who carry off young girls!' Bagirov did not at once realise what he was talking about. One can imagine what efforts my parents had to make to persuade the functionaries of the town to register their marriage!

After their wedding the young couple eventually decided to go back to Sasha to ask his forgiveness and tell him they were now married. When he saw them coming, Sasha threw himself on my mother and, seizing her around the waist, gave her a few clouts on the bottom: 'That's for your sins, past and future,' he said, laughing.[13] This matter having been settled, the bride and bridegroom set up home in Baku. My father dreamed of resuming his engineering studies at the Polytechnic Institute and then going on to a petrochemical institute in Belgium, so as to complete his training. But these dreams remained dreams as, on his arrival in the capital of Azerbaijan, the Central Committee confirmed his appointment to the Cheka. Ordzhonikidze finally closed down my father's 'civilian' plans by making him head of the department for secret Cheka operations in Georgia. The die was cast, my father had to submit. My mother was never to forgive Ordzhonikidze for that decision. She recalled later, weeping, the role he had played in her husband's fate. 'It was through you,' she said, 'that he was drawn into this accursed revolutionary activity. He would have made an excellent engineer. We should have had a normal life and been happy. Today we have no life. Nor have you, either, but *you* chose this path, whereas my husband was trapped into his career. You left your career in the Party in order to devote yourself to heavy industry. Why didn't you let Lavrenti do likewise?' Faced with these reproaches, Ordzhonikidze tried to justify himself: 'It was war. At that time we had no need of engineers.'

So my parents packed their bags again and left Baku to return to Tbilisi. They went to live with great-uncle Sasha. When they recalled that period of their lives they could not repress a smile. Sasha, who was an expansive man, liked to share his experience and, above all, could not refrain from lecturing the youngsters. It was therefore not infrequent for him to burst into their bedroom without announcing himself or knocking on the door. Fortunately, my father recalled, Sasha had a wooden leg – he had lost a leg during his expedition in the Caucasus – and one could hear him coming from far off, which meant that the young married couple had time to assume a decent posture.

The Bolsheviks got at Sasha[14] on the occasion of the visit by the Shah of Persia and his wife to Georgia. Sasha, who was a fine-looking man despite his wooden leg, made a big impression on the Empress. A group of Armenian Communists with truly Bolshevik rigorous views on morals denounced to the Moscow authorities his 'unproletarian' behaviour. Then the harassment became more intense, and insinuations and comments became more frequent. He was accused of having 'princely' ways. Sasha defended himself, giving as good as he got. 'You rat-packs!' he shouted, 'What right have you to lecture me? Who installed the Soviet regime for you, by force of arms?' In 1928, driven to the brink by these persecutions and by the suffering that his stump caused him, he killed himself. My father always told me that deeper and more serious tensions were hidden behind the gossip passed around concerning Sasha's gallantries. He

thought that Georgia should be ruled by Georgians. He was not an internationalist and showed himself to be particularly hostile to the Armenian
Communists. Though my father fundamentally shared his ideas, he
regarded his attitude as not very politic.

Vera, Sasha's wife, a pleasant German woman, told me later that her
husband had done everything in his power to get my father out of the
Cheka and let him complete his studies. 'Gifted young people should not
be sucked into that sewer,' he said to her at that time. He also made this
remark to my mother: 'An intelligent man does not have to work with
morons.' Having been Minister of Internal Affairs, he knew what he was
talking about.

So my father arrived in Tbilisi in November 1922 to take up his post in
the department for secret operations. Six months later, he became the
number two in Georgia's Cheka. When he recalled that period of his life he
was rather gloomy. He told me he had never known a Chekist who liked
his job and yet was not a scoundrel. Whoever could manage it fled that
organisation as soon as they found the opportunity to do so. Thus there
were Latvian Chekists, numerous in the Eleventh Army, who had been
ready to accept any job as long as it offered them an escape hatch. Those
who did not succeed in escaping became tuberculous. The Cheka's sanato-
riums were always full. My father tried several times to get out of his
Cheka responsibilities. He sent the Party letters in which he asked to be
released from his functions so as to resume his studies and devote himself
to the oil industry. This was, I believe, a unique case in the Party's annals.
Just imagine an official of his rank renouncing his post and asking to be
allowed to lead an ordinary life. If you wanted proof that at that time
power held no attraction for him, this would have been enough to convince
the most sceptical.[15]

My father retained only one good memory from that time. As the Cheka
lacked resources, he had managed to raise some money by selling a few
barrels of oil and had used it to organise a network in Turkey and Iran. To
reward the man who had enabled him to carry out this financial operation
my father gave him permission to emigrate to the United States.[16] 'He
danced with joy when Lavrenti gave him the news,' I was told by my
mother, who was present at the interview.

1924: The Menshevik revolt

The Menshevik revolt of 1924 affected my father profoundly. Since he was
in charge of the intelligence network responsible for surveillance of the
Mensheviks, he found himself immediately plunged into the midst of
events. At that time, my mother was pregnant with me. She was at
Abastuman, a village surrounded by pine trees, near the Turkish frontier.
She had a difficult pregnancy and could not return to Tbilisi. My father
had been about to ask for leave to go to her when he learnt of the
Mensheviks' plans. They were aware that most Georgians were opposed to

Russia and to the Soviet regime, and were organising an insurrection. But they made a mistake in relying on material support from the French and British.[17] In my father's opinion, the Western powers had deliberately deceived them – as they were to do later with the Baltic states – and the Mensheviks were doomed from the outset. However that may have been, my father wanted to avoid a clash, to prevent a mass uprising and intervention by Russian troops. He feared the repression that would inevitably ensue. With this idea in mind, he sent a report to Ordzhonikidze, who was then Secretary of the Party's committee for Transcaucasia, and he passed it on to Stalin. Doubtless with Moscow's blessing, Ordzhonikidze authorised my father to make contact with the Mensheviks. He was to let them know that their plan had been discovered and to dissuade them from going ahead with the adventure. The Mensheviks received this warning but, under pressure from the British, declared that it was a 'provocation'. The Bolshevik government's warning even seemed to them a sign of weakness. To persuade them this was not the case, my father then proposed that he should meet a representative of theirs to whom he would prove that he knew where all their caches of arms were located. They sent the former commander of the Georgian Menshevik Guard, Dzhugeli, to him.

This man came to Tbilisi secretly with the aid of my father's agents. He went to Kakhetia, then returned to Tbilisi. But then he decided to stay there instead of going back to Western Georgia. He had found a mistress in Tbilisi and, abandoning all caution, flaunted himself without any disguise in the main streets of the capital. What was bound to happen happened: one of his former mistresses encountered him and denounced him to the authorities. Dzhugeli was arrested with great to-do by zealous Chekists. My father's boss in the hierarchy, Kvantaliani, the man at the head of the Georgian Cheka at that time – who, be it said in passing, was an absolute imbecile – boasted to Moscow that he had captured the commander of the Menshevik Guard.

When he learnt the news, my father hastened to Ordzhonikidze's office. And, for the first time, Ordzhonikidze disappointed him. 'I warned you,' was all that he said, 'that if the affair became public I should not lift my little finger.' Dzhugeli was doomed and my father's efforts were brought to nothing. In order to try and save the situation despite this catastrophe, he went to the prison where Dzhugeli was being held. The Menshevik admitted that he had acted foolishly and wrote to his friends to confirm that it was his own fault that he had been arrested and to urge them not to launch the insurrection.[18] But this was in vain. The Menshevik *émigrés* were not prepared – and one can understand why – to accept Dzhugeli's statements which had been written behind the bars of his prison. Nevertheless, my father tried to save him but was not successful. Feeling helpless, he wrote an official letter to Ordzhonikidze and Dzerzhinsky, head of the GPU, in which he expressed his disagreement with the Georgian authorities. At the end of his letter he asked for leave to visit his pregnant wife. He was at last granted his request, at the end of August, a week before the revolt broke out. He had never doubted that the revolt would occur, whereas Ordzhonikidze imagined that the Mensheviks had given up their plans. My father joined my mother and awaited the start of the troubles. He did not have long to wait. Less than a week after his arrival in the village of Abastuman, on 28 August, Georgia rose.

Ordzhonikidze recalled my father in haste, admitting that, despite his youth, he had been right about the revolt, but it was too late. Russian troops descended upon Georgia, coming in from Northern Caucasia, from Azerbaijan and from Armenia, so as to seize the country in a pincer-grip. My father took three days to reach Tbilisi on horseback, accompanied by Shariko Tsereteli,[19] prince and officer of the old regime. My mother followed in a car. They passed through the rebels' lines. The rebels did not harm them, though they knew their identity. Tsereteli told me that when they reached the capital, 'all the shits in the Party were hiding behind their wives' skirts.' Ordzhonikidze alone had kept his cool. He sent my father and his comrade to Kakhetia to negotiate with Cholokashvili, the rebels' leader. Again and even though they were unescorted, they were allowed to pass unscathed through the rebels' lines. At that time there was still a sense of honour in Georgia. Though Cholokashvili refused to meet them, his representatives agreed to lay down their arms on condition that they were promised freedom from persecution. My father replied that he could give them no guarantee, as he was not in control of the situation. Accordingly he advised the Menshevik officers to flee – for which he was to be blamed at his trial.[20] During these negotiations, Tsereteli tried to persuade my father to guarantee their immunity. 'They have given their word that they have renounced the armed struggle', he argued, 'We can trust them.' To which my father replied: 'We can promise nothing. Kvantaliani will execute them as soon as he gets the chance.' Nevertheless, Tsereteli took away with him some officers personally known to him, whom he passed for Bolsheviks. Cholokashvili fled, accompanied by a group of officers, while others disappeared in Russia and the peasants returned to their fields.

The atrocities began when the Russian troops entered Kakhetia, where many rebels surrendered to them. Despite the promises they had been given they were all either executed or deported to Siberia. This was the fate of all the officers, whether or not they had taken part in the revolt. The flower of Georgia's youth was destroyed in this way.[21] In the months that followed my father's fate hung by a thread. The Party authorities looked into his case. Had he not warned the Mensheviks, allowed Dzhugeli to come to Tbilisi, negotiated with the rebels and allowed their leaders to escape? The Armenian Communists and Kvantaliani were the most furious with my father, accusing him of double-dealing – already at the time he was alleged to have links with the Musavatists[22] – and of showing complacency towards the Mensheviks on account, especially, of his kinship with Evgeni Gegechkori, my mother's other uncle who had been Minister of Foreign Affairs in the Georgian government. The hostility towards him was so intense that my father offered his resignation. However, and doubtless under the influence of Stalin, who, it seems, recognised in him a gifted young man, capable of analysing a situation and taking original decisions, Ordzhonikidze and Dzerzhinsky rejected his resignation. He was even awarded the Order of the Red Banner for the quality of the intelligence he had provided. This was the beginning of his rise in the world.[23]

After these events my father already had his own idea of the policy to be pursued in intelligence matters, considering it more worthwhile to keep opponents under surveillance than to arrest them. 'A self-respecting intelligence service', he said, 'never arrests an actual spy. We should be inspired by the example of the Tsar's police, the Okhrana. They arrested Lenin only once and then by mistake. The gendarme responsible for this blunder was punished.' According to my mother, he even became extremely angry when the Menshevik leader Khomeriki,[24] who ran an underground organisation before and during the revolt, was captured in Tbilisi.

It was during this dramatic period that I was born on 28 November 1924 in Tbilisi. The birth was a difficult one. The doctors had warned my father that he would perhaps have to choose between the mother and the child. 'Do everything you can to save the mother,' he replied. My arrival was not enough to obliterate the distress and despair my mother felt after the repression her country had suffered. One day she even threatened my father: 'Either you resign,' she told him, 'or I leave, taking the child with me.' He did not resign and she stayed – because she loved him and now had a son.

First Tensions

Two meetings which had been decisive in determining my father's destiny were those with Kirov and Ordzhonikidze, his future protectors. They trained him and inculcated in him the principles and practice of Bolshevism, even though love of Georgian traditions and of Georgia, in him and in my mother, set him subsequently against those influences. Ordzhonikidze, who saw my father as to some extent his disciple, had spoken about him to Stalin. The affair of the Menshevik revolt had caused the first disagreements between them and it was then that my father experienced his first disillusionments. When tensions became more acute between the two men, he asked for permission to appeal directly to Stalin. My mother was present during their conversation and she heard Ordzhonikidze reply: 'Do that and you'll see. You complain about me, but with him you'll know what pain is.'[25] Then, turning to my mother, he added: 'Your husband is going to learn what Russian communism is like.' My father was much affected by this clash, and fell ill. Ordzhonikidze had been his idol, and now that idol began to sway on its pedestal. He saw him in a new light, discovering an impulsive man capable of the worst foolishness.[26]

Ordzhonikidze was convinced that my father exaggerated the danger of the Menshevik revolt, that he overestimated the Mensheviks' strength and the amount of support they enjoyed among the population. For him it was enough to send in an extra division and everything would be drowned in blood. Later, he explained to my father that it had not been possible for him to act otherwise. If he, a Georgian himself, had held back the repression the Russian Communists would have seen his moderation as nationalism. So as not to arouse suspicion Ordzhonikidze had to show himself more royalist than the king. He justified thus his action in 1921: 'If I had not entered Georgia with the Red Army, someone else would have taken my place. Don't imagine that I was too naive to realise that.'[27] My father considered that Ordzhonikidze was mistaken. It would, as he saw it, have been better if a Russian had invaded Georgia: he would not have needed to go so far in order to prove that he was no nationalist. And to my mother, who remarked to him: 'At least Ordzhonikidze had the courage to admit his mistakes,' my father replied in downright fashion: 'He would have done better to understand at the outset.' While acknowledging that Ordzhonikidze had acted badly, my mother thought that he had let matters go so far because he felt that he had been betrayed. Had he not told the Mensheviks that he was cognisant of their plans? Why had they not believed him, but instead hurled themselves headlong into the revolt? Most of the times when Ordzhonikidze met my father he presented himself as someone who understood the situation, who tried to oppose excesses, but who found himself helpless. In a sense his self-portrait was true. His suicide in February 1937 was to appear as a final act of protest.

After these events my father showed himself sensitive to Georgian nationalism, if I can believe the testimony of my mother, who had always been a nationalist. Increasingly he realised that the Bolshevik policy was the same as that of the Tsars. It aimed solely at crushing the non-Russian populations and establishing Russian control. He began at that time to interest himself more closely in Georgian history and in studying Russia's colonial policy. And this he did thoroughly, as with everything he undertook.

Collectivisation

Collectivisation was imposed between 1930 and 1932. In the letters he sent to Ordzhonikidze, Kirov and Stalin, my father explained that it would be unreasonable to practise this policy in mountainous regions like Caucasia. He drew nearer again to Ordzhonikidze, who helped him to set going a plan for growing subtropical crops in Georgia. In this way he diverted the attention of the central organs of the Party and so enabled himself to preserve the Georgian peasantry from complete destruction. The state farms saved the Caucasian peasantry from deportation to Siberia and the plan for subtropical crops furnished my father with a pretext for defending the existence of private plots of land. He pointed out that such crops required a high degree of technical skill which could not be acquired otherwise than by work on private plots.[28] Unfortunately, the peasants did not understand this policy. They did not appreciate that, by making them plant tobacco and orange trees in their gardens, my father was trying to protect their farms, and they resisted as hard as they could.

Georgia has always been opposed to serfdom. Collectivisation gave rise to riots, especially in eastern Georgia, in the vine-growing region. The organisers of these movements of revolt, who were usually survivors of the 1924 insurrection, were arrested afresh, and, once more, my father took steps to save them from execution by facilitating their flight abroad, as I was told later by Shariko Tsereteli, who himself organised their escape. My father gave them clearly to understand that the moment had not come to stir up trouble and that it was necessary to save the Georgian nation from destruction. He let them keep their lives but, in return, they had to cease agitation. Implicitly, however, his address to the Georgian national-ists conveyed the following message: preserve yourselves for a more favourable occasion. He was to say the same thing later to the Ukrainian nationalists. Calm prevailed in Georgia until 1939.

Later, during the war, when I was surprised that the Ukrainian nation-alists had criticised the collective farms, my father explained to me the reasons which had prompted him to act the way he did during the collec-tivisation wave of 1930. 'Towns,' he said, 'spread cosmopolitanism, whereas the peasantry is the bearer of national traditions and characteristics. To destroy the peasantry, Ukrainian and Georgian, means to destroy the nation.' He went on: 'In Georgia the situation was the same. After creating state farms in order to prevent the deportation of our peasants I encour-aged the existence of private plots on the pretext of favouring the cultivation of citrus fruits. By doing that I saved the peasants from complete ruin, even if I failed to save cattle-rearing. See,' he added, 'how intelligently the French have behaved in refusing to ruin their peasants. Despite the steamroller of capitalism, the peasants are still here and the French government tries to help them. That's the policy we should have followed'. My father authorised the formation of associations of vine-growers, inspired by the associations of the German vine-growers who had been established in Georgia since the 18th century.[29] My nanny Ella came from one of their villages and my father questioned her closely in this connection. He tried to implant this German model in Kakhetia, in the Georgian and Tatar collective farms, but had only a limited success. The Germans worked and did not steal: one could not say as much of the others.

At the head of the Transcaucasian Federation

In October 1931, when he became First Secretary of the Communist Party of Georgia, my father gave up all hope of leaving politics. Despite the reti-cence of my mother, who urged him to take leave for health reasons, he plunged into his new career. He emphasised the needs of the economy, leaving Marxism-Leninism to good-for-nothings. He applied himself to planting orange trees, draining the marshes of Colchis, building railways and houses and developing the oilfields. In short he strove to make the Transcaucasian republics self-sufficient. He noted the extent to which Russia exploited her colonies. The republics received only one hundredth of the value they exported. The central authorities arranged things so that none of them, not even the Ukraine, was able to produce a complete product. Each republic produced parts and Russia undertook to make the finished product. I remember how hard my father had to fight, later on, to get a missile factory built at Dnepropetrovsk, so as to provide the Ukraine with an aeronautical industry. Georgia he wanted to make self-sufficient, at least for the production of bread and of energy. Moscow refused, ordering that priority be given to the growing of mandarin oranges.

The Federation of Transcaucasia

In October 1932 my father was appointed First Secretary of the Party's regional committee for Transcaucasia. In December 1922, Armenia, Georgia and Azerbaijan had been cast into a common cauldron, a republic created from scratch – the Federated Soviet Socialist Republic of Transcaucasia – so as to get the three peoples to forget their roots and thereby hasten their integration into Russia.[30] Of the Transcaucasian Bolsheviks only the Armenians had been favourable to this idea. They doubtless counted on reigning as masters over their new territory, by utilising the substantial minorities of their people living in Georgia and Azerbaijan. My father had been against the Federation from its creation and when he became its head he lost no time in causing it to disappear.[31] He operated so well that he convinced the normally obtuse Politburo and achieved the result that, four years after his appointment, the three republics which had been merged were resuscitated. He always said to me that this story was particularly revealing of Bolshevik hypocrisy. The Federation's disappearance was bound to entail territorial disputes. To cut them short my father proposed to carry out some transfers of population. This idea was not opposed, but he was told that the moment to act had not been well chosen and the settlement of the question was put off till later. 'Bolshevik hypocrisy' which my father was often to come up against in subsequent years: they never said no to you but told you that such-and-such a measure was premature. This affair also showed that it was possible to manipulate Stalin. In fact, while the latter agreed to the dissolution of the Federation in April 1937, this was certainly not for the reasons that motivated my father. He intended already at that time to make use of the territorial demands of Georgia and Armenia upon Turkey, along with those of Azerbaijan on Iran, in order to turn them into springboards into the Middle East. My father, who knew of these projects of Stalin's, encouraged him in them in order to obtain what he wanted. He said to me later: 'It's only by using roundabout ways that one can get results and do something for one's people.'

My father's rise and his new responsibilities did not make everyone happy and evoked mixed feelings among the other Bolshevik leaders in Caucasia. He was only 32, and people envied him.[32] It seems to me, though, that the way my father acted at the head of the Federation provides a further argument against those who claim that he was nothing but a careerist. If that had been his nature he would, instead, have consolidated the Federation so as to make it his fief.[33]

My Childhood

My parents had registered me in a German school because they wanted me to learn foreign languages. My nanny, Ella, was German, as I have mentioned. She had lived with us since I was a small child and was fully integrated into our family circle. She was like a second mother to me. I think, though, that if there had been an English school in Tbilisi my parents would have preferred to send me there. However, the Germans were traditionally much better implanted in Georgia than were the British. Nevertheless, my mother made me start learning English very soon. I was literally overworked, going from piano lessons to sports sessions, to courses in English, history, mathematics, without being able to draw breath for a single minute.

My father's position did not affect my relations with my schoolmates in any way. I was no different from the other boys of my age. I got beaten like the others and took part in all the usual pranks. To be sure, I saw well enough that many of my comrades led a miserable life and that my own conditions were exceptional, but our bursar, a certain Princess Takashvili, explained to me that I was descended from a princely dynasty and had absolute right to all my privileges, and I accepted that explanation. My mother blamed her for this and forbade any specially favourable treatment for me. She made me grasp that inequality had been the cause of revolution under the old regime, and that the inequality which I could perceive beginning now would not remain without effects on the Soviet regime.

The 17th Congress in Moscow

My mother liked Stalin very much and we often spoke of him in our house. For us he was a hero. He had saved Georgia from the fate of the complete 'Turkisation' which Lenin had reserved for her.[34]

My father met Stalin for the first time when he came to spend a holiday beside the Black Sea. I don't know the date when they met, as my father never told me that, but, knowing Stalin, who never appointed anyone to a post of any importance without having first met him, we may assume that it was before 1926, the year when my father was made head of the G.P.U. in Georgia.[35] As for me, I made Stalin's acquaintance in January 1934, at the 17th Party Congress. This was a big event for me. I accompanied my parents to Moscow, where the congress was being held. I was ten years old and observed avidly all that went on around me. These images remain engraved in my memory. As a rule when my parents went to Moscow they stayed with Ordzhonikidze. He had been *en poste* in the Soviet capital since 1926 and since 1932 had been People's Commissar for Heavy Industry. Like all officials of his rank, my father was entitled to a room in the Hotel Select, but he preferred staying with Ordzhonikidze. This time, however, we were assigned a flat, which we kept until we were finally established in Moscow. Giving on to Troitskii Street, it had several rooms and I must admit that it was spacious for that time.

Hardly had we settled in than the head of the G.P.U., Yagoda, called on us. He was responsible for organising the material side of our stay in Moscow. He was a skinny little man with a pointed nose and lively eyes. He showed himself very assiduous on my father's behalf, as if, already at that time, the Chekists sensed that he would one day be appointed to Moscow. My father distrusted Yagoda and kept his distance from him. He had nothing in particular against the man and regarded him as a good specialist in counter-espionage, but he thought also that he had no ideas of his own and that he excelled, above all, in palace intrigues.

Kirov, too, came twice to visit us. When he saw me he gave me a kiss and remarked that I had grown. Turning to my mother he said, with a sigh: 'My biggest regret in life is never to have had children.' My mother explained to me later that Kirov's wife suffered from a mental illness. Kirov was of average height, with a robust constitution. He dined with us now and again. A very different person from Ordzhonikidze, who was able to listen to other people, he monopolised conversations so as to be the centre of attention at an evening party.

Ordzhonikidze came to see us, intending to install us in his *dacha*. He did not want my mother and me to have contact with 'all these skunks who hang about here.' In particular he detested Yagoda. Like Stalin he always wore a military-style jacket and riding boots. His kind eyes, grey hair and big moustache gave him the look of an old Georgian prince, trust-worthy and wise. His home was open to everyone. Though his wife was a foolish woman, she had looked after him when he was in exile and he made it a point of honour to remain faithful to her. His nobility of character was shown also in his treatment of his brother, a drunkard and skirt-chaser whose only interest was hunting. Regardless of the fact that this brother covered him with insults, Ordzhonikidze tried to help and protect him as much as he could.[36] It was this same aspect of his character that explains how it was that, unlike the other heads of ministries, he never signed an order for the arrest of one of his subordinates. Once, at lunch, Ordzhonikidze asked me what I liked. I talked to him of music and sport, and stood on my head before him. 'Do you cycle?' he asked. I said no. There were only German bicycles and I could not use them – in the pre-war period it was good form to belittle everything foreign, especially whatever was German and therefore 'fascist'. 'What,' he said, amazed, 'the Soviet Union doesn't produce bicycles for children!' We left the subject there but when he got back to his office Ordzhonikidze summoned the director of the ZIL factory in Kharkov and ordered him to set up, within less than a month, a production line for children's bicycles. That's what decisions depended on in our country in those days!

I liked Ordzhonikidze a lot, and all the more because I was told that he was ill. Besides, he had protected my father and loved my mother like his own daughter. On that theme a revealing fact comes back to me. One day in 1936, when my father had sent my mother to Moscow with the task of delivering some confidential letters to him, Ordzhonikidze became extremely angry. 'How could you have sent Nina to Moscow by herself, with such documents as these? What are you thinking of?' he burst out.

He was to kill himself three years later, on almost the very anniversary of our meeting in Moscow. The fact that he had committed suicide was kept from me for a long time and I learnt of it only after we had settled in Moscow.[37] However, there can be no doubt about it: Stalin really pushed Ordzhonikidze to that point. When he made him speak at the February 1937 Plenum he offered him the choice – which was no choice – between openly opposing Stalin or endorsing all of his abominations.[38] Ordzhonikidze did not resist that pressure. According to my father he was a weak man. But my father did not stint his efforts to help him. Thus, when Ordzhonikidze was worried about his dissolute brother it was my father whom he asked to look after him, and my father did that so well that Stalin remarked to him one day: 'I can't understand why Ordzhonikidze is so much against you when you do so much for him.'[39] To which my father replied: '*You* are not pleased with me, from what I hear, yet I carry out your orders to the letter.' Stalin was beside himself. 'You've got a damned cheek!' he said to my father – who hastened, next day, to report this conversation to Ordzhonikidze.

My first meeting with Stalin

Of the stay in Moscow I remember especially one evening party, and this for good reason: I was going to see Stalin in flesh and blood for the first time. It was at the end of the congress. Our Moscow hosts gathered one evening in our flat. Molotov, Kirov, Ordzhonikidze and the rest were in excellent humour. All of them, to my great surprise, congratulated my father. My mother had to explain to me later that he had just been elected to the Central Committee on Kirov's proposal. Everybody was laughing and congratulating each other. Eventually Stalin invited us to his *dacha*. We went first to the Kremlin. We settled down, me and Svetlana, Stalin's daughter, who was about the same age as me, in front of a cinema screen, to watch *The Three Little Pigs* and other animated cartoon films in colour, until the grown-ups rejoined us and we had to watch the film a second time along with them. Then we set off for Stalin's *dacha*.

He was wearing a coat lined with wolf's fur and a fur cap. It was winter.

Outside it was freezing hard and it was barely any warmer in the car. Sitting at the back, Stalin noticed that I was shivering in my little topcoat, so he opened his fur-lined coat and pulled me against him. That was how I made the whole journey, snuggled in his bosom. When we reached the *dacha* I saw a huge room furnished with a sofa, a big table groaning under the weight of the food arranged on it, and some deep armchairs. Stalin himself put me to bed. A polar-bear skin lay at the foot of the bed. The animal's jaw was open and this made a big impression on me. As soon as I was alone I got up quietly, dressed and went to spy on the grown-ups. They were at table and singing Georgian songs. The film director Chiaureli was among the guests. My mother told me – because, though I could see and hear I was not able to understand all that was said that evening – that the conversation concerned the production of films. Stalin maintained that revolutionary films were all very well but to them should be added an epic element and he spoke at length, in support of his view, about *The Lay of Igor's Host*[40] and *The Knight in the Tiger's Skin*[41] from which, according to him, the Soviet cinema should draw inspiration. Needless to say, everyone present couldn't care less!

Next day, Stalin's younger son, Vasya, took me to see his school. Four years older than I, he was very keen on sport. He kept making fun of me, being convinced that I didn't know Russian, only German. He had been told that I was at a German school, and he took umbrage at that. He suggested that we play volleyball and lent me a pair of shorts for the occasion. I was bashful when I realised that this garment reached to my knees. Looking back, it is amusing to think that these are my sole memories of the Seventeenth Congress.

Back in Tbilisi, my father began work on a book about the history of Bolshevism in Caucasia. The idea for this did not come to him spontaneously – in fact, it came from Stalin himself. The latter, speaking in the presence of Yaroslavsky, his future biographer, of Molotov and of other members of the Politburo, had complained about the publication of memoirs which distorted the role played by Lenin and other leaders in the history of the Bolshevik movement.[42] The Politburo ordered all the republics to correct these deviations and prepare texts which would emphasise the struggle waged by the true Leninists against the Mensheviks and the Trotskyists. Stalin was no novice in the rewriting of history, but he now wanted to sculpt his image as the Leader. This was an operation carried out in parallel with the physical destruction of the Old Bolsheviks which began in 1935. The Institutes of Marxism-Leninism in each republic were mobilised to undertake the necessary readjustments. The Marx-Engels Institute in Tbilisi, where there were some good historians, received, of course, like the others, an order to produce documents authenticating the official version. It was a question of showing events 'in the correct light.' A very worthy man, Bedia, a Mingrelian from my mother's village, was chosen to perform this task.

I remember that period very well. The researchers from the Institute assembled at our place in the evening and discussed until late in the night while my mother served them tea. Sometimes my father and Bedia were puzzled and stumbled over facts that could hardly be reconciled with the account that Stalin wanted. After two or three weeks my father was at least able to read the text that emerged from this work before the Georgian Central Committee, at a meeting held in Tbilisi opera house. The Central Committee approved the text and Stalin expressed his satisfaction with this account which proved that he had played a distinguished role in the Bolshevik movement in Caucasia. Not everyone, however, shared that view. My father was blamed for having allegedly exaggerated Stalin's role, for purely careerist reasons. He considered that Stalin had indeed played an important part in the establishment of Bolshevism in the Caucasus, and he defended himself: 'Let those refute me who want to,' he said. 'Let them quote facts.' Nobody did this. All the documents referred to were authentic: only their interpretation was tendentious.[43]

My father was not at all anxious to sign this work, of which he was not particularly proud, but Moscow ordered him to do that. It was usual, in fact, for reports of this sort to be signed by the First Secretary. However, it does seem to me, from what I heard from my mother, that the editing of this book marked a new stage in my father's development. His admiration for Stalin declined. The manuscript had been submitted to Stalin so that he could amend it to his liking. My father was taken aback by the 'adjustments' that Stalin had insisted on, striking out names and replacing them with his own, not hesitating to claim for himself revolutionary exploits accomplished by others. He considered, too, that Stalin went too far when he tried to show that Bolshevism had not truly taken shape until the Prague Conference in 1912, when he had been co-opted to the Central Committee. 'He wants to be the founder of Bolshevism as well,' my father sarcastically remarked.

He foresaw that this presentation of history would arouse objections and he warned Stalin of this. The latter turned a deaf ear and, as was bound to happen, a torrent of indignant letters descended on his desk. Stalin then began to take against the witnesses. Budu Mdivani, who had played an active role in the Sovietisation of Georgia, was sent to prison because he refused to shut up. According to my mother he had accused Stalin of getting rid of the Old Bolsheviks after getting them to 'do the dirty work.' Faced with this criticism Stalin had laughed: 'We all did dirty work for the revolution,' was all he said in reply. My father respected Mdivani and his plain speaking: he perished in 1937. Another Old Bolshevik, the unfortunate Filip Makharadze, now a decrepit old man, was covered with insults. My father considered these campaigns pointless. 'Instead of persecuting them, it would have been more worthwhile to increase the pensions of these veterans and build them heated lavatories: then they would all have chorused Stalin's praises.'

The most comical thing in this entire story was that my father himself was denounced by the researchers of Georgia's Marx-Engels Institute. They accused him of having understated Stalin's role! Bedia and the rest had been so terrorised that they decided to write to the Central Committee pointing out that my father had failed to mention a series of documents which high-lighted the eminent role played by Stalin during the Prague conference. My father was not worried, but when the book was published Stalin sent for him and ordered him to add a note on the documents he had omitted to discuss.[44]

It was in connection with this work in the archives that my father began to study the character and conduct of Stalin. As he possessed intu-ition he very soon analysed certain features of Stalin's psychology even before he came to know him intimately. He began to foresee his reactions and understand what would attract his attention.

My achievement, as a militant atheist

At this time I was a Pioneer and belonged to a group of 'militant atheists'. We had noticed the Lutheran church near our school. One day, armed with inkwells, we set out to bombard it. This affair reached the ears of our headmaster, who called in the pastor. The latter, however, instead of getting angry, took us into his church and said: 'The church is not only a place for prayer' and, while making us listen to the organ, he explained what it meant. This man impressed me. He did not punish us but simply caused us to feel shame for what we had done. Intelligent people always know how to influence children. After this episode I often called on him. He never tried to convert me but merely sought to make me understand things which were remote from me. My nanny Ella, who was a Protestant, was delighted with my new association and told me, many years later, that my father had, on the pretext of equipping a sports centre, given a subsidy to our school, and the Lutheran church had been restored.

My second anti-religious exploit was carried out in the very midst of my own family. My paternal grandmother, Marta, was pious and a regular churchgoer. She had had me baptised secretly, but all Tbilisi knew of this. One day, when I had just come home from school, I went up to her icon, grabbed it and broke it. When my grandmother found the fragments she collapsed in distress. My father had arrived meanwhile. 'What's going on?' he growled when he saw his mother in this state. She said nothing. I then came forward and said that I had broken the icon. My father did not reply. He simply sat my mother on a chair, drew her portrait (he drew very well), placed it in the frame where had been enthroned the Madonna whom I had cast down to the ground and gave it to my grandmother, who hung it on the wall. Then he took me aside. 'You love your grandmother. She has faith. You who are so smart, you don't believe. Why do you want to impose your views on her by force?'

About the same time, during the summer of 1935, Stalin wanted to visit his mother in Tbilisi. My father had stayed in the capital and sent my mother and me on holiday beside the Black Sea. When he heard the news he at once rang my mother to ask her to come back to Tbilisi as soon as possible. It was all bustle in our house when Stalin arrived. Seeing my mother he exclaimed: 'Nina, what are you doing here? Why aren't you at the seaside?' He had forbidden my father to warn his family that he was coming. Turning towards my father, he reprimanded him sharply. 'When I give an order it must be obeyed to the letter,' he said coldly. Then, without any transition, he was once again extremely amiable, as he could be when he chose. He went into the kitchen to congratulate the cook, my grand-mother, who had not yet showed herself, and made her sit at the table. Stalin spotted me, crouched in a corner, and devouring him with my eyes. 'Well now! An old acquaintance,' he said, with a big smile. 'Come here.' He had forgotten that I had already met Svetlana and Vasya and began to tell me about his children. 'I have three children,' he said in Georgian. 'One of my sons is as tall as your mother and my daughter is the same age as you. You must meet her. I'll send her here.' He sat me beside him. I was as proud as could be. All the boys in the block knew that Stalin had called on us. After he left, every time we met they gathered round me and bombarded me with questions: 'What's he like? Did you touch him? What did he say to you?' At that time Stalin was a god for most children.

Ekaterina Dzhugashvili

Stalin's mother lived in Tbilisi. She had been installed in the palace of the Tsarist governor Vorontsov – in the servants' quarters, it is true. All the same, her rooms were comfortable and the palace was surrounded by a vast garden in which she could walk whenever she liked.

Stalin did not love his mother. He introduced his children to her only when Vasya, the eldest, was 15 and Svetlana, the youngest, was 10. And yet they spent their holidays in Georgia! My mother tried hard to get them to meet their grandmother, but her efforts never succeeded. Besides, the old lady did not speak Russian and they knew not a single word of Georgian. Ekaterina Dzhugashvili, unlike my grandmother Marta, was not devout. On the contrary, she had views that were progressive for that period, and never hesitated to voice her opinion on everything, although she was uneducated. She sometimes ventured into political considerations. For example, she said: 'I wonder why my son was not able to share power with Trotsky?' She was extremely sociable and lively, even in her old age. My grandmother Marta visited her from time to time, to make adjust-ments to her clothes. She was distressed by Ekaterina's lack of piety. One day, when she had exhorted her friend to pray to God, pleading for mercy for the sins of their respective sons, Ekaterina laughed in her face. Though sick at heart, my grandmother nevertheless continued to visit her.

Ekaterina adored my mother, who called on her once or twice every week, doubtless at my father's instigation. The old lady mildly reproached her for wasting her youth looking after a husband and a family, and studying. 'Why don't you take a lover?' she asked. 'You are too young to shiver at home! Don't be a goose. If you like, I'll introduce you to some young men. When I was young I cleaned house for people and when I came upon a good-looking boy I didn't waste the opportunity. Yet I was less beautiful than you.' She even went so far as to blame my grandmother for 'keeping Nina under lock and key and forbidding her to show her nose outside.' My grandmother took offence. She thereafter ceased to call on her as she had nothing to say to her. Ekaterina was interested only in sexual affairs and gossip.

Everyone knew that her husband Dzhugashvili drank and beat her because of her way of life. He had ruined himself and she had been obliged to go out cleaning, but the money she brought home did not always come from domestic work. In the evenings little Stalin witnessed scenes in which his parents fought each other, with his drunken father beating his mother. Eventually the man left his family. My parents were convinced that Stalin had been marked by his childhood. My father even alleged that Dzhugashvili, who was a shoemaker, was not Stalin's father. He would often say that Stalin must have Persian blood – he readily compared him to Shah Abbas.[45] Stalin's perfidy was not Georgian, he maintained.

Ekaterina Dzhugashhvili liked to recall her son's childhood. He was a puny boy who suffered for his physical weakness. All through his childhood years he had cherished the dream of swimming across the river Kura like his friends who were stronger. In that connection I remember a significant anecdote. We had been invited to Stalin's *dacha* beside the sea. The wind had risen that day. My father and I plunged into the rough waves. We were both good swimmers and loved to roll in the surf. We had paid no attention to Stalin, who was seated at some distance from us and was shouting, trying to dissuade us from swimming in this wild sea. 'Come out, come out,' he bawled. When, at last, exhausted and delighted, we left the water, I saw Stalin rush at my father. 'How can you risk the boy's life like that', he thundered. It was plain to see that he was furious and not joking. I realised that Stalin hated anything that might remind him of his physical weakness. For instance, he could not allow anyone to mention the fact that he had been exempted from military service in the Tsar's army. When, in 1944, his sister-in-law Allilueva was so imprudent as to mention this matter in her memoirs, my father sniggered: 'Poor woman, it wasn't enough for her to be married to Redens,[46] now she has to go and remind people of the Generalissimo's physical defects!'

Stalin did not attend his mother's funeral in 1937. He was too deeply absorbed by the political struggle to be able to leave Moscow. Later, though, he asked my parents about his mother's last days, as if he felt guilty. That, at least, was how my mother interpreted it. But he may well have been putting on an act.

First attempts on my father's life

My father's appointment as Party Secretary for the Transcaucasian Federation had offended many people's susceptibilities. In 1936, Yezhov took the place of Yagoda. Like Yagoda, he saw my father as a rival. Using a tried and tested method, he built up dossiers of evidence against him.[47] They always tried to discredit an adversary by beginning with his entourage. Later, my father obtained access to the records of the interrogation of some of the accused. They were forced to bear witness against him. They had to say that Beria was an enemy of the regime, that he had written his book in order to create a smokescreen. In 1937 the Second Secretary of the Georgian Central Committee, Kudryavtsev, was transferred to the Ukraine, arrested and tortured, for one purpose only – to extort from him something that could be used against Beria. He died without confessing anything.

The Kekelia affair took place about the same time. My father thought well of this man, a fellow Mingrelian. He had been nicknamed 'Fouché' because of his bent for intrigues. Although Kekelia participated in the activity of groups hostile to the Party my father had made him Third Secretary of the Georgian Party's Central Committee, merely enjoining him and his friends to keep a low profile and put an end to their schoolboy plotting until better times should come. When Kekelia was arrested it gave my father a shock.[48] Kekelia refused to testify against my father and was shot.

The attempt to destabilise my father failed and his enemies resolved at last to go for a radical solution, namely, his physical elimination. I personally witnessed two attempts on his life, but there were others.[49] The first took place when Lakoba was still alive, in or about 1935.

Nestor Lakoba

He was an Old Bolshevik, a member of the Central Committee of the Georgian Communist Party and head of the government of the Abkhazian autonomous region. Of elegant aspect and average height, he had refined features, a high brow and black eyes. Unlike many Communist functionaries, he took care of his person. People still don't know that Lakoba detested the Soviet regime, in which he saw the vehicle of Russian penetration.[50] He 'worked on' my father to get him to slow down and restrict so far as possible the expansion of Russia into Georgia and Abkhazia. Consequently, he was opposed to the building of a railway along the Black Sea coast because for him this meant 'opening the gates to Russia.' He was also against the building of roads over the passes of the Caucasus and he did not want there to be a tunnel linking North Osetia with South Osetia, fearing that Abkhazia and Georgia might become 'a holiday resort for Russians.' And he did whatever he could to scupper these projects. Lakoba had decided to obtain the support of my mother, being convinced that she had great influence on her spouse. As she herself told me, he confided in her when he saw the opportunity during our annual holiday in Abkhazia. 'Nina, you don't know the Russians. You've never lived in Russia, but I had that experience before the revolution. They feel at home everywhere and invade everything like locusts. Try to make your husband understand that he is committing immense folly in making himself a tool of their policy.'

'But how can one resist, in conditions such as ours?' my mother asked.

'By all and every means. It is useless to try for an open confrontation. Things have to be dragged out as long as possible and one must obey only when the knife is at one's throat.'

My father did not remain deaf to the advice of this older man, even if it seemed to him impossible, for the time being, to stand up against Russia, and he also considered that economic links between the two countries were vital for Georgia. All that could be done, as he saw it, was to restrict Russian immigration. 'We form part of a Russian grouping,' he argued with Lakoba. 'I cannot follow you when you favour an orientation upon Turkey. Don't forget that the Abkhazians became Christians after their incorporation into Georgia.' Lakoba distrusted Stalin no less than the Russians. 'Don't deceive yourself. He may be a Georgian,' he explained to my father, 'but he's a Russian Tsar, and more dangerous still because he has more power.' Later, when Stalin, faithful to his usual tactic, tried to set Lakoba against my father, he did fall for it. He went to see my father and told him everything. The two men decided that thenceforth they would co-ordinate their actions and keep each other informed of Stalin's intrigues.[51] Even though my father did not share all of Lakoba's views, he did not betray him. The Russian group among the functionaries in the apparatus of the Central Committee of the USSR who agitated behind the scenes, intriguing against Lakoba and my father alike, were convinced that Lakoba was against the attachment of Abkhazia to Georgia and that he cherished sympathies with Turkey. He had indeed formed a number of links with that country, and he also felt a certain fondness for Germany. He had reasons for this: his wife was Turkish and his brother-in-law had studied in Turkey and Germany. Unlike, however, the Abkhaz nationalists of today, Lakoba approved of the union of Abkhazia with Georgia. Or, rather, what mattered for him was the independence of Georgia and Abkhazia from Moscow. The status of Abkhazia came second in his concerns. For my part, I am sure that Lakoba did not organise a separatist trend in Abkhazia but, on the contrary, collaborated with my father in seeking to avoid clashes on this issue.

Apart from these political intrigues, Nestor Lakoba became accidentally mixed up in an affair which was particularly revealing of the corruption that prevailed in Moscow, namely the death in his house of the daughter of People's Commissar for Trade Rosengolz. She had been shot. Lakoba's wife gave this version of the facts to my mother. 'Nina, you need to keep away from these Russian women as from the plague. They turn their charm on you, settle down in your home, sleep with your husband and, on top of everything, play dirty tricks on you. Look at what's happened to me through that slut, that drunkard, that junky (in those days only Muscovites could get drugs). I invite her to our *dacha* and, believing her to be of good family, I go off to visit my sick son in Sukhumi, where I stay for a fortnight. During this time my stone-deaf husband (Lakoba was hard of hearing) takes the opportunity to go to bed with her. And there, one day when she is on drugs, she kills herself with Nestor's revolver!' God knows what actually happened. But it was well known that Rosengolz's daughter drank and took drugs.[52]

On the shore of Lake Ritsa

One day Stalin wanted to see Lake Ritsa. This was a wonderful place in the mountains of Abkhazia, but there was no practicable way to get there. Stalin decided to have an approach road laid and a *dacha* built by the lake. 'The Tsar built palaces, Stalin could do no less than they did,' said my father, ironically. The decision angered Lakoba, but he had to carry it out.

One summer we decided – Lakoba and his family, my parents and I – to travel on horseback to Lake Ritsa and see how the works were going. On arrival we pitched tents for the night. Lakoba's and ours were both at the edge of the lake. We were in excellent spirits. A fire was lit, and while the grown-ups chatted together I went to lie down in our tent. Suddenly my mother woke me and took me into Lakoba's tent. Everybody was asleep when, a few hours later, a series of shots rang out. We rushed outside to see what had happened, and found that the tent in which we were supposed to be sleeping was riddled with bullets, turned into a colander. Lakoba had been told by Abkhazian nationalists that an attempt on my father's life was being prepared, and had proved his loyalty by saving him.[53] After this experience my father was never without his Thompson submachine-gun. He liked weapons and knew how to use them. To tell the truth, he felt safer with his tommy-gun than when he was surrounded by bodyguards. He never went about with a personal guard, preferring to rely on his two drivers, Russian soldiers who had chosen to remain in Georgia and enter his service.

Lakoba's death

Before continuing I should like to describe the circumstances of Lakoba's death on 27 December 1936. My mother has been accused of poisoning him. That's stupid. The facts are quite different. At the time Lakoba was very ill. He had problems with his blood and took anti-coagulants. 'It's not blood but urine that circulates in my veins', he used to say, jokingly. When his state of health got worse he even had to go to Germany for treatment, as many Communist dignitaries did at that time. During a plenum of the Georgian Central Committee, convened on Stalin's initiative, the 'errors' of Lakoba had been severely criticised. He was then summoned to Moscow to explain himself to Stalin. He was to be accompanied by his assistants and by my father. We feared the worst. It was in this atmosphere of crisis that Lakoba called on us. He came to consult my father, hoping that, with his help, he could ward off the attacks. Some time after his visit he had a bad turn and died.[54] My father telephoned Moscow to ask for Stalin's permission to prevent the charges brought against Lakoba at the plenum from becoming public, and also to bury the Abkhazian leader with honour. His requests were granted and Lakoba was buried at Sukhumi. After Lakoba's death my father took charge of his family.

A little later a commission from the Moscow NKVD arrived in Tbilisi. My father was accused of protecting and encouraging Abkhazian separatists and nationalists.[55] My father wrote to Ordzhonikidze to warn him against returning to the Tsar's policy of setting the Abkhazians and the Mingrelians against the Georgians.[56] Ordzhonikidze backed my father, but Stalin was unwilling to listen and sent a Central Committee commission to Abkhazia to carry out an investigation of Abkhazian separatism. When autumn 1937 came, Stalin ordered the arrest of Lakoba's entire family, together with the leaders of Abkhazia.[57] My father tried to save Lakoba's son, taking steps to stop his deportation to Russia. But his efforts were in vain and the young man was executed during the war. Yet I am not too sure about that, as I remember that, during that period, Serov evacuated the prisons of Abkhazia (it was feared that Germany might invade the province) and transferred the prisoners to Poti. It is therefore not clear whether Lakoba's son was actually executed in 1942. The purges affected not only the Abkhazians but also the Mingrelians. This affair was linked with that of Mikeladze, a friend of my father's youth who had formerly been accused of making a terrorist attempt on Stalin's life when, from carelessness, he fired on the boat in which the latter was travelling.[58] My father had confined himself to dismissing Mikeladze and then getting him a job of subordinate rank. Mikeladze was eventually arrested and was promised his life in exchange for statements that would incriminate the late Lakoba and my father. He probably refused to say anything against my father, since the latter arranged for my mother to help Mikoladze's wife after his execution.

The clouds gather

The second attempt to kill my father was in 1937, organised by Yezhov who used his men in Georgia, particularly Kiladze, the head of the Georgian Cheka. My father was returning from Moscow by train, along with my mother. His two drivers came by car to meet them at Mozdok, in the Kuban. I was with them. On our way home we formed a little two-car convoy. We were in the first car, with my father in front, on the driver's right. My mother was on the back seat with, on her right, the Second Secretary of the Party, Khatskevich, a Byelorussian who wore pince-nez like my father. I was seated between these two. In the other car, following us, were Kiladze's wife and an official of the Tbilisi municipality. I was asleep when a violent braking of the car woke me with a start. The road was blocked by a tree-trunk, and this had forced the driver to pull up sharply. It was then that I heard the shots. The windows were shattered. Khatskevich cried out: he had been struck by two bullets. Fortunately the driver did not lose his head. He accelerated and drove hard at the men armed with rifles, managing to get through the ambush. We stopped 200 metres further on. My father and the men in the second car, who were armed, rushed out and went to the place where the attack had been made. I stayed in the car, covered with Khatskevich's blood. I heard an exchange of fire, then saw my father return. We drove on to the nearest village from where we could call for help. Two surgeons were sent. An hour later they were bending over poor Khatskevich. They succeeded in extracting the bullets but could not save his life, as these bullets were of the sort that fragment. Khatskevich died two days later. The assassins managed to find refuge in Turkey, from where they went to Paris. One of them had been seriously wounded in the scrimmage, and it was possible to establish his identity before he breathed his last. Although the investigation was entrusted to Kiladze, the organiser of the attack, my father managed to discover, in time and thanks to his networks among the Georgian *émigrés*, who the fugitives were. These newcomers from Georgia did not remain unnoticed in France. But my father did not let himself be deceived, and did not believe for one moment that *émigré* circles were involved in this affair. He knew precisely where the blow had come from. In Moscow he eventually identified the Russians who were mixed up in the affair. Kiladze was quickly unmasked, and then denounced by his wife, who took revenge in this way for his infidelity. However, he had time to note down the men who were close to my father and point them out to Yezhov, who ordered their arrest. Yezhov put the entire responsibility for the affair on Kiladze and lost no time in having him shot.

The purges of 1937: a family crisis

Early in 1937 a wave of arrests swept over the country.[59] The central government by-passed the local authorities in order to organise the repression more effectively,[60] and these bodies looked on helplessly as events unfolded.[61]

My friends' parents disappeared. My father's entourage, his family and my mother's family were decimated. Two of her cousins and two of her nephews disappeared at this time. On of them, who was a doctor, acted as an informer for my father through his contacts with the Mensheviks in France. He had confidence in my father and knew that he would never betray him. He was kidnapped, however, on French territory and nothing could be done for him.

I remember, too, Golublishvili, an old Bolshevik who had been put at the head of the Georgian Government. He was tall and lean and dressed with distinction. He spoke English and German. My father had much respect for him, appreciating his culture and erudition. This Georgian nationalist knew Russia well. Golublishvili expected to be arrested one day or another and was never without his revolver.[62] Even when he came to dinner with us he kept it on him. My father remarked to him one day: 'When you come to us you can leave your revolver at home. Nobody's going to arrest you here.' Golublishvili laughed and said: 'I always have good reason to carry a weapon.' Bedia, too, was shot.

The Georgian intelligentsia was exterminated. It must be realised that the Georgians were not numerous and that their intellectuals could be counted on one's fingers.[63] Liquidating twenty or thirty poets amounted to eliminating *all* the country's poets. My mother had many friends among these intellectuals and she was angry when she saw them disappearing one after the other. She found this harder and harder to bear and began to make scenes with my father because he was not preventing these repressions. I was present at some of these quarrels, the significance of which I did not grasp. My mother accused my father: 'You are the First Secretary, aren't you? How can you allow these men to be attacked? Aren't you the master here? Are you just Russia's tool?' Replying to these reproaches, my father pointed out that he tried to resist by invoking the official slogans put forward by the regime, particularly stressing that the economy would suffer as a result of the extermination of cadres.[64] He defended himself by saying that he had managed to save several people, including the writer Gamsakhurdia. But my mother would not be convinced. She even considered divorcing my father, and for reasons other than his extra-marital escapades. One day she said to me in a serious tone: 'Sergo, I can't stay with your father while he lets all these arrests go on. We shall separate'. My father was present and reacted thus: 'I don't want to contradict your mother, but she is mistaken. I do everything in my power. Decide.' I burst into tears. My grandmother Marta tried to comfort me: 'Don't cry. God will not let them separate.' My mother never revealed why, in the end, she stayed with my father. When, later I asked her about it she replied: 'I realised that I should be betraying him if I left him.'

This affair had a deeply traumatic effect on me, to the extent that I was ill for two or three weeks. I had the impression that I was personally guilty. I found it very hard to get to sleep, and when I did I suffered from frightful nightmares. Some of these were premonitory. My mother had explained to me that some people wanted to kill my father because they held him responsible for the bloodshed in Georgia. I dreamt that he had been assassinated, falling riddled with bullets. This family drama marked me forever. Although life in Moscow did mitigate the shock, I have always retained a sort of inward anxiety. It may, however, be that this anxiety reflected the perpetual anguish that held my mother in its grip. My paternal grandmother was also much affected. She said nothing to her son but redoubled her piety, praying fervently for divine mercy.

Cultural efforts

My father could not do much, overtly at least. And yet, paradoxical as this may be, he really did try to slow down repressions.[65] But the men on whom he relied, those who implemented his policy, were eliminated, and the basis for any independent national existence on the part of the Caucasian republics was destroyed.[66]

The February 1937 Plenum, which unleashed the paroxysm of the purges, gave a fresh impulse to Georgian nationalism.[67] Those Georgian Communists who had wagered on a Moscow-oriented policy understood they had been mistaken. In three-quarters of the schools in Tbilisi, where teaching had hitherto been conducted in Russian, Armenian or Azeri, the Georgian language was made obligatory. My father closed the Russian schools in the villages so as to dissuade the Georgian peasants from sending their children there. On the other hand, the teaching of Russian was made obligatory in the Georgian schools from the first year.[68] In the universities, as I heard from students, he took steps to de-Russify the teaching of history and philosophy by encouraging study of the ancient history and architecture of Georgia. He sought and obtained subsidies for the restoration of churches. My father could not act openly but had to find roundabout means to achieve his ends. Hence the characteristic tale of the folklore groups. Until this time it was enough for someone to hum a Georgian air for him to be immediately accused of being a spy for the British. But Stalin liked Georgian songs and my father turned this to his advantage. He created folklore groups, in the shadow of which choirs could be developed, and it thus became possible to sing in Georgian without being accused of a 'nationalist deviation'.

Though he was very fond of his native Mingrelia my father never encouraged separatism or particularism in Georgia, which he regarded as extremely dangerous. With a population of four million, decimated by successive invasions, Georgia could not permit herself that luxury. It was at this time too that my father prohibited publications in Mingrelian. His fellow Mingrelians held this very much against him. They did not appreciate the danger that separatism could bring upon the nation when outside forces chose to play upon it. My father's aim was to form a young generation of Georgians who would be physically strong and intellectually well-developed. He encouraged the practice of sport and physical culture, inspired by the example of England. Not a smoker himself, he strove to combat the use of tobacco in Georgia.

Applying the principle which had enabled him to authorise the folklore groups, my father proposed to Stalin that festivals be organised during which each republic would be able to present its cultural achievements. Officially, the point would be to illustrate the beneficent influence exercised by Russian culture on the cultures of the other peoples of the USSR. The true purpose was actually to preserve a minimum of the nations' cultural patrimony. Stalin took up this idea and presented it as his own. The first of these festivals, organised in Moscow, took place in early 1937, and it was the one devoted to Georgia.

My mother always laughed when she recalled my father's artistic activities. When one day they were listening together to a record of organ music my father remarked to her: 'This reminds me of the Georgian church choirs. What a pity there aren't organs in the churches here.' Then, pensively, he added: 'Perhaps I ought to think about that?' My mother trembled. 'That's all you needed! You are already mixing yourself up with the ballet and the theatre – that should be enough.' She was alluding to something which had happened during the preparation of the festival. For the purpose of 'demonstrating its cultural achievements' Georgia planned to present a ballet. The music was beautiful and the dancers excellent. The first act showed collective farmers happily living in their orange plantations. The second act saw the appearance of wicked imperialists who created in the marshes of Colchis a centre of subversion aimed at sabotaging the paradisial life of the collective farmers. In the third act everything was sorted out. The spies were unmasked and captured. Such themes were very fashionable. At that time such crazy productions were common, so general was the psychosis. However, my father could not control himself. 'This ballet must be changed,' he told the director. 'Keep the music but get rid of the spies. Besides, it's pointless to make your dancers cultivate oranges.'

'But, Lavrenti Pavlovich, what will be left?' the poor man asked.

'Leave the dances and change the story.' The ballet was altered as he suggested and had great success in Moscow.

His involvement in the country's artistic activity was not to stop there. When he settled in Moscow he was appointed a member of the commission which awarded Stalin Prizes for absolutely indigestible works of literature. Few were the members of the commission who possessed sufficient endurance to read these books. My father knew this and took advantage of it to indulge his facetious temperament, just 'to pass the time,' as he liked to say. He would buttonhole his wretched colleagues who, he knew, had not read any of the books and ask them: 'What do you think of such-and-such passage in so-and-so's book?' The poor fellow would shift uneasily, confused as to how to reply. 'You would have died of laughter,' my father would say when he told us of his little bit of fun. But the joke did not last long. The members of the commission, having been scolded, began to read the works that were submitted for their judgement. When my father noticed this he was amused. 'These people who decide what should be published have only to read the books put before them. Well, at least, they should decide on the basis of knowledge.' The writer Fadeev, who presided over the commission, tried to defend his colleagues. 'Put yourself in their place. It's impossible to stuff oneself with all that shit.' My father told me of this conversation and commented: 'That's the first intelligent thing I've heard Fadeev say.'

The transfers of populations

Just as he sought to protect Georgian culture, so my father sought to oppose the implanting of Russian populations in Caucasia. From the start the Bolshevik regime had tried to carry out extensive transfers of Russians into the Union republics. My father saw in these endeavours a policy aimed at destroying the nations. Between 1937 and 1938 he installed Mingrelian highlanders along the shore of the Black Sea. Russians, mostly de-kulakised Cossacks from Krasnodar and Stavropol, were actively colonising this region and it was necessary to restore the balance. My father did not want a situation wherein the Georgians were all concentrated in the mountains, where land was scarce, while the Russians occupied the plains. He justified these measures by means of economic arguments. He established in those coastal regions state farms for the growing of tea, vines and citrus fruits, all crops which required care and competence and justified a return to individual farm organisation without passing through the 'collective' stage. My mother was delighted with these measures. My father also favoured the building of factories, so long as these undertook to employ Georgians and Abkhazians. After the war he arranged for Georgians to study engineering in Russia and the Ukraine, so as to avoid the importation of Russian specialists into Georgia. He wanted to save Georgia from the situation that prevailed in Central Asia. Later, when he was established in Moscow and had a freer hand, he did the same for the other republics of the USSR. He completed this policy by another measure: he encouraged the rich Armenians of the diaspora to return to their country in order to establish enterprises, and this despite opposition from Armenian Communists. These repatriated Armenians introduced French technology. My father even wanted to use their capital to strengthen the Caucasian republics (the Armenians, though nationalists, showed themselves quite willing to help the whole region), just as, later, he planned to appeal for Jewish capital. The leader of the Armenian Communist Party, Khandzhian, supported this policy and was blamed for it.

My father's international networks

In the sphere of foreign policy my father very soon became interested in Turkey and France. It was in those countries that he formed networks of agents in the 1920s and 1930s. In Turkey he had agents among the Lazes,[69] while in France he made use of the Georgian Menshevik *émigrés*, whom he prided himself on controlling. 'It's thanks to me that they are still alive. Otherwise they would have been shot down like partridges,' he said. One of Sasha's nephews was among his go-betweens with the Mensheviks. He always came to see us when he returned from his trips abroad. I remember hearing him pass on to my mother an invitation from Evgeni Gegechkori, who proposed that she come and stay with him in Paris. This nephew perished later in the purges, on account of his visits to France. It was in this period, too, that my father concerned himself with Britain, which had been very active in Caucasia in the days when the Caucasian republics were independent. He had networks in France, in Britain and in America and recruited many agents among the Russian princes and princesses in emigration. These people collaborated willingly with him, not through fondness for Bolshevism or from greed but out of patriotism – for the Georgians, love of Georgia, for the Russians, love of Russia.

I have retained some memories of the discussions we had in our family about foreign policy during the period 1936-1939. My parents did not doubt that Germany was an aggressive and dangerous power. Before we went to live in Moscow my father tended to overestimate the importance of the alliance between Germany and Italy, because he was influenced by British sources. The British felt more threatened by Italian claims in the Mediterranean than by Germany's eastward ambitions. My father was convinced that Germany and Italy would plunge together into colonial adventures in Africa. When my mother expressed surprise at the stir caused by Mussolini's war against Abyssinia, he explained that 'the German jackboot is behind it.' Then he added: 'Don't underestimate Abyssinia. Don't forget that Russia's greatest poet was an Abyssinian.'[70] (When somebody enthused before my father about the greatness of Russian culture, he never failed to say: 'We should, like the Russians, learn how to borrow from the Abyssinians and the Scots the best they can offer.')[71] In that connection I recall a diplomatic incident that was mentioned in the family. Stalin had insulted the Negus by referring to him as an example of African obscurantism. The Negus wrote him a letter to tell him that he had a degree from a British university, and, furthermore, was at war with Mussolini. Stalin was somewhat embarrassed by this.

My father had long been interested in Spain because of the Basques, who, he thought, had a common origin with the Mingrelians. In his youth he had dreamed of creating a series of bases around the world, to be linked by a well-developed navy. Among these potential bases he included the Laz region in Turkey and an independent Basque country (later, also Israel). That was why he showed a lively interest in Basque separatism. He was very fond of the Spaniards and greatly regretted the victory of Franco in 1939. He blamed Stalin for betraying Spain, considering that the Soviet Union could have brought much more vigorous pressure to bear on Britain and France to ensure that they imposed respect for the non-intervention agreement of August 1936. At the outset Stalin did not want to do anything in Spain as he believed that France and Britain would be able to prevent the victory of Fascism. My father also wondered why the British had not supported the Spanish republicans, since they had every interest in preventing the expansion of Italy and Germany into Spain. Germany and Italy had sent many troops. France and Britain acted as though neutral and blocked the approaches, and the Soviet Union alone sent arms via the Black Sea.[72] I know this from Admiral Kuznetsov, whom my father met at this time. He commanded a cruiser which escorted the convoys. According to my father Stalin was wrong to poke his nose into Spain and would have done better to concern himself with our frontiers with Turkey, as he thought the moment was propitious for bringing pressure on the Turks and recovering the Caucasian lands lost at Brest-Litovsk.

Stalin confided to my father the task of creating a network in Spain when my father was still in Georgia. He was to infiltrate his agents through France, where they were already well implanted. Later I often heard my father say: 'I've known that man since the Spanish war.' He recruited a number of Spaniards and sent them everywhere in Europe and America. He knew the Spanish Communist leader José Diaz, who died in 1942 in the USSR. The Spanish war enabled my father to expand his network, which previously had been confined to the Georgian Mensheviks in France and to go beyond the purely Georgian limits of his activity abroad.

My last summer in Tbilisi

In 1938, a little before we came to Moscow my father had me moved from the German school, which had been obliged to close, to a Russian and then a Georgian school. When summer came a former grammar-school teacher of my mother's, who had been educated under the old regime and hated the Russians, was invited to come and live with us so as to prepare me for schooling in Georgian. He taught me the literary language, while my mother made me read the writings of Lermontov and Tolstoy, which gave a picture of the Russians' war in the Caucasus. My mother also asked the philosopher Notsubidze to give me private lessons for two hours each day. This teacher helped me discover the Greek myths and their similarities with the Georgian myths and then told me of the beginnings of Christianity in Georgia. For my parents the purpose of these lessons was to prepare me for the new school year. They did not know that they were going to leave home and go to Moscow.

The NKVD

Our arrival in Moscow

My father did not want to leave Georgia and become Number Two in the NKVD.[1] He was aware that this was a job in which one did not make old bones. 'You last for two years, then you go down the chute,' he said to my mother, gloomily, when he was still hoping to escape from this ordeal. One had to be totally stupid not to take account of the precedents. The fate awaiting Yezhov, the current head of the NKVD, could be foreseen. Before his appointment became effective my father tried to find loopholes. 'It's not good that a non-Russian should be at the head of the NKVD,' he argued, especially with Stalin. But nothing was any use. Stalin assured him that he would act temporarily as Yezhov's deputy and then, when things were going better, he would get another job. Stalin had decided to give up the policy of repression and wanted to appear as the initiator of this turn. A young Georgian, seemingly easy to manipulate, a tried and tested Stalinist who had shown reticence regarding the repressions,[2] seemed the ideal candidate for this project.[3]

Stalin always analysed a situation before taking a decision. He weighed up the foreign policy aspects, also taking account of them in his internal policy. When my father was promoted in July 1938 the country was threatening to explode. It was not just a question of isolated protests by a few leaders of the Party – whole regions were close to rebellion.[4] The peasantry were ruined, the intelligentsia of the republics decimated, the arms and aircraft industries devastated by the purges. Externally, the threats to us were becoming more precise, while internally everything was breaking up. My father explained to me that if this policy of extermination of the elite had continued for another two years, the Germans would not have needed to invade us because the state would have collapsed by itself. Moreover, Stalin had not yet opted to ally himself with Germany. He had, at all costs, to cut a good figure on the international scene and, if not to assume the air of a democrat, at least to stop looking like a tyrant. These foreign policy considerations mingled with internal policy factors in the decision to appoint my father.

My father summed up Stalin's motives something like this: 'Why did he call for me in 1938? Because the country was on the brink of insurrection. He decided to correct his approach, but so that the change seemed to come from him. How was he to do that? By using a Georgian. Couldn't he have appointed Malenkov or Zhdanov? No! They did not agree with this new policy. Whereas I was not yet forty. Stalin thought that I lacked experience and that he would use me and then cast me aside like the others!' However, had the Politburo to meet twice before my father would agree to accept the offer made to him.

My mother, horrified at the prospect of seeing him renew his police activity, in Moscow moreover, resolved to remain in Georgia with me. My father couldn't persuade her even though he would have liked to have us with him. As we have seen, Stalin had promised that his assignment would be temporary. He merely wanted someone in whom he had confidence to stop the purges, which had got out of his control. But when he learnt that my mother and I had stayed behind in Georgia he became very angry and sharply rebuked my father. He sent Vlasik, the commander of his body-guard, to Tbilisi to hasten our departure. We carried out our move in less than 24 hours, accompanied by my paternal grandmother, my deaf-mute aunt ... and our two cats. (My father adored animals. Our house was always full of canaries, parrots, cats, dogs and even a bear cub.) My maternal grand-mother, who lived in the same block but on the floor below, managed to avoid the 'clean sweep'. My mother and I departed, sick at heart, leaving our ties behind. For the first period of our establishment in Moscow my mother cher-ished the hope of returning to Tbilisi. However, we stayed in Moscow for good. The atmosphere in our family and the relations between my parents changed for the worse.

My father was given as his official residence a flat in the block where former political prisoners lived, which was near a bridge giving on to the Kremlin. This building was a sort of 'home' designed for a commune, sharing a cinema, a kitchen and sports facilities. This commune was a failure. Stalin came to call on us only a few days after our arrival. He inspected the premises and was displeased with them. The flat comprised five rooms – one a bedroom for Ella and me, one for my grandmother and my aunt, a third for my parents, plus a library and a living room. 'You are squeezed together here like sardines in a tin,' he said. 'I'm going to move you into the Kremlin.' My mother, who did not yet realise what he was like, burst out 'But, there, we shall be as though in prison!' Stalin laughed: 'There's an idea!' Nevertheless he did not insist, and finally lodged us in a private house.[5] We visited it three days later, the delay being necessary, as we learnt subsequently, to give time for the installation of microphones. This two-storey building at the corner of Malaya Nikitskaya Street, had belonged before the Revolution to General Kuropatkin. I was given the sunniest room. This was my first and last privilege. Apart from this advan-tage my existence was subjected to the strictest discipline. My parents no longer supervised my education, so, of course, I had to manage as best I could and do my homework unaided.

Stalin came to see us when we were at last settled. He again inspected the premises, saying this time that we lacked furniture and that our dwelling was like a bivouac. He noted with pleasure, though, that we had brought our huge library from Tbilisi.

Stalin wanted to visit our *dacha* too. This was no more than a wooden hut, but it was situated in a magnificent pine forest near Arkhangelskoye. He wanted to examine the place at leisure and took advantage of a day when we were away to have a good look round. Not long afterwards he summoned my parents to the *dacha* and at once set upon my mother. 'Why did you choose such a wretched hovel?' he exclaimed as soon as he saw her. 'Even in exile I lived in better conditions! I want your *dacha* to be nearer mine and also nearer the city. Tomorrow I'll come and pick you up and install you in a house of my choice.' Then, turning to me, he added: 'You'll see, over there you'll have the finest roads for cycling.' Next day a car came to help us move. We took over Postyshev's[6] *dacha*, a modern structure surrounded by a garden: comfortable indeed, but without beauty. As neighbours we had the Kaganoviches. We never liked it and greatly regretted having to leave our old hut, which was more isolated and, above all, far from the other members of the Politburo. But Stalin wanted to have my father under his hand.

My new school

My father took up his new functions in the NKVD at the beginning of the school year: Vasya, Stalin's son, suggested that I go to his school, but my mother refused. She preferred that I should go to an ordinary school. I joined the district school, which faced the Japanese embassy. It often happened that, when my schoolmates and I were playing football, we broke the embassy's windows. The Japanese complained to the Commissariat of Foreign Affairs and our school was transferred elsewhere. I eventually ended up in the school attended by Vasya and Svetlana. The latter gradually grew closer to my mother and spent many hours with her. She never showed much interest in learning Georgian and Stalin did not insist that she learn the language. While I was regularly in her company, I saw much less of Vasya. Older than I, he had left the college to join the aviation school.

My father was against my choosing a literary speciality. He feared that I might end up as a historian of the Party or something like that. For a time he cherished the ambition to make an artist of me – he had himself taught me to draw – but I obviously lacked the vocation. Eventually, he observed my aptitudes for science and technology, and gave up. What was essential for him was to see me with a proper job and not about to become a Party official. Whenever a member of the Politburo tried to draw me into a bureaucratic career he would get extremely angry. One day Bulganin offered me a job in the Ministry of Defence. My father knew this and summoned me: 'Don't accept,' he said. 'You like science: continue along that path.' Then he telephoned Bulganin to reprimand him for having sought to turn me into a functionary. When Molotov wanted to take me into the MID (Ministry of Foreign Affairs) and raised the matter with my father, the latter exclaimed: 'You want to ruin him!' The

Leningrad Party Secretary, Kuznetsov, also had the idea of appointing me to be responsible for scientific research for the Central Committee, and this time it was I myself who turned down the offer. The job went to Zhdanov's son.

False smiles

Despite his reticence, my father thus became deputy head of the NKVD in July 1938. The top ranks of the apparatus of both Party and State were occupied by a Russophile group who distrusted and hated their non-Russian colleagues. Only Molotov and Andreev did not belong to this group. The set of Russian chauvinists, supporters of the purges, took my father's promotion badly. Zhdanov was against it. (Svetlana, Stalin's daughter, was to confirm this to me later, having heard it in Zhdanov's family circle.) Zhdanov had begun to intrigue against my father while we were still in Georgia. He already saw in him a dangerous rival. This was also the feeling of Yagoda and Yezhov, who carried out the Russophiles' orders. Malenkov was also involved. Zhdanov did not come into conflict with him until the time came when he felt that Malenkov might evict him from the Party's top leadership. As soon as we were installed in Moscow Zhdanov put my father under surveillance by his personal guard. My father noticed this, and even discovered that people working for him were spying on him for the benefit of the Central Committee and reporting to Zhdanov. None of this prevented the maintenance of a façade of outward cordiality. Zhdanov pretended to be pleased with my father's promotion. As for Malenkov, he bowed to the ground before him. Every Sunday, and without troubling himself in the slightest as to whether he was disturbing us, he would call, accompanied by his wife Golubkova. The latter showed herself full of solicitude for my mother and urged her to persist with her research work. She even proposed to introduce her to Lysenko and to help her find a job in his institute. Mikoyan, too, pretended to be delighted at the arrival of another Caucasian. He had formerly been a friend of my father's and, observing that he was in Ordzhonikidze's good graces, he undertook to protect my father. Mikoyan always knew which way the wind was blowing. Because their father esteemed mine, at least in appearance, Mikoyan's sons invited me to join them in their sports outings. As for Voroshilov, he presented my mother with an American tape recorder and invited her and me to visit him and go riding.

It is not difficult to understand that the appointment of my father caused anxiety in that little world. Khrushchev, Yezhov and Malenkov, three inseparables, had been zealous instruments in the great purges.[7] Since Yezhov and Malenkov had gone too far, Stalin feared that they might try to exculpate themselves by putting the blame on him, for the struggle for the succession began as soon as 1937-38. Sensing that his regime was in danger, he decided on a sharp change in policy. That was always how Stalin proceeded. He launched a campaign, got what he wanted, then pretended that he had had nothing to do with it and that abuses committed without the Party's knowledge were due to provocateurs whose only aim was to stir up discontent with the government among the peoples of the USSR. He then posed as the arbiter intervening to 'correct mistakes' and punish the scapegoats.

Zhdanov and Malenkov, in particular, had reason to be worried. The former was the inspirer of the policy of repression (with Stalin's approval, of course), the second was its organiser.[8] They had good grounds for fearing that Yezhov might involve them in his downfall. Malenkov coveted the NKVD, but Stalin insisted on keeping him in the Central Committee, from where he would continue to have the right to keep an eye on the NKVD. The idea of replacing Yezhov with my father thus came not from Malenkov but from Stalin.[9]

Yezhov

Yezhov and Malenkov, urged on by Zhdanov, had brought about the disgracing of Yagoda.[10] Hardly had Yezhov succeeded him as the head of the NKVD than he set about systematically eliminating witnesses of his predecessor's crimes, the scale of which had alarmed him. He found himself caught in a vicious circle. When he spoke of Yezhov and his behaviour, my father observed that this man had done all he could to avoid suffering the fate of Yagoda (arrested, charged along with Bukharin, and executed with him), who had been accused of showing excessive indulgence. This was a reproach that could be considered largely 'unjust', since Yagoda had shot people without restraint even if, unlike Yezhov, he did not 'run ahead of the locomotive.' Yezhov therefore sought to avoid laying himself open to such an accusation. For a long time my father believed that Yezhov's attitude was due to fear. He eventually perceived that Yezhov was just cynical. Far from being a fool, he analysed the situation perfectly and it was the very monstrosity of what he accomplished that crushed him. Yezhov did not even try to hold back the rising wave of the terror: he preferred to run ahead of it. My father was also to discover that he had committed as many crimes when he was at the head of the Orgotdel.[11] People always forget to mention that Yezhov was not only the head of the NKVD, he was also Secretary of the Central Committee. When he was in the dock in April 1939, some months after our arrival in Moscow, Malenkov revealed some of Yezhov's misdeeds committed at that time.

I met Yezhov a few times after we came to Moscow. He was always drunk and always gloomy. Yezhov was a short man – a head shorter than Stalin, which greatly pleased the latter. He had a crumpled face, a yellowish complexion and shifty eyes. He seemed to be in the grip of a perpetual agitation. He felt that his position was unsteady and knew who was going to replace him. One day in the autumn of 1938 he called on us. He was already tipsy when he arrived. At table, drunker than ever, he told my father that he knew he was doomed. My father tried to calm him and urged him to trust in Stalin's wisdom, but Yezhov would not listen. 'I'm done for,' he repeated, 'done for. But you won't escape the same fate, either.' After he had left, my father voiced his astonishment to my mother: 'He treated me like an intimate friend though he knew I was informed of all the plots against me!' My father was different. He never managed to hide his antipathies.

Through Yezhov, therefore, Stalin had got rid of all his potential adversaries. Later he entrusted Malenkov with the task of eliminating Yezhov. Malenkov applied himself to the task all the more willingly because he was compromised up to the neck in the great purges and he feared the revelations about him that Yezhov might come out with.

My father made one condition for accepting his new post. He asked for and obtained the appointment of a commission by the Central Committee to investigate Yezhov's actions. Through this inquiry he hoped to compile a list of the crimes committed up to that time, so that they could not be laid to his account later on. This commission was chaired by Andreev, a weary, yellow-faced man who, according to my father, had played a considerable part in the repressions but had managed to remain in the shadow.[12] I knew and liked his son. Andreev did not drink, was in no way pretentious, and was a good skier. His wife, Jewish and a militant activist of the Party, stuffed her husband with medicaments which, so said ill-wishers, only worsened his state of health. So, Andreev had been chosen to chair the commission, and this by design. He had played a more discreet role in the purges, he was conscientious and he was close to Stalin. The latter wanted to maintain control of the whole process and limit the damage done. He did not altogether succeed, even though Andreev braked as hard as he could. My father insisted that the truth be revealed, at least to the Politburo. The commission discovered some frightful things, going back in some cases to Yagoda's time: people had been executed in a hurry and their cases investigated *after* their execution.[13] My father was shocked when he learnt of the reports of this commission. Though the purges in Georgia had given him a foretaste, he had never suspected the full scale of the repression.

Yezhov was eventually arrested, charged with plotting against the state, found guilty and executed. For some time denunciations of him had been pouring in.[14] These accusations did not stand up, of course: Yezhov had always obeyed like a dog the orders of Stalin and the Central Committee.[15] There was a rumour that he was shot only when the war began, not in 1940.[16] I do not rule out the possibility (though this is pure hypothesis on my part) that my father compiled a dossier on the period of the great purges and that this dossier was, precisely, one of the documents that Malenkov and the rest tried to find after his arrest.[17] However that may be, my father drew three lessons from the fate of his predecessors. Slavishly obeying Stalin was no use (for him, Yezhov was a weakling). It was necessary to get free of the NKVD as quickly as possible. And, in order to survive, one must find support elsewhere than in the security organs and the Party. He immediately adopted this line of action and turned his attention to economics and technology.[18]

The Cases

The Assassination of Kirov

I have forgotten what the occasion was when I asked my father what should be thought of the assassination of Kirov, which took place in December 1934.[19] 'We made a meticulous investigation,' he replied (and he said 'we'). 'There was no Trotskyist plot. Kirov was murdered on account of a woman. Stalin profited from this affair to attack the opposition. Zhdanov helped him a lot. It was even he who suggested the idea that Kirov's death could be exploited to get rid of all of Stalin's adversaries.' My father also pointed out to me that if Kirov had enemies, they were to be found in Georgia. What relation could there have been between the Georgian nationalists who had good reason to hate Kirov and, at the other end of the country in Leningrad, the Old Bolshevik Zinoviev? Even Yagoda himself, as my father knew from reliable sources, was convinced that there had never been any plot against Kirov.[20]

Marshal Tukhachevsky and the purges in the Army

Tukhachevsky was accused of being a German spy and executed in June 1937 together with a group of senior Red Army officers.[21] We knew him well. He had visited us in Georgia: he was later accused of touring the republics in order to recruit supporters. He was an educated man. He liked to make violins, and played the instrument quite well. He also had the reputation of being a phenomenal skirt-chaser. My father explained to me that Tukhachevsky had nothing against Stalin or the Party, or, at least, nothing that would justify his arrest. He could hardly be charged with anti-communism, having participated in a bloody repression of peasants during the civil war. 'His only offence,' said my father, 'was to attack that idiot Voroshilov.'[22] A few years earlier, in fact, Tukhachevsky had been summoned by Stalin when the latter wanted to put things right in the Army. Tukhachevsky had recommended that the cavalry be got rid of, and with it Voroshilov and Budenny,[23] and had gone on to transform the Army with Stalin's blessing. The latter eventually found him too enterprising and altered his attitude towards him, considering that a high position in the Army could not be entrusted to a man who was overly ambitious. My father thought this fear well-founded as, in his view, Tukhachevsky might well one day have coveted supreme power. The Germans – possibly prompted from the Soviet Union – compiled a compromising dossier against him. This was all the easier for them because, between 1923 and 1933, the Red Army and the Reichswehr had had close contacts at the highest level.[24] My father had heard talk of that when he was still in Tbilisi. However it may have been, the Germans succeeded in trapping Tukhachevsky, and Voroshilov and Co. profited by this, settling their accounts with him. Stalin hastened to impose belief in a plot by the generals against his person and launched the purge. This plot was said to have ramifications in the NKVD, but Stalin did not believe that. Frinovsky, a professional soldier who was one of Yezhov's deputies and a friend of Tukhachevsky's, was not disturbed and was eliminated only when Yezhov fell. Stalin regretted, though, that he had not had him shot at the same time as Tukhachevsky. Sumbatov, a Chekist very close to Frinovsky, told me about his arrest. Frinovsky had heard that they were coming for him and had barricaded himself in his quarters. They could have stormed the place and killed him but he was wanted alive. My father had therefore ordered Sumbatov to undertake the arrest. 'This is the only way for you to escape being involved in his case.' And Sumbatov agreed. He told me, weeping, how he had betrayed his friend. Frinovsky had let him into his house supposing that he was going to get him out of this desperate situation. Frinovsky was executed.[25]

As my father was to say to me later, treachery and the desire to bury others rotted our society and were particularly rife among the military.[26] Stalin needed only to use some of them to liquidate the others. In that milieu he did not even need to take the initiative. He just let the officers get on with it, while sometimes restraining their zeal.

Marshal Blucher

Marshal Blucher contributed substantially to the downfall of Marshal Tukhachevsky,[27] of whom he was jealous, but eventually owed his own downfall to the future Marshal Zhukov.[28] Voroshilov too was determined to have his head. According to my father, Voroshilov was pathologically jealous of officers who were more intelligent than he was. I heard about Blucher from Makhnev, one of my father's deputies after the war. He had known the Marshal in the Far East and thought very ill of him: 'Blucher exterminated his military colleagues like so many lice.' According to Makhnev, Blucher had such a thirst for power that he systematically eliminated potential rivals. I don't know if this is true, but Zhukov, who had served with him in the Far East, was of the same opinion. He hated Blucher and considered him a blackguard. He even told my father that Blucher behaved like a petty tyrant in the locality and subordinated the Party's organs to his control. He interfered in everything, including agriculture and public works. My father considered Blucher to be a very intelligent man, self-controlled, two-faced and a perfect scoundrel.

He was arrested at the end of 1938. He was accused, among other things, of being an agent in the pay of the Japanese. They took him to the NKVD's premises and there subjected him to a 'vigorous' interrogation which caused his death.[29] I asked my father one day if torture was widely practised under the Soviet regime. He replied that revolutions do away with law and establish a state of war in peacetime. At that time, he also told me, if injustices were discovered the Party corrected them. Later, he was no longer to conceal from me what he really thought about the system and never refused to answer my questions.

Bukharin

Bukharin, Stalin's former ally in the fight against Trotsky, had been arrested, judged, condemned and executed within ten days between 3 and 13 March 1938. My father did not show himself particularly moved by this, as he had no sympathy with the individual concerned. While he did not believe the charges of spying brought against Bukharin he considered that 'this bootlicker was a weakling, since he confessed. One needs to be stupid to imagine that one can save one's life by confessing,' he said. 'Some manage to convince themselves that in this way they are helping the Party. That's complete idiocy!' We were still in Georgia at this time, but my father already suspected he was going to be transferred to Moscow, so he followed events closely, especially because Georgia was compelled to follow Moscow's example.

Kosarev

My father has been blamed for the purge that was inflicted on the Komsomol in November 1938.[30] I knew two people who had worked with Kosarev, the head of the Komsomol, arrested on 20 November 1938. They were Mikhailov, who became head of the organisation, and Ryabikov, first deputy to Ustinov, the Minister for Military Industry. They enlightened me regarding what lay behind this case. Kosarev was a 100 per cent Stalinist. Impulsive and fond of good living, he enjoyed company and tours. He was a born leader of men, and was also ambitious, aiming at a great future in politics. One day, during a banquet, he said that the Komsomol should no longer be 'the Party's reserve.' It was necessary to shake the palm tree and make room for the young. This remark displeased Stalin, who saw in it one of the theses of Trotskyism. Others also felt that they were threatened. The Party organs were alarmed when they saw the Komsomol seeking a share in power, and began to set up a case. This happened before my father arrived in Moscow and the NKVD had nothing to do with this purge.[31]

For a long time I believed that the mania for informing on one another dated from the 1930s, but old Chekists dispelled my illusions on that point. One of them, Raikhman, told me that during the First World War the Bolsheviks spent their time informing on each other, and that was even before the establishment of the Soviet regime and the Cheka. 'The funniest thing,' he added, 'is that even now people don't realise that informing always ends up getting the informer into trouble.'

The NKVD

When my father inherited the NKVD this People's Commissariat was a
bloody mess in which the most absolute irresponsibility prevailed. He set
about reforming it by establishing order in the various sections. He separated off the frontier guards[32] and provided them with an effective system
of communication, together with special rifles manufactured on the model
of weapons captured from the Finns. He also restructured the administration of the Gulag.[33] From the start he considered transferring it to the
People's Commissariat of Justice, but did not manage to do this until the
spring of 1953. He organised a Technological Bureau[34] and developed
research units, the *sharashki*, so as to enable scientists and engineers in
detention to be spared physical labour and devote themselves to their
speciality under bearable conditions, while awaiting their release.

At the same time as he undertook these reforms my father had to deal
with the problem of the purges which had ravaged the country and were
still going on. He explained to me later that it had not been possible for him
to halt the machinery of repression[35] immediately when he took up his task
at the NKVD. In Georgia, for example, my mother's friends were not freed
until April 1939. He began by dismissing some of Yezhov's collaborators,
along with investigators who had been distinguished by particularly
horrible acts of torture. Many were judged by courts and not by the *troikas*
of the NKVD, and were shot.[36] Yezhov, who was still *en poste*, did not oppose
these measures.[37] He claimed to know nothing of the monstrosities that
had been committed. I even saw him show indignation regarding them.[38]

After Yezhov's resignation, on 12 November 1938, my father, having
become head of the NKVD, gave priority to replacing the cadres of the
commissariat, whom he considered were dependent on the Party, leaving
in position only those who had not been involved in the repressions. When
Andreev tried to introduce Party functionaries into the security organs,[39]
my father had no difficulty in demonstrating their incompetence and
stupidity, so that after six months they were returned to the Party apparatus. Later, he was to be accused of having made a clean sweep so as to
be able to install in key positions Georgians who were devoted to him. In
reality he had brought with him only a dozen collaborators, whereas he
had to find replacements for hundreds of functionaries.[40] He merely
needed to have ears within the NKVD, especially in the early days of his
appointment.

The prisons

Along with renewing the NKVD apparatus my father had to apply himself
to the problems of the prisoners. He listed the ones who, though
condemned to death, had not yet been executed, so as to be able to decide
their fate. At the beginning of 1938 Stalin and the Central Committee had
announced a change of policy and a slow-down in the purges. Yet in the

spring of 1938 executions were still being carried out on a grand scale, a fine example of duplicity.[41] My father nevertheless managed to save a large number of condemned men from death, such as the aeronautical engineer Tupolev. He set up special rehabilitation commissions in the republics, the regions and the administrations.[42] Thereby some hundreds were set free.[43] My father also hastened to suspend the execution of the military men who had been condemned to death but had not yet been shot. Before getting permission for this from the Central Committee he had transferred to the central prisons those who had been kept in camps.[44] In 1940, after Voroshilov had been set aside, I personally met some of those military men who had been freed. They were all trying to remember the names of the arrested men who were still alive. Timoshenko and Zhukov joined in this enterprise, whereas Voroshilov always did what he could to obstruct it. Zhukov even called for the rehabilitation of an officer who had denounced him. 'He's a skunk as a human being, but a good officer who will make himself useful.' This shows that Zhukov was free from meanness.

The mechanism of arbitrary rule

Until my father came on the scene the *troikas*, the NKVD's extraordinary tribunals, were all-powerful. The NKVD investigated cases, pronounced sentence and executed it. My father wanted to strengthen the authority of the Public Prosecutor by returning to him the power to supervise judicial procedures and the application of laws. Unfortunately he was unable to stop the Orgotdel of the Central Committee from taking decisions on arrests and the fate of accused people. Things usually happened like this. Any functionary of the Orgotdel could telephone an investigating magistrate or a section-head of the NKVD and order him to arrest someone because 'the Central Committee thinks this should be done.' Nothing more than that was needed. Lists were drawn up and submitted to the Central Committee, and, to use my father's own expression 'all those idiots signed.' Nobody except those who carried out the order bore any responsibility. Furthermore, for most investigating magistrates, expulsion from the Party was equivalent to a verdict of guilty. It was not easy to get rid of that idea, implanted in people's minds over so many years. My father was able to obtain only a watching brief where the activities of the Orgotdel were concerned. He found that 30 per cent of the functionaries in the apparatus of the Central Committee were NKVD agents. Any 'information' coming from the Central Committee was automatically taken seriously by the investigating magistrates. I remember hearing my father's deputy, Serov, joking about this situation: 'It's as though my teacher at the Military Academy was my agent: I should have no interest in ignoring his reports.' My father proposed to the Politburo that an end be put to this practice and he prepared a resolution in this sense which was adopted by the Central Committee on 27 December 1938, against Malenkov's opposition.[45]

He soon came to the conclusion that the investigation department should be taken from the NKVD and transferred to the People's Commissariat of Justice. It was wrong for those whose job was to capture criminals to also investigate their case, especially when confessions were regarded as proof of guilt. Actually, the use of torture followed directly from the perversity of the established system. My father spoke about this to Stalin, who asked him to 'clarify'. However, using the pretext of the international situation and the imminence of war the Central Committee vetoed the proposal.[46] All the same, my father did succeed in considerably reducing the number of cases where recourse was had to emergency procedures.[47]

An inquiry revealed to him also that three-quarters of the investigative magistrates and officials engaged in counter-espionage were Jews. Fearing that their too obvious presence in the organs of repression could give rise to anti-semitism, he decided to replace them with Russians. At that time one could hear remarks, according to which the Jews were oppressing and destroying the Russian people.

The Peasants

My father also wanted to grant the peasants the right to leave their collective farms. It was impossible for them to quit these institutions into which they had been put by force. Peasant refugees swelled the numbers in the camps and yet there were still many who tried their luck. In Georgia my father had solved the problem by ordering the Party organisations to allow any peasant who wanted to leave his collective farm to do so. Without changing the law he had managed to nullify its consequences. But this attempt at emancipating the peasants was blocked by the Party. Stalin did indeed wish to take some measures that would reduce the tension in the country,[48] but he did not want any reforms from which there could be no going back to his usual practices. I think that at this time, in 1938-39, my father had not yet taken the measure of Stalin, even though he guessed that the latter was using him to support and strengthen his personal power. He still thought he could bring Stalin round to his own ideas and was pleased with the measures he had managed to get passed with Andreev's backing and despite the opposition of Zhdanov, Voroshilov and Malenkov. That trio would not agree at any price to allow any softening of the political line and considered that the enemy had not yet been finally crushed. My father was therefore delighted to be able to apply on an all-USSR scale the reforms he had begun to implement in Georgia. This period was a real honeymoon between him and Stalin, but he was soon to be disillusioned. Stalin had allowed him to proceed with some local improvements which he authorised only in order to break the wave of discontent which was rising in the country.[49] His disappointment increased when in the spring of 1939 the Politburo decided to intensify labour discipline in factories, agricultural enterprises and administrative bodies, introducing custodial penalties for lateness, absenteeism and petty thefts. The NKVD was literally over-whelmed by the task thus imposed on it.[50] They had to cope with the paper-work, find accommodation for all these new prisoners and feed them. My father considered that the Gulag was the most unproductive thing ever invented: even Pharaoh's slaves, according to him, produced more. In that connection he urged me to read a book on the building of the Egyptian pyramids, *Memoirs of a Freedman*, so that I could under-stand that free men always work better than slaves.

My father had to wait till Stalin died in order to release nearly half the prisoners in the Gulag. He would have liked to do away with the entire system of forced labour, but did not have the time.

March 1939: the 18th Party Congress

By the time the 18th Congress opened, and although it was supposed to correct past errors, my father's euphoria had vanished. He realised that Stalin thought he had achieved his essential aims and was now ready to resume his usual methods. The tone adopted by the congress was in flagrant contradiction with reality. My father had to give a speech. He used this to make the point that the economic mistakes committed in Soviet society ought not to be systematically imputed to saboteurs – that incompetence was also a factor. The reaction was sharp. He was accused of 'wrongly orienting' the Party cadres.[51] Fortunately for my father, at this time Stalin had had his fill of victims and did not encourage those attacks.

Among the decisions that were taken at this congress my father was pleased with the promotion of Voznesensky to the post of Secretary of the Central Committee, but he was disagreeably surprised to see coming into leading positions in the state some people who had been responsible for the abuses that had just been exposed. The men who had destroyed the Party cadres in Byelorussia and the Ukraine and those who had directed the purges in Georgia were allowed to 'perk up', as my father put it. They had become candidate members of the Politburo at the same time as himself. He thought, of course, of Malenkov and Zhdanov.[52] He shared his anxiety with my mother: 'The thaw is ending. I'm going to be subjected to pressure, and I and my collaborators will be the ones held guilty.' It was from that congress onwards that the struggle between my father and Zhdanov became overt.

I remember a long conversation between my parents in the summer of 1939. We were on the veranda of our *dacha* and I was busy in my corner, repairing the balustrade. My parents were talking about the hunt for 'fascists' inside the country ('Trotskyists' had given way to 'fascists'). My father said: 'I'm doing all I can to hold back the repressions, but in the situation I'm in I can do no more.' He found it ridiculous to want to fight Germany by persecuting 'the enemy within.'

'What can happen to a state like the USSR? Suppose the Germans invade us. Only little territories like Armenia or Georgia can become German protectorates, but not the entire Soviet Union. Russia will remain with all her problems – the Germans will change nothing.'

Hitler

Most Soviet diplomats misappropriated the state's money and spent it without accounting, forgetting the proletarian slogans which they affected. My father had a poor opinion of Chicherin and his group in the NKID. He found fault with Litvinov for weakness of character.[1] 'When he's summoned on high and pressure is brought to bear on him, he yields. But then, when he is alone again, he tears his hair and wonders how he could have agreed to that.' A very bad organiser, Litvinov was rigid and obtuse, and did not know how to use his wide range of relations so as to broaden his horizon and form opinions of his own. He always kept to the official version. Litvinov never had a political programme. He was overestimated by the Westerners. Personally, I regard him as a mediocre opportunist, a pen-pusher who was jealous of people of talent. He feared them and intrigued against them as he had intrigued against Krassin, whom my father liked.[2] My father had a certain respect for the Vice-Commissar for Foreign Affairs, V. Potemkin.[3] 'There is something of the country squire about him,' he would say. Potemkin's knowledge of history seemed to my father a substantial asset. It was for the same reason that he thought of offering the historian Tarlé[4] a diplomatic career. However, Tarlé was so fond of good living and so lazy that he refused all such offers. My father also had nothing against our ambassador in Sweden, Alexandra Kollontai, as she never hindered his activity. He sent her agents who were young and handsome, whom she accepted with gratitude. Stalin was fond of her because of her tumultuous youth.[5] He may have fancied her at one time.

Finally, of all these functionaries, the only one my father really hated was Vyshinsky, the man who orchestrated the great trials – 'a mixture of prosecutor and diplomat who is in fact neither the one nor the other,' he said.[6] He felt a genuine physical revulsion[7] for Vyshinsky and formally forbade my mother to call on his family. Vyshinsky tried to worm his way into my father's good graces, but the latter could not conceal his disgust for the 'grovelling viper.' At the outset he had clashed with Vyshinsky when he tried to bring military jurists into the Public Prosecutor's office. My father demanded his dismissal. Vyshinsky was a bureaucrat fond of puns. If I had to describe him in two words I should compare him to an insignificant louse. His face was distorted by a permanent grin and his eyes wandered this way and that.

Among our ambassadors my father particularly esteemed Maisky. More quick witted than Litvinov, he was different from the Party functionaries, and a real diplomat who loved his job. My father knew that he was very competent and would have liked to make him Minister of Foreign Affairs before the war, when my father had not yet acquired the influence he was to have later. It was even difficult to get Maisky sent as ambassador to London.[8] However, my father needed someone of his quality in Great Britain. They kept up close relations, probably in connection with intelligence work (this was the case also with other diplomats) and, like Umansky[9], but much more frequently, Maisky, an agile little Jew who resembled a mouse, used to visit us. My father would have preferred to see him rather than Molotov at the head of the NKID, as the latter, who replaced Litvinov in May 1939, had the defect of being viewed abroad as Stalin's man. Litvinov and Maisky, as true diplomats, had managed to preserve outward appearances such that Westerners considered them to be independent personalities who were obliged to pursue a Bolshevik policy. They had a better attitude towards Litvinov and Maisky than towards the others, and my father thought that was important.

Purges in the NKID

Molotov was instructed, in May 1939, to 'purge' the NKID and change its orientation.[10] He always kept strictly to Stalin's directives, even if sometimes he disagreed with them. Once a decision had been taken he would carry it out to the letter.

Although my father lacked sufficient authority to interfere in the affairs of the NKID, he was, nevertheless, head of the NKVD and in that capacity was invited to be a member of the commission charged with purging the NKID. Stalin wanted this. He wished to emphasise the importance of intelligence work in the Soviet Union's activity abroad.[11] In the Commissariat there was a veritable free-for-all, with no holds barred. The diplomats competed in mutual denunciation,[12] with each man hoping to get rid of his superior in this way. When new appointments had to be made my father seized the opportunity to put in men of his own. It was not that he sought to influence foreign policy, merely so that he should have well-placed informers. Molotov asked him to recommend candidates for the post of Vice-Commissar of Foreign Affairs and for certain embassies which had been working very badly. My father supplied him with a list of names and advised him to have a talk with each candidate so as to form a judgement of his capacities. This was how Dekanozov's turn came. He was a collaborator of my father's who had come to Moscow with him from Georgia. Molotov received him and asked him to draw up some reports. Dekanozov did well, and Molotov asked my father to let him have him.[13] My father agreed on condition that Stalin was told. He actually thought that Dekanozov was not up to the job of Vice-Commissar of Foreign Affairs, and Dekanozov himself was intelligent enough to agree. All the same, the meeting with Stalin went well, and Dekanozov became Molotov's deputy. My father then asked Dekanozov to single out, from among the young people who had worked in the archives, those who struck him as the most competent, so as to employ them in Molotov's apparatus. Work in the archives seemed to him to be a better preparation for future experts in the NKID than cutting a figure at official receptions. In 1940, Molotov and Stalin appointed Dekanozov to be ambassador in Berlin. As they saw it, his experience in intelligence marked him out naturally for this post.

Towards the German-Soviet Pact

The Czechoslovak crisis

My father took a very negative view of the Munich agreements. He would have preferred that the USSR, France and Britain should oppose by force of arms the dismemberment of Czechoslovakia. I remember seeing him studying maps and discussing these questions with military men. The Czechs could have held out for at least six months behind their fortifications, which were excellent. Their armaments were of better quality than either the German or the French.

My father thought that the Germans would perhaps halt after acquiring the Sudetenland. However, he was worried that Czechoslovakia would be strategically vulnerable after losing that region. Marshal Vasilevsky told me that at this time our General Staff worked out plans for going to the aid of Czechoslovakia in the event of German aggression. They contemplated crossing Polish territory by force while asking how long the Czechs could hold out until reinforced. The soldiers discussed the possibility of preventive attack by Germany if our troops entered Poland, with or without the assent of the Poles. We understood that the latter found themselves in an unhappy situation. After the war I met some young Polish officers who told me that at this time a small group of military men in their General Staff drew up a project for an alliance with the USSR in the event of attack by the Germans. The second echelon of the Polish forces would be reinforced by the Red Army in defence of Warsaw. My father was always very critical of Beck, Pilsudski's successor. He considered that he behaved as though subject to the Germans and he saw in Beck's policy an obstacle to the alliance he wanted with the British and French. The Poles misinformed Britain concerning the Soviet Union and its military capacity so as to dissuade the British from getting closer to Moscow.

After the Munich agreements Stalin conceived the greatest contempt for the British Prime Minister Chamberlain. He used to say that Chamberlain's monocle should be put in a certain place which decency forbids me to name. He found a similar use for his umbrella. 'One day that madman Hitler will grab his umbrella and hit him with it. And Chamberlain will take it without complaining,' said Stalin, exasperated by the weakness shown by the Westerners. On the other hand, the Soviet leaders followed closely the career of Churchill. It was known that he wanted to resist Germany and that the group of opponents to Chamberlain's policy was continually growing. My father took a special interest in Churchill, as, secretly, he compared himself to him. Like him, Churchill enjoyed support in the intelligence services and headed the different branches of these services. Like him, he wanted to pursue a policy that was not backed by the official authorities, and, he had to act clandestinely. He, too, suffered setbacks because he was not in power. Naturally I understood this only much later.

My father said of Bonnet, the French Minister of Foreign Affairs at this time, that he was a political prostitute.[14] I remember that remark because my father had noticed that Bonnet had a nose like a Georgian's. 'Let's hope that they don't discover that he has Jewish and Georgian blood! That's all we'll need!' He also joked that 'Bonnet's long nose is always poked into Hitler's kitchen.' As for Daladier, he was generally seen as an incompetent. Stalin did not like Leon Blum any better. He found him 'amorphous' and referred to him as 'the amoeba Blum', regretting that the French Left had chosen such a leader. Blum confirmed him in his view that the Socialists were worse than the Conservatives. Generally speaking, he never missed an opportunity to cover them with sarcasm. Later, he was to prefer seeing de Gaulle at the head of the French Government rather than a Socialist. For the same reason he regretted that Pilsudski was no longer alive: he alone would have been strong enough to conclude a treaty with the USSR. With that vigorous Marshal it would have been possible to come to an understanding.[15] My father shared Stalin's opinion and thought that Pilsudski would have chosen the anti-German camp. Stalin had put many questions about him to the Polish Communist Wanda Wasilewska,[16] who knew him well. It was she who confirmed to him that Pilsudski had regretted that an alliance with Russia against Germany was not possible.

Germany

For us Georgians Germany was no unknown land. There were many Germans settled in Georgia and many Georgians went to Germany to study. It was therefore natural that the Georgian intelligentsia was pro-German. In fact, according to my father, if Germany had not gone Nazi, that was the country with most to offer Georgia and Russia. But National Socialism had altered everything. For that reason and despite what has been said about his alleged Germanophilia, my father favoured an alliance with Britain. He saw to it that all intelligence tending to show that one should not trust Germany duly came to the attention of Stalin. He felt as lively an antipathy to German National Socialism as to Russian chauvinism, and mocked the Nazis' race theories: 'Take the famous Prussians,' he said to me. 'If you dig down a little, what do you find? That these Prussians are Slavs! All those Prussian junkers have Slav blood. That's only one example, but it shows that politicians will do anything at all with history when it suits them to.'

The Germans knew that my father was against closer relations with their country. Schulenburg, the German ambassador in Moscow, a diplomat friendly to Russia and categorically opposed to a conflict between Germany and the USSR, tried to meet my father, but the latter always avoided meeting him. In general he took care not to frequent the company of ambassadors, fearing the displeasure of Stalin or Molotov, who regarded foreign policy as their preserve.[17] He knew that, during the First World War, Schulenburg had been given the task of forming a Georgian Legion.[18] He was a diplomat of the old school. Hitler distrusted him and had placed beside him a military attaché who was a fanatical Nazi and kept a close watch on him.

Down to the last moment my father tried to persuade Stalin not to sign the German-Soviet Pact. The latter hesitated, but at the end of July 1939 the British and French found nothing better to do, in order to win the Soviets to their cause, than to send some underlings to conduct the negotiations. The British behaved insolently because they believed they could arrive at an understanding with Germany. This attitude of theirs was felt as a veritable affront.[19] Stalin replied by making them deal with Voroshilov. During these meetings our General Staff supplied the precise number of tanks, aircraft and divisions that we could throw against Germany after traversing Poland, and also explained how long it would take to get them moving. The French and British were caught napping, since they could not supply any corresponding information. Poland made known its refusal to allow our troops to cross its territory, not on its own initiative but under pressure from Britain and France.[20] My father knew this from a reliable source. Meanwhile, the Germans were negotiating simultaneously with Britain, through Sweden, and with us. The British wanted us to pull their chestnuts out of the fire. We learnt that, in this double game, the Germans aimed above all to gull the British and French. Despite this, my father opposed the pact with Germany right to the end, even though he had no confidence in Britain and France. When Stalin concluded that the French and British were deceiving us, he wound up the whole business in 48 hours, without consulting the Politburo, who were faced with a fait accompli.[21] He aimed to set Germany against France and Britain. Stalin had not used my father's services or those of the NKID: he always had groups of his own operating in parallel with the established apparatuses. During his stay in Moscow, on 22 and 23 August, Ribbentrop sent enthusiastic telegrams to Hitler.[22] My father brought the texts to Stalin, who found them very amusing. I asked my father his impression of Ribbentrop. His reply was: 'He struts around like a turkey puffed up with pride.'

The Politburo was far from being unanimously enthusiastic. Stalin, Molotov and Zhdanov approved of the pact. Kaganovich and my father expressed reservations, but Stalin explained that war with Germany was inevitable and this pact was only provisional. It was necessary to win time and make sure that the USSR would not have to face Hitler alone. My father thought that this cosying up to Hitler alienated us from Western civilisation as a whole. He was especially fearful lest this entente should be reflected in a worsening of Stalin's domestic policy. With an ally like Hitler Stalin would no longer need to worry, and this alliance with Germany might well transform Russian chauvinism into Fascism pure and simple. He pointed out that France and Britain, though capitalist countries like Germany, were less aggressive. It was less dangerous to be their ally than Germany's. This pact deprived the Soviet Union of the support of the opponents of Fascism. Besides, it could not last, since Hitler was still hostile to Communism. My father sent Molotov a report from his services on the reaction of governments and financial circles in the West, so as to show the negative effects produced by the pact. If my memory is correct, Maisky supplied some of the information used. Molotov failed to react, even though the NKID's diplomats confirmed the analysis made by the NKVD. Nevertheless, he congratulated my father in a fatherly way (he imitated Stalin's manner) on his increasing ability to analyse situations. My father was pleased with Molotov's amiability, since he wished to avoid at all costs making an enemy of him.

For his part Zhdanov, who had done all he could to sabotage the negotiations with the French and British, beamed when, on 18 August, Ribbentrop reported that Germany was ready to negotiate. 'He even looked younger,' was the comment made by my father, who already hated Zhdanov. The latter had always been a keen supporter of close relations with Hitler.[23] He had even sent his wife and son to Germany for more than a year, and they never missed an opportunity to boast about this. In the little circle of the Kremlin everyone knew that the Zhdanovs admired German culture while deploring Fascism and Germany's bad relations with Russia. Zhdanov thought that the Anglo-Saxons would always take steps to prevent Russia from becoming a real protagonist on the international scene, whereas the Germans would be compelled to favour the USSR's expansion into the Near and Middle East, in exchange for Soviet raw materials.[24]

Towards the Great War

The war with Finland

Under the terms of the pact with Germany, Finland became part of our sphere of influence but the Finns refused to agree to the exchanges of territory proposed by the USSR.[25]

In Finland capital was essentially provided by the Americans and the Swedes, with the Germans playing only a small part. So, when people tried to persuade my father that an attack on Finland would be useful, arguing that if we did not do it the Germans would rush in, he always replied: 'If the Germans want to penetrate Finland they will have to go to war. The Americans and Swedes are there already and won't fail to offer resistance. Rather than trying to take over that country from Leningrad we ought to make use, as a way of infiltration, of the Americans and Swedes, by encouraging increases in their investments so as to increase our own influence[26] and improve our relations with the West.' My father also had, moreover, a poor opinion of Kuusinen[27], the leader of the Finnish C.P., and thought it would be better to seek support from the Social-Democrats or even the Nationalists, in whose interest it was to have good relations with the USSR. In any case, he was against the idea of war with Finland.[28]

Several sessions of the Politburo were devoted to the Finnish problem. On this matter the military did a lot of harm, and not only Voroshilov, who was in charge of national defence but also a very intelligent general, Meretskov, commanding Leningrad Military District. During one of these sessions Stalin asked them: 'How many days will it take to dispose of Finland?' Zhdanov and Meretskov declared that two or three weeks would be enough, using merely the forces of Leningrad Military District. The Finns had hardly any air force, no continuous defence line, no navy and no heavy tanks.[29] Stalin then asked them if Finland's lakes and rivers would constitute an obstacle. 'No problem, they'll be frozen over,' replied Voroshilov. Stalin also wanted to know how long the French, British and Germans would need to prepare a landing. My father's estimate was three months. The decision to invade Finland was taken.

The stupid idea that this invasion could be carried out with the forces of the Leningrad Military District came from Zhdanov and was endorsed by that subtle strategist Voroshilov.[30] I learnt subsequently, from future admiral Kuznetsov, [31] the course of events that followed. After the check suffered by the first offensive and the bogging down of our troops on the Finnish frontier, Kuznetsov and my father proposed to Stalin that a landing be organised, taking advantage of the Finns' lack of an air force or a navy. My father was afraid that the operation planned by the British, through Norway to Finland, might start off hostilities on the front between Germany and the Western powers. It would be better to have done with Finland as soon as possible. However, Voroshilov and Kulik, backed in this by Molotov, convinced Stalin that Kuznetsov and my father were meddling in matters that did not concern them. And they both received a severe reprimand.[32] Later, however, after the Finnish war, Stalin felt obliged to decide on the creation of a force of marines. At the time of the conflict, though, he reminded my father that he must confine himself to collecting information on the plans being made by the French and British for attacks on the Soviet Union. My father found that the British were planing a landing in Finland for which they would use forces originally intended for an operation in Norway.[33] The French were preparing an operation in Caucasia.[34] He was delighted to be able to submit a report to Stalin on these plans, which he took very seriously because of his high opinion of Weygand. When he had read these documents Stalin said: 'Do as you see fit. But I want peace with Finland within fifteen days.' We then had recourse to some Swedish industrialists, as my father had advocated from the start, and peace was signed.[35] Soon afterwards Molotov sent for my father and admitted to him: 'I was wrong,' something that Stalin never did.

After the Finnish fiasco Zhdanov's star waned. He never recovered from this, even though, later, he was to return to centre stage.[36] He lost for good the prestige he had enjoyed in the Party. This war also revealed that our military intelligence was worthless. Our military men were totally ignorant of the Finns' defence provisions. Furthermore, the Swedes supplied the Finns with the radio messages of our High Command, ready decoded.

Katyn

The men around Stalin did not immediately realise that my father would never be Stalin's slave. At the time of the Katyn affair[37] they at last perceived that he was able to defend his opinion and resist pressure. It was, in fact, on that occasion that my father had his first clash with the Politburo, in February 1940.

In September 1939 Germany had invaded Poland, and was soon followed by the USSR. The two armies had met and, in conformity with the terms of the Pact, the eastern part of the conquered territory had come under Soviet rule. It remained to settle the fate of the Polish officers who had been taken prisoner by our forces.

The Soviet authorities tried for a long time to place responsibility for the Katyn massacre on my father and the NKVD but eventually they had to publish a document from the archives, dated 5 March 1940, which showed the guilt of the Politburo as a whole.[38]

There were about 300,000 Polish officers and other ranks in Soviet custody in the Soviet Union[39] at the beginning of 1940, when the Politburo met to decide what was to be done with them. My father was certainly not moved by humanitarian considerations[40] when he urged that these officers be kept alive, but it is certain that he did try to save them, in opposition to the general feeling. According to my father, war with Germany was bound to come. Now, even if these Poles hated the USSR, they were experienced officers and should be preserved. 'It takes dozens of years to train men to that level,' he explained. 'They could form the nucleus of an army of 300,000 men to be thrown against Germany. If we want to see, in the future, a Poland well disposed towards us, we must keep this body of officers, create a Polish army and use it against Germany.' But Voroshilov, Malenkov, Zhdanov, Molotov, and Kaganovich were all opposed to this project.[41] For them ideological considerations took precedence over everything else. 'We need a Socialist Poland,' they said. 'If these men stay alive, even at our side, they will never be Socialists and will stab us in the back at the first opportunity. If they liberate Poland they will take power there. We should rather form a Polish workers' army.' Voroshilov and Zhdanov yelped that my father didn't know the Poles. *They* had had experience of them during the Soviet-Polish war[42] and knew what they were like! Molotov argued in more sententious style. For him, my father's political analysis was false. All the enemies of Socialism had to be destroyed, not just the Polish ones. This approach suited Stalin, and he gave the order to kill the officers.[43] My father then said: 'Do as you wish. But I shall not carry out this decision.'

'If you refuse,' came the reply, 'you lose your job and we shall get rid of you.' Zhdanov even proposed to replace him. All this is evidenced in the archives.[44] One can also consult a document which gives the names of the members of the *troika* charged with sentencing the Polish officers: my father's name is struck out by Stalin and Zhdanov. He had refused to take part,[45] and managed, even, using various pretences, to save 449 of the condemned men.[46]

When my father returned home and told us what had happened, he made this comment: 'I don't know how this will end.' For a whole week he remained uncertain of his fate, believing that he was going to be dismissed and replaced by Zhdanov. To avoid the worst he entrusted Shariko Tsereteli with the task of taking my mother and me back to Georgia, after a fictitious divorce that would separate us from him. But my mother was against this: 'Whatever happens we shall stay with you.'

'How can you decide for our son?' my father replied.

'That's my decision. There's no more to be said.' My mother was stubborn.

My father was sure that it would not be possible to hide this crime from posterity, as the truth always comes out in the end.[47]

He set out his opposition to the execution of the Polish officers in a memorandum. When Stalin read it he summoned my father and said: 'I'm warning you, Beria, for the first and last time. Henceforth I shall consider such steps taken by you as expressing disagreement with Politburo decisions and with my orders. I shall take it that this is your way of repudiating our policy.' He took my father's memorandum, crumpled it and put it in his safe. My father realised that he had gone as far as he could and had learnt his lesson. However, it was from that time, I think, that Stalin began to distrust him. The decision to shoot the Polish officers shows that Stalin planned to communise Europe after 1940. That is how Katyn must be interpreted.

Zhdanov took advantage of this affair, putting himself forward as replacement for my father. Stalin informed him that there would always be time to think about that, but that, for the time being, my father could still be useful. At the moment of the crisis we thought that Zhdanov, who saw himself as Stalin's heir, had attacked my father on his own initiative. After his death, however, and thanks to the indiscretions of his widow, which were reported to us, we learnt that Stalin had encouraged Zhdanov to go after my father's job. From that time, though, my father adopted a strategy for survival: he never told me this in so many words but it was the conclusion I drew from his behaviour. He saw to it, in fact, that he was constantly indispensable. He always had something in hand that would prevent Stalin from getting rid of him.

Summer 1940: the assassination of Trotsky

My father might have been dismissed in the spring of 1940 and though in the months that followed the danger retreated, he knew that his state of grace was provisional. He had understood that Stalin never forgot anything and that, one day, he would demand a reckoning for that affair.

For the moment Stalin had other things on his mind. He was not sure that the great discontent caused among the people by the wave of repression had passed away. He knew that if he put Zhdanov or Malenkov at the head of the NKVD a new era of terror would begin. My father was, therefore, particularly useful to him. The second reason why my father was spared, and this is not to his honour, was the twelfth attempt on Trotsky's life. This attempt was being prepared and Stalin awaited the results. He was quite determined to get Trotsky out of the way, being convinced that he jeopardised the foreign policy of the USSR.[48] My father tried to persuade him that Trotsky in exile presented no danger and was nothing but a 'political corpse' – not that he felt any sympathy with the man, whom he considered an extremist. I heard him explain to my mother that there was no such thing as Trotskyism: there was no difference between Trotskyist propaganda and ours, apart from the matter of 'building Socialism in one country taken separately.' But Stalin would hear nothing of this. 'Remember Spain. There we were not dealing with a "political corpse",' he retorted. 'In Spain it was the Anarchists, not the Trotskyists, who created our principal problem,' my father objected, adding: 'We observe every move Trotsky makes and have him under complete surveillance.' NKVD had indeed penetrated the entire Trotskyist movement with its agents. As my father saw it, eliminating Trotsky would nullify his efforts. He thought that it would be a better idea to undertake Trotsky's support instead of letting him depend financially on the British, the Germans and the Americans. But Stalin persisted: 'You underestimate the potential nuisance of Trotskyism.' Eventually he summoned Sudoplatov and the other officers entrusted with the operation and himself supervised the preparations. He had not forgotten the objections raised by my father and preferred, in any case, to supervise personally anything that was especially important to him. At the time my father did not appreciate that Stalin had a personal grievance against Trotsky, and the motive for his fury was in no way political. Later, my father concluded that rancour was indeed the decisive factor in his determination to have Trotsky killed. I agree. Stalin was capable of sacrificing a political interest for the mere pleasure of gratifying his thirst for vengeance. He never forgot people who had stood in his way.

The first communisation of the Baltic states

I had known the Baltic peoples since my earliest childhood. I was impressed by their sporting achievements and my father admired their efficiency. Moreover, they did not drink. There were many of them in the Cheka, first of all in Moscow, later in the republics. Lenin had deliberately encouraged the recruitment of foreigners to the Cheka and this policy (disapproved of by my father) was continued after his death.

Penetration of the Baltic states by Soviet agents went back well before 1939. The task of our agents was to support the local Communists and all the forces opposed to the established governments but also to sow dissension between the Baltic states themselves. During the autumn of 1939[49] we installed military bases on their territory. The Army had been given very strict instructions regarding the way it was to behave towards the civil population, and, at first, it respected these instructions.[50] The Germans hastened to strengthen their economic domination of these countries and also intensified their subversive activity. For a time the Soviet government hesitated as to the line to follow. Should it be satisfied with bourgeois governments which had a pro-Soviet orientation (which was my father's position) or should it proceed to the Sovietisation of these countries?

The policy to be followed in the Baltic states was the theme of a fresh discussion in the Politburo. My father suggested that their governments be left in place, with support to be given to those that might serve our interests. To him it seemed more useful to finance pro-Soviet elements rather than spend money on organising insurrections. He thought, particularly, of using the Latvian president Ulmanis, a man capable of understanding how advantageous for his country a pro-Soviet policy would be. He also pointed out that this plan would be easier to put into effect and that it had the merit of not alarming the Germans, who regarded the Baltic states as a province of theirs. Neutral Baltic states would be more advantageous to the Soviet Union. Besides, war was threatening and it would be better to avoid confrontations with the Baltic population and with Germany. Finally, if Germany attacked neutral Baltic states, that would constitute a *casus belli* much more decisive for the Anglo-Saxons than if these states had been incorporated into the Soviet Union. Confident in his argument, my father insisted that our services must apply themselves essentially to two tasks – recruiting members of the Baltic governments and exposing pro-German elements in those governments, who could then be thrown out by their own colleagues. Merkulov told me that, at the beginning of the discussion, Stalin had listened with interest to what my father had to say.

Merkulov, my father's deputy, also gave the Politburo an objective report on what he had observed during a journey through the Baltic states. He did not hide the fact that German agents and nationalists were active, but was careful to stress that the governments and administrations respected to the letter the agreements made with the USSR. He pointed out – and this, no doubt, in accord with my father – that the local Communist Parties were committing provocations, alluding, without naming him, to Zhdanov and his role in this sphere. He complained that these excesses[51] by Communists directed by Zhdanov were undermining the policy he was trying to implement through his agents. My father then remarked that he had known the Baltic peoples over a long period: if they gave their word one could rely on it. Molotov came out in vigorous opposition. According to him such arguments meant sacrificing the interests of the Baltic people, and they would not understand why the Soviet Government was not supporting them. Merkulov, who had seen with his own eyes the situation in the Baltic states, knew what the 'demands of the toiling masses' were worth, and lost his temper. 'What right has Molotov to lecture me and talk to me about "the Baltic people" when he lives in Moscow and has no notion of what is going on over there? What people is he talking about?' Zhdanov came to Molotov's rescue, arguing that our troops themselves would not understand our passivity if the local police were allowed to crush the Baltic proletariat before their eyes. Zhdanov and Molotov eventually produced a brilliant plan – to despatch to Riga our biggest battleship, the *Kirov*, carrying arms for the working class. When Merkulov heard of this scheme he returned to Moscow in panic and hastened to call on my father: 'Those morons have sent a warship and are distributing arms!' My father telephoned Kuznetsov at once and ordered him to put a stop to what was happening. However, the admiral replied that what was being done was being done on Stalin's personal orders.

Being the head of the Party in Leningrad, Zhdanov was responsible for giving guidance to the neighbouring Communist Parties. He opposed vigorously any coalition government: only one with a purely Communist policy would do. When, with his group, he succeeded in organising 'workers' demonstrations' in the Baltic states, he won Stalin's support for his policy.[52]

I remember a scene that occurred in this connection. My nanny Ella had family in the Baltic states. In the spring of 1940 she asked my father's permission to go and visit them. 'Don't go just now,' he replied. 'The situation there is very tense. To my great surprise, workers' demonstrations have been launched. Our troops are still keeping neutral, but things may change from one moment to the next.' At that time some people from the Baltic states come to see us at home. They spoke Russian very badly and expressed themselves in German. They were ministers and intellectuals whom my father intended to put into government in their native countries. Ella admired how well brought up they were and would say to me: 'Take a leaf from their book, Sergo. See how well they behave at table.' For my part I can't say that they made a good impression on me. My memory of these events is rather vague. I do recall, though, that these Baltic citizens complained that the Soviet Government had not kept its word and had put them in an impossible situation.[53]

When Stalin chose the policy advocated by Zhdanov, Molotov assembled the NKVD cadres responsible for the Baltic states, and called on them all to intensify their efforts to overthrow the bourgeois governments and put pro-Soviet elements into power. On 15 June 1940 the Soviet troops went into action. 'People's governments' were installed and were to 'appeal' in August 1940 for their countries to be incorporated in the USSR. In spite of everything, my father managed to save a few ministers of the former governments, at least those not disgusted by Soviet policy, and put them in the new governments. But the victory of the Party ideologues set the intelligentsia of the Baltic states finally against the USSR and pushed the Baltic peoples into the arms of the Germans. In the twinkling of an eye industry was disrupted. My father said to me: 'You see how one can antagonise a whole people by a few stupid measures.' He raged against Zhdanov.

Although he had supported Zhdanov's line, Molotov had not remained unaffected by my father's arguments. When some of his Politburo colleagues remarked to him that Beria had shown political immaturity, he retorted that even if he still lacked experience, he had shown undeniable subtlety.

Following these events many Soviet cultural delegations were sent into the Baltic states. I can see still one acquaintance of my mother's, a Russian, who, returning from one of these trips, asked her: 'Nina Teimurazovna, why don't you go to the Baltic states? The shops over there are magnificent and everything is so cheap!'[54] A few years later, during the war, I met some engineers from Riga in a NKVD laboratory. We conversed in German and, to my great surprise, they asked me where they were. I was still young at the time and was deeply shocked to realise that they did not know where they were. I spoke about this to my father and he replied that these Baltic citizens were privileged in comparison with some of their compatriots who were rotting in Siberia.[55]

In July 1940, a few weeks before the conclusion of the Baltic business, the USSR annexed Bessarabia. Stalin wanted to get close to the Romanian oilfields, which he had no intention of leaving to the Germans. In my father's view none of the territories acquired as a result of the Ribbentrop-Molotov pact possessed decisive strategic value. He foresaw that the war, when it came, would not be restricted to the frontiers, that it would be carried into our country or into Germany. Moreover, the Red Army would have to cope with hostile populations. Only the ignorant Party officials were unaware of these realities.[56]

The threat becomes specific

In 1940 Stalin had no fear of aggression from Japan.[57] After the thrashing inflicted on them by our troops in the previous year, in Manchuria, the Japanese realised that it was to their interest to keep out of trouble with the USSR. We had assembled considerable armoured forces and a powerful air force in the Far East. Had we wished, we could have penetrated deep into China, and the Japanese knew that. That was why the advocates of expansion southward and war with the USA triumphed in Japan.

On the other hand, from the moment when the pact with Hitler was signed, the entire Politburo was convinced that war with Germany was inevitable and could come in two or three years' time. Shortly before the 'Barbarossa' plan came into our hands Stalin burst in upon us, unexpectedly as usual, as he liked to know what was going on among the members of his entourage. He asked me: 'If you were sent to fight the Germans, would you be able to understand their dialects?' He knew that I had attended a German secondary school. Then he added: 'Do you know the Berlin dialect?' This was a very special dialect and I had not mastered it. He impressed on me that one should learn dialects, the importance of which he had realised during his stay in Austria. It was that day that I grasped how merely provisional the agreement with Germany was, in his mind. Many years later, Ryabikov, the Vice-Minister for Armaments, told me that a Soviet delegation headed by Tevosian, which went to Germany in March 1940 to order some armaments, had been told to insist on delivery deadlines not exceeding six months. 'War with Germany is coming. Try to get as much as you can as quickly as you can.' That was what was said to the delegates on the eve of their departure. The Germans had, of course, noted this point and asked the Soviet delegates for some clarifications. The reply they received was that the objectives laid down in the five-year plan had to be attained.

The lessons of the Finnish war were not without their uses. Stalin set about modernising the army. All our aircraft were renewed within two years, along with the leadership of our forces. In May 1940 Timoshenko succeeded Voroshilov at the Defence Commissariat. He was a perfectly decent man who had never denounced a colleague. Nobody had tried to compel him to take part in a trial of military men. It was well known that Timoshenko was a respectable man. Stalin also set on foot a commission of the Central Committee which he entrusted to Zhdanov. Its task was to draw up an inventory of our military resources. Why were our aircraft not ready? Why were there all these shortfalls? Zhdanov then sounded off against the apparatus of the Defence Commissariat, against military intelligence and against the armoured units. Timoshenko, who was a member of the commission, was afraid that the matter would degenerate into purges and trials. He came to see my father and share with him the anxiety he felt. My father advised him to protect the men whom he needed: as for the rest, he thought that Timoshenko should dismiss them, without being able to guarantee that this measure could save these officers' lives. A few victims had to be left as fodder for the Central Committee. This commission had not finished its work when the war began. The debacle of the first days confirmed the diagnosis made by the representatives of the Central Committee and a whole series of generals were judged and sentenced without investigation. When Timoshenko asked Stalin to spare certain officers, the reply he received was: 'You would have done better to entrust this purge to the NKVD instead of undertaking it yourself. Then you would not have been here today asking me to reprieve some officers when you don't know where the Germans are.' Stalin made it clear to Timoshenko that he had mixed himself up in something that did not concern him. He ought to have turned these officers over to the NKVD and let Beria deal with them. He was vexed that my father had been spared that dirty job. Since the Katyn affair he noted with suspicion every move my father made to avoid such base tasks.

June 1940

My father had not expected that one day all Europe would be working for Germany. The speed with which Poland fell in September 1939 had not been anticipated by us. Even more than Stalin[58] my father was surprised and put out by the defeat of France. He had been convinced of the strength of the French army[59] and thought that there would be a furious battle between it and the Wehrmacht. A group of our officers had studied in France after 1935, including two generals known to my father who were responsible for the Caucasian military region. One of them, Levandovsky, of Polish origin, was a most charming man. He loved children and when he visited us he drew me pictures of French tanks. He perished in the purges of 1937. The other, General Tyulenev, gave my father a full description of the French general staff and their military schools. In his view the French were technically weaker than the Germans, but intellectually their superiors. The German was a good executive, dull, and there was no need to supervise him. The Frenchman needed to be well officered, but he was mentally more flexible. France's defeat in 1940 came as a real shock to Tyulenev.

My father and Stalin were equally taken aback[60] by the news. I vaguely remember that Stalin even contemplated 'arming the people.'[61] He tried to understand the reasons for the disaster. Our military men, Zhukov among them I think, considered that the British had dodged combat and had several times left the French flanks exposed, so that they were surrounded. They saw this as conduct unworthy of an ally, and as another sign of British duplicity. My father, however, remarked to Zhukov that when the day came when the British wanted to fight they would prove to be excellent fighters. Stalin and my father took up the hypothesis of treason as an explanation of the French debacle. Our agent Lev Vasilevsky said that the French high command behaved more aberrantly than if it had been infiltrated by traitors, since the latter would at least have feared exposure. We knew how much the Germans had invested in order to corrupt France from within and render her leaders incapable of resistance. My father said that the press had played a considerable part in this demobilisation of society, this carelessness which prevailed even after the declaration of war. He had heard echoes of the exchanges between the

Georgian Mensheviks in Germany and those in France. The German-based Mensheviks warned the others: 'War is coming to you! Open your eyes!' Their compatriots in France replied: 'What war? Come and see us here. Everything's peaceful. There won't be any conflict ...' My father shared my mother's perplexity at the passive attitude of the French: 'Here is a European people with great traditions. As soon as it's in danger it starts to go after whores and drink itself silly instead of taking itself in hand to resist. How can we understand it?' My mother observed that it was the normal reaction of an individual faced with danger. The Georgians, too, went on a spree before going off to war. My father used the French example to highlight the danger that patriotism-to-order could constitute for us.

Nevertheless, he respected the head of the French government, Paul Reynaud, because he did try to organise resistance to the Germans. I remember hearing him discuss the negotiations between Reynaud and Churchill: how it was I don't know, but he was informed of these contacts in the fullest detail. After the evacuation of Dunkirk he and Stalin concluded that the Germans would not attempt a landing in Britain. If Hitler had had such a plan he would never have allowed that evacuation to take place. Either negotiations between Britain and Germany, aimed against us, had already borne fruit or else Hitler was doing a good turn to the British so as to promote such discussions. Stalin interpreted the Cripps mission[62] to Moscow in the summer of 1940 as a manoeuvre by the British. In the midst of their dealings with Germany the British wanted to strengthen their position by making Hitler believe that his Soviet ally was not reliable. Stalin accepted, however, that the British also wanted a rapprochement with the USSR, but Molotov, more radical, saw in the British approach merely a provocation. I say nothing of Zhdanov, who was invariably pro-German. My father thought that the British were sincere but that Churchill lacked a completely free hand, owing to the Germanophile majority in Parliament. He greatly distrusted Cripps because he was a Socialist and my father suspected that the Socialists were less patriotic than the Conservatives.

I was 16 at this time. With my comrades I followed closely the struggles that were shaking Europe and we talked about them. That year there were in my form seven young Germans, sons of Communists who had taken refuge in Moscow. What was my consternation when I saw them openly rejoicing in the Wehrmacht's victory in France, since the father of one of these boys had been executed by Hitler. 'How can you be rubbing your hands at the sight of the Germans in Paris? You know they are fascists!' I said to him. 'All the same, they are Germans,' he replied.

When I told my father this he shrugged his shoulders. 'The Germans are pleased with their victory, that's natural. But there are some idiots among us who are just as pleased.' It was not long before I had confirmation of that from my history teacher, who was fanatically pro-German. One day he shared his enthusiastic forecasts with us: 'In a few days Turkey will enter the war on Germany's side.' Turkey! We often spoke of that country at home and I considered that I knew something about it. I had, in particular, heard that in no circumstances would the Soviet Union allow Turkey to enter the war on Germany's side. We should take preventive action, sending troops into Turkey. The British, from their side, would fall upon the Turks if they dared to move. I decided, therefore, to set forth all that I knew on the subject. 'Petr Konstantinovich,' I interrupted, 'your idea about Turkey is wrong ...' and I poured it all out. My remarks spread like a trail of gunpowder. The Party and the Komsomol seized on the affair, and it came to my father's ears. He sent for me. 'Have you lost your wits? Taking to school what you hear at home! Try to understand. What Beria's son says goes straight to the ears of the ambassadors.' He did not punish me, confining himself to explaining that, if he trusted me to be present at certain discussions, then, in return, I must control my tongue. This was my first lesson in politics. Later, my history teacher was expelled from the Party on a charge of 'Trotskyism,' but my father arranged that this matter went no further.

In Berlin

In November 1940 Molotov met Hitler for a discussion on the share-out of spheres of influence. On his return to Moscow he reported to the Politburo. He said that the talk had been very difficult as he had not managed to interrupt the Führer.[63] The latter had, essentially, assured him that he was not going to dwell upon trifles such as the presence of German troops in Finland and Romania. He offered the Soviet Union a veritable partition of the world.[64] Stalin, who knew that the Germans were carrying on parallel discussions with Britain,[65] saw Hitler's proposals as a provocation. Nevertheless, he expressed dissatisfaction with Molotov's attitude during this encounter, blaming him for lack of flexibility.[66] He ought to have left the door open for negotiations and dragged things out at greater length instead of crudely informing Hitler that the USSR was not interested in his proposals.

Stalin appointed Dekanozov ambassador to Berlin in November 1940. Dekanozov had as counsellor Amayak Kobulov, an agent of the NKVD. Although not of shining intelligence, Kabulov had charm and was a ladykiller. He was given the task of seducing the ladies in the German capital so as to get as much information as possible from them. Being very stupid he continually boasted of these exploits. He prided himself, for example, on a liaison with an actress who knew Hitler's photographer. She confided in him that, one week before every military operation by his army, it was Hitler's custom to stick on the wall a map of the country where the operation was to take place. One day Kobulov noticed a map of the Soviet Union and hastened to report this. At least that was what he proclaimed after the event.[67]

The 'Barbarossa' plan

Everything that has been written about the 'surprise' attack is false. We knew about the 'Barbarossa' plan in detail before it was put into effect.[68] Our industry was actively preparing for war. Labour discipline had been strengthened and the working day lengthened.[69] I even remember jokes about the doubling of the price of vodka. All the intelligence supplied by our service showed that the conflict would come in 1941. My father had the German plans and Vasilevsky, who was then head of the operational department of the General Staff, often came to our house to study these plans with him. He stayed for nearly a month at the NKVD to study 'Barbarossa' with a group of officers.[70] At the end of this mission he reported his conclusions to the General Staff and to the Military Council led by Defence Commissar Timoshenko. In this connection Stalin showed himself extremely jealous of my father's collaboration with the military. One day, when he had tried in vain to meet Vasilevsky, at a time when the latter was in the NKVD, Stalin said to him, reproachfully: 'Why is the NKVD meddling in questions that concern only the General Staff?'

We knew, therefore that the German offensive would come in May 1941. We knew where it would strike and were ready with a counter-offensive. Two or three months before the invasion Dekanozov's wife came to visit my mother. She said she had brought her children back to the USSR with her because war was imminent. But she added that Stalin was dissatisfied with her husband's work. The information he sent to Moscow did not agree with that which Stalin had. The latter blamed Dekanozov for confirming Beria's opinion instead of doing a proper job of intelligence gathering. Dekanozov never stopped warning Moscow that war was imminent. He was thoroughly depressed. Eventually his wife returned to Berlin. In his last message he declared that only an approach at the highest level could now prevent the German attack.

The NKVD is split

Timoshenko had been friendly with my father since their joint efforts to rehabilitate the military men under sentence. He had also appreciated his proposals at the time of the Finnish crisis. He asked Stalin to appoint my father Vice-Minister of Defence, with as his pretext the importance that intelligence would have in the coming war. Stalin asked him: 'Where do you get the idea that Beria will agree to being Number Two?' Timoshenko was foolish enough to reply frankly: 'I have talked to him about it and he said he would be very pleased to accept the appointment, giving up the NKVD if you agree.' Stalin avoided replying to this by saying that he could not take such a decision on his own but must consult the Politburo. When Timoshenko told my father the result of this interview he exclaimed: 'How could you tell him that I agree? It's all up now, you can be sure of that!' Although Timoshenko had known Stalin for twenty years, he was no politician.

In February 1941 my father was deprived of control of State Security.[71] He announced this to my mother in these terms: 'Stalin has taken the first step. I've done what he wanted of me and now I'm of no more use to him.' But he reassured her by adding: 'Don't be afraid. He has other things to think about now than settling accounts.' At heart, he was glad to be rid of the security organs.

Stalin entrusted State Security to Merkulov. He explained to him: 'We have divided the NKVD so as to be able to concentrate on counter-espionage. Beria is too keen on intelligence-gathering work. He neglects counter-espionage, which doesn't interest him. I count on you to make it a priority.' Stalin was sure that Merkulov, with his air of a refined intellectual, would be a docile instrument. Stalin was soon to realise what a mistake he had made.

My father retained some responsibilities in industry. He had come to the conclusion that the best way to escape the fate of Yagoda and Yezhov was to get control of war industry. He applied himself to this as soon as Stalin released him from State Security. And it was in this way that the war saved him, for he became indispensable once again. For the same reason he interested himself very early in the atomic bomb, which became his escape-hatch.

The affair of the German submarine

A month before the war began I went by train to Leningrad, along with Admiral Kuznetsov and other officers. From there we went to the Kronstadt naval base where we were to meet, in the greatest secrecy, the captain of a German submarine. My father came by aeroplane to join us. He was accompanied by Admiral Geller, commanding the Baltic Fleet, a handsome man, one of that type found in the aristocracy of the navy. My father had not invited any representative of the Leningrad Party, his relations with Zhdanov being already very bad indeed. It is even likely that Zhdanov was not informed of the visit. Nor were there any interpreters from the NKVD or the army: we four were by ourselves, and I translated. We entered the submarine. The German officer explained that he had come from Kiel and that he had been obliged to tie up the National Socialist members of his crew, who were opposed to his move. He then gave us several sealed envelopes containing orders for his mission: they were orders for war: the German added that on receipt of a certain coded signal all German vessels in Soviet ports were to put to sea.

Later, my father had another talk with the German officer. The question was whether, after having given us all that information, he could return home. According to the young captain there was no great problem. He had kept contact with his headquarters and his mission had, in any case, been to patrol the waters near Kronstadt. As for the members of the crew who had disappeared, we need not worry about them either. He would see to them. When war came he would seek refuge in a Soviet port and, if ordered to go back to Germany, he would defect. Meanwhile he would pretend to carry out his patrol. Kuznetsov told me later that the submarine had gone. I don't know what happened to it. Very few people were informed of this ultra-secret affair.

Stalin's calculations

The description given by Suvorov of the disposition of our forces on the eve of the German attack is correct. Nevertheless, I never heard Vasilevsky, Shtemenko or Zhukov speak of launching a preventive war.[72] We merely provided ourselves with the means of hitting back in the event of a German onslaught. Some of our military men did indeed propose that we attack,[73] but Stalin was against this,[74] saying that the disadvantages of such an initiative would weigh much heavier in the long run than the momentary advantage of surprise: 'Provided that you can guarantee that we shall hold out against their assaults, it is preferable that public opinion should see the USSR as victim rather than aggressor.' It is foolish to allege, as some still do, that Stalin planned to attack Germany. His mistake was, indeed, that he did not strike a preventive blow at the moment when it was certain that war was going to break out.[75] He told the Politburo that the political disadvantages of a preventive attack were too great. He preferred to wait for the offensive, at the risk of having to retreat a very long way.[76] In a word, German aggression had to be obvious.[77]

On Molotov's motion Stalin became head of the government on 5 May 1941, so as to concentrate all power in expectation of war and to show the whole country that the execution of decisions was going to be subject to stricter checking than ever. This also sent a message to Hitler: we were ready for war, if that was what he wanted.[78] At the same time we deployed 20 new armies along our western frontiers and Stalin persistently urged the military to find new ways to strengthen our defence line. However, they told him that no improvement was needed[79] and Zhukov thought that it would be useless to establish a second line of defence. I knew about all this because, after every meeting with Stalin, the military men were invited to our place and they continued their discussions there. They argued exclusively in terms of numbers, of men and weapons, forgetting that the German army was inured to war and also had an excellent signals service. It knew how to combine operations by aircraft and armoured forces, and could rely on its middle-ranking officers.

More fundamentally, Stalin remained convinced that the Germans would not attack the USSR because it was not in their interest to do so. Hitler would not launch such a war, at least unless he yielded to British provocations.[80] In short the Germans would not of their own initiative turn against the USSR, but everything was to be feared from British provocation. The statement by the Tass Agency on 14 June 1941[81] is to be explained in this context: Stalin wanted to prove to the Germans that he was not preparing to attack them. He really hoped to put off the conflict.

He would have preferred that the war did not break out before 1943, but, this being unlikely, he hoped to hold out at least until the spring of 1942, and he would have agreed to all sorts of economic concessions to ensure that that happened, estimating that the USSR would be ready by this date.

The British position

Hitler would certainly have agreed to make substantial concessions (he would have evacuated France and Africa) in order to secure British support. Churchill was able to play upon this. He pretended to conduct negotiations with Hess and others, even discussing points of detail. The Soviet government doubtless knew the content of these negotiations better than the British government itself. When, in May 1941, the Number Two of the Nazi Party, Rudolf Hess, landed in Scotland, Stalin gave free rein to his irritation with Hitler. How could he dare to behave like that when the Soviet Union had just come to an understanding with him? He was certainly no great statesman if he showed himself incapable to sticking to one policy! The Hess affair proved that Hitler was preparing a war against the USSR.

Hess's contact with the British was followed by Stalin hour by hour, studied microscopically, analysed minutely. We were up to date in everything that was going on even sooner than the British government was, thanks to Philby. My father was particularly worried to learn that it was Hess who was negotiating. That man had several acquaintances among the British aristocracy and my father was afraid that the Germanophile lobby might use these proposals for peace with Germany in order to overthrow Churchill. However, Churchill emerged smartly from this situation. He distorted Hess's proposals in the reports he gave to some ministers. In fact he was in control of the people who were in contact with Hess. According to my father Churchill owed his escape to the support he received from the Intelligence Service. As for Stalin, he wondered how Churchill meant to act. Would he return to his old policy of an anti-Bolshevik crusade backed by Germany? He saw in the warning that Churchill sent him, about the imminence of a German attack, proof of the British leader's intention to draw the USSR into a conflict with Hitler and a sign of Britain's double-dealing. My father did not agree.

Churchill succeeded splendidly in his attempt to set Germany against the Soviet Union, and saved his own country. I congratulate him here on his political cleverness. He deceived us and the Germans alike. The latter remained convinced, to the last moment, that the British would be with them when they went to war with the USSR. I see nothing wrong with that: it was the only way for Britain to survive. But at the same time as they were urging the Germans against us the British were frightened: they feared that Hitler might not attack us, or that, if he did, the USSR would be too weak to resist. This twofold fear was part of the explanation for their ambiguous attitude. At any rate, that was my father's view.

The last days of peace

On 24 May 1941 Stalin and Timoshenko received the commanders of the military regions. Each had to report on the situation in his region. Were the troops ready to repulse an enemy attack? The General Staff sent them directives. Some had time to carry these out, others failed to do so because of their lack of experience. Stalin and our dear military men were firmly convinced that our forces were capable of resisting the German offensive, that they could stand up to the first onslaught and then reply by launching offensives into East Prussia and the Balkans. Order was given to our troops to do nothing that might cause us to appear responsible for the aggression.[82] The Germans must definitely not be provoked. My father shared that view. The head of military intelligence, Golikov, was blamed for providing incorrect information. Actually, he passed on all the facts at his disposal, even if he was unable to analyse them properly. My father considered that Golikov was neither a soldier nor an intelligence officer. Dekanozov in Berlin and our numerous agents in Germany knew the date for the German attack, but every time anyone tried to convince Stalin of this he would reply: 'You told me the attack would come in April and it still hasn't begun.'

A few weeks before the invasion I heard my father tell Kuznetsov that he had put the frontier guards on alert and was going to ask Stalin for Timoshenko and the General Staff to provide them with artillery cover. One week before the attack was launched my mother and I didn't know from one day the next whether war would break out. That same week Svetlana came unexpectedly to our house and stayed with us as she sometimes used to. On 20 June my father telephoned us: 'Don't expect me today, or tomorrow, or the day after.' He had ordered Maslennikov, the commander of the frontier-guard units, to put his men on the alert.

War

During the night of 22-23 June 1941 Stalin convened the Politburo and shared with it the perplexity he felt: how could Hitler not have realised it was to his interest to stay allied with the USSR?[1] How could he not see that the USSR had far more to offer him, economically, than America or Britain? At that moment Stalin really believed that Hitler had simply gone for a reversal of alliances and that the Anglo-Saxons would back him in his war against the Soviet Union. The statement that Stalin let himself collapse in confusion during the first days of the war is rubbish. Both my mother and the head of the Party in Moscow, Shcherbakov,[2] told me what happened in those crucial days. Once the German attack had been confirmed, Stalin, far from collapsing, set himself to receive the military and other leaders.[3] My father spent three-quarters of his time with Stalin, when not busy performing tasks entrusted to him by Stalin. Every day, however, he managed to telephone us.

Stalin and our military men had not appreciated that our senior officers were unable to command troops. The Germans broke through our lines not because we lacked weapons or men but because our army had never fought. Only the frontier guards had experience. Among our pilots, only those who had been in the Spanish war or the conflict with Japan succeeded in taking off when the German aircraft appeared. It took three or four months of war for our troops to acquire experience. It was not the German attack that took Stalin by surprise, but the collapse of our troops. Our army had not seriously begun to prepare for war until after the fiasco in Finland.

The shambles

In the first days of the war our army's communications were non-existent. This was not, as subsequently alleged, the result of operations by German commandos but quite simply the usual Russian 'balls-up'. The only exceptions were the navy, the frontier guards and some of the armoured corps. Of all the counter-offensives planned by the General Staff only two succeeded – one towards Königsberg and the other towards the south: but, as the other units fell back, we lost these armoured forces. Our military leaders made reconnaissance flights over various points on the front so as to obtain an overview of the situation. Stalin had to accept the evidence they gathered: soldiers were refusing to fight and fleeing the battlefield. One of my cousins, an officer in an armoured unit in Byelorussia, told me that, even before fighting began, his men had blown up their tanks and disappeared into the woods. One commanding officer even had the brilliant idea of sheltering his men from bombs under a bridge ... which the Germans duly bombed!

When Stalin understood that his troops were retreating without fighting he knew moments of discouragement and mad rage. 'Why this rout? Why are the military not on top of the situation?' he kept repeating. 'How is it that Beria is in touch with every frontier position while the military have lost contact with the headquarters of the army groups?'

'The answer is simple,' my father explained, wishing to calm the atmosphere. 'The frontier positions, unlike the army headquarters, have ultra-modern radio equipment.' But Stalin would not cool down, furious as he was not at the German advance but at the helplessness of our armies. 'Why? Why?' he kept demanding, frightened at the collapse of our troops. Those around him spoke of inexperience, surprise, lack of communications, 'But why? Where is your accursed working class?' My father eventually said to him that if these men had been property owners they would have fought like lions and tigers from the first days of the war. Malenkov, Timoshenko and others who were present then heard Stalin say this: 'Lenin left us a state and we have turned it into shit.' My father found this formulation excellent, and when he told me about the conversation he mentioned that, previously, Stalin had expressed himself critically about the sort of state Lenin had left us ... He said no more on that subject.

In September Stalin hit upon a solution. Since our setbacks were due to desertion by our troops, he decided to station behind them units which were ordered to fire on men running away from the battle. What can one think of an army in which one soldier is ordered to fire on the enemy and another is ordered to fire on his compatriots? There was something dirty and sticky there, like in Dostoevsky's books.

A crisis at the top

It was only several days after the invasion began that Stalin let himself go. He had needed a little time to take the measure of the disaster.[4] He then withdrew for a few days to ponder on the measures to be taken and what to do. He received nobody during those days. The Politburo continued to meet, but without him. Some of the members started to murmur. Among the most vehement was Shcherbakov. During one of these sessions when Stalin was absent, he turned to Molotov and said: 'Vyacheslav, be our leader!'[5] My father broke in: 'Calm down, or I'll hang you up by your feet.' The idea of Molotov as leader struck him as comical. Voznesensky, the head of Gosplan, discussed with my father what needed to be done. Without waiting for orders from Stalin they prepared the plan for evacuating the most important factories, using NKVD transport units supplied by my father. The latter never breathed a word about what his or others' motives were during those fateful days. Apparently, the members of the Politburo knew that they could manage without Stalin but his prestige among the masses was so great that they could not overthrow him at this moment when it was essential to mobilise the people. What seems to me most interesting is that nobody reported Shcherbakov's behaviour to Stalin. Khrushchev and Zhdanov were absent. Malenkov did not inform on Shcherbakov because they were very close and Stalin might have concluded that he had encouraged his friend to act as he did. Molotov kept his mouth shut because to tell Stalin that someone had seen him as Stalin's successor would be dangerous to him, above all. As for my father, he said nothing because he was delighted to see Shcherbakov in a state of terror. To the end of his life Shcherbakov trembled lest Stalin get wind of the matter. 'Lavrenti, what will happen to me if he finds out?' he would ask my father, who always replied: 'Nothing good, you can be sure of that.' Shcherbakov was lucky, as he stayed in Stalin's favour right down to his death in 1945. But he never again dared to oppose my father openly.

The war necessitated abandonment of the methods of government imposed by the Party. My father obtained documents on the Defence Committee which was set up during the Civil War – he always studied historical precedents – and that was how, on 30 June 1941, the State Defence Committee, the GKO, came into being. This organisation concentrated all power itself and even had priority over the Politburo. The Party's organs were subordinated to it. This structure, conceived by my father, suited him well, as it made it possible to bypass the Party's apparatchiks.

It was he and Molotov who had to take the initiative in creating the GKO. My father counted on Stalin's approval, since the situation was desperate. The members of the Politburo asked urgently to be received by Stalin, who eventually invited them to his *dacha*. He believed that they were coming to tell him that he had been relieved of his functions. Later, my father described the scene to my mother. 'I had decided to concentrate my attention on his face and not to miss any of his expressions or gestures. It was obvious that Stalin expected that anything could happen, even the worst. When Molotov told him that Malenkov and I proposed to form the GKO and make him its chairman, the tension left his eyes.' Stalin contented himself with insisting that the GKO should have a small membership[6] and he began to define the tasks of each member,[7] organised his work schedule and squeezed the members 'like lemons,' in his usual way. My father said to us, laughing: 'I understood at that moment that all present would come to a bad end.' Khrushchev was absent because he was in the Ukraine and learnt of this episode from my father.[8] When he referred to those memorable hours my father always said to his colleagues: 'We were witnesses to Stalin's moments of weakness and he will never forgive us for that. Don't forget it.' He often teased Mikoyan, who had hidden behind the backs of the others so that Stalin should not see him. The funniest thing in the whole affair was that even Molotov understood the risk they had taken. He said to my father one day: 'Iosif Vissarionovich will never forgive that move of ours.'

The first months of the war

The people's militia was called up on 4 July 1941 and the NKVD was given charge of organising the partisan movement. My father thought it criminal to involve the population like this. It would serve no purpose and would only cause massacres of civilians.[9] In his view, so long as we were retreating, resistance should be left to small, well-equipped and well-trained groups who could cause diversions by sabotaging bridges and railways.[10] Still, the decision had been taken and my father had to apply it. This he did, however, in his own way. Thus, he shocked a lot of people when he eliminated courses in Marxism-Leninism from the training programme of these partisans, considering that it would be more beneficial for them to cultivate physical fitness than to fill their heads with quotations from Lenin. These partisans were divided into two sorts of units, under Sudoplatov's command – those which confined themselves to collecting information and those which carried out sabotage operations. When our army began to win victories, everyone claimed to be a partisan.

From the beginning of the German attack Churchill offered us his help. Stalin told the Politburo that the British would regale us with fine words for a year, without doing anything, so as to see how things would turn out.[11] For his part, he made several attempts to negotiate with the Germans, so as to confuse them. The Wallenbergs, Swedish industrialists, acted as go-betweens in one of these initiatives. Molotov conducted the negotiations, making use of my father's channels of communication.[12] My father, however, thought that these moves would come to nothing, except to cause us to lose time and to expose our agents to the Germans. The Wehrmacht pressed on and Hitler did not change his mind.

On 5 July negotiations began with the Polish government in London.[13] These were closely followed by my father. Sikorski appointed General Anders to form and command the Polish army created on Soviet soil. Anders was one of the officers whom my father had saved from the massacre at Katyn. He had lived with us for nearly a month after leaving prison, on 4 August 1941.[14] At the time I did not understand what he represented. I liked him – I am not, of course, talking about his political views[15] – and he pleased my father very much on account of his independent behaviour. Anders was the same in prison and at our house. Opposed to Pilsudski's policy of creating a cordon sanitaire against the Soviet Union, he favoured an independent Poland having good neighbourly relations with the USSR.[16]

The formation of a Polish army in the USSR was approved, but Stalin was extremely reluctant when it came to equipping this army. My father showed no surprise at this attitude. He had even expected it. Eventually, since this army seemed destined never to be used, my father interceded for it to be allowed to leave the USSR in spring 1942. He knew that, otherwise, steps would be taken to exterminate it. Merkulov nevertheless asked Anders to leave behind a group of officers whom my father planned to introduce into the Polish Communist army led by Berling.[17] Anders would not hear of this, and he made a mistake there, for his men would have occupied high positions in Poland. Later he was to admit his mistake.[18]

At that time my father regarded Poland as very important. He wanted that country to be the nucleus of a confederation of Central European states[19] which would include the Baltic states.[20] He did not see Czechoslovakia playing that role. He distrusted President Beneš, whom he found shifty.[21] He thought Beneš aimed to become the head of the confederation.[22] The pre-war period had shown that he regarded Central Europe as his fief. As a real shyster he aimed to take the credit for the confederation for himself and thought that the Soviet Union would help him to do this.[23] That was why he showed himself so accommodating in his relations with us. My father, however, thought that there was nobody more suitable than a Polish patriot like Anders to carry out the plan for a confederation. He hoped that this belt of states, more advanced than the USSR, would contribute to our development and 'get the cart of the Communist economy out of the rut it was stuck in.'

On 20 July 1941 Stalin decided to merge the NKVD and the State Security Service again. He entrusted my father with responsibility for the merger, despite his objections. 'I'm fed up with these petty games,' said my father to my mother when he heard of his appointment. 'The next time he wants to give me extra tasks to do I'm going to shake off the NKVD once and for all.' But it was wartime and Stalin needed results. In that moment of crisis and despite his doubts about my father, he had more confidence in him than in the other members of the Politburo. He knew that a Georgian would be the last to plot against him. As soon as the danger was past, in 1943, Stalin was to go back on that decision.

During this critical period Stalin wanted to send Svetlana and me to Georgia, chaperoned by my mother. I revolted against this. I yearned to fight, in spite of my 17 years, and I presented myself for this purpose at the Komsomol organisation to which I belonged. As I knew German I was assigned to an intelligence school in a suburb of Moscow. My father approved of this decision. I undertook a term of probation and was then sent to Iran, after two failed attempts to parachute into Germany, in the neighbourhood of Peenemünde.[24] Personally, I had never doubted that we should win, even if I cannot say today on what I based that conviction. The masses were convinced that the Germans would quickly be routed. In the country's leading circles, though some were less optimistic, they did not let this appear and feigned the same certainty. I knew, however, that shortly before the outbreak of war my father thought that, in the long run, the Germans would succumb to the combined efforts of the Anglo-Saxons. He based this belief on an estimate of the economic capacities of the two camps. Even control of Europe and alliance with Japan could not guarantee victory to Hitler. Everybody was amazed at the Führer's stupidity. He had let himself be made a fool of by the British! As for the latter, to them we ascribed the policy which had been our own: wait until the contending powers had bled each other white, then prolong the struggle by supporting the side that was about to succumb. Even Maisky, though pro-British, shared that view: 'When the Germans have given us a good thrashing,' he said, 'the British will decide it's time to lend us a helping hand.'

The collaborating governments

After the war I met Professor Koshlyakov, a mathematician who formerly occupied a chair at Leningrad University. He was arrested during the war for 'attempting to form a government that would collaborate with the Germans.' When I knew him he was being allowed, though a prisoner, to work at his speciality. I took advantage of this to ask him to initiate me in model-making mathematics. In this way I was able to study under his guidance for nearly two years. He told me the circumstance of his arrest. 'It was at the beginning of the war. Leningrad was under siege and the Germans might enter the city at any moment. One fine day Zhdanov summoned me, along with a dozen other scholars and scientists working in various fields. He assembled us and said that the Party's regional committee had decided, with approval from higher authority, to get ready a group of people who would constitute the Russians' representatives in the administration that the Germans would set up. They would be responsible for contacting the Germans if they took over Leningrad. Most of us were far from enthusiastic. Politics held no attraction for us. But nobody asked us for our opinions, and documents were manufactured for us which were to show that, even under Soviet rule, we had been carrying out underground activity aimed at seizing power. These preparations came to nothing because the Germans did not take Leningrad, and eventually Zhdanov ordered the arrest of our whole group. We were accused of being counter-revolutionaries in cahoots with the Germans! It was no good our reminding the authorities that we had acted on their instigation, with the NKVD's full knowledge. They locked us up and we signed our confessions. The oddest thing was that Zhdanov, at the audience he gave me, denied that he had fostered this collaborationist government.'[25]

When next day I saw my father I asked him to grant an amnesty to Koshlyakov: 'The only way I can do that,' he replied, 'is to release him along with some others. If I release him on his own, that may come back on me. Appoint him director of a research project, even if he doesn't take much part in it, and I'll see what I can do.' I followed his advice and Koshlyakov was set free. This sort of affair was not unique. Governments of the same kind, made up of intellectuals, had been provided for in all the regions threatened with German occupation. It was thought that the Germans would take them into consideration and that they would enjoy the people's confidence. In Georgia, the writer Gamsakhurdia, the philosopher Notsubidze and Machavariani, a Party functionary, were to be members of the government. Gamsakhurdia was marked out for this task owing to his reputation as a Germanophile.[26] In small localities, similar appointments of *starostas* were made to serve as Russian representatives in the German administration. This measure had some tragic consequences when, very often, Soviet partisans killed men who had been put in office by the NKVD.

Zhdanov's role in Leningrad

Zhdanov was responsible for the deaths of millions of men and women in Leningrad. He had been instructed to disperse the storehouses containing the strategic reserves of food that were to enable Leningrad to withstand a siege of two or three years. New sheds had to be built and these stocks scattered amongst them, at any cost. The military and the NKVD pressed for this to be done but, through his incompetence, Zhdanov did not get this work done in time and the wooden storehouses were burnt down by the Germans. Not only did he let these reserves be lost, dooming the city to famine, he also committed errors of strategy. Thus, he provoked panic among the Leningraders by preparing to evacuate them. Zhdanov was typical of the incompetents, those men of whom my father said that they were distinguished only for their ideological ardour but knew how to do nothing except carry out witch-hunts. Voroshilov commanded the fleet, which did nothing whatsoever. It is hard to say which of these two caused the most harm.

On 10 September Stalin sent Zhukov to organise the defence of the city, which was close to panic and surrender. When Zhukov reported, he showed that there was no military leadership and that the political leadership was no better.[27] Malenkov proposed that Zhdanov be court-martialled. Zhdanov's hatred of Malenkov dated from this incident, which he never forgave. Stalin was going to agree, but my father, despite his hostility to Zhdanov, advised against it. 'This is a bad moment for judging a member of the Politburo,' he said. In my opinion, he preferred to have an opponent like Zhdanov, whom he found not very dangerous on account of his incompetence and obvious limits.

Moscow: the decisive days

I was not in Moscow in October 1941, at the most critical moment of the war.[28] People wondered if it would be necessary to abandon the capital.[29] My father was the only member of the Politburo to advise Stalin to stay. The others, notably Malenkov and, especially, Shcherbakov, the head of the Party organisation in Moscow, wanted him to leave. My father later told my mother and me that he had told Stalin: 'If you go, Moscow will be lost. To ensure your security we can turn the Red Square into an airstrip. The army and the people must know that you are in Moscow.' Stalin shared this view, otherwise he would have ignored my father's advice. And when Shcherbakov began insisting that he leave Moscow, Stalin said to him: 'Your attitude can be explained in two ways. Either you are good-for-nothings and traitors or else you are idiots. I prefer to regard you as idiots.' My father would never have acted as he did if he had not known what Stalin was like and anticipated his reactions.[30]

The Party organs were evacuated. My father was overjoyed at the departure of the Central Committee, all the organs of propaganda and the officials of the NKID. 'Ouf,' he said, delighted, 'now we can breathe. All the spoilsports and incompetents who wield a bad influence on Iosif Vissarionovich are now far away. If only this could last.' All that were left in Moscow were the GKO and the people indispensable for the country's administration and the war effort. In this period the members of the government and the military enjoyed more latitude than previously because it was simply impossible for them to consult Stalin on every decision they had to take. He confined himself to defining the overall policy.

I returned to the capital on 7 November, just in time to attend the great military parade. This has remained etched in my memory. The pupils of my schools formed part of the guard in the Red Square. The whole world thought Moscow had fallen, and here was Stalin reviewing his troops! The parade took place in the morning, three hours earlier than usual. The Germans did not bomb Moscow until the afternoon. This review restored the people's courage. It had a colossal effect.[31]

After their defeat before Moscow, however, the Germans demonstrated their superiority. Our soldiers thought they would be able to pursue their advantage as far as Smolensk, but the Wehrmacht resisted step by step. The fighting was furious. When Stalin saw that we had come to the end of our reserves, he called off our offensive. Our allies accused us at the time of wishing to make a separate peace with Germany. In reality we were unable to continue the offensive. Later I heard our military men complain that it was necessary to plead with Stalin on one's knees in order to get him to release an extra tank or aircraft. He kept an inventory of our reserves in a little notebook and displayed stubborn stinginess when they had to be distributed.[32] He had some memorable disputes with Zhukov over these reserves.

Towards the South

The occupation of Iran

Stalin agreed to a joint occupation of Iran with the British: they were to control the south, we the north.[33] He made it a condition of this agreement that the British must take responsibility for the territories under French mandate. For this occupation of Iran we had to take troops from the Turkish frontier. Stalin was not afraid to strip that line, being convinced that Turkey would be forced to restrain herself. From one side the Soviet Union could threaten Turkey from Iranian Azerbaijan, while on the other there were the Kurds. My father would even have agreed to an occupation of Iran by the British alone. He considered that a confrontation with Britain was not desirable.

After the German attack on 22 June 1941 Churchill planned to send British troops into Caucasia so as to prevent the Germans from acquiring the oil of Baku.[34] These British reinforcements would enable the Soviets to send to the front the units stationed in Caucasia. My father told me how Stalin reacted when he gave him this information, which my father had obtained through his agents. 'No doubt they want to send the troops that they had prepared to fight us at the time of the Finnish war,' he observed acidly. My father reminded Stalin that it was the French, not the British who had prepared to bomb Baku. Stalin was sceptical. My father then showed him the documents concerning the Franco-British plans of that time. One hundred thousand British soldiers were supposed to attack us through Norway while the French destroyed our oil industry in the south. He pointed out that the British were now no longer able to count on French forces which were controlled by the Vichy government, and preferred to keep them out of it ...

When the British proposal became official, Stalin laid it before the Politburo, saying: 'If we let the British install themselves in Caucasia we shall never get rid of them.' Timoshenko suggested nevertheless that some army corps stationed in Caucasia be transferred to fight on the Western front. My father went further, proposing that the troops stationed on the Iranian frontier, and intended to take the offensive, be similarly transferred, while leaving untouched those responsible for defending the frontier. Stalin refused. But not long after, at the beginning of autumn, he did authorise the transfer of two or three army corps.

My first mission in Iran

At the intelligence school where I registered at the very beginning of the war I was able to learn encryption, deciphering, radio transmission, location by compass, map reading, the use of weapons and parachute-jumping. I was 17 when my instruction ended and I was sent by the General Staff to Iran with the rank of lieutenant. Two men who graduated with me were sent to Turkey, where we had an excellent network, and from there, thanks to the passports obtained for them, they made their way to Bulgaria, then to Hungary, and eventually to Germany. One of them got a job in the Messerschmitt factories, while the other managed to infiltrate Peenemünde. I remained in Iran from December 1941 to March 1942, very disappointed at not having been sent to Germany.

I was near Kurdistan. I encoded and transmitted information to Baku, where a section of our General Staff was stationed. On the spot we were in touch with Kurdish tribes whom we supplied with enormous quantities of arms. Some Kurds were sent to Azerbaijan or Georgia to undergo special training. I met some of these men again after the war. They were leaders of the national liberation movement. The British, too, tried to form connections with them, and not without success. When I asked my father why we were interested in the Kurds, he replied: 'It was the British who had the idea. The Kurds are a dagger ready to be pointed at Turkey, Iran or Iraq. So long as things are going well, the British take steps to foment discord between the Iraqi, Iranian and Turkish Kurds. But they have their agents in each of these groups and can unite them, when they wish, into a state well armed and rich in oil and other raw materials. For our part, we cannot leave this monopoly to the British. We are also interested in keeping Turkey quiet.'

Our task in Iran was to expose the networks of German spies. We had to track down the terrorist groups who might threaten our oil installations in Baku. The British pretended to help us. But sometimes they betrayed our positions so as to let the Turkish troops intercept us. Fortunately, we had infiltrated our men among them and we managed to escape in good time. We did not tell them where our bases were, nor did they reveal theirs to us. Distrust prevailed and was very marked at our level. However, I think we did carry out some joint operations with the British against the Germans. I can't prove this, only deduce it from the information I encrypted. On the eve of the Teheran conference in November 1943 our services and those of the British together cleared Iran of German agents.

In February 1942 my comrades and I were taken to Tabriz, and from there a British aircraft conveyed us to Casablanca. At the time I did not understand why we had been sent to this town. I think now that our services were studying the places where a summit meeting might be held. We stayed two days in Casablanca and then were returned to Iran. At my very modest level I realised that we were collecting information that we had had no need of for the moment but which was to be of use to us later. After my stay in Iran I was sent to the central laboratory of the NKVD, to study new radio equipment and apparatus – British, German and American. I lived at our home in Moscow. I champed at the bit, frustrated in my warlike ardour. I was eager to fight.

The Kerch disaster

The flower of our youth fell at Kerch, where most of the divisions made up of Caucasians were concentrated. The majority died there. A handful of Germans forced them into the sea and they drowned.[35]

The military and the Georgians held Mekhlis responsible for this disaster. A member of the Military Council[36] at this time, he had substituted himself for the commanders, ruling over everything without bearing any responsibility. Mekhlis defended himself by trying to put the blame on the Azeris. According to him 'they didn't know how to fight!' The Party leader in Azerbaijan, Bagirov, took this assertion very badly and choked with indignation when anybody mentioned Mekhlis's name in his hearing. Later he took revenge by compiling a compromising dossier on Mekhlis. In spite of this setback Mekhlis was merely reduced in rank to Colonel. Through acting the informer on numerous occasions he soon regained his former rank of General and his membership of the Military Council. Stalin had confidence in his judgement and also appreciated his complete docility.[37]

Some workers in the NKVD laboratory who were specialists in 'bugs' told me that Mekhlis had installed these in the homes of members of the Politburo since the 1920s. This detail shows how much confidence Stalin had in him. My father considered him dangerous because he was able to put over a subjective viewpoint on Stalin as though it were an objective truth. The results were sometimes harmful. Mekhlis is nowadays as unpopular in Georgia as Khrushchev. Thousands of Georgians died through his fault. The functionaries who organised the mobilisation in Georgia were Russians. The percentage of men called to the colours in that region was much larger than in other parts of the USSR.

On the Caucasian front

Offensive towards Caucasia

Stalin and a section of the military believed that the Germans would not make for the Caucasus but would concentrate around Stalingrad with a view to taking Moscow. My father and Vasilevsky thought, on the contrary, that an offensive would be launched against that region and that, consequently, the central front would have to be stripped to some extent so as to reinforce the south. They remembered that, in the period of the German-Soviet Pact, hundreds of German alpinists had, with Molotov's permission, surveyed the Caucasus, although my father was expressly against this. They were accompanied by our guards but chose their own itineraries. My father had, moreover, reliable sources of information that defined the Germans' intentions. Rapava, one of the men close to him, Lakoba's successor at the head of the Party in Abkhazia, was married to the niece of the former head of state in Georgia, Noah Jordania. Stalin knew this, and my father had persuaded him that Rapava constituted an excellent source of information. Rapava had, furthermore, a brother who spoke German perfectly. My father was still in Tbilisi when he sent this man to Germany with the task of making his way into certain circles in order to glean information there. When in Germany, Rapava's brother got to know Robakidze, a Georgian who was an enthusiast for Buddhism and occult sciences[38] and who was close to Hitler. My father, who followed things closely, said that this Robakidze was dangerous, not so much for his theories as for his zeal in drawing Hitler's attention to the Caucasus. He regretted, in this connection, that he could not act as the British did – infiltrate an agent deep down and leave him undisturbed for dozens of years. He did not have the time. However, Rapava's brother remained unused right down to the beginning of the war. It was he who warned us that part of the army which was advancing on Stalingrad would be turned towards the Caucasus. Stalin did not believe him. He stayed convinced that the Germans would be content to enclose Moscow in a pincer movement, and he refused to allow any more divisions to be diverted to the defence of the south.

During the summer of 1942 the German forces passed through Rostov and were then divided. While one section moved towards Stalingrad, Kleist's army reached Northern Caucasia at lightning speed. We were taken by surprise, having no troops in the region. Stalin took fright at the prospect of losing Caucasia and called on my father to go down there and organise its defence. For the first time he spoke to him politely, before witnesses, addressing him as 'Lavrenti Pavlovich' and not as 'Beria', his normal usage. He said: 'Take with you whoever you like, and all the armaments you think necessary, but please stop the Germans.' With Stalin's authority my father sent General Maslennikov into Caucasia, as commander-in-chief of the Northern Caucasia Army Group. Before the war he had given my father considerable help in reorganising our frontier guards. His head was shaven, he had the gait of a soldier, and his expression remained austere even when he smiled. He had earlier distinguished himself in the fight against the *Basmachi*, the anti-Communist resistance in Central Asia. Stalin did not like him because he had on several occasions been contradicted by him. I knew him well and do not believe that he committed suicide in July 1953. He was not a man to hang himself. My father chose as his own companions Colonel Shtemenko and General Bodin, deputy head of the General Staff, a very cultivated man who spoke fluent German and French. He met his death in Caucasia. My father knew these men from having discussed with them the 'Barbarossa' plan when it came into our hands.

In the radio units

Shtemenko commanded the special units responsible for radio transmissions. Doubtless on my father's initiative, Shtemenko told me that he needed me and wanted to put me into one of his units. I was to be responsible for radio communications with the high command. I travelled in the same aeroplane with my father, along with Georgian officers. Several hundred men, including Sudoplatov and his shock-group, which had been formed to parachute into Germany, accompanied us in other aircraft. Our flight was to go by Krasnovodsk, Baku, then Tbilisi. The first part of the journey went without incident, but between Baku and Tbilisi our engine caught fire. The commander of our aircraft was a certain Grachev, a Russian who resembled a man from the Baltic, he was so impassive and laconic. When the engine burst into flames, Grachev left the pilot's cabin and joined my father in the back of the aircraft. He quietly announced that there was a fire. 'We have three possibilities,' he went on. 'Either the engine explodes or I try to land or, if you will allow me, I'll dive and try to put the flames out that way.' My father answered: 'It's no good trying to land in these mountains. Go for the dive.' Grachev nodded and went back to his cabin as though nothing was happening. He did his dive and succeeded in extinguishing the flames. We arrived in Tbilisi safe and sound.

After spending two days in Georgia's capital we went to Maslennikov's headquarters, near Mozdok, in Northern Caucasia. Once there, my father assembled all the military and carried out an inventory of the material means we possessed for defending Caucasia. These resources were almost non-existent: no tanks, no anti-tank weapons, and so on. We had only a frontier-guard division which my father had brought from the Far East when the Germans were only fifteen kilometres from our positions. That day I learnt how decisions were taken in wartime. There was no time for reflection, everything was improvised. I realised how important were the personal qualities of commanders in these circumstances.

They sent me to the headquarters of the Caucasian front, in Tbilisi, where I met Tyulenev again. My job was to set up a radio station, establish communication with Moscow and encode my father's orders. He always left written traces of anything he did, instructions or orders that he passed to Stalin and the General Staff. I encoded also the messages in which he asked for permission to take some measure or other.

The frontier guards

The Germans' habit was to send officers ahead of their armoured units, to reconnoitre. We then had the idea of forming groups from the frontier guards brought from the Far East whose task would be to seize these scouts and hold up the advance of the Germans' armoured armada. These small units were armed with rifles that were fitted with silencers and infra-red sights, made in the laboratories of the NKVD. I asked to be posted to one of these groups and almost got killed during an expedition. A Ukrainian comrade saved my life by protecting me with his body. We succeeded in slowing down the German advance for ten days. The Germans are good soldiers but they operate only in accordance with a well-established strategy. Our commando attacks had quite destabilised them and they took more than a week to react. Eventually they gave up reconnaissance and their tanks advanced under air cover instead. We then suffered heavy losses as we, too, needed time to adapt ourselves to this new situation. At last, reinforcements arrived from Iran and we were able to resist the offensive. My father remained, as usual, seemingly calm and level-headed throughout these terrible days, showing no sign of panic.

I remember a German prisoner whom I had to interrogate. He was a

mathematics teacher in civil life. Having participated in the building of fortifications near Dieppe before he was transferred to Kleist's army, he drew a
plan of them at our request. We needed to accumulate information that we
could use to bring pressure to bear on Churchill for a landing in France.
This German said that there were no really serious fortifications. Later,
other sappers we had taken prisoner gave us similar information, which was
confirmed by our French agents. We were thus able to send to Churchill a
complete file proving that the coast near Dieppe was open. Churchill refused
for a long time to accept the evidence, but aerial photography supported our
information and he found himself obliged to organise a landing at Dieppe.
He wanted to prove that the operation was impossible, but, contrary to all
expectation, it succeeded.[39]

The Allied forces found themselves in difficulty only when the Germans
rushed in reinforcements while they themselves were not getting any help
from Britain. It was clear that the Anglo-Americans did not want to hear
of any landing in France. They made a big mistake in putting it off.
According to my father, if the landing had taken place sooner, in 1943
rather than in 1944, we should have hardly had time to reach Poland.

The mountain peoples

The Caucasian mountain peoples brought us valuable aid by joining volun-
teer units.

During the offensive a group of Chechens who had not been given arms
seemed to be hesitating as to which side to take. Eventually they came to
see my father, who was at Grozny, to complain about the Russian military
who looked on them as traitors and had no trust in them. Our troops did
indeed distrust these highlanders and tried to keep them out of things. My
father replied: 'I give you my word that you will have arms, and to prove
my good faith I'll leave my son with you as hostage.' He said to me in
Georgian: 'Don't worry. These are our people. I'm doing that for the
benefit of the others.' And, indeed, this action of his had great resonance
among the Chechens. I spent two days with them. They came in great
numbers to see me, on various pretexts. Some remembered Sasha
Gegechkori, others spoke of Shamil. I don't know why, but they imagined
that the latter had been pro-Russian. They were given the arms they asked
for and fought bravely. When eventually I got back to headquarters and
told my father what those Chechens had said about Shamil, he burst out
laughing: 'Never in his life did Shamil do anything that could be called
pro-Russian!'

Novorossiisk

When the German advance in Caucasia had been halted my father flew to
Novorossiisk, where the Germans had made a breakthrough. Kaganovich,
as a member of the Military Council of the Southern Front, was respon-

sible for maintaining Party discipline in this region, while Budenny was the military commander. These two idiots disorganised everything. Behind the house where they installed themselves a mountain of empty brandy bottles was piled up, symbolising the activity of the Southern Front command. Panic prevailed. My father, whom I had joined two days after his arrival, was glad to dismiss them[40] as soon as he had Stalin's authority to do this. I remember a humiliating scene where Budenny, dead drunk, was in a deep torpor, while Kaganovich, sober, trembled like a leaf and crawled on his knees before my father. My father told him: 'Don't make a public exhibition of yourself.' Shtemenko was shocked to see Budenny, a hero of the civil war, in such a state. 'He drinks to drown his worries,' he said to me, trying to excuse him. Stalin did not hold it against Budenny and immediately appointed him Inspector-General of the Cavalry.

After they had gone the young officers were able to breathe. My father gave the command to a Georgian, Leselidze, and a Ukrainian, Grechko, the future Minister of Defence. They undertook to defend the sector stretching between the coast and the mountains, from Novorossiisk to Sukhumi. In that connection I remember an amusing episode. We heard, from all directions, that Novorossiisk had been given up to the Germans. Then new information reached us: Russian sailors told us that they were in the town. The commander of the Black Sea Fleet, Admiral Oktyabrsky, was sent to find out what the actual situation was. He sent us a euphoric report: 'We are resisting step by step ...' My father asked, in reply: 'But where are you?' Oktyabrsky's response was: 'In the champagne factory.' When my father heard that, he laughed. 'Now we can be at ease, the Germans will never get our sailors out of there!'

Budenny was not decorated for his exploits until Khrushchev's time. Those two were made for one another: both won battles by heavy drinking. Khrushchev carried on resistance in the Ukraine seated before a table groaning under food and drink. Zhukov said of Khrushchev: 'What is good about him is that you can always find something to eat at his place.' On the pretext that they wished to consult him the military visited Khrushchev whenever they wanted to fill their bellies and get tipsy. Kaganovich had to be replaced. My father asked Bodin: 'Do you know an officer who is not up to much as a military man but is inoffensive as a human being?' Bodin recommended an officer who was put at the head of the Military Council. After this affair Stalin adopted the practice of appointing officers to the military councils, rather than Party bigshots. Like Zhukov my father regarded the political commissars as useless and harmful. They acted the busybody and took responsibility for nothing.

The Georgians

When the situation at Novorossiisk had been more or less restored, my father set off for Baku. I asked to stay in Caucasia along with Serov, my father's deputy.

I was able to see the Germans close up in the mountains of Abkhazia. We were a hundred metres apart, separated only by deep chasms. The highlanders dragged heavy guns along steep slopes. They did not love the Soviet regime but they were unwilling to surrender to the Germans. The Georgians fought the enemy solely because a Georgian was at the head of the Soviet State. They could not betray a compatriot of theirs, however keen their hatred for the Soviet regime. My father always compared them to the Irish: 'The Irish might have taken advantage of the war to win their freedom. But their loyalty to Britain took precedence, even though the British did all they could to exacerbate their hatred.' He compared the Irish to the Western Georgians, two lyrical peoples who both play the bagpipes. This detail caught my attention.

The Georgians enrolled by the Germans in their legions were not at all active, so that eventually the Germans ceased to trust them in Caucasia and sent them to France and Italy. Rapava's brother was responsible for all the national units that the Germans sought to use in Caucasia. He was even in command of the Indian corps. As he was working for my father he passed over everything: the Germans' objectives, their plans, the state of the units, and so on. Later, at the time of my father's trial, this affair was dug up and was to have been included among the accusations against him. The Georgian Mensheviks were mostly reticent regarding Germany.[41] They had not forgotten that Germany betrayed Georgia in 1918 by withdrawing her troops.

When the German troops were approaching, some groups of young Georgians tried to organise demonstrations in Germany's favour. My father took steps to stifle this movement, so as to avoid repressions. General Bodin told me, admiringly, how he went about it. He summoned some of these young people and explained to them that their attitude would only add to Georgia's woes, and then said: 'We know all about your organisations. Now go, and pass on to your friends what I have said to you.'

Stalin was certainly pleased that the German advance had been checked in Caucasia, but his pleasure was not unalloyed. He shared his anxieties with Shaposhnikov, who repeated what he said to Vasilevsky: 'Now,' he said, 'Beria is going to imagine he's a military leader. He drove us crazy by keeping on about how the Germans were going to make for the oil-bearing regions. Yet they have gone to Stalingrad ...' Stalin was jealous of any successes by members of the Politburo.[42] Thus, in 1943, when General Tolbukhin's offensive into the Balkans seemed to be getting bogged down, Stalin sent my father to rectify the situation. But as soon as Tolbukhin managed to effect his breakthrough, he recalled my father to Moscow so that he could not claim the laurels of victory. Stalin's jealousy sometimes assumed comical forms. It angered him, for instance, to see my father reading military maps without difficulty and commenting on them with as much ease as the generals. Eventually my father gave up doing this, so obvious was Stalin's resentment.

The situation is turned upside down

I heard about the first meeting between Stalin and Churchill, on 12 August 1942, from Avakian, a colleague of my father's who had lived a long time in the United States. When Churchill told Stalin that the opening of the second front had been postponed, the Soviet leader showed his dissatisfaction. But my father noticed that he did everything he could to convince Churchill of his esteem, of his recognition of him as a real statesman, despite his grievances and the memory of the intervention of 1919. Churchill had yesterday been an adversary of stature,[43] today he was an ally of weight[44] and his word was to be trusted. Churchill could not allow himself to fail in that respect, at least in the short term. What was essential for Stalin was, therefore, to get Churchill to give a precise promise for the opening of a second front. However, he did not succeed in that during this visit.

Stalingrad

At the beginning of August 1942 I heard from the men around my father that the big clash with the Germans would take place near Stalingrad. Bodin confirmed to me that we were going to strike a great blow in a few months' time. We have since learnt that the German generals, and in particular the command of their Sixth Army, had warned Hitler against venturing to Stalingrad, but he was stubborn. The town bore Stalin's name and drew him like a magnet. Stalin, too, was devilishly obstinate on this: for him there could be no question of yielding that town. Here we had, as my father was to say, 'a confrontation between two rams.'

Vasilevsky confirmed to me that the idea of the operation came from Stalin. The town was to provide a diversionary objective for the German forces and it was there that we must crush them: Even before receiving the reports of our special services Vasilevsky said that we had to strike at two weak points, namely, the sectors where the Romanians and Italians were stationed.[45] That was what he did, and everything went as forecast, because the Romanians and the Italians bolted. Vasilevsky told me that the only non-German troops who fought to the end, like lions, were the Hungarians. The Spaniards were good in defence but were not numerous enough. As for the Italians, we usually saw their backs. The men from the Baltic states showed courage, whether fighting for the Germans or on our side. When they fell into our hands we did not take them prisoner. I know from people who fought against the Latvian guerillas[46] that the Latvians were never untrue to their flag, and this was true also of the young Ukrainian nationalists, as I was able to observe with my own eyes. The Stalingrad victory was made possible thanks to the excellent organisation of our forces, our superiority in numbers and our strategy. The Germans ought to have retreated at the outset, but they were victims of Hitler's foolish obstinacy. Also, German intelligence had not been up to its job.

At the Military Academy

Towards the end of 1942, when the situation was crucial for the Soviet Union, Stalin ordered that about a hundred young men at the front, who had received advanced training, or who showed themselves to be gifted, should be selected to fill up the military academies. The move was typical of the Soviet regime and of Stalin's personality. In the midst of war he was already preparing for the purges to come and making sure of replacements for the victims. To those who were puzzled by this decision of his Stalin said: 'When we have won the war we shall need cadres.' Bodin encouraged me to seize this opportunity to undergo training at one of these military academies. Shtemenko warmly supported him and made this suggestion to me: 'You know several languages and are a radio expert, you ought to specialise in intelligence work.' But my father dissuaded me: 'You've no need of that. Go to a military academy if you like, but study science and technology.' Later he was to ask me: 'Well, did I do well to divert you from intelligence work?'

'You were right,' I replied, 'and I'm very grateful to you for that.'

'There, you see, he listens to his elders,' my father said to my mother. 'That's not too common these days.' On that point he had no reason to complain of me. I always took account of his opinion. And so, in November 1942 I entered the Budenny Military Academy, to specialise in radio transmission.

The academy was in Leningrad but had been evacuated to Tomsk. I spent a year there. My comrades were all one or two years older than I was. They had had the time to rise to officer rank. At first they were suspicious of me. But when they saw that I lived as they did and that our teachers showed me no indulgence, they accepted me and began even to 'mother' me, by excluding me, for example, from their drinking bouts. An astonishing atmosphere prevailed, made up of extreme privation and great freedom of speech. We firmly believed in victory. Many regretted that they were not at the front, but these were the objects of sardonic remarks from their comrades who had lost limbs: 'You ought to congratulate yourselves on coming here before you got smashed up. Take your time and enjoy it, you idiots, instead of wanting to rush to the front!' The inhabitants of Tomsk were students and former political prisoners who had completed their sentences. There were also many deported Poles, including young Polish girls whom my comrades courted assiduously. Sometimes I went along with them. I heard these Poles speculate about the fate of their nearest and dearest. My comrades joined in their conversations. Common woe brought us together: at that time there was no violent Russian chauvinism or any antisemitism. Poles and Russians alike, we were all hungry. One fine day the head of the local Smersh sought me out and said: 'Sergo,

don't go with those men. They have formed secret anti-Soviet organisations.' But I continued to take an interest in them and met them at the
theatre or at concerts. I was fascinated to discover people who hated
equally the Soviet and the Hitlerite regimes and did not hide their feelings. I understood them when I remembered Katyn. At the end of 1943 a
large number of them were arrested. When next I met my father I spoke
to him about these Poles. He said that I had done well to seek their
company, since such encounters would widen my view of the world. I
mentioned the arrests. He said: 'They did indeed form anti-Soviet organisations, but that went no further than intellectuals' prattle. They didn't
commit sabotage or anything of that sort.' These Poles were deported to
Central Asia. The British did not want to take charge of them. Stalin
declared that he did not want to feed these enemies of the Soviet power.

I could perceive that most of my comrades were perfectly aware of the
defects of the Soviet regime. Many of them were of peasant origin. Some
had relations in prison and in the camps. They did not conceal their opinions. They all dreamt that the system would change after the war. Their
hope was to be felt everywhere, as much among simple folk as among intellectuals. I mentioned this to my father, whose thinking had already run
ahead: 'Imagine how these youngsters will react when they've seen
Europe!'

The winter was very hard and my mother brought me German woollen
jerseys which I could wear under my uniform. To improve our diet, which
consisted of turnips, we went shooting in the country round about. When
we passed through a village the peasants gave us food: their cellars were
crammed with honey and smoked meats. These villages, which in winter
were accessible only by sleigh or boat, were oases of opulence that were
completely ruined after the war, when it became possible to get to them by
railway. The villagers' welcome to us sometimes became a regular festival.
It must be mentioned that nearly all their menfolk were at the front, with
only women left. My comrades had great success among these ladies, who
vainly implored our political commissar to let us stay with them a little
longer. Eventually, the academy returned to Leningrad.

Field Marshal Paulus

After the surrender of Stalingrad on 2 February 1943 Field Marshal
Paulus wanted to shoot himself. He was given to understand that if he did
that the capitulation would be cancelled. Accordingly, he preferred to save
his men's lives, but was none the less bowed down with remorse and a
sense of desolation. At my father's instigation I met him several times.
Very much affected by what had happened, he was a figure of sadness. He
was worried about the fate of his son in Germany and even asked us to
kidnap him. What became of that request I don't know. Paulus was in such
a state of depression that my father sent Ella, my nanny, to keep him
company. He spoke to her about his family and his youth in Germany,

asked about my mother and, with infinite caution, about my father. He said: 'I have met Beria on several occasions. He is the only one who did not call on me to take up a position and make declarations, but advised me to do only what is allowed by military honour.' After a fortnight, however, Ella declined to spend more time with Paulus: the task was too heavy for her. My father then found some officers to take her place, men who were not informers acting for the German Communists. My father was afraid lest Paulus fall victim to provocations. He wanted to avoid that because he had ambitious plans for the Field Marshal, as he had had for Anders.[47] He wanted these officers to form part of the future government of the states of Central and Eastern Europe. These governments, he expected, would be democratic, but, as my father considered such governments to be weak, he thought that the presence in them of officers who were patriotic and alien to political intrigue would strengthen the new ruling teams. Paulus was no Ulbricht. Formerly he had been in charge of military intelligence and my father remarked: 'It is surprising that even after holding that position he has not lost his human qualities.' He knew what he was talking about. My father was sorry that Paulus was a broken man.

The Free Germany Committee

After the Germans' defeat at Stalingrad and their retreat, the German Communists who had taken refuge in the USSR set up, on Stalin's order, in July 1943, a Free Germany Committee.[48] My father had a poor opinion of these German Communists, whom he called 'idiots' and 'careerists who want to give themselves a leg-up on the ruins of Germany. They are column-dodgers who arrive back in their country in the baggage-wagons of a foreign army,' he added contemptuously. The only decent man among them, in his view, was the future president of the GDR, W. Pieck.[49] Ulbricht, the leader of the German Communists, was regarded by my father as 'a scoundrel capable of killing his father and his mother,' a nobody good only at intrigue and informing.[50] My father had not forgotten the conspiracy hatched by Ulbricht against the veteran Communist Thälmann when he accused the latter of embezzling Party funds. These Communists spent their time snitching on each other. My father's deputy, Serov, told me that when one day he reported to Stalin on Ulbricht, pointing out that his only talent was for writing denunciations, Stalin asked: 'Does he write without making mistakes?' Serov had not forgotten that episode when, in 1945, he was Zhukov's deputy in Germany. The German Communists gave him a hard time, drowning him in denunciations. When my father had some influence he saw to it that Serov refrained from following up these letters. But when Abakumov succeeded him at the head of the MGB the policy changed. These column-dodgers hated the genuine resistance fighters, who acted upon them like a red rag to a bull. It was easy for them to accuse the men on the spot of having, among other things, 'collaborated with the British.'

I had met Ulbricht before the war, at the house of one of my German friends. He reminded me of one of our actors, who specialised in the role of Lenin. 'He doesn't talk, he pontificates,' I told my father. 'That doesn't surprise me,' he replied, 'Ulbricht is a complete imbecile.'

My father tried to protect the organisation of anti-Fascist officers[51] from the German Communists. I heard him one day blaming Kruglov for allowing the Communists to approach these officers, instead of ordering them to confine themselves to spreading propaganda in the prisoner-of-war camps.

The dissolution of the Comintern

My father did not think that the dissolution of the Comintern in May 1943 would deceive anyone: 'Only the weak-minded could fall into that trap,' he said. He was therefore amazed to find Westerners taking seriously a gesture which, among us, did not mislead anyone, not even the lower functionaries of the Party.[52]

My father could not stand the Comintern, 'that nest of intriguers and informers,' he called it. 'Even our Party organs, which are a fine set of snake-pits, are beaten at that game by the Comintern.' He pitied the Comintern leader Dimitrov for having 'got stuck up to the neck in that sewer. He's certain to be swallowed up. Ercoli[53] is much more cunning, he always manages to wriggle out of a difficult situation.' It was at this time that he told me about the past 'exploits' of the Comintern, stressing particularly the role played by the Hungarian Communist Béla Kun, 'that head-case who persuaded Lenin that Germany was ripe for revolution.'

Policy on religion

While war was raging at the front Stalin agreed to some concessions in the sphere of domestic policy. The appeal to Russian nationalism became more marked. For some time already my father had been trying to convince Stalin that it was necessary to soften his policy on religion, in the interests of the Soviet war effort. He regularly put before him reports from his services which showed that the clergy was playing a patriotic role. He insisted so much that Stalin eventually said to him: 'One might think that it was you, not me, who attended the seminary.' I should not be surprised to learn that it was my father who instigated the approach by the Orthodox bishops to the Government which led to the restoration of the Patriarchate in September 1943.

Considerations of foreign policy certainly played a decisive role in this decision of Stalin's. He had far-reaching designs and dreamed of an outlet to Antioch and Greece. As for my father, his view was that the churches constituted substantial forces which ought not to be antagonised: the ideal being, of course, to be able to manipulate them. He approved of the concessions made to Orthodoxy, but he would have liked them to be accompanied by comparable gestures to the Vatican.

The Battle of Kursk

We won the Battle of Kursk in July 1943 because our arms industry had found a means of knocking out the Germans' new Tiger tanks. We used small cumulative bombs which our aircraft dropped fanwise in packets of five hundred or a thousand. The armour of the Tigers was less thick on top than in front and at the sides. When the bombs reached the tanks they burst inside and put them out of action. The gun barrels of our anti-tank weapons were also lengthened, which increased their power.

After this victory Stalin put away all his plans for assassinating Hitler. The Führer was the last obstacle to a separate peace between the Western powers and Germany, something that Stalin wanted at any price to prevent. He realised that the Soviet Union would not only win the war, it would emerge stronger from the ordeal. Once he had grasped how powerful the Red Army had become, Stalin began to draw up plans for the conquest of the rest of Europe. He then set himself to prepare cadres and to think about the composition of the future governments. Should the conquered nations go over to Communist rule straight away, or ought we to wait? My father recommended 'popular front' governments, but Stalin recalled the discouraging precedent of Léon Blum. My father retorted that Blum's government had been weak, unable to resist aggression: was that not just what we needed? He was already concerned to maintain the alliance with the West and desired that the states of Central Europe should enjoy American economic aid. As he saw it, the USSR ought to install governments that would not scare the westerners but, on the contrary, would be sure of getting support from them.

At this time Stalin was not necessarily thinking of a military occupation of the whole of Europe, even though he was giving himself the means for this. He calculated that liberation from Fascism would be associated with the Soviet state and that the peoples would rally to Socialism. Where the intellectuals were concerned we knew that this was already in the bag. The progressive elements would take power, and where they encountered obstacles they could always have recourse to the bayonets of the Red Army. As for the Americans, they would be busy dismembering the colonial empires and would not interfere in Europe.

My father's Polish policy

When the mass grave at Katyn was discovered by the Germans in April 1943 my father was unable to repress a certain feeling of satisfaction. Events had proved him right. Those who had ordered the massacre could only try to cover up their crime. Our troops quickly reconquered the area. As the Germans had committed the incredible foolishness of shooting some Poles in the same place (I recall hearing my father expressing amazement at this stupidity on the Germans' part) it was easy for us to confuse the inquiry[54] and accuse the Nazis of the crime.[55]

Sikorski, the head of the Polish government in London, was less clear-minded about the Soviet Union than Anders.[56] The latter had been in our prisons and camps and knew what a danger the USSR represented. But Stalin hated Anders, whereas he was ready to tolerate Sikorski, a man apparently more conciliatory but in reality more intelligent.[57] My father knew of the conflicts among the Polish leaders but did not intervene in them (I knew that from Merkulov). One section of the Poles who had gone to the Middle East with Anders' army considered that confrontation with the Soviet Union was not in Poland's interest.[58] My father's wish was that these Polish troops should liberate Yugoslavia[59] and he advised Tito to contact Anders, whose army was well organised and efficient. Tito did not reject the idea. Contrary to Churchill, who gave priority to liberating the Aegean Sea and landing troops in Greece, my father preferred that the Allies should land in Istria and thrust towards Vienna through the Ljubljana Gap. In the end Roosevelt scuttled the plan for a landing in the Balkans,[60] as we shall see later. My father was constantly urging the Soviet government to do things that would improve relations with the Poles. Sikorski was ready to begin direct negotiations after the break in April 1943, and was even willing to recognise the Curzon Line.[61] Churchill was against this.[62] The Americans did not interfere. My father was always convinced that the British caused Sikorski's death in an aircrash in July 1943 because he had agreed to a rapprochement with the Soviet Union.[63] In this connection he reminded me of the death of Kitchener, whom the Intelligence Service had liquidated by blowing up the ship he was in. According to my father, however, the British had made a major blunder when they got rid of Sikorski and were victims of their own manoeuvres when they overestimated his successor, Mikolajczyk, and the other Polish leaders in London. These were politicians of mediocre calibre and not true patriots like the soldier Sikorski, who was for a Poland strong and free. The British had, unknowingly, facilitated Stalin's task. My father greatly regretted Sikorski's death. *He* would not have let himself be ignominiously ejected from the government, as happened to Mikolajczyk in 1947.

My father did not like the Polish Communist Wanda Wasilewska.[64] Her first husband had been killed at Katyn, and she found nothing more urgent to do than rush into the bed of Korneichuk, a Soviet playwright who was always ready to obey the Party's orders.[65] I think my father was shocked by this behaviour on the part of a woman who had been a member of Pilsudski's entourage. He knew from the Ukrainian nationalists that no trust was to be placed in this hysterical woman given to denunciations. The Polish Communists were also wary of her[66] and had her removed from the Polish committee in 1944.

My father supervised the formation of the Czech units just as he had done with Anders's army. Our military were angry because these Czechs were not allowed to fight on Soviet soil. My father's view was that they should be preserved until the Red Army drew near to the frontiers of Czechoslovakia, which was when we should need them. But the military got their way and many Czechs died on a Soviet battlefield. Ludwig Svoboda[67] came to my father to complain. 'They deliberately exposed me to the risk of certain death,'[68] he said. He was probably right: our troops let the Czechs go forward without cover for their flanks. All that my father could obtain was a posthumous decoration for these soldiers who had been killed in action. That was a fine mess.

Towards the end of the war

The Teheran conference

The Party leaders who prepared for the conference which was to be held at Teheran between 28 November and 1 December 1943 thought that everything had already been decided at the conference of foreign ministers which had been held in Moscow in the previous month. Indeed, I heard one of them say to my father: 'Anyway, Stalin held them to the decisions that were taken at the Moscow meeting.' Stalin had in fact, said on that occasion: 'Now the fate of Europe is settled. We shall do as we like, with the Allies' consent.' Before the foreign ministers he had cleverly shown his displeasure regarding the capitulation of Italy, in which the USSR had had no part, so as to require that henceforth all regions liberated should be administered by the occupying army.[69]

Two aircraft had been provided for the flight from Baku to Teheran – one for Stalin, to be flown by General Golovanov, and one for my father, flown by Colonel Grachev. Grachev told me later that, at the moment of boarding the plane, Stalin decided to fly in the one designated for my father. As he made his way to Grachev's craft he said, when passing Golovanov, who was waiting for him, bewildered: 'Don't take it badly, but it seems to me that colonels have more experience than generals where flying is concerned.' Golovanov was a fool and Stalin knew what he was doing. I was summoned by the General Staff and sent to Teheran without knowing my destination. We stopped off in Moscow, where I was presented with the most up-to-date secret listening devices. I thought I should have to install these devices, but when I arrived in Teheran (I still didn't know where I was) I learnt that the 'bugs' were already in place and that my task would be to make summaries of the recordings. I was told to listen to everything that Roosevelt said. My father joined me as soon as I arrived. He told me that Stalin himself had had the idea of bringing me and that it was to him that I was to report. Some time later Stalin sent for me. I was moved: every meeting with him was an event for me.

'How's your mother?' he began by asking.

'Well,' I replied, wondering what would come next.

'And your academy, tell me, is it well-equipped technically?'

'Not as well as it should be. We lack equipment, and what we have is already out of date.[70] But, ideologically, everything is as it should be in our training. We study your works ...'

'On that point I have no worry,' he interrupted me, with a touch of irony in his voice. 'I have had you brought here, along with some other young men who have never had dealings with foreigners, because I want to entrust you with a mission that is delicate and morally reprehensible. You are going to listen to the conversations that Roosevelt will have with Churchill, with the other British, and with his own circle. I must know everything in detail, be aware of all the shades of meaning. I am asking you for all that because it is now that the question of the second front will be settled. I know that Churchill is against it. It is important that the Americans support us in this matter.'

Why did he make a point of impressing on me that the task he was giving me was morally reprehensible? Perhaps he wanted to captivate me. When he thought it necessary he was able to seduce a Field Marshal just as well as a young man. It was not enough for me to be obedient, I had to be completely with him.

This 'task' was a hard test for me, even though I have never done anything since with such enthusiasm. I got little sleep. From 6 a.m. I was preparing my summaries. At 8 a.m. Stalin, who had changed his habits for the occasion (usually he worked at night and got up at 11 a.m.), received me and the others. He prepared himself carefully for each of our sessions, having at hand files on every question that interested him. He even went so far as to ask for details of the tone of the conversations: 'Did he say that with conviction or without enthusiasm? How did Roosevelt react? Did he say that resolutely?' Sometimes he was surprised: 'They know that we can hear them and yet they speak openly!' One day he even asked me: 'What do you think, do they know that we are listening to them?'

'I can only say this,' I replied. 'That it is impossible to spot the microphones that we use. We ourselves couldn't do it.'

'It's bizarre,' he said, returning to his thoughts. 'They say everything, in fullest detail ...'

During his conversations with his collaborators Roosevelt always expressed a high opinion of Stalin, and this obviously pleased him. He was much more mistrustful of Churchill. One day when the latter had said that there was no way of gulling Uncle Joe, Stalin reacted by smiling into his moustache: 'The old swine is lying.' When with Stalin, Churchill constantly flattered and praised him. Stalin took malicious pleasure in reminding him of some of the anti-Soviet reflections he had come out with in the past.

Roosevelt and Churchill met Stalin separately. Each of them tried to persuade him that if they met like that they would reach a better understanding than if all three met together. Roosevelt said, again and again, that he would support Stalin in his efforts to destroy the British Empire, as that would correspond to American interests. It seems to me that this was his dominant idea and chief preoccupation.[71] Nor did he hide this from Churchill. And he returned to it at Yalta. Roosevelt did not want to isolate the Soviet Union, as Churchill did when he advocated an Allied landing in the Balkans. In Roosevelt's view this policy would not be in America's interest. Also, he wanted to spare the lives of as many American soldiers as possible and the landing in Normandy was the best option from the military standpoint. Even Churchill did not deny that. When this argument was put to him he merely blew like a seal, but could find nothing to say. I heard him beg Roosevelt not to commit himself to the landing in Normandy. I was struck by his bulldog stubbornness. He returned again and again to the attack, always bringing forward fresh arguments: 'If we allow the Soviets to settle themselves in Europe they will be able to boss the place.' Roosevelt replied that it was necessary to think about beating the Germans rather than wondering who would be boss in Europe afterwards.[72] He insisted that he would not sacrifice one American life for nothing.

The Americans were chiefly concerned with their war with Japan and their President wanted to free his hands as soon as possible from European affairs so to finish the conflict in the Pacific. The British were resigned to the loss of Singapore and had made Europe and the Near East their priority. But when Churchill warned Roosevelt that the Soviet Union was clearly preparing a Communist replacement for the Polish government, the President replied that Churchill was doing the same thing by preparing an anti-Communist government. Why, then, get excited? It was all quite fair. Roosevelt put Churchill and Stalin on the same plane and presented himself as arbiter between them.

The British and American leaders were agreed on fixing the Polish frontier at the Curzon Line,[73] but they realised that the Soviet appetite would not stop there. Churchill hoped to get Stalin to agree to an Allied landing in the Balkans in exchange for abandoning Poland.[74] 'You've dropped Poland,' Roosevelt said, teasing Churchill. Actually, he was the one who spoilt Churchill's game. According to my father Churchill handled the question of a landing in the Balkans badly. 'In his place I would not have presented it as an alternative to the landing in France but as a mere complementary operation,' he said.[75] The political mistakes made by the British always puzzled him, for he admired the way they preserved their empire by means of their intelligence alone. The Americans were so strong economically that they could let themselves commit all possible follies. Faced with the plain blindness of the British where Stalin's intentions were concerned, however, my father wondered whether this was stupidity or hypocrisy. He favoured the second hypothesis.

I was able to establish from my eavesdropping that Roosevelt felt great respect and sympathy for Stalin. Admiral Leahy tried several times to persuade him to be firmer with the Soviet leader. Every time he received the reply: 'That doesn't matter. Do you think you can see further than I can? I am pursuing this policy because I think it is more advantageous. We are not going to pull the chestnuts out of the fire for the British.'

In his discussions with Molotov and my father Stalin tried to anticipate Churchill's reactions. Whereas he was sure of being able to guess what

Roosevelt would do, it was difficult for him to make plans for dealing with Churchill. 'You can expect absolutely anything from him,' he said. My father was convinced that, even independently of any strategy, Stalin was simply curious to know what Churchill's reactions would be to a particular measure or criticism. He even said to the Politburo: 'My hypothesis is that he will do this.'

I saw little of my father during the Teheran conference. During one of our rare consultations he mentioned to me a young American of Georgian origin[76] whom he was very keen I should meet. 'He is an officer who is well up in the history of Georgia and knows a lot about Turkey and the Middle East. I understood a great deal about American policy when I was talking with him,' he said, animatedly. And he added: 'We are terribly short of young people with so broad a horizon. I would pay a lot to have a few like him around me.' In the grip of enthusiasm he even spoke of the man to my mother. I was curious to meet him, and almost jealous. But, alas, I never had a chance to make his acquaintance.

Nobody thanked me for my services. I was rewarded solely with a Swiss watch. According to my father, Stalin was satisfied with the results of the conference and considered that he had won the game. I am sure that my summaries must survive somewhere in the archives. Perhaps the recordings too have been preserved.

1944: on the way to victory

The deportation of the Caucasian peoples

The end of 1943 and most of 1944 were marked by a growing return to Stalin's usual policy of repression, especially in the 'liberated' territories, and by the deportation of some small nations.

I had been able to observe, while I was on the Caucasian front, how the Chechens and the other mountain peoples fought against the Germans. There were far fewer collaborators among them than among the Cossacks. All statements issued on this subject have been inflated by the old school of Russian imperialism.[77] The Politburo decision to deport these peoples was taken on the initiative of those who, like Zhdanov, Malenkov and Molotov, wanted to continue the war in Caucasia that had been waged by the Tsars. Stalin merely gave his assent. He was not, of course, against the idea, but it did not come from him – unless that Russophile group guessed and anticipated his desires. They exploited the misdeeds of a few individuals – for example, a village which had offered a white horse and weapons to Hitler[78] – to accuse entire populations. There were 300,000 Russians in Vlasov's army[79] yet nobody dreamt of deporting the Russian people on that account. In reality, the Caucasians' resistance to Sovietisation had not been forgotten.

It was Suslov who provided the theoretical argument to justify this deportation. My father opposed it, orally and in writing.[80] He had had dealings with these peoples, and they had trusted him. He did not want to lose face before them by seeming to be a man who failed to keep his word. Serov described to me the session of the Politburo at which the decision was taken. He had been summoned along with Kruglov because they were entrusted with implementing the decision. When my father mentioned the contribution made by these peoples to the defence of Caucasia Stalin turned to Vasilevsky and asked his opinion. Vasilevsky replied that he had never seen braver warriors. Moreover, no Caucasian unit had gone over to the German side. My father went further, warning that the proposed action would deal a severe blow to the prestige of the Soviet regime throughout the region. Zhdanov then asked, perfidiously: 'And in Georgia too, Lavrenti Pavlovich?'

'Absolutely, in Georgia more than anywhere else,' my father replied.

'You don't know your history. Georgia was with Russia against the peoples of the Caucasus,' Zhdanov retorted.

'That was not Georgia,' my father protested immediately. 'It was merely a few Georgian princes installed by Russia at the head of some Russian units.'

Stalin refused to give the floor to the Georgians who were present. He turned to my father and dryly conveyed the order to carry out the government's decision. 'So long as you are Commissar, do as you're told.' Speaking to Serov at the end of the session my father fulminated. 'I should have liked that rat Suslov, that Tsarist satrap, to be put in our place and sent to Caucasia to organise this operation!'[81] And he added: 'They wanted to soak Vasilevsky in this shit, but he was intelligent enough to refuse to take part.' When Serov told me this I asked him if he thought the deportation was justified. Being a prudent man, he expressed his disapproval. Maybe he was sincere. I don't know. He was a brave man and people of that calibre do not like low-down deeds.[82]

The troops who had fought alongside these peoples were given the job of deporting them. It was monstrous. When they heard the news the Secretaries of regional and district and Party committees, young people devoted to the Soviet state, came to see my father, to complain.[83] My father was greatly embarrassed. 'I can do nothing more than save you and your families. No more than that.' They rejected his offer and were deported with the rest. This attitude of theirs tells us much of these people and their pride. My father was particularly distressed by these events and wanted posterity to know who had really originated the decision.[84]

Kruglov told me that the NKVD had been given the job of transporting the deportees to their places of exile. The local Party organisations had to receive them and distribute them among the villages. Suslov was supposed to organise that phase of the operation. On paper everything was provided for. In reality the deportees were without food or water and epidemics broke out among them. No local official was willing to take over these hungry and sick peoples, who were left to wander, driven ever further from their homelands. Kruglov, doubtless at my father's instigation, nevertheless sent in a report denouncing Suslov's negligence.[85] Stalin read it and, as usual, agreed that there had been abuses. Suslov was then obliged to issue an order requiring the republics of Central Asia to provide housing and work for the deportees in the collective farms. He nursed a deadly grudge against Kruglov for this and eventually, after my father's death, succeeded in having his head.

The Ukrainian nationalists

During the summer of 1944 I was sent to the 4th Ukrainian Army Group, commanded by Petrov. When I arrived in Lvov I met Kruglov again. He had been given the task of setting up new frontier-guard positions and purging the rear of the SS Divisions of Ukrainian nationalists. Kruglov made me take part in pitched battles between Red Army units, NKVD troops and Smersh on one side and, on the other, Ukrainian nationalists who were waging guerrilla warfare against the Reds.[86] I encountered Mekhlis, who was then a member of the Military Council. This was the first time I had seen him since I met him in Georgia, when I was still a child and he was editor-in-chief of *Pravda*. He looked at me attentively, guessed who I was, and pretended to recognise me. He immediately referred to his stay in Georgia and said to me: 'Why haven't you got a decoration? Stay in our army and in six months you'll be covered with medals.' He imagined that that was what I had come for. I explained that I was on probation, that I had taken part in the parachuting of our men into Slovakia and that I had been given fifteen days' leave. I took advantage of this to meet great military leaders like him, I said.

He puffed himself up. Actually, I especially admired General Burmak, who had been in command of the parachuting in Slovakia and had organised the new Ukrainian frontier. I knew him through Maslennikov, who had depicted him to me as a hero. When we were alone Kruglov said to me: 'Your place is not in the Military Academy but at an embassy!'

My brief stay in Lvov was marked by several events. A division of Slovak transport planes had landed unexpectedly. The Slovaks had captured the German officers and neutralised them.[87] I noticed a British officer among these Slovaks. It was he who had organised the whole operation. I spoke to him and he at once detected that I was not a captain like the others. I asked him why he had set up this mutiny. He laughed at my naivety and replied that things were not so simple.

While in the Ukraine I witnessed the horrors committed against the Ukrainian nationalists. My comrades and I had the opportunity to talk with these young resistance fighters. They told us: 'We have nothing against Russia but we don't want to be deprived of our freedom.' We spoke about that among ourselves. Some young Russian officers were moved: 'They are not wrong, if you put yourself in their place. Can you imagine what foreign rule can be like?' I knew well what it was like, but refrained from comment. When I got back I described to my father a scene which had struck me forcibly. I had seen, in a hospital near the frontier-guard position where she had been captured, a young girl student who was badly wounded. Her face has remained etched in my memory. She had acted as a courier for Melnik's[88] group and had betrayed no one when interrogated. These nationalists were cultivated students, which surprised me. 'How is it,' I asked my father, 'that these young people are anti-Soviet?' At that time I was a complete idiot and my father laughed outright. 'Can't you draw any conclusions? Remember Georgia. Whom did they arrest? Students, of course, who had studied in Germany. They were not arrested because they had become fascists but quite simply because they understood the situation in the Soviet Union ... They were young and hadn't the blinkers worn by grownups. They had no fear of the future. They fought for what they wanted. Meaning their country's freedom.' He made me appreciate that these students were not traitors. Their sole aim was to see their country free, whatever its ideology might be, and he stressed that point. 'If the young Slovaks were to lose their illusions about the Soviet Union they would follow the example of the young Ukrainians. A good policy for the USSR would be to encourage them to reconstruct their country instead of making them take up arms.' He also said: 'All Georgians, be they Chekists or military men, have suffered inwardly at the sight of what has happened. That's why it's been necessary to bring in Chekists from the Baltic states.'

My father was well informed on the Polish, Ukrainian and Baltic nationalists through his British agents, who were involved in those movements.

The fate of the Uniate Church

While in Lvov I visited an Armenian church and also a Uniate church where I met some young priests of ascetic appearance. They had studied in Rome and did not conceal their hatred of the Soviets, but they managed to restrain themselves. When I passed near them in my Red Army uniform they called out to me: 'It would be better to worship God than to worship Stalin as you do.'

Stalin hesitated for a time before deciding what attitude to take towards the Ukrainian Uniate Church.[89] There was even quite a debate in the Politburo about what to do with the Uniate bishop Sheptitsky, who had blessed the SS Division 'Galicia.' Khrushchev insisted that he be dealt with in exemplary fashion. My father suggested that this old man be allowed to die in peace. Stalin took no notice, any more than he let himself be dissuaded from arresting the Uniate Metropolitan Joseph Slipyi in April 1945. He settled the question by requiring that the bishop be deported without any show trial. My father then tried to urge the Vatican to approach the Soviet authorities with a view to preventing the liquidation of the Uniat Chruch. But his efforts were fruitless and he could do nothing against the stubbornness of the Party functionaries, especially

Khrushchev, who were backed by Stalin.[90] The forced union of the Orthodox and Uniate churches was proclaimed by the Council of Lvov in March 1946. As my father saw it, this decision could only cause a quarrel with an institution so powerful as the Catholic Church. 'We shall kick ourselves,' he said.[91] It was no good: he failed to convince Stalin that the policy of brutal repression advocated by Khrushchev could not promote the integration of the annexed territories.

The liberation of the Southern flank and the Crimean Tatars

Stalin pondered long on who he should entrust with the operation to liberate the Crimea and the south of the Ukraine. My father suggested Tolbukhin, an officer in whom he had confidence. He liked him because, like Vasilevsky in this respect, he was not a brute. Stalin sent for Tolbukhin and put him in command of the troops that were to liberate the Crimea. At the same time he advised him to go on a diet in order to lose weight! The wretched Tolbukhin undertook to ride for an hour every day for this purpose. He gave my father two splendid horses.

The Tatars were accused of large-scale collaboration with the Germans, and when the question of deporting them came up my father asked Tolbukhin to compose, with Kobulov's help, a report on their collaborationist actions. Tolbukhin established that there had been only a few hundred cases in the entire Crimea.[92] My father passed this report to the commission investigating the pro-German and pro-Turkish activities of the Tatars. The report had no effect, except that Tolbukhin received a sharp reprimand: a military man should not mix himself up in politics. Smersh profited by the opportunity to add to the dossier it was compiling against him. The deportation of the Tatars in May 1944 was a blow aimed at Turkey.[93]

The Warsaw insurrection

When I met Rokossovsky I asked him if he had been ordered to halt before Warsaw at the moment of the insurrection in August 1944.[94] He gave me his word of honour that he had not. The Soviet forces had tried to make contact with the insurgents, but everyone sent on this mission had disappeared.[95] The Polish General Bor-Komarowski did not want to have the slightest contact with the Red Army.[96] I also put the question to my father: 'Evidently, in the eyes of Iosif Vissarionovich, this insurrection was a provocation organised by Churchill, who wanted to install the London Polish Government,' he replied.

When our troops had driven the Germans from Soviet territory and reached the frontier in April 1944, the American and British sent us news films that showed Western workers rejoicing in our victory. Stalin was pleased. He recalled that the international proletariat had saved Bolshevik Russia from the intervention of 1919.[97] My father, alluding to the talks that had taken place on the future political organisation of Europe, observed that we must not disappoint these people who were celebrating our success. Stalin at once replied: 'You know how to organise mass enthusiasms. Well you have only to go on doing that.' As a rule my father merely swallowed that sort of remark without flinching but on that occasion (when everybody was a bit tipsy), he replied: 'Are you hinting that I'm your propagandist-in-chief? Propaganda is not my line. Your pianist (and he pointed his finger at Zhdanov) is here for that purpose.' Stalin never forgot that sally. Zhdanov was delighted, to the point that, when the party broke up, he kissed my father.

The Western powers in Moscow

Harriman, Hopkins and Wallace

Harriman had known my parents in Georgia in the twenties. At that time he owned a concession for mining manganese at Chiaturi. He told me how he had met my mother. He was accosted one day in a bank by a charming young woman who asked him to make a contribution to an organisation which looked after orphans. He responded generously, not out of charity but because the young woman pleased him. One of his friends who was present warned him: 'Don't look at her too closely, she's the wife of a Chekist.' Some time later he was sent for by my father to discuss the concession. My father reminded him to observe 'the progressive laws' introduced by the Soviet Government and Harriman recalled my father's ironical expression as he uttered those words. 'I looked at him and wondered how this puny fellow could be the husband of that beauty,' he told me.

My father saw Harriman again when he came to negotiate the release of an American woman who had been caught red-handed at spying. This release was to be effected by an exchange for Soviet agents arrested in the USA. Molotov, Stalin and others had loaded him with gifts – objects stuffed with microphones which were cleverly concealed by the laboratories of the NKVD. According to my father, who ridiculed 'this amateur who prides himself on knowing about intelligence work,' Harriman concerned himself with foreign policy solely because his commercial interests were at stake. This active and enterprising aspect of the man pleased my father. Harriman wanted to win the Soviets' favour so as to do business with the USSR after the war. Again according to my father, the envoy of the British, Lord Beaverbrook, showed himself much readier than this American to respond to Soviet requests.[98]

Roosevelt's adviser Hopkins was pro-Soviet well before he met Stalin and so it can't be claimed that he succumbed to Stalin's charm. My father considered that he was a perfectly honest man but that he understood absolutely nothing about the Soviet Union and cherished illusions on the subject. 'It's astonishing,' he said to me, 'This man is not an intellectual, and he can't see things as they are.' We knew that Hopkins had very great influence on Roosevelt, who paid more attention to his advisers than Churchill did to his, so that it was easier to influence the President through the men around him. Many of the disagreements between Roosevelt and Churchill were due to Hopkins' influence on the American President and to his pro-Sovietism.

Vice President Wallace[99] was not a Soviet agent, either, but quite simply an imbecile.[100] We succeeded in throwing dust in his eyes by presenting him with a spectacle of opulence during his stay in the USSR in May–June 1944. My father appointed Amaiak Kobulov to accompany him, calculating that they would get on well together. He was not mistaken. Wallace liked wine and women, passions that were shared by Kobulov, who became Wallace's best friend. Arm-in-arm, they made a very agreeable trip to Central Asia.[101] But none of us expected that such a cretin could become President of the United States – it was already surprising that he was Vice President.[102]

De Gaulle

My father took a close interest in the leaders of the French resistance because it was Soviet policy to push to the forefront the Gaullists, who might facilitate infiltration of Communists into positions of authority. Bidault had attracted his attention: 'He's a drunkard and a skirt-chaser, he has everything that goes to make a politician without scruples,' he said. 'But he's a nationalist, and when we want to use him we need to take account of all three factors.'[103] I remember, too, hearing my father wonder why Bidault had not joined Colonel de la Rocque's Croix de Feu. My father preferred De Gaulle to Darlan and Giraud because he thought de Gaulle would defend the interests of France rather than those of the United States. He knew that he was anti-Communist but what was essential, in his view, was that he represented the national bourgeoisie and was the *bête noire* of the United States. My father respected de Gaulle's intelligence. He even advised Stalin not to drag out his meeting with the French leader during his visit to Moscow in December 1944. Stalin merely replied: 'But I'm studying him.' And my father replied: 'And don't you think that he is studying you?' Stalin was very sure of himself and had good reason for that. De Gaulle was seen by my father as a very great political figure, the only Frenchman in the Resistance who was devoted to the independence of France, someone who would not play the British game, nor, especially, the American game, and who had great strength of character – with, however, some characteristics of a dictator.[104] I too thought highly of him: When I told my father that, he approved: 'Yes, de Gaulle is the only man who can frighten Churchill.' Stalin loved to hear of all the ways that de Gaulle was able to annoy the British leader and found them great fun.

I read later the portrait of Stalin drawn by de Gaulle.[105] He was mistaken on one point, in underestimating the Soviet leader's intelligence.

I am surprised, too, that he did not mention their conversation on the history of France. I know that they spoke about the French Revolution. My father had watched Stalin soaking himself in books of French history in preparation for his meeting with de Gaulle, and he remarked, with irony: 'He wants to astonish de Gaulle, or else to catch him out in flagrant ignorance.' It seems to me that de Gaulle failed to convey the impression that Stalin was able to make at this time. He was careful not to assume a conspiratorial air, as he wished to mislead his interlocutor and lull his vigilance. He never let himself appear sad or tired before people he did not know.[106] I don't think he behaved differently with de Gaulle from the way he behaved with Churchill or Roosevelt. Perhaps de Gaulle was shrewder, but he described Stalin in relation to his policy, not under the impact of personal impressions. I think that, of all the Western statesmen, it was Churchill who best understood Stalin, because he foresaw all his manoeuvres. But when I read in his works that he was able to influence Stalin I cannot prevent myself from smiling and feeling astonishment that so intelligent a man could have entertained such illusions.

'Peace'

At the time of Germany's last offensive in the Ardennes in December 1944 some of our military men proposed that we do nothing and let the Western Allies be driven into the sea. Stalin was against this, on the grounds that it would give the Allies a pretext for a separate peace with Germany and enable the Germans to attain the objectives aimed at by this operation of theirs. The military men yelped in vain that they were not ready. Stalin ordered them to bring forward our offensive by two weeks. My father gave unreserved approval to that decision.

The Yalta conference (4-11 February 1945)

The successes of the Red Army were so impressive that Roosevelt and Churchill no longer insisted that Stalin travel abroad for their next meeting. He had, until that time, categorically refused to leave the territory of the USSR, on the pretext – because, of course, it was only a pretext – that he was the commander-in-chief of our armed forces. I knew that there was going to be a conference because we often spoke of it at home. This conference was to decide the fate of defeated Germany, the problems of Poland's frontiers and of the regime in Poland, the conditions for the USSR's entry into the war with Japan and the statutes of the United Nations Organisation. Stalin was not against the idea of the UNO. He saw it as a club of the great powers, which would rule the world with an iron hand under democratic appearances, on condition that the entente between the USSR and the USA was maintained. In any case, he did not want an amorphous organisation like the League of Nations. At this time he was wagering on co-operation with the Anglo-Saxons, even though he had his own plans for Europe. He also counted on American aid to rebuild the USSR. Roosevelt had promised him that. My father favoured the prospect of the United Nations. They would, so to speak, lay down the rules of the game, and each country would act for itself while respecting these rules and not encroaching on the interests of others.

I was once more summoned to the General Staff and it did not surprise me when I found myself at Yalta. I arrived in the Crimea before the conference opened. I met a group of surveillance specialists whom I had not encountered before. Stalin did not send for us, but he let us know that we were to perform the same tasks as at Teheran. I was again entrusted with eavesdropping on Roosevelt and his entourage. Our equipment was more advanced than at Teheran. Moreover, the engineers who had made it were on the spot and showed us how to use this equipment, which included directional microphones. These were like cameras and could pick up sounds at great distances, between 150 and 200 metres away. We foresaw that Roosevelt would have himself wheeled into the park surrounding the palace, a former residence of the Tsars, to take the air, and so we could no longer be satisfied with microphones hidden in the rooms that had been assigned to him. We had therefore planned the itinerary for these trips outside and combed the avenues of the park so as to facilitate the movements of the paralysed president. We were thus able to follow him to a considerable distance with listening devices.

I watched from afar when Roosevelt arrived. I regretted having missed Churchill's arrival. I had often been told how comically the latter behaved when he stepped out of an aircraft. He went up to the guard of honour and looked each soldier in the eyes with a stupefied air, as though he had just landed among extra-terrestrials. When I saw Roosevelt I was struck by the dignity of his entourage and by the care taken of their disabled president by his bodyguards. It was obvious that they loved him. One had only to observe the way they put him in his car, doing everything to conceal his infirmity. Even the guards who accompanied me, and who were not particularly sharp, noticed this and refrained from making jokes about the American president. As against that, they did not spare Churchill, whom they compared to a poodle wagging his tail around Stalin. At our level, we felt a benevolence towards Roosevelt which was far from being extended to Churchill. The latter complained that he couldn't get a wink of sleep at night because, as he claimed, he was being eaten by bugs.[1] I can testify that this was quite untrue and I am amazed that Churchill could allow himself to make such accusations. We had just renovated all the buildings in use and it was impossible for vermin to appear in so short a time. Churchill's insomnia was more probably due to the fact that he knew that Roosevelt had very clear-cut ideas and that Churchill was not going to get him to change them. I was witness, thanks to my microphones, to the way Roosevelt refused to talk to him when they met. I remember this very well because it was the first time that I used my microphones. Churchill was walking beside the jeep that carried the President. He tried to take up certain questions, but Roosevelt cut him short, saying that everything had been discussed and decided.

The American and British guards were well fed and had plenty to drink with their meals, which was different from the way it had been at Teheran. They often fell under the table and regularly had to be carried to their bedroom. Some of us were allowed to get drunk with them and relations were cordial. I think this permission was given with a purpose. My team had the right to eat up the leftovers, but we were happy with that because these scraps were better than our regular meals at the Military

Academy (where we followed the example of the Three Musketeers, looking for any pretext to visit someone in order to fill our bellies at our host's expense).

The conference

My work was the same as at Teheran, but I no longer had to report to Stalin. He was content to read the summaries that were prepared for him. According to my father he was no longer interested in the details of conversations. From this time onwards he was convinced that he could force the Allies to accept whatever was important for him. Still, we had to remain vigilant. If my memory is correct, Churchill made difficulties about Poland, trying to go back on decisions already taken. I recall hearing him say that the Russians wanted to swallow such a big piece that they risked choking. As for Roosevelt, he pursued the same policy as at Teheran, only more so. He explained to Stalin that the USSR and the USA would have to carry out a number of tasks in common when the war was over. As he saw it, America's post-war policy would be more in conformity with the interests of the Soviet Union than that of the British. In fact, the USA and the USSR would have to establish order in Britain's former colonies, and the United Nations Organisation would be the instrument for the dismantling the British Empire.

Roosevelt said that the American people would not let him keep his forces in Europe much longer. In the presence of my father, who reported it to me, Stalin remarked that the weakness of the democracies lay in the fact that the people did not delegate permanent rights such as the Soviet government possessed. He took account of what Roosevelt had said in all his subsequent plans.[2]

The American president was very pleased to hear Stalin describe to him the plan for his operations in the war with Japan. He assured Roosevelt that Chinese territory would be liberated by the Soviet army and that the Americans had nothing to worry about on that score. Roosevelt told Churchill that Stalin had also prepared joint participation in a landing planned in the north of Japan, in Hokkaido if my memory is correct. Stalin declared his readiness to extend naval operations if circumstances were favourable and the United States thought it necessary. All this had been discussed with Churchill absent. Roosevelt gave Churchill a detailed account of the way Stalin had dwelt on the fact that he would be obliged, not without reticence, to violate the Soviet-Japanese Pact of April 1941, whereas Japan had scrupulously respected it. Roosevelt had even felt compelled to calm Stalin's scruples by recalling the treacherous attack on Pearl Harbour. Stalin, however, observed that that attack had not been so unexpected as had been made out, and Roosevelt did not pursue the matter. Roosevelt also explained that he had been obliged to give in to Stalin on a number of points because he had shown himself so accommodating in matters concerning Japan. The British leader did not conceal his resentment and abruptly left. He must have been especially furious because he always showed great deference to Roosevelt.

In his dealing with the Allies, Stalin always sought to give the impression that he was a man of his word. He even made small concessions in order to succeed in this. Churchill had therefore drawn the conclusion that one could take Stalin's short-term promises seriously. The Soviet leader resorted to blackmail only on important matters, particularly the Polish question. On other matters he acted like a generous person. But each of his gestures of goodwill was carefully weighed and measured out in advance. Unlike Roosevelt, Stalin never yielded to an impulse. He sensed that the American president was very ill. My father noted, moreover, that Stalin had a certain respect for his adversary. 'You will have noticed,' he said, 'how full of consideration he is where Roosevelt is concerned, when, as a rule, he is dreadfully rude.' Stalin voiced his worry before the members of the Politburo: 'He has changed a great deal. Let's hope nothing happens to him. We shall never do business again with anyone like him.' And he ordered my father to inform him in greater detail about the men around Roosevelt, especially Truman and those who would be influential in the near future.

I encountered my father several times during this conference. I even spent a whole day in his bedroom, which was close to Stalin's. I asked for his view on how the discussions were going. 'Everything is going well. We have reached agreement on all points. We are going to have to go to war with Japan.' (I perceived that he did not attach much importance to this.) 'We can foresee big difficulties in China, where the situation is not simple. But on Poland Iosif Vissarionovich has not moved one inch.' And that was what worried my father. He would have liked Poland to have a bourgeois coalition government that we could control. But at Yalta Stalin opposed this: 'We shall allow one or two *émigrés* in, for decorative purposes, but no more.'[3]

My father's plans for the post-war period

His German policy

When, in January 1943, Roosevelt decided to demand Germany's unconditional surrender, my father thought that this was a huge blunder, as the Germans' resistance would be galvanised by it. He thought, too, that the Morgenthau plan for the 'de-industrialisation' of Germany[4] was an unreasonable act of vengeance by the Jews against the German people. He considered it to be all the more harmful because, at this time, he was counting on the German economy to serve as the engine for our own short-winded economy. Nor did Stalin approve this plan. He did not want the German state destroyed, as he counted on setting it against the other capitalist states. Similarly, my father thought the idea of dismembering Germany was absolutely idiotic.[5] A fragmented Germany would have but one idea – to be reunified. And that reunification would lead to another war. We must avoid inflicting national humiliation on the Germans. It was a mistake to have annexed East Prussia when it would have been enough to establish a military base there. The population transfers would be a source of future conflict. However, on the question of frontiers, the Party and the military were united. Only Admiral Kuznetsov shared my father's views. Generally speaking, my father would have preferred to go back to the frontiers of 1937, though he kept that opinion to himself. He hoped, it seems to me, that the arrangements made in 1945 would only be provisional.

In the spring of 1945 my father was angered by the anti-German propaganda of the Soviet media. Though Stalin had declared that Hitler was not forever, whereas the German people would always be there, our propaganda identified Germany with Fascism. My father was already worrying about our future relations with that country, which he did not want compromised by this sort of propaganda. The writer Ilya Ehrenburg was particularly unrestrained in this vein. At the instigation of my father, who did not like him, Stalin called Ehrenburg to order, requiring him to damp down his anti-German hatred.[6] Our troops invading Germany found that the vanquished foe led a life that was princely compared with theirs, and this redoubled their fury. It was certainly not the moment to proclaim 'Death to the Germans!,' as Ehrenburg was doing, in a tone that recalled the Black Hundreds.[7] The writer calmed down after that reprimand. In this connection Zhukov[8] pursued a good policy for which he was later blamed. He organised public executions of looters and succeeded in ending excesses by the threat of punishment.[9] My father reminded me that the Soviet army had behaved in exactly the same way in Georgia when Budenny was retreating before the German advances. It was an uncontrollable mass which destroyed everything as it passed. Budenny, that abortion steeped in alcohol, cried: 'What's the point of giving one's life for mandarin orchards and vineyards! Don't hold back, plunder and burn!' My father gave him twenty-four hours to get out, saying: 'Be grateful if I don't tell Iosif Vissarionovich what I've seen.'

There was little plundering and raping while fighting was in progress. These activities began only when hostilities ceased. The NKVD drew up many reports on the question,[10] which showed that commanders, far from checking their men, encouraged their excesses. Only one idea prevailed, to fill our pockets and stomachs in preparation against future shortages. My father suggested to Stalin that each man be given, on demobilisation, a share of the trophies brought back from Germany, instead of turning these over, uselessly, to the state. The purpose of this measure was to direct the Red Army men away from plundering the German population. Stalin agreed in principle, but this decision got stuck somewhere in the various administrations and was never put into practice. Very soon, Stalin sought to remove my father from German affairs, and he eventually lost all hope of influencing policy on German reparations through Maisky. So long as he was in charge of the reparations commission, in 1945-46, Maisky had to carry out Molotov's orders. And in 1946 he lost his post as Vice-Minister of Foreign Affairs. He was blamed for sending memoranda to my father as well as to Molotov.

His Polish policy

My father did not wish to see either a Soviet military presence or the implantation of a Socialist regime in Poland. He wanted the London Poles to be represented in the future government of their country. In other words, he favoured a genuine coalition government.[11] In his view, it would be best to have a pro-Soviet Poland, governed by men who had fought against the Germans, even if they were not Communists, in coalition with the Communists. He even, through third parties, sounded out the Polish Communist Bierut to see if he would accept Anders into his government. He spent some time trying to convince Molotov that people like Mikolajczyk would be quite harmless. Such bourgeois liberals were totally unfit to do anything but swank about and make fine speeches. Our own men would do the work and we should be able to supervise everything. This solution had seemed elegant to Molotov, and in June 1945 Stalin ended by accepting Mikolajczyk and a few others. They were so stupid that they took to quarrelling among themselves.[12] My father realised that his plan for Poland had miscarried.

His Jewish policy

My father had worked with Jewish intellectuals when he was a Chekist in Baku. I have already told how, in order to finance his service and the Soviet administration, he had sold two consignments of oil with the help of a young Jew who received, in return, a percentage of the gains and the right to emigrate to the United States. One of my father's close collaborators, the future Vice-Minister of Foreign Affairs in the Ukraine, Milshtein, was a Jew whom he had known in Georgia. His brother lived in the USA but often came illegally to the Soviet Union.[13] So my father had not needed war and fascism in order to learn how to make use of Jews. As he saw it, the country needed them. However, he did not encourage them to go into politics and occupy leading positions, lest this foster anti-Semitism. He had no sympathy for Zinoviev, Kamenev, Trotsky and the rest. He blamed them for their unscrupulous ambition, their pushiness and their tendency to judge people by their race rather than their ability. In politics he found the Jews to be opportunistic and he had no hope of openly seeking support among them. He did not blame the Jews for this, however, and explained their attitude by the centuries of persecution they had suffered. Provoked beyond endurance by Tsarist policy, the Jewish intelligentsia had favoured revolution and Socialism. Jews had formed the most aggressive wing of

Bolshevism. For lack of a state of their own they wanted to establish Bolshevism all over the world. They had begun to change their attitude only after Trotsky had been sidelined.

According to my father, Stalin was totally indifferent to individuals' nationalities, as he judged men in relation to the usefulness or the danger they could constitute. In his eyes a Jewish revolutionary was closer to Trotsky than to him, and this was what had made him so hostile to the Jews. My father considered that the struggle against Trotskyism was utterly harmful. Very early he was appealing to the American Jews who had roots in the USSR. He wanted to use the Jewish lobby to incite the USA to enter the war, because only the influence of that lobby could shift America out of its isolationism. Its weight enabled Roosevelt to get round the neutrality laws. The British, who had reasoned in the same way, acted similarly. They had even begun before we did. During the war my father cherished the hope that the entire Jewish community throughout the world, with its scientists and its bankers, would work for the Soviet Union. He wanted not merely to obtain financial and military aid from the United States but also to create a network of 'agents of influence' and even of ordinary agents. A great number of Jewish *émigrés* worked for the USSR out of anti-fascism. Stalin authorised this policy.

The Jewish Anti-Fascist Committee

During the war my father initiated the creation of anti-fascist committees, including the Jewish Anti-Fascist Committee, which came into being in April-May 1942.[14] The Jewish intellectual élite helped him to organise this committee, which was intended to form a permanent lobby that would mobilise Jewish capital, financial and political, throughout the world and influence American policy. The substantial sums that the Soviet Union received during the course of the war came to us thanks to the Jewish financial group that supported Roosevelt. Morgenthau[15] and Lilienthal[16] are the two names that I remember from this group. Lend-lease and the provision of warships almost free of charge were benefits resulting from this lobby. These Jewish financiers were not necessarily pro-Communist, though there were Socialist-inclined elements among them: they simply wanted to see Germany destroyed. My father and the Soviet government of the time were able to exploit that feeling thoroughly.

However, my father made a blunder when he wanted to give the leadership of the Jewish Anti-Fascist Committee to G. Erlich and V. Alter. They were real leaders[17] and had contributed a large number of suggestions regarding the organisation of the Committee.[18] But my father did not know that they had formerly been critics of Stalin. In general he knew little of the conflicts between the Bund and the Bolsheviks. When Stalin saw their names on the list of future members of the Committee he became violently angry: 'What's this? You've taken people from the Bund,

Trotskyists!' And he ordered their arrests. After this gaffe my father delved into the history of the Bund: I saw Merkulov bring him huge files about it. Any Party could derive inspiration from the Bund's remarkable organisation, he remarked. I heard my father express regret at the deaths of Erlich and Alter, talking to the actor Mikhoels, who then became the leader of the Jewish Anti-Fascist Committee.

Mikhoels did not have such widespread connections as Erlich and Alter. Nevertheless, he was sent to the USA with the poet Fefer, between June and December 1943.[19] At the same time, my father sent over there a Georgian film director named Kolotozov, accompanied by a very beautiful Leningrad actress. They were supposed to reactivate my father's old contacts in Hollywood. My father advised Kolotozov to warn Mikhoels that his every move would be reported to the Soviet authorities by his closest colleague and friend Fefer,[20] and to urge him to control his tongue and conceal even from his nearest companions the real purpose of the visit, keeping secret some of his meetings with Americans. The informer was not reporting to my father but to Abakumov and Merkulov. He was therefore unable to get rid of him and could influence Merkulov only at a very high level (which explains why Stalin dismissed Merkulov). Such a move would have attracted suspicion. Fefer was an enthusiastic skirt-chaser, so he was kept busy with women. In his absence, Mikhoels, accompanied by Kolotozov, was able to meet a certain number of influential financiers. Unfortunately he could not stay discreet. The results of this visit were extremely profitable. They concerned aid for the reconstruction of the USSR after the war. Stalin approved of this policy. He remembered how the first Five-Year Plan had been fulfilled with American capital,[21] and saw nothing untoward in Americans investing in the USSR. Later, one could always take the necessary measures.

During his visit to the United States Mikhoels discussed with American Jews the project for creating a Jewish State in the Crimea. This had been an old idea of the Zionists before the revolution.[22] After the revolution they obtained the right to set up there a number of Jewish communes, like kibbutzim. The project failed because the Jews preferred to live in big cities. My father was at first in favour of the Crimea scheme, as he hoped to develop the Black Sea region with the aid of Jewish capital. But it did not take him long to perceive that Stalin was hostile to the scheme, and he then tried to dissuade Zhemchuzhina, Molotov's wife, from getting involved in it. 'Russia will never allow the establishment of a Jewish state in Crimea,' he told her. Zhemchuzhina did not heed my father's warnings.[23] She counted on him more than on Molotov to bring the project to a successful conclusion, whereas he had already realised that this was quite out of the question.[24] At the start Stalin said neither yes or no.[25] But he soon gave preference to the creation of a Jewish state in Palestine – a Socialist state, which, as he saw it, would become an advanced satellite of the USSR in the Middle East and enable Moscow to expand its influence forward in this oil-rich region.

Raul Wallenberg

My father never spoke to me of Raul Wallenberg.[26] What I know of him I learnt from Serov, who was in charge of counter-espionage in Germany, Austria and Yugoslavia. I met him in Germany at the end of the war and we travelled together in Austria, Czechoslovakia and Hungary. I liked Serov, who was only a dozen years older than me. He readily confided in me and always boasted of the importance of his networks. He mentioned a powerful organisation which, during the war, had helped certain Jews to get out of the concentration camps in return for large sums paid to the Reich. These transactions were enacted through Sweden. Serov, who was anti-Semitic, saw British manoeuvres in all this. He told me that an important group of Swedes was engaged in wiping out traces of its past activity in Europe. Two or three years later, after his return to Moscow, he told me that Abakumov's Smersh had seized Wallenberg in Budapest in January 1945.[27] Like me, Serov did not know of the connection between Wallenberg and my father. I mentioned the matter to my father as though this had been an exploit of our services. He looked at me and asked: 'where did you hear that name?'

'Serov spoke to me about him.'

My father then telephoned Serov and covered him with invective. 'What got into you to spread such gossip? And before my son, too!' At the time I did not understand this reaction. Later, when the affair of the Jewish Anti-Fascist Committee was used to undermine my father's position, he explained to me that Wallenberg had been kidnapped for the same reason. My father was the target aimed at through Wallenberg.[28] The Wallenberg family had acted as intermediaries with the Finnish government in the armistice negotiations with the USSR. Raul Wallenberg had connections with the British, German and Soviet services and had used these relationships to save Jews.

Maintaining the Grand Alliance

From 1943 my father tried to persuade Stalin not to impose Communist governments in the countries of Central and Eastern Europe and the Baltic states. He argued that it would be enough if these countries had pro-Soviet governments and an economy oriented towards the USSR. Our country's priority after the war was to restore its economy. At the beginning Stalin allowed him to entertain some hope that he would be listened to. But the further our troops advanced into Europe, the more Stalin became convinced that force would enable him to attain the objectives corresponding to the interests of the Soviet Union as he conceived them from his ideological standpoint. After having for a long time hoped that Anders's army could return to Poland, my father realised at Yalta that Stalin would not listen to him. In any case, from the Teheran conference he had had a presentiment that his Polish project would not come off. He had pricked up his ears when Roosevelt had, so to speak, asked Stalin to provide him with excuses that he could use with his Polish electorate. It was clear that the Americans were going to give in to Stalin's demands regarding Poland.

My father disagreed with Stalin on many points, though I never heard him say that Stalin was unable to give a lucid judgement on facts reported to him. Stalin often drew the same conclusions as my father but oriented them differently because their objectives were different. My father wanted genuine peaceful co-existence. He wanted to avoid repeating our mistaken policies. He declared, for example, that we should not organise the weakness of the democracies. We ought not to raise up against us a solid bloc of adversaries, but must avoid forcing our enemies to unite. 'Let's leave them, rather, to their natural weakness,' he advised. 'The more aggressively and provocatively we behave, the more we shall unite them and incite them to increase spending on arms when they would prefer to reduce that expenditure.' In his view we should have no illusions about the divergent interests of the capitalist states: faced with what they perceived as a common danger they would forget their quarrels and form an alliance. The democracies would eventually react and we should unquestionably be the losers in a protracted war. My father recalled that Churchill had managed to become an effective leader, capable of taking rapid decisions, in a democratic Britain. He referred to the example of Hitler, who had won only blitzkriegs. 'We may win some momentary successes at the start, but we can't win a long-term war.'[29] To which the scientist Abrosimov, of whom my father was fond, retorted that man's life was short.

I remember well those discussions in which Shtemenko tried to convince my father that he was mistaken. My father flared up. 'You know nothing about our economy. Given time we shall always lose.' These discussions have stayed in my memory because they took place on several occasions after the war, right down to 1951-52. The further our forces advanced into Europe the sharper these discussions became. Shtemenko told me that in 1944-45 plans for the invasions of France and Italy had been drawn up by our General Staff.[30] The accession of the Communists to power would take place at the same time as the advance of the Soviet troops. A landing in Norway was provided for, as well as seizure of the Straits. A substantial budget was allocated for the realisation of these plans. It was expected that the Americans would abandon a Europe fallen into chaos, while Britain and France would be paralysed by their colonial problems. The Soviet Union possessed 400 experienced divisions, ready to bound forward like tigers. It was calculated that the whole operation would take no more than a month.[31] The Yugoslavs would lay siege to Italy and Austria. I was amazed that Tito consented to participate in our operations, as I knew that he had leaned towards Britain since the war. (Churchill's son spent a long time at his side.) All these plans were aborted when Stalin learnt from my father that the Americans had the atom bomb and were putting it into mass production. Without the Americans' will to resist, Stalin would have taken over Europe. He said that if Roosevelt had still been alive, we would have succeeded. America would have been content to inherit British colonies and would not have moved against us. Stalin was convinced, moreover, that Roosevelt had been assassinated and he blamed my father for having nothing to tell him about that matter.

I do not wish to claim that my father was the only one to defend this moderate line. Some of the military shared his view. I am thinking particularly of Vasilevsky, Antonov and other officers of our General Staff. Malenkov, too, was for moderation, at least so long as ideological considerations did not cause him to change his position, as was to happen when the Yugoslav crisis came. Malenkov, my father and a group of the military thought that the United States was potentially the most dangerous of our enemies, whereas Britain was less to be feared: we could neutralise that country by encouraging it to conserve its strength to keep its empire. According to this group we should avoid provoking Britain's hostility and wager on its conflicts with the United States.

Stalin, therefore, had his reasons when, at Yalta, he presented my father to Roosevelt as 'our Himmler.' He knew that my father was a convinced advocate of maintaining the Grand Alliance and that he had his own contacts and channels with the Allies. (He had, for example, met Cripps and Harriman with the agreement of the Politburo.) And Stalin, as always, distilled his drop of venom to discredit my father, so as to dissuade anyone from engaging in talks with him. My father never mentioned this episode to me: it must have hurt him to the quick.[32] I often saw him discontented at being kept out of negotiations with the Anglo-Saxons by Stalin. Stalin was extremely jealous of any contact between foreigners and the men around him. At the end of October 1945, Harriman was invited by Stalin to Sochi. He was to stay in our *dacha*. I was on holiday. One day, when I returned from my daily ride, I came upon men engaged in installing microphones in the house, including my father's bedroom. But my father knew his Stalin and, so long as Harriman was staying at our place, he did not go to it, and even spent his nights at Stalin's.

The beginning of the Cold War

Towards the end of the war Zhdanov got back into Stalin's good graces. Ideological claptrap came to the forefront once more. Zhdanov, of course, encouraged Stalin in an aggressive policy. Even while Roosevelt was alive he strongly opposed our accepting American aid after the war, a plan dear to my father. He did everything he could to sabotage our alliance with the Anglo-Saxons. At first Stalin did not go along with him. America was absorbed in dismantling the British Empire while Britain was obsessed with the danger threatening her colonies, and was consequently not much concerned with Soviet activity. In short, things were going splendidly.[33]

After Roosevelt's death (13 April 1945), Stalin was soon made to realise that American policy was now going to be different. His analysis and my father's were the same. Truman represented a different financial group. Roosevelt had been supported by international finance and Jewish capital. Those groups encouraged him to promote decolonisation, because they wanted to take over the French and British possessions. The group which supported Truman was not isolationist, but it favoured other methods. In particular, it wanted a rapprochement with the Arabs, on account of their oil. A turn in American policy was therefore to be expected. My father had to resign himself to the ousting of the American lobby in which he had influence. I remember hearing him say to Serov, who was an anti-Semite: 'Ah well, it's now the turn of your favourites.' All his plans for economic reconstruction of the USSR with the aid of Jewish capital were scuttled. Stalin, who had agreed to accept American aid while Roosevelt was alive, changed his policy and said that we should get ourselves out of the economic mess by our own efforts. My father regretted this in turn, because, under these conditions, any rapid improvement in our economy was out of the question, especially as military expenditure continued to enjoy first priority.

When Hopkins was sent to Moscow by Truman on 26 May 1945, he reported to Stalin that Roosevelt had been very disappointed by Stalin's conduct during the last days of his life, and warned him that the change in American policy had already begun. Hopkins said that Truman, knowing that the Soviets had confidence in him, wanted to make use of him, and added that he refused to play that game and misinform Stalin.[34] Had he passed that message at his government's request or had he done it unknown to them? I favour the second hypothesis. At this time the worsening of relations between the USSR and the Western Powers was still covered up.

Kruglov told me about the conference he attended at San Francisco. It was held between 25 April and 26 June 1945 and its purpose was to inaugurate the United Nations. On his return he gave us his impressions. 'I found San Francisco marvellous,' he admitted, in a sprightly way that astonished me. I had known him during the war and he seemed to me not the sort of person to get excited about anything. That day, though, he found words of enthusiasm for describing America. But that was not the main thing in his account. He went on: 'I was strolling in the United Nations Organisation when, suddenly, I spotted someone I knew. Looking more closely, I recognised one of our agents. Walking further along, I was surprised to encounter another familiar face. In a single day I was able in this way to count a score of our agents who were not members of our delegation but of foreign delegations. I was flabbergasted,' he concluded. My father did not fail to wax sarcastic about the conduct of our delegation. Instead of fighting to obtain concrete benefits, especially in the economic domain, they had spent their time casting ideological thunderbolts. 'It's as though the Westerners had knowingly provoked our people to channel all their zeal into diatribes against any mention of God!'

Defeated Germany

In May-June 1945 I went to Germany for the first time. Before I left, my father gave me some advice: 'Try to meet as many German scientists as possible. Get an idea of what they are thinking. See if they will agree to work for the Soviet Union and try to convince them that it would be more to their interest to collaborate with us than with the Anglo-Saxons even if they are not Communists. Make them understand that the USSR has at heart the restoration of Germany, and play upon that theme.'

I took advantage of this stay in Germany to familiarise myself with German technology. I was protected by Serov, the head of the NKVD in Germany, and I had obtained the necessary permits from Zhukov. While others concerned themselves with nuclear research, which was not my field at all – my father had set up special commissions to evaluate Germany's armaments and industry – I particularly looked at radio equipment and the technology of missiles and anti-aircraft defence. I was enthused by some of my discoveries, such as the remarkable guided missiles which the Germans had managed to manufacture for anti-aircraft defence but which they had had no time to use. Among the German scientists I met, Dr Pose made an excellent impression. Though he did not know who I was, he showed me the work he was engaged on. He explained that he had not been forced to make an atomic bomb, though he would have been able to. Speer had said that Germany had greater need of nuclear engines for her submarines than of hypothetical atomic bombs.

I remember that at this time the main concern of the Soviet administration of our zone of occupation was how to feed the Germans. All the conversations at which I was present dealt with this problem. We had also to get the drains functioning again, so as to prevent epidemics. Our soldiers expended great efforts in this domain, and not only for humanitarian reasons. What our leaders were thinking I don't know, but, on the spot, those responsible had already understood intuitively that a contest with the Allies for the goodwill of the German population had begun. [35] I heard Sokolovsky[36] lament on several occasions that we lacked the means to rival the Americans: 'When I see the huge sacks of food that they bring in! One has the impression that it costs them nothing.' We seized large reserves of food that the Germans had set aside, especially canned goods from France. Serov had the idea of distributing this food on the spot instead of sending it to the USSR, and I believe he obtained permission to do this.

The Germans were demoralised by defeat and by what they saw happening. Serov told me that the Communists were just as depressed as the Nazis. The bad behaviour of our troops worried him a lot. He asked Zhukov to intervene, so as to stop the excesses and punish the guilty. Our soldiers were plundering and raping sometimes whole villages at a time.[37] In the towns there was certainly less abuse of power, thanks to the presence of the *Komandatura* which enforced something like discipline, but in some regions I saw girls whose knickers were held up by cords with complicated knots. I was told the reason for this ...

On my return from Germany, my father asked me to stay in Moscow for a week before I went back to Leningrad, so that he could question me on my stay. Every lunchtime he asked me about what I had seen. He asked if I had noticed differences between our scientists and the German ones. I said that the German scientists seemed to me more balanced. And that was all I could think of to say! This made him laugh. 'You can make some profound observations,' he said, teasingly. I took umbrage: 'You have thousands of people there, and look at the result.' He went on laughing and said: 'They will spend years making an inventory of the Germans' inventions and then they'll need more time assimilating what they've seen.' I then told him that I had overheard fragments of conversation between the military, Sokolovsky and others, which gave reason to suppose that we were mounting an offensive in Europe. 'This is something we have been preparing over a long period,' he said. 'There are people who imagine that it is to the interest of the Soviet state to project an operation of that sort.' I must say that the prospect of reaching the English Channel in a week enchanted me. I showed my father my enthusiasm. He cooled me down at once. 'I don't want to discuss that with you now and I hope I shall never have occasion to.' He never returned to the subject but I noticed several times subsequently that he was unhappy when I displayed my will to conquer. He said nothing but, some time later, one of his subordinates telephoned me and asked me to go and see him so that he could make me understand certain matters. Even with me my father could not reveal all that he was thinking, and preferred to use a go-between for the purpose.

My other visits to Germany

I had the opportunity to visit the Reich Chancellery during my stay in Germany, and was struck by the absence of luxury in Hitler's rooms, compared with what one saw in films. My impressions did not interest my father, who found this in no way surprising. He explained to me that Hitler liked outward pomp but lived modestly. He lacked the appetite for receptions and parades but used them as a way of acting upon the masses.

Serov gave me a dagger which had belonged to Dönitz and a writing-pad with Hitler's heading. I showed them to my father, who said: 'Give them to our big child, it'll make him happy.' He was referring to Molotov to whom I offered these objects for his collection. He accepted them, embracing me, and was very happy. Molotov kept inviting my father to visit the Chancellery. He agreed eventually, but took care to warn Stalin, knowing that he interested himself in everything in the behaviour of those close to him which might catch the attention of the press. Stalin showed lively disapproval. Any independent action by one of his subordinates irritated him deeply. He too had been invited to visit the Chancellery, but he had refused, saying that it did not interest him. Actually, Stalin had not forgiven Hitler for his foolishness and, above all, he was particularly vexed with himself for having overestimated Hitler's capacities and having been mistaken in him. That was, anyway, how my father explained Stalin's attitude when talking to my mother.

Serov brought my father a lot of German books and archives. He had hunted out works dealing with the Basques because he knew of my father's interest in that subject. I remember that I spent hours devouring these books.

I had a third stay in Germany, of about two months, in May 1946. I went with Pugachev, a mathematician who taught at the Air Force Academy, Keldysh and other teachers at that academy. Our group was to be billeted on Germans. My father had advised me to make this trip and encouraged me to spend as much time as possible with the Germans: 'That will be useful for you.' But Keldysh and Pugachev spoilt everything. Like most Russians they felt at home everywhere and behaved with such arrogance towards the Germans that the latter took against them. Keldysh was a skunk of the worst type, as I had plenty of chances to learn during our trip. My father did not understand how so gifted a man could aspire to become a functionary in the scientific field, and he kept away from him. Keldysh was able to make a career only under Khrushchev, who systematically promoted scientists whom my father had rejected.

I drew no conclusions from this last visit, except that the Germans expected no good from us. I told my father that and he said: 'You are quite right. All that we can do is to show the Germans that, unlike the Western Powers, we favour the unity of their state.'

My successive visits to Germany partly decided my professional orientation, but I can say that Svetlana also played an active role in this. She spoke to her father about me towards the end of 1946. He summoned Ustinov and said: 'I've been talking with Beria's son, who is finishing his studies at the academy. He has told me interesting things about what he saw in Germany, and his version does not correspond at all to what you have written in your reports to me.' Stalin never missed an opportunity to check on his subordinates. He went on, 'See what you can do with him.' It is interesting to observe that Stalin went directly to Ustinov, acting behind my father's back. Having failed to make me an artist, my father had vigorously encouraged me to go into teaching. He wanted me to be happy in my life and as free as it was possible to be in our country. He knew all too well that a career in armaments meant isolation and secrecy to the end of my days. I finally decided to follow a career as an engineer in the military sector.

The Potsdam Conference

The British and Americans were in a hurry to solve the problems set by Germany in defeat. The Soviet Union was less so.[38] But the Americans changed their attitude when they learnt that the atomic bomb was almost ready. They then decided to wait, so as to strengthen their position when negotiations took place. Stalin knew that Truman came to Potsdam with the hope that the bomb would go off during the conference. He decided not to change his plans and to see how things would turn out.

I asked my father to let me go to Potsdam with him and he consented. This time I was not concerned with eavesdropping, though this was still on the programme. During the journey my father told me that the Americans were getting ready to test their atomic bomb. He expected the news to reach him from one moment to the next. He urgently instructed Serov to send the news without delay, so that he could immediately warn Stalin. Truman was also on tenterhooks, awaiting the news. The funniest bit in this affair is that twice before the Potsdam Conference, Stalin and my father had speculated about how Stalin should react if the Allies announced the existence of an atomic weapon. They agreed that he should pretend not to understand. My father warned Stalin, however, that the Americans had captured some of our agents. They might know that we were interested in the question and even that we had started to work on it.[39] I had already heard my father touch on this problem when, in the presence of Serov and others, he was checking on the results of the commission which had the task of carrying off the German scientists who were working on the atomic project.[40] We wondered how to reply if the Americans sounded us out on the question. We had carried off, under their very noses, a group of scientists whom they had intended to take home, so that it was now impossible to conceal our interest in nuclear matters. Stalin decided, in spite of everything, to act the innocent. He waited, therefore, for the Allies to tell him the news, curious to see what they would say. He thought that the Americans might supply him with some technical details so as to intimidate him the more.

I remember too that there was discussion then about the possibility of a setback to the Americans' test. This was thought to be slight. My father said, jokingly, that for a setback to occur in these conditions would require an extraordinary twist of fortune. However, we knew from our information services that Stimson, the American Secretary of State for Defence, was sceptical about the effects of the nuclear weapon.

On 17 July my father at last announced to Stalin that the bomb had been exploded. He explained to him that it was a weapon of unheard-of destructive power. I learnt from Serov how Truman had given Stalin the news the next day. He began to whisper something to him. Stalin had asked no questions and merely congratulated Truman. Our secret recordings enabled us to hear Churchill asking Truman how Stalin had taken it and Truman replying that Stalin had apparently failed to understand.[41] Stalin sent for Molotov, my father and a few others after the end of that session. He related, sniggering, how they had shared the news with him and watched his reaction: 'Churchill was standing by the door, his eyes fixed on me like a searchlight, while Truman, with his hypocritical air, told me what had happened in an indifferent tone.' Stalin ordered that a complete documentation of the American atomic bomb should be put together. My father confided to Serov, with satisfaction, that Stalin was fully aware of the capacity of this new weapon. He now understood the absurdity of the military operation he had planned in Europe and the uselessness of his 400 divisions. Serov was as much opposed as my father to a Soviet offensive in Europe because he had had military training and estimated quite well what the Americans could do. The decision to cancel these plans was taken late, between the end of the Potsdam Conference and the USSR's entry into the war with Japan.[42]

After the bomb had been exploded, Truman began to hesitate between two policies. Should pressure be brought to bear openly on Stalin, or was the Russians' help still indispensable?[43] He consulted General Marshall and Defence Secretary Stimson. The latter was not an enthusiast for the nuclear weapon. Perhaps he feared that the policy of the United States might become aggressive now that they had the bomb.[44] According to my father and Serov, Stimson dissuaded Truman from taking a hard line because the Americans still had need of the Russians.[45] Truman was very unhappy about this. Byrnes, the head of the State Department, was unhappier still. He asked the General Staff for a note of the economic and human consequences that a Soviet refusal to join in the war with Japan would have. My father told me that Byrnes behaved very rudely to Truman and dictated to him what he should say in an absolutely indecent manner. The British had noticed this too and even talked about it among themselves. Churchill advised Eden to work first upon Byrnes while he tried to get a decision from Truman.

It emerges clearly from the Potsdam Conference that the Americans would have used the atomic bomb on Japan even if military circumstances had not required this: they wanted to intimidate the Soviet Union and put a brake on its appetite in Europe.[46]

Plans for conquest

Stalin foresaw the change that would follow the explosion of the atom bomb and thought he would need to renegotiate all the agreements he had made with Roosevelt. But this did not make him more prudent. He continued to press forward, retreating only when he came up against resolute resistance. He knew no other way of proceeding.[47] In reality, he had never wanted peaceful co-existence and had counted on the weakness of the democratic states. Parliamentary governments seemed to him incapable of rapid and concerted reaction to lightning moves and accomplished facts. He considered that he could exploit that situation by moving his chessmen forward. Stalin had studied Hitler's example: the latter had nothing in the 1930s and brought off his coups by means of intimidation. He ascribed the success of Hitler's actions not to Chamberlain's weakness but to that of democratic governments. They had to be assured of support from public opinion and were, he thought, unable to react quickly, using force. He never gave up, despite repulses, and remained convinced that this inertia of the democracies had not changed. Stalin did not abandon his usual methods even if they led to reverses.

Attlee replaces Churchill

Churchill had left Potsdam confident that he had won the British General Election. My father had information that gave him cause to expect that it would be close fought. We presumed that Churchill would win, but only just. When Churchill made difficulties for us Stalin thought that this was understandable. 'He defends Poland like a lion, but he is not thinking of Poland – he is wondering what awaits him tomorrow.' Stalin contemplated the possibility of defeat for Churchill: 'In the minds of the British he is associated with war. The people are tired with fighting and that's what will tell against him.' Stalin felt a sort of satisfaction when Churchill was defeated. True, nothing of that kind could happen to him! But he was not pleased that Churchill had been replaced by the Labour Party leader, Attlee. He knew Churchill and had learnt to calculate what his reactions would be. He was going to have to sound out a different set of men. Perhaps he realised that from now on he would be dealing with people who were harder to handle. Subsequently, I heard Stalin say that any Conservative government, and especially a British one, was more committed to its country's interests, and it was therefore easier to do business with Conservatives than with Socialists, whoever they might be. He meant that Socialists who were not rich were not interested in the development of their nation's productive forces. Being more cosmopolitan than the Conservatives, they were more subject to American influence. I have the impression that this was also my father's opinion. Moreover, since he was always concerned to intensify the contradictions between the capitalist states, Stalin thought that Conservative governments in these states lent themselves more easily to that game and would sow discord more effectively in the imperialist camp. I think he wanted to erect a bridge between the Conservatives and the national Communists. He was therefore very strongly prejudiced against Socialist governments. He even referred to some remarks by Lenin (citing Millerand[48] as example, if I remember rightly) and liked to repeat that any Socialist movement did more harm to the Communists than any Conservative government. He saw the French Socialists and the British Labourites as particularly noxious. Every month Stalin received a report on each Western statesman. My father mentioned to him one day in 1951 that Bevin[49] was seriously ill. Bevin was a key member of Attlee's cabinet. Stalin replied, sceptically: 'He's only pretending, because he's thinking of making a turn in his policy. And your useless fellows aren't up to telling me what it is that Bevin is preparing!' Two weeks later Bevin died. My father casually announced this news to Stalin: 'Bevin has accomplished what he was preparing: he's dead.'

'You are playing with a tiger,' my mother said to him when he told us of this witticism of his.

'I couldn't resist it,' he replied, laughing. He beamed like a child.

Hitler and National Socialism

According to my father, Stalin commented thus on the fall of the Führer: 'He appeared on the political scene as an adventurer unable to see far ahead,'; he took the Führer seriously, above all, because of his powerful Wehrmacht. My father noticed that Stalin felt no personal irritation when he was dealing with a Western statesman, whereas Hitler always got on his nerves because of his inconsistency. At first, he believed that Hitler was the unconscious tool of French and British policy. He never wanted to meet him and dreaded lest, at the time of the Pact, the German leader might invite himself to the USSR. He spoke to Molotov about his fears, and Molotov told my father.

Stalin considered that Nazism would not last. I think he found irritating the analogies that were drawn between him and Hitler and, especially, between Nazism and Communism. Stalin was intelligent enough to be aware that these analogies were more valid than was supposed in the West but he wanted to present the image of being a man full of kindness. He did not like to be reminded of the Communist tones of Goebbels' early writings and put an end to discussions that turned on to that subject. He even chided my father when he began to speak about the similarity between National Bolshevism and Nazism, even though he quoted Bolshevik Georgia in the first years of the Soviet regime as an example. Stalin shut him up, saying that he confused it with Trotskyism. I must mention that my father liked to stress the fact that many National-Socialist leaders came from the Communist camp, quoting especially Goebbels and his youthful articles in which one felt the spirit of War Communism. My father thought that if Bolshevism was an extreme system, then Fascism was the highest development not of capitalism but of our Socialist system. Comparing the two systems, he nevertheless pointed out a difference. 'In Germany the National-Socialist Party is only an instrument for supervision, in the hands of the dictator. With us the Party is not merely an instrument for supervision, it is also the means that Stalin uses to carry out his policy. That's the only difference.' And he added: 'We are better able to manoeuvre and improvise, despite our stupidity and that of our officials. The Germans can't adapt themselves to new circumstances. They carry through to the end whatever they have begun, even if the dynamic of events has changed. There is an element of inertia because they need to understand why they must alter their conduct, and that's a handicap for them.' This kind of reflection exasperated my mother. I remember that one day Stalin had behaved badly to Ella, our nanny. He arrived out of the blue at lunchtime and said to Ella, who always ate with us: 'Are you Hitler's representative?' The poor

woman went pale and my mother came to her rescue: 'She is nobody's representative. She has been part of our family since 1929.' Stalin quickly
changed his tone: 'I did not mean it like that. I highly esteem the German
nation. I have even lived in Austria.'[50] And he talked about the country, even
using some German words. In short he turned the thing into a joke. Next
day, at lunch, my father asked my nanny: 'Ella, how do you feel after that?'

'You know very well how I feel.'

'Well, then, since you are Hitler's representative, I will tell you what he
is like. That fanatic is worse than Iosif Vissarionovich. He is a man
possessed, a man who is extremely gifted, since he manages to control
those around him better than Iosif Vissarionovich can ...' I have forgotten
what his next words were exactly, but I do recall that, for my father, Hitler
was a man possessed. Though gifted, he felt that he was a failure and so
was frustrated. 'I, too, love the arts,' my father went on, 'but, for all that,
I don't envy artists: on the contrary, I delight in their works. Whereas he
cannot forgive those who could not appreciate his talent.' My father did
not speak of Hitler as a degenerate or an idiot, though he considered him
abnormal. 'He is not only able to hypnotise crowds or subjugate those close
to him. He subjects himself, and that is the cause of his mistakes because
he stops analysing with his reason.' Hitler ended by believing his own lies.
My father was surprised that he was able to subjugate intelligent people
and not only imbeciles. 'He is near to being a genius, like our man (he
meant Stalin), but with this difference, that he is mad.' In the end, Hitler
could not win.

The attempt on Hitler's life in July 1944 gave rise to a comment by my
father the significance of which I can now understand. According to him,
the German conspirators' failure was due simply to bad luck. Their plan
was based on the physical elimination of Hitler, and if they had succeeded
in killing him all the rest of their plan would have followed without a
hitch. But Hitler had survived and his grip on the country was so firm that
nothing could be done. The considerable support that the conspirators
enjoyed in the army was no help.

Among the dignitaries of the Third Reich my father found Schacht
especially interesting. He saw in him a financier of genius, a man
connected with American capital who nevertheless lacked the practical
spirit of Speer, the organiser of the German economy. 'Speer is intelligent,
but he wasn't intelligent enough to appreciate the importance of the
nuclear weapon the German scientists would have made if they had been
given the means. My father thought that Schacht and Speer would play
important roles in post-war Germany.

The Pole Radziwill kept us regularly informed about Goering. One day
when we were talking about his obesity, his gluttony and his passion for
precious objects, my father turned to Bogdan Kobulov and said, laughing:
'I think that's you, to the life.' Kobulov was fat and disgusting[51] with a
fondness for luxury and works of art.

Speaking about Goebbels my father also pointed out to me the contrast between his repulsive physical appearance and his talent as an orator. He told me that Goebbels had once said, in a speech: 'You wonder why this monkey is playing Apollo. It's because in my soul I am Apollo.'

My father compared Martin Bormann to Molotov. 'He is a workaholic totally devoted to Hitler. He owes his influence over the Führer not to his ability but to the fact that he is always close to him. He has become indispensable by his presence.' I never heard anything either from my father or from anyone else that might show that Bormann was a Soviet agent.

Churchill

Stalin considered Churchill a much more formidable opponent than Hitler. 'He will never change. It was he who tried to destroy Bolshevik Russia. He will give us a lot of trouble,' he said at the beginning of the war. Churchill sensed this and that was why he sent in Cripps and Beaverbrook, who he thought would be more acceptable to us. When, at Teheran, someone remarked to Stalin that Churchill had changed his attitude to the Soviet Union, he replied, ironically: 'He has already tried to crush us, now he is trying to isolate us behind a cordon sanitaire.' This had already been Curzon's policy. At the time of the capture of Berlin, when he learnt that Churchill and Montgomery were urging their forces eastward in order to get there before ours, he exulted and vigorously lectured Zhukov. Serov was present and reported the scene to me: 'Are you going to let yourself be overtaken by that Montgomery who wasn't able to beat Rommel? Are you going to let him take Berlin before you? If you can't manage it, I'll send Konev to help you.' Stalin knew that Zhukov and Konev loathed each other. He put his threat into effect and Konev was able to share with Zhukov the glory of taking Berlin. Stalin never missed a chance to play upon the rivalries between the men around him.

My father had a quite different opinion of Churchill. He was not afraid to say that he was Britain's greatest statesman since Disraeli. He did not hide his admiration for him, even in Stalin's presence. 'He is a man dominated by feeling and capable of making mistakes when he acts under the influence of his emotions,' he said. 'He has a stubbornness that is dangerous for a statesman, but his political flair is incredible.' My father thought the British people very ungrateful when Labour proved victorious in July 1945. For him Churchill was not an ideological adversary but, above all, the defender of the British Empire. If the USSR had let it be known that it had no designs on Britain's possessions it would have come to an understanding with Churchill and would not have thrust Britain into the arms of America, as it did through the fault of Stalin alone. Churchill was able to rely on the intelligence services and always took account of their views, which pleased my father greatly. 'Churchill is the soul of the British secret services,' he observed. He did not fail to highlight this aspect in the reports he made to Stalin. The latter drew the conclusion in his own way. 'Henceforth I will take charge of intelligence,' he told my father.

Eden and Roosevelt

We had files on every foreign statesman. These files drew attention, particularly, to their weaknesses. We had observed that Eden, the head of the Foreign Office, had a high opinion of his looks and was very susceptible to flattery, which he readily encouraged. My father considered him a dandy. He did not like men who attached excessive importance to their dress and spent their time admiring themselves in a mirror. When Stalin learnt that Eden had this weakness he did not miss the opportunity to apply his favourite tactic. Churchill had total confidence in Eden and Stalin made use of Eden's weaknesses to create rivalry between the two men. He set himself to indicating to Eden that he preferred young people like him, who did not drag a heavy past behind them. Eden purred with delight as he drank in Stalin's words, and we heard him tell those around him that Stalin had understood him. And when Churchill had to fight like a lion on matters dear to his heart he received no support from Eden.[52]

As for Roosevelt, my father took him to be purely a politician who nevertheless had to be taken seriously on account of his alliance with the Jewish financiers. Besides, on the American scale, Roosevelt ranked as a statesman.

The Soviet generals

Our military leaders were extremely jealous of each other and each of them kept an eye on his colleagues' careers, with the exception of Vasilevsky, who was above these petty passions. They all had a high opinion of Stalin's capacities, because he knew how to select and utilise men. While they detested Malenkov, I never heard them accuse him of incompetence, as he was intelligent enough not to involve himself in matters that he did not understand. Their opinion of Molotov was less flattering, as they thought him a narrow-minded person who knew nothing about military matters.

Zhukov

Zhukov had a strong face with roughly cut features. His look was attentive and severe. Of average height, he had a robust constitution. He was always impeccably dressed. I liked him a lot and still esteem him despite what has been written about his part in my father's arrest. Stalin also appreciated him and did not hold his setbacks against him, despite Zhdanov's insinuations against the General Staff at the beginning of the war. Zhukov was above all a fighting soldier and Stalin realised very soon that the place for him was not at the head of the General Staff.

My father got on well with him. They were pretty frank with each other. Zhukov often came to see us during the war. He complained about the political commissars. One day my father teased him in my presence: 'You talk about nothing but the political commissars. I agree with you, they do harm. But the whole structure of your army is built like that. You should blame, rather, the army regulations that you have had adopted. Compare your procedures with what happens with the Germans. Among them there is no question of verifying the execution of orders. If an officer gives an order there will be no doubt that it well be carried out. Whereas, in your regulations, everything depends on many checks being applied.' And he waved the relevant document under Zhukov's nose. The general was furious, all the more so because he had not participated in the drawing up of these regulations, which were mainly Shaposhnikov's work. After the war, he became still more vehement against the Army's political organs. 'What good can they do? They take responsibility for nothing and busy themselves entirely with collecting gossip in order to compose denunciations. They create divisions among the military. At bottom, they are the ones guilty of the repressions in the Army.' That was my father's opinion on the Party's organs in general.

In June 1945 Serov was appointed second-in-command to Zhukov and sent, at Zhukov's request, to Germany. Zhukov had told my father that he wanted as his deputy a decent man who would not invent calumnies against him. My father had offered him Serov, while warning the latter to control his tongue (Zhukov did not hide his opinions) and to distrust military men who were jealous of him. There were limits to what Serov could do for him. Zhukov accepted Serov, who saved him from much unpleasantness.[53]

Abakumov took it into his head to expose enemies within our armed forces. When he replaced Merkulov as chief of State Security in May 1946, he started to initiate investigations, and was given plenty of encouragement by Stalin. The military stationed in Germany became his favourite target. It has to be said that they plundered for all they were worth, sending back to the USSR whole convoys of stolen goods. When Stalin ordered that these practices must be stopped, and at whatever price, Abakumov tried to compromise Serov, without being able to prove anything.[54] He merely wanted to take him away from Zhukov. Serov was in an uncomfortable situation because he had refused to work for Abakumov, and, at Zhukov's side, he represented the intelligence services in Germany. He told my father of his worries and was advised to stay with Zhukov, being assured of my father's protection in the event of trouble. Stalin knew that Serov had been recommended by my father. Through Abakumov, he proposed that he be dismissed. My father opposed this, using the pretext that Serov was useful to him in Germany for his research in the atomic field. At Potsdam he had already taken care to get Serov to send reports to Stalin on the state of nuclear research in Germany, at a time when he did not yet know much about it.

This affair took off when dirt began to be written about the men around Zhukov, beginning with the Military Council: Zhukov was not an admirer of that institution and he made the mistake of failing to defend his people.[55] The ring closed, and every pretext was employed to compromise him. Zhukov had decorated a singer named Ruslanova, who gave concerts in army units. What was wrong with that? They made it a matter of state concern. Zhukov was also accused of stealing precious objects in Germany, whereas he lived like a private soldier. These charges of debauchery and plunderings were 100 per cent inventions.[56] One day, Stalin summoned Serov and Zhukov to Moscow. He read them a report signed by Marshal Sokolovsky which described all the abuses that were going on around them. Zhukov and Serov explained that they themselves had organised the commission which produced this report. Stalin did not know that, as Abakumov had intercepted their conclusions and sent them to him. Stalin realised that Abakumov had manipulated him. Serov told me that Stalin telephoned Abakumov in their presence. Abakumov was no fool and immediately guessed what had happened. 'I gave you a report composed by a commission that Zhukov and Serov set up when they were told that I was concerned about the corruption in our military administration in Germany and knew what was going on.' Stalin hung up and said: 'A draw.' Zhukov did not grasp his meaning, but Serov did, at once, and, seeing that his companion was about to speak, he gave him a nudge, to warn him not to say anything out of place. Stalin noticed this but said nothing. The two men hastened to tell my father what had happened. 'I don't know about you, Georgi Konstantinovich,' he said, 'but you, Serov, are in danger.' He advised Zhukov to write, without delay, a request for Serov to be withdrawn, stating that his mission had been completed. Zhukov did this, and gave my father the document, and the two returned to Berlin. That same day Stalin said to my father: 'I've seen Zhukov and Serov. They are obviously hand in glove.' (Since the war period Stalin had closely watched my father's relations with Zhukov. He even asked Zhukov what he found to talk about at such length with Beria.) 'You surprise me greatly, Iosif Vissarionovich. I have just received a request from Zhukov that Serov be recalled.' Stalin was flabbergasted but said nothing. Some time later my father approached the government with a view to reinstating Serov. Stalin suggested that he be sent to prison. Wasn't he a thief whom even Zhukov had not wanted with him? My father pointed out that, on the contrary, Zhukov had said only good things about Serov, and showed Stalin the relevant document. In the end Stalin left it to Malenkov and my father to decide whether or not Serov should be reinstated in the MVD. However, Abakumov still pursued him with his ill will. His closest collaborators were arrested, including his aide-de-camp, who was horribly tortured.

Abakumov also accused Zhukov of arranging unofficial meetings with Western representatives and, when with them, talking too freely and criticising Stalin. Zhukov was called to Moscow and Stalin made him read Abakumov's report. He said: 'You deserve to be prosecuted for all that. But

I have confidence in you and I accept that there may be exaggerations. I'm tired of rummaging in your dirty washing, but I shall set up a commission of inquiry and recall you to Moscow.' Zhukov lost countenance and said some foolish things. I don't know all the details, but I do know that he referred to his private life. With hindsight he was ashamed of his behaviour at that interview, and he told my father so. My father advised him to try and discredit accusations that might do him harm if they were brought up later. My father was not made a member of the commission of inquiry because Stalin knew that he was well disposed towards Zhukov. The commission established that Zhukov had not committed any political crime but that he had let himself be caught up in corruption. He was therefore recalled from Germany in April 1944 and sent to Odessa Military District. He was replaced in Germany by Sokolovsky, a competent soldier who was all the more dangerous for his competence. Stalin had first inflicted him on Zhukov as second-in-command before he left Germany. He took him everywhere: very unwillingly, because he could not stand the man. Stalin knew that and had chosen Sokolovsky for that very reason. Zhukov was so sickened by those insults that he wanted to resign. But my father warned him: 'Above all, do nothing. You can be sure that your resignation would be accepted with the greatest pleasure. They will give you a fine *dacha* before they arrest you, and this time you will be charged with a political crime. And don't think that anyone will defend you. Accept the post offered you and be patient. This situation won't last forever.' Zhukov was arrogant. He denigrated his subordinates after his victorious campaign against the Japanese in August 1939, saying that, had he not been there, all would have been lost. Perhaps that was true. In my view Zhukov's rudeness was purely superficial. He liked to make people fear him, but, in reality, he was able to see when he was wrong and was open to reason. It has been alleged that my father was behind his disgracing, because my father was associated with Abakumov, who pulled the strings. But Abakumov was dependent on Stalin alone. Those around Stalin had tirelessly hinted to him that Zhukov was a potential military dictator. That had been enough for him to send Zhukov away. When, in the summer of 1948, the situation in the Balkans became tense, because of the quarrel between Belgrade and Moscow, Zhdanov said that we ought not to leave someone so unreliable politically as Zhukov in that neighbourhood, and he was recalled from Odessa and sent to Sverdlovsk.

Bulganin

Zhukov counted a lot on my father's help in becoming Minister of Defence. My father wanted him to obtain that post. He thought Vasilevsky more competent in the military domain but appreciated Zhukov's strength of character. Stalin, of course, chose instead the plumber Bulganin, who had formerly been in charge of maintaining the drains for the Moscow Municipality.[57]

Bulganin was a pretentious imbecile and incredibly illiterate. He tried to assume the air of an aristocratic officer, but did not succeed. The military had a poor opinion of his capacities, and he had never shown the slightest desire to improve himself in that domain. When shown a map he stared at it with an idiotic air but never thought of asking for explanations of what he did not understand. One day he was told that the Americans now had substantial air forces in Norway. Instead of asking for details, as any soldier would have done, Bulganin pontificated: 'And what can we put against them?' I learnt this from Shtemenko: 'We were so irritated by his silliness that we loathed reporting to him. He was really an arrant fool – whereas, when we had been with Stalin we left in a sweat, he grilled us so thoroughly about the smallest details.' However, Bulganin had an undeniable flair for intrigue (you don't crawl in a snake-pit for twenty years without something rubbing off on you) and Stalin was without fear when he went on holiday leaving Bulganin at the helm.

Vasilevsky

I have never met a milder and more civilised man than Vasilevsky. Even physically there was nothing of the soldier about him. He was very calm, with eyes full of kindness. One could not imagine him shouting orders. Of average height, he had an awkward and sickly air. I liked him better than Shtemenko, though I spent more time with the latter. I heard him talk at length about the First World War, when he commanded a Mingrelian cavalry regiment. He described with humour the poverty-stricken way of life of those Georgian squires who had to pool their clothes when one of them had a rendezvous with a lady. When he was an officer in the Tsar's army he took an interest in his men and came to know their customs minutely.

He told me how he had been forced to join the Party. He was already on the General Staff when Stalin began to interest himself in him. When Stalin was told that Vasilevsky had no Party card he politely asked him the reason. Vasilevsky replied that he had never been invited to join the Party and, most important, that he had not wished to draw attention to his social origin, being a priest's son. Stalin looked at him and said: 'Mikoyan and I were seminary students, yet nobody has expelled us from the Party on that account.' And he ordered him to join the Party. My father, who knew this story, said to him one day, laughing: 'And you have become a convinced Communist. I've even heard that you have been put in charge of a Marxist study group ...'

'That's no laughing matter, Lavrenti Pavlovich – I spent a hell of a time preparing for those meetings. It was harder for me than planning battles,' Vasilevsky replied.

Of all the military men he was my father's favourite. Zhukov did not like him much, finding him too delicate. 'He's one of those people who don't want to get their hands dirty,' he said with a certain contempt. Stalin respected him sincerely. He appreciated his way of thinking and his manners that bore the mark of the old school.[58] Vasilevsky resembled Marshal Shaposhnikov, who had, to some degree, trained him. Like Shaposhnikov he was non-political. I never heard him express a judgement on the Soviet regime, though my impression was that he didn't think much of it. Shaposhnikov had something of the old regime about him. He was not a Communist upstart.

My father thought that Vasilevsky had made a greater contribution to victory than Zhukov, because he was more intelligent, more gifted. 'He has only one fault,' he said, 'he can't firmly defend his point of view. In a normal society that would not matter much. Here it is a serious short-coming, since the logic of arguments doesn't weigh heavily with us.' And, to be sure, Vasilevsky was unable to stand up to Stalin. He told my father one day that he was terrified by what he saw around him. He was well aware that Stalin was the cause, but always found mitigating circum-stances for him. Knowing his character, I have the feeling that, at the bottom of his heart, he condemned Stalin. Vasilevsky was much affected by the disgracing of Zhukov in 1946. He told my father that he feared a rerun of the purges in the General Staff. My father replied that everything depended on how the soldiers behaved: 'If you start to tremble and groan you will have everything to fear. Continue to behave as you did during the war, show that you are able to resist.'

Vasilevsky loved Russia. He was a true Russian intellectual who had become a soldier through the chances of life. But he was no chauvinist.[59] When Khrushchev and the rest plotted against my father they were careful to say nothing to Vasilevsky, who would never have gone along with them. Zhukov had a quite different temperament. He told me that he once had to give a decoration to an officer who spent his time writing denunci-ations of him. 'All the pleasure of victory was spoilt when I saw that clot, and then I had to decorate him!' Vasilevsky would never have allowed himself to come out with anything like that.

When Vasilevsky was Minister of Defence my father tried to bring Zhukov to Moscow as commander of our land forces. Vasilevsky spoke about this to Stalin. Stalin looked at him suspiciously. 'Since when have you and Zhukov become friends? I well remember Zhukov speaking about you in an uncomplimentary way.'

'I know that, but I think Zhukov will be useful to us.'

'Comrade Vasilevsky' [when Stalin was angry with one of his circle he used the word 'comrade'], 'the Central Committee will decide about that.' Some time later, Stalin said to my father: 'So, Beria, am I to suppose that you don't dare to put your proposals yourself to the Central Committee? Why do you push forward that miserable Vasilevsky?'[60]

Shtemenko

Shtemenko was extremely vain, yet free from arrogance. My father liked him for being a good executive and for being not Russian but Ukrainian.

When Shtemenko reached the rank of colonel he made a point of honour of being impeccably turned out. When he became a general he strove to adopt a solemn manner but his boots were not so well polished. He remained no less elegant than before. He also changed the shape of his moustache, having it cut to look like Budenny's, which made me burst out laughing the first time that I saw him. My father teased him about it: 'One might think that you were an actor in search of a role.' I liked Shtemenko and he liked me. We saw each other quite often. The poor man! When I think of the letter he wrote to Khrushchev after my father's death, in which he claimed that he had nothing to do with Beria, it really makes me pity him.

Shtemenko could not stand Zhukov, blaming his arrogance and ambition. I have remembered all my life this disenchanted comment he made to me one day. 'The lowest of underlings is more important than all the generals and marshals put together. He'll play dirty tricks on you which all the big chiefs will be unable to undo.' I have subsequently always tried to impart this truth to my young colleagues

Kulik

Marshal Kulik was an old friend of Stalin's. They met during the civil war. I can't remember anything about him except that he was as strong as a Turk. One day my father tried his strength with Kulik and threw him to the ground, thanks to his mastery of karate, which he practised assiduously. Soldiers have told me that he was as stubborn as a mule. When he got an idea into his head there was no way of making him give it up. They took a poor view of his abilities. Of mediocre intelligence, he did enormous harm.[61] But Stalin had complete confidence in him, even though he began to doubt his competence after the Spanish war. Which did not prevent him from ordering my father to arrest Kulik's wife, as he had heard rumours that she was a spy. 'Take her away and bring all that to light,' he said. Merkulov, who took part in this affair, told me what happened. The poor woman was arrested, but the charges against her proved to be unfounded. My father reported to Stalin to that effect, recommending that she be released and engaged to work for us. Stalin did not agree. 'No question of that. That fool Kulik is mad about her. She would tell him everything and he'd be lost for the Soviet regime.' She was executed.

Konev

It was from Zhukov that I first heard of Konev, in 1941. Vasilevsky told me later that he was well in with Stalin, who entrusted him with important tasks. Konev had wicked little eyes, a shaven head that looked like a pumpkin, and an expression full of self-conceit. He showed his aggressiveness by the way he gesticulated when speaking. According to Vasilevsky,

Konev was extremely rough and cruel, competent as a soldier and ready to sacrifice lives without limit in order to carry out an order. I sensed at once that Vasilevsky did not like him. He judged people by their human qualities, not by their talents as strategists. Konev gave his generals a drubbing when they reported losses so as, hypocritically, to show how much he cared for his men's lives. He made great efforts to obtain Stalin's permission to take part in the capture of Berlin, and succeeded. But Stalin assigned him only an auxiliary role, which was worse than anything for Konev, and caused him to nurse undying hatred for Zhukov. He did not even conceal this feeling, unlike the other military, who licked Zhukov's boots. Konev felt that he was a superior person, and was devoted to Stalin. He became a Marshal and made a fine career after the war. He was systematically on the side of whoever was in power, never hesitating to betray his colleagues. His reputation in the army grew worse and worse. My father never invited him to our house.

I had occasion to meet him, with my mother, in 1949. We were staying in a rest home in Czechoslovakia. He hardly knew me, but said without any preamble, that the Czech doctors were all 'bastards', so that he was amazed that my father had allowed my mother to stay in this nest of bandits. He had already been poisoned by them. I had a very hard job to get away from him. I avoided him like the plague thereafter, and warned my mother. She already knew what he was like, as the head doctor had complained to her that he did not know which way to turn, Konev was giving him such a hard time. The general was, in fact, not ill at all. His paranoia played no small role in the 'Doctors' plot.' He was to bombard the authorities with denunciations of various doctors and his letters facilitated the invention of the 'Doctors' plot' to a greater extent than the letter from that idiot Timashuk.[62] Konev believed that he was the target for various assassins and attributed his survival to his robust health. After Stalin's death my father read these letters. It turned out that Konev had denounced not only doctors but also his military colleagues. He had got his hand in already in 1937 and had continued by reporting to Stalin horrors concerning Zhukov and Vasilevsky. My father drew the conclusion that Konev was more of a shit than a madman. When Khrushchev began to denounce Stalin's crimes Konev wanted to attack him, but Khrushchev shut him up by showing him the packet of letters that he had written.

Rokossovsky

Rokossovsky was a very handsome man. He had the eyes of Charles Boyer and a pleasant voice. He was well proportioned and had great charm, even when on horseback. He made himself accessible to everyone without being ostentatious about it. It seems to me that, at the bottom, he was shy, and that was probably what I found attractive in him. He came out of prison thanks to intervention by Zhukov and Timoshenko. He was not in too bad a state, even though they had tried to extort from him testimonies against

Zhukov. Rokossovsky began to visit our family when he came to ask my father for troops for the defence of Moscow. My mother liked him and found him 'almost as charming as Vasilevsky,' with his way of being at once lively and shy. My father had to let him have the regiments of the Kremlin guard, and reconstituted the internal guard by posting to it middle-aged minor officials of the NKVD.

Of all the soldiers, Rokossovsky was the only one who spoke to me of the Germans with admiration. 'Their General Staff suffered from Hitler's influence, but at that level of the command of armies and army groups this influence was less felt and the officers were remarkable. They knew what their forces could do and never gave an order that could not be carried out.' Rokossovsky did not feel Polish. He did not speak the Polish language. When he was given the post of Poland's Minister of Defence, in 1949, he told my mother that he was not keen to go there. He felt himself a stranger there and did not like this role as Moscow's creature. There was something aristocratic about the Polish officers which made him feel ill-at-ease among them. He ended his days in the USSR, bitter and disappointed with life.

Stalin

After my father's death my mother never wanted to talk about Stalin and she did everything to dissuade me from doing so. 'You must realise, Sergo, that in people's minds and memories Stalin and your father are inseparable.' She did not imagine that, one day, the archives would prove the contrary. For my part I have very contradictory feelings about Stalin. I admire his prodigious intelligence: I see his inhumanity.[1] In order to tell the truth about him I have to overcome a taboo. I am a Georgian, and it is not easy for me to attack a compatriot. I know, indeed, that the Georgians will not forgive me for this book.[2] But it is enough for me to remember some of his vile actions for the barriers to come down.

There was a time when I thought Stalin was better than Lenin and different from the way I see him today. It has taken me years to understand that he could have changed many things if he had wanted to, instead of aggravating the defects of Leninism. He could have preserved that centralised system but without the fanatical zeal to destroy the human personality. He could have exiled his opponents instead of sending them to rot in the camps. Actually, human life meant nothing to him, and he lacked Lenin's excuse of mental disorders. While he was alive I never immersed myself in his writings. Today I have his complete works and have read them three times. Stalin succeeded in formulating any idea simply and clearly: but it is that very schematism of his that frightens. He believed in Marxism with a fanaticism that was quasi-Islamic.[3] He had transformed the idea of the encirclement of the USSR by the capitalist countries[4] into an instrument of struggle against his own people. For a long time I wondered whether his behaviour was determined by features of his character or whether the system itself forced him to be like that. My impression is that the two factors combined. Without that personality of his Stalin would never have won out within the system. Trotsky, the arch-revolutionary, failed not for ideological reasons but because he lacked the art of intrigue, and thought himself above that sort of thing. Lenin, however, had that art, and perhaps to a greater degree than Stalin.

Stalin was Satan incarnate. He did not just commit crimes in order to achieve his aims. He took a wicked pleasure in striking blows, in trampling on people, in destroying whatever resisted him. It gave him a sort of inward joy. I believe that he was perfectly aware of his wickedness – otherwise he would not have made an art of dissimulation and would not have striven systematically to appear different from what he was. Only a villain conscious of his villainy can pretend with such skill. And Stalin was a born actor. It cannot be said, either, that through lack of intelligence he failed to understand the consequences of his actions. I met him several times towards the end of his life, and I was able to observe the facility with which he went straight to what was essential, even in technological spheres he knew nothing about. He had the gift of putting his finger on the weak points. An organiser of genius, he was able to create a service in a few minutes, give it a mission to perform, and obtain the result he wanted within the deadline fixed by him. In that he was better even than my father.

It's astonishing, but I am unable to give a physical description of Stalin, although I saw him often! Like many Caucasians he had a way of moving with suppleness and grace. He stepped lightly. His face was expressive and mobile. He always locked himself in when he slept, but it would be wrong to put that down to cowardice. My father said that Stalin did not fear death. He simply did not want anyone to see him asleep and defenceless. When he was ill he concealed his weakness.

Stalin liked simple food, especially soups and fish. He was not an alcoholic. He was happy with a dry wine which he mixed with Georgian lemonade, and never drank vodka with meals. He did not employ servants, even when he had guests. He always had a buffet set out on a big table. The drinks were placed on small round tables. Everyone served himself. Some of his guests drank themselves under the table, and Stalin loved that. He delighted in the spectacle of human weakness.

My father never ate the food that was served at Stalin's, as he found it too fatty. He was brought Georgian dishes that were rich in vegetables and herbs, along with his favourite wine, *khvachkara*. One day Khrushchev grabbed the bottle. 'Let's try this wine that Beria treats himself to all alone!' And he filled a big glass and swallowed it in one gulp, like vodka. My father asked him: 'Did you get the taste?'

'No.'

'Very well, take another glass.' Khrushchev swigged the bottle with this comment: 'It's like vinegar.' This was the typical reaction of a man accustomed to stuffing himself with pork fried with garlic. I don't want to say that my father had luxurious tastes, it was just that he preferred simple food and had no fondness for alcohol.[5] Whatever has been said, he was no drinker, except on account of the nephritic colics to which he was subject as the result of a chill, and not, as has been alleged, through a liking for the bottle.

Youth

Stalin liked to call up memories of his youth. I think he did this not merely to charm the people he was with. I was at an evening party to which he had invited some Georgian intellectuals. The ambience was cheerful but nobody got drunk. At that time Georgians drank only wine. The mere presence of Stalin induced a sort of inebriation in those who approached him. He began relating episodes from his past.[6] I listened, hanging on his words. He told us of his escape from exile in Siberia.[7] Everything was ready, except the money he was to receive from the Party. 'A Mingrelian bandit had stolen it,' he guffawed, 'and when I met that rascal after the revolution he had the cheek to ask me for help!' Stalin therefore had to escape on foot in the midst of winter. 'I fell into a frozen river. The ice had given way under my weight. Chilled to the bone I went to knock at a door, but nobody invited me to enter. At the end of my strength I had at last the luck to be welcomed by some poor people who lived in a miserable hut. They fed me, set me by the stove to get warm again, and gave me some clothes before helping me to reach the next village.'

Stalin liked simple folk, in his own way, but this did not stop him from ruining the peasantry. He retained a lively memory of the prosperity in which the Siberian peasantry lived, and of the profits they made from trade. I am sure that his hatred of the kulaks went back to his time in exile. Furthermore, he remained firmly convinced that, even today, the Siberian peasants were as rich as before.

He told my mother one day now he had spent a month preparing a strike, having all the difficulty in the world to get together those who were to bring it to a head. 'And now there turned up your handsome uncle Sasha, with his gift of the gab. In ten minutes he managed to ruin a month's work. He addressed the public, pointing to me and saying, "Look at this wretched creature who can't put two sentences together. Are you going to follow him or stay with me?"' My mother never got over this. She had never believed my father when he said that Stalin forgot nothing and never forgave. 'Just think, he still remembers that affair after so many years! He has cherished a grudge against Sasha because he was handsome and was able to speak to crowds! How fortunate that the poor man is no longer with us.'

I never heard Stalin say anything bad about Lenin. One day, though, he told us of this episode. 'I was in the office of the Central Committee when I saw Krupskaya[8] arriving, in tears. She gave me a paper and said, weeping: "I'm at the end of my tether." I asked her why and she replied: "Vladimir Ilyich has slept with all his secretaries, but that's not enough for him. Now he has designs elsewhere. I demand that the Central Committee take measures, because he is discrediting the government."' I was thunderstruck. I knew, of course, that Vladimir Ilyich was hot-blooded. In those days a leader didn't have to worry about indiscretions from his guards. So I told Krupskaya that I would call the comrades together to discuss this business with her before taking action. The meeting was held. I explained the problem and everybody burst out laughing. Actually, we sympathised with Vladimir Ilyich. It has to be said that Krupskaya was no gift of nature and had not improved in looks as she grew older. But we had to do something and I found a way of dealing with the problem. We invited Vladimir Ilyich and he at once understood the purpose of the meeting. He looked at us mockingly when I told him that we had examined a complaint from Krupskaya concerning his escapades and had concluded that he was certainly guilty, but that Krupskaya was guiltier still. Through taking on so many Party duties she had neglected her husband. We released her from these duties, calling on her earnestly to consider that her chief duty to the Party was to be Vladimir Ilyich's wife and to perform her conjugal obligations. Lenin, to whom we nevertheless recalled that the family was sacred, laughed heartily. Krupskaya slammed the door as she left. We drew up a resolution. Nobody blamed Vladimir Ilyich.'[9]

According to my father, who closely studied Lenin's archives, Krupskaya took against Stalin after this affair and never gave up setting Lenin against him. When Lenin was unable to write, because of his illness, she arranged for a tendentious twist to be given to whatever he dictated, and Lenin's secretary Fotieva reported this to the Politburo. Relations between Lenin and Stalin, which had hitherto been excellent, now deteriorated.

My father said that an attentive reading of Lenin's 'Political Testament' shows that he saw nobody but Stalin as fit to succeed him.[10] Stalin described, in my presence, the last months of Lenin's life. He suffered a great deal and often asked Stalin for poison. 'When I saw him in that state I couldn't sleep at night,' Stalin said, and I think he was sincere. The Politburo decided that everything must be done to prolong his existence, even though it was clear to everyone that his condition would not improve. Rumour had it that Lenin had fallen ill as the result of the dissolute life he had led during his studies in Petersburg. He had received treatment but had never managed to recover completely. He had retained an extreme irritability which he tried to overcome by means of physical exercises. Having said that, it may be that he was by nature, and not through illness, someone whose nerves were always on edge.

From Stalin I also learnt that Lenin hated the Church virulently. Stalin was surprised at this: 'Mikoyan and I wondered what the reason for this could be. In our case such a feeling would have been comprehensible – we were former seminarists. But, unlike with Lenin, our hostility to religion has nothing personal about it. Something must have happened in his life to make him so hostile to the Orthodox.'

Stalin and Russia

My mother long imagined that Stalin adored Georgia, and, to be sure, appearances are deceptive. He liked Georgian songs, read Georgian and knew the country's history well. In his youth he even wrote excellent verses in Georgian. When he did things that displeased my mother she thought at first that he was acting under pressure from the Russians. But she had to accept evidence that the initiative came from him. I remember her saying:

'He will be even more pitiless towards the Georgians than towards other peoples, because he is furious that his own people should oppose his policy. Resistance would irritate him less when it came from Russians.' My father shared this view. He too had believed that Stalin was attached to his homeland because he had opposed Lenin when the latter wanted to offer Georgia to Kemal Atatürk. But the evidence was clear. Stalin had ceased to love his little homeland, he had grown too big for it. His heart was given to Imperial Russia. He insistently stressed the continuity between the Russian state and the Soviet Union, going so far as to present the latter as the heir of Tsarist Russia. He saw himself in the lineage of Ivan the Terrible and Peter the Great. One evening, at a dinner where there was plenty to drink, he allowed the actors who were present to sing in his honour the old Tsarist anthem. With his usual irony my father said that it would, nevertheless, be hard for Stalin to compete with the great Catherine II. 'She had herself screwed by Russian *muzhiks*, whereas Stalin has screwed all Russia.' Despite my devotion to and boundless admiration for my father, I have to say that I did not greatly enjoy that sort of joke. Actually, Stalin loved nobody. For Stalin the Russian people were merely a tool that enabled him to achieve his aims. It was by design and not through lack of intelligence or mere thoughtlessness that he reduced the peasantry to serfdom and deprived every Soviet citizen of all rights.

But he did ostentatiously emphasise the priority of Russia and his reverence for Russian history. He chose traditional Russian names for his children. I remember a significant anecdote. Alexei Tolstoy, when working on his book about Peter the Great, explained to Stalin that he had found in the archives some documents which suggested that Peter's father was a Georgian king.[11] Stalin's reaction was immediate. He replied that one could not imagine a worse service rendered to him than this allegation, and he forbade the writer to talk about it, even in private conversation. He later ordered my father to get hold of these archives and put them in a safe place, 'so that bootlickers like Tolstoy don't get the idea of using them.' Stalin followed attentively what was written about him, without, however, trying to hint to the writers what they should say. He was content to take note of their silly mistakes. In one of his books Tolstoy had described the arrival of Stalin at Tsaritsyn during the civil war. Stalin invited him, along with others, and said with an air of not alluding to him: 'There are good descriptions and there are others which make the hero look like an imbecile. I'll show you an example.' He went to his library, took Tolstoy's book and began to read a passage aloud. Tolstoy's portrait was so idyllic that it sounded artificial and Stalin commented that it would be better to write nothing than resort to such crude flattery. 'Stalin achieved two aims,' said my father, laughing. 'First, he showed, in public, that he rejected flattery. Second, he demonstrated that he could read aloud very well. And, as a bonus, he made Tolstoy lose his appetite.'

Tolstoy ended by going up to Stalin and asking; 'Iosif Vissarionovich, what must I do?'

'Write about normal things.'

'I have a good subject. I'm going to write about the adventures of Senka in Paris.'

'Excellent idea,' said Stalin. 'But don't make too much of the mess that any Russian can create if he wants as he passes through.' A peasant girl who became a countess, Senka was a character in Tolstoy's book on Peter the Great. As a good courtier, Tolstoy sensed that Stalin's love for Russia was artificial and that Stalin himself secretly mocked it.

The theatre

Stalin loved the theatre. He sometimes invited actors to his *dacha*. He had in his living room a large portrait of the famous actor Kachalov. One day I asked my father why Stalin had felt the need to put it up so prominently. He replied: 'It's so that everyone may see how much he loves the Russian people. But he doesn't know that Kachalov's real name was Chverubovich.'

'He was a Byelorussian,' added Malenkov, who was present.

'I know,' retorted my father, 'but I admit that you are a greater specialist than I am where Byelorussia is concerned.' I did not appreciate the subtlety. In fact, my father was alluding to the repressions organised by Malenkov in Byelorussia.[12] The story of Kachalov's portrait shows how Stalin left nothing to chance and calculated everything. According to my parents although Stalin pretended to adore the hysterical songs bawled by Pyatnitsky's choir, in reality he could not bear this music, and my father again could not refrain from mockery. 'He pretends to swoon with pleasure so that the masses will imagine that he loves this Russian simplicity.'

I was very fond of *Tsar Fyodor*, which I saw at the theatre. Stalin made my father accompany him to the theatre to see it. He had already seen the play three times and groaned. The famous Moskvin played Tsar Fyodor. When Stalin expressed delight at his acting, my father said to him: 'Iosif Vissarionovich, you are always praising Russian culture. But you must know that there is no Russian theatrical tradition. The Maly Theatre was created by the Georgian prince Sumpatashvili and Moskvin's real name is Tarkhnishvili.' Stalin did not know that. He replied: 'They are Russified Georgians. Not like you, who stink of Georgia to high heaven.'

Stalin and women

The wives of the Politburo members were not invited to evening parties at Stalin's. After the death of his wife Allilueva in 1932, he had no official family. He had two more children after the war. One day at the theatre I glimpsed their mother, a large redhead who was sitting near the government box. Stalin cultivated the spouses and families of those close to him, and had the custom of making impromptu visits to them. He once summoned Zhdanov's wife to hear her view on the state of the Party in

Leningrad. Flattered to be asked, this foolish woman fell into the trap and babbled away for all she was worth.

I don't think he was a misogynist, though many rumours circulated to that effect. Stalin went often to the opera. He had a weakness for certain singers, and not only for their talent. My father had taken note of them and did not fail to tell smutty stories about the relationships. They were all very big, well-endowed blondes with blue eyes who were at least a head taller than Stalin: Valkyrie types ... The German actress Spiller was one of his passions. Serov's wife claimed at one time that Stalin was not indifferent to the wife of the Moscow Party Secretary, Popov, a pretty shock worker who was not shy. But at that time there was little talk of such matters.

His physical appearance

Before the war Stalin did not bother much about his appearance. His physical decline began after our victory.[13] He became tired sooner, especially as he wanted to keep everything under his own hand and delegated less than before. His distrust increased parallel with his will to supervise the actions of those near him. Stalin felt that he was ageing but did not want this to appear. He therefore tried to conceal his age. He began to take an interest in uniforms, trying them on, and modifying them to suit himself. He wanted his dress to be impressive without being ostentatious. According to my father and others around Stalin, he liked to be photographed by Vlasik from every angle and in different uniforms, so as to check on the effect produced.

In or around 1932 Stalin built us a *dacha* at Gagry, where we spent our holidays. One day he paid us an unexpected visit. 'I know that I didn't warn you I was coming,' he said on arrival, 'but I've had nothing to eat since morning and I should be glad if you could dish up a snack for me. Meanwhile I'll take a look around.' And he went all over the house. When he returned to took my mother aside. 'You haven't even found room for my portrait in this big house!' he growled, with a discontented air. My mother went pale but did not lose her composure. 'You haven't had a proper look, Iosif Vissarionovich,' she replied. 'My son has drawn a portrait of you which he has put up in his room.' I had in fact made a sketch of Stalin as a young man, taken from a photo, and hung it on the wall. 'Let's go and see,' said Stalin, wishing to check that my mother was telling the truth. 'That's better than an official photo,' was his only comment. After this incident my mother wanted to acquire an official photo of Stalin to put up in our *dacha* but my father formally forbade it. Stalin often presented portraits of himself, signed, to members of the Politburo or others whom he wished to single out. Outside the ranks of those close to him, the people who received this gift saw it as an inestimable favour.

Stalin's costumes and those of the other members of the Politburo were made in a special workshop. I was authorised to order a uniform from this workshop and took the opportunity to ask Stalin's tailor if he tried his on. He told me that he had a model made to Stalin's measurements which was modified every year. Stalin was concerned about his weight. He weighed himself regularly and went to the sauna to keep his figure and stay fit. I heard him explain to some military men that, for him, the sauna was a substitute for physical exercise. Though his movements were always slow and furtive, so that he was sometimes compared to a tiger approaching its prey, he made it a point of honour to mount the steps of the Mausoleum at the double during the revolutionary ceremonies, followed by my father and, at a distance, by Malenkov, who was sweating and breathing hard. My father made fun of this childishness. He was exasperated by Stalin's affectations, which he regarded as a waste of time when the country was collapsing under its problems.

Stalin and those around him

Stalin did not miss a chance to criticise the appearance of the men around him. He detested negligence and carelessness. He criticised Malenkov for his face swollen with fat, because he thought it inexpedient, ideologically, to appear before the people with so much flesh on one. He ordered him to go regularly to the sauna and do exercises, so as 'to recover the look of a human being.' Now and again my father would ask Malenkov: 'That human-being look, where is it? Have you lost any weight?' Poor Malenkov had to take up horse-riding, but all his efforts were in vain. Stalin also teased Khrushchev about his square build. However, he did not impose any regime on him, doubtless considering that his case was hopeless. Mikoyan he blamed for not knowing how to fasten his tie. Kaganovich should shave his beard off. 'I don't need a rabbi near me,' Stalin said to him.[14] He also found something to say about Bulganin's beard. The latter did not yield completely: he kept a thin little goatee in the French style. My father and Khrushchev pulled his leg. 'Well, now! You've trimmed your beard again! But we can still see a few hairs ...'

Stalin did not allow himself remarks of this sort when talking to my father, though he made him wear a tie and a hat, both of which my father hated. When in Georgia he preferred to wear round-collared shirts and caps. Molotov was ordered to supply him with ties, and sent a boxful. Where hats were concerned the struggle was more protracted. Stalin asked Harriman to buy some broad-brimmed hats like those worn by cowboys. He did not say who they were for. I inherited this collection. My father did not like spectacles, and had worn pince-nez since his youth. Stalin tried to dissuade him: 'It makes you look like a Menshevik. Only a little chain is needed for the picture to be complete!' The first time that Stalin made that remark my father said nothing. But Stalin did not give up, and one day, when he returned to the charge in the presence of others, my father replied drily: 'I shall not put a chain on my pince-nez. And you will not chain me up.' Stalin changed the subject. When my father told my mother about this incident she said: 'Why do you oppose him over trifles? Wear spectacles if that will appease him.' But my father replied: 'You don't know him. If I give in to him on little things he will trample over me still more.'

My father was not fond of uniforms. He wore one on one occasion only, the Victory Parade. Unlike Stalin, he did not consider his appearance important. He looked above all for comfort and preferred loose clothing. My mother saw in this attitude a lack of respect for other people and warned me not to copy his bad example. Caring for one's appearance, according to her, formed part of European civilisation.

Stalin did not hesitate to humiliate those around him. To Mikoyan, for example, he said: 'What a moronic remark you made just then!' In a small committee he often said to Voroshilov: 'Shut up, imbecile.' He was more indulgent to Budenny, though he was stupider than Voroshilov. It was said that Stalin chose Poskrebyshev as his secretary because his hangman's look could inspire terror.[15] Actually, this man's appearance was more comical than frightening. He was a narrow-shouldered dwarf. When he sat at table you could see only his head. Dreadfully ugly, he resembled a monkey,[16] but he had an excellent memory and was meticulous in his work. No one but Stalin would have tolerated such a creature by his side. Stalin kept him for thirty years. He was equally attached to the chief of his bodyguard, Vlasik, a debauchee and the worst of scoundrels, who was devoted as a dog to him.

Poskrebyshev set up some practical jokes.[17] One day he and Khrushchev, when a little drunk, threw Marshal Kulik into the river. His uniform dripping with water, the Marshal pursued Poskrebyshev to get his own back, but the latter hid in the bushes. Kulik treated the affair as a joke, but my father was indignant. As for Stalin, though he pretended to have seen nothing, it amused him greatly. 'If anyone had tried something like that on me' my father thundered, 'I should have made mincemeat of him.' Stalin would, indeed, never have allowed my father to be insulted, whereas he regularly called Khrushchev 'degenerate' and 'idiot.' He always used the respectful form when speaking to my father, although he was much younger. He knew that my father would never forgive an affront.

I was never witness to such practical jokes as, for example, putting tomatoes on someone's chair. I only saw vodka being poured instead of water (or vice versa) and pepper galore being shaken on guests' food. That was rather vulgar. I don't think Stalin greatly enjoyed these jokes. He liked humiliating people but preferred to do this in a more intellectual way, so to speak. He wanted his victim to feel cut down to nothing. If one of those near him allowed weakness or a tender spot to appear, Stalin never forgot it, nor missed an opportunity to remind him of it. My mother told me of an episode which, though seemingly insignificant, was characteristic. Stalin was giving a reception at his *dacha*. There were about thirty guests – the members of the Politburo with their wives, actors, dancers and opera singers. The atmosphere was relaxed. Stalin noticed that my mother was standing apart and looking unhappy. She had no taste for these social events. Knowing that she did not like to dance he went up to her and asked her: 'Why aren't you dancing?' She replied that she was not in the mood for it. Stalin went away, but she saw him talking to a young actor while still keeping his eyes on her. The young man came over and asked her to dance, insisting to the point of insolence, with an allusion to the approach made by their host. 'I watched Stalin out of the corner of my eye,' she told me. 'He was looking at us with an ironical smile. Lavrenti was observing the scene with an irritated air.' My mother got rid of the actor. The purpose of this manoeuvre had been to annoy my father. Stalin found the failure of his marriage hard to bear, and that, perhaps, accounts for this sort of joke on his part. He went so far as to rebuke my father for allowing his collaborators to stay with him beside the Black Sea, together with their families.

My mother suffered another affront from Stalin one day when he had invited some Georgian actors to our *dacha*. Among them was one Bogashvili, a very handsome man, slightly eccentric, who played Stalin in various films. This Bogashvili proposed a toast: 'I drink to the health of our beautiful hostess, charming Nina, I drink to her liberation from the gilded cage she is in now.' My mother looked at my father, but he did not react. Stalin smiled slyly. She rose and said: 'I greatly enjoy Bogashvili's films, but I don't take him seriously, as I think he is an imbecile. I presume that Iosif Vissarionovich and my husband share that opinion, since they have not thought good to defend the honour and dignity of the mistress of the house.' Stalin pulled himself together, went up to my mother and kissed her hand. 'Nina, this is the first time I have kissed a woman's hand.' As for my father, he got a severe reprimand that evening. 'The next time that you allow me to be insulted without saying anything I shall consider that the insult comes from you,' said my mother.

Yet Stalin was able to charm people,[18] as I can testify from experience. He managed to give the people he was with the impression that Jupiter had come down from his Olympus for them, deigned to speak with them in a familiar tongue, and was taking an interest in their problems. This was his great strength and, as a child, I was already susceptible to it. He found subjects of conversation with everyone, young or old, scientist, engineer or actor. One day before the war he asked me: 'What recent Georgian books have you read?' At that time I read nothing in my mother tongue. He was annoyed and telephoned my mother: 'What sort of education are you giving your son? He's a grown-up now and yet reads nothing in Georgian!' My mother was delighted with this intervention. He said to me on another occasion: 'If you want to know the people around you, find out what they read.' He followed this rule to the letter. When he visited someone from his circle he went straight to the man's library, and even opened his books to check whether they had been read and even reread. He reproached my mother for having collected works that were suspected of 'nationalist deviation.' Noting that their pages had often been turned, he asked if they were her bedside books. My mother explained that we had found them in a second-hand bookshop, which accounted for their condition. Stalin liked to give advice on reading and was indignant at the gaps in my knowledge of literature. For example, I had not read *Germinal* (I had read only *Nana*) whereas he worshipped Zola. One day he gave Svetlana and me a regular course on the history of Byzantium. On several occasions he advised me to plan strictly the way I used my time. When I complained of being overworked he said: 'You have only to lead a regulated life. Take my own use of time. It is fixed for days ahead and I keep to it rigorously. People who lack self-discipline are good-for-nothings.' He told me that he read some 500 pages every day. He hated the practice of underlining or writing notes in books. He used bookmarks.

I was not bad at chess. My father loved the game and made me read about it in handbooks for beginners. 'Then you won't be satisfied any longer to play only two moves ahead.' His favourite chess master was Capablanca. He knew whole games. One day I succeeded in beating Stalin's elder son Yasha quite quickly. He was good-natured but fiery-tempered and rather vain. His siblings Svetlana and Vasya laughed at him. I won a second time, then a third. He was very annoyed. Stalin learnt that his son had been beaten by such a greenhorn as I was, and said to me: 'Right, then, will you take me on?' I lost. I did not lose deliberately, on the contrary, I wanted to win, but I was too excited. Stalin said to me: 'Let's have that again another time.' He had human reactions, but they were rare.

Stalin's ascendancy over others was also due to the fact that he left each person he spoke to anxious to see him again, with a sense that there was now a bond that linked them forever. This honour did not intoxicate everyone. My father had appointed a certain A. I. Berg to be in charge of intercepted telephone calls. The man paled when he heard the news: 'My God, what will happen to me? I'll never get out of this alive.' A colleague congratulated him 'Now you have access to Iosif Vissarionovich.' You should have seen Berg's expression! I told my father about this, and he laughed heartily: 'Ah, yes indeed, the good man is at the highest pitch of happiness! To have access to Iosif Vissarionovich ...'

I knew that Stalin had told Abakumov to create a dossier on me. (He confirmed this at his trial.) When nothing criminal was found, not even connections with abroad, Stalin had grumbled: 'He married a Peshkov against my will. Have a good look, there must be something.' Though I knew that he was spying on us and preparing to arrest us, I could not prevent myself from falling for his charm again when he invited me to his place and began talking to me. I don't know how he did it. If he had asked me to sacrifice my life for him I would have obeyed without hesitation. Then, when I left his presence, I remembered that this same Stalin was plotting to arrest my mother.

In or about 1951 I was present at a meeting at Stalin's place which was devoted to problems of armament. When the business was concluded most of those present left. Malenkov and my father remained. I had not been told to leave. Stalin wanted to discuss the problems of youth and the inadequacies of the Komsomol. He asked me my opinion. As always when I was face to face with him I felt both tense and euphoric. Without thinking I said that our Komsomol suffered from excessive formalism, that members wasted a lot of time on futilities and that it would be better to develop sporting and cultural activities or to form clubs. I did not see the look that Stalin gave me, but my father noticed his change of expression. His initial benevolence vanished as though by enchantment. Suddenly I had the impression of receiving a tub of cold water over my head: 'You have just heard a description of the method by which England's aristocratic youth are educated. To be sure, we need sport and also to concern ourselves with the military training and patriotic education of our young people. But we must not neglect the class point of view.' And Stalin got on to his hobby-horse. I cursed my thoughtless eloquence. I looked at my father, who did not conceal his exasperation. Later he said to my mother that he had feared the worst when he saw the way Stalin was looking at me. 'A cobra about to strike,' he said. It was indeed said that Stalin had deliberately chosen the nickname 'Koba,' which was close to 'cobra.' My father lectured me: 'Haven't you realised yet that he cannot stand the slightest contradiction? I'm not suggesting that you act the hypocrite, or lie, but, for heaven's sake, keep quiet and never take the initiative.'

'But I had to reply, since he asked my opinion.'

'You should have said that it was a difficult problem and you hadn't yet made up your mind about it.'

'Yet you give him your opinion when he asks for it.'

'He would not believe me if I replied in that way. My principle is to say what I do, otherwise he wouldn't believe me.' My father did not urge my mother and me to practise dissimulation. It would be better that Stalin should know what we really thought than that we should give him grounds for suspicion. My father could not, of course, follow that line himself, as he was unable to reveal to Stalin what he really thought, even though he did try from time to time to make him understand certain things: he waited for the propitious moment with Stalin to take up matters that were close to his heart. After this episode I set myself to observe Stalin in a new way during meetings at which I happened to be present. His look could change in a fraction of a second. Mild and even affectionate, it became spiteful, even murderous, at the slightest contradiction.

My father, Vannikov, Ustinov and other ministers that I met had all undergone the same process of evolution regarding Stalin. They had gone through a phase in which they worshipped him madly. Stalin had held them under his charm for a certain time. Gradually, however, they became aware that he was using them before rejecting them with cynicism, depending on the aims he was pursuing at the time. Love did not necessarily turn into hate. Vannikov, for instance, continued to admire him. 'Why does he put this uncommon intelligence of his at the service of a diabolical policy?' he wondered. Stalin made a clear distinction between those who had seen through him, and before whom he no longer took the trouble to play-act, and the rest of mankind. When he was dealing with ordinary people his close collaborators could not refrain from admiring his talent as an actor.

The statesman

What were Stalin's methods of government? His first principle was to multiply the apparatuses. He encouraged the parallel development of the Party apparatus and that of the government, each of which was watched by a third apparatus, that of State Control, while State Security watched them all. The leader of the Party had at his disposal control organisations within the Party itself. Stalin did not create this system based on universal suspicion. Having inherited it from Lenin he had been able to use it to take power. He utilised the apparatuses against his rivals, whom he succeeded in supplanting because he had much more information than they had. Eventually, this arrangement promoted his personal power. The Party had the organs of repression under its orders, but it was the Party's leader who wielded the sword.

Stalin's second principle was to set those around him one against another. He was a master of this art. He whispered to one man something bad about another, then did the same with the latter. After our arrival in Moscow some members of the Politburo, such as Malenkov, Khrushchev or Shcherbakov, who wanted to win my father's approval, started to repeat to him some disagreeable remarks that Stalin had made about him. Khrushchev said that one day when he was boasting to Stalin about his successes in Ukrainian agriculture the latter had barked: 'Stop boring me with your plantations, like Beria with his rubbish about citrus fruits!' Now my father's citrus fruits were like his own children to him. In cultivating them he had sought a means of consoling himself, so far as possible, in the period when he had had to exterminate his compatriots. My father took the blow. Khrushchev was quite pleased, I thought. When he had left my mother said: 'Don't take that to heart, Lavrenti. He may have made up that story.'

'No, Nina,' my father replied. 'That was no lie. Khrushchev told the truth.' Malenkov reported another wounding remark aimed at my father, which he had from Poskrebyshev. Stalin was re-reading the proofs of the *Short History of the Communist Party (Bolsheviks)*. He criticised the plan of the work. When someone pointed out that this was the same as the plan of my father's work on the history of the Bolsheviks in Caucasia, Stalin interrupted drily: 'Don't confuse history and my biography.' This remark showed what he thought of this work which he had ordered to be written and had personally corrected.

It was Stalin's rule to nip in the bud any attempt at forming a bloc against him, to sow discord among those around him and to play the arbiter. He had the art of harnessing together men who could not stand one another and practised this policy at every level. In the armaments sector, he set the engineers and the researchers against each other. In the aviation sector, Yakovlev, Mikoyan, Gurevich and Lavochkin all worked on the same type of aircraft, each with his own team, but in different organisations, which Stalin refused to merge. This competition was not very healthy: each team strove to surpass the others, and the methods used did not always concern technical performance. Informers' tales and calumnies flourished. Stalin was skilled in destroying the self-esteem of each, heaping favour now on one, now on another. Yakovlev got a divorce when his father-in-law was condemned as an enemy of the people. He remarried, to a woman pilot, a shock worker, which did not prevent him from meeting actresses at the Bolshoi. I do not cast a stone at him. Stalin's manoeuvres transformed men into robots or hypocrites. Poskrebyshev was devoted to him body and soul, yet Stalin had his wife arrested, before the war, because she was Jewish and her sister had connections with Jewish organisations.[19]

Using every means, including blackmail and attacks on wives and close friends, Stalin incited people to commit base actions. To Beso Lominadze,[20] who had had the courage to oppose him and had never done anything contemptible in his life, as Stalin well knew, he promised pardon if he would denounce his supporters in Georgia. 'Do what you like with me,' Lominadze replied, 'but you won't get a single name out of me.' Stalin released him in return for a promise to give up all political activity. He liked intelligent people. Lominadze was gifted but had gone too far, in Stalin's view: 'We put him at the head of the trade unions and they became a bloody mess. We shoved him into the Kuomintang, he wreaked havoc all around and turned the Communists into opportunists and Trotskyists ...'

Mikoyan applied himself to setting Stalin against Lominadze, who confided in him, thinking Mikoyan to be a friend. Mikoyan however ran to report everything to Stalin. The latter ordered the provocateurs of the NKVD to implicate him in a case, then sent for him. 'I can do nothing more for you,' he said, leaving it to be understood that things did not depend on him. Lominadze killed himself in 1935. My father thought highly of him and considered him infinitely more intelligent than Ordzhonikidze. He would have liked to work for several years under his leadership, he told my mother. Poor Lominadze had a soft spot for her, and had chosen for a wife a woman who looked like her and was also called Nina. My father was blamed for being on friendly terms with a man who had fallen into disgrace.

The fate of Sergo Ordzhonikidze also tells us much about Stalin's methods. At the end of his life, Ordzhonikidze had become an opponent of Stalin, though remaining personally attached to him. He totally disapproved of the policy which was leading to the extermination of the cadres of our economy. He could not be removed like a Bukharin or a Rykov as he was popular, a fact that stirred Stalin's jealousy. The latter had Ordzhonikidze's close collaborators arrested and showed him the records of the interrogations in which these wretched men accused themselves. 'Here, look. You don't believe these confessions? All right, I invite you to a confrontation with witnesses ...' Sergo was ill: he had only one kidney. Stalin pestered him. 'You want to play the noble role, leaving me that of the skunk.' Driven too far by this little game of Stalin's, Ordzhonikidze ended his life, leaving a letter for Stalin, the content of which I learnt from my father. He wrote that he wanted, as a dead man, to make him read what Ordzhonikidze had never had the courage to say to him, face to face, when he was alive. 'My friendship for you, the fact that you are a Georgian, and my position in the Party all forbid me to take any steps against you. That is why I discharge you from the measures that you think necessary to adopt regarding me, and which I find hateful. But understand one thing: you are spreading harm all round you.'

'He let it all come out,' said my father, with satisfaction, years after these events. Stalin was deeply affected by Ordzhonikidze's suicide and by his letter. Did he feel remorse? I can't be sure. In any case, under the effect of his emotion, he showed the letter to the members of the Politburo. But grief did not prevent him from trying to wipe out the very memory of Ordzhonikidze, just as he had done with his wife Allilueva, whose death had nevertheless overwhelmed him, if we are to believe Kirov and Ordzhonikidze. In both cases, he found explanations which soon consoled him. His wife had betrayed him. As for Sergo, he should have been born in another century, in an epoch when the chivalric virtues were appreciated. He too had betrayed Stalin.

The fate of Stalin's brother-in-law Svanidze is also eloquent. He was arrested and condemned to death for no reason. He confessed nothing and signed no appeal for mercy. Before the firing squad he cried: 'Long live Stalin!' When these words were reported to Stalin he commented: 'The swine! He lied with his last breath.' He knew neither pity nor compassion. He was as callous as a robot.

In his life both private and public Stalin avoided pushing himself forward. When he launched a new campaign or negotiated a new turn in his policy, he was careful to put other people out in front, so that he reserved complete freedom to manoeuvre. They served as scapegoats if things should go wrong. Above a certain level in the hierarchy of Party and State Stalin appointed only individuals he knew personally. He was not guided by ideological criteria. He reasoned as a statesman. He knew personally every Secretary of a regional Party committee, every Central Committee Secretary in the republics, every head of government. He sent for them from time to time and never ceased studying them. Before promoting a cadre he spent a long time analysing him. When he thought of making my father the Number Two of the Transcaucasian Cheka, he consulted his superiors Pavlunovsky and Redens, to obtain their view of him. He had one unchanging rule: one can never be too suspicious.

The real Stalin

Far from being the head-case he is described as nowadays, Stalin was supremely intelligent. He had a cold heart, calculated every action and remained invariably master of himself. He took all his decisions after having carefully weighed them. He never improvised. He always had ready-made plans which he carried out point by point. When he was obliged to depart from his original plan he never risked doing it until he had worked out a replacement strategy in full detail. It was not that he was slow in his reactions, but he undertook nothing lightly. Every one of his actions formed part of a long-term scheme which was to enable him to attain a particular aim at a particular moment. With him nothing was gratuitous: every conversation pursued an objective. If he invited someone to give his opinion on a book, it was because he wanted to test his state of mind, to capture his intimate thoughts. He never gave up an aim once he had decided on it. He knew how to get round an obstacle and, if necessary, to await an opportunity. Though clever at hiding his thoughts when he thought this useful, he was sometimes unable to control brief flare-ups of hatred. But one did not really perceive his full wickedness except as the result of his actions. He took care to make those near him realise that he forgot nothing, that a Sword of Damocles was always hanging over their heads. When in a morose mood he came to us as though seeking a little human warmth. That did not stop him compiling at the same time a dossier against my mother in which she was accused of nationalism because she corresponded with her uncle, the Menshevik Evgeni Gegechkori. Stalin could wipe out with a sweep of his hand any person whom he imagined was against him, and he hesitated no longer when millions of people were the target. My mother compared him to the Eastern prince Shadiman who also ruled by eliminating all his adversaries. My father pointed out to me that none of the men who had contradicted him at one time or another had managed to keep his wife.

Methodical in the extreme, Stalin's vast memory constituted a veritable collection of archives, and he drew from it at will the data he considered he needed in order to achieve an aim. He prepared carefully for every meeting, studying the questions he meant to raise. He swotted at his books like a good pupil, said my father, who did the same himself. Stalin's life was just as ordered, despite the distressing timetables that he inflicted on his collaborators, because he worked late into the night. He took the air regularly, even in winter when the temperature was under thirty degrees. He stuck to his habits and nobody would have got him to change them.

Stalin and his image

He had a dual approach to the intelligentsia: one part he exterminated and the other he attached to himself by coaxing them. His success was total. Writers and artists vied in idolising him unreservedly. But the admiration of the crowd irritated him. I remember an evening at the Bolshoi. Words of welcome had been addressed to all the Party organisations except, inadvertently, that of Moscow. Wishing to correct this omission, Stalin entered the government box, loosing a thunderstorm of applause. I did not abstain but reacted like the rest, in spite of what I already knew. He lifted his hand and silence was restored: 'We must also greet the Moscow Party organisation' he said. More ovations, interminable this time. He made an exasperated gesture as though to say: 'Gang of idiots.'

Stalin cared much for the judgement of posterity. He wanted to enter history as a model ruler. That was why he caused all the witnesses and instruments of his crimes to disappear. He wanted to pass, in the world's eyes, for a wise, reasonable man, full of kindness and intelligence. He realised that shrewd people might perceive that this persona did not correspond to reality if they were to see too much of him. Accordingly he restricted the number of his close associates. He never admitted officials of the apparatus to this circle. That, at any rate, was the opinion of Khrushchev, Malenkov and my father. My mother did not agree: she believed that this was, rather, a feature of his character. She was always trying to find justifications for Stalin's behaviour, not on the political but on the human plane. She did not want to hear him spoken of, even in private, as a monster. My father, irritated, would lecture her: 'If a man shows himself a villain on one point he will be a villain all down the line. There is no such thing as a semi-swine.' He was against Stalin precisely because the latter knew what he was doing. 'He's not a man possessed, he is a cold and calculating intelligence.'

As, today, we behold the morons and scum who have proliferated on the ruins of the Soviet empire and now govern it, I am sometimes gripped by a doubt. Perhaps I am wrong to condemn Stalin? Perhaps he knew these people perfectly well and was right to consider that they understood nothing but the cudgel? After all, had he not, during his youthful tribulations, explored the depths of Russia, with its gendarmes and its good-for-nothings?

The People around Stalin

Svetlana

Stalin had ascetic tastes. He never spoilt his daughter and would not have allowed anyone else to spoil her. He was sometimes incredibly rude to her.[1] One day when Svetlana was looking through an album of photographs of her mother she asked him: 'Was Mummy beautiful?' 'Yes, except that she had horses' teeth,' he replied, and rebuked her for continually looking at those photographs. Angrily, he added that he had married Svetlana's mother because the other women in the Alliluev family would not leave him alone. They all wanted to go to bed with him. 'Your mother was at least young, and she really loved me. That's why I married her.'

Choking back her tears Svetlana ran to tell my mother what Stalin had said. My mother wanted to speak to Stalin, to remind him that one can't say to a child what one can say to an adult, but my father was categorically opposed to this. 'He will realise that you have glimpsed his true nature, and you must avoid that at all costs.'

Svetlana suffered from seeing her father so infrequently. She loved him and he showed her affection while she was very small. But a mother's tenderness was lacking. When she was a child she would snuggle up in bed against my mother, to whom she was very attached. She never spoke to me about her own mother. As for her grandmother and her uncles, she regarded them as crazy people.

In 1942, when she was fifteen, the film-maker A. Kapler succeeded in getting her to fall in love with him – for careerist reasons, of course. Svetlana was not really pretty, but she was intelligent and, above all, charming, with her flame-coloured hair and her freckles. Kapler took her to museums and explained paintings to her. For the first time she felt she was a woman, and that turned her head. But her father discovered what was going on and sent for her. 'Have you gone out of your mind? You've seen how old he is? Couldn't you find a younger admirer?' It was said later that Stalin was hostile to Kapler because he was Jewish, but when this was happening that did not matter. He was, above all, furious that a man had presumed to pay court to his daughter. He took this as a personal insult and blamed my father for failing to prevent the situation from developing. But it was wartime and my father had other fish to fry. Svetlana came to my mother, complaining that Stalin had slapped her and had stopped speaking to her.[2] She wanted to meet Kapler at our place. My mother exclaimed: 'Svetlana, do you realise what you're asking me to do? Do you want your father to do away with me? Anyway, I too think you are too young ...'

'But how old were you when you married?'

'Sixteen, but my husband was only twenty-one.'

Svetlana took me into her confidence as well. I merely asked her what she could find attractive in that old goat. I was seventeen and a man of forty-three seemed to me to be aged! Kapler was made to understand that he must stop courting her. But he knew that Svetlana was in love with him and thought he was in control of the situation. He left Moscow and became a *Pravda* correspondent at the front. From there he published 'Letters to my beloved', in which a soldier remembered his sweetheart, all written in a sublimely patriotic style. Svetlana's name did not appear, but when she read these 'Letters', the girl nearly went mad. She rushed to show them to my mother, who tried to reason with her. This time Stalin became seriously angry and instructed Merkulov to see to it that Kapler never returned to Moscow. Merkulov sent for him and demanded: 'Where have you stuck your nose in? What are you after?' Kapler did not lose countenance: 'So what? I fell in love with Svetlana and she with me.' Merkulov described the scene to me with humour: 'What was I to do? I had been ordered to get him out of Moscow. I advised him to leave if he didn't want to be beaten up. He didn't move and so we beat him up. But he persevered ...' Kapler engaged in speculation with some foreigners, so they seized the opportunity to prosecute, and he was exiled. Later, during the anti-Semitic campaign, he was accused of participating in a Zionist plot and was arrested.

This episode shows how much Stalin was attached to his daughter but he held it against her. When she began to live her own life, Stalin treated her as an adult, responsible for her actions although she was still only a child. He required that she show perfect equanimity, without allowing for the enthusiasms of youth. He made her dress austerely and forbade make-up. She had to understand that an adolescent must not allow herself to flirt with a man of forty, because, for him, there was something perverse in that. I think that, at bottom, he had realised that Svetlana had glimpsed his real nature and he gave her the cold shoulder for that reason.

During the war I was sent for two months to Sverdlovsk, with three teachers at my academy. We were to examine the apparatus that the British had installed in their Spitfires to intercept enemy aircraft at night. When we got our hands on that sort of innovation we took it to a special laboratory where they appraised it. After that, it was passed to the institutes whose task was build comparable devices for our own use. My level of competence offered no justification for my inclusion in this mission, and I was well aware of that. Nevertheless, I seized the opportunity to widen my knowledge. I had told Svetlana where I was, and one fine day she asked her brother Vasya, who was a pilot and already in command of a regiment, to put an aeroplane at her disposal. She landed at Sverdlovsk. None of us knew that she had acted without telling her father. A room was made available to her in our hostel. I was pleased to see her. My commander and I were celebrating her arrival when my mother turned up, having been sent by my father when he learnt of her escapade. 'That's all we needed. If our young fool does anything silly ...' My mother said to Svetlana: 'Don't you realise what you're doing? When your father knows about this he'll skin Sergo alive.'

'But I was getting bored without him.'

I learnt much later that Svetlana had fallen in love with me and wanted to marry me. My mother reasoned with her: 'You are both young. You must get a job first. And he looks on you as a sister. He'll never marry you.'

'I'll see about that.'

My mother took her back to Moscow after two days and the affair had no consequences for me, apart from a sermon from my mother. 'Above all, don't marry her. She would make you unhappy. You know her character, she would wear the trousers. I don't want that to happen to my son.' She said nothing about the girl's father. Years later, however, she told me what she had not spoken of at the time. 'Stalin would have interpreted the marriage as an attempt to worm your way into his family. And anyway, I did not want you to fall under his influence. I wanted you to have a normal family life. With Svetlana that would have been out of the question.' We lived in such a milieu that we were both doomed to suffer, whether we were together or separated, whatever course events had taken. Evil surrounded us and had taken us over, even if we did not participate in it directly. Hypocrisy and lying contaminated all human relations, and this not only in politics. Without my mother's presence my character would have been quite different. She stopped me from becoming a cynic. If I have acted according to my ideas, I owe that to her.

In the spring of 1944 Svetlana married G. I. Morozov, a fellow student of Vasya's. I knew him well. He loved her for herself and not because she was Stalin's daughter, that was plain to see. He was a weak man whom she dominated, but she was happy with him. Once she was married, Stalin's attitude changed, and he helped her materially by obtaining a flat for her. He did this not with public money but out of his private purse. Svetlana's way of life was fairly modest. She hadn't enough money to buy a fur-lined coat. When she had a son, Osya, her father did not come to see the boy.[3] He merely sent a present to Svetlana. For years he refused to receive his son-in-law and his grandson, as if they were not part of his family. Svetlana visited her father by herself, and even then had to give notice of her coming, by telephone.

It was Svetlana who wanted to separate from Morozov in May 1947. Yuri Zhdanov[4] then appeared as suitor. Stalin tried to dissuade him. 'You don't know her character. She'll show you the door in no time at all.' But, faced with Yuri's insistence, he changed his opinion and said to his daughter: 'I like that man. He has a future and he loves you. Marry him.'

'He made his declaration of love to you? He has never looked at me.'

'You have only to talk to him and you will see.'

So, in 1949, she married Yuri, who was in charge of the science department of the Central Committee.[5] And when she did it she did not fail to
mock me. 'You didn't want me? Right, I'll marry Yuri Zhdanov.' I did not
know him well, but my wife Marfa and I were invited to the wedding.
Svetlana had a little girl, Katya, round and dainty like a doll.[6] Three or
four years later she confided to us: 'My cup is full,' she said. 'I can't stand
this degenerate any longer. Really, it's impossible to love men. You have to
treat them as the bees treat the bumblebees.' Svetlana brought her children up well and had a sense of discipline. Her daughter became a
volcanologist, her son a doctor. They did not suffer from de-Stalinisation
so far as their material well-being was concerned.

My mother said that Svetlana turned out better than her brothers
because she was a girl and Stalin had kept her under his eye. If he had
shown the same indifference to her as to her brothers she would have
turned out badly. Mother forgave all the stories she told about my father
in her books.[7] 'You have to understand why she did it. She is trying to
exonerate her father as best she can.'

'But why do it at my father's expense? Why him?'

'Because it is the version of the C.P.S.U., a version that lends itself easily
to embellishment. Svetlana has always been a Russophile above all. She
grew up in Russia, surrounded by Russians.'

Personally, I think Svetlana should not have fled abroad and should not
have written what she did. She ought not to have spat on her father like
that if she loved him as much as she claims.

Yasha

Stalin's elder son, Yasha, had style. His father teased him for his slow-
ness. He had been forced to join the Party in the same way as my mother,[8]
whom Stalin had sent for one day. 'You are married to Lavrenti Beria, you
are a researcher, you meet a lot of people, and you don't want to belong
to the Party. What am I to conclude? Is this a way of showing that you
don't agree with the Party's policy? Join the Party in the next two days.
If necessary, I'll be your sponsor, even if the Central Committee advises
me not to.' She spoke to my father about it. He had to insist. 'Listen.
Don't make life more difficult for me than it is already. Join that shitty
organisation and don't make yourself conspicuous. Don't forget that
Stalin suspects you of harbouring sympathy with the Mensheviks. Don't
underestimate him.' That was how my mother entered the Communist
Party. Yasha stubbornly refused to join and did not hesitate to say why.
When he finished his studies at the Academy Stalin sent for him and
rebuked him for being the only non-Party man among the graduates.
'And you are my son! What do I look like, me, the General Secretary of
the Central Committee? You can have all the opinions you wish, but think
of your father. Do it for me.' And Yasha gave in. He told my mother that

without that argument nothing would have made him change his attitude. He hated the Party.

His entire short life shows that he stayed loyal to his father. When the Germans took him prisoner in July 1941 they wanted to make use of him, but Yasha was inflexible. They offered to exchange him for Paulus. Stalin refused, saying that mere officers were not exchanged against Field Marshals.[9] Svetlana told me how her father felt when he took that decision. He was in such anguish that he asked her to stay with him in his bedroom several nights in succession, something he had never done when she was small. He couldn't sleep, talked to her about his youth, his first marriage, Yasha's childhood. He also recalled her childhood. 'I felt then that he did love us, in his own way,' she told me. He aged a lot in that period. Later I asked my father how he thought Stalin should have acted when faced with such a dilemma. 'You know, he could not have acted otherwise,' he replied. 'Had he accepted the exchange offered, that would have dealt a terrible blow to the symbol he had become. He did not take that decision out of concern for justice but for political reasons. As a head of state who had to think of the image he wished to present, Stalin could not act in any other way. Other historical personages have also sacrificed their children without being monsters on that account.'

'And if I were in the same situation as Yasha, what would you do?'

'I would never have let you stick your nose in there.'

'Yet I was parachuted into Germany.'

'Don't talk about what never happened.'

Vasya

Stalin's second son, Vasya, was a good and brave man. He would have given his shirt to his friends. He never held it against me that his father was always referring to me as a good example. During the war he shot down several German aircraft and took part in twenty or thirty battles. He was quickly promoted, without his father having anything to do with it. There were always boot-lickers who wanted to be seen in a good light. On two occasions Stalin opposed a promotion for Vasya[10] and refused to let him be given command of a division, giving as his reason that the young man lacked the necessary experience. He gave in, though, when it was pointed out to him that men less gifted and less deserving had obtained higher appointments than this.

During the war Stalin and Churchill agreed that British universities should open their doors to a group of young Soviet citizens. Alas, Stalin put me in charge of the group. When I heard that Vasya was going to be with us I took fright. I realised at once that he would go his own way, refusing to attend lectures, and I should be obliged to report to Stalin on all the scenes he might create. I told him why I objected to my assignment and he grew angry. I had never seen Stalin so furious. He said that I was as stubborn as the rest of my family but he would make me bend to his will and he gave me a few hours to pack my bags for the journey. I went back home, sick at heart. My father was out. I told everything to my mother, who was frightened. For the first time in her life she took the initiative of telephoning Stalin. She begged him urgently not to send me to Britain with this group referring to my inexperience. He listened, laughed, and said: 'Good, send him back to his studies.'

Stalin showed himself more indulgent towards Vasya after he lost the older boy. He confined himself to growling at him. 'You should have got your diploma from the Military Academy long since,' he said. And Vasya retorted: 'Well, you haven't got a diploma, either.' After the war, however, from Stalin's point of view, his career took a bad turn. Bulganin, Marshal Novikov and Marshal Golovanov competed in servility. They all sought Vasya's favour, inviting him to banquets where plenty of liquor flowed. Actresses hung on his neck and jostled one another to share his bed. It may be that his guards incited him to excesses so as to strengthen their influence. As nobody checked him, he ended by knowing much more about life than I did, still getting my knowledge from books. He tried to draw me into his adventures but my vigilant mother restricted my freedom of action. It has to be said, though, that I was not too much inclined to lead that sort of existence.

Vasya held a high position in the air force.[11] He had little ambition, being interested above all in sport, horse-riding and football. He married three times. He fell in love, married, had children, fell in love with somebody else and started over again. I saw him after his father's death, on the eve of the funeral, and a month later. He took to drinking immoderately, shouting everywhere that they had sent his father to the other world and Beria would be next. When the foreign press began to publish photos of Vasya and to report his words, Molotov and Khrushchev raised the problem in the Presidium and declared that his behaviour must cease. Vasya told my mother that Molotov had sent for him and made clear that severe measures would be taken against him if he continued to spread all sorts of rumours. He had not yet been dismissed. Vasya wanted my father to intervene in his favour, but did not want this to be known. To my mother he said: 'Tell Lavrenti that it's not only me they're aiming at. His turn will come.'

'But nobody can accuse you of being a Georgian nationalist, you don't even speak the language,' my mother retorted.

'I have lots of Georgian friends.'

And that was true. Vasya had many Georgian sportsmen among his friends and they caroused together. My mother reported to my father the conversation she had had with Vasya and insisted that he must understand the need to be more careful. Already in Stalin's lifetime he was uncontrollable. He had not changed and Bulganin wanted to dismiss him. My father ordered me to find him. I eventually found him, quite drunk, surrounded by a disgusting rabble, celebrating in his own way the memory of his father. He was shouting: 'I'll make them pay, those bandits who killed him!' I had all the trouble in the world to get him away from that company. His wife of the moment, a swimming champion with an impressive bottom, helped me put him in my car. I took him to our *dacha*, where he slept for 24 hours. It was not till the next day, when we had returned to town, that my father said to him, over lunch: 'In all things you need to exercise self-control. If you have suspicions about your father's death you must support them with arguments and get to the bottom of the affair. You can talk to me about it, or else to Molotov, since you have confidence in him. But spreading these rumours before foreigners is stupid. Travel, change your ideas, take a rest from women and recover your spirits. Look at yourself in a mirror: you look as though you are my age, whereas you could be my son.'

'But, Uncle Lavrenti [that's what he called my father], you yourself are in danger.'

'Dear boy, am I a man to be unaware of the situation I'm in. Do you think I need your warning? I know exactly how I'm placed, and that's my problem. For the moment I can still help you. Molotov and Khrushchev are well disposed towards you.' Where Khrushchev was concerned he was wrong.

Vasya behaved himself for two weeks. When sober he was friendly and quite reasonable. Unfortunately he plunged back into his orgies. They then began to investigate his military record. It turned out that in 1952 he had forced some airmen to fly in a fog and caused accidents. On 28 April 1953 he was interrogated and put away.[12] My father having been ousted, he resumed his drunken cries, worse than ever. 'I said so! They're going for the real Communists!' Vasya was sentenced first for his past faults. While in prison he stopped drinking. Khrushchev let him out in January 1960 and gave him a general's pension and a flat. But he was surrounded by Chekists who led him back into drinking. One day they put him at the steering wheel of a car when he was intoxicated and he caused an accident. In April he was condemned to five or six years of detention. He asked to be allowed to work. He liked carpentry and applied himself to it. He was released before his term was completed, in the spring of 1961 and exiled to Kazan. There he fell ill and the KGB sent him a nurse who regularly gave him injections. He got weaker by the day. The nurse made him marry her (his previous wife was Timoshenko's daughter). I tried to visit him in Kazan. My mother and I wanted to propose that he come and live with us in Sverdlovsk. Svetlana told us that nothing more could be done for her brother. A fortnight later, in March 1962, a Georgian football champion called us and told us he had just buried Vasya in Kazan, the expenses paid by the Georgian sportsmen. He had been found stabbed before the door of his house. I have always thought that odd, as he was so weak that he could hardly walk.

My mother was always indulgent to Vasya. She forgave him much because he had grown up without a mother. 'Think of all that trash there was around him, think what would have become of you if I hadn't been there. You would have ended up like him. Don't imagine that you had sufficient character to hold out. If you had been surrounded by girls from the age of 14, you would never have experienced real feelings.' A weak person like Vasya was unable to resist. The sorrow caused by his father's death ought to have incited him to react, since he believed in him. But the contrary happened. I have tried to find out what happened to the children he had by his various wives. From what I have heard they are ordinary people. I regret that somewhat: if only Stalin's intelligence had appeared again, free of his wickedness! But that did not happen.

Generally speaking, the offspring of members of the Politburo had to behave properly because they were closely watched. The degradation of morals was noticed first among the children of the middle ranks of the *nomenklatura*, the sons of heads of departments of the Central Committee or of Vice-Ministers, for example. On the other hand, writers and artists were able to lead a bohemian life because the regime cultivated them artificially. But Stalin imposed his own asceticism on all who were near him. The dissolution of morals, which had been camouflaged or repressed while he lived, burst out publicly after his death.

The Politburo

Under Stalin's rod

Stalin succeeded in subduing all the men around him and I do not believe that he allowed anyone to escape from his control until his last breath. He worked twelve hours a day and everyone was ruled by a rod of iron, my father included. That was no small achievement, given the men who made up his entourage – Zhdanov, for example. Stalin held all of those close to him in a grip of fear. The leaders distrusted each other. Intrigue, ambushes, hidden motives made men like Malenkov or Khrushchev, who were perhaps not wicked by nature, what they eventually became. The first one to strike a blow was the winner.

Stalin knew his circle perfectly, foreseeing everyone's reactions. He had not raised many intelligent people to the rank of his closest associates because he feared that such would hinder his actions. But neither could he allow himself to choose only imbeciles if he wanted results. My father explained to me one day that there were two groups in the leadership, those who wanted to strengthen the economy and modify foreign policy and those who could not imagine doing without the Party apparatus. These two factions hated each other, and the worst thing, my father thought, was that Stalin encouraged this antagonism.

Stalin was also always closely interested in the private lives of those near him. He often arrived unannounced at their homes and tried to establish what the hierarchy was in their families. He was very surprised to find that we all ate at the same table, including Ella, my nanny. He was vexed at never managing to worm his way into our affairs, being so fond as he was of playing the arbiter. He also made sure that the families of Politburo members did not see too much of each other, as he feared that such friendships might give rise to coalitions aimed against him. He busied himself setting some husbands against others by distilling his poison drop by drop, but if there was a bond between the families concerned, this strategy became harder to follow.

He did not allow Politburo members to be absent even for a few hours without his knowing where they were. A conversation of any length aroused his suspicion. He also disapproved of the evening parties they organised in their houses, fearing the thoughts and actions that might develop when he was not there. Any meeting held without his supervision was suspect in his eyes. For example, my mother loved to receive visitors from Georgia, to bring back memories of her youth. Stalin took umbrage at this. 'One might think that you have turned Georgia into your personal fief. Why do you need to frequent all these remains of princely families? Some leaders of the Party in Georgia think this is undesirable.' My mother was even obliged to give up entertaining her family (the 'remains' in question) and my father had to stop receiving the writers and artists he had known when he lived in Tbilisi. My father explained to me one day: 'As soon as he saw something like friendship beginning among the men near him, he crushed it. He distrusted everyone. This was not paranoia but a method he had employed over a long period, as I realised when I studied the archives.'

Unlike the other Politburo members, who outstayed their welcome with Stalin so that he had to shoo them away, my father tried to avoid his company as much as he could, using his work as excuse. Stalin was irritated by this, and said: 'You have plenty of time.' Contrary to what was alleged by Khrushchev, who did not always understand Stalin, he liked to have people with him only in order to keep an eye on them and not from fear of solitude.[13] My father grumbled about this, as it was hard for him to get his work done under the conditions imposed by Stalin. One had to sleep during working hours, and when with the boss it was practically impossible to make a phonecall.

When the members of the Politburo visited us, they railed against Stalin. 'He really takes us for kids. He doesn't let us move a single step without supervising us. If only he'd get a little sleep,' Khrushchev moaned. My father took up the theme: 'He could settle down by the Black Sea. We would take him a report once a week. What a wonderful life!'

He happened to say some bad things about Stalin in Malenkov's presence. Needless to say, Malenkov reported everything. When one day I expressed astonishment at his impudence he retorted: 'It makes no difference. Everyone knows what I think. It would seem suspicious if I were to act otherwise.' I think that this was a way he used to get himself understood by Stalin, to make him grasp certain things. In any case, Malenkov was not behindhand: he, too, criticised Stalin right and left. Molotov showed more restraint, yet he could not forgive Stalin for arresting his wife in 1949.

The criticisms made by my father, Malenkov and Khrushchev related, as a rule, to precise questions. They all knew about the listening devices and spoke only about what could be known from other sources. 'Him or the Party and the Politburo, there's no difference,' my father reminded the others. 'We sign all the decisions. If we don't agree, we should tell him instead of being content to run him down among ourselves.' He had spoken to Stalin about the objections to the cult of his personality, and Stalin had expressed agreement. Nevertheless, his whole entourage encouraged him in that direction – then, later, declared him guilty of everything.

I must say that I read with stupefaction the interviews that Molotov and Kaganovich gave to Chuev. It seems to me that their virulent orthodoxy must by attributed to a self-defensive reaction or else to senile decay. When I knew them the members of the Politburo were aware, I thought, that something was not going right. They knew that. It is significant that none of their children wanted to make a career in the Party – not even the Zhdanov boy, who chose to become a chemist and did pretty well in that field.

My parents

My father was different from Stalin's other close associates. He acted as he meant to act. He considered that this did not change anything essential. He explained to my mother: 'At our level people's behaviour does not depend on what we are or on what they are. All that counts is one's career.' Another time he said to me: 'There can be no question of friendship between members of the Politburo, it's a snake-pit.' When I spoke of the universal mendacity he replied: 'Don't look at the others. Look at our family. Have we changed since you were small? You can see that we don't conform to orders from on high ...' And it is true that we never went in for luxury.

At Politburo meetings my father drew the men sitting opposite him or those he thought most comical. He often brought his sketches home and I even made a collection of them. They were not caricatures but portraits. He succeeded in recording their expressions. In his leisure moments he did gouaches. He would have liked my wife, Marfa, to become an artist, but when he realised that she lacked the vocation, he advised me not to press her. When he was with his colleagues my father never spoke of what he was reading, and our conversations at table then were nothing like those we had *en famille*. Our guests were usually visitors from Georgia and the other republics, with their families, but we hardly ever visited my father's colleagues. This was a deliberate attitude on his part, I think.

My mother, too, differed from the other wives, not having the same areas of interest. She was a chemist (she had defended a thesis before the war) and worked at the Timiryazev Academy without benefiting from any favouritism. She was merely rebuked for having, when she fetched samples of soil from different parts of the Soviet Union, used state transport. She did not like official banquets. The atmosphere that prevailed in Moscow disgusted her. She was young and beautiful, and all the other Politburo wives hated her. She admitted to me: 'I feel that hatred. I can't stand them. I'm afraid they'll put a curse on me.'

Zhdanov

Stout and of average height, Zhdanov had bloodshot, expressionless eyes. He gave the impression of not having washed properly and his shoulders were covered with dandruff. His face gave off self-conceit. He was known as 'the grey eminence'. He imagined that he had an immense influence on Stalin whereas the latter merely made use of him. When Zhdanov took steps to exploit the assassination of Kirov he certainly acted on Stalin's behalf. He was a sinister type of person, chauvinistic and a furious anti-Semite.[14] Too much emphasis has been put I think, on his role in the ideological campaigns such as the fight against cosmopolitanism, while people have forgotten the active role he played in the repressions. He struck his blows discreetly, sheltering behind Stalin. The Zhdanovs prided themselves on their culture, especially their German culture. You should have seen their faces when they discovered that I spoke German well and knew Goethe better than they did. They had not expected that of a provincial. Their son Yuri cordially detested me.

My father never concealed his antipathy for Zhdanov and made fun of his artistic pretensions: 'He can just manage to play the piano with two fingers, or to distinguish between a man and a bull in a picture, and yet he holds forth on Socialist Realism and abstract painting.' His wife, a stout woman with short legs, a perfect sourpuss, wanted one day to leave her husband. Stalin sent for her. 'Go back home at once.' She complained that Zhdanov was no good in bed. 'Take as many lovers as you want,' said Stalin, 'but stay with him.' It was the woman herself who told this story to my mother during a cure at Karlovy Vary!

The rumour ran that Zhdanov had been assassinated, but this did not stand up. He drank like a fish and suffered from colossally high blood-pressure.[15] When he died, nothing changed. Others inherited his role, which shows that it was Stalin who pulled all the strings. His successor was Suslov,[16] a 'Party rat' according to my father, a man all the more dangerous because of his phenomenal capacity for work. My father compared him to a tapeworm: he felt a physical revulsion when with him such as he felt with Vyshinsky. Suslov's grating castrato's voice made his hair stand on end and he did all he could to avoid him.

Malenkov

Physically, Malenkov resembled a woman.[17] He was pear-shaped, with narrow shoulders and a big bottom. He often came to see us before the war, but our families did not mix much. He had a daughter who was undoubtedly his, and two sons, all three well brought up by a maternal uncle who had at one time led a fast life but did not lack talent. Malenkov's wife installed him in her *dacha* so as to keep him from doing silly things and ending up in prison. Malenkov asked me to interest his children in technology. They were still at school at this time. They came to see me at the Institute and were delighted when I showed them some rockets. They told their father about this and he telephoned to thank me. I don't think, though, that he was trying to please my father by acting in this way: he was genuinely concerned for his children.

His wife, an authoritarian woman always dressed up to the nines, used to visit us sometimes before the war, but my mother never went to their place. My father had warned her. 'Don't see in her an elder sister or a friend. She's dangerous, a gendarme in skirts. She has a very much stronger will than her husband. It was she who set his foot in the stirrup, thanks to well-placed relatives, and she got him into the Central Committee.' Furthermore, my father could not stand anti-Semites, in whom he saw products of the ideology of the Black Hundreds. He often quoted their watchword: 'Kill the Jews and don't forget the Georgians,' but reacted more violently to remarks aimed at the Jews than those aimed at the Georgians. While Malenkov's wife was anti-Semitic, he himself did not display such gut anti-Semitism. He may not have been anti-Semitic to start with. Was there a personal element in his policy towards the Jews[18] or did he act in that way at his wife's instigation?[19] His daughter married a Jew named Shamberg and when the anti-Semitic campaign began she was forced to get a divorce. I was sorry for her, as she adored her husband.[20]

Malenkov was one of the Russophile group on whom Stalin relied. When my father teased him about his Russian nationalism he replied: 'Lavrenti, you know very well that I am Macedonian. How can you suspect me of Russian chauvinism?' And my father grew still more sarcastic: 'You certainly look to me like a descendant of Spartacus.' As for Spartacus, Malenkov was timid, easily influenced, incapable of independence, a weakling who carried out with zeal the instructions given him by Stalin. My father had put together a dossier on his past activities and the crimes he had committed on his own initiative. I was present when he passed this task to Kruglov and Merkulov. Malenkov had participated in the collectivisation and all the repressions. He had been a member of Stalin's Secretariat, then of the Politburo's Secretariat, and had been chairman of the Orgburo. My father showed him the dossier: 'Think yourself happy that these documents are in my hands,' he said. 'But behave reasonably in future.' That was how my father neutralised him. I have never been able to distinguish in the positions adopted by Malenkov, what was due to my father's influence on him, and what were his own beliefs. Malenkov was always crushed by the strong personalities around him. Yet he was not a man to get aboard the train when it was in motion: on the contrary, he ran ahead of the locomotive. Being intelligent enough to foresee what was expected of him, he performed his tasks with the servility of a lackey. 'When Stalin orders him to get rid of a man, he does away with a thousand so as to be more sure,' said my father. Another feature of Malenkov's character gave rise to jokes. He could not stand it when others succeeded in their undertakings without going through him. My father said to him once: 'You remind me of the baboon who dies of a stroke when he is isolated from his troop in a nearby cage and sees other males taking the females. Stalin has, a hundred times, given me new tasks to perform when I had just established order in a sector. That's happened to many others, but nobody takes it to heart as you do. Watch out, or you, too, will one day die of a stroke.' Malenkov looked at me. 'What do you think? Are we all baboons?' My father drove in the nail: 'Don't think that these youngsters who seem to worship us look on us otherwise than as ignoramuses who can't wield anything but the cudgel.'

Malenkov had humour, even though he confined it to a limited circle. He was really only concerned to strengthen his position in the Central Committee. In inner-Party intrigues he was distinguished by a certain originality. His wife encouraged him to assume the image of a cultivated and charismatic leader. At the time, I was taken in by this. I thought that he shared my father's views but was sometimes, under pressure from Stalin, obliged to distance himself from them. My father put it down to cowardice.

I had personal experience of Malenkov's duplicity. When I was appointed chief engineer at my institute, he became, in a way, my superior in the hierarchy. He shoved his nose in everywhere on behalf of the Central Committee. We enjoyed a degree of latitude owing to the priority task assigned to the Institute, namely constructing missiles. When I had to recruit my collaborators I followed my father's advice and chose students at the military academies, as he had done for his intelligence network. He had advised me to avoid well-known scientists who would try to take all the credit for our work. 'Form a team of young officers of your own age. They have a sense of discipline, without being obtuse.' I also needed experienced specialists who would be able to cool our youthful ardour and prevent us from committing follies. Here, however, I came up against a few difficulties. One specialist had lost his father in the purges, another was Jewish, the third came from occupied territory. If I had applied the criteria for recruitment used by the Party's cadres department I should never have had anyone but idiots in my Institute. This time I acted like my father. I engaged these specialists regardless of their 'blemishes'. The central Committee took note of that. When I had already recruited about a hundred of these 'criminal' elements I was summoned by Serbin,[21] who was in charge of the heavy constructional engineering sector and was close to Malenkov. He told me: 'I have a dossier showing that you are following an incorrect cadres policy. You recruit former prisoners and people whose relatives were victims of the purges, and you give them access to state secrets of the utmost importance. Take, for example, Raspletin, your deputy. He is the son of a merchant who was shot in 1919, his uncle died on Solovki, and he got himself false papers in order to join the institute ... Then there's your second deputy, Kochman. He is a graduate of the Military Academy, but his father led a Zionist organisation.' All that was true. In the last case mentioned Abakumov had 'advised against' recruiting the man. He snitched to the Central Committee. 'And this Lifshits?' Serbin went on. 'His father was a millionaire Jewish industrialist. He has a regular museum at his place.' I did not deny the facts but I guaranteed the competence of these men who made it possible for me to perform the tasks that had been entrusted to us. 'You've gone too far,' he replied, 'dismiss them.' I exploded and made an enemy of him from that moment. He did not let this appear, which was typical of the hypocrisy of the Party functionaries. 'I did not speak to you about this matter on my own initiative. Malenkov told me to do it, but don't speak to him about it.' He hastened to explain when he saw how I reacted. Malenkov did not want to show his face in this affair. I told my father everything. 'My dear boy,' he said, 'you'll have to fight for each of your collaborators. Don't abandon a single one, or nobody will want to work with you any more. Ring Malenkov. He will promise to help you. He will call me. But everything will depend on the special services. This dossier is on Stalin's desk, you can be sure of that. Perhaps you ought to appeal to him. We'll see.' So I telephoned Malenkov, and he invited me to visit him. I explained everything to him as though he knew nothing about it. 'How can we find the people we need when you rule out half of our fellow citizens for the sole reason that they lived under German occupation or have relatives who did?' He promised me to see to the matter. 'As for my deputies, they worked with your wife [they were assistant professors in her institute]. That is for me the best of references,' I added, maliciously. His expression changed and he immediately sent for his wife, who confirmed what I had said, complaining that I had, by recruiting those men, stripped her establishment of staff.

'All the same, we can't let such charges pass uninvestigated,' he said.

'Just let us finish the work we're engaged on. Then you will decide.'

'We'll have to think about all that, and get to the bottom of it. The Central Committee will have to do something.'

I left and, as arranged, telephoned my father. 'Do as you wish,' was all he said. A few days later that same Serbin sent for me, along with my director. The latter was a very competent Armenian who had previously been in charge of a huge ordnance works in Gorky. He loved me like a son and had persuaded me to spend an hour every day in study with him and other specialists, so that I could master all phases of our production. We were summoned to a room where all the sector heads were assembled, together with some officers of the MGB. Malenkov announced that the usual criteria for recruitment of cadres would not be applied in my institute. I saw some faces lengthen, as some of those present waited impatiently for the upstart daddy's boy that I was to be put in his place. I heaved a sigh of relief. A resolution was adopted, condemning my cadres policy and calling for intensified surveillance of my institute but recognising the extraordinary nature of the task which had been entrusted to us and the priority of our results over considerations of political orthodoxy. When everybody had left except the members of the Central Committee's Secretariat, Malenkov said to me, with his usual perfidy: 'Actually, Sergo, you are right. One has to fight for each of one's collaborators. It is possible to make use of the worst bastards.' A few minutes earlier, speaking in public, he had said the opposite. Though I had already witnessed all sorts of hypocrisy, this shocked me. We complain today about the dual morality of our fellow citizens. At that time this was the norm in our leading circles, and people have inherited it.

I had another opportunity to observe Malenkov's duplicity. We had to test a missile for use against warships. An antiquated cruiser had been provided for us to measure the effect of our charges. The crew were to leave the vessel just before the experiment, so that we needed special radio-control equipment, which took time to make. We planned to carry out our test in the following month. My father directed military industry through the special committee he chaired, which did not prevent the Central Committee from sticking its nose in. The special committee was invited to discuss the problem. Malenkov, who was a member of the committee, spoke, declaring, in an affected tone that, since human beings were our most precious possessions, we must ensure complete safety for the members of the crew. He asked how we intended to proceed. After the meeting my father asked him why he had involved himself in these problems. 'Lavrenti,' he replied, 'you know very well that I care as little about them as about my first shirt. But I had to take up a position in the presence of the others.' He had wanted to display his philanthropy, he who had sent tens of thousands into the other world. My father never acted in this way, trying to appear better than he was. Malenkov was a real hypocrite, like Khrushchev, whom only stupidity prevented from using this feature of his character in a consistent way in politics. He always ended by showing his true character. Malenkov was more artful, which explains why he was able to deceive the Westerners. In my view, Khrushchev did less harm, and I say this in spite of the infamous role he played in my father's fate, because he was less sly and less intelligent than Malenkov, that master of intrigue.

In foreign policy, Malenkov did not preach an aggressive Russian imperialism. During the Korean War he maintained a waiting attitude at the sessions of the Military Council where I was present. On the other hand, he took an active part in the anti-Tito campaign. Like my father, he thought that the Party ought not to control the economy. I heard him with my own ears expounding this view during Stalin's time. Himself without convictions, he deeply hated the man who had made him commit infamies and his hatred grew more intense when Stalin attacked his collaborators. This feeling brought him closer to my father.

Voroshilov

Voroshilov's stupidity was not to be read in his face. He had laughing eyes and a jovial temperament. Vain as a woman, he took great care of his appearance. In February 1936 Stalin sent him to Georgia for the 15th anniversary of the Sovietisation of the republic. A house had been got ready for him, but he preferred to stay with us, like Stalin and Ordzhonikidze. I must say that he knew how to put us at our ease, he was so free of haughtiness. But my father could not stand him, because he considered Voroshilov an absolute cretin. Because of his stupidity he was not an adversary to be feared, but he always made thorough use of his capacity to cause harm. Stalin had no illusions about him. Always extremely irritated by the man's stupidity he treated him like a dog. He would never have behaved like that with Molotov or Zhdanov, or even with my father. Voroshilov let himself be bullied by his wife, a large lady with three chins, who never missed an opportunity to make public display of the contempt she felt for him – even before Stalin. It was said that Stalin was only mimicking her when he treated Voroshilov as an imbecile. Voroshilov was promoted by Stalin as a great patron of the arts, even though Stalin was aware of his ignorance. My father did not fail to see in this a manifestation of Stalin's wicked sense of humour.

Kaganovich

A Jew from Central Asia, Kaganovich was a handsome man, tall, well turned out, with long eyelashes. He had a fine voice, and knew it. We visited him because our *dachas* were close together, but my father never showed any esteem for him. He had had a great friendship with Kaganovich's brother Mikhail, Minister of Aviation, whom he had known from Ordzhonikidze's time. Mikhail was a cheerful man with a sharp sense of humour that my father liked. The Politburo criticised him on the grounds that our aircraft were not ready.[22] That was true, but the situation could not be blamed on the Ministers, since, had one moved heaven and earth, it was impossible to attain the Central Committee's objectives in the period laid down, and though Kaganovich was Mikhail's brother he spoke not a word when my father tried to defend him. The unfortunate man left the room and put a bullet through his head. My father never forgave Kaganovich for that.[23] My mother asked him, later, how he had been able to sacrifice his brother. He replied that, for the sake of Communism, he was ready to sacrifice his entire family. Nor did my father forgive him for having refused to participate actively in the Jewish Anti-Fascist Committee which he set up during the war. I was present at their conversation about this. 'Some of our Jews respect you, in spite of everything,' said my father. 'Well, they're wrong,' replied Kaganovich.

Kaganovich was a prudent man, much more so than my father. He never let himself be blinded by the interests of the moment and never lost sight of the future. This was why he showed his antipathy for Zhemchuzhina, so as to make clear that, for him, there was no question of Jewish solidarity. This attitude irritated my father, who did not hesitate to promote talented Georgians. Between a gifted Jew and a mediocre Russian, Kaganovich always chose the Russian. For him, considerations of personal safety outweighed concern for efficiency. He was a rather servile creature, not stupid, a good executive, always ready to anticipate Stalin's wishes, and a crawler before my father. On that point I remember a story. One day when my father proposed to organise a volleyball match between our family and Kaganovich's, the other man backed out, giving as his reason: 'I won't play against Beria's family. I'd rather be in your team.'

He was proud of his literary and historical culture. He had undeniably read a lot. He talked about Gorky to Marfa and me, though I detested Gorky's novels.

Kaganovich's family was patriarchal and profoundly Jewish. His wife looked after those close to her. She was an intelligent woman and my father, who liked the family spirit, was very fond of her. Kaganovich had an adopted son, an Eastern-looking boy who could have passed for Jew or Georgian. My mother and I thought he was his natural son. My father revealed to us that Kaganovich had acted as go-between in a relationship between his niece and Stalin and that the little boy was actually the son of Stalin[24] and the niece, who, I must admit, was very pretty. I found his daughter Maya no less attractive. She resembled Liz Taylor, though her curves were less generous.

Khrushchev

Khrushchev was in the Ukraine when we arrived in Moscow, but he spent two days of every week in the capital and he often visited us, inviting himself to stay the night. He was afraid that my father might use his former friendship with Yezhov against him.

Khrushchev was not intelligent, though cunning as a peasant. He acted the fool, pretending to enjoy the jokes that Stalin made at his expense. He had the habit of singing doggerel, and he drank. It may be that he cultivated this image without pleasure. My father said that one should not take him for a harmless cretin. He thought Khrushchev was crafty and perfidious, extremely dangerous despite his illiteracy. After the war he made a show of passionate friendship for my father, who thought this funny, but eventually let himself be taken in by it. Khrushchev never contradicted him openly.

He won Stalin's confidence through Allilueva, whom he had met at the Industrial Academy where she studied. He was first distinguished by his zeal against the Trotskyists.[25] This he carried so far that all the teachers at the Academy were put in prison. Once made head of the Party organisation in Moscow he extended his struggle against Trotskyism to

Bukharin. All the leading personnel of a certain level were arrested: not one escaped.[26] Now, the NKVD could not arrest a Party functionary without approval from the higher instances, which, in Moscow, meant Khrushchev. Serov, whom my father made Minister of Internal Affairs in the Ukraine, told me before the war about the role that Khrushchev played in the repressions. In Yezhov's apparatus there was a functionary[27] who prepared the dossiers that were to go to Khrushchev. As they were close (their wives were often together), Khrushchev took this man with him when he went into the Ukraine. The functionary summoned the Ukrainian leaders, told them that he had the impression that he was in a synagogue and said that this situation must be ended. A furious anti-Semite, Khrushchev subjected the Ukraine to a regime of terror such that even Stalin felt obliged to cool his ardour. The functionary took fright and fled to Siberia. Perhaps he was encouraged to leave by being warned that his arrest was imminent. However that may be, Khrushchev, panic-stricken, telephoned my father, who advised him to speak to Stalin about the matter. Stalin called him everything under the sun. Eventually the man was tracked down. My father entrusted the investigation to Khrushchev, who, in turn, passed the job to Serov. Serov said that Khrushchev, at the head of the *troika*, had actively promoted repression. And it was he who insisted that the functionary be executed, whereas Serov proposed a ten-year prison sentence. He even arranged with Malenkov for the man's wife also to be condemned to death. Khrushchev continued to order the assassination of Ukrainian nationalists even after Stalin's death.[28]

Khrushchev had a son from his first wife. At the age of 17 or 18 this young man took to drink and ended by getting mixed up with gangsters and murderers. When Serov arrested the gang he discovered that Khrushchev's son belonged to it. He telephoned my father, and was advised to speak to Khrushchev himself. Khrushchev asked that his son be treated separately from the rest of the gang, but Serov replied that the investigation was already under way and my father had been informed. Thereafter, Khrushchev began to exert continual pressure on Serov. He even telephoned my father to demand 'dismissal of this imbecile who can't tell the difference between the son of a Politburo member and gangsters.' My father explained that the case had gone to the Public Prosecutor's office and no longer depended on Serov, then reassured him by saying that his son would get off with a light sentence which he would serve in good conditions. The young man would stop drinking and return to the right path.[29] Khrushchev could only bow to this, but he maintained a grudge against Serov. He was to remind Serov of the case when he got rid of him.

During the war Khrushchev wanted an appointment in Moscow, but found himself exiled to the front, in the Military Council, on Stalin's orders. Stalin said: 'Remain with the supply services until you have liberated the whole of the Ukraine.' When that was accomplished, Khrushchev proceeded to systematically exterminate the intelligentsia of the Western Ukraine, instead of making use of it as my father wished. He wanted to boast to Stalin that the Sovietisation of that part of the Ukraine was going well. My father, Serov and Gatoshka, the Secretary of Khrushchev's apparatus, told me how he had organised the assassination of numerous nationalists. He had also deported Ukrainian priests and prelates, despite opposition from my father, who was keen on preserving channels of communication with the Vatican. Khrushchev posed as champion of the Party line against Ukrainian nationalism. In foreign and domestic policy alike he always supported the same aggressive line.[30]

Khrushchev was physically repulsive.[31] When I knew him he had a sagging belly, a double chin, a spluttering, ever-open mouth and little pig's eyes. He not only drank, he also chased skirts and was a notorious debauchee. They say that about my father, too, but he at least was handsome and had charm.[32] He teased Khrushchev about his successes with women. 'Look at Nikita, he's nothing much to look at, but what a ladykiller!' My mother rebuked him for that: she hated his way of wounding people. She tried many times to make him understand that a person could forgive a justified criticism, but by chaffing them in this way he made implacable enemies. When he visited us, Khrushchev often got drunk. He knocked back large glasses of brandy. We always had to put him to bed because he couldn't stand. One day our bursar could put up with him no longer. 'Don't invite him to stay the night again. He wets the bed, and even worse. I'm tired of cleaning up after him.' My mother complained to my father: 'Why do you encourage that creature to drink?' I too was shocked to see my father competing in vulgarity with Khrushchev, and I told him so. 'You have to put yourself on the same level with the people you're with,' he said. 'If you don't, they hold it against you. In that connection, let me advise you never to show that you know more than they do.'

Nina Petrovna, Khrushchev's wife, brought up their children. Her daughter attended my school. Unlike Molotov's daughter she was not skittish and did not draw attention to herself. My mother knew the mother of Adzhubei, Khrushchev's son-in-law, and got on well with her. She was a dressmaker. She had not approved of her son's marriage to Rada Khrushchev. She thought that he did not love her and had married her for the sake of his career. 'It's a frightful family,' she told my mother. And, in fact, the Khrushchevs kept her at a distance because she was only a dressmaker. She choked with indignation when she spoke of them. 'Those mugs who can't put two words together without making mistakes think I am not good enough for them!' Nina Petrovna readily praised to her the qualities of her Nikita. Adzhubei's mother, struck by the hypocrisy of that family, warned my mother, her friend: 'They are dangerous people. I'm afraid for my son. Watch out, they hate you, I know that from my son.' After my father's death, when we were in exile, she wrote to us: 'You should have told Lavrenti what I told you ...'

Molotov

Always dry and formal, very careful of his appearance, Molotov had claims to elegance, but his bristling moustache had something comic about it, and he stuttered. I liked him well enough and my father's relations with him were good. Before the war Molotov was the country's Number Two, even its Number One, since he was Russian. That did not please Zhdanov, who saw himself as Stalin's heir. There were many intrigues against him from that time, but as he was a docile instrument of the Party[33] it was hard to incriminate him for anything. However, his wife Zhemchuzhina, a member of the Central Committee, who was Jewish, provided an ideal target. Anti-Semitism was deeply rooted among most of the higher Russian functionaries of the Party, though little was said about it before the war. Stalin had already begun a witch-hunt among his collaborators' wives in the 1930s. In Yezhov's time the Party organs began to compile a dossier on Zhemchuzhina. Malenkov busied himself assembling the items and my father was ordered to investigate Zhemchuzhina's links with the Zionists.

One day Stalin showed him the Central Committee's dossier which proved Zhemchuzhina's anti-Party activity[34] and told him to check the accusations, making it plain that they were to be confirmed. 'He did not doubt that I would do as he wished,' my father told me. He examined all the reports, dating back to Yezhov. Zhemchuzhina's only sin was to have helped some Jews.[35] She had indeed met representatives of Zionist organisations, but officially and with the permission of the Politburo, and so of Stalin. They wanted to make this a crime on her part. 'These charges don't stand up. They only want to organise a provocation against Molotov,' said my father to Stalin, who took his report and did not mention the matter again. 'But I felt that he made it a grudge against me,' my father concluded. Stalin threatened to pass this dossier to Shkiryatov. My father then sought to make an ally of Molotov, and sent him reports drawn up by his services. Molotov considered my father a young man with a big future. My father warned him of the danger that hung over his wife, regardless of Stalin's order that nothing be said about the affair to Molotov. 'You must see to it that your wife doesn't do anything imprudent,' he said. But Molotov dared not say anything to Zhemchuzhina, because he was afraid of her. Knowing her volcanic temper, he feared that she would go and make a scene before Stalin. However, he complained to Stalin, who naturally blamed my father. When Merkulov took my father's place at the head of State Security in February 1941 Stalin brought up Zhemchuzhina's case again.[36] He wanted her to be kidnapped. Had Merkulov not managed to organise the kidnapping of Marshal Kulik's wife? Merkulov objected that they must first set a watch on her circle, and then ran to ask my father's advice, which was to warn Molotov. Merkulov was frightened and so my father did this himself. In February 1949 the initiative for Zhemchuzhina's arrest came not from Stalin but from people who were competing for his succession.

Molotov loved only Zhemchuzhina,[37] who was herself madly in love, all her life, with Stalin. 'There's a man!' she said to Molotov. 'You are nothing but a simpleton.' At bottom, though, she loved her husband. Unlike my mother, who was much younger, she did not shun worldly vanities. She was not beautiful but dressed with taste. My mother was very fond of her. She admired her intelligence. She said that, beneath her prima donna's ways, Molotov's wife was not a bad lot. And the other woman felt an affinity with my mother. Perhaps she knew that my father had helped her in 1939. In any case, she would have liked my mother to be more active socially. She said to her: 'When will you leave your academic lair?' Zhemchuzhina often visited us, even accompanied by Golda Meir. She arranged to come at times when she was sure of finding my father at home. She knew that there were no anti-Semites in our family. But when she began to cultivate my mother's friendship, my father revealed to us that Molotov had applied Party policy like an automaton and had had people shot, in great numbers, on the basis of mere suspicion. He told us all that in a quite objective way. He warned my mother that Zhemchuzhina was an independent woman with her own ideas. Molotov put up with this, though his attitude was disapproved of by his Politburo colleagues. During the war Zhemchuzhina took an active part in the Jewish Anti-Fascist Committee despite my father's warnings. Later she sharply criticised Stalin's anti-Jewish policy. How could he not understand that the Jewish people deserved help after all they had done for the revolution? Ought the proletarian state not to show its gratitude? Molotov said nothing. My mother was embarrassed. She would have preferred to do without this sort of conversation, knowing well what the consequences would be.

Relations between my father and Molotov remained formal and official, but equable. I never heard, before the war, of any clash between them. There were certainly divergences of view, but these did not degenerate into personal conflicts. My father felt a kind of sympathy with him. Stalin had noticed this and reproached my father for supplying Molotov with information which he should share only with him, Stalin. During the war Stalin made a scene because my father had taken measures to ensure the security of Molotov's visit to London in May 1942 as though he had been the Chairman of the Council of Ministers. He had rejected two aircraft which seemed to him not to provide the necessary guarantees of safety. 'Don't play at being a little craftsman fascinated by unimportant details. It's not for you but for your deputy to bother about such matters,' said Stalin, in Molotov's presence. This remark particularly annoyed my father. Yet poor Molotov was terrified of flying, I was told by Kutepov, an air-force officer who served as my father's liaison with Tupolev and our aircraft industry. Provoked beyond endurance, my father ordered Kutepov to take Molotov to the airport and show him all the preparations made for his flight, so as to reassure him and calm him down.

Molotov never had any ideas of his own. He merely repeated what

Stalin said. He was never interested in anything. I would even say that he was a phenomenon in this respect. He lived for nearly forty years after retirement and did absolutely nothing during those decades. He did not even have a hobby but was satisfied to live like a vegetable. Perhaps longevity was his only aim.

Saburov and Kovalev

Saburov was a Tatar. I knew his family because one of his sons had married the daughter of Kovalev, the Minister of Transport, who was quite close to us and had a nearby *dacha*. He often visited us, or vice versa, and so I came to know Saburov. I learnt that he had worked closely with my father, on whose recommendations he became Vosnesensky's successor as chairman of Gosplan. He was a calm, level-headed person, like Pervukhin, a type my father liked. As he was inclined to be impulsive he had to surround himself with placid people who could restrain him. To Saburov he confided his conception of foreign policy and his ideas on our internal affairs. They talked at length about these things.[38]

Saburov and Kovalev consulted my father on various economic questions and made sure of his support. Among other matters they discussed the oil industry in Tatarstan, in which my father had begun to take an interest before the war. One day when he was speaking of these immense resources (he had studied the question with Professor Gubkin), Saburov complained that the Tatar population had gained nothing from their oil that had been exploited during the war. On the contrary, the peasants had lost their land and become proletarians, and the country had been polluted. My father said to him: 'You are responsible for Gosplan. Act. I await your proposals.'[39] He would have liked to give Tatarstan the status of a union republic, with access to the Caspian Sea. After all, Astrakhan was a Tatar, not a Russian town, and to give it to Tatarstan would only be just. Unfortunately he did not achieve his aims.

The Bomb

His taste for technology always inclined my father towards scientific espionage. He boasted that he was able to obtain any secret whatsoever from anywhere in the world. As he saw it, it would have been criminal not to profit by the sympathy that the USSR and Socialist ideals enjoyed in the West.

In 1939 he received from French scientists[1] documents concerning work on the nuclear project. He reported on this to the Politburo, who did not react however. We were not yet concerned at this time about the nuclear weapons in the hands of the USA and Britain – or, at least, we had no state programme for the matter. In the Soviet Union scientists were working on it only at the level of theory. Eventually in 1940 a commission was set up.[2] It concluded that an atomic weapon was a possibility but that it would take ten to fifteen years to make, whereas war was expected to come in three or four years. Accordingly, this project was abandoned in November 1940.

1942: The British precedent

My father continued to collect information about nuclear weapons through his agents. He did not conceal his admiration for the British effort in this field[3] and for the intelligence of the British. 'They are poor,' he said to me, 'and yet they have found the resources needed to develop radar, sonar, jet aeroplanes and the nuclear project. Whereas the Americans, though they are rolling in money, haven't lifted their little finger. The British know how to wait, and think of the future; the Americans dream only of immediate profit.' Here he perceived the influence of Churchill who, while in opposition, already inspired, more or less secretly, Britain's armaments policy. The fact that such a policy could be carried out in parallel with the government's, and independently of it, made a big impression on my father. 'A country capable of that is a strong country and such a thing would be inconceivable with us,' he said. I did not fully understand at the time what was in his mind.

Eventually, in March 1942, he was able to prove that the British were working tirelessly on the atomic project. He knew also that the Germans were at the stage of preparing the reactor vessel and the Americans, instigated by Szilard and Einstein, were starting to move. He therefore put forward his proposal again,[4] and this time the Politburo approved. A new commission was formed, headed by Molotov. From 1943 we aimed at making the bomb.[5] True, Stalin did not think of making it till after the war, but he wanted to take measures in the meantime so that our research should not lag behind that of the Western powers. And we knew that the Germans would not succeed in surpassing our allies in this field.

Young researchers who were interested in nuclear fission were recruited. The physicist Ioffe pointed out the ones he thought most promising.[6] The same cannot be said of his colleague Kapitsa, who thought that we should not have the bomb. Every month my father submitted to Stalin a report on the state of our work and another about the Americans, the British and the Germans. From 1943 onwards we mobilised physicists, engineers and metallurgists. We had to find scientists who were able to utilise the information obtained by our agents. We then concentrated on the specialised equipment needed, as our scientific development was inferior to that of the Western countries. That was what my father was working at, with passion, in 1943-44.

1943: the reorganisation of intelligence

My father recommended that the NKGB be separated from the NKVD and that military counter-espionage be put under the control of the Defence Commissariat. This was done on 14 April 1943, as Stalin was pleased with the idea. My father was left with the NKVD: all the extraction industries (uranium and nickel) came under that authority. My father's deputy Kruglov actually ran this commissariat, and had been warned from the outset that he must be ready to take it over formally at any moment. My father counted on getting free of the NKVD after one year. Unfortunately he had to remain responsible for it until December 1945, which he regretted, as he did not want to concern himself with the camps. Nevertheless, from 1943 he no longer had to supervise the investigation of cases or anything in that field. State security was Merkulov's task. At the end of 1943, I spent fifteen days staying with my mother, as she was ill and my father thought my presence at her side was indispensable. I remember that when Merkulov arrived, my father said: 'Let me present a new Minister.' Merkulov laughed and said: 'Thanks for the gift, Lavrenti.' Counter-espionage, directed by Abakumov, was put under the Defence Commissariat, and so under Stalin himself. He wanted to keep an eye on the heads of the armed forces. Contrary to what has been said, the men in charge of this organisation had not been recommended by my father, and Abakumov was his enemy. Later, an investigation established that Abakumov had nothing to do with 'the Beria gang' but was nonetheless a rotter. From the day he took on the job he began to spy on our family and compile dossiers against us.

1945: my father is put in charge of the atomic project

Molotov was removed from the atomic project at the request of the people who worked in it.[7]

During the Potsdam conference I saw my father making notes on a sheet of paper one evening. He was organising the future commission[8] and selecting its members. When I saw the names of Malenkov and other Party functionaries I asked him: 'What need have you to include those people?'

'I prefer that they should belong,' he replied. 'If they stay outside they will put spokes in our wheels.' Though he knew that Kapitsa[9] was very reticent he had also put his name down, in the hope that patriotism would carry the day with him. Stalin had frowned: 'Kapitsa said that we were not capable of making the bomb; he would obstruct the others' work.' My father explained that, on the contrary, the presence of a critical mind would stimulate the scientists. Later, when Stalin tried to use Kapitsa against my father, he sent for him and said: 'I understand that you did not want to take part in the project, but why are you creating problems for me?' Kapitsa replied that when he gave his views and advice he was merely making his contribution. 'I see,' replied my father, with irony. 'Thank you very much for this misinformation which undermines my work.' Kapitsa was removed from the commission and, from one day to the next all those who had worked him up now abandoned him.

Stalin came back from Potsdam discontented. After the conference he sent for my father, Serov and other people connected with the atomic project, including those who were involved in the rounding up of scientists in Germany. Calmly, he asked them to tell him the overall state of our work and asked my father to write a memorandum with proposals which might hasten the making of our bomb. He ordered that all the resources of our economy be mobilised in order to attain that end. Finally, on 20 August 1945, the project was entrusted to my father, who then said that, under these conditions, he wished to be freed from the NKVD. In December, having decided to use extreme measures, Stalin agreed to his request, and transferred to him the entire sectors of energy, metallurgy and transport. The tasks entrusted to my father were of first priority, and he was made Deputy Prime Minister. Around this time I asked him: 'Why have you abandoned Smersh and State Security to others in order to devote yourself to the atomic project?' There was a flavour of reproach in his reply: 'This was the only way to rid myself of those terrible structures. At your age you ought to understand.' Thereafter, down to 1953, he devoted himself entirely first to making the atomic bomb and then to making the hydrogen bomb. He was also responsible for building ballistic missiles, guided missiles for anti-aircraft defence and missiles for use by our navy.

He created a new intelligence network to serve the atomic project. He separated it from the Ministry of State Security, which was controlled by Abakumov,[10] and gave it to Sudoplatov, while retaining nevertheless his parallel network, to the great resentment of the latter, who was not given access to it. Before the war my father had succeeded, not without effort, in persuading Stalin to create a second intelligence network which was not dependent on any apparatus and was not attached anywhere. Thereafter he ran this network personally and Sudoplatov had to make do with what he had. It was necessary to place it out of reach of a bandit like Abakumov, my father explained. Sudoplatov must have learnt that lesson by the time he completed the thirteen years of prison that he mentions in his book. I don't say that maliciously. I am grateful to him for not attacking my father.[11]

When they learnt of the explosion of the American bomb, my father and his colleagues realised at once that Stalin would exert constant pressure on them until the USSR possessed its own bomb. We then began to kidnap German scientists whom the Americans had moved into their zone, something we had previously hesitated to do.[12] We even managed to attract into the Soviet zone a certain number of von Braun's collaborators.[13]

My father never overestimated the role of intelligence work in scientific research, as in other domains. 'Spying is all very fine, but you have to be able to digest the information obtained, to understand it and use it. Organisations and men are needed. All we have is Gosplan, a sewer which is incapable even of assembling and analysing the statistics of our economy. And we claim to understand the economies of other countries!'

Task Number One

My father told me that Stalin had more than doubled the budget for the nuclear project, as compared with the initial estimates that he himself had proposed when he returned from Potsdam. This forced Voznesensky, the head of Gosplan, to find extra means for hastening the construction of the military bases provided for. My father was well-informed on the country's actual capacities. He knew, as did the heads of Gosplan, Voznesensky and, later, Saburov, the pitiful state our economy was in, the extent to which it resembled a rope too tightly stretched, which could break at any moment, and what great need we had for resources with which to reconstitute the country's infrastructures. 'I wanted to preserve our resources so as to invest them in the coal and oil sectors and, especially, in our railways. But Stalin told me, brusquely, that it was not for me to play the economist. The whole country had to be mobilised to solve Problem Number One.'[14]

My father never ceased repeating that we had to change our policy, because our economy was collapsing. We had to cut off the electricity from whole towns because this was assigned, as a matter of priority, to Project Number One! After 1949 especially, he would have liked to slow down the pace of research and make economies. He particularly wanted to inject capital into the sectors for which he was responsible, but was unable to do this. Makhnev reported certain words of my father's on this subject. 'Compare the share of the GNP devoted by the Americans to their military budget with the share that we allot to it. We spend twenty or thirty times as much. At this rate we shall destroy ourselves,' he said in response to criticism, including some from Zavenyagin, who wanted still more spent on the nuclear project. This attitude of his was interpreted in 1953 as a further proof of my father's dealings with the enemy. This is only one example among others that show what imbeciles he had to reckon with. And Zavenyagin was not the most obtuse of them.

As Malenkov served on the commission Stalin was doubly informed, by my father and by him. Now, Malenkov did not support my father, although he did not contradict him either. Voznesensky, on the other hand, another influential member of the special commission, helped him as much as he could. When, after the Leningrad affair in 1949, he was removed from the commission, my father replaced him with Bulganin, who was then Minister of Defence. He wanted the military to participate in the nuclear project, as in other armaments projects, and from the earliest stages, even if they did make stupid remarks. In this way, he thought, they would be able to familiarise themselves with new developments. Besides, it was they who built the test-bases. Bulganin's signature enabled him to get from the military whatever he wanted. After the war Stalin entrusted the construction of missiles to Bulganin, and this proved disastrous. My father, who succeeded him, got things going fast. Annoyed at this setback, Bulganin looked for the reasons for it. Had his decisions not been sabotaged? He admitted his perplexity even to me. By appointing him to the commission my father sought to console him a little, and he did, in fact, show himself satisfied with this position.

My father was an enthusiast for anything he undertook. He undoubtedly liked power, though not so much power in itself as the chance to launch operations or to plan stratagems. My mother said that she guessed at once when he was cooking something up. He was as though transfigured. 'He puts his whole soul into what he is doing,' she said. When he was in charge of Georgia, Armenia and Azerbaijan he never left off developing their economy. During the war he immersed himself in questions connected with oil. With Bagirov he proposed to the government that the oilfields of Tatarstan be exploited, although this ran contrary to the interests of Azerbaijan. One day, at table, he described to us with enthusiasm the 'little Russian Switzerland' that could be created around Moscow. 'With these landscapes, hills and lakes, all that would be needed would be to build cottages ...' My mother interrupted him angrily. 'Think of Georgia, rather. There, everything has already been built. All that's needed is to let the people live as they do in Switzerland.'

When my father wanted to understand something he sent for specialists and made them explain it. Thus, he asked Kapitsa for clarification on a technological point, and the scientist said to him, jokingly: 'You know, Lavrenti Pavlovich, these lessons have to be paid for extra.' To which my father at once replied: 'But I've no need of you for anything else.'

The nuclear project took up three-quarters of his time. He was very fond of technology and though he had no education in physics he knew what he had to learn from the scientists in order to obtain results. He was a better organiser than his American equivalent, Groves. He chose the scientists he needed and got rid of the 'oldies' of the project, taking on only youngsters who began by using the data furnished by intelligence and went on to build the hydrogen bomb a year ahead of the Americans. It was on the very day that we were to decide on testing this bomb that my father was murdered.

The researchers

Stalin took no interest in the scientists who worked on the project. My father wrested from him audiences for these men, knowing that to them these meetings were infinitely more precious than decorations and prizes. For a long time Stalin refused to see them. He did not want to give away his ignorance of atomic matters. Helped by Kurchatov, my father composed regular reports on these matters, and Stalin eventually said he would like to meet the atomic scientists. It became a habit with him to receive my father and Kurchatov two or three times a month.

Among the researchers who surrounded my father there was not a single scientific official, only scientists who were enthusiasts for their discipline. Aleksandrov agreed to become President of the Academy of Sciences only when he felt that his career as a scientist was over.

It has been said that when my father was not satisfied, he would insult his collaborators in a very crude way. He did worse than that. He had a very mordant tongue and made fools of them, which was more wounding than if he had covered them with invective. My mother continually warned him that his tongue was too sharp. It has also been claimed that he threatened the scientists and used violence against them. These are nothing but inventions. Among all the thousands of people who worked on the nuclear project, not one was arrested or penalised.[15] It was said, contrariwise, that Beria protected bandits and British spies in order to attain his ends.

It was my father who engaged Sakharov. A special commission looked for young scientists of talent. They were invited to colloquies also attended by older scientists, and there a second selection was carried out. Sakharov was rejected by the physicists Tamm and Fock at this last stage, not for scientific reasons but on account of his quarrelsome nature, as Makhnev was to tell me. They considered that the trouble he would cause would outweigh any contributions he might make to the project. My father heard about this. He invited Sakharov and asked him what set him against his elders. Sakharov explained that they could not abandon their accepted ideas and disliked new approaches. My father liked him and included him in the research team. Sakharov and his young colleagues were even allowed to carry on with their original work. My father called on well-known scientists only in order to consult them. They took umbrage at the rapid promotion of their young colleagues and sent denunciations to Stalin. Abakumov used all these old academicians in his attempt to undermine my father. One day Stalin sent for my father and said: 'According to my sources, Khariton is a British spy. Here, Beria, read this.' And he handed to him a letter written by a group of physicists in Moscow. They said that Khariton had once visited Britain and so must be a spy. It was the usual delirium. 'I have thousands of papers of that sort,' my father replied. 'I guarantee that the men who work with me are honest and do their best. I answer for them.' 'State in writing that Khariton is not a spy,' replied Stalin, adding that my father would answer with his life for the truth of this. My father replied that he was ready to answer with his life for the whole nuclear project.

The physicist Kikoin was also very close to my father. One day this man's brother boasted in public that he had read Bukharin and Trotsky. He took advantage of his elder brother's position to allow himself to say that sort of thing. Of course our vigilant organs did not fail to report everything to Stalin, who thereupon sent for my father and accused him of protecting a Trotskyist. Brandishing the report of the search made at young Kikoin's place, Stalin had not realised that the person concerned was the physicist's younger brother. My father reacted and succeeded in calming him. A little later he ordered Sudoplatov to talk to Kikoin Junior. The conversation left Sudoplatov with a very bad impression. As he saw it, the young man was a pretentious snob.

My father had to fight the old scientists, especially those in Moscow, in order to have Kurchatov admitted to the Academy of Sciences. At first they rejected his candidature almost unanimously. My father sent for the Minister of Education, Kaftanov, and the President of the Academy, Vavilov, with whom he was on good terms, and ordered them to see to the matter. Vavilov assembled the academicians and told them that only those who were against Kurchatov's candidature would vote secretly. That looked like a practical joke, but the scientists understood that resistance was useless, and Kurchatov was duly elected in September 1943.

Research centres and laboratories were built near Moscow and at Sverdlovsk, Tomsk and Chelyabinsk. But Stalin grew greedier. After the explosion of the atomic bomb in 1949 he wanted to speed up the making of the hydrogen bomb and never ceased harassing my father. The bomb that we exploded in 1951 was no longer a mere copy of the Western bombs. Made with original Soviet technology, smaller and more powerful, it already employed the principle of fusion of hydrogen and paved the way for the H-bomb. When I say that I do not wish to detract in any way from Sakharov's merits, but facts have to be recognised.

My father was also responsible for a project which concerned atomic engines for submarines. We had invited to the USSR a German scientist who was a specialist in this question, Dr Pose. He had already made great progress in it. But it was only after Stalin's death that my father wanted to bring this project to fruition. Our first nuclear power station was built in my father's lifetime, though it did not begin to operate till after his death. It was an experimental power station in which he took great interest. For him, nuclear power was the energy of the future.

The men around my father

There were many around my father who hated the Soviet regime. He said that this did not matter. He chose people always for their capacities, and only competence counted in his eyes. Nor did he attach any importance to nationality. There has always been friction between Armenians and Georgians, yet his closest collaborators were Armenians. For instance, he brought Safrasian from Baku to be Vice-Minister of Construction.

He had put Petr Sharia in charge of ideology in Georgia. Sharia was a professor of philosophy, a specialist in Hegel, whom he tried to serve up with a Communist sauce. It must be said that he was a dubious Marxist. He detested and despised the Russians, considering that they had no civilisation and were parasitical on other peoples.[16] I liked him and often saw him in Moscow before the war.

While Stalin shared my father's philosophy where the selection of cadres was concerned, he was more cynical. He squeezed men like lemons and pitilessly scrapped them when they were no longer of use to him. He gave them a precise task to perform, then rejected them and did not hesitate to destroy those who knew too much. When it was proposed that he get rid of someone, as happened with Voznesensky, Stalin agreed. 'It will be your turn soon,' he thought, concerning the one who made the proposal. My father, on the other hand, did not look on his collaborators as favourites of the moment. If he was satisfied with them, he kept them.

From the beginning of his career he had adopted an original method for testing somebody he thought of recruiting. He asked the man to set out orally what his conception was of the tasks he was to take on, and then to put this in writing. If the candidate showed himself incapable of precision, he rejected him.[17] He systematically ruled out Party intriguers, considering that people who had no serious speciality could do nothing but harm and spoil paper. Even less could he endure Party fanatics who hid their incompetence behind slogans, and he used any pretext to show them the door. I remember that a Georgian friend came to him to complain of having to put up with sessions of Marxist-Leninist indoctrination. 'It's hard to endure that in wartime,' he said. And my father replied: 'Do you mean that in peacetime you find it endurable?' When he was blamed for having put a Menshevik in charge of the Georgian railways he retorted that if the post had been given to a Party cretin the trains would have ceased to run.[18] He often preferred to have around him people who did not like him, or even plain rascals, provided that they were efficient and intelligent. He did not hesitate to entrust them with important tasks. Nothing was worse in his eyes than a devoted imbecile. Of all his collaborators I think that Merkulov was closest, as he had, in a way, trained him. But he did not reveal to anyone what he was really thinking, not out of a spirit of dissimulation but simply because he was forced to measure out carefully the information he gave to each individual.

Serov

When my father was appointed to Moscow he insisted on being allowed to recruit youngsters fresh from the military academies. He wanted restore order in the NKVD with the help of people who had never in the past had anything to do with the organs. Serov was a product of the Frunze Military Academy, where he had studied intelligence work and, more particularly, Japan. He was a lively, athletic man with an open face, typically Russian with his alert grey eyes and his light auburn hair. He did not want to join the NKVD, preferring a military career. The NKVD already had a bad press at that time.

Serov told me that Vasilevsky had brought him to my father's notice. He had begged Vasilevsky not to authorise his transfer to the NKVD. In vain, for a week later Serov was received by my father, whom Vasilevsky had put in the picture. 'Tell me, Serov,' my father began. 'Why don't you want to work in the NKVD? Do you think that here you will meet only cannibals?'

'Since I know Japanese I thought that my place was rather in military intelligence,' Serov stammered.

'I'll tell you something. The hieroglyphics that you will have to decipher in the NKVD are infinitely more complex than the Japanese ones. Here you will read in Russian what you would never dream of finding in Japanese.'

Serov told me that he thought his initial resistance had won him favour with my father. When he began to have trouble with Khrushchev in the Ukraine my father said to him: 'You know Japanese. You are capable of resisting!'[19]

Zavenyagin

I can mention men for whom my father had no esteem but whom he made use of. This was the case with Zavenyagin, a good organiser, a specialist in metallurgy. As a person he was disagreeable, two-faced, morose, with unbounded ambition, and he hated everybody. These features of his character may have resulted from the ordeals he had suffered. He had been arrested in 1936 and in 1937 his wife had left him. Appreciating his capacity for work, my father put him in charge of the metallurgical combine at Vorkuta. Later he associated him with the atomic project, eventually entrusting him with its administrative management.

Ustinov

My father also supported Ustinov, an unassuming Leningrad engineer. When Stalin made him commissar for the arms industry he ordered the Vice-Commissar of that time, Mirzakhanov, to help him at the start. Ustinov revered my father and I don't think he was disappointed in him as he always helped me. He even rescued me from a scrape after a failed test which had given the Central Committee's rats a pretext to have a go at me. Nevertheless, throughout his life, his association with my father was a veritable Sword of Damocles hanging over him. After my father's fall they wanted to get rid of everyone who had worked with him. In the end, though, they had to resign themselves to calling on some of the men he had promoted. The country had to be kept going!

Vannikov

Vannikov, my father's deputy and the Number Two of the atomic project, was short and thick-set. Intelligent and kindly eyes brightened his big bald head. Three times a Hero of Socialist Labour, he had known many vicissitudes. When he was Commissar for Armaments he was arrested, in June 1941, and condemned to death. My father succeeded in preventing the worst from happening. When war broke out Stalin remembered him. 'What a pity, an intelligent man like him would have been useful today,' he remarked. 'Who knows, perhaps he may have survived somewhere in the camps,' said my father. Stalin was not deceived by this reply and blamed him for it later. A fortnight after this conversation Vannikov was presented to him and he was made Minister. My father thought highly of him. He was the very stereotype of the wise Jew. He liked me and I kept his confidences to myself. I did not want interference by my father in our relations. Vannikov, who came from Baku, was over 50, and I was 25 years old. He tried to educate me. 'What feelings do you think this regime arouses in me?' he asked. 'I hate it and yet I work for it. And I work honestly. What else can I do?' One day he said to me: 'I soon gave up my career in the Party. I went to Moscow, studied engineering while living from hand to mouth, and got a diploma. But I liked power at that time. Instead of shutting myself up in research I had to go into politics and end up as a Minister. Thereafter, I was done for. Our system creates only hypocrites. We are deprived of everything and we have no right to be ambitious. Stalin doesn't give a damn for wealth, only power interests him. Don't let yourself be impressed by his asceticism.' Stalin never overcame his antipathy for Vannikov. Every time he saw him he saw fit to remind the man that he regarded him as an opportunist and a scoundrel. He allowed himself to treat any people who had seen through him like that. At the time of the atomic project he tried to have another go at Vannikov. My father, who had had difficulty in fitting him into the commission, told him about this. He always kept his collaborators informed of Stalin's views, so that they should not overestimate his influence over Stalin and would be careful. There were, in fact, a lot of people who supposed that my father had only to whisper a few words in Georgian in Stalin's ear in order to get whatever he wanted from him. He never stopped telling them: 'You are under threat, and so am I, even more than you.'

Vannikov and Zavenyagin cordially hated each other but were always mutually polite. The former was Jewish, the latter a furious anti-Semite.

One day Vannikov warned my father against Zavenyagin. My father wanted to create, in connection with our universities, centres of research in physics and advanced technology, endowed with material resources, like the American and British universities. His plan was to establish them not only in Moscow, Leningrad and Sverdlovsk but also in Riga, Kaunas, Kiev, Lvov and in Caucasia. There was a good mathematics school in Georgia and the Armenians were well up in astrophysics. However, Zavenyagin was against this. According to him these republics were not trustworthy, and one of these days those research centres would fall into the hands of nationalists. My father replied in terms that decency forbids me to repeat. Vannikov and others wanted to take this opportunity to get rid of Zavenyagin. Nevertheless, my father refused to dismiss him and urged them to co-operate with him despite what he was like. It was useless for Vannikov to keep on about how Zavenyagin was a bad man, a Russian chauvinist. My father remained deaf to his pleas. Vannikov complained to me about this. 'What's he waiting for, to have a reason to dismiss him?' I replied, wittily: 'He has to keep the man, otherwise people will accuse him of having only Jews around him.'

'Your father told you that?'

'No.'

'He would be quite capable of it!'[20]

It was Vannikov who introduced Pervukhin to my father. He was another member of the special commission. He liked meals where there was plenty to drink, but usually showed himself extremely prudent, though Vannikov told me that when he was drunk he invented obscene jokes about Stalin and could never be stopped once he got going.

Tupolev

In 1938-40 my father saved from the camps and from death,[21] Tupolev,[22] Mints, Petlyakov and Korolev.[23] Tupolev liked the Communist regime no better than Vannikov did: it was, he said, a 'regime of dogs and skunks.' He dreamt of being a private businessman. 'Why can Sikorsky and Grigorevich [two of his *émigré* friends] be bosses in America while I am still a petty functionary paid by the state?' He told me that for two months my father had tried to make him repudiate his confessions and he, suspecting a trap, had stubbornly refused to do this. Fed up, my father said to him: 'Fine, if you want to remain a German spy, so be it. Tell me what you need in order to work. Here is a list of people who were arrested at the same time as you. Who do you need? Draw up a project for me, I'll present it to the government, and then I'll release you.'[24] This was in 1938, when my father had just arrived in Moscow. He was in a hurry as Yezhov was still shooting people right, left and centre. It was only two or three months later that he won the right to co-sign with Yezhov the lists of people condemned to death. Thereafter an order was not valid unless it bore both signatures. When Tupolev finished his aeroplane project my father showed it to Stalin. When he came out of prison Tupolev found it hard to readjust to freedom. 'I felt like a defenceless kitten thrown out into the street,' he told me. He also confided in me: 'I don't care a damn for the Soviet regime. I work only for your father … You don't realise it, but he runs enormous risks. All those bastards in the Politburo are only waiting for a chance to squash him.' Tupolev did not mince his words. He did not crawl before Stalin, whom he had not forgiven. 'That good-for-nothing hasn't learnt a thing,' said Stalin to my father. Vannikov was more cunning and knew how to put on an act.

Tupolev changed as he grew older. The man who in 1959 accompanied Khrushchev to the United States was no longer the same. When I saw him on his return, he thought he needed to justify himself. Was he sincere? In his position he could have been. 'Khrushchev dragged me along with him so as to be sure that his plane wouldn't fall to pieces during the flight.' He told me how, on the journey, Khrushchev kept pestering the writer Sholokhov to write a book in praise of him. But the writer took refuge in his alcoholic torpor. Khrushchev came back at him. 'Well, then, write something about that blackguard Beria.' Sholokhov eventually gave in and, with great difficulty, wrote one or two chapters before his inspiration dried up. Referring to Khrushchev, Adzhubei and the rest, old Tupolev said: 'They are the same scoundrels as before, but of inferior calibre.'

Mints

My father thought well of Academician Mints, a specialist in radio-communications – not to be confused with the historian of the same name. He teased him. 'When I think that we're having to search for economists, and I've got Mints under my hand. A real Morgan, a born banker. He's a scientist in spite of himself. Actually he'd prefer to work at something other than science.' Mints praised private property to me. He also talked about the Bund, about Jewish organisations. He even showed me documents dealing with the kibbutzim which Golda Meir was to describe to us later.

The scientists

Most of my father's collaborators tried to make me think. A specialist in building missiles, I was involved in the nuclear project when the time came to put nose-cones on these missiles. The scientists were fond of me. They saw that I was not a corrupt young man and that I was interested in what I was doing. Looking back, I am amazed at how frankly spoken some of them were. They were even imprudent, unless it was that they thought my father shared their views. I am glad that they opened my eyes on to the world around me. Thus, Kurchatov, a man very close to my father, said to me: 'We are working on an atomic bomb. I am doing this willingly, unlike those American scientists who break out into humanitarian jeremiads.

But all of us need to be clearly aware of the consequences of this weapon. From now on may God preserve us from war.' And he read me a Hindu poem which described the atomic bomb. This was the first time anyone had broached this subject to me. Previously I had not thought about these questions. I now began to ponder on the fate of civilisations.

I was able, after my father's death, to judge the real esteem that the scientists felt for him. It was they who practically saved my life. They got me out of prison, then supported me morally and offered me material help, which I declined. I have never had an exaggerated idea of my talents and realised that this solicitude for me merely reflected their attachment to my father. They talked to me a lot about him after his death. Of course they wanted to console me, but I think they meant what they said. They described my father as a man of exceptional talent who was able to grasp instantly the problems his work presented. They considered him a peerless organiser who did not force people to work from fear of repressions, as was later alleged, but who, on the contrary, passed his enthusiasm on to them. He protected his collaborators from Party intrigues and tyranny and sheltered them from the MGB. In the sectors of industry that came under him, particularly the military complex, he saw to it that Party functionaries kept their mouths shut. The Party organisations had to be satisfied with mumbling their way through the *Short History*, without interfering with anything else. Kurchatov told me, after my father's death, about an amusing episode. He had the idea of making the Party meetings that were held in his institute more interesting. Since they had to be held, why not combine the useful with the unavoidable? And these meetings were devoted to Kant, among others. Denunciations rained down, so that my father sent for him. 'Stop studying Kant. Dive into the writings of Suslov and the other cretins. Try to understand what country you are living in!' he said. 'He treated us like children,' Kurchatov told me, 'because we were, in fact, very naïve.'

When I asked my father how men like Tupolev, who had been in prison, were able to work for the Soviet regime, he answered: 'They hate it, but they are scientists, they can't not work. Man needs to create, it helps him to shut his eyes to what he would rather not see. His soul finds peace only when he absorbs himself totally in his work. And since they are Russians they believe they are serving their country.' Subsequently I convinced myself of the truth of his judgement. It is true that, if you want to bring something to fruition, it is impossible not to do that. And if I had not been educated by my mother, the influence of Russian culture would have predominated in me.

I should like to emphasise one last aspect of my father's policy in the scientific domain. He was always keen on developing the periphery of the Soviet empire. In that connection, I was given a description of the following scene. One of his Russian collaborators, who had been given the task of setting up an institute of nuclear physics in one of the Baltic republics, came to make his report. My father asked what researchers he had recruited. The man presented a list of Russian names. 'Where did you find these men?' my father asked.

'I took them with me,' the man replied. My father became extremely angry. 'Imbecile! I told you to select students from the local universities. If their education is inadequate, let them go on courses in Moscow and Leningrad.'

'But I found no one ...'

'Don't lie to me. You are behaving like a typical Russian. You distrust other peoples.' My father was literally beside himself. I was not present at this scene. My father refrained from reprimanding his subordinates in the presence of third parties. He would never have let himself go before me.

Post-war expectations

My memories of the immediate post-war period contain little of political interest. I had to complete my studies at the Military Academy. I dreamt of building a missile for use against aircraft-carriers and examined closely all the documents we had obtained from the Germans and the British. I married and started a family. It was only in 1948-49 that my work led me to mix with our top military hierarchy and my horizon was widened.

Attempts at reform

After the war my father was made Deputy Chairman of the Council of Ministers and given responsibility for the sectors of coal, oil and metallurgy, for heavy industry and for the military-industrial complex. He even took charge of the production of watches, because he adored all mechanisms, and he made our industry learn from the Swiss models. If the Swiss progressed further and improved their production, we should be left marking time.

My father surrounded himself with the young leaders of industry who had, along with him, operated the war economy. They knew that the country had been bled white. We had neither normal resources of energy, nor a machine-building sector worthy of the name, nor any electronic industry. Our entire economy was cracking up. And we could no longer require our young people, now returned from Europe, to go on living in filthy holes. 'People have nothing more now but their dirty, ragged trousers,' said my father. They must be given something of their own, be it a house or a bit of land, and a little money. Nobody can live forever on revolutionary enthusiasm!' It was absolutely imperative to raise the standard of living, even if only modestly. To that end it was indispensable to release people from serfdom, to renounce the imperial Russophile policy and to restore the national states in the USSR. In short, reforms were needed. My father thought that so long as we did not have the bomb, he could try to get his proposals accepted by Stalin. At the end of 1945 he began to press Stalin to come round to his ideas.[25]

As he regarded Party congresses as superfluous, Stalin imposed his will without going through that formal stage, and took no account of the Party's apparatus[26] – which did not stop him from relying on it and regarding it as his fief. My father pointed out to him how harmful it was to retain, operating in parallel, the apparatus of the Party and that of the government. The economy suffered the consequences. It was abnormal that a Party cadre should take decisions and the ministerial functionary charged with implementing them should bear responsibility for them. The situation had become intolerable. The Party cadres informed on the governmental cadres and the latter objected that they had only carried out orders that came from the Party. For a time Stalin was willing to listen to observations of this sort, until the disgracing in 1949 of Voznesensky. He had shared my father's views on the economy and supplied him with examples to illustrate the harmful effect of interference by the Party in the economy.

Before handing the NKVD over to Kruglov in December 1945 my father wanted to see a number of reforms realised, such as separation of the Gulag from the NKVD. He did not have the time. I heard him talk of these plans with Kruglov. He said that it would be hard for him to put them into practice and advised him to try to seek help from the Party organs. Kruglov's attempt at reform came to naught.

My father also wanted to do away with the passport system.[27] However, this produced a strong protest from the Party. The Communist functionaries realised that this measure would toll the knell of the collective farm system. As soon as this became possible, the peasants would flee from the collective farms. My father then tried to abolish the collective farms in certain regions of the USSR so as to enable the peasants to breathe. 'If we must have collective farms,' he said, 'then at least refrain from imposing them on the Western Ukraine, the Baltic provinces or Georgia.' But Malenkov withheld his support. This measure went against the whole system whereby agriculture was kept under the thumb of the Party's organs.

Where industry was concerned, my father defended his reform plans more energetically and he enjoyed wider support. The Council of Ministers and the heads of Gosplan understood very well that centralised methods of managing the economy, which had perhaps been justified in the first years of the Soviet regime, had become anachronisms. They appreciated that we were holding back our economic development.

Our youth had seen Europe

After all, my father thought, the status of victor over Fascism ought fully to satisfy Stalin's pride, and he ought henceforth to be able to tolerate a few concessions, as he had done during the war. Had he not dissolved the Comintern? Had he not mitigated religious persecution? Had he not become sensitive to international public opinion? Although my father had lost his youthful illusions after Katyn and had understood that Stalin never took account of the opinions of those close to him, even if he listened attentively to them, he nevertheless tried, right to the end, to get him to share his views. He was convinced that the only changes possible in the USSR would be those to which the dictator had consented, for a palace revolution was unthinkable. Stalin's prestige was so great and the power of his apparatus so unlimited that one could not dream of fighting against them by normal methods. And then my father found another reason for hope. Many Soviet citizens had seen free Europe. Our soldiers, in rags, had observed that European countries ruined by the war were living better than their own victorious motherland. These young people would open their eyes and rise up to demand a normal life such as they had glimpsed in the conquered countries. In his struggle against the Party my father thought that he would find support in that army returned from abroad. Stalin would have to agree to reform, willy-nilly, under pressure from these millions of soldiers who had been in Germany, Hungary and Austria. His hopes were dashed. The soldiers of the Red Army, after plundering and raping, went back submissively to their prison cell. There was not even the slightest movement to secure a better standard of living, except perhaps in the non-Russian areas. Those who understood the need to change the economy and our way of life in order to draw nearer to civilisation received no support from the Russian masses. Worse, they came up against their lack of understanding. My father concluded that there was nothing to be got from that people. What would he say now?

The atomic scientists who were close to him told me, long after his death, that he shared with them his astonishment at this time. 'Is it possible that around you there is no sign of rising discontent?' 'Lavrenti Pavlovich, you are dreaming,' they replied. 'Fear has conditioned their brains. For twenty years people have been so terrorised that now they are afraid of their own shadows.' My father did not know the real situation because he kept company with men like Vannikov, whose thinking had not been frozen by fear. He imagined that fear had merely fostered opportunism – he did not realise that it had also affected people's intelligence. He underestimated the hypnotic effects of terror. I have seen men transform themselves in Stalin's presence. Their eyes went glassy, they even became speechless. I think that today, still, we are suffering the consequences of that fear.

The cold shower

Stalin was perfectly well aware of what the people expected. He put those who returned from Europe under surveillance. Acting with his usual cunning he began by presenting as traitors prisoners-of-war and people who had lived under German occupation. He brought continual pressure to bear on them to ensure that they would not be tempted to tell what they had seen. At the same time he made some concessions, launched a few trial balloons. He found that he could win if he based himself on Russian chauvinism, and so was able to persevere in his policy after the war.

My father had to give up his illusions. Stalin evidently meant to persist in his errors. In February 1946 he announced a programme providing for reinforcement of our war economy and a confrontation with the capitalists, whereas even our military knew that the people were tired of fighting. It was clear that repressions would be resumed, as the struggle for the succession to Stalin became ever more furious.[28] The ideologists took advantage of this to lift their heads again. My father kept away from these intrigues, being convinced that a Georgian had no chance of succeeding Stalin. The first wave of repression affected the aircraft industry[29] and the economic cadres. This was a blow struck to neutralise Malenkov, who was in a fair way to supplanting Zhdanov in closeness to Stalin. Molotov, with his Jewish wife, was no longer regarded as a danger by the pretenders. In any case, he was not possessed by the same thirst for power as the others. He was the only one of them who sincerely wept for Stalin when he died. He took his setbacks calmly and always had the air of not worrying about them.

In May 1946 Zhdanov had Malenkov sent to Central Asia.[30] His removal from the scene enabled the ideological apparatus to redouble its pressure. As spokesman for the anti-governmental groups, Zhdanov was responsible for cultural policy and relations with the intelligentsia. No doubt my father had few illusions about Malenkov, but he thought he could control him, and it was through Malenkov that my father acted on the Party apparatus. By sending Malenkov away they wanted to deprive him of that possibility, so my father made great efforts to bring him back to Moscow.[31] Stalin teased him about this: 'Why are you taking so much trouble for that imbecile? You'll be the first to be betrayed by him.' My father thought that Stalin wanted to sow discord between them but, in fact, he had perceived Malenkov's true nature. Stalin agreed promptly to recall Malenkov to Moscow, to the Central Committee's Secretariat, because Zhdanov was beginning to take himself for the hub of the universe. Did he not propose, in February 1947, to draw up the agenda for the next Party congress? Stalin found that he was not lacking in cheek. The rule was for the General Secretary to chair the commission which prepared the agenda. But he merely said, between clenched teeth: 'Very well, let him do that. We will simply criticise what he produces.' Stalin was irritated when he saw a member of his circle playing a prominent role, even when it was a matter of committing infamies.

The exiling of Malenkov made my father realise that the policy he proposed had been rejected. But at that time he enjoyed such strong support in the military-industrial complex and among some of the military that it seemed difficult to get rid of him without first compromising his popularity in those circles and in Georgia, Armenia and Azerbaijan. He set himself to await Stalin's death, concerned only to survive until then, sheltered in the niche made available for him by the nuclear project and the arms industry.

In 1946 I had been given the job of conducting courses of political indoctrination for first-year students at the Academy. I had to explain to them
the progressive character of our foreign policy. In order to make my talks
less boring I was so rash as to read the Western press and to refer to it.
That was how, one day, I explained how we had dropped the Greek
Communists as the result of an agreement with Churchill. Naturally, the
political section mentioned this to the Leningrad Party organisation,
though without naming the guilty man. The Party chiefs made a terrible
row about this until they learnt the name of the troublemaker. Kuznetsov
sent for me urgently. He talked to me about this and that, then said,
straight out: 'What got into you to give these political lectures?'

'What do you mean? I did all I could to avoid giving them. It's a chore
the Party has imposed on me.'

'You see how you have departed from the theses you were to expound,'
he said, showing me a paper. 'What are we to do now?'

Eventually he found the solution. He went to the Academy and held a
Party meeting, restricted to a small committee. I then understood how
perfectly the machine worked. Had I been just anybody they would have
expelled me on the spot and I should have ended up in the Kurile Islands.
I grasped at last the nature of the dictatorship of the proletariat, which
does not say much for my perspicacity. I had a comrade who was no good
at mathematics, but was a giant when it came to Marxism-Leninism. I did
his maths homework for him, and in return he showed me all the tricks
for passing my exams in Marxism-Leninism. He was such a virtuoso in
this sphere that we always tried to be present at his vivas. One day when
the examiner faced him with a poser to which he had to reply he held forth
on Stalin's strategical genius during the battle of Stalingrad, comparing it
with Hannibal's in the battle of Cannae. The examiners stayed silent,
while we shook our sides with laughter.

I was disgusted by the hypocrisy all round me. Drunkards and
debauchees looking as if butter wouldn't melt in their mouths discoursed
learnedly on how useful it was to go to the theatre and to read the classics.
When, later, I was director of an institute, I had again to deal with this
situation. My deputies were summoned to the Central Committee to listen
to this sort of nonsense (they also wanted to discover what spirit I
promoted in the institute). These men who were constantly overworked
were going to lose half a day in order to listen to a semi-literate
Communist instructor talking about culture and the latest play to be
announced and to answer questions such as: 'Do you discuss politics with
the head of your institute? Do you sometimes feel doubt over the need to
create this or that weapon?' My colleagues were sharp and replied in the
right way: 'Why should we be worried when the weapons we are making
are purely defensive?' They attacked particularly my friend Shabanov, an
exceptionally intelligent man, who later became Vice-Minister of
Armaments under Ustinov. The head of the political section at my institute was ordered to reprimand him because he did not go to the theatre. I

counter-attacked by threatening to accuse the bureaucrat of trying to distract these people from their work. It was clear that if I gave way on this point we should never again have a minute's peace.

Change in the special services

In 1943 Stalin had put Merkulov at the head of State Security. He was one of those closest to my father, who had expressly advised him never to carry out orders given orally. He should demand written instructions and try to ensure that these came not just from Stalin but from the Politburo as a whole.[32] If the worst came to the worst, he must see to it that written evidence proving that the initiative did not come from him was available in Poskrebyshev's Secretariat.

Having imagined that everyone whom he had raised to power was devoted to him, Stalin found that Merkulov was not submissive enough for his taste, since he opposed the most monstrous measures he was called on to apply.[33] Accordingly, he was dismissed on May 1946 and replaced by Abakumov,[34] who lacked such scruples. My father nevertheless managed to save his life. Abakumov did not dare take steps against Merkulov, possibly fearing that Stalin and my father might have some understanding behind his back. You never knew with those Georgians! Nevertheless, Stalin deprived my father of any right to oversee the intelligence services, or at least those which belonged to the apparatus, since he retained his personal network. And while fiascos accumulated in the official network once he had been removed from it, there was not the slightest falling-off among the men who were directly associated with him. He was against the fragmentation of our special services. From his point of view nothing good could come of it. Stalin soon perceived that our services were rapidly going to the bad. He now had only one idea – to redress the situation, but without appealing to Beria.

In the spring of 1947 he decided to merge the intelligence organs of the MGB with military intelligence in an information committee which he entrusted to the faithful Molotov so as to be able to control it directly. This proved a catastrophe. All the riff-raff in the Party involved themselves in intelligence work and imagined themselves up to it. My father rejoiced: it was a long time since I had seen him so cheerful. He never ceased being sarcastic about 'agent Vyshinsky' and 'resident Molotov.' As he saw it, there could be nothing stupider than to bring these people together in a single organisation. He prophesied a series of disasters. The odds were that this new organisation would try to show what it was capable of by activating the networks, thereby alerting the West's counter-espionage services. And this was just what happened.[35] That was the reason for the reverses we suffered at that time, not any improvement in the American and British services. A moment came when Vyshinsky found himself appointed head of the information committee. Terrified, he overwhelmed Stalin with entreaties to let him go to a different job. Before Stalin

Vyshinsky cringed even more than Molotov, if that were possible. The latter did sometimes dare to take the initiative: with Vyshinsky no question of that.

My marriage

My mother did not much approve of my marriage in 1946, which she thought too early, but she was pleased that I was in love and safe from Svetlana. 'I wanted you to marry a Georgian girl,' she told me later, 'though I gladly accepted your wife. To tell the truth, I had already found you a fiancée of good family. But you did as you wished.' I met Marfa, Gorky's granddaughter, before the war, through Svetlana, who was in the same class at school. I thrashed boys who were annoying her during breaktime. I liked her because she was dainty and, then, did not talk much. When my studies were over I went to my father and said I wanted to get married. He asked with whom, but, when he heard the answer he at once added: 'She's a good girl. But Iosif Vissarionovich won't like your getting connected with that family. It's for you to decide: I'm only warning you. He may even send for you and ask what's got into you.'

'Why?'

'You must know that Gorky was not at all like the way he is depicted nowadays. He hated the Bolshevik dictatorship. He was a Russian patriot who had supported the revolutionary movement before the revolution. And even though he wrote "if the enemy does not surrender he is destroyed," he did have other opinions.'

'What do you mean?'

'How can I explain it to you? Let's say that he rejected dictatorship and violence set up as a system.' In short, though Gorky had been presented as an apostle of Communism, Stalin distrusted those connected with him. We did not have a normal wedding. I simply asked the commander of my father's guard to be our witness. He just asked: 'Lavrenti Pavlovich knows about this?'

'Of course.'

'You're not lying to me?'

'Ask my mother.' And he did!

The day we were married there was a military parade which we attended. All the Kremlin elite were present. These people knew Marfa but did not consider her as belonging to our world. After all, she was only Gorky's granddaughter. Writers and artists were an inferior species. Svetlana alone did not share this snobbery, being influenced by her father, who, outwardly, showed great deference to the intelligentsia. They asked me why I had brought Marfa. 'Because she's my wife.' She came with her little suitcase to settle in with me. My father received her kindly and even suggested we had a meal. So we celebrated our wedding strictly *en famille*. My father was pleased with our discretion, as he foresaw Stalin's disapproval.

When she learnt of my marriage Svetlana made a scene. I reminded her vainly that she had herself just married and had children, and that I had met my future wife through her. She told me that her father was furious. I retorted: 'If he had wanted me to marry you, he would have summoned me and ordered me to. I could only have obeyed. So, he won't say anything.' A year passed, and Stalin invited me to his *dacha* with my mother. My father and Malenkov were to join us later. Stalin liked walking and asked me to accompany him. As usual he wanted to pump me. He began by asking me about certain scientists. When I replied I kept in mind my father's warning never to say anything bad about anyone, even if I thought it, because one did not know what use Stalin might make of it. Then he changed his subject: 'Do you know your wife's family?' I replied that I did not and told him how I had met her through Svetlana. He then told me what he thought of that family: 'Gorky himself was not bad in his way. But what a lot of anti-Soviet people he had around him! Think about that. Don't fall under your wife's influence.'

'But she is quite non-political.'

'I know that. But I regard this marriage as a disloyal act on your part. Not disloyal to me but to the Soviet state. Was it perhaps an idea forced on you by your father?' he concluded; always direct and abrupt in such connections.

'No, I didn't even consult him on the subject.'

'You want me to believe that you didn't even speak to him about it?'

I decided not to mention my conversation with my father. Stalin resumed: 'I see your marriage as a move to establish links with the oppositionist Russian intelligentsia.' This idea had never even crossed my mind. My wife was pretty, plump like a quail, but not very intelligent and with a rather weak character, as I was to discover later. Stalin went on: 'Your mother would never have done that. She is a nationalist and an aristocrat. It must be your father who urged you into this marriage, so as to infiltrate the Russian intelligentsia.'

'Iosif Vissarionovich,' I replied. 'The guilty one is Svetlana. I met my wife at your place, and it was Svetlana who brought her. We fell in love. Svetlana knew it. And when I finished my studies Svetlana was married.'

I deliberately stressed that. Stalin grew very angry. 'You never breathed a word about it to Svetlana, she told me that herself.' Then he looked at me and changed completely. 'Don't take any notice, old people are always peevish. But tell your mother what I said. As for Marfochhka, I saw her grow up. I understand you. I should like to give your wife a present. Do you think she'd like a book?' He never missed a trick. Knowing that Marfa was not exactly brilliant, he wanted to denigrate someone who was dear to me. Eventually he gave her a book of reproductions of pictures in the Hermitage, and me a Russian translation of Shota Rustaveli, with a dedication. The translator was a Georgian nationalist philosopher whom my mother wanted to appoint as my tutor. He had been arrested and, as he did not conceal his opinions, my father failed to get him out of prison. He therefore suggested that he undertake a new Russian translation of *The Knight in the Tiger's Skin* and managed, after showing the man's work to Stalin, to improve the conditions in which he was held. Stalin had personally corrected the translation. His dedication of the book read: 'You would do better to form bonds with the Georgian intelligentsia!' I showed this to my father. He burst out laughing. 'That's Iosif Vissarionovich for you. Even there he couldn't resist the temptation to make a point.' Nothing could shake Stalin's conviction that it was my father who had pushed me into marrying Marfa. Anyway, there was never any way of making him give up anything.

The listening devices

Dissatisfied with my father, Stalin had us spied on more than ever after the war. Vasilev, a specialist in listening devices linked to the Central Committee, warned us: 'Your house is bugged.' My mother had been under surveillance since the beginning of the war. A young assistant had confessed to her one day that she had been ordered to report everything she did to the section of the Central Committee that dealt with surveillance of the country's leaders.

When Abakumov took charge of State Security, Makhnev warned me personally that my wife and I were also bugged. 'Your wife's grandmother invites all sorts of swine. I know that she loves you and you love her. Try to put her on her guard.' She had indeed welcomed to her home four families who were each more open than the next to criticism from the Soviet standpoint. Former Trotskyists, former Bukharinists, a real nest of counter-revolutionaries. She was a remarkable woman.

Makhnev revealed to me that Abakumov had tried, by means of threats, to turn him into an informer. He told my father, who said he should tell me himself. 'I won't say anything to him.' I then believed that I was being played with as a mouse is played with by a cat. When I asked my father why he had not himself passed on to me the message from Makhnev, he replied: 'What guarantee have we that he isn't an informer for Abakumov?' And he was talking about one of his closest collaborators! He was doubly careful when I and my family were involved. He advised me to invite Ekaterina Pavlovna, my wife's grandmother, to live with us, which I did, making it seem that the initiative came from Marfa.

I must say that I found it extremely disagreeable to know that I was being bugged, day and night, including in my bedroom and engaged in conjugal intimacy. I wanted to remove the microphones, but my father dissuaded me. 'They'll think you have something to conceal. Don't do anything. On the contrary, utter abuse now and again.' He was not bothered, even though some of his conversations took place only in the open air. In private he bad-mouthed Stalin, to the point that my mother took fright: 'Be careful, you know that walls have ears.' He replied, as usual: 'If I spoke differently they would be suspicious.' Another time he told her:

'You remember our conversation the other day? Well, Iosif Vissarionovich knows about it already. I noticed that he looked at me reproachfully. I must have upset him.' Such were the little games played between my father and Stalin.

Disillusionment

Churchill's project of a European union[1] had greatly attracted my father, though he thought it hardly realisable, because of the strength of national feeling in the European states. 'Germany, France, continental Europe will form a united economic whole,' he said one day. 'But that doesn't mean that each country will lose its sovereignty. National feeling is one of the most powerful of feelings, and hundreds of years will have to pass before the frontiers disappear. Actually, they are dug so deep that perhaps they will never be obliterated.' While my father thought it reasonable for the countries of Europe to unite their economic interests, the Soviet Union, according to him, needed to go in the opposite direction. The country was already united economically, but the nations ought to be revived. And if Europe saw the Soviet Union adopting a correct policy it would turn not against us but against the USA. Not that my father was hostile to the latter. But in his eyes agreement between Western Europe and the Soviet Union was more important than anything else. When this was accomplished the Americans would leave Europe.

He did not favour the Sovietisation of Europe. He had studied history well and was sure that all the empires would disappear one day. 'See how intelligently organised the British Empire was and what political experience the British had! In spite of which, that empire has collapsed. This was inevitable, moreover. In the next 25 years the Europeans are going to have to give up their colonies,' he explained. As for the Soviet Union, he thought that the only desirable system was a voluntary union, and that, in order to arrive at that, it was necessary to proceed step by step: first of all, emancipate the republics economically, then make them independent states, united by their economy. Regarding the countries of Central Europe he did not want them to become burdens on our economy; he wanted them, on the contrary, to be able to help us. For this reason he was categorically against the Red Army continuing to occupy these countries. The presence of those troops was indeed necessary if our intention was to plunder, but if we wanted to make these countries our friends and economic supports for the Soviet Union, we must give up pillage. As my father saw it, these states could perfectly well remain bourgeois, provided they worked for us. In fact, non-Communist governments economically oriented on the USSR were even preferable, and they would certainly be easier to control than Socialist or Communist governments.

Project for Central Europe

My father would have liked to form two blocs, uniting the neutral countries of Central and Eastern Europe – one around Poland, the other around Dimitrov's Bulgaria and Tito's Yugoslavia. In his mind this arrangement should be completed by a unified and non-Socialist Germany. This was the idea he had suggested to the men who later tried to put it into effect. But none of those on whom he had relied showed sufficient strength of character to oppose Stalin.

My father looked for men capable of implementing his policy. This was no easy task, especially as they would need to be approved by Stalin. The Ministers of Information in the peoples' democracies had links with my father: during the war he had put his men into the Radio Committee formerly attached to the Comintern.[2] Now, though all were more or less favourable to Socialism, none inclined towards Bolshevism, which made a big difference. They wanted a community of Socialist states, but these states had to be democratic and free from domination by the USA. My father also relied on the resistance fighters who had remained in their own countries. He thought that Dimitrov would understand that we should not implant communism by force in Bulgaria, and that he had status enough to carry out that policy. The Hungarian Nagy, the Czech Slansky and the entire Yugoslav group of Tito, Djilas and Rankoviæ had endorsed his view but most of them let him down. Togliatti and Dimitrov frequently came to see us, but I never saw Thorez, the French Communist leader, at our house. My father did not think much of him. Another he could not endure was Jacques Duclos, who reminded him of Rákosi: 'reptiles,' he called them.

Romania

So long as he was commander-in-chief of our forces in Romania, Tolbukhin applied the policy advocated by my father, who counted on support from certain Romanian officers (Romania had an excellent officer corps). Tolbukhin had established contacts among these men. He and some others even managed to persuade Stalin to award the Order of Victory to King Michael. But the Romanian Communists found nothing more intelligent to do than to complain to Stalin that 'reactionary anti-Soviet military men connected with Britain are coming to power.'[3] They were, of course, unaware that my father was behind this policy. He was shaken by Tolbukhin's death because this meant he now had nobody to put his policy into practice. The task was going to be difficult in Romania, where the Communists, few in numbers, were fanatical. I think my father had some hope of the Minister of Finance, V. Luka, who later fell victim to the purges. When Transylvania was transferred to Romania in March 1945 he regretted that a first breach had opened in the alliance of Balkan and Central European countries that he wanted to see.

Hungary

I well remember the Hungarians Nagy, Kadar and Rajk. They were Communists but they understood that Communism could not sit on bayonets in their country. Some agreed with the idea of a coalition with the Social Democrats, which would have allowed them to get close to Austria.[4] My father was very friendly with Imre Nagy. He had been evacuated to Georgia during the war and had enjoyed his stay! It is said that he had behaved badly when he was in the Comintern.[5] I never heard my father say anything about that. He simply told me that Nagy was one of the people on whom he could rely in carrying out his plans. Lena Sturua, who worked in the Radio Committee during the war, told me what Nagy thought of my father. 'He thinks in a modern way. He's not at all like the Comintern people.'

Yugoslavia

In Yugoslavia, my father's networks and those of the British had collaborated with Tito during the war. My father followed with attention the affairs of that country. One day, when the Yugoslav leader Kardelj complained to him about Tito's tyrannical character, he replied: 'Don't you think that we are all in the same boat?' He took care to add, however, that heads of state who mattered always had negative sides. Rankoviæ, the head of Yugoslav security, was more primitive than Kardelj, but Tito had total confidence in him, which was why he often acted as intermediary between Tito and my father.

Poland

My father wanted to see a strong Poland, possibly because he had many agents there. He cultivated relations with the Polish Catholics in the hope of reaching, through them, the Catholics of Germany. He tried to use Prince Radziwill[6] and put him into the Ministry of Foreign Affairs. He had saved the Prince's life and hoped to make him an agent of influence. Rich and noble, Radziwill had excellent relations with the Germans and the Americans, including business contacts with Harriman. However, Stalin did not agree. Neither did the British, because the Prince had compromised with the Germans. There was also Gomulka,[7] who fell into disgrace in 1949. To lead the Polish Communist Party Stalin chose Bierut, a tank of the Russian type, crushing everything in its path.

My father had difficulty in persuading Stalin not to impose collectivisation in Poland. He made him understand, though, that the Polish intelligentsia would never be pro-Soviet and that, consequently, we could not allow ourselves to do without any support we could find among the people.

Czechoslovakia

In Czechoslovakia my father could rely on a number of leaders – those, for example, who disapproved of the expulsion of the Sudeten Germans in 1945.[8] In his eyes, Beneš was not quite with it, unable to arrange for his escape from Czechoslovakia after the Germans' coup: 'He wasn't even capable of making sure of an aeroplane.' Beneš was at heart with the West, flexible and ready to make concessions, even if he did not inwardly agree with them, for he was a democrat and not a Soviet agent, as Sudoplatov suggests. He played with the British, the French and us. He and Masaryk had not forgotten Munich and were ready to deal with the Soviet Union rather than with France or Britain, so long as it did not seize them by the throat. Beneš's chief fault was that he was self-infatuated and did not realise in time what his limitations were.[9] My father, who never wanted to do business with people suffering from illusions as to their real abilities, had noticed this fault in him from the outset. Having respect only for people who were able to make themselves respected, he also wrote off Masaryk, the Minister of Foreign Affairs as a weak man who followed the policy of the USSR.[10]

My father did not favour the Communist coup d'état in Prague in February 1948, even though his men had to take part in it, since Stalin had so decided. One of his Czech agents told me: 'Your father did not encourage Gottwald[11] to carry out that coup d'état.' For my father, Gottwald was merely a pawn. On the other hand he later thought well of the head of the Czech Government, Zapotocky.[12] I was friendly with General Ludvik Svoboda. He came to relax on the shores of the Black Sea and we took walks together. My father knew him well[13] and approved of my association with him. Svoboda was a very artless man. When, later, I travelled in Czechoslovakia I always went to see him.[14] I also met Fierlinger,[15] a slimy character. He resembled an Austrian civil servant. He was never invited to our place.

Struggle for influence in the Kremlin

Some of the military shared my father's ideas, as also did a few Party leaders, mostly those from the Baltic region, Caucasia and the Western Ukraine. These men understood the concept of the nation, but such were very rare in the Party apparatus, which was full of Russian chauvinists. The *apparatchiks* of the economy supported my father.[16] Saburov, Pervukhin, Tevosian, Ustinov and Voznesensky favoured his views. Later, Saburov even composed a plan for the progressive integration of the countries of Eastern Europe into a united economic whole. However, it would be wrong to speak of a tendency. Any political or economic proposal that ran contrary to the Party line entailed arrest. These conceptions were rejected by the Party's leaders and the Marshals (except Zhukov and Vasilevsky.) They considered that we absolutely must retain at least three or four hundred divisions.

Stalin chose cold war

Victory had confirmed Stalin in his assurance that his policy was the right one. Had he not built Socialism in one country and won a world war? In 1945 he thought that he already controlled Europe.[17] When he perceived that the states of Central Europe had been surrendered to him he had no longer hesitated, but sided with the other Party leaders. Stalin and Molotov looked on Europe as conquered territory, to the point that any non-Communist regime, in Poland or elsewhere, became for them out of the question.[18] Curiously, Stalin had, nevertheless, only contempt for the governments he installed in the peoples' democracies. He spoke of those Communists who had taken refuge in Moscow as 'column-dodgers.' Yet it was he who ordered the elimination of the real resistance fighters, those who, like the Yugoslavs, were unwilling to copy the Soviet model and wished to retain links with the West. There was this difference, though: Yugoslavia was not occupied by our troops.

Stalin refused to listen to my father and those who advised against making enemies of the British. He was allergic to Bevin, doubtless under the influence of Molotov, who had had sharp clashes with the British minister. In that connection my father, who, like all the members of the government, received the despatches of the Tass Agency, felt obvious pleasure when he came upon accounts of how Molotov got what was coming to him from Bevin. He read them to my mother: 'Vyacheslav has had a ticking-off again. It's plain to see that Bevin is no degenerate aristocrat but a man of the people, as aggressive as our lot.'

Truman showed himself as weak in Europe, as Roosevelt had been. I once asked my father what would happen if the Americans were to try to dislodge us by force from Central Europe. 'We should give up these states without a fight,' he replied. At that time he was still of the opinion that Stalin would do everything to avoid war: only from 1950 did the situation change. My father was astonished at the West's policy. Why had they taken so long to land in Normandy after renouncing a landing in the Balkans? 'Churchill ought to have pushed for the landing in France as soon as it became clear that Roosevelt and Stalin did not want the Balkan project. If the Westerners had landed a few months earlier they would have got to Poland while we were still far to the east,' he said. 'Though they realise what consequences follow from their mistakes they shrink from accepting minor sacrifices, and do not see that they risk paying dear for that.' He made these remarks in a perfectly objective tone, as though putting himself theoretically in the place of the Westerners, without revealing his own opinion.

For the moment, Stalin did not want to engage in another war, but he settled in wherever he had been able to advance. In my view, he was less interested in Marxist doctrine and more concerned to annex territory. Communists simply seemed to him the best instrument of control. He therefore renounced, for the time being, his plans for the military conquest of Europe even though he strengthened our army, counting on having his hands free when the day came when he would possess the atom bomb. As always when he came up against an obstacle, he at once worked out another strategy that would make it possible for him to continue advancing towards his fundamental objective. He passed from direct confrontation to little wars that would disperse the economic and military resources of the United States and Britain. In 1946-47 nobody yet thought in terms of inevitable conflict. Our economists kept telling Stalin that America was on the brink of economic collapse. For instance, the Hungarian Varga forecast an imminent crisis in the supply of energy in that country. In which connection, a detail comes back to me. My father had appointed a deputy, Topchev, to be Vice-Minister of the Oil Industry. This Topchev was a pupil of Varga's and was very keen that my father should meet him. However, my father refused: he considered that, while Varga was probably a good theoretician, he had no sense of reality. The allegations about an imminent economic collapse of the USA made him laugh. He supplied Stalin with analyses that tended the other way, proving that the American economy was getting stronger and stronger. Stalin was angry when he received these reports.

Turkey

Stalin was violently anti-Turk, though with him this was more of a tradition inherited from Russian imperial policy. Expulsion of the Tatars from the Crimea seemed to him the radical solution of the Turkish problem in the region. My father was always passionately interested in Turkey, considering that it would have a capital role to play in Georgia's future. In his view we should avoid antagonising the Turks and should adopt a more delicate policy towards them so as to get them to agree to some territorial concessions in return for a promise from us to drop our demand for the Straits, to renounce Communist subversion in their country,[19] and to help Turkey to get control of the oilfields of Kurdistan. He often talked to me about how Turkey had grabbed parts of Georgia and I have the impression that he was not indifferent to the fate of the Mingrelians living in Turkey. Hostile to pan-Turkism, he wanted to recover the Georgian and Armenian lands annexed by Turkey and repeople them with Lazes, who had been driven out into the mountains. He looked forward eventually to an economic association between Turkey, Iran and the Balkan bloc, into which Caucasia should be integrated.

For their part the Turks followed a prudent policy, hesitating to put themselves firmly in the Anglo-American camp. Stalin paid no heed to this. He ordered the Black Sea fleet to manoeuvre ostentatiously off the Turkish shore and urged Dimitrov to make demands for Turkish territory near the Straits. Poor Dimitrov did what he could to get out of this. Stalin orchestrated our territorial demands[20] in the press, and historians were called upon to justify them. My father then asked historians who were specialists in the history of Turco-Georgian relations, Professor Dzhanashia and Berzinishvili, to publish articles in Georgian journals so as to let the Turks understand that matters were not so simple as they might seem and that Georgia, at least, was not presenting them with an ultimatum. He had long known these historians, as it was his custom to invite them when we were visited by Lazes from Turkey, in the period when he wanted to increase contacts between the Mingrelians and the Lazes. These articles displeased Stalin. He sent for the two professors and ordered them to write the opposite of what they had written. The two, who were intelligent men, spoke of Georgia's interest, but Stalin advised them to rise above parochial sentiments and, in fact, to adopt the standpoint of Russian imperial policy.[21]

From the summer of 1945 Armenian *émigrés* were invited to return to the USSR. Stalin then summoned the leader of the Armenian Communist Party, Aryutunov and said: 'Armenia's national emblem shows Mount Ararat. Do something to turn that emblem into reality.' Aryutunov asked my father's advice and was recommended to speak to Mikoyan, with whom he reached agreement. With his usual guile Mikoyan succeeded in persuading Stalin that the Armenian demands should be put off until later. But the diaspora had been invited to return to Soviet Armenia. I remember hearing Aryutunov moaning to my father: 'How I am going to house all these people?'[22]

'You are really not very bright. Act as we did in Khandzhian's time, make them cough up. They have relations all over the world: use them,' my father advised him.

In 1946, at the height of the Turco-Soviet crisis, some Lazes brought a complaint to my father. They said that the Soviet Union was stirring up the Kurds in their region. This was not the case, as my father knew well. The British were inciting the Kurds to make incursions into Turkish territory, making out that the USSR was behind these actions. To tease me, my father asked me for my expert opinion on the Kurds. I said, with a learned air, that the young Kurdish leaders I met during the war had all studied at British universities and were not at all pro-Soviet. In the end my father advised these Lazes to take up arms, if the Turkish government gave them permission, and resist the invaders. He thought that we should not play the Kurdish card unless the British decided to. Actually, any attempts to create a Kurdish state would cause a tension in the Middle East which would not be to the advantage either of the USSR or of the Caucasian countries. But Stalin wanted to press on this tender spot.[23]

My father never gave up his aims in spite of adversity. Even when his situation was at its most precarious, when Stalin was after his head, he discreetly pursued his Turkish policy. His men in the Ministry of Foreign Affairs, including Vice-Minister Kavtaradze, applied his line in the Middle East – so far as possible, as Stalin left him little latitude, and Kavtaradze, who had tasted prison, was not disposed to take risks.

Iran

Iran, too, had invaded Georgia many times. My father considered that we ought to keep an eye on this neighbour whose territory gave access to the Indian Ocean. He was greatly interested, as well, in Iran's oil.[24] He proposed that we let Iran have the benefit of our technology in exchange for a very modest percentage of the profits. This would have been the beginning of our penetration into Iran. The Iranian bourgeois parties would have supported us, finding it more advantageous to deal with us than with the British, who invested only a tiny share of their profits. He advised, along with this, that we put a damper on the demands of the Iranian Communists and lend our support to the parties that represented the national bourgeoisie. He was convinced that a British presence in Iran was better than an American one, and consequently urged that we avoid damaging the interests of the British. Unlike the Americans, the British were ready to recognise Soviet aims in the Middle East, as they knew they had little to fear from an economically underdeveloped country like the USSR. America had the appetite of youth and would not hesitate to jostle both the British and us.

Stalin took great interest in this question, possibly influenced by my father. One day he summoned Kavtaradze and told him that we had been handling Iran with kid gloves for too long. We must now strengthen the Iranian workers' party with Iranian Communists who had been trained in the USSR and must support the Communist insurrection in Iranian Azerbaijan, while explaining to the Westerners that we had no designs on southern Iran and its oil resources. He wanted to unite the north and south of Azerbaijan just as western Ukraine and western Byelorussia had been united with Soviet Ukraine and Soviet Byelorussia.

Whereas the British withdrew their troops from Southern Iran in the summer of 1945, ours stayed on in the north of the country. As though by chance, we had problems with transport.[25] In December that imbecile Pishevari[26] – even Ulbricht was more intelligent – established a Communist regime in southern Azerbaijan. My father, exasperated, warned Stalin in vain, trying to make him understand that he should not employ idiots as emissaries. His anger reached its climax when he found that the First Secretary of the Party in Azerbaijan, Bagirov, dreamt of creating a Greater Azerbaijan and was doing all he could to help Pishevari, alleging that the instructions came from Stalin. One day he called on us, bringing a fish. My father gave him a memorable dressing-down. 'If you think you can win me over with that, you are mistaken. You are behaving like the worst of cretins. On the excuse of acquiring a little piece of land you are turning Iran into an enemy for centuries to come. You would do better to think of attaching your Azerbaijan to Iran!' He was mad with rage. Bagirov stayed silent.

We had thus managed to get hold of Iranian Azerbaijan without firing a shot. This time, however, Stalin hit a snag. The British and Americans reacted vigorously and Stalin had to abandon the Iranian Communists.[27] I think, but this is only a hypothesis, that Pishevari was assassinated because he knew too much and was too stupid to seek obscurity. He kept complaining about being dropped. The USSR got absolutely nothing in the sphere of oil concessions. Stalin then had the idea of overthrowing the Shah, using the merchants and industrialists, so as to bring to power a more or less democratic leader such as Mossadegh,[28] pro-Soviet without being Communist. It was not a question of annexing Iran to the Soviet Union but of ensuring access to the oil triangle.

Soviet policy towards Turkey and Iran was thus entirely determined by Stalin. Molotov carried out his orders with zeal, delighted at the prospect of Soviet expansion to the warm seas.[29] Zhdanov and the rest were not greatly interested in the Middle East. They simply took over Milyukov's[30] idea that Russia ought to establish herself in the Straits. Any Great-Russian imperial ambition won their support at once.

After the Turkish and Iranian affairs Abakumov and Stalin suspected my father of friendly feelings for Turkey and Iran.

The German question

My father wanted the four-Power occupation of Germany to be terminated as soon as possible. He proposed that a few *komandaturas* be left in place to watch over the de-Nazification process and, for the rest, that the Germans be allowed to manage their own affairs. At first, Stalin viewed this solution with favour, but soon changed his mind. He was, to be sure, for a united Germany ... provided that it was Communist.

My father had approved of the agrarian reform of autumn 1945 in the Soviet occupation zone, which aimed at expropriating the junkers and creating a large number of small property owners, but he opposed, vainly, the merging of the Communists and Socialists in Germany and the creation of the SED[31] in April 1946. In his view it would be better for the Socialists to remain independent and he had tried to persuade Stalin of this, in the presence of Zhukov and Vasilevsky when they came to report on Germany. It was from Vasilevsky that I learnt this. My father said to Stalin: 'You want to force the Communists and the Socialists to unite. The Socialists are stronger, more intelligent and more numerous. They will transform your Communist Party into a Socialist Party.' This was an argument designed to appeal to Stalin but he replied, drily: 'Have no fear. Those Socialists who won't conform to the line will be eliminated.'[32] And that was all. My father did not insist. Once they were out of Stalin's office, Zhukov asked my father: 'Why are you interfering? What difference does it make to you if the Communists and the Socialists are together or separate?'

'It makes no difference to me,' he replied, 'but it's of capital importance for Germany. If we keep the Socialists we shall have a developed country of the Western type. Otherwise we shall have a fief in which to squander our money and which will be of no use to us.' He said no more to Zhukov. He was more inclined to share his ideas with Vasilevsky.

On policy concerning reparations and removal of plants to the USSR, my father saw as indispensable deliveries of German coal, as our mines had been destroyed. But he had proved, with figures to support his case, when he submitted these studies of his to Stalin, that it was much more onerous to dismantle a factory, transport it and re-erect it elsewhere than to build a new one. A large proportion of Germany's heavy industry equipment was out of date. The Westerners did not bother to dismantle and take home this old equipment. On the contrary, they helped the Germans to modernise their industry.[33] Moreover, my father, in agreement on this with many leading personnel, preferred to send Soviet people to Germany rather than bring Germans to the USSR. While we had been justified in inviting major scientists to our country, men who could create a school, what was the point of importing factory workers? Far better to send our young people to Germany, in the hope that there they would acquire the taste for a good job well done. In the end, a few young people were sent to Czechoslovakia and Hungary.

My father showed me the documentation that the Americans had put together on the state of scientific research in Germany. 'You see how they go about it. When I think that our wretches can think of nothing better than stealing women's underwear and stripping museums!' In my presence he furiously rebuked the group we had sent to Germany to compile documentation on patents. 'If you hadn't sense enough to understand for yourselves how important this work was, you should at least have followed the example of the Americans.'

'But we have no need of patents, we do as we like,' one of them objected. He retorted: 'To steal intelligently you need to know what there is to steal. We send agents abroad when we have here trunks full of documentation with everything we are looking for.'

The German reparations question set Malenkov against Voznesensky at the end of 1945 or the beginning of 1946.The former headed the commission for the restoration of the occupied territories, the latter was the chairman of Gosplan. Malenkov wanted to supervise the proceeds of the dismantling carried out in Germany. Voznesensky considered that it was for Gosplan to administer reparations.[34]

This reparations question reminds me of the time when I was studying in Leningrad. I was visiting the Hermitage when one day a man of a certain age who saw that I was not Russian spoke to me. He was the director of the museum, Orbeli, who was an Armenian. He took me into the cellars of the Hermitage, where I was able to admire statues by Phidias and the altar of Pergamum, brought from Germany by our troops. Orbeli was in love with a statue of a young man which he never tired of contemplating. I told my father what I had seen. 'How can one hide masterpieces in a cellar?' I demanded indignantly. I was struck by the acid tone in which my father replied: 'Iosif Vissarionovich wants to be like Napoleon – who did not, however, touch the museum in Dresden.' It had been decided to return Germany's works of art, and this was done, but only after the death of Stalin.[35]

The Marshall Plan

We were tempted to accept the Marshall Plan[36] in June 1947. We would have willingly taken the money and the material aid, but there was no question of giving political concessions. All those in charge of the economy, Voznesensky and my father, for example, and those who administered German reparations, favoured acceptance of American aid and authorised the peoples' democracies to do the same. Like my father, they thought that we should have been able to manoeuvre and were not at all in favour of a categorical refusal. Besides, preliminary contacts had shown that the Americans were ready to make concessions. They merely wanted to be sure that their aid would not be used in the military sector. Some of our leading personnel even thought that we might allow the Americans in to supervise certain sectors. I remember that the Minister of Transport, Kovalev, and his deputy Beshchev, argued in that sense. The Americans were offering special equipment which enabled railways to be built more quickly. 'Why refuse them a right to supervise? After all, there's no way you can conceal railways.' The leaders of agriculture were also much attracted by the American offers, especially of fertiliser factories and technologies to improve yields. My mother told me that there was discussion of this at the Timiryazev Academy. In short, all those in charge of the economy saw at once the advantage they could gain, each in his own sphere, from the American proposals. But they were overcome by the isolationist apparatchiks of the Party. Stalin had contemplated accepting American aid in 1945, because he was not sure of being able to subdue the country when the war was over. By 1947 he was confident that he could do that and so he rejected the Marshall Plan without even trying to negotiate. He thought that the less contact the USSR had with the Westerners, the more effectively it would achieve its aims. As he saw it, this plan aimed at American control of Europe. My father, too, thought that the Americans were seeking to make Europe dependent on them, but he believed that, with a Germany freed of occupation troops and allied to the Soviet Union, France and Britain would prefer an independent Europe to submission to America. Provided there was no confrontation, the Americans would soon lose their power over Europe.

The Berlin blockade

In the spring of 1948 my father thought that creation of a West German state by the Western powers was unavoidable, thanks to the mistakes made by the Soviet Union. It would have been enough to allow a unified, peaceful and democratic Germany to exist for this to become an ally of the USSR. Such a Germany would have agreed to revive the ruined Soviet economy, for the Soviet Union would have been the sponsor of German unity, in opposition to America. Its huge economic power would have been neutralised by the Soviet Union and China.

My father was very fearful that the Westerners would split and retreat when the blockade of Berlin began in 1948.[37] Stalin held a meeting and put three questions to those present, while making clear that his decision had already been taken. How long could the Americans sustain the airlift without ruining themselves? What could they do when they realised that they no longer had the means to sustain it? What might be the negative effects of the blockade of Berlin? My father, supported by Voznesensky, tried to dissuade Stalin from plunging into this enterprise, pointing out that the blockade would have disastrous consequences for our economy. But Stalin replied that it would be the American economy that would succumb. There was always a substantial group of warlike military men.[38] Some of them had convinced Stalin that the Americans would be unable to keep the airlift going for long. The information supplied by Abakumov's services pointed in that direction. My father had other information which allowed him to predict that the Anglo-Saxons would hold out and that this whole affair would backfire on us.

Among our military, men like Konev and Air Marshal Rudenko declared that we could perfectly well prevent the Western aircraft from landing, squadrons of our bombers were all ready. Our special services claimed that the Americans would not start a war if we destroyed their aircraft. But Stalin rejected that option, though not because he thought there was a risk of escalation, for he believed Western public opinion would remain indifferent to the fate of Berlin. After all, we were not invading the Western zones. My father assembled a group of military men whose moderate views were known to him and said: 'How has the situation changed since the summer of 1945, when we abandoned our expedition into Europe? Our position was much more favourable then. We had four hundred divisions in the heart of Europe, with nothing in front of them. We stopped because we did not have the bomb. We still haven't got it. Do you want the Soviet Union to be devastated by atomic bombs?' He was supported by Vasilevsky, Zhigarev, Vershinin and Yakovlev. They thought, also, that the blockade of Berlin would strengthen the solidarity between the Westerners[39] and would inflict a stinging rebuttal to Stalin's favourite thesis according to which the imperialists would always be unable to act together. This group approached Stalin to urge him to be prudent. Eventually Stalin did realise that he had been defeated, and lifted the blockade in the spring of 1949. But he drew no lesson from this experience, for at the same time, he was already preparing for the Korean War.

My father never believed in the aggressiveness of the American leaders. He explained to me many times that in democratic regimes a warmon-

Lavrenti Beria, *centre*, and
his classmates at Sukhumi college.

Below: Lavrenti Beria in 1927.

Georgian period in the Thirties.

Nina Beria in 1928. She was famed for her beauty.

In 1938.

At Gagry in Abkhazia, 1952.

The same year.

Lavrenti Beria with his mother, Marta, and his wife, Nina.

Father and son, Lavrenti and Sergo Beria. Tbilisi, 1936.

The young Sergo, aged 6, in 1930.

Aged 13, Tbilisi, 1937.

Sergo in 1938 and 1941.

Sergo and the son of Bagirov in 1934.

Svetlana Stalin, around 1938.

Vasya Stalin in 1939.

Above: 1948. Sergo, Marfa and their eldest daughter.

Right: 1950. Sergo, his wife and their two daughters.

From left to right: Sergo, Nina, Lavrenti and Marfa, around 1950.

Mother and son, Sergo
and Nina Beria, 1946.

Marfa, Gorky's granddaughter and
Sergo's wife, and Nina Beria, 1950.

Nina Beria, her granddaughter and Sergo's German governess, Ella Almendiger, 1948.

Nina Beria and Sergo's eldest daughter, 1949.

Marfa's mother Ekaterina Peshkov, Nina, Lavrenti Beria, and their granddaughter, 1948.

Stalin in 1897 and 1908.

In 1908 and in 1915.

Voroshilov and Stalin
in 1920.

The first Stakhanovite
conference in Moscow:
Molotov, Stalin
and Andreev,
November 1935.

Yagoda, Kaganovich, Ordzhonikidze, Stalin, Kuibichev, Schmidt
the explorer and Zhdanov.

November 1935: the first Stakhanovite in Moscow. Here,
Zhdanov and Stalin.

Stalin and Kaganovich.

Ordzhonikidze and Stalin.

Ekaterina Dhugashvili, Stalin's mother, 1937.

The young Sergo Beria and his father at the funeral of Stalin's mother, 1937.

Beria announces the Great Purge at the Georgian Communist Party Congress. Tbilisi, 1937.

The 'decade of Georgian art' in Moscow in 1937. Reception in Moscow. *Centre*, Stalin and Beria.

Beria in 1939.

ს.ს.რ. კავშირის შინაგან ორგანთა სახალხო კომისარი, სსკ.კ.პ(ბ) ც.კ.
პოლიტბიუროს წევრობის კანდიდატი ამხ. ლ.პ. ბერია.
Народный Комиссар Внутренних Дел С.С.С.Р. кандидат в члены
политбюро ЦК ВКП(б) тов. Л.П. Берия.

1937. Beria receiving
an Uzbek delegation
in Tbilisi.

Stalin and American Vice-President Wallace during his visit to Moscow in 1944.

Kruglov, Molotov, Beria and Serov in Berlin in 1945.

Official portrait of Stalin.

The Presidium at Stalin's funeral in Moscow in 1953.
From left to right: Molotov, Kaganovich, Bulganin, Voroshilov, Beria, Malenkov.
Second row: Khrushchev (*first from the left*), Mikoyan (*second from the left*).

gering attitude resulted in the political death of a statesman. I was sceptical every time he said this, under the influence of our propaganda about
warmongering imperialism, until the time came when I learnt that we had
launched the Korean War, whereas I had been convinced that it was South
Korea that had attacked first.

The German Federal Republic

My father hoped for a long time that Pieck[40] would succeed in exercising a
moderating influence on the imbecile Ulbricht. However, Pieck was old
and it was easy to set him aside. The only way to prevent the creation of a
West German state was, in my father's view to replace the Communist
government by a Social-Democratic one in the German Democratic
Republic. 'We need Germany. We should admit that and stop behaving like
slobs,' he said. When the German Federal Republic was created in 1949,
he could not refrain from chaffing his colleagues in the Politburo: 'In a few
years we shall be faced by a well-armed economic colossus which will not
be our friend. All because we stupidly refused to make concessions that
were perfectly acceptable for us.' He described this scene to my mother,
being very pleased to have told those 'idiots who well deserved what's
happened to them' just what he thought of them. Events proved him right,
but his pleasure was only relative. He understood also that the creation of
the German Federal Republic would open a new phase in Stalin's policy.
His own position would be weakened and repressions would again be
multiplied.

Chancellor Adenauer was, according to my father, one of the greatest
statesmen of the post-war years. He admired his strength of character and
compared him to Bismarck, for whom my father had great respect. 'He is
a born leader,' he said. 'That is something that the Americans, the British
and the French have not understood. If you show him a possible way to
unify Germany, he is intelligent enough to harness himself to that task
and take it to fruition, just as Bismarck did in his day. At his age he has
retained an astonishing clarity of thought and, above all, he has his own
conception of the future German state and its foreign policy. Adenauer will
never allow Nazism to reappear in Germany. If we help him to unify
German he will reward us.' My father was thinking of economic assistance
to the USSR, not political concessions. 'Adenauer has firm convictions and
is as stubborn as a mule.' This appraisal of Adenauer has remained in my
memory. My father was sure that the German Chancellor would never give
up the alliance with the United States but Stalin was a hundred miles
away from this policy. He liked repeating that a reunified Germany would
lead to another world war.[41] He had always had a high idea of the
Germans' capacity as soldiers, and was impressed, I was told by Marshal
Shaposhnikov, by the fact that nobody in Germany felt the need to check
on the execution of an order, it was so universally accepted that an order
had to be obeyed.

The state of Israel

My father and Stalin thought that by helping the state of Israel to come into being they would ensure the support of international finance for the Soviet Union. They saw in this state a base from which to influence the world of Jewry, with all its financial resources, in the interest of the USSR. It mattered little to my father that the new state's leaders were not Communists, provided that they were useful to us. We should put our money on Israel and not on the Arab countries as we had resources enough. He tried to help the Jews to create their state,[42] in the first instance with Stalin's approval.[43] He succeeded in giving military aid to Israel.[44] Stalin did not know everything and did not necessarily approve of everything that my father did in this connection, in a sphere where he could act discreetly and without asking for permission,[45] by using his personal network of agents. In return the Jews gave him information about the Arab world. I have met Israelis who received military training in the Soviet Union, certainly with Stalin's approval. But Stalin later abandoned the Jewish policy advocated by my father,[46] which he had supported at the outset.[47] My father wanted to continue with it, believing that it might prove fruitful in the less immediate future.

The Yugoslav Crisis

Tito

Stalin had borne a grudge against Tito since the war.[48] He did not forgive him for his links with the British, especially because they evaded Stalin's control.[49] He constantly pestered my father on the subject: 'Tell me, what's Churchill's son doing at Tito's side? Why are the British helping him so much?' My father tried to make him understand that Tito was forced to appeal to the British since we were so unwilling to help.[50] 'And you claim that he is one of us?' demanded Stalin. One day when Stalin repeated for the hundredth time that Tito was a British spy, my father could not hold back any longer and burst out: 'You're surely not going to say that you believe that story!' When Stalin openly asked Tito about his relations with the British, the Yugoslav leader replied sharply, defending his position. I asked my father about these connections. 'The British want to have him on their side,' he explained. 'Nothing surprising about that. Tito is a Communist, but he wants his country to remain independent. He practices a balancing policy, and he is right to do so. As for Stalin, he would agree with British aid for Tito, provided that everything went through Moscow.' Stalin was very much against my father when he advocated a joint Polish-Yugoslav operation in the direction of Austria.

Stalin even proposed to Tito that he keep the King of Yugoslavia. 'With all your caprices, I'm beginning to wonder if that wouldn't be better for the Soviet Union ... You would be Prime Minister for life.' To the members of the Politburo he said, jokingly: 'With the King, life would be easier for me.' Tito became angry and replied that the Yugoslavs had not fought in order to go back to the monarchy. Whereupon Stalin treated the subject as a joke.[51] After this interview Tito came to see us, accompanied by Malenkov. He waxed ironical about 'revolutionaries who need Tsars.' They both made fun of Stalin's idea. Tito then spoke of his plan to establish collective farms in his country. My father broke in. 'What are you doing? All the peasants will run away.'[52] He explained to Tito that Yugoslavia reminded him of Caucasia. In those mountainous regions, individual work was much more to be recommended than collective undertakings. Eventually the Yugoslavs decided against collective farms.[53] When the break with Tito took place Stalin brought this matter up again and threw it at him.

I asked lots of questions about Tito, because this man who had fought in the resistance instead of hiding away in Moscow appealed to me as a romantic figure. In May 1946 he visited us, bringing many presents: hand-woven carpets, bronze statuettes … At that time he was slender and had a musician's brow. In the USSR he behaved with modesty and dignity. He drank little. He made a powerful impression on me. My father asked him ironically: 'Why don't you offer me a signed portrait of yourself?'

'But of course,' Tito replied, not having noticed the irony, 'I'll go at once and get one.'

'Definitely not! I already have entire stocks of portraits given me by Iosif Vissarionovich.'

The Soviets had no grounds for reproaching the Yugoslavs. They acted openly and even suggested that the USSR establish military bases in their country. They simply wanted to strengthen their influence in the Balkans and to decide for themselves what their internal policy should be. But when Stalin ordered him to stop supporting the Greek Communists' guerrilla war, Tito took it very badly. He would lose face in the international Communist movement. My father thought that, at least, the frontier should remain open so that the Greek Communists could escape reprisals. But he had never believed that a Communist insurrection would succeed in Greece.

The Balkan Federation

Zhdanov favoured Tito's plan for a Balkan Federation.[54] His conception of it differed, naturally, from my father's. He saw this federation as a copy of the USSR and an extension of the Soviet state. My father wanted an economic union of the Balkan countries, led by Yugoslavia, which would later join up with a unified Germany and a free Austria.[55] He hoped that Tito would come to renounce the monopoly of the Communist Party and agree to a people's-front-type government.[56] On the other hand, he saw no reason why Yugoslavia should not annex Albania.[57] From the summer of 1948, not long before his death, Zhdanov played a decisive role in the anti-Tito campaign. For this dogmatist, in whom Bolshevism and Russian chauvinism lived happily together, the peoples' democracies ought to be exact copies of the USSR.[58] My father mocked his claim to involve himself in Balkan affairs and to be teaching Dimitrov his job. He told me that he had heard Zhdanov express amazement that there were so many countries in Macedonia. How could bits of Greece, Bulgaria and Yugoslavia be included in one country? Zhdanov was mixing up Macedonia and Thrace. Malenkov resembled him in this respect. I saw my father reading one of his reports, which swarmed with references taken from encyclopaedias and works of rudimentary popularisation. He wrote on it. 'Georgi, tell your wretches to find you sources that are a bit more reliable.'

In September 1947[59] Stalin made Malenkov take part in the foundation meeting of the Cominform, though he knew him to be opposed to this enterprise. He always tried to humble those around him by publicly imposing on them tasks which they hated. A few years later he sent my father to crush Mingrelian nationalism in Georgia. After the break between Tito and Stalin in June 1948 my father explained to me that he had never disapproved of Tito: 'Every state has the right to pursue the policy of its choice.'[60] He was conscious of the analogies between Yugoslavia and Georgia. Both countries had fought the Turks for centuries. 'An understanding can always be reached between highlanders,' he said. I recalled this comment of his when Tito was condemned: 'A period is beginning now such as we knew after 1934.'[61] Malenkov, doubtless influenced by my father, who was against that condemnation and often cursed the Cominform, hesitated where the Yugoslav question was concerned. He did not like the anti-Tito campaign but said that he was obliged to take part in it. That was not enough for Stalin, who stuck the label 'Titoist' on him as well as on my father.

My father liked Dimitrov, with his southern temperament, impulsive and at the same time trusting. He reminded him of Ordzhonikidze when he was young. He did not see in him one of those intriguers who swarmed in the Comintern. But Dimitrov disappointed him when he dropped the Balkan Federation plan as soon as Stalin had shown himself against it.[62] He joined in the anti-Tito campaign even though, in private, he expressed reservations regarding this policy.[63] He was not a man of totalitarian bent. I knew him in Georgia, where he went for his health after leaving Germany. He was very solitary and did not speak Russian. He enjoyed my company, though I was only a boy, and declaimed passages from Schiller by heart, which left me stupefied with admiration.[64] The Comintern found him a partner so that he shouldn't sink into melancholy. I believe he died in 1949 because of all the black deeds he had witnessed. I don't believe he was assassinated.

Stalin opposed the Balkan Federation project[65] as soon as he realised that it could give rise to a third force in Europe.[66] He soon saw that he could not manipulate Tito as he wished. Tito was too much like him. For Stalin, his judgement of men had priority over every other consideration.

The great turn

1949 was the year of the great turn. Stalin multiplied his blows against the old guard, dismissing Mikoyan, who was Minister of Trade and removing Molotov from Foreign Affairs. The purges carried out in the peoples' democracies struck at people linked with my father. Anna Pauker[67] and Slansky belonged to the Jewish group. Vannikov, too, was worried, fearing that the wave of accusations might reach him again. As a Jew and a protégé of Beria's he had everything to fear. My father explained to me the purges in the Army, the Leningrad affair and the anti-Semitic campaigns as being Stalin's desire to liquidate all potential opposition, by getting rid of elites and intellectuals who might take the lead in such an opposition. Relations between my father and Stalin now worsened permanently.

The fight against 'cosmopolitanism'

For my father, anti-Semitism opened the way for Russian chauvinism and national socialism.[68] Before the war there was no anti-Semitism in the Soviet Union. It was created by the country's rulers shortly after the victory,[69] the authorities feeling sure that it would immediately meet with the approval of the masses.

As I have said, my father did not believe that Stalin was anti-Semitic,[70] even after his struggle against Trotskyism. He had many Jewish friends and mistresses. In 1947 he sent Kaganovich[71] to the Ukraine because of the virulent anti-Semitism which had developed there and which risked discrediting the USSR, whereas Khrushchev encouraged these anti-Semitic tendencies in the Party in the Ukraine.[72] Calculation governed all of Stalin's actions. He realised that the Jews were needed in that period. Mekhlis was for a long time his personal secretary, and became editor of *Pravda* before being given charge of propaganda in the Army and, finally, charge of State Control. Stalin kept him close to himself and retained his services for years.[73]

Stalin could, by nature, have been a Georgian nationalist, but he chose internationalism. If he had been Russian he would never have permitted anti-Semitism, which was one of the concessions he made to Russian nationalism.[74]

The assassination of Mikhoels

I well remember the death of Mikhoels in January 1948. I had seen him playing King Lear in Yiddish. I found this rather comic, the Yiddish sounding to me like some deformed dialect of German. Our newspapers alleged that he died in a car accident. One day, over lunch in our *dacha*, I asked my father what actually happened. In the presence of our guests he pretended not to hear me, but when we were alone again he scolded me. 'Why must you always be opening your mouth when you ought to keep quiet?' Then he added, laconically: 'Mikhoels was assassinated by terrorists.' He said no more than that.

Some years later he explained to me that Mikhoels had been assassinated on Stalin's orders, because he had become an eminent personality in Zionist circles. He enjoyed immense prestige among the Jews, no doubt partly undeserved. But Stalin could not put up with a Soviet citizen who was popular abroad as well as at home. He ordered the Tass Agency to supply him with complete texts of all articles about Soviet individuals that appeared in the foreign press. Unlike Gorbachev, he was not interested in what was written about himself but woe to the wretched Soviet citizen who attracted the attention of foreign journalists. Mikhoels had, more or less, found himself in the same situation as Trotsky.[75]

The campaign

The Jewish Anti-Fascist Committee was dissolved on Stalin's initiative, though to do it he made use of Malenkov.[76] For my father, the campaign against cosmopolitanism which began in January 1949 was 'the last nail driven into the coffin of co-operation between Europe and the Soviet Union.' The Party organisations at district level were ordered to check the number of Jews in every research establishment. I had experience of this – I was sent for and was asked, straight out, why I employed so many Jews. The head of my institute admonished: 'Why are you afraid of Beria's son? Is that why you are not going for his comrades?' The wife of a Jewish engineer who had been dismissed wrote to my father. She listed the services rendered by her family to the Soviet Union and the exploits of her near relatives during the war. 'I am addressing myself to you, Lavrenti Pavlovich, because I know that you are not an anti-Semite.[77] I want you to pass this letter to Comrade Stalin. I dare not address him directly as I know he is surrounded by anti-Semites.' It was a very intelligent letter. My father said laughing, that the entire Jewish family must have got together to compose it. He showed the letter to Stalin, who remarked: 'It's like the Song of Songs.' (He was fond of that work and often referred to it.) The engineer got his job back.

Although I was usually prompt to swallow our propaganda, this time I did not go along with it. I knew a number of 'cosmopolitans' and was aware that they were close to my father. At the same time, I had the opportunity to see for myself how effective were the appeals being made to chauvinism and Judeophobia. Some of my comrades, whom I had known for a long time, and whom I would never have suspected of this sort of behaviour, began to complain that the radio and culture were in the hands of the Jews.

In this affair, Abakumov, who was not an anti-Semite, was merely a docile executive. He even became afraid of the scale of the provocation. Fearing lest he be made a scapegoat when Stalin died, he started to show hesitation. That was why he was at last dismissed, in my view. My father said of him: 'He's a poor creature who obeys Iosif Vissarionovich blindly. He won't last long.'

Lysenkoism

Stalin set himself to talk up Russian science, the most progressive of all. He ordered our intelligentsia not to underestimate our achievements and not to 'bow down before the foreigners.' His main purpose was to isolate our intellectuals from the Western world. Henceforth 'the flood-gates of Russian chauvinism were open.'[78] I had heard of Lysenkoism from my mother, who was an agricultural chemist. Lysenko got away with it at the start because he had observed the peasants and presented as his personal discoveries some procedures which had long been used by cultivators. He boasted that he could produce rubber in the USSR and had obtained the support of the Party and of Stalin. The latter compared him to some starving rural deacon, ready to scrounge whatever was going, but admired him for his enormous activity. My father said he ceased taking Lysenko seriously after the rubber fiasco. Lysenko played on the theme that he was 'a man of the people and a Bolshevik,' forcing the scientists on to the defensive. Like a pack of wolves, Lysenko and his disciples persecuted the biologist Vavilov, multiplying their denunciations. They feared him because he did not hesitate to call them charlatans. Eventually, in August 1940, he was arrested and charged with counter-revolutionary sympathies. He did indeed have associations that were dangerous from the Soviet standpoint.[79] My mother's colleagues begged her to speak to my father in his favour. Vavilov's brother, the president of the Academy of Sciences, told him that the accused was no sort of conspirator – on the contrary, if he did not like something he said so openly. When he was condemned to death by the Supreme Court, my father succeeded in discrediting certain testimonies and the sentence was commuted to twenty years' imprisonment. My father then had the idea of creating a biology *sharashka* with Vavilov in charge. But the war had begun. Vavilov died from dysentery in prison in January 1943. My father nevertheless remained friendly with his brother, who was grateful to him for his efforts.[80]

When we moved to Moscow my mother chose Academician Pryanishnikov as supervisor of her thesis. She knew all the ins and outs of the struggle among the biologists. Now, Pryanishnikov was close to Vavilov and in her thesis my mother attacked Lysenko's theories without naming him. Lysenko tried several times to contact her, but she could not stand him and he met with a blank refusal. My father did not intervene. It was his principle to let her do as she pleased, even where Stalin was concerned.

After the war Lysenko was used to prove that Russian science existed and that some academicians came from the peasantry. In short, Lysenko was a pure product of Russian chauvinism and Communist illiteracy. My father regarded him as a typical Party careerist, an ambitious ignoramus. 'I knew men of his kidney in Georgia, but down there we quickly discovered what they were worth. We gave them experiments to perform under the supervision of scientists who had my support. Generally speaking, we found, from the first year, that their results were lamentable.' The most comic thing was that Lysenko surfaced again under Khrushchev. He had promised to produce a new race of cows which would give ten times as much milk as others.

My father took under his wing a certain number of scientists who had been persecuted in these campaigns, arguing that he needed them for the nuclear project. He welcomed chemists who had been harassed by Zhdanov's son, specialists in the resonance phenomena in chemical reactions. Stalin was suspicious and summoned Kurchatov, who assured him that these chemists were indispensable to the project. When Zhdanov Junior started to denounce relativity on the grounds that it was 'Jewish science,' Vannikov and some Jewish scientists asked my father to watch out for danger. He decided to teach young Zhdanov a lesson so as to calm him down for the future. 'Give me the text of his report in advance,' he said. When he had all the documents in his hands he sent for some Moscow physicists, all fanatical Russian chauvinists, and gave it to them to read, saying: 'You see, they want to prevent us from making an atomic bomb under a show of struggle against cosmopolitanism. I need your help.' They agreed with alacrity. 'Prepare a report. I'll arrange for you to be received by Stalin.' When the matter was raised, my father said to Stalin: 'We ought not to involve ourselves in these theoretical questions which have nothing to do with real life. Let the physicists have their say, including Kapitsa and Kurchatov's opponents.' Stalin sent for the scientists, who refuted the lucubrations of young Zhdanov. And that was how the affair was ended. The Moscow physicists were able to take part in the atomic project, even if their contribution was modest. When Vannikov complained that they cost a lot, my father said to him: 'Better to pay them a lot of money and have peace than make enemies of them.'

I only knew by sight the philosopher G. Aleksandrov, who was responsible for ideology at this time. But I met him years later in Sverdlovsk, where he had been exiled in 1955 after a rather comical misadventure. When participating in an orgy with other *nomenklatura* members he had been photographed by a British journalist in the company of naked women, and the British press had had great fun with this picture. He had been sent to teach philosophy in Sverdlovsk and it was there that he said to me: 'When I think that that bastard Mikhalkov managed to be photographed from behind!' However, I was unable to get to know him better, as I was forbidden to socialise with him. The authorities thought that two exiles might well hatch plots together.

The Leningrad Affair

Stalin had encouraged the rise of the Leningraders Kuznetsov and Voznesensky. He wanted to make sure of replacements for the men who had run the country during the war. Being well disposed towards Kuznetsov, he had appointed him Secretary of the Central Committee without obtaining the plenum's approval. Despite the post he now occupied, Kuznetsov wanted the Party reorganised. Like my father, he wanted to end the Party's interference in the economy. Voznesensky also understood that we needed to reduce the hypertrophy of the military-industrial complex, which distorted our system, and my father thought well of him for that. But it was just this which brought him into conflict with the Party's organs, whose ultra-chauvinistic notions, incidentally, he shared. My father never saw Voznesensky as a rival; on the contrary, they were always allies.[81] And Voznesensky did not have the makings of a leader. He would never have been able to head an apparatus or even a ministry. He was, instead, an economist, and his rudeness to his subordinates was not enough to make him a talented administrator. My father had no reason to persecute the two Leningraders; he had other things to worry about.

Kuznetsov was very close to my father, contrary to the widely-held idea that he was Zhdanov's man, or Voznesensky's. My father had already sometimes made use of him during the war. I knew him well, as he came to see us at the Military Academy, discussed matters with us and attended Party meetings. He was subsequently accused of seeking support among the youth. I remember things said by young men returned from the front, who belonged to Communist organisations in Leningrad, when I was still a student and Kuznetsov was Secretary of the regional Party committee. Why did Russia not have its own Party organisation: Why was Leningrad, a cultural, political and economic centre which might count for more than Moscow, reduced to this humiliating status?

Kuznetsov sometimes, though very rarely, visited us in Moscow. I discerned that he had a hidden dissatisfaction with Stalin. He felt that he was vulnerable through owing his appointment as a member of the Central Committee's Secretariat only to a decision by Stalin, and he bore a grudge against the latter for not regularising the situation. He spoke about this to my father, who declared himself ready to raise the matter at the next meeting of the Central Committee's bureau, though he warned Kuznetsov that this was a risky business.

A few days before his arrest, in August 1949, Kuznetsov came to our house. He told us that he knew he was being watched. 'I am, too,' my father replied. 'I advise you to be careful what you say to your friends in the Party.' There were, in fact, provocateurs among them, working for Malenkov, who was already busy getting rid of all his potential rivals.

Whenever he saw my father was getting close to someone he began intriguing against that person. He wanted to be the only one close to my father, knowing well that he would never seek the first place and would always put Malenkov in front. Worse still, he had believed that he could make Kuznetsov one of his creatures, and now the man had taken up a position against him.[82]

The affair began when Abakumov composed a report on 'anti-Party' tendencies in Leningrad. The pretext used was that the city had organised a trade fair without consulting Moscow,[83] from which it was concluded that the Party's local organisation wanted to rival the Central Committee. The Leningraders were accused of separatism.[84] The Orgburo decided to investigate and the machinery started working. Malenkov and Abakumov had already been whispering to Stalin over a long period that all heresies started from Leningrad; didn't Zinoviev and Kamenev come from there? Wasn't this Leningrad anti-Party group reviving the old Trotskyist platform? People were arrested and the desired confessions extorted. These referred to spying and speculation in foreign currency, but nobody took them seriously, even at that time.

It was Malenkov who wanted the heads of Kuznetsov and Voznesensky,[85] not because he saw in them the successors of Stalin but because he resented the support they enjoyed.[86] Kuznetsov made a show of his friendship with Abakumov. They were constantly seen together. Accordingly, Malenkov decided to destroy the Leningrad Party organisation and began by compiling, with Shkiryatov's help, a dossier which compromised Kuznetsov. Together they established a special prison attached to the Central Committee and created an investigation department associated with the Orgburo and the Party's Central Committee, in which torture was practised.[87]

Voznesensky was not a target, originally, but as he supported the Leningraders he went down with them. Malenkov used his Leningrad origin in order to condemn him along with the rest, deceiving Stalin on this point. The latter thus abandoned Voznesensky despite his regard for him.[88] My father was amazed that he had withdrawn his protection from Voznesensky. Stalin said to himself: 'Since I have been supplied with such a good pretext, I am going to repeat the operation of 1934-35 and liquidate the entire Party organisation in Leningrad, where, I'm told, there are malcontents.' He set himself to put pressure on Abakumov. The latter was no fool and began to take fright at the scale the affair was assuming. He understood the risks he ran in the event of things going wrong and tried to manoeuvre and temporise.[89] He enjoyed direct access to Stalin but the latter often entrusted tasks to Malenkov, who hastened to tell my father everything – concealing only the actions of which he was himself the instigator. He warned my father of what Stalin was fomenting against him. Abakumov used to moan to Malenkov when Stalin resorted to the services of other people for operations that he considered his business. Malenkov repeated all that to my father.

Having seen that Stalin was dissatisfied with the way Abakumov investigated the Jewish Anti-Fascist Committee, Malenkov accused Abakumov of trying to hush up the affair of the Jewish plot, along with the Leningrad affair, and proposed that he be replaced by Ignatiev, a man devoted to him. He it was who, in June 1951, dictated Ryumin's letter accusing Abakumov.[90] This Ryumin was an illiterate imbecile. Malenkov's secretary, Sukhanov, had to make sixteen attempts at correcting that letter. When he was made head of State Security in July 1951 Ignatiev behaved as a docile tool of the Central Committee.

After Stalin's death Abakumov told my father what had happened. He claimed that he had only been obeying formal orders from Stalin to complete a dossier against my father. Abakumov protested his devotion to my father and claimed to have done nothing about it.

To return to Ignatiev, he carried to their conclusion the Leningrad affair and the Voznesensky affair and expanded the anti-Semitic campaign. Subsequently, Ignatiev and Ryumin were forgotten and responsibility for all these horrors was heaped upon my father. But Abakumov's testimony showed the role played by Malenkov, who put one Andrianov at the head of the Leningrad Party. My father rescued Saburov, one of Voznesensky's men who, however, lacked his strength of character and what my father called his 'innate intelligence'. My father reproached Malenkov for his part in the Voznesensky affair. 'You risk paying for that one day,' he told him. Malenkov answered, defending himself: 'All I did was obey Stalin's orders.' My father was not convinced. 'No, you went into it with enthusiasm.'

'It's easy for you to say that. You managed to get yourself excluded from the Central Committee's commission dealing with those affairs, whereas I was the chairman of that committee.'

'It was Stalin himself, if I am to believe what I have been told, who didn't want me to be a member of that commission.'

Such a discussion shows how frankly they spoke to each other.

In 1948 Stalin began to bring pressure to bear on Rapava, Georgia's Minister of Internal Affairs, to provide him with a compromising dossier on my father. Rapava was very close to my father, and his wife, a niece of the former Menshevik President Noah Jordania, was my mother's best friend. So, without explicitly refusing to do as Stalin ordered (following my father's advice in this), Rapava did nothing and was dismissed. Another Georgian Communist, Georgi Sturua, refused point-blank to comply with a similar request, doubtless to Stalin's great surprise, as he supposed that people would be ready to do anything in return for promotion.

Bulganin

In March 1949 Stalin replaced Bulganin with Vasilevsky as Minister of Defence. As war plans were becoming more precise he needed to have a real soldier in that post. My father tried to dissuade Vasilevsky from agreeing: 'Sooner or later you will be replaced. But God knows what will happen to you then. It's doubtful that you'll get your old job back.' Vasilevsky did what he could to avoid the appointment and seeing that he was not serviceable to Stalin's warlike aims, the latter dismissed him and brought Bulganin back as Minister of Defence in April 1949.

Khrushchev

Khrushchev was not unconnected with the dismissal of Popov, the head of the Party in Moscow, whom he succeeded when Stalin brought him back to Moscow in December 1949. He had done so many foolish things in the Ukraine that Stalin preferred to have him under his eye. 'With him you need to have a short leash,' said Stalin, using the German word for a leash which tightens round the neck when the animal pulls on it. He also wanted someone to act as a counterweight to my father (not to Malenkov, who had no need of one). Stalin knew that he could count on Khrushchev in everything and that the latter would even anticipate his wishes, especially if some plot had to be hatched against Malenkov or my father. Khrushchev does not tell, in his memoirs, how, barely arrived in Moscow, he hurried to our house and asked my father if he knew why he had been brought to the capital. My father replied that he did, and Khrushchev replied that he did, too, but this did not mean that the scheme would work out.

One day, when Khrushchev was drunk and was delivering himself of a torrent of crazy nonsense, my father told him to shut up, at least in front of me. Khrushchev replied: 'How can you reproach me? Don't you remember how Stalin wanted to use me against you when I came here from the Ukraine and I refused to play that game?'[91] From the outset, Khrushchev wanted to play the double-dealer. It was from him that I learnt of this episode, for my father never told me that sort of detail.

Stalin's 70th Birthday

Stalin's 70th birthday was solemnly celebrated in December 1949. Delegations from all over the world succeeded one another at the lectern, each delivering in their own language a speech of homage to Stalin. Every speech was at once translated into Russian. When Togliatti's turn came and he began his address in Italian, Stalin lost patience and shouted in a stentorian tone: 'That's enough! Speak Russian!' Togliatti did not lose countenance and continued in Russian. It was comic.

Stalin received a mountain of presents, some of which were priceless. The Chinese, for example, had sent magnificent objects made of old jade. Stalin took none of them and did not even want to look at them, despite Malenkov's insistence. He did not feel the need to surround himself with beautiful things. Later, a museum was created for these presents, which was stupid, because splendid antiques appeared there side by side with drawings and paintings that showed Stalin as seen by Mexicans or Chinese. The wives of the Politburo members also brought presents. My mother offered a jar of walnut jam which she had made herself. Stalin's mother had taught her the recipe. She attached a note: 'I send you this little souvenir of Georgia and of your mother ...' Stalin was touched and my mother was the only one he took the trouble to thank. 'As I eat your jam I remember my youth.' My father, who never missed a trick, made this comment: 'Now you're lined up for the jam-making chore every year.'

Mao came. I remember that my father called on my mother and me to go to the concert given on this occasion. 'Go, it will be better than usual,' he said. My mother objected that she did not feel like going, but he insisted. 'Even if the concert doesn't appeal it will be worthwhile seeing those two idols set up opposite each other.' I must admit that this remark displeased me. How could one say such things? But when we saw them, side by side, my mother and I looked at one another and burst out laughing. Mao, who found it hard to keep his balance, I don't know why, and Stalin, with the rheumatism in his hands, looked like two Asiatic despots and murdered each other with their looks! I can see it all even today. My mother and I had difficulty in recovering our seriousness and people asked us what the matter was. Hardly had we got back home when my father, who was in a good mood, asked us: 'Well, tell me frankly, was it worthwhile?' He had guessed what our reaction would be, because he himself found that Stalin and Mao had much in common, which accounted for their mutual mistrust.

Stalin and Mao

The Kuomintang

Before the war my father was very interested in the Kuomintang,[92] which tried to combine capitalism with elements of Socialism. The principles of its peasant policy seemed good to him, though their application left something to be desired because of a corrupt bureaucracy. The peasants supported this party and if the USSR had not helped the Communists the Kuomintang would have held on to power. That would have been better for China even though, in my father's view, Chiang Kai-shek was infinitely more dangerous to the Soviet Union than Mao was, not for political reasons but on account of his personality.

Some men close to my father perished through their collaboration with the Kuomintang. I am thinking of the Georgian Lominadze, who did much to help the Chinese nationalists. He was recalled to the USSR and Stalin blamed him for our failure in China.[93] My father tried to defend him, recalling that Chiang Kai-shek had studied in the USSR.[94] It was enough, indeed, to remember the precedent set by the Georgians who, in Tsarist times, had lived in Moscow and returned home violently anti-Russian, to understand that our disappointments in China should not be imputed to

Lominadze alone. Through his agents my father knew a lot about the Chinese leader and his family.

We gave up our attempt to reach an understanding with Chiang[95] when we realised the extent to which he was controlled by the Americans, especially through his wife. In Europe one could leave the bourgeois governments in place. In Asia, American influence was so strong that if Chiang Kai-shek won in China, the USSR would have no means of penetrating the region, since the Kuomintang ruled monopolistically. After the war my father and Malenkov, considering that China was a potential ally of substantial weight against America, had concluded that we should cast aside the Kuomintang. Instead, we should give far-reaching aid to the Chinese Communists, satisfy all their demands, strengthen China's economy and use China against the United States and Japan. My father once said to me that if China and Japan came together, Japanese technology and organisation combined with the gigantic human potential represented by China could constitute an irresistible power. My father wanted the closest possible economic and political bonds with China to be restored.

I found it hard to understand why the Americans abandoned Chiang Kai-shek and allowed Mao to take power. The British would never have allowed such a thing to happen, I thought. I asked my father to explain. 'The Americans think like merchants,' he said. 'They believed that Mao was no worse for them than Chiang Kai-shek. As for Mao, he is an opportunist who has sided with the Soviet Union because he needs our help. But as soon as he has obtained what he wants he will turn his back on us and go over to the Western side.'[96] I was scandalised. Mao enjoyed immense prestige among the Soviet people. He had behind him a country with a billion inhabitants!

Mao

My father obtained a list of the books that Mao read, just as he did in the case of other leaders. We thoroughly analysed all the people in whom we were interested. I think my father read a number of these books, because he wanted to know for himself the works listed. Mao's lists, very detailed, showed the notes he made, the direction of his interests and how these evolved. My father's conclusion was that though the man was very well educated he remained nevertheless 'a librarian, nothing more.' Accordingly to him, Stalin was right to call him a 'margarine Communist', for there was no trace of ideology in him. He had one passion only, power. Mao was a very good organiser and an intelligent man, 'but he was a dictator even worse than ours. Beside him, Iosif Vissarionovich is just a Little Red Riding Hood.' My father preferred Chou En-lai, in whom he saw the only one of China's leaders who was able to appraise soundly the internal situation of China, its capacities for external action and the real possibilities for co-operation between China and the USSR. He thought that Mao would inevitably come to follow the policy of the Kuomintang.[97] The only difference that was left was his attitude to the United States. My father considered that the Americans had made a monumental mistake in speculating on the Kuomintang instead of seeking support from Mao, who wanted to come to an understanding with them.

Mao's presents

The officer responsible for supplying us with necessaries arrived at our house one day with a lorry-load of rice. There was a tonne of it. As a rule, we received in accordance with a decision of Stalin's, a certain sum for foodstuffs and bought what we wanted. My mother said to the officer: 'I haven't the money to pay for such a large amount.' He replied that the rice was a present from Mao. 'But I won't know what to do with so much!' He insisted. 'It's an order from Iosif Vissarionovich, it's he who has allotted the rice among the members of the Politburo.'

My father arrived during this conversation and, when he saw the heap of rice, asked what it was. My mother replied that it was a present from Mao. 'So, then, you expected that he'd send you a Chinese print? He has sent you something at his own level.'

Stalin's China policy

My father and Malenkov disagreed with Stalin's China policy, to such an extent that he described them one day as 'Sinophiles.' He did not want to give generous aid to China[98] and the Chinese knew that very well. My father explained the reason for this to Malenkov. Secretly, Stalin envied Mao for being Chinese and at the head of the immense Chinese people, whereas he, the Georgian, reigned only over a disparate collection of Russians, Tatars and Caucasians, and consequently felt less sure of himself.

Mao, on his part, hated Stalin. We knew that from our listening devices.[99] We followed everything that was said in the Chinese Politburo, just as in the British Cabinet. Mao expressed himself in unflattering terms on Stalin and Khrushchev. The latter he regarded as a buffoon, and he held it against Stalin that he was a poor theoretician of Marxism-Leninism and a politician of limited intelligence.

When the Chinese asked for Soviet aid to make their atomic bomb, Stalin refused. On this point, my father agreed with Stalin. He made a remark in that connection which has stayed in my memory. 'We must understand it is not to Mao that we are giving this weapon but to China. Tomorrow Mao will be gone, but China will remain.' Malenkov, on the other hand, would have liked to give the bomb to the Chinese.

After Stalin's death, Malenkov and my father at once began negotiating with the Chinese. Malenkov had a photograph published in *Pravda* in which he appeared at Mao's side, a montage for which my father ticked him off: sooner or later it would be exposed. He should rather have waited for an actual meeting with Mao in order to publish a picture like that. Khrushchev exploited this episode to the full in order to set Malenkov and my father at variance. All the men who gravitated towards Stalin suffered from morbid self-esteem, because Stalin treated them like dogs and had turned them into mere puppets permitted only to announce: 'His Majesty is served.'

Stalin's Grand Design

The Korean War

When, in 1949, we acquired the bomb, this was far from calming Stalin. On the contrary, it convinced him that everything was henceforth permitted to him and we would soon to be able to go over to the attack.[1] Realising that our totalitarian system had the advantage over the democracies in that it could quickly concentrate the maximum of resources in a chosen sector, he wanted to use this provisional superiority to achieve a definitive success, on not only the European but the world scale.

The operation to reunify Korea, which was launched in June 1950, had been planned with the North Koreans and the Chinese. It is claimed nowadays that the initiative for it came from Kim Il-sung,[2] but this is quite mistaken. The North Koreans were so weak economically and so poor, their only ambition was to keep what they had. Kim was a cipher that we used. He put into effect the policy decided by Stalin, who sent for him and indicated what his duty was. As ever, Stalin did not do this directly: he never acted 'barefaced.'[3] After Kim's visit to Moscow in the spring of 1950[4] I remember hearing my father say ironically: 'All that we needed was a big war in the Far East.' He did not believe that this conflict would stay localised.[5] He did not want this war – not for humanitarian reasons, of course, but because he feared that it would unite the West.

In 1949 the USSR and China had trained a large number of North Korean officers, and not just senior ranks. Vasilevsky told me that he himself drew up the plan for aggression against South Korea.

After the initial successes,[6] the General Staff and our intelligence services warned Stalin that conquest of all Korea should be avoided, as otherwise a Western counter-attack would not be long in coming.[7] But Stalin did not want to listen, so that he was obliged to call on Mao to come to the rescue of the North Koreans.[8] He did not yet feel ready for a world war and wanted to gain time for putting the final touches to his preparations. Therefore it seemed to him preferable to make use of the Chinese.

My contribution to the Korean War

At this time I was working on missiles for use against warships at a distance of 100-150 kilometres. These missiles could be given a conventional or a nuclear charge. They weighed three tonnes. I had adapted the nuclear nose-cones to the missiles. Before that task I had had no contact with nuclear technology. During a test at the beginning of 1950 I had trouble with eight of my rockets, which turned over every time. My father telephoned me to express his concern. 'Try to find a reason for these failures, otherwise things will get bad.' Fortunately, the personnel of the research centre, headed by Mikoyan Junior (the aircraft specialist), pointed out the cause of the accident. When the bomb broke away, a draught of air struck the gyroscope and the rocket was thrown off balance. Eventually, Vannikov got me out of trouble by coming to terms with Gurevich, another 'wise Jew' who worked with Mikoyan. The latter testified before the inquiry that the rocket itself had nothing wrong with it. My comrade Shabanov and I pretended to have discovered for ourselves the cause of the disaster. Vannikov greeted us in a merry mood: 'So then, young fellows, have you found where the problem lies?' In short, everything was put to rights and in the autumn of 1950 the missiles were tested with success.

In 1951 Stalin decided to lend a hand to the Chinese troops who were in difficulty after the American push in the spring. He convened the Politburo and ordered that preparations be made to send part of our air force to China, equipped with these missiles, which would be attached to the undersides of the aircraft. He wanted to use them against the Americans' aircraft carriers and warships. Some hundreds of aircraft were also to be sent to protect our forces.

While I was rejoicing to see that weapons made by me were going to be put to use, my father spoke up to say that by acting like this we were going to start the Third World War. If we destroyed the Western forces the Americans would be obliged to launch nuclear war so as to keep their position in the world. Vasilevsky, Bulganin and other military men supported him. Stalin reacted with irritation. 'Our aircraft and our anti-aircraft defences will finish off the Americans,' he replied.[9] My father, Vasilevsky and Ustinov then told him that we had no system for shooting down the American bombers. Our MiG 15s and other jet fighters were not able to intercept those bombers because they flew at a very great height. Stalin turned to me to get confirmation that we possessed the necessary missiles. I had to explain that we were certainly in a position to destroy the aircraft carriers but not the bombers that the Americans would send over our cities. They did indeed fly too high. He ordered me out of the meeting. I learnt afterward how it proceeded. Stalin had forced the military to agree that they did not have an effective system of defence against bombers. I was called in again. 'How long will you need to construct a system that would protect Moscow and our principal centres?' Stalin asked me. I stammered that this was a complicated task. Furious, he replied that the Politburo never dealt with simple tasks and that, if I had not understood that, my place was not there. I assumed that he was dismissing me and I got up to go, but he stopped me and, in an unusually rough tone, said that this system must be ready within a year. Responsibility for the task lay with Beria and Malenkov. All the country's resources would be mobilised. The project was thus linked with the atomic commission of which my father was chairman.

Vasilevsky was given the job of keeping the military informed of the progress made, so that they might take this into account in their plans. After the meeting Stalin met him in private and asked him what he thought of the new weapons systems on which we were working. He wanted, without letting it seem so, to know whether he could trust me. Was I capable of 'defending our military interests'? Vasilevsky replied that I was doing my best to perfect my knowledge. Stalin suggested that I be sent on a six-month course at the General Staff Academy, but Vasilevsky objected that the moment seemed to him inopportune. I was one of the principal engineers in charge of the anti-aircraft defence system.

As for me, I had been coldly put in my place. As Vasilevsky liked me he personally explained to me the consequences that would follow the utilisation of my weapons. He described the American response that was foreseeable and what our reaction would be: in short, he made me realise what damage a war would cause. My father emphasised his point, saying that we could not allow ourselves to break with the Western world and that a new world war would mean the end of Europe. I understood the lesson.

The lessons of the Korean War according to Stalin

I remember a discussion that took place in our house during the Korean War, in the presence of Marshals Vasilevsky and Zhigarev. We were wondering whether the Americans would bomb China. My father and Vasilevsky thought this might happen.[10] Zhigarev, who was naïve, objected: 'But Comrade Stalin said that the Americans would never take such a decision.' My father smiled and said nothing.

For Stalin, there was a lesson to be drawn from the Korean War. China had attained the desired objectives with the help of our aircraft. The Chinese army had been able to 'liberate' North Korea. And that became an argument that he frequently used. 'Even the Chinese troops' – when he spoke of China it was always 'even China' – succeeded in solving the problem in six weeks.[11] The Korean War taught Stalin nothing. He continued to gamble on the dissensions between the democracies. My father said that this was a fixed idea with him. From this war he got the impression that the United States was the only country able to wage war, the others merely having walk-on parts, so to speak. Nothing could shake this conviction of his, not even the many reports, written for him by my father and the military, which emphasised the contribution to NATO made by America's allies.[12]

Towards the Final Conflict

Threats of war and threats of purge

None of the members of the Politburo, not even Khrushchev, I must honestly acknowledge, wanted war with the West. To carry that enterprise through, Stalin needed to be absolutely sure of his rear, and this put the Politburo's members in a precarious position.

I frequently heard Bulganin, Khrushchev, Malenkov and my father discuss how, at whatever price, they could succeed in preventing this war. As they saw it, there was no question but that the initiative in such a war would come from us.[13] After 1949 nobody believed any more in the likelihood of American aggression. On several occasions my father advised Bulganin to take steps to submit to Stalin reports from the Chief of General Staff and the commanders of the various armies and to urge him to ask if they could answer for their forces and resources, so that they might make him realise how far from assured was our success in such a war. Though cowardly, Bulganin did not like to put forward his subordinates, unlike my father who readily did so, inviting them to submit reports to Stalin.[14] Actually, Bulganin was afraid that his incompetence would be exposed if he had recourse to the expert knowledge of his subordinates. Consequently, my father had to exert all his powers of persuasion in order to get him to turn to Vasilevsky, to the commander-in-chief of our air force and other military leaders. Bulganin eventually acted on his advice.

It was then that the Americans organised a leak, and a document describing their plans fell into our hands. It was a warning, intended to let us know that any attempt at aggression on our part would unleash a reaction from them. My father thought, however, that the Americans had not conveyed their message vigorously enough. More than that was needed to cool Stalin's ardour.

War preparations

Our military expenditure kept rising. Famine raged in the country, yet the Central Committee had ordered, in 1950, that enormous strategic stocks of foodstuffs be created. All the canned goods that we produced were stockpiled. Stalin accumulated maniacally, not for himself but for the state. My father said that his relationship with his people was like that of a gypsy with his horse: he economised on its food to the point where the animal died. My father proposed in vain that, at least, the oldest stocks of canned goods should be put on sale. Stalin stubbornly refused and there was no way of making him see reason. He quoted the experience of 1941, when our strategic reserves had been of immense service to us.

Vannikov thought of a stratagem which he proudly explained to my father. The industries controlled by him published production figures that fell short of reality, so that we could freely dispose of the surpluses that did not appear in the official data. Many people knew of this subterfuge, but nobody brought it to Stalin's attention. Unfortunately, it was impossible to apply this system to foodstuffs, a domain in which it was harder to fiddle the figures.

Economic problems

In 1949-50 the decay of our economy because of the age of our infrastructures and the equipment of our basic industries provided my father with an excuse to go back on the offensive. He initiated economic discussions, using the argument of efficiency, which safeguarded him from accusations of ideological deviation. He urged that Germany be reunited at all costs, that our military expenditure and the size of our armed forces be reduced, and that our production of conventional weapons be cut down in favour of concentration on new types of armament. Only an agreement with Germany would furnish the resources needed to rescue our economy. The East European countries should be integrated into our economic system and the burden weighing on our shoulders shared with them, but on condition that they were made totally independent and freed of our armies of occupation. We could dominate Europe by other than military means. This time, my father was supported by Gosplan, by the energy-producing complex and by the arms industry. Together with Saburov he advocated releasing light industry and building work from state control. He was careful not to break cover when trying to get a measure passed. He pushed others forward and never acted on his own. It was the same when he was promoting a policy or a stratagem: he always arranged matters so that nobody could form an idea of the big picture.[15]

The bomb in 1951

The preliminary steps in Stalin's programme had already been taken. In 1946 I happened to be working at Institute No. 108, which specialised in wireless telephonic interceptors. They came under the listening-devices committee. The employees, who were quite non-political, were interested in their work and talked freely to me. I learnt from them that Stalin had ordered new systems which made it possible to intercept radio communications over very long distances (on US territory), especially between airfields. The engineers realised that these were not to be defensive systems. In 1946 it was already clear that Stalin's aims were not confined to defence of the USSR. To be convinced of that you only had to analyse the type of orders presented to the research departments.

We exploded our second bomb in 1951. This was already more than just a copy of the American bomb.[16] To persuade Stalin to be patient my father dangled before him the prospect of something still better – the hydrogen bomb, very much more effective. But he was not in a hurry to explode it. In my opinion, it was ready in 1952 but my father waited till Stalin died before deciding to test it, in July 1953.[17] He knew very well that Stalin wanted to have the H-bomb before the Americans so as to be able to start a war with them.

Stalin began to harass my father and Kurchatov, demanding that they speed up manufacture to the utmost. (It had begun while we were still working on the two previous bombs.) When they both explained to him that at least three or four years would have to pass before the project was complete, he suspected that Kurchatov was hand in glove with my father. Stalin had begun involving himself in the affairs of the atomic committee in 1946, at the time of Malenkov's disgrace, which also marked a weakening of my father's position. It was then that he started to send for scientists.

After 1951[18] he became really unbearable and, seeing how close Kurchatov was to my father, he redoubled pressure on him. In his usual hypocritical style, pretending to show a paternal interest in this representative of the intelligentsia, he sought to remove him from the project by making him President of the Academy of Sciences. Faced with Kurchatov's refusal, Stalin commented: 'I see that Beria has been at you.' Kurchatov tried to explain that he did not like purely administrative jobs and was quite happy to be head of the nuclear project, but Stalin interrupted him: 'I've heard all that from Beria.' Eventually Stalin appointed Nesmeyanov, who had been recommended to him by Yuri Zhdanov, to be president of the Academy. This affair increased his suspicions. How was it possible that anyone could reject such a distinction? He could not get over it. He then sent for Pervukhin, who later described this interview to my father, in detail. 'It seems to me that manufacture of the H-bomb is not going fast enough,' said Stalin. 'I could have asked Vannikov about this [Vannikov and Pervukhin were old friends], but I've chosen to speak to you. How much time do you need?' Stalin wanted to give Pervukhin the impression that he had chosen him for the honour of his confidence. 'Then you and I will take the measures necessary for reorganising work on the H-bomb together.' Pervukhin replied: 'But I must put Lavrenti Pavlovich in the picture.' Stalin stayed silent, then replied: 'Yes, of course, tell Beria. But that changes nothing in my orders.' My father advised Pervukhin to make his report to Stalin, describing the actual state of the project, but to submit this report first to Kurchatov and Vannikov.

So Stalin might spur his people on as much as he liked, but the work on the H-bomb went no faster. According to Kurchatov, he and my father feared that acquisition of the weapon by the USSR might incite the Americans to do the same. However, my father did not confide the fundamentals of his thinking to Kurchatov, or to me either. I remember a conversation that took place in that period. Kurchatov knew nothing of politics, but my father tried to make him understand certain things, without seeming to be trying to teach him. As Kurchatov was rejoicing in the fact that we should soon have the H-bomb, my father said to him: 'Haven't you understood yet that nobody will thank either you or me for that? They will take this weapon and we shall have the right to a kick in the backside.' Kurchatov was thunderstruck. Embarrassed, no doubt, by my presence, my father turned the subject into a joke.

The German scientists

We were working at the same time on the construction of nuclear power stations, still on the basis of German plans. We took six years to complete the first of them, which came into service only in 1954. It should be realised that the general impulse came from work done by the Germans, even though the Soviets made their contribution: it was necessary to affirm that Russian science existed.

As regards missiles technology, which was my sphere, I should say that we owed 99 per cent of our achievements to the German engineers. The only exception was the atom bomb, which was developed on the basis of British, American and Soviet research. I once asked my father why the Germans had chosen to work for us – speaking, of course, about those who had come voluntarily to the Soviet Union.[19] He explained that they doubtless had little sympathy with the Communist regime, but in the USSR they felt they were in the front rank, whereas in the USA[20] they would have been given only an inferior role.[21]

Stalin was interested in all the technical means that would enable our nuclear weapons to reach American soil. He wanted our submarines and aircraft to be able to fire cruise missiles, if not ballistic ones. When in 1950 I perfected my anti-warship rocket, with a range of 150 kilometres, he asked me if this could be used against America's coastal cities.

The Germans had had the same type of concern and Stalin knew of their plans. One of these conceived of an aircraft that could fly all round the globe, the Sanger. Stalin ordered that this project be reactivated.[22] He also learnt that the Germans had begun work on the ballistic missile R10. They had not been able to produce it because their bases had been bombed but the conception of the missile was there and the engine ready. A group of several thousand Germans was made responsible for reactivating the project and, towards the end of the 1950s, these missiles went into mass production under my father.

By means of a forced march our military-industrial complex was endowed with ballistic missiles,[23] and we were ahead of the Americans in this field.[24] I was very proud that they had not thought of making a missile similar to mine. I thought myself very smart until the day when I realised that they simply had no need of such devices, since we had no navy! Research centres were set up to invent engines for rockets, under the direction of Luzhov, Sevryuk and Isaev. Luzhov developed the German system, propelled by alcohol and oxygen. Sevryuk looked for other fuels. Isaev studied the use of paraffin-oil and sulphuric acid. These engines had to be perfected first, for everything depended on their power.[25] Consequently, factories for producing missiles were built even before the projects reached completion. I remember going with Yangel to Dnepropetrovsk where we chose a motor-car factory to be transformed into one for producing rockets.[26]

The Germans, particularly Dr Pose, built for us atomic engines for submarines which, on my father's insistence, were produced in the Baltic provinces, though the Russian ministers wanted all military industry concentrated in Siberia and the Urals. The projects were already complete, and the submarines should be able to fire two or three ballistic missiles.[27] But we did not yet have operational atomic submarines, only an atomic icebreaker. Stalin insisted that, at any cost, we must get some. He wanted to send them to patrol the Pacific and the Arctic Ocean. He was not aiming at communications between Europe and the USA, a task that fell to our air force based in the airfields of occupied Europe. What interested him and the military were the flanks. I knew Butoma, the Vice-Minister of Naval Construction, well, a nasty character. He boasted before me that he had been personally summoned by Stalin, who had enjoined him to harass without mercy the engineers under his orders until the atomic submarines were operational.

The bombers

Compared with our four-engined Pe-8 bomber[28] the Tu-4, an exact copy of the B-29 (Stalin had ordered Tupolev and my father to conform to the American model in the smallest details[29]), represented a leap forward. It could reach the United States and, in principle, could be refuelled in the air for its return flight. However, this possibility remained illusory in the real conditions of combat.[30]

The Tu-95 was tried out at the beginning of the fifties. The first of these aircraft caught fire. A commission of enquiry, headed by the Vice-Minister of Aviation, Dementiev, was set up to find the causes of the accident. At this time I was testing my rockets in the Crimea, at the Bagyrovo airfield, Vannikov having intervened to obtain authority for me to work in that sunny spot. Nuclear bombers were also tested, in Zhigarev's presence. We were already at the third or fourth squadron, each made up of 28 Tu-4s. We then had a dozen atomic bombs copied from the American model. Only lack of plutonium still restricted our production. But we already had reactor vessels and an isotopic separation plant.[31]

In 1951 we perfected bombers that could reach the USA and return without needing to be refuelled. They flew at 700 kilometres per hour. The following year we had jet bombers.[32] The engines were produced in the Ukraine[33] by Lyulka. Stalin had planned to have fighter planes accompanying the bombers which flew in the European theatre of operations, having been inspired by the British example in the Second World War.[34] With an arsenal like this he counted on sweeping up Europe with the back of his hand. Then he would neutralise the United States, should that country attempt reprisals.

Anti-aircraft defence

I have described earlier the circumstances in which Stalin ordered us to provide missiles to defend Moscow from attack from the air. A ringroad equipped with artillery batteries was built.[35] At the end of 1952 the bulk of the work had been completed, protecting the 900-kilometre belt of Moscow to a height of 25 kilometres and with a radius of 45 kilometres. The system had been tested and its effectiveness proved. What remained was to finish building roads and barracks and install reserves of missiles and technical stations, and this was done in 1953-4. Not long before he died, Stalin ordered that decorations be prepared for the engineers who had participated in the effort. The system was tested again after my father's fall. As he and I had become enemies of the people, there was need to check with vigilance whatever we had built.

Along with this we had already begun working on mobile anti-aircraft defence systems. Stalin intended to provide protection for the major centres of arms production – Chelyabinsk, Kharkov, Leningrad and Sverdlovsk. Moscow was, in any case, considered to be safe from a nuclear strike.

1952: clearance for warlike action

In 1952 the whole country was on a war footing. The objectives of the Central Committee were quite clear: we were preparing for the third world war and it would be a nuclear war. All the country's resources were mobilised. We already had several squadrons of Tu-16 bombers. Myasishchev was working on an ultra-rapid bomber which could reach America and was better than the B-52. However, it had not yet been tested.[36] At the end of 1952, Korolev was decorated for having created missiles with a range exceeding 1,000 kilometres.[37] One has to remember that our forces were in Germany, so that all Europe was within our reach. Factories were getting ready to mass-produce intercontinental missiles that did not yet exist. As a general rule we began to mass-produce weapons before we had tested them. Stalin took this risk in order to gain time. Subsequently, Khrushchev needed only to utilise the bases created by Stalin in order to launch his 'strategic revolution,' which consisted of abandoning traditional weapons and stuffing the whole world with missiles.

Our superiority in Europe was crushing.[38] We could destroy all the American airfields in Europe and make nuclear strikes on any European country, Britain included. We possessed the primary elements of weapons capable of inflicting reprisals on the USA. The West's anti-aircraft defences consisted only of guns, radar and fighter planes, whereas at least 600 projectiles had to be fired in order to bring down a Tu-16.[39] And our bombers flew at such a height that it was hard to intercept them.

Our objective was to destroy communications between the United States and Europe. We could easily take command of the Mediterranean and, through our missile launching ramps in Bulgaria, ensure our control of the Straits. As we could no longer count on Tito[40] we provided for special units to seize Trieste. And we must occupy Spain and Italy so as to prevent an American landing. In East Prussia and the GDR, where aviation fuel was already stockpiled, the superiority of our conventional weaponry was beyond doubt.

What, for Stalin, was essential was to take Germany, the only country in Europe he thought of as formidable. Elsewhere he did not expect much resistance from NATO. Though still disarmed, Germany had an economic potential so dangerous that he preferred to destroy it. He summoned me on several occasions around May 1952 to ask if our missiles would be able to demolish the bridges over the Rhine or wipe off the map this or that industrial centre in Germany. We had nose-cones with infrared sights that were perfectly well adapted to that task. He wanted also to know if we could destroy the dykes of the river Ruhr. The British had thought of doing that during the Second World War, but had not attempted it.

At this time our armament industries were working as in wartime. Our preparations clearly showed that what we had in mind was an offensive war.[41]

The reign of the absurd

My father and Saburov presented a study which showed that if we had assigned to current consumption 10 per cent of the resources devoted to the military sector and 'the great construction works of Socialism,' our standard of living, though not becoming equal to that of the people in the West, would have been three or four times higher than it was. The Soviet people would have had no more worries about food or housing. 'With all this wealth,' said my father, 'we could enjoy a paradisal existence. Then the Soviet people would defend the regime, tooth and nail and we should have no more need of atom bombs. For this it would be enough for our foreign policy not to provoke the Western countries, for us not to try to impose our regime on others but to be content with what we have, to let people breathe instead of treating them like slaves and animals, and to grant equal rights to the republics.' He considered, too, that the 'peace campaigns' we organised entailed a useless squandering of money. 'We invite these peace activists to be our guests at great cost, we finance congresses, we place articles in the foreign press. And all that we achieve thereby is to irritate those who are really in charge of policy in the West and to move around a lot of air. Don't let's deceive ourselves as to the support we enjoy in those countries. The masses refused to elect Churchill in July 1945 without our having anything to do with it and faith in the USSR has substantially declined since then.' It would have been enough to invest one-tenth of the sums spent on those campaigns in agents of influence and we should have got more decisive results. My father thought it was just as stupid to interpret the trouble in the Third World as a sign of the advance of Communist ideology in those countries. 'They are totally different phenomena, peasant revolts such as have occurred over centuries. And we claim to see in them a revolutionary movement!'

Stalin's last manoeuvres

Everything was ready. Stalin was on the point of playing the final chords of his symphony. The prospect of war did not make him recoil.[42] As he saw it, best get on with it at once and have it over with.[43] Perhaps he sensed that he had not much longer to live. Also, he thought that time was working in the West's favour, that the relation of forces was at this moment as favourable to the USSR as it could be. So he set himself to prepare, not public opinion but those close to him, by repeating to them that war was inevitable, and that the Americans would start it.[44] He claimed to have documents that proved his assertions. There were indeed American plans for a preventive war.[45] We used our knowledge of them to justify a preventive strike by ourselves. My father tried in vain to prove to Stalin that the Americans were not at all ready to go to war, even though we had mobilised them through the Korean War.

When he was asked, one day, why he made so much of the perfidy of the Germans in violating the pact of August 1939, Stalin answered: 'It was important to me to emphasise that we were not the attackers.'[46] He had not spared his efforts in that direction, for at that time the relation of strength was not in his favour. For the Third World War, likewise, public opinion had to be made to swing our way. He therefore decided to put everyone on the wrong scent by means of a series of initiatives. He was able to gull friends and enemies in the same way, seeing in this a manoeuvre and not perfidy. He proposed to organise elections in Germany[47] and to resume international trade. He even authorised a conference on that theme, held in April 1952. Malenkov's pacific declarations at the 19th Party Congress, held in October, also reflected his intention to delude the West.[48] This was no personal initiative on Malenkov's part, anything like that being impossible while Stalin was alive. Needless to say, Stalin had not yielded to the arguments of my father and the group who favoured a conciliatory policy. He thought only of lulling the vigilance of the West while he got on with making the H-bomb and missiles and speeding up the communisation of the GDR with a view to war.[49] He said as much in my father's presence. My father had begun to hope that Stalin was changing. At each of Stalin's turns he imagined that this might indicate a new orientation, but they were all only manoeuvres. These measures, 'more provisional than those of the New Economic Policy,' served only as camouflage for our actual plans, Stalin explained.

Invasion plans

It was intended that in 1954-55 the USSR would assume a more aggressive attitude. The mass-scale development of conventional weapons, the multiplication of bombers, tanks and missiles, all our military preparations pointed to the imminent launching of an offensive.

During a meeting, Stalin declared that he alone possessed the means to ensure that the Soviet Union won the war. When he was gone, victory would be inconceivable. Once we had the H-bomb the USA would think twice before provoking us. In the event of their risking it, we would reply with devastating strikes. Conquest of Europe would enable us to solve our economic problems without affecting the foundations of our system. Stalin even cited the precedent of Nazi Germany, which had considerably increased its economic potential by seizing Czechoslovakia and France.[50] He had already thought out precise plans for exploiting the conquered countries. My father objected that, for this idea to work out, it would be as well for the countries concerned not to have suffered too much, for communications to have survived, and so on. He also sought to show that, even given military success, things would not necessarily turn out as foreseen, quoting the example of China, which possessed huge resources but would need many years of assistance from abroad in order to build an economy.

Stalin planned to use Europe as a hostage, assuming that the Americans would not dare to drop atom bombs on the European continent. My father did not share that opinion. I was not present at these discussions but I heard echoes of them from Vannikov and Shtemenko. The latter told me that our invasion plans included Spain and Italy. They calculated how long it would take for our troops to reach these countries, allowing for the nuclear strikes forecast. The military potential of our allies in Central Europe would have to be utilised in the operation, and summit meetings were held at which the finishing touches were put to these plans. Shtemenko was delighted with the prospect of war, seeing himself already with a Marshal's baton. When my father learnt that he had talked to me about all that, he gave Shtemenko a sharp reprimand. Furthermore, he forbade him to tell Stalin that we were militarily ready. 'And yet I've already sent him reports to that effect,' the general said to me, very worried. I realised that this was a controversy that had been going on for some time. Not long after, my father had to send Shtemenko away in order to shelter him from Stalin's anger.

A number of military men and Party leaders declared that we could win the war, provided that we got in a preventive strike and enjoyed the advantage of surprise. This theory was still in force under Khrushchev and Brezhnev. The commanders of the land army were especially bellicose. The naval officers were much more reasonable. They realised that our navy amounted to little compared with the American navy. They knew that they could not destroy NATO's communications otherwise than by landing operations and that they were not in a position to do much against the communications between Europe and the United States. The land army commanders swept these objections aside: 'Why should we trouble ourselves with these communications when, in a matter of days, we shall have reached the English Channel, Spain and Portugal and closed off the Mediterranean?' Even Zhukov was affected, though he did not like Stalin. I overheard a fragment of conversation between my father and him in 1952: 'The balance of forces has changed. We now have an anti-aircraft defence system. We can win,' said Zhukov. 'All right,' my father replied. 'And afterwards? Soviet territory will be devastated by American atom bombs and Europe will be destroyed. What good purpose will that serve?'

The Great Works

Meanwhile, it was necessary to put people off the scent by showing the world that the Soviets were absorbed in peaceful construction. Great trumpetings announced the launching of each 'construction work of Socialism.' Stalin and the Party thought that, everything else having been done, the time seemed to have come to transform nature. Yet they knew the people were hungry and wretched. How could one forget that all these initiatives were being taken at a time when the country was making the colossal effort in armaments which I have just described?

There was a plan to irrigate Central Asia by digging canals. In 1948 Stalin became infatuated with forest belts. My father opposed to the best of his ability the 'great works for transforming nature' which were to finish off our economy. The entire Council of Ministers backed him. What was the good of turning the country into a garden if its inhabitants were naked and starving? In my father's view, we ought to begin by developing the inhabited areas, where there were roads, and put off till later the opening up of virgin lands. There was, consequently, a violent clash with the Party organs. All the First Secretaries of the republics, except the Baltic and Caucasian ones, declared themselves for the 'great works.' My father and his supporters, Saburov and Malenkov, lost the battle.

My father never reconciled himself to seeing our meagre resources assigned to Pharaohonic projects.[51] 'For a long time now the Soviet state has been too small for Iosif Vissarionovich,' he said. 'Henceforth his plans are to be not world-scale but on the scale of the universe. He wants to dig canals like those on Mars so that, from space, people can admire our canals and forest belts.' I was shocked by this sarcasm. I did not like to hear Stalin spoken of in that tone. But my father was especially bitter because he could see that Stalin understood the situation yet nonetheless did as he pleased, repressing reality and refusing to abandon his grand projects. He prided himself on reducing prices so as to improve the people's well-being and show that our economy was on the up and up. Production was indeed rising steeply – but our war preparations swallowed everything. Stalin decided to show the people how much the Party cared for them by reducing prices at regular intervals. The heads of Gosplan just had to get busy finding the means to put this decision into effect. The entire economic machinery was thrown out of order.

I was present at Stalin's *dacha* when Stalin said: 'We make cars but people can't buy them. We simply have to reduce the price, let's say to 3,000 roubles.' It must be realised that these cars, produced in very small numbers, were distributed among the various branches of the administration and never put on sale. When he learnt that an American could buy a small helicopter for himself, Stalin ordered mass production of helicopters, so that every Soviet citizen might be able to have one of his own. Saburov, overwhelmed, began to object that he would not be able to meet this wish. My father came to his aid. 'It's an excellent idea from which we should obtain a tremendous propaganda effect. But, for the immediate future, we lack the means to implement it.' Later I heard him fulminate: 'He has lost all sense of reality. It reminds me of the time he ordered that the ceiling of his flat in Moscow be raised and the walls shifted. He did not appreciate that the whole building would have to be reconstructed. He imagines that it's enough for him to give an order and things will happen by themselves.' This was the time when Khrushchev was riding his hobbyhorse, the agro-towns.[52] My father advised him to re-read Saltykov-Shchedrin.[53] 'Your agro-towns are like Fooltown. Artificial creations are not viable,' he said, However, as my father had no responsibility in the agricultural sphere, he caused Aryutunov and Bagirov, men who were close to him, to intervene in the spring of 1951 and oppose this plan for regrouping the collective farms.[54] They went about it tactfully, by showing that this scheme would not work in their respective republics. The First Secretary of the Party in Georgia shared their view but hadn't the courage to take a stand.

Stalin becomes linguist and economist

This is how, in this same period, Stalin turned out to be a distinguished expert in linguistics. One fine day, he organised a discussion between two schools of linguistics, encouraging the specialists to squabble among themselves. He then took on the role of arbiter, reconciling the angry children by showing them the truth of the matter. At the start he did not want to involve my father in this undertaking, but when he needed linguistics specialists to prepare his work *Marxism and Problems of Linguistics* he turned to him. At that time my father had under his aegis a group of Georgians who were specialists in the Basque group of languages. My father was extremely unwilling to let these men become involved (in general he did not like his collaborators to be diverted from their work and become exposed to political adventures) but he had to do as he was ordered. Accordingly, he called the linguistics expert Chikobava to Moscow. My mother knew him well and he used to visit us every day. He was not a supporter of Marr.[55]

I must confess that I never understood Stalin's work on linguistics. I had the cheek to ask Chikobava if he had written it. 'No,' he replied, 'Stalin wrote it himself. He used some of my criticisms of Marr, but without actually quoting. Then he presented his work to me, not for me to correct but so that I should take account of his views in my own writings.

Which is what I have done.' I think he spoke the truth. Stalin wrote his speeches and reports himself.

Commenting on Stalin's excursions in the linguistic field, my father told a joke. It was about someone who, when asked what his dearest wish was, replied: 'To be in a theatre wearing a white dinner-jacket as the curtain rises, while all the other people around me are splashing about in shit.' Stalin, he went on, had built Socialism in one country, carried out collectivisation, and industrialisation, and won the war. He had reached the summits in philosophy and linguistics and put the final touches to a masterpiece on economics. There was nothing left for him to do but give a kick in the pants to all the rest.

Stalin provided a theoretical foundation for the new stage opened by the 19th Congress in his work *Economic Problems of Socialism in the USSR*. He did not write this from vanity. He thought himself above all that and felt no need to prove he was not senile. He launched the discussion on economics just as he had done the one on linguistics, and compelled my father to take part in the composition of this work. He knew what my father's ideas were and one of his favourite tactics was to prevent those near him from acting as they intended, to impose his own view and to make them expound it as theirs. He did this because he had noticed that a large number of leading cadres supported Beria. He therefore ordered his apparatus, my father's and that of Gosplan to assemble the basic data. My father was to draw from this a summary dealing with scientific research and the oil industry. He tried in vain to get out of this task on various pretexts but eventually gave in. I know nothing more about the circumstances in which Stalin's work was written. The conflict between Stalin and my father was so serious at that time that we no longer talked of such trifles among ourselves.

Stalin against my father

I don't think the relations between them worsened as the result of a particular episode. It was a slow process which remained for a long time hidden from third parties. Stalin became more and more polite and formal with him, which was a clear sign of increasing alienation. Beginning in 1949, he allowed his hostility to show in a wider circle, while my father began to express himself more frankly about Stalin in conversation with me. He was so irritated that he could no longer contain himself. His nerves were frayed.

My mother told me that at this time he asked her to sit silently beside him when he came in, exhausted, from his office. I think there is only one word that describes what my father felt in those days: hatred. Stalin was hateful to him because he expected a death-blow to come from that quarter at any moment.[56] 'The harm he is doing he does knowingly, not from stupidity.[57] He thinks he is a god who can do whatever he likes. He is no longer human,' he told me. And to my mother he confided: 'You know,

I was wrong. I ought to have insisted on Sergo becoming an artist. In that job one isn't dependent on anybody.' He was always aware of the precariousness of his position. That was why he encouraged me to become an artist even when I was still a child. And he was right, for the speciality I chose made me dependent on the state.

Threats to our family

One day at the end of 1949 or the beginning of 1950 my father sent for me and said: 'Iosif Vissarionovich is preparing the conclusion of his biography. Disciple of Lenin, initiator of industrialisation and collectivisation (and who will ask at what cost all that was achieved?), victor in the war, liberator of Europe ... But there is a seamy side to it, and witnesses to that are still alive. He has already eliminated some strata of them: now he is entering the final phase. He will begin by attacking me and all our family, then he will go for the rest of the Politburo. He is intelligent and knows how to select people. He will choose youngsters who know nothing of the crimes of the past and he will destroy the records. New leaders will appear, no witness will be left. He wants to enter history as a demigod who created a state, overcame Fascism and spread Socialism over the whole world.[58] Nothing else interests him. And for the sake of that he will sacrifice the whole world – millions of people, including those closest to him.'

My father had learnt to foresee Stalin's actions and reactions, in small matters and great, with infallible precision, because he had studied his behaviour in detail and knew what his aims were. In small matters as in great, Stalin's tactic was the same. My father told me that the operations against himself that had started some time earlier had entered a new phase and a direct attack was becoming possible: 'Now it's not just me any more,' he added. 'Your mother and you are also targeted. I know that statements against me have been collected, showing me as an enemy and a wrecker. I will take the necessary measures so far as I am concerned. As for you, I suggest that you make friends with the crews of the test aircraft. In case of necessity, when I give you the signal, take with you your mother and your family. Otherwise he will destroy you all.' He gave me the names of men in the air force and the frontier guard to whom I could apply. I was in a state of shock. It stunned me to learn that Stalin was preparing to get rid of my father. 'Doesn't he realise that you are devoted to him?' I stammered. 'Where did you get the idea that I was devoted to him?' he replied. 'The age of vassals and suzerains is past. Many times I have had to act under constraint. Now, though, he has gone too far. One is devoted to someone because one loves him or because one shares his ideas. How can you think that I am devoted to Stalin? No question of that.' My father was irritated to find me so obtuse and immature despite the efforts he had made to broaden my outlook. However, he was kind to me. 'Don't you understand why I have to tell you these things, so that you can be ready for anything, and one day, if necessary, you can do what you must in order to stay alive?' It was not that he lacked confidence in me, but he saw how young I was. That evening Svetlana called on us. I remember that as I looked at her I wondered if she knew what was going on.

In the summer of 1950 I had a chance to flee abroad with my wife, my mother, my children and Ella. Our whole tribe was at Gagry, ready to take flight at the first sign of danger. My father did not think of doing this himself, doubtless because he realised that, while Stalin was alive, he possessed no 'political personality' abroad. Besides, neither America nor Britain would ever have forgiven him for the fiascos he had caused in their intelligence services. Then the alert passed, for the moment. Stalin's tactic was to make my father feel that the ring was tightening round him, as around a bear cornered by hunters. And, at the same time, he dangled rewards.

The 'gang of four'

In 1951 the members of the Politburo, Bulganin, Malenkov, Khrushchev and my father, began to appreciate that they were all in the same boat and it mattered little whether one of them was thrown overboard a few days before the others.[59] They felt a sense of solidarity once they had faced the fact that none of them would be Stalin's successor – he intended to choose an heir from among the younger generation. They therefore agreed among themselves not to allow Stalin to set one against another,[60] and that they would immediately inform each other of anything Stalin said about them, so as to frustrate his manipulations. They recalled their former intrigues and buried their old grievances. Khrushchev told my father that Stalin had asked him for reports on the national question when he was in the Ukraine, though, in principle, policy on that matter was still a preserve of the NKVD. This solidarity among the members of the Politburo increased as time went by. They also confided in Mikoyan, who understood the situation. But Stalin's intrigues left traces which were not completely wiped out. It must be said that Stalin constructed his provocations around an element of truth, so that even an intelligent person found it hard to see through them.

After about six months Stalin guessed what was going on and unceremoniously demanded of the members of the Politburo: 'Tell me, are you forming a bloc against me?' He took the steps he thought appropriate and began to meet Ignatiev, the head of State Security, without going through the Politburo.

The speech of 6 November 1951

On the eve of 6 November 1951 Stalin, who was on holiday, asked my father to give the address on the eve of the 34th anniversary of the October Revolution. 'Write whatever you like. You needn't send me your text in advance.' My father came home in a good mood that evening and told my mother: 'Iosif Vissarionovich definitely takes me for a fool. He imagines that I'm really going to believe that he has confidence in me, whereas this is a diversionary manoeuvre. Now I know what to think: there's something in the wind.'

I saw my father write his speech and then distribute it to his colleagues, requesting their opinion. Their reply was unanimous: 'You haven't buttered Stalin up sufficiently.' We were all convulsed with laughter. My father observed, gravely, that this defect must be corrected, but he did nothing. As Malenkov and Khrushchev, pretending to be solicitous for him, advised that he send the text to Stalin, he offered to bet: 'I won't do anything, but you'll see that an order to send it to him will arrive very soon.' Stalin waited as long as he could, then two days before the event, unable to hold back any longer, he asked Poskrebyshev to obtain the text from my father's secretary, Lyudvigov. Much amused, Malenkov and Khrushchev would not give in: my father had lost his bet they insisted, because Stalin had not given the order in person. Naturally, Stalin telephoned my father: 'Why have you sent me your speech? I'm trying to rest and here you are, bothering me with these details ...' I remember even today how funny we found this affair.[61] Three days later, however, on 9 November, a resolution of the Central Committee denounced 'the Mingrelian conspiracy.'[62]

The Mingrelian Conspiracy

The government had been fragmented.[63] Nobody could take a step without Stalin's agreement. All those who had enjoyed seeming independence were deprived of it, losing all direct contact with their subordinates. For the time being, Stalin did not touch his ministers, but henceforth he was to call up a second echelon. However, he had overlooked one thing. While he postponed the disgracing of my father, the latter was strengthening his influence over a certain group. Stalin undertook to discredit him, first of all in the eyes of the Georgians, so as to destroy the support he enjoyed in that republic. The Mingrelians were targeted first and foremost. Dynamic, quick, fairly intelligent and cultivated, they had acquired a dominant position in the republic.

To achieve his purpose Stalin revived the Tsar's policy of setting eastern Georgia against western Georgia. He did not want a united Georgia backing my father. So he appointed a new First Secretary for Georgia, Mgeladze. This man was not directly connected with the head of State Security, Ignatiev, one of Malenkov's men. Ignatiev's tool in Georgia was Rukhadze, who headed the local MGB. Stalin knew that this wretch hated my father and had chosen him for that very reason. Mgeladze was not against that policy but did not actively engage in it. Stalin sent for the Georgian leaders, including Rukhadze, and told them to compile a dossier.[64] From this resulted the 'Mingrelian conspiracy'.[65]

At this time Vasya, Stalin's son, said to me: 'You know, my Georgian friends tell me that relations between Iosif Vissarionovich and Lavrenti are very tense. They think these clashes are due to intrigues by those Russian chauvinists who want to make trouble between them.' He didn't know that it was his father who had organised the 'Mingrelian conspiracy'. My father was warned in good time, by Malenkov, of what Stalin was up to. Khrushchev said to my father, chaffingly: 'Iosif Vissarionovich hasn't forgotten the spokes you put in my wheel when I had the job of combatting the Ukrainian nationalists.'

The purges in Georgia

Tens of thousands of people in Georgia were arrested and tortured in order to get them to bear witness against my father, so that he could be accused of 'bourgeois nationalism' and sympathy with the Mensheviks. Nor were my mother and I forgotten. The Georgian Minister of Internal Affairs, Rapava, was arrested and Ignatiev wanted to extort from him confessions directed against my father. Later, after he had been released following Stalin's death, he told my mother that Stalin had sent for him and said: 'I'll make you head of the Party in Georgia here and now if you will tell me everything that Lavrenti has done.' Rapava had acted stupid: 'But what is it he's done?' Stalin wanted to obtain material that would support the accusations of 'bourgeois nationalism,' 'links with international Zionism,' along with 'spying for the British.'

Stalin tried to persuade Evgeni Gegechkori, my wife's uncle, to return to the USSR.[66] No need to say what would have happened to him! My father never, if he could manage it, sacrificed people who worked with him and were useful to him. He warned Gegechkori that he was going to be invited to come to Georgia and that he must on no account agree. He also sabotaged the repatriation to Georgia of the Menshevik leaders, and prevented the return to the USSR of all the Georgian national treasures which, he claimed, might be embezzled. Sudoplatov mentions the operations connected with the recovery of these treasures. My father did not have complete confidence in him and refrained from entrusting more delicate missions to him. There are many things that Sudoplatov doesn't know, and other things that he knows but doesn't talk about.

Stalin sent my father to Georgia at the beginning of April 1952, when the purges were in full swing. He wanted to crush all opposition in Georgia, making use of my father in order to discredit him.[67] I have read the speech my father made to the Georgian Central Committee Plenum in Tbilisi. In substance he said: 'Since I have had nothing to do with Georgian matters since 1938 and the Central Committee dealt with all important questions of Party life, the Party's Central Committee has given me the task of conveying to you its views and those of Comrade Stalin ...' In short, he distanced himself from what he had to announce.[68] Everyone understood. My father allowed himself sometimes to insert some allusions into his speeches which would indicate that he disapproved of what he was obliged to do. Stalin noticed this and made him pay for it.

The Nineteenth Congress

Stalin had, in 1952, a plan of action for the years ahead. He had defined his objectives and the means to obtain them. He was perhaps less interested in current affairs precisely because he was concentrating all his efforts on his grand design. He was neither senile nor mad. Until the last months of his life Stalin was in good physical condition and his mind and will were intact. His iron grip was not relaxed for an instant. He had important plans for the 19th Party Congress, which was held in October 1952, but he was unable to complete them fully. He expelled Molotov[69] from the Politburo, also discrediting Mikoyan, in order to disguise what he was up to. As ever, the former accepted his fate with equanimity. The same could not be said of the latter who, very upset, came to pour out his heart to my father, who advised him: 'Look at Molotov and learn from his example.'

'What do you mean?'

'Take a holiday.'

'I'd like to see your face when the day comes that you're sacked.'

'That happened to me years ago.'

This was the first step towards realisation of Stalin's programme.[70]

It had been very difficult to compromise Molotov. Stalin had already tried to before the war. He would have liked to get rid of the other four as well, but he was no longer in control of all the levers of power. All that he had was Ignatiev, the head of State Security. Stalin had always taken care to have the police apparatus under his personal control. My father had had experience of that in 1938-43. 'I couldn't take a step without being watched by him. I tried to get round that by vigilance but rarely did I succeed, and then at great risk.'

Stalin could not, therefore, carry out the sort of coup d'etat he contemplated. He had to be satisfied with creating an enlarged Presidium of 25 members and 11 deputies, which was to provide him with support for the coming purges. In order to intimidate the Politburo and the Central Committee, he started to talk about 'strengthening the Cheka,' and bringing Chekists into the Central Committee. He praised 'Cheka methods' and so on. It is my opinion that he temporarily abandoned his design because the Politburo members he targeted gave him to understand that they would not surrender without resistance. The next stage was to unfold a few months later, with Kaganovich and Khrushchev suffering the same fate. No great problem there. Stalin would have left no witness in place. He would have got rid of the old Politburo and promoted new people, idiots like Brezhnev. After winning the Third World War he was determined to correct all the 'mistaken' interpretations of historical events which had been current in the West.

What was Stalin's dream? From some of his remarks I imagine that he was tired of the people around him, tired of his existence, and that he looked forward to a new life once the war was won. But perhaps these remarks were not sincere, either; perhaps he was trying, right to the end, to put everybody off the scent? One day he came to our place and said to my mother: 'You can't know how tired I am, how much I am fed up with these people who aren't interested in anything. Sometimes I ask myself why I am wearing myself out for them. I'm exhausted. I see Lavrenti eating pimento and I envy him. I can't eat it. I've something wrong with my gums. He enjoys walnut sauce, but I can't sleep at night if I eat it. I can't even stretch myself out in the normal way. I have to sleep like a gundog.' My mother pitied him. I still wonder today if he had a purpose in taking her into his confidence like that. Was he a scoundrel to the extent of pretending in these moments of apparent forlornness? Who knows? He was capable of anything. These confidences were imparted while he was preparing to arrest my mother and my father. I believe, all the same, that he was sincere at that moment, as otherwise he would not have mentioned his private miseries.

The Doctors' Plot

My father was at bay. Our second alert came at the end of 1952. 'This time, you know, it's irreparable,' he said to me. 'But why didn't he dismiss you along with Molotov and Mikoyan?' I asked. 'That was a tactical manoeuvre,' my father replied. 'He fears to confront me openly because he fears that I might resist. And, also, he is waiting for our H-bomb to be tested.'

To this was added the Slansky affair in Czechoslovakia.[71] I was with Vannikov when we heard the news on the radio, on 22 November 1952. He commented: 'It's set out like in 1937.' Stalin supervised and directed the great trials in Eastern Europe just as he had done with the great trials in the USSR. As the Mingrelian conspiracy had not gone as well as he had expected,[72] the Doctors' Plot was added on to it so as to speed things up.[73] Stalin made use of the stupidest of the military, Konev, who wrote a denunciation accusing some doctors of wanting to send him to the other world. He was flattered at being taken to be a person sufficiently important for someone to want to assassinate him.

The doctors concerned were divided into two categories, the British spies and the American spies. All the Jewish doctors, described as British spies,[74] were alleged to be Beria's men. Subsequently the survivors told my father and then, after his assassination, me that they had been savagely beaten in order to obtain statements that compromised him. Among them were Egorov,[75] who was in charge of medical services in the Kremlin, and Professor Vinogradov, our family doctor.[76] They survived. They had confined themselves to testifying against people already dead. Professor Vinogradov, whose son died during this period after going mad, told us how, under torture, he racked his brains to remember names of deceased people whom he could denounce. 'That was a lesser evil,' he said.[77]

The entire intelligentsia took part in that shameless campaign against the Jews, whatever they may say nowadays. (My father waxed ironical on that theme.) I say nothing of the masses, who had no need for encouragement. We came close to pogroms. The hounds were unleashed. I saw apparently normal people transformed into mad dogs. The most fantastic stories were spread. The Jews were said to have deliberately inoculated children with diphtheria, to have poisoned vaccines, to have killed newborn Russian babies in the maternity hospitals so as to annihilate the Russian people, and so on. The human vileness and baseness described so complacently by Dostoyevsky (a writer whom I detest, since I consider myself to be a normal man) burst forth in every journal. This was the first time that I experienced evil in a purely unreasoned form. It was unbearable, worse than the Nazis' murders. An entire people was being conditioned to kill.

We regarded Professor Shcherbakov as a decent and highly civilised man. One day when he came to attend to my daughter and, as was our custom, he was invited to take tea with us, he began lamenting the fact that Jews occupied all the posts of responsibility in his clinic. The Jewish doctor at the head of his department had inoculated children with bacteria. My father rose and left the room without saying a word. Shcherbakov, embarrassed, took leave of us. After he had gone my father said to my mother 'I never want to see that shit here again.' Professor Shcherbakov obtained the department headship he coveted.

There were rumours that the Jews of the Soviet Union were about to be deported. My father never spoke to me of concrete measures taken in order to carry out that project. If there had been any he would have told me of them because, after Stalin's death and after he had taken charge of the MVD again, he described to me all the crimes in preparation which he had discovered.[78] Lyudvigov, whom my father ordered to write an account of the anti-Semitic persecutions, did not tell me anything like that, nor did Milshtein.

While in Moscow they were denouncing the Jews and the doctors, in Georgia a parallel campaign was being waged against the Mingrelians. One day my father came in with a stack of newspapers and said to me: 'Here, read. You'll gain from it for your study of Soviet politics. Don't forget one thing: these two affairs are aimed at me and therefore at our family.' He was not expressly named as the guilty man, but he knew from his contacts that every accused person was interrogated regarding his relations with my father and about any orders received from him. Stalin was assembling a dossier and waiting for the right moment to bring it into play. I asked my father if we should wait like sheep going to be slaughtered. 'Things won't go that far,' he replied.

My mother threatened

Stalin looked on my mother as his daughter. He was very fond of her. He agreed to be treated only by doctors whom she recommended. However, that did not stop him from ordering her arrest. Svetlana warned her. She told my mother everything she knew, because she too loved her, to the point of betraying her own father. My mother, who did not dabble in politics, was not greatly surprised. If Molotov's wife had been arrested there could be no doubt as to her own fate, with a Menshevik uncle in Paris![79] She realised that this decision of Stalin's formed part of his plan regarding my father. The latter, I can say with certainty, did not react like Molotov. When he saw that things had gone too far he declared that if the people involved in this affair were not dismissed, he would himself take certain measures. These would not be political measures, or measures affecting himself, but measures affecting his wife. He meant that they would arrange to save her by sending her abroad somewhere. There was a scene between Stalin and him, the details of which I don't know. 'Don't worry,' he said to me. 'Do as I told you the other day. I am going to take steps to ensure that nothing happens to your mother.' He knew that Stalin wanted to live in history as the noblest, most intelligent and most honest of rulers, and not with the reputation of a bloody tyrant. After this episode Svetlana visited my mother much more frequently than before.

Not only did Stalin order my mother's arrest, he later planned an attempt on my father's life, to be arranged by Ignatiev. My father expected this. I know that because our guards found a cache of weapons near our *dacha* just beside the road that my father walked along every morning. After Stalin's death he wanted to arrest Ignatiev so as to get to the bottom of that business.

Marfa did not understand the danger that hung over our heads. She made jealous scenes when Svetlana came to see us. 'Why does Nina let her in?' she complained. 'She's like her father, why can't you see that?' She did know, though, that her mother's second husband, Popov, had been arrested. Ignatiev and Ryumin interrogated him personally, seeking to make him confess that he was a terrorist specially trained by my father to assassinate Stalin.

My father

I have the very clear impression that in 1952 my father acted so as to make Stalin realise that he would not let himself go like a lamb to the slaughter but was ready to declare open war on him should Stalin decide on his liquidation. He let Stalin know that he did not want to attack him, as this would mean an unprecedented clash in the top leadership. He spoke to this effect in the hearing of people who, he was sure, would report everything to Stalin. Previously he had been extremely cautious with them but now he began violently criticising Stalin's policy when they were present!

Eventually I asked him: 'Why do you say all that in front of them?' To which he replied: 'I want them to pass the message on.'[80]

I have read in the writings of Khrushchev and others that Stalin had begun to fear my father. Actually, he feared no one. He was quite aware of his power and did not know fear, but he was able to judge people's characters. It was not possible to attempt anything against Stalin in his lifetime. He was so strong, he had succeeded so well in setting those around him against each other, and had so effectively multiplied apparatuses which watched each other, that he had erected insurmountable obstacles. But my father knew that he no longer had anything to lose.[81] It was possible only to sacrifice oneself in assassinating Stalin. My father, being neither a coward nor a sheep walking submissively to the slaughterhouse, I do not rule out the possibility that he may have thought of doing something like that.[82] 'I will never lift a hand against him,' he said, when I asked one day if we were going to wait for the guillotine blade to fall. Did he say that sincerely or did he think that he ought to make that reply? In any case, he took account of one thing, namely, that Stalin's prestige in the country was so great that whoever lifted a hand against him signed his own death warrant and compromised for good the cause for which he acted. One had to wait for Stalin to discredit himself. It may be that my father sometimes helped him in that direction, though I lack formal proof.

In 1952, my father felt able to face up to Stalin. He had not sat with folded arms but had put his men into key posts. He had appointed one such to head Moscow Military District, Artemiev, who had previously commanded the frontier guards. With Vasilevsky's help he had Shtemenko made chief of General Staff. He twice attempted to fetch Zhukov from the provincial holes where he was stagnating. He wanted to make him commander of the land army, a discreet nomination that Stalin would not think called for opposition on his part. But Zhukov, a proud man, did not agree to go along with this. I overheard the end of a conversation between him and my father at the time when Zhukov was transferred from Odessa to Urals Military District. He was asking my father's permission to form special forces in the military district he commanded. Later, when he was Minister of Defence, he put this project into effect, and this was the cause of his fall. Speaking of Stalin he said: 'He'll have all our heads.'

Although my father did not control the security organs he had men in place who kept him informed of whatever was happening. Also, and above all, he had his own intelligence network, which was not dependent on any existing structure. Stalin had allowed him to form it (part of his tactic of using some against others) and had never gone back on that decision. He supposed that my father supplied him with all the information obtained by this network, whereas he passed on to Stalin only facts compromising the organisations which were intriguing against him.

Final manoeuvres

Malenkov, Khrushchev and Bulganin were doubtless not so direct with Stalin as my father was, but he could have no doubt that my father enjoyed their support. I remember hearing all four of them refer to a statement Stalin had made after the 19th Congress, when he spoke of withdrawing from public life.[83] They recalled that he had already, several years earlier, hinted at retirement, but concluded that, this time, they should call his bluff – and must be stopped before he started a war and killed off his entourage. They toyed with the idea of offering him an honorary position which would allow him to end his days in tranquillity, haloed with glory but without real power. They wanted to save their skins, of course, but they did also genuinely want to prevent war, which would have meant the end of them.

Stalin had never made a mistake before: he always struck first and hard enough to knock his opponent down. I believe that if the Soviet Union had started a war, it would have won. It may be said that Providence took a hand here, for nobody could have arrested Stalin. At the same time I must emphasise that opposition was very much stronger in 1952 than it had been in 1945. If Stalin had decided at that time to conquer all Europe my father could not have stopped him, whereas in 1952 the group opposed to war was more numerous, more organised and more resolute.

Doubtless at Stalin's instigation, Malenkov undertook to discredit Vlasik[84] and Poskrebyshev, though they were fanatically devoted to their master. He wanted to replace them with his own men and ordered Ignatiev to compile a compromising dossier that would show them to be corrupt. It appeared that they used Stalin's name to enrich themselves. Poskrebyshev rushed to my father to seek his help (this man often came to our house and my father put up with him). He proclaimed his innocence, certainly lying. My father replied that he could do nothing, as he was in a much worse situation. 'Have you ever lifted your little finger for me? You can only rely on the wisdom of Iosif Vissarionovich.' Poor Poskrebyshev was ready to climb up to the ceiling. Eventually he was made to retire. Nevertheless Malenkov succeeded only partly in gaining control of Stalin's immediate entourage. He did not manage to infiltrate the Secretariat completely.

Stalin's death

The last months

Death gave Stalin short notice. His health, the only thing that escaped his forecasts, began to totter, and he took fright when he noticed this. He sent for a doctor from Georgia. This man swelled with pride at the honour, but my mother persuaded him to return home at once as she was fond of him. When I saw Stalin in December 1952 he looked well and had a perky air.

Svetlana told me that he was keeping to a diet and had stopped smoking. However, in January 1953, most exceptionally, Stalin did not attend the commemoration of Lenin's death, held at the Bolshoi Theatre. Everyone was struck by his absence. My father told me that Stalin was ill. When I questioned my mother in the hope of learning more she told me that Stalin had had a flutter in his heart as he was getting into his car. I met him, for the last time, a few days later. He had sent for me to talk about the decorations he meant to award to the engineers responsible for the system of anti-aircraft defences built around Moscow. I found him, contrary to habit, lying on a sofa. He had lost his usual liveliness. He explained to me that these decorations had to remain secret. 'Don't be in a hurry to show off all the stars you're going to be given,' he advised me, in a tired voice. At the time, however, I was so angry with him that I felt no pity. Svetlana celebrated her birthday on 28 February. I remember the preparations. She came to consult my mother about the dress she was having made for the occasion. On 2 March I saw my mother in tears, her face swollen from sorrow. 'What's up?' I asked. 'Iosif Vissarionovich has had a very serious heart attack,' she replied. Still remembering the threat that hung over us and the conversations I had had with my father, I felt great relief. 'This may save our lives. There's no call to get into such a state.' She was indignant. 'How dare you talk like that? A man is dying, a Georgian. I want never again to hear such words from you.' My father did not come home for lunch that day. I told Marfa. She did not feel sorry either, though she was unaware of what great danger we were in and only vaguely guessed that something was wrong. As I was thinking to suggest that she telephone Svetlana my mother called to her in the corridor: 'Marfa, let's go and see Svetlana!' She did not want to go that day and my mother left by herself.

'A fatal outcome is unavoidable'

Svetlana has embroidered the story of her father's death. He died without recovering consciousness. There were no winks or anything of that sort.

This is what I learnt from my father. The Politburo members had visited Stalin in the evening. He had sent them away early because he felt unwell and wanted to lie down.[85] Next day his guards noticed that he stayed shut in his room longer than usual (he locked himself in, so as not to let anyone take him by surprise). They knocked, but got no answer. They were afraid to break down the door and telephoned Malenkov and my father, who told them to do that and then hastened to Stalin's *dacha* along with Khrushchev. They found Stalin lying unconscious on his sofa, barely breathing. Contrary to what has been said, they at once sent for the doctors – Myasnikov, a well-known heart specialist, and three or four other specialists. The resuscitation service arrived, and gave Stalin heart massage as he lay on his sofa. The doctors examined him and made their diagnosis. My father was very pleased with Myasnikov. While the others were running hither and thither in a great state of agitation, he sought out the members of the Politburo and told them, calmly, as though what was a stake was an ordinary death: 'Comrades, I have to disappoint you. A fatal outcome is unavoidable.'

None of the Politburo members present shed a tear nor did any of them want to sit at Stalin's bedside. Seated in a nearby room they came to an agreement on the succession[86] and discussed future reorganisation of the government. They decided to send for all the other members of the Politburo, to warn the Central Committee, and to do everything possible to save Stalin's life, so that nobody should accuse them of negligence. Then they took turns in watching over him.

My father had plans which he had formed years earlier. I did not see him during those days. We even gave up the physical exercise we took together in the mornings, for the first and last time in my father's life. Two or three days later he came to lunch and told me that Stalin would never return to political activity, even if he recovered. 'He is completely unconscious. It will be better for him to die. Because, if he survives, it will be as a vegetable.' When my mother cried, he added: 'You're a funny one, Nina. His death has saved your life. If he had held out a year longer, no member of the Politburo would have survived.' To which she retorted: 'That would have been no great loss – except for you, of course.' She was exasperated against everything and everybody after the years of tension we had been living through.[87]

Stalin's death-agony went on. My mother visited Svetlana every day. She did not like the people who gathered round her, 'people who hated Stalin and now pretended to weep for him.' She would have liked to tear her away from that company, but did nothing. Marfa went with her on one occasion and came back saying she would never go there again. As she was pregnant we did not insist. Stalin died on 5 March, in the evening.[88]

My father advised us not to go and say farewell to the body laid out in the Kremlin. 'Anything may happen. The people have lost their heads. All these fools press towards him in their thousands as if they hadn't had the opportunity to show their love when he was alive. He's dead, so what!' There was indeed a frightful crush.[89] I was one of the guard of honour at the funeral, which took place on 9 March. The sarcophagus was set down in front of Lenin's mausoleum. It was a terrible sight. You could see Stalin's face through a glass panel. I examined attentively the faces of those around me. Nobody was crying. There was a sense of relief. People seemed to have been rejuvenated. For me this was a revelation. Suddenly I spotted my director: his face was swollen, his eyes too, and he was weeping. I wondered if this idiot was feeling sorrow. I went up to him and looked at him quizzically: 'I've just had an accident,' he whispered. When his car braked suddenly, he had been thrown against the windscreen.

Malenkov, my father and Molotov delivered their funeral orations standing on the mausoleum. I listened attentively. I detected no emotion in my father's address. Molotov alone visibly felt sincere sorrow. I saw my father next day. My mother criticised him for the dryness of his address. 'People won't understand,' she said. 'On the contrary, I hope they will understand me,'[90] he replied abruptly. 'Nina, you really ought to take a less narrow view of things. See what will be published in the press. That will be my view.'

'Do as you wish,' she said, 'but on no account sign those articles. Your position now is even more precarious than it was when Stalin was alive.'

Svetlana

My mother was concerned for Svetlana. My father assured her that it had been arranged that the girl should lack for nothing. 'When Lenin died the people around him, all except Krupskaya, were thrown into the street. People have short memories.' Measures had to be taken quickly so that this did not happen to Svetlana. There were some who objected, but Molotov insisted, with my father's backing, and the necessary decision was adopted.

I saw Svetlana again at the session of the Supreme Soviet which was to ratify the changes made in the structure of the government. She came up to me. 'Ah, well, Sergo, it's all over.' I asked her what she meant. 'It's all over, my father's not there any more, others are taking the decisions, everything will be better.' I told her that I shared her sorrow, but she went on, bitterly: 'And you have no further duty to perform where I'm concerned.' I suggested that I visit her with my mother so that we could talk more calmly. 'Very well, come, both of you, but don't bring Marfa.' I was so stupid as to say that, anyway, my wife was hardly in a condition to travel, and this brought the comment: 'Oh yes, of course, you are expecting a son.' When I told my mother about this incident she said that Svetlana had never forgiven me, and advised against my visiting her. So she went there alone. Svetlana asked her: 'Will you hate his memory because he wanted to arrest you?'

'Don't you see what a state I'm in? For me, your father was a great Georgian and someone very close to me.'

'But aren't people going to forget what was good in him?' Svetlana concluded.

The First de-Stalinisation

Once Stalin was buried, the Politburo members started to swagger around. 'Now we'll put the country on its feet again.' My father was pleased because he could now implement reforms that previously had been inconceivable. My mother never stopped warning him: 'You were thought to be very close to Stalin. You took advantage of that, and now that he's dead your position has been weakened. Your plans lead you straight into confrontation with your colleagues. I don't believe they are sincere. They haven't changed overnight.' But he persisted: 'The people who work with me know what the real situation is,' he explained. 'I want to rely on them. As for my colleagues, they aren't stupid. They know that the country is in a critical condition, worse than in 1937 because people today see things clearly. That's why they've made me take charge of the MVD again.' But my mother would not be persuaded. She was very frightened for him, and for me, too. Being more intuitive she did not share the optimism of my father, who thought that after Stalin's death we were no longer in physical danger.

It has been alleged that my father set himself to promote reforms with great energy because he had committed more crimes than anyone else and was afraid he would be called to account for them. Nothing could be more mistaken. It is enough to recall his previous attempts at reform in order to be convinced of that.

The new government

Malenkov as head of the government

Even before Stalin fell ill, Khrushchev, Malenkov, Bulganin and my father had agreed on how to share power when the moment came.

My father proposed that Malenkov be Prime Minister because he thought he would be able to control him totally.[1] He started from the idea that a Georgian could not take the helm of the Russian state a second time.[2] If Stalin was successful that was because, when he came to power, he had only Jews around him. No Russian was in a position to take power, possibly because of the policy followed by Lenin, who preferred to have non-Russians around him. As the Jews could not agree among themselves, they preferred a Georgian. In my father's view such a conjuncture of circumstances would not recur.

He knew what Malenkov amounted to but considered that he was good enough for the role he meant to let him play.[3] He would have found it hard to have to obey an imbecile. He had put up with Stalin because he admired his ability.

Bulganin and Zhukov at Defence

Bulganin had to be implored to accept the Ministry of Defence. He objected that the military did not regard him as one of their own, and, indeed, he understood nothing of military problems. My father suggested that Zhukov be made Vice-Minister, to understudy Bulganin, and he made the latter accept this decision.

The idea was to undertake a reform on the American model, by establishing a main General Staff and giving the Ministry of Defence to a civilian. Zhukov caused conflict from the start. He never missed an opportunity to highlight Bulganin's incompetence, arrogantly ignoring his orders to an extent that evoked complaints from the Minister. Zhukov was summoned before the Central Committee. He had to listen to a sermon on the leading role of the Party. Malenkov pointed out that the Americans appointed civilians as Minister of Defence and that Vasilevsky had accepted Bulganin's nomination without flinching. Zhukov clenched his teeth and said nothing. At the end Khrushchev asked him, in a joking tone: 'Well, now, have you learnt the lesson?'

My father had occasion to rebuke Zhukov in my presence: 'You make things harder for yourself and harder for me.'

'So you're asking me to tolerate an idiot like that!' Zhukov exclaimed. 'Have a little patience, you will be Minister,' my father replied.

In April 1953 Zhukov tried to get my father to abolish the political organs in the army. He was very hostile to those organs, losing his temper at the mere memory of the Military Council and political supervision in the army. He broke out into obscenities (it was for that that he was to be dismissed in 1957). 'What use are they?' he asked my father. 'When it was necessary to keep watch on the Tsarist officers, fine. But today?' He added that our army would become effective only when unity of command was restored. 'Be a little patient,' my father replied 'We can't do everything at once. Patience, patience.' He tried to make Zhukov see that the decision he wanted would become possible when the Party's role had been reduced in other spheres. Zhukov loathed the Party and that was what created an affinity between him and my father.

My father as Minister of Internal Affairs

It was not without hesitation that my father accepted the Ministry of Internal Affairs, which had been reunified with State Security. As he saw it, Vice-Prime Ministers ought not to be simultaneously Ministers. It took a week for Khrushchev and Malenkov to persuade him to accept the post.[4]

'You have experience of reorganisations in this sphere. After all, you managed it in 1938 and 1939, under much less favourable conditions. This time we'll all help you, and after a year we'll release you from the MVD. You can then take charge of the economy and co-operation with Europe.' In reality they wanted to compromise him before getting rid of him. Besides the MVD, my father inherited the military-industrial complex.

He thought he had reassured his colleagues by leaving the most important roles to them and making it clear that he did not aspire to them. He was convinced that the members of the Presidium wanted, as he did, to end the confrontation with the outside world and to improve the standard of living of the Soviet people. He was mistaken as to their real intentions.

Khrushchev at the head of the Party

Khrushchev himself suggested that he take over the Party leadership. In their plans my father and his colleagues had agreed to abolish the post of General Secretary and free the economy from Party tutelage.

My father said that the old system was justified so long as there were still people who had been brought up under the Tsarist regime and received a bourgeois education. But now, when we had already reached the third generation of Soviet people, we could not entrust the country's administration to the Party apparatchiks. They should confine themselves to activity in their cells. It was not up to the Central Committee to run the country; that was the job of the Council of Ministers. The experience of the Soviet Union and of the other Socialist countries showed that the Party ought to devote itself exclusively to ideology, education and culture, to everything that went to form the new man, without interfering in the economy.

My father was basically convinced that everything depended on the economy. Once that was emancipated, ideology would follow. In private he summed up his position in a witticism. 'Iosif Vissarionovich taught us that events precede the development of consciousness. That's absolutely correct. And the Party organs have only to devote themselves to the development of consciousness. Nikita Sergeevich [Khrushchev] attaches great importance to the harmonious development of the human being. He is himself a model of harmony internal and external. That task is his by right.'

He explained to me one day. 'Look at the rest of the world. Even in Fascist Germany it was not the Party that governed but the state apparatus, and the Nazi Party was quite separate from that. Hitler transformed the Party apparatus into a machine for control and repression. Iosif Vissarionovich did the same thing. But here the Party decides everything, both harvests and arrests. Its leaders dominate everything and are responsible for nothing. What I want is for everyone henceforth to be answerable for his actions.'

He realised that the Party could not be made to disappear overnight. To begin with, he had to deprive it of any real function, to prevent it from doing harm. He imposed his point of view because he was able to, but he did it with the agreement of Malenkov, Molotov and Khrushchev. I really insist on that point. True, some people raised objections. I've forgotten what they were. But that trio agreed. A commission was formed to transform the Party's organs and wind up its agricultural and industrial departments.

Reform of the government

In the last phase of Stalin's reign, ministers multiplied like mushrooms. After his death my father proposed that they be regrouped. There was not the slightest political motivation in this proposal: he simply wanted to lighten the administration. When, after the war, he was Vice-Chairman of the Council of Ministers and in charge of a number of ministries, he observed that the Party's tutelage, and indeed that of the Vice-Prime Minister, was a burden on the ministries. These ministries were, generally speaking, run by efficient people who ought to have elbow room within their sphere of competence. My father had started to practise this policy de facto, without authorisation from the Council of Ministers, in relation to the ministries for which he was responsible. After Stalin's death he extended this autonomy and these enlarged powers to the remaining ministries, and had laws passed to cover the change.

Thenceforth economic and foreign policy decisions were taken at ministerial level, whereas previously they had had to be approved by the Central Committee. The Central Committee's economic departments were abolished.[5] The only supervising organ was now the Presidium. The Central Committee was, naturally, much displeased with all this, since it lost its imaginary control over the economy – imaginary because what control meant was mainly intrigues and dismissals. The whole Party apparatus hummed like a beehive. All that was left to it was ideology![6] The Party now had charge of education and culture only! It was, above all, the top of the Party pyramid that was aimed at. Later, it was alleged that my father wanted by this means to take power for himself.[7]

The MVD

My father immediately formed a special section within the MVD. Its mission was to prepare dossiers of rehabilitation, to rid the MVD of all its repressive functions, and to set up 'think tanks' inside the ministry for working out national and economic policies and formulating recommendations to put before the Council of Ministers. He composed a series of notes on these points.[8] He wanted to build a real Ministry of Internal Affairs which would no longer spend its time imprisoning or trapping people and blowing their brains out. In order to mount major reforms it was necessary first to deal with a large number of minor matters, such as the right of foreigners to move freely about the territory of the USSR, and reform of the internal passport system. He got down to this without delay and set going groups with the task of elaborating proposals on the basis of directives he gave them. The major reforms were to be ready for introduction at the beginning of 1954.

My father also began to clear the decks in the intelligence sector. His aim was to get rid of all the incompetent Party functionaries with whom our services abroad were lumbered. He wanted to concentrate intelligence work on economic and technological matters. Rapprochement with the Western countries made our traditional methods of blackmail and terror pointless. This, too, was held against him.[9]

Censorship

As he did not want to leave the press in the Party's charge, my father put the censorship under the control of the MVD. 'Our censorship,'[10] he told me, 'is so clumsy that we publish only idiotic books, especially in the political domain. These books are so unreadable that they deserve to be thrown down lavatory pans. I want to lift the restrictions and allow some fresh air to circulate.'

Some time later he brought me a pile of books in English. 'We are going to publish all that,' he said. He gave me, among other books, works by British economists and war memoirs. I did not have time to read them all. He intended to publish translations of foreigners' writings about politics and economics. He wanted to print, in large numbers of copies, the memoirs of foreign statesmen which had already been translated by Tass for internal use, and also historical works, not necessarily confined to 20th century themes, so as to remove the blinkers from the eyes of our intelligentsia. He wanted, also, to publish the writings of Bukharin and Trotsky, so that people should realise that they represented genuine political tendencies and were not agents recruited by foreign intelligence services.

He had already put together a team to rewrite the history of the USSR and that of the Party. What was wanted above all was to 'de-Stalinise' this history.[11] My father insisted that the real debates and dissensions between the various groups should be described instead of being dismissed, as before, under labels like 'British spy' or 'agent of imperialism.' Lyudvigov was put in charge of this project. Pospelov, too, was to participate. My father had helped him to rise so as to counterbalance Suslov. This does not say anything for his judgement, for Pospelov proved to be narrow-minded.[12] My father was keen for Sharia to take part in this work but, being too much weakened by his spell in prison, he declined. Alas, my father had no time to bring these schemes to fruition.

The Pantheon project

One day my father told me of his plan to build a Pantheon, an idea he had begun to discuss while Stalin was alive. Amazed, I asked him, 'But have we the money for that? 'I want to clear the Mausoleum and all the tombs from the Red Square,' he replied. Seeing my expression, he laughed. 'Well, now, isn't that a good idea?'

'One doesn't disturb the dead,' my mother intervened. 'True, when they are buried in a cemetery. But I don't see why the principal square in our country should be a cemetery.'

He wanted to entrust this task to the architect Abrosimov, but he ducked out. The project was evidently assigned to others. They had to find somewhere in Moscow where they could build a burial-place for the occupants of the Mausoleum and the Red Square.

Decorations and portraits

Another time, when there was talk of introducing an Order of Stalin, to immortalise his memory, my father opposed this, saying that it was time to put an end to this flea-market. He proposed decorations of a quite different style, honouring the national heroes of the republics. He was to be blamed for this later. He made things worse for himself by suggesting that a ban be imposed on the displaying of portraits of the leaders of Party and State during popular demonstrations. 'Aren't you tired of seeing your touched-up mugs everywhere?' he asked his colleagues. 'I am. I look like an idiot in my pince-nez. And you look like a piglet. Does it give you pleasure to see yourself at every street corner?' he concluded, turning to Khrushchev. He also wanted to rename the innumerable places and enterprises that bore the names of our leaders. 'In the United States a great President like Roosevelt hasn't even a monument. We should copy them if we want to seem civilised.' This charge was also laid against him, that he wanted to deprive the masses of the possibility of contemplating their guides.

The *dachas*

Our *nomenklatura* possessed no personal property. My father proposed to each of his colleagues that they have a *dacha* built at the state's expense. An architect would make plans in conformity with their wishes. The *dachas* they had had up to that time would be turned into kindergartens. He suggested that these new residences be built at Sukhumi. 'That way,' he guffawed, 'I'll have you all together, I'll put a wire fence all round, and I'll be able to keep an eye on you.' They laughed in chorus but were not to forget that joke of his, either. These plans were not to my mother's liking. 'You are going to spoil those lovely landscapes,' she said. My father did not give ground. 'We've already built a zoo there. Do you think they'll spoil the scene worse than the monkeys?' My father had a strong dislike for those animals, though he was very fond of bears and the cat family.

The Jewish doctors given amnesty

My father had the Jewish doctors released without waiting for the approval of his colleagues, who were extremely displeased.[13] He confronted them with a fait accompli, knowing as he did that Malenkov and Khrushchev would have continued the anti-Semitic persecution, though doubtless in a less exaggerated form. Khrushchev reproached him for acting on his own and too precipitately. 'The masses are not ready,' he insisted. My father retorted that if he had waited for Khrushchev to agree, the situation would have been the same in a year's time. Khrushchev also considered that it was wrong to emphasise the anti-Semitic character of the persecution. Better to say nothing about that, he thought. The accused could have been released without publicity. When my father told my mother of this conversation she said: 'Have you still not understood that Khrushchev participated in the anti-Semitic campaign not because he was forced to by Stalin but because he is himself a furious anti-Semite.' 'If that were all,' my father replied, laughing, 'things wouldn't be so terrible.'

Malenkov and Khrushchev did not expect my father to move so quickly. They did not have time to remove Abakumov and Ryumin, thanks to whom my father put his hand on documents dealing with the anti-Jewish campaigns.[14] He then opened an enquiry into the assassination of Mikhoels, in the face of fierce opposition from Khrushchev, who became the spokesman of the Russian chauvinists. My father wrote a report on that assassination and sent it to the Presidium of the Central Committee, causing a lot of reticence among those who had been directly involved in the affair.[15]

When he studied the trial of the activists of the Jewish Anti-Fascist Committee he was astonished at the hatred breathed by certain witnesses and informers, especially regarding Mikhoels. These were sometimes voluntary testimonies given before arrest, so that torture and pressure had no part in them. 'The worst anti-Semites are to be found among the Jews,' he told my mother.

Reviewing the conspiracies

My father had time to reveal the truth about the Doctors' Plot despite obstruction from Khrushchev and the whole Party apparatus. He also opened up the Mingrelian Conspiracy[16] and the Leningrad Affair and had enough time to release half of the inmates of the Gulag.[17] He had the investigation department of the MVD and the Gulag transferred to the Ministry of Justice.[18] He had always been against the inclusion of these administrations in the MVD. Some of these measures were later annulled. The speed with which he put them through aroused suspicion among his colleagues, probably because they had already formed the intention of attacking him. They were particularly anxious that he should not reap the benefit of these decisions, or else they simply wanted to drag things out as long as possible.

They might have put up with all that if my father had not proposed, at the end of April, to convene a congress at which each one of them would describe what part he had played in the repressions, without putting the blame on Stalin. He wanted to establish the responsibility of every member of the Politburo and to be able to explain to the country how such things could have happened. The Party would then have taken decisions accordingly. Such a congress should analyse the whole history of the repressions, from the Bolsheviks' seizure of power onward, and then explain the changes in internal and external policy that were planned.

My father at once suffered a rebuff. 'Do you want us to engage in self-criticism Chinese-style?' demanded Molotov. 'The Chinese merely imitate us. Let's not give up our prerogative,' my father replied. And he returned to the fray, proposing that, at least, an enlarged plenum be convened, so as to settle this question not by a vote of the Presidium but of this assembly. They agreed, but reluctantly. This plenum was to have been held in November or December 1953.When my mother heard that, she said to my father: 'Believe me, you've just signed your own death warrant.' I remember that my father replied: 'I had no choice.' Until April 1953 Khrushchev had behaved as a docile ally of my father. The break between them took place on account of this congress.

Ignatiev's role

Kruglov and Serov told me that my father had strongly insisted that responsibility for the Doctors' Plot and the Leningrad and Mingrelian conspiracies must not be attributed exclusively to Stalin. He wanted an inquiry that would reveal the role played by Ignatiev, an inquiry that might incriminate the apparatus of the Central Committee, as my father realised very well. Malenkov, having been up to his neck in those affairs, became alarmed.[19]

One evening in May, while drinking his tea, into which he had sliced some pieces of apple, my father said to my mother, in a weary voice: 'You can't imagine all the dirty deeds I've come upon in the course of this inquiry into Ignatiev's doings. The picture that emerges is exactly like the situation following Kirov's death, with the same sort of provocations concocted by the Orgotdel of the Central Committee. All my efforts before the war were in vain. Many in the Party apparatus are implicated, and not only as executives. All that needs to be cleaned up. Ignatiev must be punished and this must be announced publicly.'[20]

'But you are going to incriminate Malenkov,' my mother objected. 'Malenkov played a double game. On the one hand he warned me of intrigues against me, but, on the other, just as earlier in Byelorussia, he was putting his shoulder to the wheel of repression.'

Ignatiev was recalled from exile. He pretended to be ill and took refuge in hospital. 'He's trying to gain time,' my father remarked. And my mother said: 'If so, you need to understand what that means for you.'

How far should glasnost go?

It seems strange today, but at that time I was not at all that interested in the discussions between my father, Malenkov, Bulganin and Khrushchev at which I happened to be present. I listened without paying attention, waking up only when they spoke about the coming congress, as I was curious to learn how they were going to treat the various periods of our history since the 1930s. Khrushchev, for example, thought that nothing should be said about the trial of the 'Industrial Party.'[21] 'Impossible!' objected my father. 'That trial began the series of persecutions of scientists.' This shows the extent to which they were already going into details.

My father was against personifying what was evil. He put it to Malenkov and Khrushchev that 'the evil was in the system itself,' and that this system had to be reformed. Malenkov and Khrushchev did not contradict him, but said that we must proceed slowly, lest our external enemies exploit the situation. My father replied that if we lost time we should discredit ourselves definitively and would never again be able to restore the economy. We must, on the contrary, make the change sharply and show what was wrong in the foundations of our system. 'We must open all the abscesses. What are we afraid of? We shall, perhaps, lose our jobs, be demoted. We shan't die of that.' Khrushchev and, especially, Malenkov, gave their assent. The latter declared that he had long dreamt of giving up any position in the Party. This drew down my father's sarcasm: 'I do indeed remember what a burden Party tasks were for you.' Malenkov replied in the same vein. Khrushchev boasted of his 'humane' policy in the Ukraine. 'I am ready to give an account of all my actions before the congress, I have nothing to blush about,' he proclaimed. Malenkov and my father refrained from comment. 'We all have things to reproach ourselves for, but we prevented things still worse from happening,' my father concluded. On that point there was complete consensus.

Some time later my father drew up the instructions for the committee charged with rehabilitations. He recommended that all the trials be reviewed, including the pre-war ones, and that Trotskyism be treated as a political tendency and not as spying. Malenkov, Saburov and Pervukhin sided with him, but Khrushchev and Kaganovich opposed, presenting a resolution to the effect that this would be premature. This was a problem that called for special study. Rehabilitation commissions had to be set up, the people had to be prepared, saved from shock, and we must avoid harming the international Communist movement.[22] On that last point my father, irritated at being blamed for 'hastiness,' replied drily that the Party had everything to gain in taking the initiative in exposing past crimes, if it wanted to be respected world-wide. Only Bulganin and

Malenkov agreed. I suppose the latter was not afraid to reveal the past because he counted on my father's protection.

The Presidium adopted a resolution that judged the proposal to be correct, but it made the point that precipitancy in this field could only harm our image in the international movement.

Nationalities policy

I never heard my father say anything to suggest that he wanted to break up the Soviet federation. However, he considered that the national policy pursued up to that time was bad and that immediate changes were imperative.[23] The republics had to be rid of their Russian 'overseers' and ruled by local cadres.[24] He proposed that the USSR be ruled by a Soviet, the presidency of which should be held for six months at a time, taking turns, by one of the heads of the republics. This idea comes back to me because my father referred to Cadogan, the Permanent Secretary of the Foreign Office, and to the British civil service from which he wished to draw inspiration. He pointed out that in Britain parties and governments succeeded each other in power while the state apparatus stayed in place and ensured essential continuity. (The situation in the USA was different, but there economic and financial interests maintained stability.) 'Here,' said my father,' the opposite applies. The same party stays in power but it is enough for one functionary to be removed and his entire apparatus is replaced. We need competent people who stay in place whatever happens.' My father had arrived at this conclusion through interesting himself in Cadogan's career. He was connected with the secret services and stayed in his post under all governments. Our bugs once intercepted a conversation between him and Churchill. We heard him railing violently at Churchill for having been too conciliatory with Stalin. I happened to be in the MVD's laboratory where these interchanges were recorded and a friend played me the recording. We were thunderstruck. Imagine a Vice-Minister being able to speak to Stalin in that tone! While still stunned I told my father what I had heard. He began by being angry because he thought I should not have heard the recording, but then he explained that Cadogan had spoken like that because Churchill had made promises to Stalin without consulting the British government and getting its agreement. In Britain, he said, the members of the government could express their divergences of view without fearing a stab in the back. If one of the ministers found himself in a minority on a question, he need not fear that this would one day constitute a charge against him. 'In that country,' he said, 'relations within the government are not at all as they are here. People think there's more freedom in America, but that's not so. There, it's always capital that lays down the law: in Britain the government is less subject to the financiers.' He added that men like Cadogan were the real rulers of Britain. They were independent of political intrigues and served the state. Churchill and Cadogan had known each other over a long period, through their connections with the British secret services. That also explained their familiarity with each other. However, my father warned me: 'Don't breathe a word of what I've said to anybody. It would be taken as a criticism of our system.'

The former president of the Ukraine, Kravchuk, was one of a group of young men from western Ukraine whom my father had wanted to bring forward. The machinery of repression had destroyed them, Kravchuk escaping by a miracle. In Poland, I met Ukrainian nationalists who had spent fifteen or twenty years in the camps. Our ambassador was much afraid that my meeting with these men might turn sour on me. He warned me: 'I know what you're like. Try to control yourself this time.' These Ukrainians were older than I was. Imagine elephants advancing towards one another! But these men fell into my arms. 'These people know nothing,' they told me. 'In 1953 your father summoned us to Moscow with other leaders of nationalist movements and told us "I consider that your criticisms of the Soviet regime are fundamentally correct. Every people has the right to defend its interests within the Soviet state. I propose that you enter the government and put together a policy for the well-being of your people." And when that happened to him which you know about, we were tortured for three months to get us to tell what he had said. But we held out, and collected fifteen extra years.' My father had spoken also of bringing back the *émigrés*, without obliging them to become Communists.[25]

Zhukov and my father had a dispute about territorial formations and national armies.[26] My father thought them necessary. Zhukov replied, saying that admitting this principle would lead to the destruction of the Soviet Union. There must be only one army. At most one might tolerate a regiment that carried a Ukrainian flag, comparable to the Ukraine's Ministry of Foreign Affairs. Even that, though, he thought went too far. My father saw nothing inexpedient in authorising the creation of national guards. They would look grand at receptions for foreign heads of state. He could very well picture a Ukrainian national guard dressed in Cossack costume and carrying sabres. The police, too, he thought, should be autochthonous.[27]

Foreign Policy

Arms reductions

My father, who was still in charge of the military-industrial complex, put a brake on the arms programme, reducing the mass-production of tanks, guns and aircraft. Here too he met with strong resistance, especially from Bulganin. The war party in the Ministry of Defence, especially the commanders of the land army, howled that this was treason, and began to hate my father. This group continued to rage after his death, and Khrushchev had to use Zhukov to combat them.

My father was blamed for deciding to explode the H-bomb without informing the Politburo.[28] This is false. The question had been discussed in the special commission of which Malenkov and Bulganin were both members.[29] There was nothing secret or unilateral in my father's decision.

After Stalin died, my father proposed that negotiations be begun immediately with the Western powers in order to eliminate subjects of discord and initiate a rapprochement. The members of the Presidium preferred to wait for the end of the Korean War before embarking on fundamental discussions. However, as soon as Stalin's funeral was over the situation eased. Here, too, it was my father who took the initiative. He wanted to make clear to the Westerners that the USSR did not want confrontation and was abandoning its previous policy. He made a certain number of approaches in that sense. The Westerners did not realise straight away that it was possible for a radical turn to be made.

Malenkov and my father proposed that Soviet troops be withdrawn from Austria. Molotov objected that we ought to make something out of that concession. We should end our occupation when we were offered something in exchange. Malenkov and my father pointed out, to no effect, that the economic advantages to us would be immediate. But Molotov dug his heels in.[30]

German reunification

My father returned to his idea of reunifying Germany. He argued for this by stressing that the United States would be kept busy for a long time with decolonising the British Empire and the other colonial empires. While that was going on the German-Russian tandem would carry through an economic transformation. Reunified Germany would be grateful to the Soviet Union and would agree to help it economically. We could even put up with a bourgeois Germany. Malenkov and Saburov saw nothing against that. Khrushchev and Molotov had to be persuaded.[31] My father was surprised to find Molotov so obtuse. 'I thought he was more independent-minded,' he told me. 'I attributed his hidebound behaviour to Stalin. But now I can see that his brain has gone sclerotic.'[32]

He produced a report on the measures adopted in July 1952 with a view to strengthening Communism in the GDR. He showed the disastrous consequences of these measures and in May 1953 called for the dismissal of Ulbricht. Everyone agreed, making only one objection, namely, that we must not seem to be retreating. My father replied that we had every interest in seeming to be reasonable people. He had to insist very strongly that Ulbricht and the other East-German leaders be summoned to Moscow. His colleagues were convinced only when he showed them that the GDR was on the brink of insurrection.[33] My father criticised Ulbricht vigorously, supporting his argument with proofs.[34] The East German leaders acknowledged their mistakes, while stressing that they had only been applying the policy dictated by Moscow. They were told that a new line had been adopted and they must change direction forthwith.[35]

Initial measures were taken. The Central Committee's resolution mentioned 'abandonment of the accelerated building of Socialism' and not, as my father wanted 'abandonment of the building of Socialism'. But the decision to reunify Germany had been taken. Ulbricht was to be dismissed. My father had already sent signals in that sense to the Western countries. He thought that reunification would take place before the end of the year, on the Soviet Union's initiative. Some Socialists could be included in the future government of Germany and the hostility of the German Social-Democratic Party towards the Soviet Union would disappear after reunification. Malenkov, who may have shared his views, supported my father, but Khrushchev and the rest tried to win time by putting him off the scent.

The German case was one among others. Several times it happened that important decisions sought by my father were put off. The opposition by Khrushchev and others to abandoning the building of Socialism in the GDR was due not to ideological considerations but to Russian chauvinism, Russian desire to control the Germans. Communism was always, for the Russians, a pretext for interfering in the affairs of other countries and setting themselves up as a superpower. Ideology was merely an instrument that enabled them to claim hegemony.

Reconciliation with Tito

My father's second project in the sphere of foreign policy was to bring about reconciliation with Yugoslavia. He pointed out to his colleagues that Tito had not joined the Atlantic alliance in spite of the extremely difficult situation his country was in. He had held out. The USSR ought, therefore, as soon as possible, to admit the wrong it and the Cominform had done, and reveal the whole truth on that affair. Here again he heard the same refrain from his colleagues. We had to go slowly and avoid losing face. However, Molotov agreed with my father and he was given the task of restoring ties with Belgrade, as he had retained networks in that country. He did that and reported that the Yugoslavs had agreed, for their part, to admit some of their own mistakes (purchasing arms from America), so that the Soviet leaders should not lose face completely. All that remained was to make this decision public. The text of the letter to Ranković, which was attributed to my father had received Molotov's approval.[36]

Hungary

In Hungary, as in Germany, tension grew. Rákosi was pursuing the usual Communist policy of collectivisation and suppression. He came to Moscow 'to obtain advice.' He was not quite so stupid as Ulbricht, though of the same type. He sensed that change was in the air and came to learn the news.

Malenkov and Molotov started to mutter some obscure formulas.[37] Irritated to perceive that they dared not announce what had been decided, my father told Rákosi that the Party must no longer interfere in the economy and that domination of the Council of Ministers by the Party ought long ago to have been ended in the Soviet Union and, a fortiori, in the People's Democracies. 'Busy yourselves with ideology and the education of the masses if you want to stay in politics in spite of your health problems. But you would do better to resign,' he said. That evening my father, greatly amused, described to us how Rákosi reacted. 'Thank you, Lavrenti Pavlovich,' he had replied. 'I've long dreamt of withdrawing from politics, but I was afraid to propose it.'

'You were wrong, there are no irreplaceable people,' my father had shot back. Rákosi therefore had to submit to the decision of the Presidium by which he was to devote himself to ideology, leaving the government to Imre Nagy.

Meetings were held with the leaders of the other peoples' democracies at which the coming reforms were discussed. Some prisoners who had survived the trials were set free. I met some of them at our place. My father told us that he was now going to succeed in applying the policy which he had wanted to apply after the war and which Stalin had prevented: to go back to governments of coalition with the socialists and to withdraw our troops from Central Europe.[38] The peoples' democracies had allowed us to station our missiles on their soil and to supervise their anti-aircraft defences and that should be enough for us. He had talked about this with Zhukov, who agreed that we must reduce the establishment of our army and modernise our armaments. According to Zhukov, what we needed were forces small in number but mobile and well-trained. He insisted, however, that we maintain military bases, airfields and munitions depots in the peoples' democracies.

Seeing how stupidly obstinate Molotov was, my father proposed that he be replaced by Maisky at the Ministry of Foreign Affairs. 'If you don't agree, you can resign. Times have changed and the spirit of the Council of Ministers must also evolve,' he told Molotov. Maisky would clear up our position in relation to the Western powers.

The insurrection of 16 June in the GDR[39] diverted my father from his projects. Most of his trusties were there. Some had been sent to Iraq because a coup d'etat was being prepared in Iran, with the return of the Shah and removal of Mossadegh:[40] others had gone to Georgia to prepare for the 15th Party Congress.

The 15th Georgian Party Congress

My father wanted to speak in person at this congress, which was to be held in May. (It was eventually postponed and my father had no time to do this.) He attached very great importance to it, as it was to begin the process of de-Stalinisation throughout the USSR.[41] He intended to bring up the Mingrelian business and the repressions during and after the war, but also the Sovietisation of Georgia, the 1924 revolt, national policy, the annihilation of the intelligentsia and the role that he had played in all that. When he told my mother of his plans, she said: 'But aren't you afraid of these revelations? Your role was hardly brilliant.' He said: 'I want to disclose everything. I shall bring witnesses from France and Britain who will describe what actually happened. They will testify that I did everything possible.' My father wanted a distinction made between the unwilling scoundrel and the willing one. 'The same thing will be done in Moscow.' But my mother said that we must not even think of that.

My father's plan

My father counted on shaking off the MVD before the congress met, or at any rate he voiced that hope to my mother. He wanted to pass the following measures without delay: to attach intelligence and the frontier guards to the Ministry of Defence, at the head of which he would have put Zhukov, and to abolish the MVD's own armed forces. He dreamt of being able to devote himself to administering the economy, thanks to his good relations with Zhukov. He was in a hurry because he realised that the time he had in which to act freely was limited. I think that he certainly had a hidden motive when he proposed the calling of a congress. He wanted to get rid of his colleagues because he knew that something was being hatched against him. He foresaw that the test of strength would take place at that congress, and he prepared actively for that. He could count on the support from the leading personnel in the economy, from the scientists, from some diplomats, from the military and from the heads of the republics. It was in the non-Russian periphery that the monstrous aspects of Bolshevism were most obvious and most grotesque. He intended to set forth before the delegates in the name of the country's leadership a coherent programme of reforms in domestic and foreign policy. He thought that, when they had learnt the truth about past events, the congress majority would rally to him and give him their support. I remain convinced that he was not mistaken. Once his colleagues had retired he would be able to proceed legitimately with his reforms.

He did perhaps intend to make certain revelations. I have only indirect signs of this: some of his collaborators mentioned to me dossiers that he had entrusted to them. Before he died, my father's secretary Lyudvigov, a man of Polish origin, was able to tell me that my father had ordered him to compose a report on anti-Semitism in Russia and the world. Clearly, my father was preparing to write an article or deliver a speech on the harmfulness of anti-Semitism.[42]

But the members of the Presidium forestalled him. They knew that my father was more intelligent and stronger than they were. If he managed to carry through the reorganisation he had begun, they would become redundant. My father's mistake was to have revealed some things too soon.

Zhukov's warning

My father did not believe his life was threatened, or at least he did not say so to me. He may have confided more to my mother, but if so she never said a word about it. Anyway, he was not one to be afraid. He had already had six attempts made upon his life with firearms. I don't conclude from this that he was a fatalist. But, for him, to live in fear was a sort of servitude.

However, Zhukov had warned him: 'You've lived in Russia for years and yet you don't know the Russians. You underestimate those people [he meant the Presidium], they are scum who understand nothing. With them there is only one argument that matters, the cudgel, and only one method, the accomplished fact.' He advised him, too, to be especially suspicious of Khrushchev: 'Don't believe that it is possible to be friends with him. Military colleagues have told me that he drew up a list of his enemies in the Ukraine while the Germans were still occupying that country. Those men were liquidated at once. Khrushchev used the political organs to perform this task of marking down his enemies. That was how my friends in the army learnt about it.'

Towards the break

It will be remembered that Malenkov had published in *Pravda* a falsified photograph in which he appeared side by side with Mao. The members of the Presidium considered that he ought not to have done that without consulting them and my father rebuked him: 'What got into you? You know very well that sort of thing always comes to light eventually, and that your enemies lie in wait for you at the turning of the road.' Malenkov then admitted his mistake. 'I committed a folly. Shepilov talked me into it.' But Khrushchev profited by this error to draw his own conclusions. 'This is the result of your protection of him. He takes himself for a Mao and imagines he can dominate us all,' he said to my father. I think that, at the same time, he set Malenkov against my father, claiming that he was using this incident against him.

After his disagreement with Khrushchev over the rehabilitations my father said that my mother was right – a clash had become inevitable. However, he thought in terms of a *political* clash and was still optimistic as to the result, counting on support from the economic cadres. My mother, less calm, decided to stay in Moscow to look after him. She expected that he would be put out of power on some pretext or other. She had, it is true, wanted for a long time that this would happen, but never imagined that things could reach the point of assassination.

Again she begged him to use the pretext of poor health in order to resign. 'There are a lot of things you don't understand' was his reply to her scolding. As for me, I thought my father would succeed in managing the congress as he wanted. I ascribed my mother's fears to exaggerations due to feminine sensitivity. I was sure that Khrushchev and Malenkov would endorse my father's initiatives because I believed they were sincere.

Plans for a coup d'etat?

Zhukov thought that only a military coup d'etat could get things going. My father objected that this would not do at all, that legality must be respected and public opinion appealed to. Besides, such a step would harm us internationally. 'You are wrong, Lavrenti,' Zhukov insisted. 'You are mistaken all along the line.' Because of these discussions I do not believe in the accusation that my father was preparing a coup d'etat.[43] Besides, I should have known. He could not suppose that my mother and I would survive him, even if we had known nothing about it. I admit, nevertheless, that he might have attempted something during the congress. My father never confided his real intentions to me.

With hindsight it seems to me that he made the following mistakes: he believed that his colleagues' declarations were sincere and he believed that they were ready to accept extremely radical reforms. He was wrong to reveal his desire to refer to the pre-war repressions. He ought to have taken his colleagues by surprise at the congress.[44] He underestimated Russian chauvinism and forgot the Russian way in politics, consisting as it did of intrigues, plots and coups d'etat. He acted thoughtlessly, overlooking the fact that his colleagues were a pretty crude lot. No doubt he also made the mistake of dispersing his activity among numerous projects instead of devoting himself to a single objective, taking power.[45]

Fall

My mother and I have sometimes looked back over these events. She did not do this willingly, her memories were too sad. But I could not prevent myself from returning again and again to the same questions: how had my father let himself be trapped by such nonentities? That thought I found unbearable. My mother shared my view on that point. It would have been less infuriating if we had all died by Stalin's hand. She said to me. 'If you knew how often I warned him! He would answer: "We can change nothing. Whatever happens there will be a clash." And then he laughed and said that we must trust in fate.' My father had escaped from so many dangerous situations in the course of his career that he had ended by counting too much on his good luck.

Arrest, Death, Exile

26 June

We spent that last day with him at the *dacha*. On 26 June we went for our morning walk together. He had a preoccupied air and told me that he expected difficulties in connection with the Ignatiev affair, which was due to be discussed at the end of the morning.[1]

I went back to the city at 8 a.m. At 10, my colleagues and I were preparing a report on the hydrogen bomb which we were to submit to my father, Malenkov and Bulganin at 4 p.m. My father arrived in Moscow at 9 a.m. His meeting which had been fixed for 12 noon was cancelled on the pretext that Ignatiev had fallen ill and had been taken to hospital.

As a rule we lunched together, but as I was at Vannikov's with the papers and the session was to begin at 4 p.m., I stayed there. My father came home to lunch at 12.30.

At about 1 p.m. an airman friend, a Tatar named Amitkhad, telephoned me. He shouted: 'Your father's dead, your house is surrounded. I have a plane ready, I'm coming to look for you and we'll take you to somewhere safe.' I did not believe my ears. It was unthinkable. I tried to telephone, first to our home, then to my office. The lines had been cut and I realised that something was wrong. I spoke to Vannikov, Kurchatov and others, six people in all. It was as though a thunderbolt had fallen on them. They all, like me, took to the telephone. Meanwhile, the car came for me. I had told my colleagues of the proposal from my airman friend and they thought that I would not return. Nobody tried to dissuade me: they thought my life was really in danger.

As I walked to the car I thought of my pregnant wife, of the baby due to be born in a month's time, and of my two other children. If my father was alive, my flight would prove that he and I were guilty. So I told the airmen that I would not leave. They went mad. I don't rule out the possibility that these friends had acted on my father's order. We had made test flights together and had permission to fly over the Baltic and Black Seas. I have never written anything on that subject, because people might draw hasty conclusions: if Beria had prepared his escape, then he must have been a British spy. Later, after I had been released from prison, these airmen came to see me at Sverdlovsk.

Having decided to stay, I went back to the office. Kurchatov threw himself upon me. 'Be confident,' he said, 'we'll do everything we can to save your life.' They tried to contact Malenkov, without success, and then Khrushchev, who replied: 'Don't worry. I'm going to send a car to take him to his mother's. Don't get ideas.' Some men did indeed come for me. I don't know why they took me first to our house. I saw that the windows of my father's bedroom were riddled with bullets. The doors had been forced. One of our bodyguards who was still there called out to me: 'Sergo! Someone was carried out on a stretcher.' That could only have been my father! Subsequently I spoke with all our servants. They confirmed that everything had happened at our place and not during the meeting of the Presidium.[2]

That same day, tanks had been sent to Moscow. They had taken up positions around the capital at 8 a.m. The Vice-Minister of Internal Affairs, General Maslennikov, telephoned to Shtemenko and Vasilevsky, who did not know what was going on. Nobody could make sense of the situation. Eventually they learnt that the order had come from Bulganin. And it was my father who was accused of having attempted a military coup d'etat!

My father's arrest

There are at least six different versions of the arrest and death of my father. Khrushchev himself provided several variants.[3]

In one of them the principal role is played by Zhukov.[4] The effect is all the better. Hero of the Soviet Union Zhukov arresting Beria! Many years later Zhukov, to my great surprise, asked to see me. 'I have no reason to lie to you,' he said. 'I took no part, direct or indirect, in the arrest of your father.[5] If he had been alive I would have been at his side. I want you to know that. Do you think that, otherwise, I should have gone with those shits?' He added that if my father had still been alive at the time of the July Plenum, most of the delegates would have sided with him. Mikoyan confirmed that.[6] He, too, arranged to see me after my return from exile. 'I'm not trying to excuse myself,' he said, 'but if your father had been alive everything would have been different.'

In my opinion, Zhukov supported Khrushchev in June 1957 against the 'anti-Party group' because he had chosen the policy of 'the worse the better.' He was preparing a coup d'etat and thought that Khrushchev's policy would soon stir up general exasperation and facilitate his aims.[7] In the end, Zhukov made the same mistake as my father – he overestimated the strength of his supporters. My father thought that the middle echelon of the industrial apparatus supported him, and this was true. But that did not save him. Zhukov thought he enjoyed the support of the army. They all let him down, except Shtemenko and Vasilevsky. Khrushchev, fearing for his life, dismissed him. Everyone joined in the persecution. He had to suffer their changes of 'Bonapartism,' like a sheep covered with spittle.[8] It would have been better for him to die. His retirement was protracted torture. When a man is on his own his capacity for resistance gives out. When I saw him years later he was no more than the shadow of his old self. 'I got out of it even worse than your father did,' he said. The fact that they had let him live, he took as an insult. Those swine were sure that he would put up with everything. I think that it was to tell me this that he tried to meet me. He felt that I alone could understand him. I wondered why he apparently did not leave anything in writing to defend his point of view, and thought that, if he did, then somebody got rid of it. Now, though, I think that he kept silent out of Russian chauvinism: what Russian wants his rulers to appear in a bad light?

As for Malenkov, he did not betray my father. When he was assassinated Malenkov was faced with an accomplished fact.[9] He chose the policy of least effort.

The Plenum's official version

It is interesting to analyse each of the themes that were developed at the July Plenum which condemned my father.

During a session of the Presidium which preceded this enlarged meeting, Kaganovich remarked that my father was being blamed for decisions which had been taken collectively.[10] If I am to believe what I have been told, before and during the Plenum Bagirov and some Georgian delegates asked that Beria be present,[11] but the minutes do not mention this request. They were told that Beria was not in a state to attend the Plenum. At the same time a rumour of his death was put about, without official confirmation. Many people believed it. Khrushchev and his clique knew that my father had many supporters and they spread this rumour deliberately.

The allotment of the themes to be expounded at the Plenum was decided at the earlier meeting. Agreement was reached on what was to be said by Malenkov, Khrushchev, Bulganin and the others. Some of the grievances against my father were intoned in chorus but each speaker also had a particular theme to develop. If we sum up the speeches that were made, we see that my father was being blamed for a programme of *pere-*

stroika, an intelligent *perestroika* that would have led very quickly to political and economic progress. It is enough to compare the charges against him with the measures he had had time to take, in order to form a clear idea of his programme of action. We had to wait for forty years before finding that he was right.

It was announced later that my father was in prison and would be tried. Then his trial was announced, a trial in which he would be found guilty.[12] He was accused of being a spy for Britain, Turkey and Iran. The unfortunate Petr Sharia, the specialist in Hegelian dialectic who had acted as my father's contact with the *émigré* Georgian Mensheviks, was accused of having, on my father's orders, negotiated with French collaborators and German agents, of having destroyed the evidence of this collaboration and of preparing (still on my father's orders) the secession of Georgia. I don't know how he behaved under interrogation but, in any case, he emerged a broken man, as I found when I met him years later.

My father and his accomplices were executed in December 1953, according to the official version.[13] As I was in prison, I knew nothing of all that.

My father's execution

There are also several contradictory accounts of my father's death. Volkogonov has recently revealed that Beria was executed as he left the room where the tribunal sat. He heard this from General Moskalenko.[14] The account given by the officer Khizhnyak, who claimed to have been present, does not coincide with Volkogonov's. Khizhnyak is, perhaps, not a bad man, but what he has written is in error on two points. First, he has lied about the execution, as Volkogonov shows. In his account he – or, rather, those who wrote the account for him – says too much about it. And he says that, after the execution, Colonel Zakharov came to see him in the bunker with two bottles of brandy, which they drank as they discussed the event. I know who this Zakharov was: the chief of Malenkov's guards. Later he became the Number Two of the KGB. Actually, he came to make sure that Khizhnyak had not guessed that the condemned man was not my father. If Khizhnyak had expressed doubt, he would not have left the bunker alive. Personally I am convinced that they shot a double of my father.[15] My father was shot at our home. They killed him then and there and took ten days to assemble the Plenum, so that everyone might have time to realise that he was dead.

My mother and I

My mother and I were accused of having wished to overthrow Socialism, assassinate the party's leaders and restore capitalism. And, of course, we could not have undertaken this threefold task without also being British agents; we had that label stuck on us as a bonus.

My mother was present when our *dacha* was searched. The officers found only children's clothes and some dresses. When they spotted a locked cupboard they hurled themselves upon it, full of hope – our hidden treasure must be there. They broke the lock – and found only two old rusty chandeliers. My mother didn't even have any jewels.

Our imprisonment

The Deputy Procurator-General was one Tsaregradsky. He carried out the investigation of my mother. He was correct, in the style of a Russian official. My mother said he never insulted her. He found that the charges against her did not stand up.

Two Procurators-General interrogated me: a military man named Kitaev, who was a right bastard, and Kamochkin, who was also a bastard, though somewhat less so. I was not tortured, only prevented from sleeping for two weeks. When I went on hunger strike they forcibly fed me. I was asked to repudiate my father in writing. I had the good fortune to spend several days at a stretch unconscious.

When we were arrested I was much afraid that they would bring up my mother's kinship with the Paris *émigrés*. However, my father had been extremely prudent where relations with the Mensheviks were concerned. He had composed formularies for all the letters, all the journeys and all the meetings with the Georgian Mensheviks,[16] and Stalin had copies. I knew from Tsaregradsky that there was a correspondence which was attributed to my mother. Every letter had been registered and there was a substantial dossier. It was easy to establish that these were forgeries. As for the actual correspondence they had no way of knowing anything at all about it.

One day, about six months after my arrest, a squad of soldiers with an official came to look for me. They chained me to a wall and read to me my sentence of death. I was so stunned that I understood nothing of this. I merely had a furious thought and feeling: 'Am I going to die at the hands of these swine?' I shouted: 'Soon it will be your turn!' I have heard that the officer in charge of this farce took fright when he heard that. After all, he was a witness. They had organised the scene where my mother could see it, from a window. They wanted by this means to make her sign confessions. She fainted and stayed unconscious for a whole day. I noticed that the guards were staring at me in an odd way, whereas usually they avoided looking at the prisoner. When, a week later, I was given a mirror I understood the cause of their astonishment: my hair had turned white in a few hours.[17]

I underwent many interrogations. I denied the accusations against me. The investigating magistrate, the Procurator-General and his deputies came to see me. 'Your father has confessed, your mother has confessed. Why be stubborn? We are thinking of your good, we want to save your life. Your duty and your interest are to confess,' they repeated. 'Show me just one document signed by my father or my mother that confirms your version of the facts,' I replied. 'I realise that you did not want to show them to me alive, but at least show me the minutes of an interrogation, signed by my father.'

Every accused person has to initial each page of the minutes of his interrogation. They were unable to produce any document at all. Today people can write letters and allege that the handwriting is my father's, but I don't believe it because I knew his handwriting very well.[18]

The people outside

Malenkov visited me twice at Lefortovo prison. He wanted me to confess to all the crimes of which I was charged. 'You must think of yourself. You are intelligent. You must help the Party. We want to help you. The Central Committee knows you, values you and wants to save you, but the Party needs your collaboration. Confess that your father was against the Party and that the Party has done well in getting rid of him. We will set you free and you can rejoin your family.' Fifteen days later he returned to the charge. I told him that I did not wish to save my life at that price. He then came back with: 'All right, but at least tell us where the archives of your father and of Iosif Vissarionovich are.' I replied that I didn't know. He was annoyed, made a gesture, and said: 'If you don't want to help yourself we can do nothing for you.' That was the last time I saw Malenkov.

The scientists who worked with my father began to move heaven and earth to get us out of prison. They sent a petition in my favour to the seven members of the Presidium. This they did out of gratitude to my father. Molotov used this petition when he intervened for us. He had not forgotten that my father had tried to protect his wife. Mikoyan, Pervukhin and Saburov supported him. Meanwhile, Kurchatov, Tupolev and some others took steps to obtain permission for me to work. Four months before my release, in November 1954, I was brought my books and my uncompleted projects.

I am still convinced that we survived for another reason, namely, that they were looking for my father's archives. There was nothing to stop the members of the Presidium from making mincemeat of me. But they had concluded that it would be easier for them to find these documents if we were at liberty. So we were kept under surveillance for over ten years. This surveillance may continue today, in another form. But I think myself lucky to have remained alive.

My release and exile

One fine day the members of the Presidium said to themselves that they might release us and send us away to perish in some corner. They thought we should not be able to adopt ourselves to ordinary existence because we had been spoilt, and that we were ignoramuses and good-for-nothings.

What could I do, taken in a cattle-truck to Sverdlovsk for a ten-year exile? They were sure that I would not be able to overcome the difficulties of my new form of existence.

They thought at first that they could separate me from my mother. They proposed to install her in Moscow or Tbilisi, guaranteeing to provide her with housing and a pension. 'I couldn't care less about your housing and pension,' she said. 'Where have you put my son? I'll go and join him wherever he is.' And she came to live with me. If she hadn't I should certainly have done something silly. I was only 29 years old. When we were let out of prison in 1954, my mother managed to visit Tbilisi clandestinely, in search of my grandmothers. Her mother had just died. My father's mother was in an old people's home, blind and isolated from everyone. She recognised her daughter-in-law by touching her hand. She stroked her face and felt her tears. 'Don't cry, I'm happy to know that you're alive.' She died before we obtained permission for her to come and live with us. My mother was forbidden to attend the funeral.

When I was released, a decision by the Presidium and the Government authorised me to have access to the most secret work and to complete the projects I had begun working on. I could settle in any town except Moscow. If they had really believed I was a spy they would surely not have done that. I learnt with satisfaction that none of my colleagues at the Institute had betrayed me. Despite all kinds of pressure they had refused to expel me from the Party and the Central Committee had had to impose that decision on the Party organisation in my Institute in defiance of the Party rules.

My version of the facts

I have good reason to believe that my father was murdered on 26 June, 1953.[19] Why did they want to extort testimony from my mother, and why did they find it necessary to fake my execution if they knew something? I agree that they were imbeciles, we see those everywhere nowadays, but they could not be stupid to that degree.

When I was released, Tsaregradsky came to fetch me from my cell. Once we were outside he said to me: 'It was I who wrote the minutes of the interrogation of your father.'

'Why didn't you show them to me?'

'There was nothing to show. I wrote them.'

'What do you mean?'

'Hundreds of people were interrogated.'

So, then, it was on the basis of those testimonies that he had composed the minutes ... without even seeing my father! Then he added: 'The picture that emerges is such that I have only one piece of advice for you. Succeed in your job, because you can never hope to get anything else.'

He wanted to convey to me, indirectly, that one could reveal nothing because that would have exposed the crimes committed by the Party and its apparatus. This man wanted to make me realise that, for the sake of my future and that of my children, I must show that I was a normal person. I had to prove that I was not an Asiatic bandit who had acquired diplomas through favouritism, nor an illiterate brigand who could only howl and bite, but someone who could make rockets for the Soviet Union. This was the most I could do to rehabilitate my father, because I could say nothing. I have remembered that all my life. In conclusion, Tsaregradsky urged me not to become 'an enemy of our country.' There was a certain nobility about that man, or at least that was the impression he made on me at the time.

The former Chairman of the Supreme Soviet, Shvernik, was a member of the tribunal which allegedly tried my father. During our exile he made it his business to reassure our Georgian friends who were worried about our fate and made inquiries. He explained that we were safe and sound in exile, sheltered from the anger of the Russian population. I met him when I returned from exile. He was sincerely pleased to see me in good health. He was not a bad man. He told me, with a sad smile: 'I was a member of the tribunal, but I did not see your father even once.' Shvernik did not dabble in politics, he was neither a Communist nor a Bolshevik, just an ordinary apparatchik.

Another member of the tribunal, Mikhailov, was the Secretary of the Central Committee of the Komsomol or of the Party organisation in Moscow. His son worked at my institute. I invited him to my mother-in-law's *dacha*. 'Sergo, I don't want to give you details, but we did not see your father alive,' he confessed to me. After that meeting with him, his son said to me: 'You can believe my father. All the time the trial was on, he was gloomy and silent.' Having been fairly close to my father, Mikhailov feared that he would have to testify.

The provocations

One day in 1959 I found in my letterbox the review *Vokrug Sveta*, to which I did not subscribe. In it was a photograph showing my father in Buenos Aires, in front of the Presidential Palace and accompanied by a woman. I examined the picture with a magnifying glass. No mistake, it was him all right! I showed it to my mother, who was filled with joy at the idea that my father was alive. 'Provided he isn't recognised!' she said. 'How was he so rash as to let himself be photographed?' She was firmly convinced. After a certain time we received a letter giving us a rendezvous at Chelyabinsk if we wanted to have 'further information.' I went there by bicycle. Nobody there, of course. Another message gave us a rendezvous in Georgia, by the Black Sea. My mother, decided to go there, helped by our airmen friends. There, too, we were stood up. Nobody commented, though we were not supposed to leave Sverdlovsk. I have never understood the purpose of these manoeuvres. Right down to her death my mother remained convinced that my father was alive. 'If only he would send us something, even just one word! Why doesn't he show himself?' she repeated. I did not try to undeceive her.

My interest in politics dates from this experience. I could not accept that those swine should saddle my father with their crimes. It was too unjust. To be sure, my father had plenty of things on his conscience, and my mother often reproached him for that. And he always asked, in reply: 'What do you think I ought to do?'

'Pretend to be ill, go on leave' she insisted. 'You don't understand, Nina, that wouldn't help. At my level there are only two exits – one straight into the other world, the other into prison till they send you into the other world.'

One day, replying to her chiding, he referred to those Georgians who fled from the Tsarist regimes into the mountains. 'It was possible at that time, because the Tsarist regime was more humane and it lacked the means to rout people out from the mountains. But if I were to take refuge in the Caucasus they would dig me out, wherever I might be.'

The successors

Khrushchev

Khrushchev quickly made some of my father's ideas his own, only a few months after denouncing them as proofs of treason.[20] He became reconciled with Yugoslavia in 1955, and had the cheek to attribute the break to my father! Tito ticked him off, saying that Khrushchev must not take him for a fool. The Yugoslavs knew quite well who had attacked them, and it wasn't Beria.

In February 1956, at the 20th Party Congress, Khrushchev denounced Stalin's crimes, but did this selectively, so as to strengthen his position by exculpating the Bolshevik Party and Lenin, though the blemishes of Bolshevism had been apparent even before the October Revolution. Khrushchev was really a Stalinist through and through – it is enough to look at his agricultural policy to realise that. He also pursued a policy of detente with the West, but, again, was content with half measures. Though confrontation diminished in his reign, he did not hesitate to provoke grave crises, as in Berlin in 1959 and in Cuba in 1962. And let's not forget the Berlin Wall, built under Khrushchev in 1961 ...

However, I want to do him justice. We had been living for ten years in Sverdlovsk when my mother fell ill. I asked to be assigned to a different place. Khrushchev told me, through the head of the KGB, Semichastny, that I could live wherever I liked. That was in 1964. I was summoned to Moscow as the plot against Khrushchev entered its final phase. Semichastny spoke frankly, supposing that this would please me. He had ordered that Adzhubei, Khrushchev's son-in-law, be put under surveillance and that Khrushchev's son be prevented from leaving for the USA. A week later, Khrushchev was removed from office, and burst into tears when he heard the Politburo's decision. I confess that I was happy to hear that. But his decision to set me free was one of his last good actions, and I do not forget it.

Kosygin and Andropov

In 1965 Kosygin took up some of my father's ideas on the economy, but applied them only partially. Among Stalin's successors the only one who was not an idiot was Andropov but he was cruel. Like Stalin he wrote verses, and, like Stalin, he was wicked. At the time of the Hungarian rebellion in 1956 he was Soviet ambassador in Budapest. Molotov had recommended him for this post, being convinced that any Party functionary made a good diplomat.[21] He took an active part in the repression. At Sverdlovsk I met military men who had participated in the crushing of the rebellion. One of them told me that Andropov had given the order for the tanks to charge the crowd. Some tank crews refused to obey this order and were shot on the spot. Recalcitrant officers of higher rank were shot in the embassy courtyard, in Andropov's presence. The officer who told me escaped the same fate because he had a nervous breakdown and was declared to be not responsible for his actions.

When he became head of the KGB Andropov had his secretary bring him my father's reform proposals. He sent for me one day to discuss the Americans' plans for anti-aircraft defence. I had written a report based on information supplied by the KGB. Andropov wanted to know if these plans were technically realisable and if we could create a system of that sort in the USSR. He made a remark which wounded me, saying that he 'appreciated my behaviour.' I replied that my silence on the matter did not mean that I approved of the fate suffered by my father and my family. He changed the subject. 'I have closely studied your father's proposals in the economic and foreign policy fields. Many of them are absolutely correct.' He asked what I thought of German reunification: I replied that I shared my father's views. 'You went to a German school, so you know the Germans well. What do you think of them?' he went on. I answered that it was better to have them as friends than as enemies. Andropov was obviously not concerned with getting advice. He simply wanted to show me that he was interested in my father. He never contemplated for one moment the reunification of Germany. A Russophile, he thought that one must support the Party in all things. He was sure that war with the USA was inevitable – I draw that conclusion from several interviews I had with him – and so we had to prepare our economy for that ordeal. He was therefore able to draw inspiration from my father's projects only as regards details. One of the ideas that Andropov borrowed from my father was the creation of an intelligence network in the Ministry of Foreign Trade.

Gorbachev

When Gorbachev and his men launched their *perestroika* I believed that they meant to carry out my father's programme. They knew of his proposals, for these were found in Gorbachev's archives: Gorbachev had at last understood that the Party's control of the economy must be ended. Shevardnadze indicated to me that he had studied my father's plans for Germany.

The initiators of *perestroika* had better luck than my father. They were not shot and they became idols in the West. Gorbachev even received the Nobel Peace Prize. And yet they were only mediocre epigones. They went about their work in such a way that they failed in everything. The reunification of Germany has had no beneficial effect on our economy. Even the Party has remained in power under a different label, which would not have happened in my father's time. At that time the state apparatus included talented administrators, men of character who wanted to get results. In the course of forty years that apparatus degenerated, became full of swindlers and thieves, and the Party had no difficulty in throwing them out and taking control. To sum up, the system was not reformable from within.

Who Was My Father?

The reader may be surprised that I have remembered so many of my father's remarks, but I was so very fond of him that every word of his is imprinted forever in my memory. I did not respect him as a father only. I loved him because he had been close to me since my earliest childhood and had looked after me. And when I did not understand what he was saying to me I tried to sense the meaning. If he did not finish telling me something confidential, I strove to read the conclusion in his face. I have tried here to reproduce his words without developing the interpretations of them that I may now have – and God knows that I have some, with hindsight.

When I was only a lad my parents spoke frankly in my hearing. Later they paid attention to what they said when I was present. Unlike, however, the other members of the Politburo, my father wanted to be able to confide in me, to leave his imprint in his son's mind. He suffered and was irritated to find me so naïve. I remember how he once became very angry indeed when I made a remark that showed the extent to which I had swallowed the propaganda put out by our newspapers. It was stupid but effective, dealing with the campaigns being waged against Georgian nationalism. My father said, drily, that one had to keep one's head on one's shoulders and analyse what lay behind these campaigns. 'Remember the Tsars' policy of setting the peoples against each other – Mingrelians against Imeretians, Georgians against Armenians. But I wanted to do the opposite.' He complained about me to my mother, who always defended me: 'Remember what you were like at his age.'

I remained in Stalin's thrall much longer than he did, and that prevented me from following the stages of his development. My father explained his outlook to me when he saw that I was ready to understand him. He was always a long way ahead of me. Experience of life had shaped him: at 40 he was a minister, while I had everything to learn.

For a long period he spoke to me in allusions. Perhaps he considered that I was too young, or he was afraid of turning me into a cynic. I understood only fragments of criticism that I happened to catch from his conversations with others. He began to be open with me when I was 24, considering that I ought to know the setting we were in and be aware of what awaited us. He bore a grudge against my mother for hindering my development: she thought that the more my eyes were opened, the more risks I would run. She well knew that I was unable to conceal my feelings and thoughts. She was afraid, too, lest I become a cynic, and protected me from the world so far as she could. She grew angry when my father let fall some sardonic remarks in front of me, and spoke sharply to him in Mingrelian, which I did not understand well. After my father's death I reminded her of those episodes. She told me that she had been trying to make my father see reason, explaining to him that I should have to grow up in our society as it was, and had no choice. He had replied: 'You are wrong to act like that. He must be able to understand what's going on. The younger he is when he understands things and what people are worth, the better he'll stand the shock. If he believes everything, like a fool, and then reality suddenly opens in front of him like an abyss, that will be a very hard ordeal for him.' He was convinced, from experience, that he was not making me run more risks by taking that attitude than if I were to remain an obtuse Stalinist. What a lot of men had cried 'Long live Stalin!' as they faced the firing squad. My mother eventually gave me the clue to her thinking, many years later. 'As you know, I have Russian friends but I have always hated Russia and always will.'[1]

My father wanted me to be an educated man. He made me learn foreign languages, history and mythology. It has been alleged that he had difficulty with the printed word, but I can bear witness that, in Tbilisi, I grew up amid books annotated by him. He advised me early on to make summaries of books that had interested me, and to keep a card index. 'You'll see, you'll learn to bring order into your thinking,' he said. I never did that, whereas he accumulated masses of notes from his reading.

He could read and write French, though he confessed to speaking it poorly ('worse than the French of Nizhny Novgorod'). He had read and reread Stendhal and liked Tolstoy's *Hadji Murad*, the *Thousand and One Nights* and the Turkish tales of Nasreddin Hodja. He was interested in Goethe's scientific works. But he had no time for Shakespeare or for poetry in general, apart from Omar Khayyam in Edward Fitzgerald's English translation. I remember hearing him tease Gamsakhurdia, who was proud of his descriptions of royal feasts in his historical novels. 'Dumas describes banquets much better than you do.' He was fond of reading translations aloud to my mother when he had a few hours' leisure. I remember, especially, *Gil Blas*. My father was not very good at music, it must be said. He sang out of tune and my mother ridiculed him when he sang Mingrelian songs. 'You make up for it with enthusiasm, but it's no good, you'll never have the ear for it,' she said. He embellished his speeches with Greek and Latin words and I often teased him about that. My mother rebuked me for this: 'Stop making a fool of him, you'll hurt him. Leave him at least that pleasure, he hasn't a lot of it in his life.' She pitied him for having to play Himmler and executioner, and thought that we ought not to deprive him of the few satisfactions he could still find in his position. When tension increased my father sought, to cheer himself up, much lighter reading. He thus plunged into Grimm's *Tales*, which made him laugh heartily, and I saw him absorbed in a novel by the German writer Eichendorff, *Scenes from the Life of a Good-for-Nothing*, the hero of which had many disappointments with the ladies.

My father and history

Unlike most Chekists, who thought that their job was to run around everywhere clutching a revolver, my father always considered that the study and analysis of archives brought in more useful information than cloak-and-dagger operations.[2] Already in Georgia he began studying the documents of the Okhrana. Then he immersed himself in the archives of the Third Reich which had been confiscated by the NKVD. He had thick dossiers on all the leaders of Nazi Germany. The connections between the Germans, Britain and France were the object of close attention on his part. And he was particularly interested in the Soviet Union's nearest neighbours, Turkey and Iran.

My father liked memoirs and was extremely fond of history. From his journeys he always brought back books and manuscripts. People knew what his tastes were and gave him appropriate presents. He received books about the Basques and their migration into Spain and the south of France, books published in Britain and Germany. He entrusted them to me, asking that I place them on the shelves of our library devoted to Spain. Later he read them with pleasure. We also had an impressive collection of books on the history of Georgia, many in German. His areas of interest varied with his priorities of the moment. I was able to keep track of his concerns through the advice he gave me on what I should be reading. Thus, when he was thinking about establishing contact with the Vatican he read a lot about the history of Christianity. He asked me once if I had heard of Taine. I had seen his works in our library but had not read them. He explained to me that such books were not textbooks but that it was impossible to understand the spirit of an epoch without having read them. Taine and Carlyle were writers of that order, he considered. We had editions of their works from before the revolution. My father kept coming back to that theme, I think he had hidden motives when he shared with me his thoughts on history.

France

He liked France, which he knew well through his Georgian Menshevik networks. He said to me: 'You like *The Three Musketeers*? Well, they're Gascons. And who are the Gascons? Basques. And who are the Basques? Georgians!' Which did not prevent him from holding France responsible for all our troubles. If there had not been the French Revolution there would not have been the revolution of 1917. For him Bonaparte had only one merit, that he crushed the revolution. Remarks like that made my mother indignant.

When I studied the *Short History of the Bolshevik Party* I made comparisons with the French historians. The way Robespierre is depicted, for example – a monster for some, a hero for others. But their descriptions were talented, whereas our *Short History* was a textbook for weak-minded people. I asked my father: 'Why can't we tell the history of the Party in as interesting a way?' He laughed and called on my mother to help me out.' Tell me,' he said, still laughing, 'how should I answer him? How can we depict Iosif Vissarionovich with the pen of a Tarlé describing Napoleon?' My mother did not appreciate that sort of humour. She was always afraid that I might drop clangers in public. My father concluded by explaining to me: 'The *Short History* was written so that the masses can assimilate the facts it records. The works of Tarlé that you speak of are read by cultivated people. One day, perhaps, we shall have good books about our history.'

Britain

He began interesting himself in Disraeli's career when he planned to unite the Jewish intellectuals in associations to work for the Soviet Union. Disraeli succeeded in concentrating all the Jewish capital in Europe in order to build the British navy and develop a powerful colonial empire. He pursued a British policy while relying on the Jewish lobby and the Jewish banks which playèd a big role in Britain's politics, both domestic and foreign. 'Just think,' he said to me, 'a country with long-standing traditions of anti-Semitism, a county where the aristocracy is as proud as can be. And a Jew turns up at the head of that state!' He kept wondering what forces had favoured Disraeli's rise to power, when there had not been a revolution. He thought it must be the Jews. I don't know where my father got this idea: in the biographies of Disraeli he made me read I couldn't find it anywhere.

He was always finding interesting analogies. For example, he put posers to me about Flavius Josephus:[3] was he, in my opinion, an objective witness to the events he describes, or was he an observer committed to a certain viewpoint?[4]

Russia

He studied assiduously the history of the Ukraine, the history of Kiev Rus, and that of Ivan Kalita[5] and the formation of the Russian state. In that connection he made unflattering remarks about Muscovy, pointing out that Kiev Rus was a state, whereas Muscovy was merely the product of usury. The Moscow princes lent money and bought land. He said, too, that these princes were allies of the Tatars, whose yoke could have been thrown off much sooner had the Russian boyars not supported them.

I remember hearing Stalin and my parents discussing two books about the Mongols, one on Genghis Khan and the other on Batu. Stalin liked them very much, despite the disapproval of Russian intellectuals. These books did not depict Genghis[6] and Batu[7] as bandits: on the contrary it was the Russians who figured as blackguards.

At one time my father immersed himself in the history of Peter the Great and annotated a large number of books which he had been able to read on that subject. He admired the emperor who, while still young, had conceived far-reaching plans and attacked Russian backwardness and laziness in order to try and create an economy. When he encountered resistance he resorted to violence, and, since in Russia's history violence always assumes barbarous forms, Peter the reformer combined his thirst for civilisation with frightful savagery. That was a terrifying combination, said my father, and our epoch greatly resembles Peter's. Bolshevism was the Russian form of European social-democracy.

Georgia

A Russian writer named Antonovskaya wrote an exciting book about George Saakadze, a Georgian military leader in the time of Shah Abbas.[8] When Turkey and Persia were quarrelling over Georgia, that country was so divided that its princes entered the service of one or other of those powers in order to pursue their personal aims. Saakadze was not of princely origin but he was a noble and he was a patriot. He strove first to unite the Georgians to fight the Persians. He won several battles but, as a result of various intrigues, the Georgian princes betrayed him. The King of Georgia turned away from him and he found himself isolated in a fragmented Georgia. The Persians then invited him to lead their forces on an expedition into India. He agreed and for five or six years waged war successfully at the head of their army. At the same time he formed a Georgian guard of ten to fifteen thousand men. Convinced of his loyalty, the Shah made him his favourite. When troubles broke out in Georgia the Shah sent him there with his men. Saakadze fought the Persians, organised a powerful Georgian army and in 1623 won great victories over the princes who had collaborated with the invader. But the Georgian princes betrayed him again. He and his men were encircled and massacred.[9] All his life he had tried to strengthen the royal authority in Georgia against the Persians.

My father liked this biography very much and eventually knew it almost by heart. Stalin read it too and spoke about it to my parents so as to provoke them. Stalin never discussed anything on which he had not already made up his mind. He brought a subject up not in order to make clear his own thoughts about it but in order to force the person he was with to reveal their views. He wanted to know how, in their opinion, a Russian could have written such a fine book about Georgia. My mother admitted that she found it hard to believe. 'This Antonovskaya must be a Georgian, a Russian could never have brought off anything like it.' The author had, in fact, lived for a long time in Georgia. Finally, my father advanced an hypothesis which Stalin liked: if she was not a Georgian, at least she had a Georgian lover. My father even insisted that her book win the Stalin Prize, though usually he did not concern himself with such matters.

In the family we recalled discussions among Georgians about Saakadze. Among the Georgian Mensheviks some thought he had served his country but others considered him a traitor, as Stalin took malicious pleasure in reminding my mother. When she told my father about that interpretation of Saakadze, he went red with anger. The Mensheviks had eventually agreed that, for the sake of one's country, one could make a temporary pact with the enemy, he recalled. 'Saakadze even sacrificed his two sons,' he said. When the Shah sent him into Georgia he had had to leave them as hostages, and they had been beheaded. The Shah sent their heads to their father. One day, Stalin asked my father, 'Do you think I am like the Shah?' He put the question in a humorous tone, but he had already made allusions of that sort before the war. My father had once said to my mother, at the time when he feared for my life, that Stalin might well seize the son of one of his circle, have him beheaded, and send the head to the young man's father.

During these family discussions I asked him why the Georgian princes, such proud warriors, had entered the service of the Tsars. He replied that this was a Russian tradition, to enrich one's own culture by absorbing foreign elites. Thus, the Tatar aristocracy had been assimilated. 'Compare the two cases. On the one hand the Tatars, who dominated Russia for four centuries and were conquered by force, on the other enslaved Georgia asking for Moscow's protection. And see the result: the two peoples were suppressed in the same way.' He told me that Moscow University was not founded by Lomonosov but by a Georgian prince who paid a large sum of money for it to be built. In Tsarist times a commemorative plaque recorded this fact, but it had been removed during the Soviet period. Historical truths were concealed.

My father also shared with me various reflections of his concerning our fellow Georgians. According to him, they were gifted but impatient, bad at systematic action and impulsive. While capable of performing heroic exploits they were incapable of day-to-day resistance. This was an innate feature of their character according to my father. He observed also that Georgia had never had a strong central authority, that the influence of the several kingdoms of former times could still be felt, and that central authority came into being only in face of an external enemy. Centralisation was desirable in Georgia because it became harder and harder for small peoples to defend their independence and even the existence of their nation. Though the Soviet regime was so hostile to 'feudalism,' it transformed some of the Georgian principalities into autonomous republics, so that the antagonisms between them should continue. My father regretted this, and tried to introduce a regional organisation based on the economy, but this attempt was nipped in the bud. It was forbidden even to discuss the project. I still wonder why Stalin took up that attitude, for the reform proposed by my father would have weakened Georgian nationalism.

However, it was Stalin indeed who insisted that the autonomous formations be maintained.

My father blamed the Georgian Mensheviks for importing into their own country the empty chatter of the Duma. The outcome of their economic policy left him sceptical. The Mensheviks made the mistake of not basing themselves on the Georgian peasantry, the most numerous section of the population, and of giving priority to the proletarian minority out of ideological prejudice. They had also made the mistake, as narrow-minded nationalists, of quarrelling with the Armenians, whereas the three Transcaucasian states ought to have presented a united front against the states that were most dangerous to them – Russia and Turkey.

The Ukraine

My father liked comparing the history of Georgia with the history of the Ukraine. He had obtained a lot of books on the latter country, varying his sources because Soviet books presented a tendentious version of its history. He read the writings of Polish authors which he caused to be translated. Tass had a translation department and Politburo members could order books to be translated for their personal use. These translations were sometimes reproduced in a hundred or so copies, sometimes in no more than a dozen. One had to sign a receipt in order to obtain a copy. Stalin received all such translations and knew what every one of his colleagues had asked to be translated.

My father was interested in Bogdan Khmelnitsky[10] and also, especially, in the personality of Mazeppa.[11] 'Think about the history of Georgia and of the Ukraine,' he said to me. 'For Russians, Mazeppa is an enemy. He betrayed Peter, he allied himself with the Swedes and he threw himself into the arms of the Turks. For Ukrainians, he is a national hero, like our Saakadze in Georgia. Well, look at the history of Georgia. Didn't the Georgians serve the Shah and the Turks? Saakadze allied himself with Persia. Why? To destroy the feudal powers and build national unity. And what about Khmelnitsky? And King Irakli II? Do you think they were blind or had their eyes closed when they turned to Russia? No, they were both trying to save their countries from the situation they were in.'

The Georgians had sought the protection of Russia against the Turks and the Persians because Russia was distant. They wasted their time, as the Russians did not lift a little finger to defend Georgia against the Muslims, even after the Russo-Georgian treaty of 1783.[12]

On Mazeppa my father read works that gave a version diametrically opposite to Pushkin's. Even the story of Khmelnitsky, he told me, was less simple and less idyllic than as presented in Soviet historiography. He was not completely pro-Russian, far from that. He even had time to regret his alliance with Russia[13] and understand what a mistake he had made before the Russians poisoned him. My father had no doubt that he had been assassinated by the Russians, since the Poles had no interest in his death.

Khmelnitsky had simply tried to release the Ukraine from Polish rule. He had no wish to bind the Ukraine to Russia.[14] He felt closer to a Polish nobleman than to a Russian. According to my father, the Catholic Church had won him over, because Khmelnitsky regretted having adopted so resolutely a pro-Russian orientation. From the beginning the Russians had broken all the treaties with the Ukraine, and more flagrantly than in the Georgian case, where appearances had been preserved.

My father observed that the Ukraine possessed a serious advantage in becoming a state because it was homogeneous, unlike Georgia, which had been divided historically into several kingdoms. On the other hand, Georgia possessed the advantage of having existed as a state for many years, whereas the Ukraine lacked that experience. It had remained squeezed between Russia and Poland, though this had not prevented it from becoming, at the end of the Tsarist period, one of the most dynamic industrial regions of the empire, attracting German, Belgian and French capital. My father spoke also of the first Ukrainian Communists. 'They realised from the start that Russia would not tolerate an independent Ukrainian Soviet republic. They thought they were serving a just cause, but at the same time, unlike Sergo Ordzhonikidze, they knew that it was a lost cause.'

On Communism

My father never expounded to me his views on our regime. They were conveyed in little strokes, one after another, in response to my reading and questions and on particular occasions.

Marx and Engels

When I was deep in a book about the model friendship between Engels and Marx I asked my father what he thought about that. He replied that this was a one-way friendship, and quoted examples of Marx's tactlessness. Thus, he had not taken the trouble to send condolences to Engels when the latter lost the woman he loved. Engels had been wounded by that and had understood that Marx did not care about other people.

My father also explained to me that Marx had begun to interest himself in the labour movement only after receiving advice from his father. The latter had realised that his son had no literary or artistic talent. The workers' cause was the only promising career for him. I remember all these remarks because my father concluded, laughing: 'He had an intelligent daddy, and that man was principally guilty of writing *Das Kapital*.' He held Marx in poor esteem. For him the whole of economics was to be found in Adam Smith. 'What's this story about "surplus value" in Marx? What does it contribute? Nothing. Even Engels wrote more interesting things. And he at least remained decent on the human level.' My mother, who listened to this discussion, broke in. 'Anyway, Sergo has a link with

Engels. The day he was born Lavrenti wrote in a book by Engels: "Today we have had a little boy." That's his only contribution to Marxism.'

Lenin

My father never met Lenin, but he studied his writings thoroughly. He was blamed for not being a Leninist. That was true. But he had read everything by Lenin and not in a scholastic way either. He pointed out to me once that none of Lenin's works was, strictly speaking, theoretical. All his books were aimed at other works or opponents. One did not sense that any of them was a creation of thought or of personal motivation. His writings were born of reactions to someone or something. Lenin had invented the term *khvostist* (tailist, tailendist) for a person who reacts to already accomplished facts. 'In that case,' said my father, 'the first *khvostist* was Lenin as a theoretician.'

Stalin was indeed the continuator of Lenin. It was said that the elections at our last congresses were fiddled. Well, said my father, all the Bolshevik Party's congresses, from the start, were manipulated. The only difference was that, in the beginning, people had the right to hold forth a bit more freely, but the resolutions were adopted in advance. Moreover, it was before they came to power that the Bolsheviks worked out their strategy for internal struggle. The technique of stealing their opponents' programme was practised before the revolution. We owe to Lenin the first steps in constructing the barracks-Socialism that was Bolshevism. And democratic centralism? A pure imposture. My father even put it to me one day when I mentioned the assassination of Trotsky that, if he had succeeded Lenin, things would have been still worse. It was he and Lenin who had created the concentration camps[15] and the system of political commissars in the Red Army. They had begun the shooting of hostages. And Trotsky thought that the revolution should not be confined to Russia but should be spread all over the world.

My father considered our trade unions harmful and utterly superfluous. He compared them to an Eskimo dance in which a solitary dancer mimes a fight between two wrestlers. A slogan like 'trade unions are the school of Communism' evoked his sneers.[16] Those who had taken the trade unions seriously, like Lominadze and Shatsky, had been labelled opportunists, because fighting for workers' economic rights meant coming into conflict with the state. As for the Komsomol, my father compared it to a harness. I was not the only one to hear his reflections. Before other people, however, my father would make observations without pronouncing judgements. To me he let his disapproval appear. He also said many things to Stalin, who did not contradict him but refused to act as my father proposed, saying that it would be premature.

Once, before the war, my father sent me to the library of the MVD with orders to summarise certain works for him. Actually, he had no need of these notes, but he wanted me to learn to read books in foreign languages.

He advised me to apply to Avakian, who came from the US and could introduce me to contemporary American literature. He encouraged me to read historical works. In short, he wanted to train me. In this way I made the acquaintance of the librarians and archivists of the MVD. Although they were Chekists, not all were stupid. Among them were Georgians, Russians and many Jews. They suggested that I read certain books, awakened my curiosity and showed me all the documents I could ask for.

During the war, doubtless on the initiative of my father, who wanted to sophisticate me, Sharia helped me discover Lenin's unpublished writings. In them another Lenin appeared, different from the idealised one I was used to. I soaked myself in these archives, while taking an interest, from the purely technical standpoint, in the way they were preserved, which shows how immature I still was. I discovered how Lenin organised the crushing of the social groups which might offer some resistance, such as the officers and the clergy, and I saw how barbarous his methods were. This was my first contact with the 'humanism' of Vladimir Ilyich. I told my mother, to whom I confided everything, about my edifying discoveries. She turned pale and rebuked my father: 'Don't get our gosling involved in those matters.'

Later, after the war, Mamulov and Lyudvigov, my father's secretaries, procured for me the documents that I wanted to see. They were cultivated people. They prepared reports for my father and compiled dossiers on questions that interested him.

My wife's grandmother, Ekaterina Peshkov, told my father and me interesting things. She had been present at Yagoda's trial in March 1938. When he was accused of having murdered Gorky he looked at her and with his head made an almost imperceptible negative movement. When she was young she had also known Chernov,[17] the leader of the Socialist-Revolutionaries, well, and also the agent-provocateur Azef.[18] But it was in the archives that I discovered the role played by the Tsarist Okhrana in the assassination of Stolypin,[19] the links between the Russian police and the Georgian revolutionaries, and the role of the police in the assassination of the Georgian national hero Ilya Chavchavadze.[20] A poet and writer, he was also one of the creators of the banking system and capitalism in Georgia. His activities drew down on him the hatred of both the Russian authorities and the Georgian revolutionaries, while the latter accused the Okhrana. In fact, both were in it together. Ordzhonikidze had been involved in that affair. My father once asked him why. 'Lavrenti, don't twist the knife in the wound,' he replied.

I was interested in the Okhrana provocateur, Malinovsky,[21] but they would not let me see the documents relating to him. I had to be content with reading Lenin's letters in which he vigorously defended Malinovsky. I mentioned what I had been reading when I returned home and my father sometimes made remarks which made me think. He said that, thanks to Malinovksy, everything Lenin and the Central Committee did was known to the Okhrana. When I asked why the Okhrana had not liquidated Lenin he answered: 'They behaved more wisely than Stalin when he had Trotsky assassinated. Yet I told him that we were going to deprive ourselves of a unique means of surveillance of his organisation. But he replied that without Trotsky there would be no more Trotskyism. The Okhrana didn't arrest Lenin, and that was clever of them, since they were able to keep a check on the entire Bolshevik Party.'

'But see how things turned out,' I objected. He replied: 'It was the Germans who helped the Bolsheviks – a brilliant idea from their point of view.' And he told me the story of Parvus, adventurer and financier, who acted as go-between for the German General Staff and the Bolsheviks[22] and succeeded in swindling everybody. Stalin knew about all these contacts. He never used that knowledge against Lenin but did so later in his struggle for power, when he had to dispose of his rivals.

My father had a very high opinion of the Okhrana's professionalism. He blamed it only for failing to analyse properly the implications of Bolshevism and underestimating it by giving priority to the fight against terrorism and the Left Socialist Revolutionaries. The Okhrana saw Lenin and the Bolsheviks as chattering intellectuals who would drown themselves in their own speeches. As my father saw it, the Okhrana had some excuse. It took account of the influence of different groups of revolutionaries on the masses and concluded that the Bolsheviks had none. It was unable to foresee that the war and the incapacity of the Duma and the Provisional Government would raise to the saddle this handful of well-organised agitators. On the other hand, my father was full of sarcasm at the expense of the Cheka's founder, Felix Dzerzhinsky. He saw him as a fanatic who was mentally ill. Stalin told him once that Dzerzhinsky got physical pleasure from interrogations.

Bolshevism

As I mentioned earlier, Bolshevism was for my father the Russian version of European Social Democracy. Unlike my mother, however, who attributed the negative features of Bolshevism to the Russian temperament, he perceived the ideological elements of the system. Nevertheless, he did consider that the Soviet leaders thoroughly exploited Russia's primitiveness and underdevelopment. 'Why did Social-Democracy stay civilised in Europe – in France, Germany, Austria? Why did the revolution take place in Russia? Because the population of Russia was ignorant.' When speaking of Stalin he would often say: 'He is a Russian autocrat.'

He disapproved of the practice of violence and the dictatorship of a minority. When once I observed that he himself participated in this violence, he replied that in order to change the situation one had to be in command of the levers that made action possible. During the war, when I was studying at the Academy, we touched fairly frankly on the subject of the repressions and he explained: 'A state so extensive as the Soviet Union can survive only by a rigorous policy. The situation would be tolerable if

these measures conformed to a legal framework. However, every dictatorship turns into a personal power which makes no distinction between
enemies of the regime and personal enemies.'

Stalin

My father was profoundly influenced by Stalin, even though the latter
never paralysed his will. He admired the way Stalin was able to plan and
carry through his projects, though Stalin's aims differed from his own.
When he gradually began to open my eyes to certain facts and to get me
ready to understand that there was a conflict between Stalin and him, he
always took care to emphasise that there was no-one equal to Stalin when
it came to perseverance and capacity to achieve his aims: 'Read the history
of Byzantium, see the intrigues it's full of,' he said. 'Well, that's nothing
compared with what Iosif Vissarionovich has managed to accomplish in a
state that was not his own, with a people who were not his own.
Circumstances helped him, but he also has genius. Evil genius,' he added.

For my father, Lenin was much inferior to Stalin. He was 'very intelligent, a remarkable intriguer, but incapable of practical organisation. Had
Lenin lived longer he would have destroyed the state, or wasted it, and
would never have accomplished what Stalin did, because he didn't know
how to administer. He was perfect in the art of setting some against others
or in triumphing in Party intrigues, but he understood nothing about the
economy.' Stalin had turned Lenin into a fetish. 'That's in conformity with
his system: he creates gods and lower divinities in order to dominate the
masses. Take those ridiculous names – Kaganovich Street, Beria Stadium
... It's nothing but magic for the purpose of hypnotising people's minds.'
Stalin had won the battle for the succession because he knew how to
organise men and subject them to his will. Trotsky was full of his own
personality. He, Zinoviev and Kamenev despised Stalin (my father made
the same mistake with Khrushchev). They squabbled among themselves.
Stalin stayed in the shadow and controlled the Party from top to bottom
by placing in it men like Molotov or Kirov, who were devoted to him body
and soul. Only the intellectual elite of the Party supported Trotsky. My
father had met Trotsky in his youth, when he had to ensure his protection
during a stay beside the Black Sea. Trotsky had talked with him as he
always did with youngsters who seemed to have a future before them. My
father found him extremely arrogant. In that respect the contrast with
Stalin was striking. 'In Trotsky's company one felt like an insignificant
worm. Stalin, on the contrary, knew how to listen to someone and make
him feel he was important.' That was his strength.

I find it difficult to trace the development of my father's opinion of
Stalin. Putting together what I heard from my mother and what I heard
from him directly, I can say that he took his time in measuring the degree
of Stalin's wickedness. For a long time he saw in it only a political strategy,
without perceiving the perversity hidden behind it. It is obvious that the

perception of things that he could have at the age of 23, when he was in Baku, and his understanding of the same phenomena at the age of 40, when he was at the summit of the system, were completely different. In Moscow he was often close to Stalin. Already in Georgia he was critical of the system, and gradually realised that responsibility for all sorts of excesses lay not only with the Central Committee and Russian chauvinism but with Stalin himself. How many of his approaches and letters to Stalin had remained without effect or had even produced the opposite effect to what he had counted on! To some extent he excused Stalin by explaining his behaviour by the need to take account of Russian policy as inherited from Lenin. The letters he sent to Stalin from Georgia when he was 26 years old show that naïvety of his. He wrote that one should not use Russian soldiers to put down insurrections in Georgia and that these interventions were not necessary: as for the Mensheviks, they could be utilised rather than destroyed. As time passed, however, he became able to see that the system and Stalin were one and the same. Yet he never completely overcame his first impression. He remained fascinated by Stalin's personality 'He dominates his entourage by his intelligence,' he said. 'Look at Molotov. In Stalin's presence he doesn't exist, it's as though he's dissolved. You could say: a rabbit in front of a boa.' And also, of course, Stalin was a Georgian. That was an essential factor in my father's attitude to him.

My father eventually realised that the aims Stalin had set himself from the start would not change. Stalin might make temporary concessions (my father had found that to be the case with Jewish and Georgian nationalism, for instance) but he always came back to his original line and eliminated the people he had momentarily made use of. He once declared that the Bolshevik Party was a sort of military-religious order. My father found that thought very revealing: Stalin had indeed caused Bolshevism to evolve from Jacobinism into a military-religious order. When he told me of Stalin's remark, he added, laughing: 'The Teutonic Knights had iron discipline and democratic centralism, and it's the same with us.'

On religion

In Georgia the Bolsheviks had to proceed carefully in their attack on the Church. A frontal assault, as in Russia, was unthinkable.[23] The population was strongly attached to its religion. In Georgia there were fewer churches destroyed than in the other republics, and these were destroyed before 1930, because, when my father had influence, he took steps to preserve them on grounds of their architectural and archaeological value. He sacrificed only the recently-built churches. This I know from witnesses of the time.

When we were living in Tbilisi my father often invited dignitaries of the Georgian and Armenian churches to our house. He tried to establish order among the Georgian clergy, starting by expelling all the homosexuals. The agents he put among the clergy were at least educated men. Of course he wanted to use the Church for his own purposes. He said to me once: 'You detest repressions and persecutions. Well, remember the Inquisition. The Church practised all that on a grand scale.'

Catholic priests stayed with us on several occasions. I don't know where they came from, but they spoke Russian well. They may have been Italians or Germans, but more probably were Poles. My father said that there were no more cultivated people than those whom one met in the Catholic hierarchy, and none cleverer in politics and more expert in collecting information, thanks to a centuries-old tradition. 'The Catholic hierarchy is as efficient and well organised as an intelligence network, with this difference, that the men it consists of have been educated and trained for dozens of years.' He particularly admired the Jesuits. 'They're the ones that diplomats and spies should learn from. The Jesuits have a system for shaping and preparing people. They even open colleges in the provinces and are good at attracting students to them. Every state should learn from them how to govern.' He gave me books about Ignatius de Loyola and other writings about the Jesuit missionaries to read. I devoured them like adventure stories. 'A missionary is a resident,' he explained. 'Religion is a colossal force, especially Catholicism in Europe. And the Orthodox Church has outlets in the Balkans and the Near East.'

He had read some books given him about Luther and the Reformation in Germany. One day I revealed to him my total ignorance concerning Protestantism and its importance in that country. This irritated him and he made me understand that if I wanted to grasp what the driving forces at work in different countries were, I must interest myself in the struggle between religious tendencies and their influence in society. Study of religions enabled one to understand societies better. For example, it was impossible to follow the development of Germany and Europe if one failed to give due weight to the impact of the personal role of Luther on the Reformation. Russia did not experience a Reformation (one could not compare Avvakum's banditry[24] to Protestantism) and was to pay for that for a long time yet. People who, like the Protestants, are concerned with their prosperity on this earth are less inclined to prostrate themselves before a Tsar or a leader. The person who is aware that his fate is in his own hands will not believe blindly in a Führer.

Regarding Islam he said: 'There is nothing original in that religion, everything in it is taken from Christianity.' And if, in fact, it was the most tolerant of all religions (something the sects had taken advantage of), he attributed this to the circumstance that Islam, late-born, had absorbed elements of Judaism and Christianity, its predecessors.

In his view it was a mistake to try and destroy the Church by force. It should be infiltrated and used in the state's interest. Religion was still a powerful factor in the maintenance of morality. For him only differences of form, not of doctrine, separated the various religions. When he talked to me of such matters it went over my head, for I was a hundred miles away from concerns like that, as, earlier, I had been to the music which my mother made me absorb.

Economic ideas

My father did not believe in self-regulation by the market and thought that the state must fulfil a certain number of duties towards the population. Even in America, France and Britain the state retained means of influencing the economy. Capitalism, when it began, had neglected the human factor. But that had been true only during the unavoidable phase of primitive accumulation of capital. The capitalist world had learnt how to avoid crises by intervening in the mechanisms of the market.

In our country, he explained, what we had was not Socialism but a form of state capitalism. 'The state controls everything and exploits people to an incredible degree. If according to Marx, the capitalists pocket surplus value, here the State grabs absolutely everything,' he joked. All the Taylorisms imaginable in the West were nothing compared with our system, our collective farms, our factories and our regulations. 'Look,' he said, 'it's enough for people to be late for work to be punished. Their wages aren't worth a hundredth part of what they produce. Everything else goes into the state's pocket. In the period when we had to create armaments that was, perhaps, justified, more or less. But, today, we should provide people with more normal living conditions.' He said that after the war, but may have thought it already before then. He tried to improve the situation of the workers employed in those sectors of industry, metallurgy and coal-mining, which came under him. He obtained subsidies for that purpose, possibly to the detriment of other branches of the economy.

My father was also well-informed on the situation in agriculture, as many leading personnel from the agro-industrial sector came to see him, as well as agronomists from the western Ukraine. He several times tried, in vain, to convince Stalin and his Politburo colleagues that the collective-farm system was the worst possible system for regions like the Baltic provinces, the Ukraine and Caucasia. Immediately after the war he obtained works dealing with Stolypin's reform.[25] 'Be quick and read these books,' he said to me, 'while they're here.' He had observed that this reform had enjoyed remarkable success in the Baltic and Western provinces of the Empire, whereas in Central Russia it had suffered sharp defeat. The situation had been a little better in Siberia. My father put this down to the fact that the most active and enterprising individuals had fled to Siberia, rather like the American far West. He advocated a differentiated policy for agriculture. There was little chance, he thought, that individual farms could develop in Central Russia, where collective responsibility was a rooted, centuries-old tradition. He once suggested to Stalin, jokingly, that land be given to the Jews in Birobidzhan: 'They are individualists. Give them farms and they'll settle there for good.' He discussed with my mother his plans for agricultural reform. The state's monopoly in agriculture would be abolished. The state would be responsible for main-taining regional agronomic institutes where the best species and seeds would be produced, for advising farmers and for setting up agricultural credit-banks. Land would be made over to the peasant for life. (To speak of private property at that time seemed as fantastic as a novel by Jules Verne.[26])

Political ideas

'There are two dominant forces in man: love and national feeling,' he said to me. Any attempt to eradicate them would be a grave mistake. One should, on the contrary, base oneself on them. 'People fought in the war not for ideas but because their country and their nearest and dearest were threatened.' Britain devoted centuries to subduing Ireland, and Russia did the same with Caucasia, even if Bolshevism effectively destroyed the national element. (My father could not foresee that the Caucasian peoples were going to be ravaged by drugs.)

The social order is founded on the family. If the family is in a bad way, the state will feel the consequences. Traditions and virtues are trans-mitted by the family: the school passes on knowledge only. 'We should imitate the English educational system. They don't fill a child's head with concrete items of knowledge before the age of ten or twelve. They try to develop first his capacity for comprehension and his physical and moral powers. Only after that do they inculcate learning.'

There were no divorces in my father's circle. When, once, Merkulov was so taken with a lady that he wanted to leave his wife for her, my father sent for the lady in question and said to her: 'Being so beautiful, you can easily find yourself a bachelor. If you think your choice is poor in Georgia, go to Moscow, where the game is plentiful.'

His entire policy can be summed up in a single phase: he wanted to free the Soviet people from serfdom. And it can't be claimed that he wanted to take power in that way, because the shortest route to power lay through the Party. His concerns for efficiency brought him continually into conflict with the Party. After his post-war disappointment, when he realised that the Soviet people, while wanting an improvement in their standard of loving, were incapable of demanding the conditions needed for that to come about, my father decided to wager on the non-Russian republics. He counted on both their national aspirations and the thirst for prosperity. Russia would arrive at the required reforms, he thought, if she saw them bearing fruit in the neighbouring regions.

The Ukrainian nationalist movement might have been destroyed a hundred times. My father did not destroy it. He wanted to have all the nationalist movements on his side. He criticised the custom by which Russians were appointed to leading positions in the republics. This he saw as a continuation of Tsarist policy: governors were sent out, no account was taken of local economic interests, and relations as between metropolis and colonies were maintained. One day he said to me: 'Just think, the First Secretary of the Communist Party of Lithuania or Estonia doesn't even speak the local language and can express himself only in Russian. And that's the norm! A Georgian can speak to the ruler of the republic only through an interpreter. It's hard to imagine a more abnormal system. Imagine the Americans putting an intelligent man who speaks only Abyssinian in charge of California. The British appointed in their colonies officials who spoke English but also had a perfect command of the local languages.' He took a keen interest in the British Empire and always praised to me the experience, shrewdness and guile that the British showed in politics.

My mother blamed my father for forgetting his own people and thinking exclusively of the Soviet Union. He would merely laugh and not let himself be drawn into discussion. He once said to her: 'You are closer to your relatives in Paris than to me. It's easy to criticise at a distance. I should like to see what our *émigrés* would do if they were in my place.' Perhaps he realised that, at that time, the republics could not survive separately.

When the nationalism of the Georgians or that of the other peoples of the USSR was mentioned in his hearing he never failed to observe that it was a reaction to the imperial policy of the 'Russian chauvinists' (he used that expression). He regretted that this reaction might degenerate into narrow parochialism. He saw the danger of nationalism quite clearly, perhaps because he had thought over the experience of the Georgian Mensheviks and of Nazi Germany. I never heard him speak of destroying the Soviet federation. He merely wanted to move the centre of gravity from Moscow to the republics without questioning the union, because he thought that the economic prosperity of the USSR would be the quickest way to independence for the republics. The Soviet federation had to be decentralised. Only defence, transport and foreign policy should remain the responsibility of the central administrations, while everything else would fall within the competence of the local authorities. The various territorial units which had been delimited arbitrarily by the Soviet power should be redrawn in conformity with ethnic criteria, but without harming economic connections. He discussed these questions fairly frankly with Khrushchev and Malenkov. Those two rascals were not so foolish as to contradict him.

The Party

My father declared straight out, even in the presence of important cadres, that reform should have been undertaken immediately after the war, and even earlier. The Party had become a superstructure that accomplished nothing concrete yet controlled everything and involved itself in everything without being responsible for anything. He did not use these terms, but the sense of what he said went even further. I heard him expound his idea to Malenkov and he also spoke of it to Stalin. When he told Stalin that intrigues flourished in the Party because its members had no real occupation, Stalin did not contradict him. That situation suited Stalin. For him the Party was his instrument for violence and control.

In my father's view the country's leaders should feel responsible and the economy should be managed by people trained for that task. In no other state could one find a system in which decisions were taken by one group of people and carried out by another group, who were held responsible for those decisions. The Party imposed decisions on the Council of Ministers and gave them the force of law. The ministers were mere executives, yet bore responsibility. My father explained to Stalin (several witnesses told me of these discussions) that this system seemed, perhaps, tolerable so long as those who took decisions belonged to the only groups that were devoted to the state, while the others remained mercenaries drawn from among the nobles and capitalists. But that age had passed. We could no longer treat the whole population as though they were White Guards. Stalin remained deaf to these arguments.

The masses

My father respected the individual but not the crowd. He taught me never to go along with the desires of the masses. I did not understand him at the time, but today I think he was right. One certainly ought not to impose on them anything totally alien to their aspirations, but neither ought one to follow their wishes where state policy was concerned, because they always looked for an immediate result. Yet there are measures that are good for the masses though they run contrary to their desires. According to my father, most people have no time for ideology. For them having enough to eat, having a roof over their heads and living quietly with their families matters more than anything else. That minimum has to be ensured for them before entering into ideological subtleties. People must not be treated like cattle. The individual must be given at least the illusion of freedom. We must not forget that, at that time, three-quarters of the Soviet people were bound to their collective farm and had no right to leave them.

My father was a deeply unhappy man. His character drove him to creativity. He avoided intrigues and manoeuvres in the apparatus, seeking refuge in domains in which he could build. He told me that one must always try to find something interesting in every occupation, and for him this meant finding a possibility to create. He had very little satisfaction in his life, since the only field in which he was allowed to deploy his talents was that of armaments, instruments of destruction. In a word, I pity him. What has he left behind him? A dreadful reputation, and the atomic bomb in the hands of those wretches.

Author's Epilogue

I did not write this book in order to rehabilitate the memory of my father – or, at least, that was not my prime purpose. I am perfectly well aware now that it was not possible to be one of the leaders of the USSR without soiling one's hands. There was always a choice to be made.

My father was a member of the Politburo and of the government. He was responsible, like the rest, for all the acts of that government, even if he disagreed with some of them. But a certain Russian intelligentsia, which I shall call chauvinist, presents the Stalin period in a way that I want to challenge. If we are to believe the representatives of this tendency, the unfortunate Russian people fell victim to non-Russians who had seized power and begun to exploit the Russians. Communism and Leninism would have borne a human face had they not been deformed by two uncouth Asiatics from the Caucasus and, above all, by the monster Beria. Well, I maintain that, whatever they may say, the Russians bear some responsibility for what happened. They welcomed with enthusiasm the plundering and expropriation preached by the Bolsheviks. They accepted the slaughtering of officers and priests. A handful of Bolsheviks would never have managed to impose this monstrous policy from 1917 onwards had they not enjoyed the active support of the Russian people. True, non-Russians were numerous among the first Bolshevik leaders. But without the backing of the Russian masses, these leaders would never have implemented any of their programmes. Besides, the influence of individuals on the Bolshevik system was always limited. The personality of one leader or another might emphasise certain features but could not modify the foundations of the regime.

My father was accused of responsibility for everything that went wrong so as to exculpate the Bolshevik system and the Party. Since he had put the Party in jeopardy it was necessary to conceal at all costs the fact that he had been a political adversary. The simplest thing to do was to show him to the masses as a bandit at all levels – traitor, spy, rapist, ignoramus and oaf into the bargain. Yet it is enough to take cognisance of the minutes of the July 1953 Plenum to see that the charges brought against him were essentially political in nature. He was accused of having wanted to reunify Germany by abandoning the construction of Socialism in the GDR, of having sabotaged the collective-farm system, of having sought to emancipate the republics and to reduce the role of the Party – in short, of not being a Communist. Today, the Party and Bolshevism have vanished from the scene, but where my father is concerned the same line is followed, this time owing to the incurable chauvinism with which the Russian elites are infected. The notes and reports that my father addressed to the Presidium, with his proposals for reforms, have still not been published. I await with impatience the opening of the archives, as this will make it possible to determine the actual degree of his guilt.

He has been depicted as a careerist without any conviction. I consider that if he had wanted to take power, he could have done that in Stalin's lifetime as well as after his death. I want to show that, from the start, my father had a policy. Sometimes he was able to put it into effect, at other times this was not possible. This policy was pursued through opposition, sometimes masked, at other times open, to the leaders of the Party. He was certainly no humanist who dreamt of the people's well-being. He was a pragmatic statesman who wanted to get results. He was against the repression not out of humanity but because he considered men were not to be won over by fear. This concern for effectiveness dictated his policy in every sphere: in agriculture, industry, foreign policy, national policy, which were all interlinked.

The conflict crystallised around foreign policy. My father did not want the Soviet Union to dominate the world – a useless and stupid project, in his view. He was beaten, and paid with his life. His mistake was perhaps to have gone beyond the framework of Georgia. He wanted to rescue Russia from the Bolshevik noose that was strangling her. He overestimated the common sense of those around him and underestimated their perfidy.

In this account I have based myself on what I was myself witness to. I have also mentioned fairly frequently things told me by my mother and others. I do not always remember the exact words of my informants, but I have tried to reconstitute the correct meaning of statements that have stayed in my memory.

Sergo Beria

Appendix

The Transcaucasian Republics after the upheavals of 1937

Armenia: Aryutunov

The central apparatus of the Georgian Party included numerous Armenians and Russians. The Armenians, in particular, were in general more competent and more aggressive than the Georgians whom they ousted.[1] This problem had to be solved and my father succeeded in doing that in masterly fashion. Making it seem that the initiative for this came from Mikoyan, he persuaded Stalin of the need to 'strengthen' the Armenian Communist Party by an increase in its numbers through transferring five thousand Armenian communists who were resident in Georgia. At the same time he caused Grisha Aryutunov to be elected head of the Party in Armenia. He came from Kakhetia (many Armenians fleeing from Turkish persecution had settled in that region) and was the same age as my father. They were very close, to the extent that my father had installed him in a flat near ours. They remained close, to the end. A calm, mild man with pleasant manners, and an excellent organiser, Aryutunov had a sobering influence on those around him. Tall and slim, he had a handsome face. My mother was very glad of his peaceful temperament, which counterbalanced my father's, always overflowing with activity. She was always relieved when she learnt that Aryutunov was accompanying him on journeys where she could not follow. Aryutunov was faithful all his life long to his wife, who returned his love.

He was recommended to Stalin for the post of First Secretary of the Armenian Communist Party. Personally, he did not want the job, and it was without enthusiasm that he let his name be put forward. Stalin chose him eventually, although Mikoyan tried in vain to advance the claims of other candidates. Mikoyan came to Tbilisi to fetch the new First Secretary and the two of them set off together for Armenia. Aryutunov was a 'Georgian' Armenian and it was to be expected that his nomination would give rise to reactions. Two days had not passed since they left when my father received an appeal from Mikoyan to go to his rescue. There was an outcry among the Armenian Communists! My father refused to move and told Mikoyan to solve his problem himself. Mikoyan then telephoned Stalin, who ordered my father to go to Armenia at once. Mikoyan himself told me what my father said when he arrived.

'You liked Khandzhian. We all liked him. Yet you drove him to suicide through refusing to obey orders that he could not fulfil.[2] Do you want to drive these two, as well, to suicide? The Politburo has sent you Mikoyan, whom you like and respect. Because you do like and respect him, don't you?' Silence in the assembly. My father had enjoyed putting that question, so as to take a rise out of Mikoyan. 'You will not leave the hall until you have settled this question.'

The Armenians did not want a man parachuted in from Tbilisi and who, into the bargain, did not speak Armenian. But they ended by giving in. After this difficult enthronement Aryutunov often came to Tbilisi to complain to my father.

'Lavrenti, you played me an abominable trick. Those people are frightful. I understand now why the nationalists hated them so much during the revolution. Yes, I understand the Dashnaks now.'[3] And, indeed, the Armenian Bolsheviks, many of them formed in emigration, were particularly fanatical. There had been Communists of that stamp in Georgia, but most of them had perished during the revolution. Aryutunov, a convinced internationalist, was nevertheless obliged to pursue, to some degree, an Armenian national policy. All the same, he would not learn the language. My father, very displeased, eventually gave him an ultimatum.

'The next time I see you I want you to make a speech to me in Armenian!'

So the unfortunate First Secretary swotted away at textbooks for ten or fifteen hours a day. The next time he saw my father he was able to make a ten-minute speech in Armenian. But my father, who knew a little Armenian, interrupted him suddenly.

'But these are verses that you are declaiming!'

'They're easier to remember,' was Aryutunov's reply. My father let go his hold when Aryutunov showed himself capable of writing a report in Armenian for the congress of the Armenian Communist Party.

Despite these little raggings he remained very close to my father, who had to remind him to call on Mikoyan first, before visiting us, when he came to Moscow. Aryutunov did not like Mikoyan. However, when my father fell it was Mikoyan who saved Aryutunov from the firing squad. He suffered many humiliations, even so, and was accused of plotting against the Soviet state. He lost his job and his flat and died soon afterwards.

Azerbaijan: Bagirov

My father's relations were excellent with the First Secretary of the Azerbaijan Communist Party, Jafar Bagirov. The two men had no secrets from each other.[4] Although my father – especially towards the end of his life – preferred Aryutunov on the human level, he recognised many good qualities in Bagirov. This man spoke Turkish and Iranian perfectly, had a lively mind, was able to find his bearings quickly in the most diverse situations, and had shown himself to be a competent administrator, well informed about the oil industry.[5] He did not drink and believed in neither God nor the Devil, and still less in communism. His first wife died giving birth to a son. He remarried, to an animated German woman who brought with her three sisters and their mother.

'It's a real harem,' said my mother, laughing at all these women, of whom she was nonetheless very fond. In order to house his tribe Bagirov had to have a house built, and this brought down on him a shower of criticisms. Bagirov was reviving the Turkish way of life, he was organising a brothel, and so on ... whereas the persons involved were perfectly civilised German ladies.

Bagirov had a lot of trouble during the war and my father did what he could to help him. Also, his elder son, who became a pilot, was killed in an air battle. His aircraft crashed with such violence that it was impossible to put together the scattered pieces of his body. The loss of this boy affected Bagirov terribly and he aged ten years. In 1942 I happened to be in a train with him. Having joined me in my compartment he began talking about his son, weeping and regretting all that he had not done for him. At that time I did not understand how one could torment oneself like that, and I told my father of my perplexity. He said: 'He is remorseful because he thinks he neglected his son and realises that it's now too late to put that right. But you are still to young to appreciate things like that.'

In 1951 Bagirov was incensed because a prize had been awarded to Guseinov, who had praised Shamil[6] in a poem allegedly marked by 'bourgeois nationalism'.

He was indignant, though his own bedroom was decorated with a portrait of this hero! My father was furious with him and I heard him lecturing Bagirov over the telephone. He said that Bagirov should have woken up earlier if he wanted to oppose the award of that prize, adding that even if he acted thus on Stalin's orders he ought never to have attacked Shamil in those terms. My father interpreted this 'Shamil affair' as the sign of a bending of Stalin's Caucasian policy, a return to the old recipe of turning some peoples against others.[7] In my opinion Bagirov's conduct was explicable rather by the fact that, aware that my father was threatened and afraid that the disgracing of my father might reflect on him, he wanted to take precautions and save himself.

Many people disliked Bagirov, especially the Russians in Azerbaijan whom he tried to remove from important jobs so as to replace them with Caucasians. After my father's death he was blamed for that policy as well as for his support of 'the spy Beria'. I heard that he bore himself with exemplary dignity at his trial in April 1956. It was even said that everyone in the room stood up when he came in.

Notes

Appendix: The Transcaucasian Republics after the upheavals of 1937

1. Before 1914 Armenians formed the majority of the population of Tiflis (Tbilisi) where they owned 60 per cent of the enterprises and of the land. When independence came the Georgian leaders tried to re-nationalise their capital. The action described here followed logically from that policy.

2. It was rumoured that Beria killed Khandzhian, the secretary of the Armenian Communist Party, with his own hand, in July 1936. However, the testimonies collected at his trial, far from suspect of partiality towards Beria, support the thesis of suicide. (*Voenno-istoricheskii zhurnal* 1/1990). Khandzhian died in Beria's office after having had several clashes with him. He was opposed in particular to the rewriting of the history of the Bolsheviks in Caucasia, to the predominance of the Georgian apparatus in the Transcaucasian Federation, and to the way the frontiers of the Armenian republic were drawn after the dissolution of the Transcaucasian Federation. (C. Mouradian, *De Staline à Gorbatchev, histoire d'une république soviétique: l'Arménie*, Ramsay, 1990, p. 48.

3. The Dashnakatsutyun (Armenian Revolutionary Federation) was the Armenian nationalist party. Founded in Tiflis (Tbilisi) in 1890 and advocating a Jaurès-style socialism, it dominated the first independent republic.

4. According to a persistent rumour, Bagirov, like Beria, was a former adherent of the Musavat party. After the Bolsheviks' victory it was said that he usurped the identity of a Bolshevik brother, whom he assassinated for this purpose. (V.F. Nekrasov, op. cit., p. 82). Bagirov got Beria into the Azerbaijan Cheka and set his foot in the stirrup. Subsequently Beria always protected him. He was executed in 1956.

5. However, he owed Stalin's favour to other services. When at the head of the Azerbaijan GPU he used, in 1924, such brutal methods that he received a reprimand from the Party's Control Commission (24 September 1929). He had not taken steps against 'the intolerable measures of the GPU' and was warned that 'as chairman of the Azerbaijan GPU he will bear full responsibility if such incidents recur in the GPU apparat'. But on 21 August 1929 Stalin wrote to Molotov, 'Bagirov (despite his past sins) will have to be confirmed as chairman of the Cheka in Azerbaijan: he is now the only person who can cope with the Musavatists and Ittihadists who have reared their heads in the Azerbaijan countryside.' (*Stalin's Letters to Molotov, 1925-1936*, 1995, pp. 170, no. 8, and 168.

6. Legendary hero of North Caucasian resistance to Russian colonisation. A Daghestani by origin, Imam Shamil took refuge in Chechnya in 1840, and from there led the guerilla war of the highlanders against the Russian invader. He surrendered in 1859, after 25 years of struggle. The war in the Caucasus, which ended (temporarily) in 1864, cost the Russian army 77,000 dead.

7. Before 1951 Soviet historiography treated Shamil as a progressive figure. In 1934 Stalin had even called for publication of studies on Shamil. From 1951 Bagirov imposed a version of Shamil as a reactionary paid by foreign powers

(*Rodina*, No.3/4 of 1994,pp. 20-21). The affair of Guseinov's prize took place in May 1951. In February 1953 Bagirov, doubtless still anxious to distance himself from Beria, who was in difficulties, published in *Kommunist* an article entitled 'The elder brother in the family of Soviet peoples'.

Chapter 1: In Stalin's Shadow

1. The Georgian princes were poor, their title to nobility consisting of glory won on the battlefield. In order to preserve their homeland they were obliged to put themselves at the disposal of Byzantium, Persia and Turkey, offering concessions now to one, now to another. When threatened by Persia or Turkey, Georgia opted for seeking the protection of the Tsar, believing this to be the lesser evil. The Georgian princes thought themselves smarter than the Russians, but they were deceived. Russia allowed them to retain the outward forms of royalty but deprived them of their country's independence and its throne. The princes were deported to Russia and replaced by governors who established a tyrannical regime. (Author's note.)

2. If we are to believe Thaddeus Wittlin, Beria's first biographer, Erkomashvili was assassinated by Beria in 1923. Wittlin, T. *Beria* (Paris, 1972) 100. Some of the allegations in this work are, however, fantastical, as we shall see.

3. At Beria's trial he was accused of having lied about the date that he joined the Bolshevik Party, saying that it was March 1917. He claimed to have been the treasurer of that Marxist group. This date was not supported by documents earlier than December 1919. Unfortunately, the minutes of Beria's trial are not available, though some extracts were published in *Voenno-istoricheskii Zhurnal*, 5-6 (1989); 1-3-5 (1990); 1 (1991).

4. Transcaucasia (Georgia, Armenia and Azerbaijan) formed an independent government on 11 November 1917. Turkey, allied to the Central Empires, took advantage of the collapse of the Russian armies to advance into Caucasia. In March 1918 the Treaty of Brest-Litovsk gave Turkey the districts of Kars, Ardahan and Batum. As Georgia and Armenia refused to accept these amputations, Turkey invaded the disputed territories. Azerbaijan having taken up a pro-Turkish attitude, Transcaucasian unity broke up. Georgia, backed by Germany, proclaimed its independence on 26 May 1918.

5. Turkey's first attempt to expel the Commune installed in Baku in April 1918 was blocked in June by Germany, urged by Bolshevik Russia. Lenin arranged with Berlin for Moscow to keep control of Baku while Germany established a protectorate over Menshevik Georgia. A quarter of Baku's oil production was to go to Germany. On 9 August the British occupied Baku. On 15 September the city fell to the Turks, who were, this time, backed by the Germans. But the defeat of the Central Empires made this success ephemeral. The Mudros armistice obliged Turkey to give up Transcaucasia to the British. Azerbaijan's first national assembly opened in Baku on 7 December 1918, a few days after the British entered the city.

6. The Musavat, an Azerbaijan nationalist party created in 1911, was the dominant political force in the country during the British occupation.

7. Beria's interest in Great Britain and British imperialist policy may go back to this period. After the revolutionary follies of the Baku Commune, the British occupation was welcomed with relief by the inhabitants of Baku. The British ended inflation, denationalised the industries and re-established the supply of food.

8. Beria was entrusted by the Baku Bolsheviks with the task of conveying secret letters to Georgia. See Mikoyan's address at the Plenum of 2-7 July 1953.

9. A North Caucasian people related to the Chechens.

10. This early sympathy for the Mensheviks was also one of the charges levelled against Beria at his trial. According to a witness, 'Sergo Ordzhonikidze related with indignation that Beria had destroyed the compromising archives of the Menshevik government of Georgia, and that when that government was finally breaking up, Beria exhorted the Mensheviks to hold on and resist Bolshevik pressure.' *Voenno-istoricheskii Zhurnal* 3 (1990) 83.

11. Until February 1921 Beria was in charge of the Commission, attached to the Cheka, for expropriating the bourgeoisie and improving the lives of the working people. In February 1921 he obtained a scholarship to continue his studies but was immediately sent to Tbilisi. In April 1921 the head of the Azerbaijan Cheka, D. Bagirov, appointed him chief of the Secret Operations Department of that organisation.

12. Ordzhonikidze insisted on this intervention despite the reticence shown by Lenin and by Chicherin, the People's Commissar of Foreign Affairs, who favoured a tactic of subversion, as they feared the bad effect abroad of a Bolshevising of Georgia by bayonets. The Georgian Mensheviks were, in fact, supported by the socialists of Europe and did much to open the eyes of the latter to Bolshevik methods. Khlevnyuk, O. *Stalin i Ordzhonikidze* (Moscow, 1993): Kvashonkin A.V. (editor) *Bolshevistskoe rukovodstvo, Perepiska 1912-1927 (Moscow, 1996)*. Not long before they left Georgia the Menshevik leaders sent for the Bolsheviks who were being held in their prisons and said that they were going to release them so that they might take power and recover Batum from the Turks. That duly happened, during the night of 17-18 March 1921. The Mensheviks fled after releasing their Bolshevik prisoners. This was how Georgia retained Batum and Adzharia. Blagoveshchensky, F. 'V gostyakh u P.A. Sharii', *Minuvshee* 7 (1918) 470.

13. Beria's first biographer, Thaddeus Wittlin, gives an incredible account of the marriage in which we see Beria carrying off young Nina, raping her in a railway carriage and then holding her prisoner and deciding to marry her for career reasons. Wittlin, op. cit., 119-20.

14. From 1922 Sasha Gegechkori was Vice-President of the Georgian Government. He was accused of embezzling public funds for his many orgies. Knight, A. *Beria*, (Princeton University Press, 1993) 44.

15. One of these requests, dated 23 November 1923, which has survived in the archives, has been published. Beria wrote to the Party authorities pointing out that, through his work in the Party, and particularly in the Cheka, he had fallen behind in his training as a specialist. He asked the Central Committee to allow him to go on with his studies. Beria openly indicated that, for him, work in the Party and the Cheka was so much waste of time. *Voenno-istoricheskii Zhurnal* 1 (1990) 73.

16. This was probably D. Z. Tyomkin, who became a composer in Hollywood. Karyagin, V. *Diplomatichiskaya zhizn za kulisami i na stsene* (Moscow, 1994) 235.

17. In 1924 the USSR was trying to obtain diplomatic recognition from the Western powers. The Georgian Mensheviks calculated that Moscow would not dare to crush the Georgian revolt while it was seeking to present a civilised image to the West and that Georgia would win independence through these exceptional circumstances.

18. Dzhugeli arrived in Georgia in mid-April and was arrested on 4 August. On 9 and 12 August he sent two letters to the Menshevik Party's Central Committee which have been preserved in the Georgian Archives available on microfilm at the B.D.I.C. In the first of these letters he tells of his interview in prison with Kvantaliani. The latter had told him: 'We knew about your preparations. The documents in our possession show that nothing will come of them but a crazy adventure.' Dzhugeli goes on: 'That evening he showed me these documents and I must say, comrades, that the reality went far beyond anything I expected ... They have a serious intelligence service. I have finally become absolutely certain that this great matter must be cancelled, and that this is something very urgent and indispensable. I am fearful that you may think that "the air of the Cheka" has had a bad effect on me, but I swear on my honour that I would never have faced death as calmly as now ...' Dzhugeli was shot in September.

19. Shariko Tsereteli had also been a lieutenant-colonel in the Georgian Legion created by the Germans in 1918. He was to remain Beria's confidential agent to the end. Bugay, N.F. *Iosif Vissarionovich Lavrenti Beria: ikh nado deportirovat* (Moscow, 1992) 11.

20. This is what we read in the minutes of Beria's trial. 'Beria knew that insurrection was imminent, but not only did he do nothing to oppose it or to warn the leaders of the Party and the Cheka in Transcaucasia, he actually supported the Mensheviks ... The insurrection was crushed only through the vigorous intervention of Ordzhonikidze, Myasnikov, Atarbekov and Mogilevsky ... The last-named three died in an air crash in August 1925. The inquiry conducted by Beria into the dubious circumstances of this accident produced nothing ... There were many who saw Beria as the assassin.' *Voenno-istoricheskii Zhurnal* 3 (1990) 83. Sergo Beria's story that his father had warned Ordzhonikdze, bypassing the leaders of the Cheka, explains why Beria managed to save his career after this affair.

21. More than 7,000 Georgians (12,000 according to some estimates) were shot and 20,000 deported. The Menshevik revolt of 1924 was the biggest revolt that the Bolsheviks ever had to face. In its first days the Western half of the country fell into the hands of the rebels. A Georgian Communist commented thus on the massacres: 'It must be said that the Mensheviks showed themselves to be weak and characterless. They did not dare to shoot a single one of our comrades whereas we had shot hundreds of theirs, members of their Central Committee included.' (Wehner, M., 'Le soulèvement géorgien', *Communisme* (1995) 161).

22. Beria never denied that he worked for the Musavat Party's counter-espionage service during the British occupation of Baku. He said that he did this on the orders of the Bolshevik Party. His enemies did not fail to point out that no witness came forward to confirm his statement. Between July and December 1953, during Beria's trial, all these past events were closely examined. Beria was accused of having forced two Armenian Bolsheviks to certify that he had been with them in a clandestine Bolshevik organisation in 1919 (testimony of Captain Balanyuk). Beria was stated to have been a 'British spy' because the Musavat's services were supervised by the British.

23. According to the Chekist Mikhail Shreider, Beria's enemies in the Cheka gave a different version of the facts. 'Redens told me that he had information proving that the armed rising by the Georgian Mensheviks which Beria was supposed to have brilliantly crushed was actually organised by him for his own self-advertisement. Stalin had been told, but for incomprehensible reasons he had particular confidence in Beria and would hear nothing said against him.' Shreider, M. *NKVD iznutri* (Moscow 1995) 111. The Georgian Archives show that the insurrection of 1924 was the subject of a lively polemic among the Paris *émigrés*. The Mensheviks' opponents blamed them for having chosen a bad tactic by not undertaking operations in Tbilisi, where the opposition was particularly strong, and for making believe to the rebels that Western aid was on the way. Some went so far as to affirm that the Mensheviks had been manipulated by the Cheka in this affair. And how to explain why Dzhugeli's letters reached Paris only after the insurrection had begun?

24. Khomeriki was one of the founders of the Social-Democratic Committee in

Mingrelia and Imeretia, and Minister of Agriculture in the first independent government of Georgia. In exile he worked actively for closer relations between the Caucasian peoples. He was executed after being taken prisoner.

25. A letter from Zinoviev to Kamenev, dated July 1923, seems to confirm that Ordzhonikidze was not entirely blind where Stalin was concerned, from this time onward. Zinoviev wrote: 'Stalin has established his dictatorship ... For you, that's not news. But what has amazed me is that Voroshilov and Sergo hold almost the same opinion.' Khlevnyuk, op. cit. 13. Ordzhonikidze was to show great unwillingness to give up leadership of the Transcaucasian Federation and 'ascend' to Moscow in order to head the Central Control Commission, in which he would become the one who did Stalin's dirty work for him.

26. After the events of 1924 Beria appears to have said that, had he allowed him, Ordzhonikidze would have decapitated the Georgian people. When Ordzhonikidze heard this he was very angry. Beria hastened to write the following letter to him on 8 February 1933. 'Dear Sergo, Bagirov has told me of things that are so monstrous that it is hard to believe them. How could you suppose, even for one moment, that I could have made allegations that are so fantastic, absurd and altogether counter-revolutionary? How could I have said: "Sergo would have shot all Georgia in 1924 if I had not held him back," how could I have spoken of "interference" in Transcaucasia?' RTsKhDNI, f. 85, o. 413, d.29.

27. It must be recalled, however, that Ordzhonikidze forced the Red Army's invasion of Georgia upon a hesitant Lenin, who feared what the effect might be on international opinion. Ordzhonikidze was at that time constantly in favour of a hard and centralising policy. This was still true at the time of the 1924 insurrection. He and the Transcaucasian Party leadership carried out massive reprisals, despite the objections raised by some members of the Politburo who were anxious about world opinion. Ordzhonikidze replied: 'Perhaps we did exaggerate a little, but nothing can be done about that now.' Wehner, op. cit., 165.

28. According to the propaganda of the time, Beria and Lakoba aimed to turn Georgia into a 'Soviet Florida'.

29. There were 20,527 Germans in Georgia in 1939. They were deported during the war. Bugay, op. cit. 36. In an interview with Italian Communists on 10 July 1956 Khrushchev spoke about Beria's agrarian policy: 'A wrong economic policy was followed in Georgia. Beria fixed higher prices for the grapes of Georgia and Azerbaijan and caused collectivisation to be carried out in such a way that the peasants drew most of their income from their private plots.' *Istochnik* 2 (1994) 87.

30. This decision, imposed by Stalin and Ordzhonikidze,was the occasion for Lenin's last major struggle, at the end of 1922. The Georgian Bolsheviks, Budu Mdivani, Sasha Gegechkori, Sergo Kavtaradze and Filip Makharadze, were indeed vigorously opposed to it, preferring that Georgia should enter the Soviet federation directly. They appealed to Lenin, who wanted to intervene on their behalf but was prevented from acting by illness. On 6 March 1923 Trotsky wrote to Stalin that 'the conflict between the Great-Russian nationalists and the "nationals" has come into the open and is turning into a factional struggle.' *Izvestia TsKKPSS* 9 (1990) 147-64.

31. Beria was accused at his trial of having 'fallen under the influence of Budu Mdivani when he arrived in Georgia,' that Mdivani who had 'done all he could to prevent the creation of the Transcaucasian Federation' and had advanced the slogan: 'Let's turn towards Constantinople.' It was Mdivani who planned the expulsion of Armenians from Tbilisi (which Beria tried later to carry out). *Voenno-istoricheskii Zhurnal*, 3 (1990) 83. Mdivani had, indeed, described the Transcaucasian Federation as an 'artificial creation'. At the Twelfth Party Congress, in May-June 1923, where the organisation of the Soviet Federation was decided, Mdivani had argued for the republics entering the federation to remain 'independent'. The autonomous republics and the independent ones should enjoy the same status. In other words, Mdivani was also proposing that the Russian Federation be liquidated. *Izvestia TsKKPSS*, 3,4 (1991).

32. The Chekist M. Shreider reports the evidence of this given by the former head of the Communist Party of Kazakhstan, Mirzoyan. 'He spoke of Beria with hatred. He told me that when Beria was proposed for secretary of the Party in Transcaucasia, Sergo Ordzhonikidze and a group of Caucasian Bolsheviks showed strong opposition. They claimed to have information proving that Beria was a traitor, about his links with the Musavatists and the role he played in the Menshevik revolt ... They also referred to his debauchery. In Caucasia Beria was nicknamed the Turkish Sultan, and it was almost as though he kept a harem ... Stalin knew all about that, but insisted on Beria being nominated.' Shreider, op. cit. 175.

33. However, Beria took care to put his own men in charge of Armenia and Azerbaijan. Transcaucasia continued to be his fief even after his transfer to Moscow in 1938.

34. In the summer of 1919, Bolshevik Russia began to draw closer to Turkey. Kemal's revolution seemed to Lenin the first revolution in Asia. Collusion between anti-British Turkey and Bolshevik Russia facilitated the Bolshevising of Caucasia. Afanasyan, S. *L'Arménie, l'Azerbaidjan et la Géorgie de l'indépendance à l'instauration du pouvoir soviétique* (Paris, 1981). Conquest of Transcaucasia did not, however, figure at all in the plans of Kemal Atatürk, a resolute opponent of Pan-Turanianism. Turkey gave considerable help to the Bolsheviks in their destruction of independent Azerbaijan, which was governed between December 1918 and April 1920 by the Musavatists, whose pro-British orientation was as repugnant to Kemal as to Lenin. 'If the states of Caucasia become a barrier against us, we shall make an agreement with the Bolsheviks to co-ordinate our offensive against these states,' Kemal wrote to his army commanders at the end of 1919. Swietochowski, T. 'Russkii Azerbaijan', *Khazar*, 3 (1990) 33-62. Sergo Beria says: 'This story entered into our family folklore. "Take little Georgia," said my father. "In 1919 Lenin agreed to let Kemal have Turkestan, with Georgia as a bonus. Just think! The Caucasians had fought for thousands of years to win their independence and now, with a stroke of the pen, history was to be altered. Heaven be praised, Stalin intervened to dissuade Lenin and that was a good deed." '

35. The first encounter for which documentary evidence exists took place in the summer of 1931. Stalin was so impressed that he immediately arranged for a session of the Central Committee to be devoted to the Transcaucasian Federation. The leaders of the Federation were summoned to attend this meeting, at which Beria would be appointed head of the Georgian Communist Party. Stalin's proposal met with vigorous protest. Ordzhonikidze was not present, but Mikoyan said to one of those who were astonished by the proposal: 'Sergo will never agree to go along with the coronation of Beria. He knows him well!' Only Kaganovich supported Stalin and spoke in praise of Beria.

36. Ordzhonikidze's brother was sentenced to death in November 1937.

37. Khrushchev says in his memoirs that he learnt the cause of Ordzhonikidze's death during the war. According to Molotov, he 'was a person of strong feelings and passions. Stalin often said this wasn't the way to be.' Chuev, F. *Molotov Remembers* (Moscow, 1992) 259.

38. Sergo Beria stresses this because his father was accused of having driven Ordzhonikidze to suicide. The latter was alleged to have said to Mikoyan a few days before he died that he attributed Stalin's hostility to 'Beria's intrigues' (the July 1953 Plenum). Recent studies exonerate Beria from this charge. Khlevnyuk, op. cit. When Stalin set himself to persecute one of his circle his favourite tactic was to insinuate that he had been 'wrongly informed', that he was being manipulated by mischievous persons around him.

39. This is what Beria wrote to Ordzhonikidze on 2 March 1933. 'A few words about Papulia. I have had several conversations with him and have sent people to him in the hope that they would have some influence on him. I suggested that he become People's Commissar for Light Industry or for Railway Construction. Perhaps I went about it wrongly, but my efforts were in vain. He refused to take a job, he is fed up, he swore and threatened to go on hunger strike. Today I had another talk with him and he agreed to be Director of the Department of Inspection of Railways ...' RTsKhDNI, f.85, o.29, d.414.

40. A famous epic describing a battle between Russians and Polovtsians in 1185. The date and the author are unknown.

41. A famous Georgian epic of the 12th century.

42. He meant the works of the early Bolsheviks, Budu Mdivani and Filip Makharadze. In their writings they flattered Stalin, but the latter thought they did not go far enough. Those veterans tended to exaggerate their own role and to present Stalin as their disciple, whereas he was the disciple only of Letso Katskhoveli and, above all, of Lenin. (Author's note.) The falsification of the history of Bolshevism in Caucasia began with the appearance in 1929 of a life of Stalin edited by Ordzhonikidze, Yenukidze and Kaganovich. For the history of the Social-Democratic groups in Transcaucasia and Stalin's actual role, see Nicolaysen, H. 'S.D. Networks in Transcaucasia and Stalin: the Rise of a Regional Party Functionary (1887-1902)' (Hoover Institution, July 1991).

43. According to Helen Nicolaysen, Beria's work was based on authentic political documents and the falsehoods in it were misinterpretations rather than forgeries. Ibid., 68.

44. And Beria did publish an article on the Prague conference, in *Pravda*, 26 October 1935.

45. A Shah of Persia who came to power in 1587. He quarrelled with the Ottoman Empire over Transcaucasia.

46. Head of the GPU in Transcaucasia from 1925 to 1931. Beria became his deputy in 1927 and quickly acquired a dominant position, so that people spoke of the Cheka chief as 'Berens'. Beria got rid of this inconvenient superior by encouraging him to get drunk in public and then reporting the scandal to Stalin. Redens was arrested in November 1938 and shot in January 1941. Anna Allilueva was arrested in January 1948.

47. In 1937 Yezhov sent M.I. Litvin, head of the Secret Section of the NKVD to Transcaucasia, with the task of compiling a dossier that would compromise Beria. Litvin arrested some officials and extorted by torture the confession he needed. He became the head of the Leningrad NKVD and killed himself in November 1938. Lurin, E. 'Palachi', *Leningradskaya Pravda*, 5 August 1989.

48. The writer of these notes obtained in 1996 the testimony of A. Mirtskhulava, a Komsomol leader who in April 1953 became First Secretary of the Georgian Communist Party and a strong supporter of Beria – one of the few Georgian apparatchiks to have survived from that time. He said that 'when Lavrenti Pavlovich learnt that he had to arrest Kekelia he almost fell dead on the spot.' Kekelia was interrogated in Moscow: the investigation of high-ranking officials always took place in the capital.

49. Beria's enemies accused him of having himself organised these attempts on his life, so as to improve his standing with Stalin. In 1925 Beria's car was ambushed near Tbilisi. One of the Chekists with him was killed. However, it is unlikely that the attempts witnessed by Sergo Beria were organised by his father. Nekrasov, V.F. *Beria: Konets karery* (Moscow, 1991) 13.

50. In 1929 Lakoba was accused of failing to take account of 'the leading role of the Party,' but Stalin opposed his dismissal. Later, he was blamed for dragging his feet during the collectivisation campaign and for setting the Party aside in Abkhazia, transferring all power to the governmental structures – which was what Beria was always wanting to do.

51. Lakoba enjoyed great prestige among the Caucasian Communists He promoted Beria's career. During the trial of the latter, Goglidze said: 'Lakoba and Beria met very often. One had the impression that they were inseparable friends.' *Voenno-istoricheskii Zhurnal* 3 (1990) 86.

52. This differs markedly from the version of the event given by T. Wittlin, who describes young Rosengolz as a pure virgin abused by Beria and his henchmen. Wittlin, op. cit. 149. The death of the Rosengolz girl does not appear in the indictment of Beria. Here is what Goglidze declares on this matter: 'Beria ordered me to carry out a meticulous inquiry into the death of the Rosengolz girl, so as to establish whether Lakoba was responsible for it. We suspected that Lakoba had raped the girl and she had killed herself afterwards, but no proof of this version turned up. The investigation showed that Rosengolz had come to Lakoba's place on the day of her suicide, had dined with him and his friends, had drunk a little wine and had then retired to a bedroom where she killed herself with Lakoba's gun. We discovered nothing more than that.' *Voenno-isoricheskii Zhurnal* 10 (1991) 47-8.

53. Sergo Beria stresses this point because, at his posthumous trial, Lakoba was accused of having wanted to murder Beria.

54. The rumour ran in Georgia that Beria had poisoned Lakoba. The latter's descendants are still convinced of this.

55. There was some truth in this. My father had, in fact, introduced the alphabet in Abkhazia and in Ossetia Russification was going strong – two regions which until then had no written literature. Georgian writers had published books in Abkhaz, manuals had been produced and teaching in the schools was conducted in Abkhaz. Lakoba had supported my father in his efforts at alphabetisation, and, indeed, their only disagreement concerned the alphabet. My father favoured the Georgian alphabet whereas Lakoba would have preferred the Latin one. (Author's note.)

56. On 7 November 1937 Beria published an article in *Pravda* entitled 'The united family of the peoples'. In this he denounced the national policy of the Tsars: 'To maintain its domination Tsarism resorted to the proven tactic of setting some peoples against others.'

57. The trial of the 'Abkhaz nationalists' took place in October 1937. Lakoba was accused, posthumously, of having sought to murder Stalin and Beria, and his family was ruthlessly exterminated.

58. This affair took place in August 1933 in Abkhazia. Mikeladze was the head of the GRU in Abkhazia. Beria's enemies alleged that he had organised the attempts so as to discredit Lakoba in Stalin's eyes. This incident was dug up during the trial of the Abkhaz nationalists. Evidence was extorted that was designed to show that this was indeed an attempt to kill Stalin and that Lakoba had covered up for Mikeladze.

59. The opening of the archives has made it possible to perceive the mechanism of the 'great terror'. It was launched on 7 July 1937 by a directive from the Politburo to the local authorities, calling on them to draw up lists of 'enemies of the people' who were still at liberty in their districts and to set up, within five days, *troikas* to try them expeditiously. The local authorities got busy and on the basis of the information they supplied the NKVD fixed the quotas for death sentences and prison terms between eight and ten years, these being made obligatory for each local leader. The operation was to begin in August and to last four months. Naturally, the local leaders asked for their quotas to be increased in order to demonstrate their zeal. Khlevnyuk, O. *Le Cercle du Kremlin* (Seuil, 1991) 206. The document laying down quotas was published in Albats, E. *La bombe à retardement* (Paris, 1995) 369-76.

60. At the 10th congress of the Georgian Party, Beria declared: 'We must act intelligently, so that one extreme does not lead to another. If we treat without distinction, in the same way, all former nationalist deviationists and former Trotskyists, some of whom ... have honestly distanced themselves from Trotskyism long since, we risk compromising the struggle against the real Trotskyists, enemies and spies.' Next day *Pravda* subjected the Georgians' 10th Party congress to severe criticism. Beria was called to Moscow and met Stalin. On his return he launched the purge. Knight, op. cit., 76-7. Here is the testimony of Goglidze, People's Commissar of Internal Affairs in Georgia in 1938, given at Beria's trial: 'In the spring of 1937 we were beginning to beat the accused systematically. One day Beria came back from Moscow and asked me to summon all the district leaders of the NKVD. He assembled us and declared that the security organs in Georgia were not fighting the enemies hard enough ...' *Voenno-istoricheskii Zhurnal*. 7 (1989) 86-7.

61. On this point Sergo Beria departs from the truth. The local authorities were active in carrying out the purges and often took the initiative in them.

62. It was not long before Golublishvili was in prison, accused of 'factional activity'.

63. Intellectuals were not the only victims of the Communist regime in Georgia. Between 1921 and 1941 60,000 persons were executed and 200,000 deported, out of a population that barely exceeded four million.

64. According to A. Mirtskhulava, 'One day Beria got a certain number of us together (one couldn't speak freely before everyone) and said: "Things are going badly." He was unhappy about all these arrests, but could do nothing.'

65. Most of the leaders of the republics were themselves victims of the purges, with Beria as a rare exception. He owed his escape to the loyalty of Goglidze, the NKVD chief in Georgia. When, in July 1938, Yezhov sent Goglidze the order to arrest Beria, he warned his boss. Beria hastened to Moscow and persuaded Stalin to annul Yezhov's order. (Nekrasov, op. cit. 60-61.) Only a few Georgian leaders were in the know about this affair, as was confirmed by Mirtskhulava's testimony. According to some sources, Yezhov had supplied Stalin with a dossier on Beria's links with Musavatist spies and the British secret services. Magnanimously, Stalin declared that he was not going to withdraw his confidence from Comrade Beria, whom, as we shall see, he appointed deputy to Yezhov.

66. Goglidze stated that Yezhov had decided on a norm of 1,500 sentences of death for Georgia (actually 2,000, according to the instructions of 30 July). The number of persons judged by the NKVD *troika* was 30,000, of whom 10,000 were sentenced to death. Beria had substantially surpassed the objectives of the plan. Nekrasov, op. cit. 34. *Voenno-istoricheskii Zhurnal* 7 (1989) 86-7.

67. This may have been due also to a reaction against the constitution of 1936, which considerably reduced the rights of the republics of the USSR. Faced with the threat from Germany, Stalin played up Russian nationalism. Thenceforth the Russian people became the 'big brother' of the peoples of the USSR and Russification was intensified.

68. A Central Committee resolution dated 13 March 1938 made the study of Russian compulsory in all the schools in the republics and national regions of the USSR.

69. A people who originated from Colchis, related to the Mingrelians. They were conquered by the Turks in the 17th century and converted to Islam. At the time of the Peace Conference of 1919 the Laz region was coveted by Greece,

Armenia and Georgia. Kemal pursued a policy of assimilation of the Lazes. In 1945 a census gave the number of Laz-speakers in Turkey as 46,987. Tumarkine, A. *Les Lazes en Turquie* ((Istanbul, 1995).

70. Allusion to Pushkin, whose grandfather was Ethiopian.

71. An allusion to Lermontov, who had Scottish ancestors.

72. In Spain Stalin was above all concerned to hunt down the Trotskyists. The Soviets installed a substantial network of the NKVD and, wherever they could, caused Communist terror to prevail.

Chapter 2: The NKVD

1. Beria said to Khrushchev when the latter congratulated him on his promotion: 'I don't accept your congratulations ... It would be better for me to remain in Georgia.' And Khrushchev comments: 'I think Beria was probably sincere when he said this.' Khrushchev, N.S. *Khrushchev Remembers* (1971) 96. Regional leaders often had no desire to 'go up' to Moscow. When, in February 1934, Stalin wanted to bring Kirov to the capital, he encountered a stubborn refusal to leave Leningrad.

2. According to A. Mirtskhulava, Stalin said, at a preparatory session of the January 1938 Plenum, denouncing 'mistakes' and 'excesses' in the purges: 'It was in Georgia that arrests were fewest in 1937. Do you know why? Because the secretary of the Central Committee in Georgia, and the head of the NKVD there, Goglidze, are honest functionaries and not wreckers.'

3. This calculation of Stalin's proved correct, if we are to judge by the testimony of Shreider, already quoted: 'I was very pleased when I learnt that Beria had been appointed head of the NKVD. I thought that if Stalin had chosen a compatriot for that post one might hope that he would correct the situation which Yezhov had created.' Shreider, op. cit. 154.

4. It seems that the Bukharin trial in March 1938 produced a reaction in the country. V. Vernadsky wrote in his diary for 19 March. 'The trial was a big mistake. People are starting to think, and believe less than they used to.' On 24 March he wrote: 'Discontent is growing and finds expression in spite of fear. I observe a big change in people's psychology.' Quoted in *Sovershenno sekretno* 8 (1990).

5. 'Whereas nearly all the top leaders of the USSR lived in the Kremlin, Beria enjoyed a certain degree of freedom and was relatively outside Stalin's control,' notes Stalin's translator Berezhkov. *Kak ya stal perevodchikom Stalina* (Moscow, 1993) 350.

6. First Secretary of Kiev Region. Accused of having belonged to a 'military-fascist centre,' he was executed in February 1939.

7. In his memoirs Khrushchev confirms that he thought highly of Yezhov: 'He was diligent and reliable. I knew he'd been ... a Party member since 1918, which was a mark in his favour.' Khrushchev, op. cit. 94. The historian Roy Medvedev evaluates Malenkov's role in the great terror in the same way as Sergo Beria does. 'Malenkov operated in the wings, but he was decidedly one of those who, under Stalin's direction, activated the most important secret mechanisms of the terror.' Medvedev, R. *All Stalin's Men* (Blackwell, 1983) 143.

8. This was also Khrushchev's opinion. Malenkov, he wrote, 'had been in charge of personnel for the Central Committee during the purges and had played a pretty active role in the whole business. He had actually helped promote people from the ranks only to have them eliminated later on.' Khrushchev, op, cit. 345. As for Zhdanov, he had 90 per cent of the Party cadres in Leningrad arrested and launched mass terror in the city. Courtois, S, ed., *Le Livre noir du communisme* (Paris, 1997) 215.

9. Yezhov had, in fact, asked Stalin to give him Malenkov as deputy.

10. Yezhov's career really took off when Stalin entrusted him with the task of 'proving' that Zinoviev, Kamenev and their supporters had organised the assassination of Kirov. Yagoda's NKVD had shown a certain lack of zeal in carrying out Stalin's instructions. Yezhov did this job to Stalin's complete satisfaction, so that he was convinced that Yezhov would be the ideal man to set up the great trials. Khlevnyuk, op. cit. 217-8.

11. The department of the Central Committee responsible for the appointment and supervision of cadres (and consequently for purges).

12. Andreev had already chaired a commission created in 1931 to devise an effective way of managing the labour of deportees. Courtois, op. cit. 175.

13. At the June 1957 Plenum Zhukov gave the number of persons sentenced to death by Stalin, Molotov and Kaganovich (the list bore these three signatures) between 27 February 1937 and 12 November 1938: 38,679. The persons concerned were handed over to the tribunals of the Military Collegium, which was equivalent to a death sentence. On 12 November 1938 Stalin and Molotov sent 3,167 persons to their death. *Istoricheskii Arkhiv* 3 (1993) 17. Molotov never, to his last day, expressed the slightest remorse.

14. According to Sudoplatov Beria himself contributed something. At his instigation two officers of the NKVD wrote to Stalin that Yezhov planned to arrest the members of the Soviet government on the eve of the 7 November holiday. Sudoplatov, P. & A. *Special Tasks* (London, 1994) 59. No doubt Beria was in this way returning a favour to Yezhov, so to speak.

15. Ordzhonikidze's widow said of Yezhov: 'He was a puppet. He could be manipulated at will.' Khlevnyuk, op. cit. 220.

16. He was executed on 4 February 1940. The indictment filled eleven volumes. *Sovershenno Sekretno* 4 (1992).

17. Yezhov's trial was held in March-April 1939. At the June 1957 Plenum Zhukov said that Beria had used the opportunity to get him to testify against Malenkov. Yezhov wrote twenty pages in his own hand against Malenkov. *Istoricheskii Arkhiv* 3 (1993) 22. This explains the curious solidity of the Beria-Malenkov tandem: Beria blackmailed Malenkov. When Yezhov's safe was searched it was revealed that he had compiled dossiers on numerous members of the Central Committee, including Stalin. It can be assumed that the significance of these archives was not lost on Beria. (Malenkov, A.G. *O moiom otse Georgii Malenkove* (Moscow, 1992) 34.

18. It does seem that, from the start, Beria chose to behave towards Stalin differently from Yezhov. The latter 'ran to see Stalin on any pretext whatever, thinking he would like that. Beria came to see Stalin only when summoned.' Golovanov, Ya. *Korolev. Fakty i mify* (Moscow, 1994) 281.

19. At the 20th Congress Khrushchev accused Stalin of organising Kirov's assassination. Recent research tends to suggest that it was an individual act committed by an unbalanced person who wanted to emulate the terrorists of the Tsarist period. Kirilina, A. *L'Assassinat de Kirov* (Paris, 1995). Stalin seized the pretext of Kirov's assassination to attack the Bolshevik Old Guard.

20. This was, moreover, how he began to lose favour.

21. See de Lastours, S. *Toukhatchevski* (Paris, 1996).

22. The allusion is to the revolt of the peasants in Tambov region in 1921. Tukhachevsky ordered, on 12 June 1921: 'With poison gases clear out the forests in which the bandits are hiding, taking care that the suffocating cloud covers the entire forest, exterminating everything within it.' *Obshchaya Gazeta* 22 (1994).

23. In 1928 Tukhachevsky sent Stalin a memorandum in which he advised modernising the Soviet forces, with emphasis on aircraft, armoured units and artillery. He encountered stubborn resistance from Stalin's two favourites, Voroshilov and Budenny. The latter came out with a formula that was soon legendary: 'Wait, the horse has not yet spoken his last word!' After the Finnish fiasco Stalin adopted, without acknowledgement, the views expressed by Tukhachevsky, who had been executed in June 1937. 'Modern war will be a war of engines,' he said on 17 April 1950, to the State Defence Council. Golovanov, op. cit. 225-6.

24. This military collaboration with the USSR enabled Germany to get round the disarmament clauses of the Treaty of Versailles.

25. Frinovsky was Yezhov's right-hand man. Stalin entrusted him with the purges in the Navy. At the 18th Party Congress, on 10 March 1939, Frinovsky, scenting that his patron was about to fall, sent Stalin a letter denouncing the 'abuses' committed by Yezhov. However, this tactic proved useless. Frinovsky was arrested on 6 April 1939, four days after Yezhov. Soskov, E. 'Ne v svoikh sanyakh', *Rodina* 5 (1997) 91-4.

26. Khrushchev makes the same observation, comparing the Defence Commissariat after the purges to 'a kennel of mad dogs.' 'Once Comrade Timoshenko pulled me by the sleeve into a session of the Defence Council. He wanted me to see how these people whom he had to work with were tearing at each other's throats.' Khrushchev, op. cit. 163-4.

27. He agreed to be a member of the tribunal which sentenced Tukhachevsky to death.

28. Blucher fell victim to the intrigues of the head of the Army's Political Department, Mekhlis, and of Frinovsky. They had gone to the Soviet Far East in the summer of 1938 in order to 'eradicate nests of counter-revolutionaries' and Blucher had complained of their conduct. Mekhlis and Frinovsky did not forget. After the defeat of the Japanese at Lake Khasan they had him arrested, 22 October 1938. *Voenno-istoricheskii Zhurnal* 4 (1994) 77.

29. According to a witness the Chekists plucked out one of his eyes.

30. Of the 63 members of the Komsomol's Central Committee 48 were arrested. See Shelepin's speech at the June 1957 Plenum in *Istoricheskii Arkhiv* 6 (1993) 57.

31. The rumour ran that Kosarev had proposed, in Bagirov's presence, a toast 'to true Bolshevik leadership of Transcaucasia, which we don't have now.' Knight, op.cit. 99.

32. Some documents relating to the reorganisation of the NKVD undertaken from January 1939 have been published in Yakovlev, A.N. Kokurin, A.I. Petrov, N.V. and Pikhoya, R.G. (eds.), *Lubyanka* (Moscow, 1997) 291-258. On 2 February 1939 the Principal Directorate of NKVD Troops (frontier guards and Interior forces) was abolished. It was replaced by six independent principal directorates: frontier guards, camp guards, escorts, railway, military supplies, military building work.

33. Beria set out his programme for reorganising the Gulag in a note to the Politburo on 10 April 1930. He called for 'sound economic management' instead of the 'hunt for enemies' practised by his predecessor, Yezhov. He advocated an increase in food rations, no more releases ahead of time, punishment for 'disorganisers of production' and the lengthening of the working day to eleven hours. Courtois, op. cit. 229.

34. This was one of the first measures taken by Beria. The special Technical Bureau was set up on 10 January 1939. Yakovlev, A.S. *Tsel zhizni* ((Moscow, 1987) 219-20.

35. In Khrushchev op. cit. 96, we read that Beria often said to him when he came to Moscow: 'What's going on here? We're arresting and imprisoning people right and left, even secretaries of regional committees. This whole business has gone much too far. We've got to stop before it's too late.' Before the Politburo Beria said, astonishingly: 'If we keep on arresting people at this rate there will soon be nobody left to arrest.' A. Maksimovich, in Nekrasov, op.cit. 141.

36. This was the case with the sinister Frinovsky, Zakovsky and Berman. Nearly all the NKVD chiefs in the Union and autonomous republics and the regional sections of the NKVD were arrested and sentenced: 2,079 NKVD officers were found guilty of 'violation of socialist legality' in 1939-40. Chebrikov, V.M. *Istoriya sovetskikh organov gosudarstvennoy bezopasnosti* (1977) 290.

37. On 8 October 1938 a commission was set up to formulate the NKVD's new policy regarding repressive measures. Yezhov presided and Beria, Vyshinsky and Malenkov were members. This was how the 17 November resolution originated.

38. On 17 November 1938 the Sovnarkom and the Central Committee adopted a secret resolution 'regarding arrests, supervision by the Public Prosecutor's office and the conduct of investigations.' This put an end to the mass purges, by abolishing the NKVD *troikas*. Henceforth arrests had to be authorised by the Public Prosecutor's office. Chebrikov, op. cit. 289.

39. Yezhov was accused of having sought to subject the Party's organs to the NKVD, just as Beria was in 1953. During the period of the great purges 'the Party started to lose its authority and to be subservient to the NKVD.' Khrushchev, op. cit. 81. A piquant detail: in February 1937 Yezhov had presented his appointment to head the NKVD in these terms. 'This was the first time that the Central Committee had tried to establish its control over the Cheka's organs.' Khlevnyuk, op. cit. 218.

40. It is clear that Beria at once began to turn the NKVD into a personal fief. He used his influence over Malenkov to get his candidates for office accepted. 'The lists of candidates presented to the Central Committee were not checked as they should have been by the C.C.'s apparatus ... Taking advantage of this situation Beria was able to introduce into the NKVD a large group of persons whom he needed.' Zhukov at the June 1957 Plenum *Istoricheskii Arkhiv* 3 (1993) 22.

41. Indeed, on 14 January 1938 a Plenum called for 'correction of mistakes and excesses during the purges,' following a report by Malenkov. Malenkov, op. cit. 33. But at the end of January the quota for arrests was again increased by 90,000. Khlevnyuk, op. cit. 210.

42. In 1936-37 1,372,392 persons were arrested and 681,692 executed. In 1939 there were 33,924 arrests and in 1940, 87,109. The number of executions in 1939-40 was 4,464. *Istochnik* 1 (1995) 120. These figures do not give a complete picture of the Stalinist terror – for example, they do not take into account those who died under torture or who perished while being transported.

43. According to the data provided by the Russian archivist R. Pikhoia, in 1938 there were 700,000 political prisoners. In 1939 they numbered 40,000. *XX syezd*, 9th broadcast, Radio Svoboda, 1996.

44. A quarter of the military prisoners were released.

45. It forbade the NKVD to recruit agents from among leading personnel of the Party, the State or the economy, or from members of the Central Committee's apparatus and the apparatuses of the party in the republics and the regional Party committees. The NKVD was to destroy the dossiers it held on persons in these categories whom it had recruited. GARF, f. 9401, op. 2, d. 1, 10-11.

46. Nevertheless, Beria's arrival at the NKVD was marked by a certain softening of the prison regime. Prisoners were given the right to have games and books and they were accorded proper medical care. But torture continued and was intensified. Accused persons were now beaten on the soles of their feet. Antonov-Ovseyenko, A.in Nekrasov, op. cit., 71, and Shreider, op. cit. 180 sqq.

47. On 22 December 1938 the investigation departments of the operational directorate were abolished. A unified investigation department was created for the

NKVD, 'so as to put an end to violations of socialist loyalty.' The number of dossiers handed over to the Special Collegium was reduced. Complaints by prisoners who had been sentenced by the *troikas* were to be examined within 20 days of reception. However, the Special Collegium was maintained in being, together with the emergency laws of 1 December 1934. *Kvashonkin*, op. cit. 289-90.

48. Thus, on 22 December 1938 deported kulaks were given permission, in return for good conduct, to return to their home region. At the beginning of 1941 these deported kulaks numbered 930,220. In 1933 they had numbered 1,317,000. Bugay, op. cit. 19.

49. To return to Khrushchev's testimony: 'At the beginning of 1939, in February, a Central Committee plenum was convened to discuss a resolution condemning excesses and abuses in the NKVD. The slackening of the terror ... was attributed largely to Beria's influence. People concluded that Beria had made an investigation into NKVD practices after he took over as commissar and then convinced Stalin to approve a series of recommendations. However, there were a number of incidents ... indicating that the terror was by no means over – it had just become more subtle and discriminating.' Khrushchev, op. cit. 98-9.

50. Arriving late for work was punished by a year in the Gulag. In three months a million workers were punished.

51. Beria said, notably, that 'it would be an error to explain the breakdowns that occurred in various segments of our national economy solely by the subversive activity of our enemies. These breakdowns were due, to a certain degree, to the unsatisfactory, unskilled work of a number of our Soviet economic leaders who have not yet mastered adequately the fundamentals of Bolshevik management. Knight, op. cit. 94. According to Khrushchev, Malenkov accused Beria of being 'complacent,' the term used in the Party's special jargon to denounce those who thought that the enemy had already been eradicated and therefore let their revolutionary guard drop.

52. Zhdanov became a full member of the Politburo in March 1939. Malenkov and Voznesensky became secretaries of the Central Committee.

Chapter 3: Hitler

1. Sergo Beria: 'My father has been blamed for trying to give Soviet diplomacy a pro-German orientation. At this time my father was a young People's Commissar who had just arrived in Moscow. What influence could he exert alongside someone like Molotov? He had nothing to do, for example, with the disgracing of Litvinov.' The replacement of the Jew Litvinov by Molotov in May 1939 was a very plain hint to Germany. Molotov declared that the purge of the NKVD aimed at 'putting an end to the synagogue' in that commissariat. Investigation of Litvinov's case was closed in October 1939. According to A. Vaksberg, Stalin prepared a grand trial of the Jewish diplomats in the NKVD which he was, however, unable to bring off for foreign-policy reasons – he did not want to burn his bridges with the Anglo-Saxons. Vaksberg, A. *Stalin against the Jews* (NY, 1994) 34-5.

2. Krassin negotiated a trade agreement with Britain in March 1921. He was the USSR's ambassador to France in 1924-25 and to Britain in 1925-26.

3. V. Potemkin had an academic career before 1914. He was ambassador to Greece and to Italy, then, from 1934, to France.

4. In 1931 Tarlé had been accused, along with other historians, of intending to organise foreign intervention and overthrow of the Bolshevik regime, and for this had been exiled to Kazakhstan. However, Stalin spared and protected him, even in 1949, when he was accused of having presented Kutuzov in an 'anti-patriotic' light in a book about Napoleon published in 1938.

5. Kollontai, an ardent Bolshevik, had fought vigorously for women's emancipation and free love.

6. As public prosecutor Vyshinsky distinguished himself during the great trials. To him is due the famous formulation: 'We must keep in mind Comrade Stalin's directive according to which there are periods in a society's existence, and in that of our society particularly, when laws are obsolete and have to be set aside.' Golovanov, op. cit. 245.

7. Vyshinsky seems to have realised this, if we are to believe the testimony of Stalin's translator V. Berezhkov: 'Vyshinsky had a panic fear of Beria and Dekanozov ...' Berezhkov, op. cit. 225.

8. Maisky was a former Menshevik. Churchill wrote in his memoirs that he had friendly relations with Maisky and that his son Randolph met him often. In 1948 the MGB accused Maisky of 'favouring the imperialist interests of Britain.' He was arrested in February 1953. A witness against him said that 'Maisky was close to Churchill, whose own links with the Intelligence Service were well known.' Kostyrchenko, G. *V plenu krasnogo faraona* (Moscow, 1994) 236. He was released after Stalin's death but fell into disgrace again after Beria's arrest.

9. An agent of the GPU and ambassador to the USA and then to Mexico. He was to die in a suspicious air crash in January 1945.

10. Here is Molotov's version: 'Stalin said to me "Purge the ministry of the Jews." Thank God for those words! Jews formed an absolute majority in the leadership and among the ambassadors. It wasn't good.' Chuev, op. cit. 192. The purge was entrusted to a special commission made up of Molotov, Malenkov, Beria and Dekanozov. Berezhkov, op. cit. 169. One of the victims, the head of the NKID press department, E. Gnedin, has given a striking account of what happened. Gnedin, E. *Vykhod iz labirinta* (Moscow, 1995).

11. From the middle of 1939 onwards the NKVD tried to reconstitute its network of agents abroad which had been destroyed by the purges of 1937. Forty residencies were set up in 1939-40, involving 242 officers of the NKVD. *Istoria*, op. cit. 307.

12. V. Potemkin denounced Gnedin, for instance, as a 'German agent,' and used the opportunity to blame the lack of vigilance shown by Litvinov, who had failed to expose this spy in time. Nekrasov, op. cit. 79.

13. The American ambassador Bedell-Smith, who met Dekanozov after the war, described him thus: 'This little man, blond and pale, seemed to me to have a negative personality.' After the war Dekanozov 'concerned himself mainly with the affairs of the British Empire.' Bedell-Smith, W. *Trois années a Moscou*, (Paris, 1950) 32. One day when somebody mentioned Marx's work *The Holy Family* before Dekanozov, he asked: 'What have those saints to do with Marx?' Nekrasov op. cit. 19. Gnedin describes him thus: 'He was like a shopkeeper trying to be seen as a big businessman or a policeman trying to seem a colonel of gendarmes.' Gnedin, op. cit. 14.

14. France's Minister of Foreign Affairs from April 1938 to September 1939, Bonnet was a strong supporter of the 'appeasement' of Germany. In December 1938 he assured Ribbentrop that 'France showed at the Munich conference her lack of interest in the East.' Schmidt, P. *Sur la scène internationale*, (Paris, 1950) 183.

15. Poland, under Pilsudski, had signed a treaty of non-aggression with the USSR in 1932.

16. A writer and journalist who was awarded the Stalin Prize in 1943, this fanatically Stalinist Polish woman adopted Soviet nationality and became a deputy to the Supreme Soviet in 1940, later acquiring the rank of colonel in the Red Army. She was one of the leading members of the organising committee of the League of Polish Patriots formed in February 1943, the group of Polish Communists whom

Stalin aimed to substitute for the Polish government in London. In July 1944 this committee was transformed into the Polish Committee for the National Liberation.

17. Some diplomats noticed this. See the account of the Potsdam conference by the British Ambassador Sir William Hayter. 'Maisky ... came into the conference room one day and was warmly, too warmly, greeted by Churchill and Eden: Stalin turned a cold, basilisk glare on him and he was never seen again by Western eyes until many years later, after Stalin's death.' Hayter, W. *The Kremlin and the Embassy*, (London, 1966) 29.

18. Schulenburg was at that time Germany's consul in Tbilisi. The Georgian Legion was soon broken up owing to opposition from the Turks. Schulenburg was actively in favour of proclaiming Georgia's independence.

19. Here, and in what follows, Sergo Beria faithfully reproduces the opinion that prevailed in Soviet ruling circles. Actually, Great Britain had undertaken, in March 1939, to defend Poland in the event of German aggression, thus ending the policy of 'appeasement.'

20. On the contrary, from the beginning of 1939 Bonnet called upon the French ambassador in Warsaw to press the Poles to authorise passage of Soviet troops across Poland, and the British ambassador associated himself with this move. On 23 August, General Doumenc told Voroshilov that France was ready to back the Soviet demand for passage through Poland. Karski, J. *The Great Powers and Poland* (UP of America, 1995) 356-7.

21. The military negotiations between the USSR, France and Great Britain, which began on 12 August, were suspended on 17 August.

22. 'Ribbentrop and his companions returned to the embassy in a state of great enthusiasm ... The German minister took to talking deliriously about Stalin and "men with strong faces",' wrote Hitler's interpreter, Paul Schmidt. Schmidt, op. cit. 205.

23. On 29 June 1939 Zhdanov published in *Pravda* an article which stated that 'the French and British governments do not want a treaty with the USSR on a basis of equality.' He was one of the supporters of the pact with Germany and had the wind in his sails after its signature. Raanan, G. *International Policy Formation in the USSR* (NY, 1983) 14.

24. Zhdanov insisted that the slogans for 1 May 1940 should denounce by name the British and French and 'their Social-Democratic lackeys' as 'warmongers.' Even so late as April 1941, when frictions with Germany were multiplying, he declared: 'The events in the Balkans do not change our policy in relation to the imperialist war and the two opposed groups of capitalist states. We do not favour Germany's expansion in the Balkans, but this does not mean that we turn away from the pact with Germany and towards Britain.' Quoted in *Komintern i vtorya mirovaya voina* (Moscow, 1994) 45-46, 340.

25. In October 1939 the USSR proposed to Finland a pact of mutual assistance. Finland rejected this. The USSR then asked for bases on Finnish territory and was again rebuffed. On 1 December a 'Democratic Republic of Finland,' led by the Chekist and Comintern official O.V. Kuusinen, was proclaimed and the USSR began military operations against Finland.

26. We can imagine how much these views of Beria's may have angered the orthodox Communists when we read, for example, in a directive by the Comintern to the Swedish Communist Party, dated 16 January 1940: 'The big capitalists of Sweden, who are closely linked with the British imperialists, are interested in keeping Finland as an advanced base against the Soviet Union.' Quoted in *Komintern* ... op. cit. 241.

27. He was backed by Zhdanov, a keen supporter of the invasion of Finland. In December 1936 Zhdanov had threatened to invade Finland and the Baltic states. Raanan, op. cit. 13-14.

28. In October Mikoyan said to a Finnish diplomat: 'We Caucasians in the Politburo are having a great deal of difficulty in restraining the Russians.' Bohlen, C. *Witness to History* (NY, 1973) 93.

29. Khrushchev wrote that Stalin 'was sure all we had to do was fire a few artillery rounds and the Finns would capitulate.' Khrushchev, *The Glasnost Tapes* (Moscow, 1990) 54.

30. The Soviets did not declare war and tried to present the matter as a local incident, a response to a request for help received from the 'Kuusinen government' created on 1 December. On 4 December Molotov declared: 'The Soviet Union is not at war with Finland.'

31. He had been military attaché during the Spanish war and was close to my father, who had brought into the central intelligence apparatus a large number of officers from naval intelligence, the most effective branch of the USSR's intelligence service. (Author's note.)

32. In his diary Admiral Kuznetsov frequently mentions the Finnish war. 'I was stupefied by the methods of preparation and planning for the offensive in Finland. The results confirmed my feeling.' *Voenno-istoricheskii Zhurnal* 3 (1993).

33. In December 1939 the French considered sending troops to Finland but were dissuaded by the British. Starting in January 1940 the British began drawing up plans for a landing at Narvik. On 16 January Admiral Darlan proposed a landing by Polish, French and British troops at Petsamo and suggested the creation in Karelia of 'a base at which all the anti-Stalin nationalist elements could gather.' On 5 February 1940 the Supreme Military Council of the Allies approved a landing in Scandinavia. Stalin feared more than anything else that all Scandinavia might enter the war on the Allied side on the pretext of lending a hand to the Finns. However, the Norwegian and Swedish governments declined to give up their neutrality. Nevertheless, on 11 March 1940 the French and British decided to ignore this. Korobochkin, M. 'Opozdavshie', *Rodina*, 12 (1995) 107-110.

34. Between October 1939 and May 1940 the French and British General Staffs contemplated bombing the oil wells of Baku, because the USSR was supplying Germany with fuel. The British and French dreamt of involving Turkey in operations in Transcaucasia. They also counted on an anti-Soviet revolt by the Caucasian peoples. Sipols, V. Ya. 'Tainie dokumenty strannoy voiny', *Novaya i noveishaya istoria* 3 (1993).

35. Peace was signed on 12 March. It had been negotiated not by diplomats but by agents of the NKVD, which confirms the role played by Beria in this matter. Under German pressure, the Soviets made only quite modest demands. The frontier near Leningrad was pushed back by 150 km. However, Stalin's intentions for the future were clearly shown in the decision on 30 March 1940 to transform the autonomous republic of Karelia into the Karelo-Finnish union republic, Semiryaga, M. *The Winter War* (Moscow, 1990).

36. Beria did not forget his grievances against the Finnish Communist Party, which was under Zhdanov's patronage. He patiently put together a dossier on Kuusinen. He protected a 'dissident' in the Finnish Communist Party, one Bergman, who in July 1940 accused his party's Central Committee of all imaginable faults: bourgeois nationalism, social-democratism, anti-Sovietism. It did not work: the Zhdanovites and the Comintern counterattacked and expelled Bergman from the Communist Party as a 'provocateur.' *Komintern*, op. cit. 424.

37. On Katyn see N. Lebedeva, *Katyn*, Moscow, 1994, and the collection of documents (*Katyn*) published in Moscow in 1997 by the International Foundation 'Democracy', in the collection Yakovlev A.N. (ed.) '*Rossiya XX vek*'.

38. Gorbachev denied that this document existed, although he had seen it in April 1989. He had ordered his secretary, V. Boldin, to bring him the papers dealing with Katyn on the eve of a meeting with General Jaruzelski. He gave back the documents saying: 'Put them in a safe place and don't show them to anyone without my permission. They are dynamite.' Boldin, V. *Krushenie pedestala* (Moscow, 1995) 257-8, and the documents published in *Voprosy Istorii* 1, (1993). Not until 1990 did the Soviet authorities admit the USSR's responsibility for the massacre of the Polish officers.

39. On 17 September 1939, in conformity with their agreement with Hitler, the Soviets attacked Poland, which had already been crushed by the Wehrmacht. The German-Soviet agreement of 28 September 1939 provided for collaboration between the NKVD and the Gestapo in the struggle against Polish nationalists. A joint instructional centre for officers of the NKVD and the Gestapo was opened at Zakopane in December 1939. In February, April and July 1940 the Soviets deported 496,000 Poles from the eastern parts of Poland which went to the USSR under the terms of the secret protocol signed on 23 August. These deportations continued until June 1941. Altogether, 1,700,000 persons were removed from the territory annexed by the USSR: more than half of them died in the process. Some of the prisoners-of-war were released. In the autumn of 1939 there were still 124,000 of them, and these were handed over to the NKVD. Raack, R.C. *Stalin's Drive to the West 1938-1945* ((Stanford,1995) 65: Lebedeva, op. cit: Brandes, *Grossbritannien und seine osteuropäischen Alliierten*, 1988.

40. Recently declassified archives and testimony by survivors show that Beria took a keen interest in the Polish officers from the outset. He sent a trusted officer of his, V. Zarubin, into the camps in order to discover each one's political opinions, with a view to possible recruitment by the NKVD.

41. On 15 September 1939 Moscow forbade Czech Communists to join the anti-fascist national legions fighting with the Anglo-French coalition. In February 1940 the Comintern repeated its refusal to encourage the formation of a Czech army abroad, stressing that the slogan 'Restoration of Czechoslovakia' was now anti-Soviet. *Komintern*, op. cit. 95-278.

42. The reference is to the Soviet-Polish war of 1920, which ended in a fiasco for the Red Army.

43. The Katyn decision was taken after a conference of high officials of the Gestapo and the NKVD held in Cracow at the end of February 1940. While the Soviets were exterminating the Polish officers the Germans carried out, from 31 March, a parallel 'Operation AB' aimed at destroying Poland's elites. This claimed 2,000 victims. Lebedeva, *Katyn*, 137. Khrushchev refers to this co-operation. 'Serov's duties required him to have contacts with the Gestapo. A German representative used to come to Lvov on official business. I don't know what sort of a network the Germans had in the Ukraine, but it was extensive. The cover for this network was an exchange agreement ...' Khrushchev, *Khrushchev Remembers* 141.

44. There is no trace in the available archives of the debate described here by Sergo Beria. On the contrary, the accessible documents are crushing for Beria, since the order to shoot the Polish officers appears to have emanated from a proposal signed by him and then initialled by the Politburo members (the document of 5 March mentioned *supra*.) For those familiar with Soviet bureaucratic practices, this nevertheless does not show that Beria originated this decision. An initiative by Stalin is often presented in the archives as an approval given to the administration charged with implementing this initiative. The editors of the *Katyn* collection mentioned above put forward this hypothesis: 'It is not out of the question that Beria's letter to Stalin dated 5 March 1940 was preceded by a conversation between the minister and Stalin during which the latter revealed a decision somewhat different from what had been provided for until then, namely, execution of all the prisoners without distinction, on the basis of a decision by a *troika* and not by a Special Collegium. This hypothesis seems confirmed by the fact that Beria's proposals were approved on the same day, practically unaltered.' Yakovlev, ed., op. cit. 35.

45. This document exists but Beria's name seems to have been struck out by Beria himself and replaced by Kobulov's. Another piece of information confirms indirectly, the existence of different views among the Soviet leaders regarding the fate of the Polish officers. In March 1940 the Polish Government in London, which had been in contact with the Soviets through the NKVD since late in autumn 1939, received news that Moscow intended to create a Polish Legion and recognise Sikorski's government. Parsadanova, V.S. 'Vladislav Sikorski', *Voprosy istorii* 9, (1994).

46. On Beria's order Professor S. Swaniewicz was taken off the train at the last moment. His evidence was to prove important later. Polish historians have wondered about the criteria used in choosing who was to live. That group did, of course, include both agents already recruited by the Soviets and men whom the Germans wanted. But it also included some who had engaged in anti-Soviet activity, notably members of the 'Prometheus' movement created by Marshal Pilsudski in order to support the nationalities of the USSR. Lebedeva, op. cit. 179. On 2 November 1940 Beria proposed to Stalin that a Polish army be formed in the USSR, emphasising the anti-German outlook of the Polish officers, but Stalin refused.

47. After July 1941 representatives of the Polish government in London made several approaches to the Soviet authorities to discover the fate of the vanished officers. Stalin replied imperturbably that they must have escaped into Romania or Manchuria. Beria and Merkulov, however, replied: 'It will not be possible to find them. We made a big mistake.' Parsadanova, V.S. 'K istorii Katynskogo dela', *Novaya i noveishaya istoria* 4 (1990) 30.

48. After the German-Soviet Pact Trotsky could have monopolised, to his advantage, the banner of anti-fascism.

49. In September-October 1939 the USSR concluded 'pacts of mutual assistance' with the three Baltic states. The USSR had the right to station 10,000 men in Lithuania. In return for this Lithuania was given Vilnius.

50. On 25 October 1939 Voroshilov categorically forbade the Soviet military in Estonia to interfere in the country's political life, to spread Communist propaganda, to establish contacts with 'the workers,' or to mention Sovietisation. Molotov had, on 21 October, given similar orders to the Soviet representative in Lithuania: 'I categorically forbid you to get mixed up in party-political affairs in Lithuania and support oppositional tendencies ... We must cease this harmful and provocative chatter about "Sovietisation" ...' Komplektov, V.G. *Polpredy soobshchayut* (Moscow, 1990).

51. In February 1940 the Communists in the Baltic states (who were few in number, only one thousand in Lithuania, for example) were ordered to play down their slogans of 'Sovietisation' and work to create Popular Fronts. *Komintern* op. cit. 314.

52. Zhdanov had advised his Estonian collaborators: 'Avoid the impression of external interference and create the appearance of a spontaneous movement of the people instead.' Raack, op. cit 49.

53. One of these Baltic notables was, perhaps, Professor Vincus Kreve-Mickevicius, the Rector of Kaunas University, who was Foreign Minister in the Lithuanian government installed by the Soviets in June 1940 – a typical pro-Soviet left-wing intellectual. Kreve went to Moscow on 2 July 1940 to ask the Soviets not to communise Lithuania. He was received by Molotov and Dekanozov. Molotov gravely explained to him that there could be no question of allowing a bourgeois

Lithuania to continue, as the Soviet Government planned to communise all Europe. Kreve lost all his illusions. Raack, op. cit. 183-4.

54. The rate of exchange of the rouble had been fixed at an arbitrarily low level. After the annexation of the Baltic states the Soviets indulged in frenzied plundering of them, a foretaste of the Red Army's depredations in Europe in 1945. Raack, op. cit. 50.

55. At the beginning of June 1941 the NKVD set about systematically arresting all the old-regime elites in the Baltic states – officers, landowners, industrialists, civil servants. During the night of 13-14 June 1941 their families were deported to Siberia: 25,000 persons were crammed into cattle-trucks and carried off eastward. A second round-up was planned by the NKVD for the night of 27-28 June. Courtois, op. cit. 236.

56. Stalin justified his conquests by 'defensive' considerations. In reality the USSR was implementing the first phase of its plan for European hegemony. On 31 August 1940 the Comintern set up a special school at which cadres of the 'brother parties' were to be given a crash course, Stalin was already preparing the satraps he intended to install in Europe as a result of the Red Army's victories. *Komintern*, op.cit. 424.

57. On several occasions Japan offered the USSR a pact of non-aggression. Moscow laid down as conditions for such a pact recognition by Japan that Outer Mongolia and Sinkiang should be included in the Soviet sphere of influence; retrocession of South Sakhalin and Kurile Islands; and abandonment by the Japanese of their concessions in North Sakhalin.

58. The defeat of France was a hard blow for the Soviet leadership. They had counted on a long, exhausting war in the West which would have enabled them to introduce the Red Army into the conflict at an opportune moment. Stalin's disquiet at this turn of events was reflected in a change of attitude by the Comintern. Down to June 1940 the priority task of Europe's Communists was to fight 'against Franco-British imperialism.' After that they received the order 'to avoid anything that might be interpreted as showing solidarity with the occupying power.' *Komintern*, op. cit. 27.

59. When the German-Soviet Pact was signed, Hitler's interpreter Paul Schmidt observed that 'Stalin seemed to have a higher opinion than Ribbentrop had of the strength of France.' Schmidt, op. cit. 206.

60. Khrushchev recalls how deeply Stalin was affected by the events in France, how, 'swearing like a trooper,' he denounced both the French and the British for allowing Hitler to beat them.

61. A draft instruction from the Comintern to the French Communist Party, dated 11 June, provided for the creation of a 'popular militia.' Manuilsky, one of the Comintern's leaders, suggested on 19 June that the French Communists living in Moscow be sent back to France 'in order to raise up the people against the bourgeois traitors.' This idea was seriously discussed in the Kremlin. *Komintern*, op. cit. 30-31, 367.

62. Churchill sent Sir Stafford Cripps to Moscow in May 1940. Cripps was a man of the left, firmly pro-Soviet. He justified the Soviets' annexation of Poland's eastern provinces and was distinguished by his extraordinary propensity to swallow Moscow's propaganda. Raack, op. cit. 55. Nevertheless, he was welcomed with icy coldness. Churchill noted that he had not yet fully realised that the Soviet Communists hated left-wing politicians even more than Conservatives or Liberals.

63. 'During our first conversation he spoke a monologue most of the time while I kept pushing him to go into greater detail ... Hitler said: "What's happening? An England, some miserable island, owns half the world and they want to grab it all – this cannot be tolerated! It's unjust!" I answered that it surely was intolerable and unjust, and that I sympathised with him. "This cannot be considered normal," I told him. He cheered up. Hitler said, "You've got to have a warm-water port. Iran, India – that's your future." And I said: "Why, that's an interesting idea, how do you see it?" I drew him into the conversation, giving him an opportunity to speak out. For me this was not a serious conversation ... He had little understanding of Soviet policy – a myopic man, he wanted to involve us in risky policy. And he'd be better off after we got stuck in the south. We'd depend on him there when England went to war with us. You had to be too naïve not to realise that.' (Chuev, op. cit. 15.

64. Ribbentrop proposed to Molotov that pressure be brought to bear on Turkey to modify the statute of the Straits, and also that Japan be pressed to sign a pact of non-aggression with the USSR in exchange for the Soviets joining the Tripartite Pact concluded on 27 September 1940 between Germany, Italy and Japan. In reply, Molotov set out a catalogue of Soviet demands: withdrawal of German troops from Finland, a pact between Bulgaria and the USSR with the granting of a Soviet base in Bulgaria, a Soviet base in Turkey, and abandonment by Japan of her concessions in North Sakhalin.

65. Stalin's suspicions were increased by Cripps. He hinted that any closer collaboration between the USSR and Germany might induce 'influential circles' in Britain to seek a separate peace with Hitler.

66. According to Stalin's translator, V. Berezhkov, Stalin severely reprimanded Molotov for the rigidity of his attitude in Berlin and hastened to send for Schulenburg in order to tell him that the USSR was ready to adhere to the Three-Power Pact 'on certain conditions.' Berezhkov, op. cit. 54-5.

67. The Germans had in fact not been slow to perceive how limited were the capacities of Amayak Kobulov, and they used him to disinform the Soviet Government. Konstantinov, A. 'Zakhar – resident Lavrentia', *Sovershenno sekretno* 10 (1993).

68. It had come into the possession of the Soviets on 29 December 1940. The head of military intelligence, F. Golikov, reported on it on 20 March 1941, concluding that the information about an imminent attack 'should be regarded as disinformation.' Matrosov, V. 'Na pervom rubezhe voiny', *Krasnaya Zvezda* 5 June 1991: Vishlyov, O.V. 'Mozhet byt, vopros eshche uladitsya mirnym putyom', in Rzheshevsky, O.A. *Vtoraya mirovaya voina* (Moscow, 1995) 40.

69. On 26 June 1940 it was increased from six days of seven hours each to seven days of eight hours each.

70. If Sergo Beria's memory is correct on this point we have here one of the mysteries of the pre-war period. In his memoirs Zhukov categorically denies that the general staff knew about 'Barbarossa' – neither he nor Timoshenko had heard of it. Stalin was stingy in passing on to the military and his Politburo colleagues the information supplied by the intelligence services. Zhukov, G. K.*Vospominania i razmyshlenia* (Moscow, 1995). Khrushchev writes: 'Information was carefully selected, limited and weighed by Stalin before it was passed on to the Politburo. He had no right to do this according to the Party statutes.' Khrushchev, op. cit. 133. Had Beria informed Vasilevsky on his own initiative? Why were the other military leaders kept in the dark?

71. At the 18th Party conference, held in January-February 1941, it was apparent that the 'rising stars' were Malenkov and Voznesensky. Along with A. Shcherbakov they were elected candidate members of the Politburo. These changes confirm that Beria had lost the favour he previously enjoyed.

72. V. Suvorov's book, *The Icebreaker*, published in 1993, which seeks to show that Stalin was on the point of attacking Germany in June 1941, continues to provoke lively polemics among Soviet historians.

73. The reference is to the plan put forward on 15 May 1941 by A.M. Vasilevsky and N.F. Vatutin, advising that 'the German army be attacked when it is at the stage of strategic deployment, before it has had time to organise a front and co-ordinate the armies.' Bobylev, P.N. 'K kakoy voine gotovilsa generalnyi shtab RKKA v 1941 godu?' *Novaya i noveishaya istoria* 6 (1995).

74. Analysis of the Red Army's manoeuvres in January 1941 showed that it was preparing to repel attack by the Wehrmacht and not to launch an offensive. In March 1941 the Soviet general staff had concluded that the main German offensive would come in the south, towards Kiev, and they decided to prepare a main counter-offensive by the Red Army towards Lublin and Cracow. However, in the face of the magnitude of the German preparations, the Soviet general staff modified its plans on 15 May 1941. The military measures taken thereafter seem to show that Stalin had approved this plan, since they conform in all respects to the recommendations made by Vasilevsky and Vatutin. But it may be that Stalin was merely trying to frighten Germany while at the same time multiplying gestures of goodwill that showed his desire to negotiate.

75. 'We had proof enough that Germany was preparing to attack us. We should have overcome our fear that the West would start to shout about Soviet aggression. We had come to the Rubicon through circumstances independent of our will and ought to have gone ahead without hesitating,' Marshal Vasilevsky said later. Bobylev, op. cit. 15.

76. On 7 August 1923, analysing the situation in Germany at that time, Stalin wrote to Zinoviev: 'It is more to our advantage that the Fascists should take the initiative in attack. That will rally the entire working class round the Communists ...' *Izvestia TsK KPSS* 4 (1994) 204.

77. Sergo Beria does not mention the turn made in May 1941. On 5 May, addressing graduates of the Military Academy, Stalin said: 'Hitherto we have pursued a defensive policy, because we were re-equipping our forces and giving them modern weapons. Now, however, our army has been reconstructed and is capable of fighting a modern war. Now we have grown strong and the moment has come to go over to the offensive.' *Istoricheskii Arkhiv* 2 (1995) 30.

78. It was also in April 1941 that the Comintern began to organise 'national anti-fascist fronts' in the countries occupied by the Axis. Stalin considered abolishing the Comintern in order to make it easier for the Communist Parties to go over to a 'national rhetoric.' *Komintern*, op. cit. 46-51.

79. Khrushchev says the same. 'We had set aside huge financial resources for arms, and I never heard of a single instance when Stalin refused a request for funds. Voroshilov simply didn't make the necessary requests.' Khrushchev, op. cit. 159.

80. Stalin was convinced that a powerful pro-British lobby existed in Germany. The Comintern's directives to the German Communists in December 1939 urged them to fight above all against 'the second front constituted by certain circles of the German bourgeoisie and a section of the Social-Democrat and Catholic leaderships, a front oriented against friendship with the Soviet Union, and enslaved to the Anglo-French bloc ...' *Komintern*, op. cit. 19.

81. It said: 'According to information possessed by the USSR, Germany is conforming to the conditions of the German Soviet Pact of non-aggression just as strictly as the Soviet Union, Consequently, according to Soviet circles, rumours about Germany's intention to violate the Pact and attack the Soviet Union are without any foundation.'

82. During the night of 21-22 June, when the Germans attacked, Stalin ordered his troops 'not to yield to any provocation, so as to avoid complications.' Total mobilisation was not declared until 12 hours after the German attack.

Chapter 4: War

1. According to Zhukov, during the first hours of the war Stalin refused to let himself believe that the Germans had attacked. The German offensive began at 3.15 a.m. and Zhukov woke Stalin at 3.25 a.m. to give him the news. Stalin's reaction was: 'It's a provocation by the German generals. Don't open fire, and try not to let the fighting spread.' Stalin convened the Politburo at 5 a.m., but did not give the order to return fire until 6 a.m. *Istochnik* 2 (1995) 147.

2. Khrushchev says that he was 'one of the most contemptible characters around Stalin during the war. He was a poisonous snake.' Shcherbakov was one of Malenkov's group, opposed to Zhdanov. He was among the pioneers of the anti-Semitic purges: as early as 1943 he dismissed the Jewish members of the editorial team of the Army's newspaper *Krasnaya Zvezda*. Kostyrchenko, op. cit. 16.

3. Neither Stalin nor the army command were aware of the seriousness of the situation during the first three days. Order was given to the Soviet troops to 'crush the invader with overwhelming blows.'

4. It was on 28 June, when the Germans took Minsk, that Stalin's prostration began. He feared that the Politburo would make him a scapegoat. According to some sources he even offered to resign. Pechenkin, A.A. 'Gosudarstvenny Komitet Oborony v 1941 godu', *Otechestvennaya Istoria* 4-5 (1994). On 17 July the Wehrmacht took Smolensk. Three weeks after the invasion began the Germans were in occupation of the Baltic countries, Byelorussia, part of the Ukraine and nearly all of Moldavia. In August they took Kiev.

5. In his unpublished memoirs Mikoyan attributes this outburst to Voznesensky. Yakovlev, A.N. & Pikhoya, R. *1941 god* (Moscow, 1998) Vol. 2, 498.

6. In July 1941, besides Beria only Molotov, Malenkov and Voroshilov were members. According to Mikoyan it was Beria who insisted that the State Defence Committee (GKO) should not be large.

7. Beria was put in charge of the production of aircraft and engines. He had also to supervise the production of weapons and ammunition.

8. Khrushchev returned on several occasions, in his speeches and memoirs, to this moment when Stalin showed weakness. Beria must have enjoyed telling the Politburo members who were absent about it. In February 1946 he could not resist the temptation to recall those fateful days, in the sarcastic doublespeak which characterised all his speeches. In an address on the occasion of the elections to the Supreme Soviet he said: 'If our country was not taken by surprise by the war ... we owe this to our wise leader, Comrade Stalin ... At the moment when our ferocious enemy attacked, and was enjoying his first successes, Comrade Stalin showed courage and decisiveness without precedent in history ...'

9. Beria opposed this measure from the outset. The first partisan units were formed on the initiative of the Army command of Leningrad Region. Beria tried to suppress this initiative.

10. After his fall, Beria was accused of having systematically sabotaged the partisan movement. He arrested nearly every member of the partisans' General Staff, formed in November 1941. Nekrasov, op. cit. 96.

11. The Western powers were afraid that armaments supplied to the Soviets might fall into the hands of the Germans. On 8 July a Soviet military mission arrived in London. The British gave the USSR 200 Tomahawk aircraft. Churchill notes in his memoirs that the British were obliged to jeopardise their own security in order to satisfy their new ally – who, only recently, had shown indifference to Britain's fate.

12. These contacts were made at the end of July. Sudoplatov, op. cit. 145-8. At Beria's trial an enquiry into Beria's secret dealings with the Germans was set up. It came to nothing, either because it proved impossible to make the witnesses talk, because the affair was too compromising for Stalin himself, or else because Beria had covered his traces too well. At the June 1957 Plenum the Procurator, Rudenko, referred to this affair. 'Beria said at his trial that he had sent Sudoplatov to see the Bulgarian ambassador at Stalin's request. We have not been able to prove this, it's difficult to do that, but Beria said that Molotov was present when this conversation took place.' *Istoricheskii Archiv* 1 (1994) 60.

13. After the destruction of the Polish state by the Germans and the Soviets in September 1939 the Polish government, headed by General Sikorski, took refuge first in France, then in Britain. Negotiations culminated on 30 July 1941 in the Maisky-Sikorski agreement. By its terms the USSR promised to release the Poles detained on Soviet territory, to help create a Polish army in the USSR, to give up its project for a Polish national committee on Soviet soil, and to recognise the London Polish government. The Poles agreed to leave open the question of Poland's eastern frontiers, as they thought the scenario of World War I would be repeated – Germany would crush the Soviet Union and would then be itself overcome by the Anglo-Saxons. For the relations between the Anglo-Saxon powers, Stalin and the London Poles, see Albert, A. *Najnowsza historia Polski (London, 1994)*; Raack, *op. cit.* and, especially, the very complete work by Brandes, op. cit.

14. Anders does not mention this detail in his memoirs, but he does say that he left prison 'in the car of the NKVD's head man.' Anders, W. *Mémoires* (Paris, 1948) 78.

15. Anders was a typical Polish patriot, vigorously anti-Communist and anti-Russian.

16. In Beria's reports to Stalin on Anders between November 1941 and March 1942 he made great efforts to depict Anders as 'pro-Soviet,' which was obviously untrue. *Novaya i noveishaya istoria* 2 (1993) 59-90. The attitudes attributed here to Anders were, rather those of Sikorski. In his memoirs Anders reports that Beria and Merkulov told him they were very pleased that he had been made commander-in-chief, because 'I was the most popular Pole in Russia' – something he found 'enigmatic.'

17. General Zhukov, whom the NKVD had put in charge of the Polish army, expressed a wish that the troops who had been evacuated should return to the USSR. Kot, the Polish ambassador in Moscow, considered the departure of Anders and his men a disaster, as he foresaw that the Red Army would now be on its own in liberating Poland. Brandes, op. cit. 259.

18. As the Soviets made ever more clear their unwillingness to equip Anders' army, in October 1941 the British asked the Soviet Government to allow the Poles to leave the USSR, so that this army could be used in the Middle East. Stalin gave his assent to this in March 1942. In April-May 1943 Stalin began to form a new Polish army, this time under Communist control. Parsadanova, V.S. 'Armia Andersa na territorii SSSR', *Novaya i noveyshaya istoria* 5 (1988).

19. The idea of this confederation was first discussed between Poles and Czechs in the summer of 1940. General Sikorski and President Beneš published a joint declaration on 11 November 1940 which advocated a Polish-Czech federation that would be open to the other states of Central Europe. At that time Beneš thought that a Bolshevik revolution was imminent in Germany and he wanted such a Germany to be cut off from the USSR by the Polish-Czech bloc. In January 1941 a Polish-Czech co-ordination committee began drawing up the future statutes of this federation. As the Poles saw it, this Central European federation was to form a door to be bolted against any Soviet advance into Europe. For Sikorski the 'good-neighbour relationship' with the USSR on which Beneš was so keen was possible only if Poland and Czechoslovakia formed part of a Central European bloc supported by Britain and capable of keeping Moscow in awe.

20. In Sikorski's eyes close relations with the Baltic states constituted one of the foundations of Poland's security. In 1942 the Polish Government's Foreign Minister, E. Raczynski, published in the *Sunday Times* a project for a Central European federation open to the Baltic states. The first blow struck at this project was Churchill's recognition, in March 1942, of the annexation of the Baltic states by the USSR. The Soviets had already made plain their opposition to the project in January 1942.

21. Beneš refused to condemn Soviet aggression against Finland in November 1939, whereas Sikorski advocated giving substantial help to the Finns (Brandes, op. cit., pp. 69-70). He dropped the federation project when Moscow vetoed it because, for him, it would be viable only if given Soviet backing. From fear of Moscow's reaction he turned down the union of Poland and Czechoslovakia and, especially, rejected inclusion of Lithuania in such a bloc. In November 1942 Beneš finally buried the federation project by proposing to replace it with a tripartite pact between Czechoslovakia, Poland and the USSR. In December 1943 the Czech Communist leader Gottwald told him that Stalin intended to communise Hungary when the Red Army got there. Beneš did not see fit to warn the British. Raack, op. cit. 214: Marina, 'E. Benesh: vtoroi visit v Moskvu', in Rzheshevsky, op. cit. 151-6.)

22. Beneš's reticence regarding the project for a Central European confederation was due partly to his fear of the preponderance of Catholic Poland in such a grouping, and partly to his centralising temperament, which made it hard for him to tolerate a political structure that would have allowed a high degree of autonomy to the Slovaks and the Sudeten Germans. The representatives in exile of these two peoples were warm supporters of the confederation idea.

23. This was the view of the London Poles, who bore a grudge against Beneš for his obstruction of their confederation plans and his blind pro-Sovietism. We shall have several more opportunities to observe the extent to which Beria's remarks, as reported here by his son, coincided with the views of the London Poles and their British protectors. This may be explicable by the close links that existed between the *émigré* Mensheviks and the Poles. In 1920 Georgia had signed a military alliance with Poland. In 1921, after the establishment of the Bolshevik regime in Georgia, Poland welcomed several hundred Georgian officers who were absorbed into the Polish Army. Evgeni Gegechkori served as the connection between the Paris Mensheviks and the Georgian officers in Poland. Several of these officers joined Anders' army. The writer of these notes is grateful for this information to Akaki Ramishvili, the son of Noah Ramishvili, Minister of the Interior in the Menshevik Government of Georgia.

24. The centre where missiles were constructed. It was bombarded on 18 August 1943 by the British.

25. Thirty-two Leningrad academics were condemned to death between November 1941 and March 1942 for having formed a 'committee of public safety' which, in reality, had been set up by the NKVD. Five were executed and the rest received long prison sentences. *Istochnik* 6, (1966) 72-8.

26. The rumour ran that in Georgia the collaborationist government was to be headed by Rapava, the Commissar for Internal Affairs, with Beria's blessing. 'Communist Takeover and Occupation of Georgia,' 85: *Special Report No. 6 of the Select Committee on Communist Aggression*, House of Representatives, 31 December 1954.

27. The animosity between Zhukov and Zhdanov dates from this period. Zhukov was made to pay for the humiliation of Zhdanov when he found himself prey to intrigues by the Soviet military administration in Germany, dominated by Zhdanov's men. Raanan, op. cit.

28. Only on 27 September did the Soviet high command realise that they had to give up offensive operations and organise defence. At the end of September the situation was crucial. The Soviets had lost 94.4% of their aircraft. On 24 September the Germans began to apply their 'Typhoon' plan for taking Moscow, and their offensive opened on 30 September.

29. On 15 October the organs of Party and State were evacuated from Moscow (they returned in August 1943). On 19 October defence of the capital was entrusted to Zhukov. A state of emergency was proclaimed in order to stop the panic that prevailed in the city.

30. This is how V.P. Pronin, who was then chairman of the Moscow Soviet, describes these events: 'On 16 or 17 October Stalin asked Zhukov for his opinion: was it possible to defend Moscow? Zhukov replied that he needed two more armies. Stalin concluded that it was possible to defend the capital.' *Izvestia TsK KPSS* 4 (1991) 218. 'During the night of 19 October Beria tried to convince us all that Moscow must be abandoned. He considered that we had to withdraw behind the Volga. Malenkov agreed. Molotov muttered objections. The others stayed silent. I remember Beria's words. "With what are we going to defend Moscow? We have nothing. We shall be shot down like partridges." ... When we arrived at Stalin's place he asked us: "Must we defend Moscow?" Everyone maintained a gloomy silence. Stalin waited a few moments, then said: "If you don't want to speak I shall ask each one of you to give his opinion." He turned to Molotov, who said "We must defend Moscow." Everyone gave the same answer, Beria included.' *Voenno-istoricheskii Zhurnal* 10 (1991) 39.

31. The German offensive was launched on 15-16 November. The Germans were 27 kilometres from Moscow but their advance was halted, with heavy losses on both sides. That was the end of the 'Blitzkrieg.' On 5-6 December the Soviets launched their counter-offensive.

32. The vice-minister of aviation, A.S. Yakovlev, relates in his memoirs that Stalin said to him in October 1941: 'Germany won't be able to stick it out for long. She will soon run short of raw materials, in spite of having the resources of all Europe at her disposal. A state cannot survive without reserves.' Yakovlev, A.S. *Tsel' zhizni*, 229.

33. The partition followed the line of the Anglo-Russian convention of 1907. What was aimed at was getting rid of the Germanophile Shah of Iran and ensuring that supplies got through to the USSR. On 8 September a treaty was signed with Iran by which the occupying powers undertook to leave Iran within six months of the end of the war.

34. The proposal was put to Stalin by Beaverbrook at the end of September 1941. Stalin replied, drily, that the fighting was taking place in the Ukraine, not in Caucasia. Sherwood, *Roosevelt and Hopkins* (NY, 1948) 387-8. On 12 October Churchill returned to the charge, suggesting to Stalin that he withdraw his troops from Iran and send them to the front against the Germans. At that time he contemplated entrusting the defence of Caucasia to Anders's army. Brandes, op. cit. 252.

35. It was in November 1941 that the Red Army was driven out of most of the Crimea. Counter-offensives between 25 December 1941 and 2 January 1942 enabled the Soviets to recover Kerch. However, on 15 May 1942 they were forced to quit the Crimea. They had lost 160,000 men. The Crimea was reconquered in May 1944.

36. An organ with the task of ensuring 'unity of command,' it was made up of military and Party leaders.

37. Khrushchev's opinion was the same. 'Mekhlis was one of the worst. He had a particularly strong influence on Stalin.' Khrushchev, op. cit. 164.

38. This was doubtless the poet Grigol Robakidze, the author of essays on

Hitler and an ode to 'Mussolini, the chosen one of the Sun.' Mühlen, P. von *Zwischen Hakenkreuz und Sowjetstern* (Düsseldorf, 1971) 32.

39. The reference is to a reconnaissance operation carried out on 19 August 1942. Five thousand Canadians landed at Dieppe: 3,400 men were killed or taken prisoner there. The 56 RAF squadrons committed to the operation succeeded in forcing the Luftwaffe to become fully involved, and protected the landing, but lost twice as many aircraft as they shot down. Bryant, A. *The Turn of the Tide* (London, 1958) 487-8. 'It was a deplorable venture from the propaganda viewpoint, as it seemed to confirm all Hitler's boasts about the impregnability of the European Fortress ...' Sherwood, op. cit. 626.

40. He replaced Budenny with Tyulenev.

41. This is not quite true. The Georgian Mensheviks hoped that the Wehrmacht would liberate Caucasia from the Bolsheviks and restore the national states. They were disappointed by the Germans' policy, as were all the representatives of nations of the USSR who had looked to Hitler to free their countries.

42. Beria must have wounded many susceptibilities, for his role in the defence of the Caucasus was vigorously challenged by some of the military and the affair resurfaced at the time of his trial. General Tyulenev summed up his role like this: 'Beria's trips to the defence lines ... boiled down to showiness and noise, to the creation of a façade of concern about the organisation and strengthening of defence. In fact ... he only disorganised, hindered and disrupted our work.' Knight, op. cit. 121. Beria was accused of having forbidden the commander of 40th Army, V.F. Sergatskov, to switch the NKVD's troops from the Batum region so as to defend the passes through which the Germans could reach the sea. 'You want to hand Batum to the Turks!' Beria said to him threateningly. Sergatskov ignored him and was struck by Beria, who then wired Moscow to say that reinforcements had been, on his orders, sent to the mountains. Antonov-Ovseenko in Nekrasov, op. cit., 97.

43. In 1918-19 Churchill was one of the most fervent advocates of an anti-Bolshevik crusade. He seems to have understood the nature of Communism better than most of the West's leaders. In November 1918 he spoke of the Bolsheviks as 'baboons,' and on 23 January 1919 he said that recognising the Bolsheviks would be like legalising sodomy.

44. The danger from Germany led Churchill to display an imprudent indulgence towards Stalin at least until the spring of 1945. In May 1942 Churchill said to Molotov, 'We should win the war and after the war Great Britain, Russia and the United States would share the responsibility for guiding the forward movement of the world.' Raack, op. cit. 203.

45. Hitler blamed his allies for this, if we are to believe what his interpreter writes: 'When Hitler tried to put responsibility on the Romanians, Hungarians and Italians for the collapse of the front which made possible the encirclement of Stalingrad, Antonescu protested energetically ... Hitler reproached Ciano regarding the attitude of the Italian troops on the Eastern front, whose lack of fighting spirit enabled the Russians to make the breakthrough into Stalingrad.' Schmidt, op. cit. 318 and 336.

46. The reference is to the anti-Communist guerrillas who fought in the Baltic states and Western Ukraine after 1945, in some cases until the 1960s.

47. Beria seems to have pursued this policy systematically. Djilas mentions that the Soviets transformed into a 'Yugoslav Anti-Fascist Brigade' a Croat regiment sent by Paveliæ to the Eastern Front. 'My impression was that Mesić (the Croats' commander) was deeply demoralised and that, like many, he had simply turned his coat to save himself from a prisoner-of-war camp.' Djilas, *Conversations with Stalin* (London, 1963) 36. Beria gave active backing to the German Officers' Union, having succeeded in rallying a number of conservative-minded officers by promising to maintain, after the war, a strong, non-Bolshevik Germany through its Wehrmacht. Schoenhals, *The Free German Movement* (Greenwood Press, 1989): Bungert, *Dis National Komitee und der Westen* (Stuttgart, 1989).

48. It was formed on 12 July. One third of the 32-man leading committee consisted of German *émigrés* (i.e., Communists), one third of officers and one third of rankers. The Committee's purpose was to call for resistance to Hitler inside Germany.

49. Pieck was as orthodox as Ulbricht, but more concerned to preserve the unity of Germany and also readier to pursue a 'popular front' policy. Moreover, he did not like the Russians. Badstûbner, R., Loth, W. *Aufzeichnunzen zur Deutschlandpolitik* (Berlin, 1994).

50. The Comintern archives have preserved the 'informer' letters sent by Ulbricht to Dimitrov and which Dimitrov passed on to Beria. In February 1941 Ulbricht asked the Comintern chief to prevent the wives of German political *émigrés* from returning to Germany, because they might engage in anti-Soviet activity. He provided a long list of examples. *Komintern*, op. cit. 508.

51. This organisation was dissolved on 30 September 1945. However, Beria was doubtless behind a second attempt which was made in June 1945, when Kruglov proposed that a Democratic Union of German prisoners of war in the USSR be formed, and Paulus drew up a scheme for it. This project also failed. *Istochnik* 3 (1994) 102-7.

52. Stalin commented thus to Djilas on this decision: '... There was something abnormal ... about the very existence of a general Communist forum at a time when the Communist parties should have been searching for a national language and fighting under the conditions prevailing in their own countries.' Djilas, op. cit. 67.

53. Palmiro Togliatti, leader of the Italian Communist Party.

54. The Polish Government entrusted the investigation to an international commission which established without difficulty that the victims had died in 1940 and not in 1941, as the Soviets claimed.

55. The Soviets set up their own commission, which tried to prove, in January 1944, that the Germans were guilty of the crime. However, at Nuremberg the massacre of the Polish officers was not included in the indictment. The Allies remained very discreet about the affair until worsening relations with Stalin led the Americans to reopen the enquiry.

56. Anders blamed Sikorski sharply for presenting relations with the USSR in too optimistic a light, for reasons of personal prestige. London backed Sikorski. Brandes, op. cit. 304.

57. In November 1942 Sikorski warned the West that Stalin meant to Bolshevise Europe. Sikorski was criticised by his colleagues in London for his concessions to the USSR. In reality, he tried to defend Polish interests with stubbornness under conditions which grew steadily more difficult as the Red Army won more victories and the West capitulated ever further to Stalin.

58. Such were rare! The Poles evacuated from the USSR were even more anti-Communist than their compatriots who were refugees in the West, and wanted their government to be more anti-Soviet, especially after 16 January 1943, when Moscow announced that all the inhabitants of the territories annexed in 1939 were to be given Soviet nationality.

59. In November and December 1942 Sikorski, worried by the growth in Russia's power, tried to win Roosevelt and Churchill for a plan to open a 'second front' in the Balkans. He said that the Polish army could take part in this, helped by the Greek and Yugoslav partisans. Romania and Hungary would then come over to the Allies and the Anglo-Saxons could liberate all Poland up to its eastern frontiers. Brandes, op. cit. 377. Beria, like the British, had illusions about Tito if Sergo's memory is correct on this point. In March 1943, Tito entered into negotiations with the Germans for co-operation between his partisans and the German divisions in Croatia in the event of an Anglo-American landing, to repel the invaders. Malcolm, N. *Bosnia* (Papermac, 1996) 183.

60. Despite the efforts of General Sikorski, who stayed in the USA between 28 November 1942 and 13 January 1943, and tried in vain to convince the American administration to support the creation of a Central European federation, an Allied offensive in the Balkans and defence of Poland's eastern frontier. The State Department, concerned not to isolate the USSR, remained deaf to his arguments, as Beneš hastened to inform Moscow. Brandes, op. cit. 421-448.

61. An 'ethnic' frontier which left the USSR in possession of the territories conquered in September 1939. After May 1943 Sikorski's attitude on the question of Poland's eastern frontiers, which until then had been intransigent despite British pressure, began to change. A few days before his death Sikorski met Anders and succeeded, apparently, in overcoming his mistrust.

62. In reality, he never stopped pressing the Poles to bow to Stalin's demands.

63. The circumstances of Sikorski's death have still not been clarified. But Beria's explanation, as given here, is certainly not correct, for the British did everything to make the Poles stop rocking the boat of the Grand Alliance.

64. See note 16 to Chapter 3.

65. Korneichuk was suddenly appointed Deputy Commissar for Foreign Affairs in April 1943.He had specialised in denouncing ill-treatment of the Ukrainians by the Poles. Brandes, op.cit., pp. 424-431.

66. Wasilewska favoured the attachment of Poland to the USSR.

67. General Svoboda commanded the Czechoslovak unit on the Soviet front. On Gottwald's order he refrained from joining the Party. He was a sentimental Russophile. Minister of Defence from June 1945, he brought the army over to the Communist side at the time of the Prague coup. Fejtö, F. *Le coup de Prague* (Paris, 1976).

68. This detail is interesting. Actually, Svoboda and Beneš's ambassador in Moscow, Fierlinger, a Comintern mole, had advocated premature commitment of the Czech battalion, in opposition to Pika's view. The unit was engaged in the battle of Sokolovo in March 1943, losing more than a third of its men. It also took part in the liberation of Kiev in November 1943, being reduced to half-strength. Soviet propaganda made much of the Czechs' sacrifices, which it contrasted with the Poles' retreat. Brandes, op. cit. 388-9.

69. It was at that conference that the principle of a three-power occupation of Germany was adopted. At this same gathering Stalin finally made Eden renounce projects for confederation in Europe and agree to the treaty of alliance between the USSR and Czechoslovakia which Beneš had been wanting to sign since April 1943 but for which he had had to wait because of British opposition.

70. I don't know if it was a result of this conversation, but when I returned to Leningrad the Academy received, on Stalin's orders, a plentiful quantity of Canadian and British matériel. (Author's note)

71. Stalin's translator, V. Berezhkov, reports these words of Roosevelt's: 'I take the opportunity from the absence of our brother-in-arms Churchill to take up a theme that he prefers not to discuss. The United States and the Soviet Union are not colonial powers and it is easier for them to talk about these problems. I think that the colonial empires will not survive for long after the war.' Berezhkov comments, 'I was stupefied by Roosevelt's initiative, especially because in November 1940 I had heard Hitler propose to Molotov partition of the British Empire between the USSR, Italy, Germany and Japan.' Berezhkov. op. cit. 189.

72. Here one can only recall Kennan's judgement on Roosevelt, that 'when [it came] to foreign policy, [he was] a very superficial man, ignorant, dilettantish, with a severely limited intellectual horizon.' Raack, op. cit. 189.

73. All this behind the back of the Polish government in London which, meanwhile, had moderated its territorial demands in the West, considering that the greater danger came now from the East. Mikolajczyk, Sikorski's successor, was not told of this decision until October 1944, while visiting Moscow.

74. Churchill personally proposed to Stalin that Poland be shifted westward, without requiring in exchange that Stalin resume diplomatic relations with the Polish government in London and promise to allow that government to return to Poland, as Eden had suggested to him in a memorandum written on 22 November. Did he really hope that Stalin would repay him by agreeing to a landing in the Balkans? This issue was the more important because Turkey made her entry into the war on the Allied side depend on such an Allied landing. At Teheran, Churchill proposed sending two divisions to Rhodes in order to draw Turkey into the conflict and provoke the defection of Germany's allies, Bulgaria, Romania and Hungary. Brandes, op. cit., 491-518.

75. This probably refers to the dispute between the British and the Americans over the landing on France's Mediterranean coast suggested by Stalin at Teheran, a project which Roosevelt approved. The British argued, instead, for a landing at Trieste which would have enabled the Western powers to reach Vienna. The debate went on till June 1944. The British lost the argument and the landing in Provence began on 15 August 1944.

76. This was, doubtless, Nicholas Kvitashvili, who has left this description of Beria: 'Beria made a tremendous impression on me right from the first meeting ... There simply cannot be any doubt that he was an extremely intelligent and shrewd man with tremendous will-power and ability to impress, command and lead other men. He may have been too sure of himself. He seemed to completely disdain any opposing view, was quite intolerant of anybody else's opinions and became very angry if anyone strongly opposed any of his proposals. Not that any of the Soviets dared – they behaved like slaves in his presence.' Knight, op. cit. 131.

77. The NKVD reports show, however, that there was anti-Communist guerrilla activity in Chechnya before the war. A 'Party of the Caucasian Brethren' was formed, with the aim of overthrowing the Soviet power with German aid. The peoples of the Caucasus were very favourably impressed by the Germans' permission to open their mosques. The Sicherheitsdienst's reports speak of the 'support' received from the highland peoples. There were sporadic attempts at rebellion throughout the war. Karyagin, V.V. *Kavkazskie orly*, (Moscow, 1994): Mühlen, P. von op. cit. 190-2.

78. On the occasion of the Muslim festivals organised on 11 October 1942 at Kislovodsk and on 18 December at Nalchik.

79. A Soviet general taken prisoner by the Germans in 1942. He headed the National Liberation Army which fought alongside the Wehrmacht.

80. Nothing in the available archives confirms this story. On the contrary, one of Beria's men, B. Kobulov, composed in October 1943 a report on the conduct of the Chechens and the Ingushes which could have served well to feed Stalin's paranoia. Vitkovsky, A. 'Chevhevitsa', *SB* 1-2 14. Other NKVD reports recalled that 'at the beginning of the 1930s there was real risk of mass insurrection in the Chechen-Ingush republic,' and that 'private property has been retained in the region,' with collective farms existing 'only formally.' Bugay, op. cit. 98.

81. However, Beria himself requested to be sent to organise the operation. In a note to the State Defence Committee dated 17 February 1944 he wrote: 'Given the importance of this operation I request permission to remain in the area concerned until it is completed.' Bugay, op. cit. 102.

82. Sergo Beria shows great indulgence to Serov, who seems to have been above all an opportunist endowed with a good instinct for survival, passing serenely from Beria's clique to Khrushchev's.

83. In a letter to Stalin, Beria described the reaction of the head of the Chechen-Ingush government, Mollaev: 'When I gave him the news, Mollaev burst into tears, but he pulled himself together and promised to carry out the tasks involved in the deportation.' Karyagin, op. cit. 2.

84. On 20 February Beria went to Grozny to organise the deportation of the Chechens and Ingushes: 478,479 persons were deported to Central Asia. On 24 February Beria suggested that the NKVD troops stationed in the area be used to deport the Balkars, which was done on 9 March. He called on the mullahs to persuade the population not to resist. The territory of the Balkars was assigned to the Kabardas and the Kabardo-Balkar republic was renamed the Kabarda Republic. Its frontiers with Georgia were altered, with the region south-west of Elbruz district being transferred to Georgia. GARF, *Osobaya papka Stalina*, f. 9401, op. 2, d. 64. However, with Malenkov's support, Beria managed to dissuade Stalin from deporting the peoples of Daghestan. Stalin had decided to divide Daghestan between Russia and Azerbaijan. When he learnt of this, the Secretary of the Daghestan regional committee, Danialov, hastened to Moscow to see Beria, who had stayed with him when he was in charge of the North Caucasian front. He begged him to intercede with Stalin. Beria and Malenkov reminded Stalin that he had himself proclaimed the republic of Daghestan in 1922. Sarnov, B. 'My sideli u Lili Brik ...' *Literaturnaya Gazeta* 26 February (1997).

85. In July 1944 Beria sent a note to Stalin, Molotov and Malenkov on which he wrote: 'The authorities in Kazakhstan have not paid sufficient attention to the settlement and employment of the deportees ... The latter have not been given an allotment, a garden or housing ... Only in rare cases have they found a job. They have fallen victim to epidemics of typhus. Their living conditions are unsatisfactory and there have been instances of theft and other crimes.' The deputy Commissar for Internal Affairs, Kruglov, was sent to Kazakhstan in May to put this situation right.' Bugay, op. cit., p. 118.

86. The Ukrainians waged a real war against the Soviet forces. According to data given by Stalin on 12 December 1944, 50,925 Ukrainians were killed and 42,984 taken prisoner between February and November 1944. Bugay, op. cit. 178.

87. In September-October 1944 the resistance in Slovakia organised a revolt which the Soviets allowed to be crushed by the Germans at the end of October. Fejtö, op. cit. 37.

88. One of the leaders of the Ukrainian national resistance.

89. In 1596 the Ukrainian church split between a Uniate church (Orthodox in ritual but accepting Rome's authority) and an Orthodox church which was subordinated to the Moscow Patriarchate in 1686.

90. At the end of 1944 the Soviet authorities pretended to adopt a tolerant attitude towards the Uniate Church, hoping to obtain its support against the Ukrainian guerrillas. In March 1945, however, the Uniate Church was suspected of being 'an agent of the Vatican' and persecution was resumed. In March 1946 Stalin obliged the Uniate Church, already beheaded by the systematic arrest of its clergy, to scuttle itself. *Otechestvennye Arkhivy* 3 (1994) 56-71.

91. After Stalin's death Beria summoned the Uniate Metropolitan Slipyi to Moscow and began secret negotiations aimed at normalising relations with the Vatican. Knight, op. cit. 189.

92. The Germans' policy in the Crimea was to rely on the Tatars who formed 23 per cent of the population, against the majority made up of Russians and Ukrainians. The Tatars were given the right to have a militia, which numbered

9,000 men in January 1942. Altogether, 20,000 Crimean Tatars fought alongside the Germans, out of a total population of 300,000. However, they were soon disillusioned and understood that they could expect nothing good from the German occupation. One of their leaders, Ozenbasli, was imprisoned by the Sicherheitsdienst when he sought to engage the Tatar Muslim Committee in political activity. Mühlen, op. cit. 186-7.

93. The Crimea was subjected to a real 'ethnic cleansing,' with the deportation of 225,000 Tatars, Bulgars, Armenians, Greeks and Germans. The available archive documents do not confirm Sergo Beria's version. In a note from the NKVD signed by Beria and dated 10 May 1944 we read: 'Given the acts of treason committed by the Crimean Tatars against the Soviet people and given that it is not desirable that the Crimean Tatars should occupy a frontier region of the USSR, the NKVD submits to you the draft resolution of the State Defence Committee concerning the deportation of the Crimean Tatars.' Bugay, 'Pogruzheny v eshelony ...,' *Istoria SSSR* 1 (1991) 143-160. In a subsequent note dated 9 July 1944 Beria wrote to Stalin: 'In accordance with your instruction the NKGB of the USSR has, between April and June 1944, cleared the Crimea of spies and persons of foreign nationality.' Bugay, op. cit. 144.

94. The insurrection was launched by the non-Communist Polish partisans when the Red Army was nearing Warsaw. The London Polish government wanted the capital to be liberated by Polish patriots, not by the Soviets. The Germans crushed the revolt ruthlessly in a bloody battle that went on for 60 days. The Red Army made no move and Stalin refused the Anglo-Saxons permission to use Soviet airfields to parachute arms to the Poles.

95. The Red Army had at first been marching on Warsaw and seemed about to bring help to the rebels. But Rokossovsky did not tell the truth. The Soviet troops were indeed ordered to let the Polish resistance fighters be massacred by the Germans.

96. Untrue. He several times appealed for help to Rokossovsky.

97. Greatly exaggerated. There were some strikes by British dockers and a mutiny by French sailors at Odessa but the Entente was above all deficient in political will and the means to act.

98. When Roosevelt died, in April 1945, Harriman hastened to Washington to warn President Truman that the Soviets aimed to dominate Eastern Europe and infiltrate Western Europe. He advised Truman to tell Moscow that the USSR would not receive American aid if it persisted in trying to impose its hegemony upon Eastern Europe. Leffler, M.P. *A Preponderance of Power* (Stanford, 1992) 31.

99. Henry Wallace had been Vice President of the United States since 1940.

100. According to Wallace's biographer, Dwight Macdonald, the Vice President was not a Soviet agent, he just behaved like one. (Beichman, 'In a Smoke-Filled Room ... Stalin's Defeat in 1944', *Working Papers in International Studies*, Hoover Institution August (1994).

101. Wallace also visited the Gulag. He went to Kolyma and was impressed by the show put on for his benefit. Nekrasov, op. cit. 114.

102. In July 1944 Roosevelt chose H. Truman as Vice President. Wallace became Secretary of State for Commerce until September 1946, when he was dismissed by Truman for his pro-Soviet sympathies.

103. Down to the spring of 1947 the Soviets considered Bidault 'loyal to the Soviet Union.' Wolton, T. *La France sous influence.* (Paris, 1997).

104. This is the portrait of the French leaders drawn by the Soviet ambassador Bogomolov to Molotov on 17 January 1944: 'Although de Gaulle is trying to include the Communists in the National Committee he does not want to collaborate sincerely with them, merely to secure himself against them ... de Gaulle fears the

Communists and the USSR ... He understands that the Communists are not like the Socialist herbivores who can be harnessed to do as one wishes ... Giraud is much stupider as a politician than de Gaulle.' *Voenno-istorichesky Zhurnal* 2 (1995).

105. 'Stalin was gripped by a will to power. Trained by a life of plots to conceal his characteristics and nature, to do without illusions, pity or sincerity, to see in every man an obstacle or a danger, with him everything was manoeuvre, mistrust and obstinacy.' De Gaulle, C. *Mémoires de guerre*. (Paris, 1959).

106. At the end of their meeting Stalin said to de Gaulle: 'After all, only death wins in the end.'

Chapter 5: 'Peace'

1. Churchill was furious because Stalin, who had always refused to go to any territory not under Red Army control, had compelled his Western colleagues to travel to Yalta.

2. Stalin cherished the hope that he would be able to take over all Germany once the American troops had left.

3. Reorganisation of the provisional government was entrusted to a commission made up of Molotov and the ambassadors Harriman (USA) and Archibald Clark-Kerr (Britain). The Soviets stubbornly opposed the candidates proposed by the Anglo-Saxons.

4. The Morgenthau plan was the official doctrine of the USA's German policy between September 1944 and May 1945.

5. Molotov was of the same opinion. Speaking of the Americans' plan to break Germany up 'into small states' he described this as 'a stupid idea.' (Chuev, op. cit. 52.)

6. The turn was made plain in *Pravda*. On 4 April 1945 it carried a violently anti-German article by Ehrenburg. On 14 April an article signed by G. Aleksandrov repudiated Ehrenburg's thesis that the German people as a whole were responsible for the crimes of Nazism.

7. Activists of the Union of the Russian People, a proto-fascist movement which appeared in Russia after October 1905 and was responsible for pogroms. It was a real mass party, with more than 358,000 members in 1907-08.

8. When he was head of the Soviet military administration in Germany, between June 1945 and April 1946.

9. On 9 February 1945 *Krasnaya Zvezda*, the daily newspaper of the Red Army wrote: 'The fact that the Germans have plundered us and raped our women does not mean that we should do the same to them.' On 20 April the Red Army was ordered to 'change its attitude to the Germans and treat them better.' Nevertheless, raping and plundering went on into 1946 at least.

10. Stalin's personal archives contain an NKVD report dated October 1945 which denounces the exactions committed by the Red Army and the shortcomings of Smersh. GARF, *Osobaya papka Stalina*, f.r.- 9401, op. 2, d.100.

11. On 1 January 1945 the Lublin committee, i.e., the Committee for National Liberation created in July 1944, dominated by the Communists, had been proclaimed by Stalin 'the provisional national government of Poland.'

12. The London Polish Government had been split since the Maisky-Sikorski agreement of July 1941. Some members thought that it was futile to try come to terms with the Soviets. After Yalta General Anders withdrew his forces from Italy as a mark of protest. Mikolajczyk accepted the Yalta decisions, which accentuated his difference with the Polish government, from which he had resigned in November 1944.These disputes simply reflected Poland's tragic situation, deserted by her allies and poisoned from within by Moscow.

13. After my father's fall an attempt was made to arrest Milshtein. He shot down five or six persons and then blew his brains out. (Author's note.)

14. However, Beria was careful to remain inconspicuous in this matter, so that Khrushchev attributes the creation of the Jewish Anti-Fascist Committee to Molotov. Khrushchev op. cit. 247. The Central Committee's propaganda department, which was headed at this time by Shcherbakov, showed great reticence towards the idea, and Beria had to force its hand. Kostyrchenko, op. cit. 27.

15. America's minister of finance from 1934 to 1945. Henry Morgenthau was a tireless supporter of the Allied cause, according to Churchill. He favoured the granting of Lend-Lease in March 1941. Between 1951 and 1954 he organised economic aid to Israel.

16. Chairman of the Tennessee Valley Authority. He was one of the inspirers of the Baruch Plan, put forward in June 1946, for placing production of atomic energy under international control. He later became chairman of the Atomic Energy Commission.

17. Erlich had been the representative of the Bund, a Jewish Socialist party, in the Petrograd Soviet of 1917. Alter was a member of the Executive Committee of the Second International and of the London Polish government. Both men were arrested in October 1939, taken to Moscow and imprisoned in the Lubyanka. They were accused of being Polish spies and sentenced to death in July 1941. They were freed in August following the Maisky-Sikorski agreement, installed in the Polish embassy in Moscow and chosen by Beria to organise the Jewish Anti-Fascist Committee. Vaksberg, op. cit. 106-7.

18. For example, they suggested that a Jewish Legion be formed in the United States, to fight against Germany alongside the Red Army. Alter also undertook to recruit for Anders's army the Poles who had been deported to the Urals.

19. They were invited by the (very pro-Soviet) American Committee of Writers and Scientists and given the task of raising enough money to buy a thousand aircraft and five hundred tanks. Their tour was a triumph. Vaksberg, op. cit. 118.

20. The Number Two of the Jewish Anti-Fascist Committee, the poet Fefer, was in fact an agent of the NKVD. According to Sudoplatov Beria sometimes met him privately. Sudoplatov, op. cit. 291.

21. Sudoplatov said that Stalin counted on getting ten billions from the American Jews for post-war reconstruction. Kostyrchenko, op. cit. 32.

22. At the end of June 1943 Mikhoels and Fefer met, with authority from Molotov, N. Rosenberg, the chairman of the American Jewish Joint Distribution Committee. He expressed readiness to finance, in part, the implementation of a plan to create a Jewish autonomous region in the Crimea. According to Fefer's testimony at his trial, Rosenberg spoke of making the Crimea 'a Jewish California'. This idea had already been discussed in 1924. Kostyrchenko, op cit. 33-57.

23. On 22 February 1944 the Jewish Anti-Fascist Committee wrote to Molotov to ask for a Jewish republic to be established in the Crimea. Vaksberg says that in March 1944 Moscow was humming with rumours of the imminent creation of this Crimean republic.

24. It is hard to believe that the leaders of the Jewish Anti-Fascist Committee, which was completely subject to the NKVD, should have risked writing to Stalin to request the formation of a Jewish republic in the Crimea if Beria had shown opposition to the project. More probably, he had himself put forward the idea and then distanced himself from it when he perceived Stalin's reaction. The project was conceived as offering an alternative to the creation of a Jewish state in Palestine. Perhaps Beria, in this way, wanted to do a favour for the British.

25. However, as Khrushchev tells us, it was not long before he 'saw behind this proposal the hand of American Zionists operating through the Sovinformburo' (the information service created in July 1941 to carry on propaganda during the war).This organisation was said to have a plan 'to set up a Jewish state in the Crimea in order to wrest the Crimea away from the Soviet Union and to establish an outpost of American imperialism on our shores.' Khrushchev, op. cit. 260. The leaders of the Jewish Anti-Fascist Committee were shot in 1952, having been accused of spying for the USA and Great Britain.

26. A Swedish diplomat who was *en poste* in Budapest in 1944. He saved tens of thousands of Jews.

27. Wallenberg was executed by the Soviets in July 1947. The Soviet Government always claimed to know nothing of his fate.

28. E. Sinitsyn, a former agent of the NKVD, reveals in his memoirs that the NKVD tried to 'wrest Wallenberg from Abakumov's talons,' on the pretext of recruiting him as a Soviet agent. In an interview with Abakumov the NKVD officer recalled that 'the diplomat Wallenberg was in Budapest on a mission from the Swedish Government, in order to represent the interests of the USSR ... At the beginning of the war the Wallenberg factories conscientiously furnished the Soviet Union with ball-bearings and tools without which our aircraft would not have left the ground ...' Abakumov rejected the request, alleging that Wallenberg was an agent of the Zionists and the Americans. Sinitsyi, Y.T. *Rezident svidetelstvuet* (Moscow, 1996) 255-264.

29. This was exactly the analysis made by the American experts until 1952. Beria was perhaps influenced by the documents obtained by his spies. In April 1949 Truman cut America's military expenditure. A report from the US Embassy in Moscow had shown that the Soviets would not resort to force in the near future, despite their sudden increase in military expenditure in 1948, because they lacked the capacities needed for waging a long war successfully. Leffler, op. cit. 308.

30. A session of the Politburo was devoted to the question of whether the USSR should conquer all Europe. Marshal Budenny said that the Red Army had made a bad mistake in halting at the Elbe, that they ought to press on and that this was not very complicated from the military standpoint. Stalin objected: 'But how are we going to feed them?' According to an officer of the First Byelorussian Army Group, D. Samoilov: 'Conquering the rest of Europe and going to war with our allies did not seem at all unrealistic either to me or to my comrades-in-arms. Our victories, our feeling of invincibility, our offensive spirit which had not yet been weakened, all encouraged us to suppose that conquest of Europe was possible.'Aksyutin, Yu. 'Poslevoennye nadezhdy', *Rodina* 12 (1993) 42.

31. A group of convergent pointers does seem to confirm Stalin's ambitious plans in Europe. An NKVD defector tells that on Victory Day a colonel of the NKVD addressed his men thus: 'For some people, perhaps, the war was over, but for us Chekists this was not so in any sense. The real war, to bring about the final destruction of the capitalist world, was only just beginning.' Romanov, A.I. *Nights Are Longest There* (Boston, 1972) 144. It was only in June 1945 that Stalin issued orders to the German Communists regarding their action in the Soviet occupation zone. He may have been dissuaded from seizing the whole of Germany by the rapid advance of the Allied forces. Raack, op. cit. 218. In November 1947, Stalin told the French Communist leader Maurice Thorez: 'If the Yugoslav comrades have done a very good job that is largely due to the fact that their country was liberated by the Red Army. If Churchill had put off opening the second front for a year, the Red Army would have got to France. We had the idea of reaching Paris.' Narinsky, M.M. 'I.V. Stalin i M. Torez', *Novaya i Noveishaya Istoria* 14 (1996). Recently declassified British archives show that Churchill feared the Soviets so much after the end of the war in Europe that on 22 May 1945 his military experts presented to him, at his request, a plan for a preventive attack on the USSR entitled 'Operation Unthinkable.' This plan was considered impracticable and abandoned on 8 June. Churchill then went over to a defensive strategy. Fenton, B. 'The Secret Strategy to Launch Attack on the Red Army', *Daily Telegraph* 1 October (1998).

32. Gromyko, who was witness to this scene, said: 'I saw that this comparison upset Roosevelt, especially as Beria had heard it ... Beria himself said nothing, just smiled, showing his yellow teeth ... That evening Beria was even more taciturn than usual. The foreign guests appeared not to notice his presence ...' Nekrasov, op. cit. 221-2.

33. In January 1945 Molotov wrote to Harriman asking for a loan of six billion dollars at two per cent. He repeated his request at Yalta. Bohlen, op. cit. 186.

34. Truman had sent Hopkins to Stalin in the hope of restoring good relations with the USSR. At the same time Hopkins had to warn Stalin, which he did, but with such reticence and self-censoring that Stalin concluded, on the contrary, that the United States was so weak that he could press home his advantage. Hopkins told Stalin that the Americans would accept the Lublin Government with only a slight change. After this visit Stalin understood that the West had abandoned Poland.

35. Stalin said to the Soviet plenipotentiaries on the eve of their departure for Germany: 'Germany has been conquered militarily, but we still have to conquer the souls of the Germans.' Koval, K.I. 'Zapiski upolnomochennogo GKO na territorii Germanii', *Novaya i Noveishaya Istoria* 3 (1994) 124-147; 2 (1995) 101-14.

36. Marshal Sokolovsky succeeded Zhukov at the head of the Soviet military administration in Germany in April 1946. He was to show himself much more anti-Western than Zhukov. Raanan, op. cit. 95-6.

37. According to Djilas, when this was reported to Stalin, he replied: 'We lecture our soldiers too much: let them have some initiative!' Djilas, op. cit. 88.

38. Churchill wanted to meet Stalin before the Americans evacuated the regions of Leipzig and Erfurt which their troops had occupied but which had to be handed over to the Soviets under the terms of the 1944 agreements. He wanted to have something with which to negotiate with Stalin. But the Americans did not listen to him and withdrew their troops at the beginning of July.

39. Actually, Secretary of State for Defence Stimson had warned Roosevelt of the interest shown by the Soviet services in the atomic project, on the eve of the Yalta conference. Malkov, 'Razvedka soyuznikov v gody voiny', in Rzheshevsky, op. cit. 199.

40. According to A. Mirtskhulava, who was then head of the government of Abkhazia, Beria ordered that a sanatorium situated on the Black Sea coast be transformed into an institute as early as April 1945, before the capture of Berlin. This institute welcomed the physicist Manfred von Ardenne and his team who, in May 1945, accepted Zavenyagin's invitation to spend a fortnight in the USSR ... and stayed there for ten years. Zaloga, S.J. *Target America* (Presidio, 1993) 39.

41. Churchill was quite deceived by Stalin's act. 'I was sure that he had no idea of the significance of what he was being told. Evidently in his intense toils and stresses the atomic bomb had played no part.' Churchill, W. *Memoirs* (London, 1959) Vol. V 580.

42. On 29 June 1945, to the great surprise of Western observers, the Red Army was suddenly redeployed. Did this mean that the plans for invading Europe mentioned here (and which must then have been abandoned a little earlier than the date given by Sergo Beria) had now been cancelled? Fenton, B. 'Churchill's plan for Third World War against Stalin', *Daily Telegraph* 1 October (1998).

43. In fact Truman tried to preserve the Grand Alliance as long as he could.

44. Stimson favoured an exchange of information with the Soviets about nuclear weapons, being afraid that relations between the two countries would worsen if the United States brandished their monopoly too ostentatiously. Leffler, op, cit. 94-5.

45. Stimson, Harriman and others considered that Stalin would have proved more conciliatory in other fields, particularly in the application of the Yalta agreements in the East-European countries, if open discussions about the nuclear weapon had taken place.

46. The American leaders were, of course, happy to possess an additional means of moderating Soviet appetites in Europe. But their principal preoccupation was with sparing the lives of their 'boys' and being able to demobilise as soon as possible. Such aims were alien to the Soviet.

47. Djilas gives a striking picture of the victorious Stalin: 'His country was in ruins, hungry, exhausted. But his armies and marshals, heavy with fat and medals and drunk with vodka and victory, had already trampled half of Europe under foot, and he was convinced they would trample over the other half in the next round.' Djilas, op. cit. 84.

48. President of the Republic between 1920 and 1924, a former socialist, he supported military aid by France to Poland in 1920, which must have made him an object of persistent spite on the part of Stalin, who had then been political leader of the Soviets south-western front and so shared responsibility for the Red Army's humiliating defeat.

49. Foreign Secretary in the Attlee Government. A robust anti-Communist.

50. Stalin had stayed briefly in Vienna in 1913.

51. Gnedin, who was tortured by Kobulov, gives this picture of him: 'He had a big head, the fat face of a man who likes good living, globular eyes, large, hairy hands and short bow legs.' Gnedin, op. cit. 22.

52. This tactic was also used by Stalin with Truman and his Secretary of State, Byrnes, if we are to believe what Khrushchev writes. 'Stalin courted Byrnes and flattered him with compliments, while saying all kinds of things against Truman ... We were indignant. Even Beria said: "How can he do that? As soon as Byrnes leaves, Truman will know everything that happened." ' Khrushchev, *The Glasnost Tapes* 67.

53. This version of the relations between Serov and Zhukov is confirmed by the archives and contradicts the opinion hitherto held by historians, according to which Zhukov's participation in the fall of Beria was due to Serov's intrigues against him in Germany. In April 1946 Abakumov extorted a confession from Air Marshal Novikov to the effect that 'Serov was hand-in-glove with Zhukov.' This good relationship between Beria's man and Zhukov could not but worry Stalin. For the Zhukov affair, see *Voennyi Arkhiv* (1993) 175-245 and *Voenno-istoricheskii Zhurnal* 12 (1992); 6 and 8 (1994).

54. Abakumov had Serov's entire team in Germany arrested at the beginning of 1948. General Sidnev reported on 6 February: 'Everyone in Germany knew that Serov was foremost in grabbing whatever had been plundered in Germany and that he helped others to plunder.' Two days later Serov replied by sending Stalin a letter in which he denounced Abakumov: 'For the sake of his career Abakumov is ready to liquidate everyone who stands in his path.' ibid.

55. Abakumov went to Germany in December 1945 and arrested some officers who were close to Zhukov. The latter sent for him and demanded that he release them, threatening to send him under guard to Moscow if he did not obey. Abakumov knuckled under but was thereafter full of hatred for Zhukov. Kutuzov, V. 'Mertvaya petlya Abakumova', *Rodina* 3 (1998) 88.

56. On 10 January Abakumov sent Stalin a report on the results of a secret search of Zhukov's flat and *dacha*. He was happy to describe the many gold objects, the 323 furs, the 400 metres of velvet and silk which had been found. 'We can simply say that Zhukov's *dacha* is a museum. There are so many pictures by great artists that four of them had to be put in the kitchen. Zhukov even went so far as to hang over his bed a huge canvas depicting two naked women ... We did not find a single Soviet book in the *dacha* ... When you go into these places it is hard to imagine that you are not near Moscow rather than in Germany ...' *Voenny Arkhiv* (1993).

57. Khrushchev held the same opinion about Bulganin: 'I couldn't understand at all the reason for Stalin's relationship with Bulganin.' Khrushchev, op. cit. 39. Sudoplatov also: 'His incompetence was striking ... Bulganin was notorious for avoiding decisions ... When Stalin made Bulganin Minister of Defence he achieved his goal of making himself the arbiter between the real commanders of the armed forces – such as Vasilevsky, Zhukov, Shtemenko, Konev, Rokossovsky and Bagramyan – and Bulganin ... Neither side, the real leaders or the figureheads, could act independently. This stimulated rivalry among the military, for whom there was no longer a clear-cut hierarchy.' Sudoplatov, op.cit. 312-13. In 1918 Bulganin had organised the Red Terror in Nizhny Novgorod, executing hostages on a grand scale. Courtois, op. cit. 89.

58. Stalin said to him one day: 'Comrade Vasilevsky, you command so many men and you don't do too badly, though you've never hurt a fly.' Marshall, *Duel* 25 (1997).

59. Vasilevsky was one of the few senior officers to defend the Jews in the Army when the anti-Semitic campaigns reached them. Vaksberg, op. cit. 147.

60. This remark of Stalin's shows that he had understood Beria's methods. Beria liked to make others take responsibility for his initiatives, so that he could distance himself from them if things went wrong.

61. Khrushchev said of him: 'He turned out to be totally incompetent as a military leader.' Khrushchev, op. cit. 165.

62. Timashuk was a heart specialist who alleged in 1948 that Zhdanov had been the victim of a wrong diagnosis. Her letter was disinterred in 1952 and served to give credit to the 'Doctors' Plot.'

Chapter 6: Stalin

1. 'He didn't simply come with a sword and conquer our minds and bodies. No, he demonstrated his superior skill in subordinating and manipulating people ... In everything about Stalin's personality there was something admirable ... as well as something savage.' Khrushchev, op. cit. 6.

2. In one of her rare interviews with the press Nina Beria said: 'If Stalin did bad things it was not for Georgians like us to criticise him.' *Sovershenno sekretno* 9 (1990).

3. Kaganovich returns several times to this point during his interviews with F. Chuev: 'I feel indignant when people allege that Stalin sought personal power. They forget that Stalin was above all a man of an idea ... All that he did he did for Socialism.'

4. In 1937 the theme of 'capitalist encirclement' was used to justify the great terror. In August 1951 the Central Committee's journal *Bolshevik* noted that the establishment of the Communist regimes in Central Europe 'has been mistakenly interpreted by some comrades as meaning the end of capitalist encirclement ... Capitalist encirclement is not a purely geographical notion, it is a political notion.'

5. Khrushchev, Djilas and others have testified to Beria's drunkenness. Stalin is alleged to have said to Khrushchev: 'Before Beria arrived, dinner meetings used to be relaxed, productive affairs. Now he's always challenging people to drinking contests and people are getting drunk all over the place.' (Khrushchev, op. cit., p.

101.) Yet, according to Molotov, 'Beria didn't like to drink, though he had to do it quite often.' Chuev, op. cit. 177.

6. Khrushchev and Djilas both report these tales of his childhood with which Stalin regaled his guests. A less sympathetic audience than Sergo, they attributed such trips down memory lane to Stalin's senile decay. Khrushchev tells how the Politburo members, having had enough of this, were 'spitting with scorn' as they exchanged sarcasms about Stalin's boastings when they met in the men's room. The picturesque detail is interesting as it shows that there was a sort of solidarity among the Politburo members, at least at the end of Stalin's reign, with hatred of the tyrant overcoming fear of being informed upon. Khrushchev, op. cit. 302.

7. Stalin was exiled to Siberia in 1903 for inciting the workers of Batum to storm the prison. He escaped after a month and in January 1904 was back in Tiflis. In 1909 he was exiled afresh in the Vologda region. He escaped, was recaptured, and escaped again in the spring of 1910. In the spring of 1913 he was deported to Turukhansk in Siberia whence the revolution released him. The ease with which Stalin organised his escapes strengthened many Caucasian Social-Democrats in their conviction, ever since the Batum affair, that Stalin was an *agent provocateur* of the Tsarist police.

8. N. Krupskaya was Lenin's wife.

9. Stalin's animosity towards Lenin's widow is well known. 'He allowed himself to say all sorts of outrageous things about her,' says Khrushchev, op. cit. 46. Stalin was alleged by Molotov, who was rather shocked by this, to have demanded, regarding Krupskaya: 'Just because she uses the same bathroom as Lenin, do I have to appreciate and respect her as if she were Lenin?' Chuev, 133.

10. One's impression is, rather, that Lenin could not see anyone as his successor.

11. A. Tolstoy received in 1940 the Stalin Prize for his (unfinished) novel, *Peter the Great*. The Stalin Prize had been created in December 1939.

12. In 1937 Malenkov and Yezhov had been sent by Stalin to Byelorussia in order to organise the purge there. A large part of the Byelorussian Communist Party's apparatus was exterminated. In the same year Malenkov and Mikoyan were sent to Armenia for the same purpose.

13. When he saw Stalin in January 1948, having previously been to Moscow in 1945, Djilas observed: 'There was something both tragic and ugly in his senility ... His intellect was in even more apparent decline ... I could hardly believe how much he had changed in two or three years.' Djilas, op. cit. 118.

14. Kaganovich told Chuev that Stalin had personally cut his beard off in 1932. Chuev, *Tak govoril Kaganovich*, 59.

15. Poskrebyshev himself related, in an interview of 1964, how Stalin had engaged him. 'One day Stalin sent for me and said: "Poskrebyshev, you have a frightful look about you. You'll terrify people." And he engaged me.' *Vechernyi Klub* 22 December (1992).

16. Khrushchev draws this portrait of him: 'He was Stalin's faithful dog ... He behaved haughtily with everyone and downright despicably with any member of the Presidium who had fallen out of Stalin's favour ... Poskrebyshev could be unbearably offensive.' Khrushchev, op. cit. 274-5.

17. Djilas saw Stalin mocking the doddery old President Kalinin: 'Stalin laughed and the expression on his face was like a satyr's.' Djilas, op. cit., p. 84. Khrushchev makes the same observation: 'He found the humiliation of others extremely amusing.' Khrushchev, *Khrushchev Remembers* 301.

18. The American ambassador Bedell-Smith noted that, when met face to face, Stalin was not at all antipathetic, but, on the contrary, could be very charming. Bedell-Smith, op. cit. 49.

19. His wife was the sister-in-law of Lev Sedov, Trotsky's son. When Poskrebyshev wanted to know what she was accused of Stalin told him: 'Get on with your work. We'll find you another wife.' Vaksberg, op. cit. 51; *Vechernyi klub* 22 December (1992).

20. A Georgian Bolshevik, a friend of Ordzhonikidze, and a Comintern agent. In 1929 he became guilty of heresy by writing that a Party member had the right to possess a personal opinion, and he criticised collectivisation. In 1930 he was accused of 'Right deviationism' and of 'factionalism.' Ordzhonikidze tried to protect him (something for which Stalin never forgave him) but Lominadze killed himself in 1935 in order to avoid imminent arrest. Khlevnyuk, *Stalin i Ordzhonikidze* 21-9.

Chapter 7: The People around Stalin

1. Khrushchev saw Stalin pull his daughter's hair to make her dance: 'His behaviour towards her was really an expression of affection, but in a perverse, loutish form which was peculiar to him ... [Stalin] was brutish and inattentive. He never showed any parental tenderness. When he wasn't being downright abusive to her he was cold and unfeeling. He broke the heart first of a child, then of a young girl, then of a woman and a mother.' Khrushchev, op. cit. 290-2.

2. Svetlana has related this episode in her book., Stalin began by shouting: 'Your Kapler is a British spy!' And when Svetlana protested that they loved each other, he retorted: 'Take a look at yourself. Who'd want you? You fool! He's got women all around him.' Allilueva, S. *Twenty Letters to a Friend* (London, 1967) 191-2.

3. Morozov was a Jew. When the MGB told Stalin that Mikhoels had met Morozov in 1946 at the Alliluevs' place, his paranoia broke loose. International Zionism was trying to get into his closest entourage! Kostyrchenko, op. cit. 87

4. 'A bright, well-educated, sensible fellow,' according to Khrushchev, who says that Stalin had forced Svetlana to give up Morozov out of anti-Semitism. Khrushchev, op. cit. 293.

5. Having opposed Lysenko, he was made to perform self-criticism in 1948.

6. When Svetlana announced to her father the difficult birth of her daughter, feeling wounded because he had not even deigned to visit her in the maternity hospital, she received this curt reply: 'I got your letter. I'm very glad you got off so lightly. Kidney trouble is a serious business. To say nothing of having a child. Where did you get the idea that I had abandoned you? It's the sort of thing people dream up. I advise you not to believe your dreams. Take care of yourself. Take care of your daughter too. The state needs people, even those who are born prematurely. Be patient a little longer – we'll see each other soon.' Allilueva, op. cit. 209.

7. Svetlana presents Beria as Stalin's 'evil genius'. 'Beria was more treacherous, more practised in perfidy and cunning, more insolent and single-minded than my father. In a word, he was a stronger character ... [Stalin] could be led up the garden by someone of Beria's craftiness. Beria was aware of my father's weaknesses ... He was a born spy and provocateur.' Allilueva, op. cit. 148-9.

8. According to Molotov Yasha 'was not Party-minded. He was handsome, a bit of a dandy.' Chuev op. cit. 209.

9. Yasha was killed by a camp guard at Sachsenhausen in September 1943, during an attempt to escape which amounted to suicide. *Rodina* 5 (1992) 61-3.

10. Here is Stalin's view of his son, given in a letter to one of the boy's teachers in 1935, a view which tells us as much about the father as about the son: 'Vasily is a spoilt boy of average ability, a bit wild (a real Scythian!), who often lies, likes blackmailing weak teachers, and is sometimes insolent, with a will that is not so much weak as disorganised.' Lobanov, M. *Stalin* (Moscow, 1995) 286.

11. In 1947 he was appointed commander of the air force in the Moscow Military Region. His father dismissed him in the summer of 1952 after a serious accident caused by Vasya during the First of May Parade.

12. He was sentenced by the Military Collegium to eight years' imprisonment.

13. In his memoirs Khrushchev mentions more than once that Stalin had a horror of solitude and used to keep people with him on various pretexts.

14. Djilas draws this portrait of Zhdanov: 'Zhdanov ... was rather short, with a brownish clipped moustache, a high forehead, pointed nose, and a sickly red face. He was well educated and was regarded in the Politburo as a great intellectual ... Although he had some knowledge of everything, even music, I would not say that there was a single field that he knew thoroughly – a typical intellectual ... He was also a cynic, in an intellectual way, but all the uglier for this because behind the intellectualism one unmistakably sensed the potentate who was "magnanimous" toward men of the spirit and the pen.' Djilas, op. cit. 116.

15. Khrushchev writes: 'One of his ailments was that he ... wasn't able to control himself when it came to drinking ... In the last days of Zhdanov's life Stalin used to shout at him to stop drinking. This was an astounding thing because Stalin usually encouraged people to get drunk.' Khrushchev, op. cit. 284.

16. Suslov was a protégé of Zhdanov, who brought him into the Central Committee in 1946.

17. Malenkov, says Djilas, 'was even smaller and plumper' than Beria, 'but a typical Russian with a Mongol admixture – dark, with prominent cheekbones and slightly pock-marked. He gave one the impression of being a withdrawn, cautious and not very personable man. It seems as though under the layers and rolls of fat there moved about still another man, lively and adept, with intelligent and alert black eyes.' (Djilas, op. cit., p.86.) 'Essentially, he was a typical office clerk and paper-pusher. Such men can be the most dangerous of all if given any power. They'll freeze and kill anything that's alive if it oversteps its prescribed boundaries.' Khrushchev, op. cit. 79.

18. In June 1944, 'Party committees at various levels received a memorandum (later known in Party circles as the "Malenkov circular") which listed those jobs which it was thought undesirable to give to Jews.' Medvedev *op. cit.* 146.

19. Malenkov refused to reprieve the condemned members of the Jewish Anti-Fascist Committee. To the Procurator Cheptsov, who asked that the verdicts be annulled in view of the lack of proof, he said: 'You want us to go down on our knees before criminals. The verdict has been approved by the people – carry out the Politburo's decision.' Borshchagovsky, A. *Obvinyaetsa krov* (Moscow 1994) 375.

20. Khrushchev on this episode: 'I'm not ascribing this sentiment [anti-Semitism] to Malenkov. On his part it was just a lackey's servility to his master. Stalin had made his daughter divorce a Jew so Malenkov had to do it, too.' Khrushchev, op. cit. 293. It appears that Stalin made Malenkov act in this way. Malenkov ensured that Shamberg and his family were not arrested. Kostyrchenko, op. cit. 132.

21. I. D. Serbin was taken into the Central Committee in 1950 after 'unmasking a Zionist plot' in the ZIL motor-car plant in 1949. The episode related by Sergo Beria is typical of the atmosphere and practices of the years 1949-50 when, following the purge of the cultural realm, the Soviet economy was systematically 'de-Judaised.' Vannikov and his deputy kept their places only through Beria's protection. Kostyrchenko, op. cit. 269.

22. In 1941 M. Kaganovich and Vannikov were accused of being hand-in-glove with the Germans. According to Lazar Kaganovich, Vannikov bore witness against his brother, Mikhail. Chuev, *Tak govoril Kaganovich*, 74.

23. Khrushchev's reaction was the same: 'He was the kind of man who wouldn't say a single word on behalf of his own brother.' Khrushchev, op. cit. 47.

24. Yuri Kaganovich became an officer and died in 1944. In his confidences to Chuev, Kaganovich said that the boy came from an orphanage.

25. It was for this reason that Kaganovich recommended him to Stalin. Chuev, op. cit. 99. Khrushchev never expressed the slightest repentance for his past actions. In 1957 when he was denouncing the 'anti-Party group' for the repressions of 1937, he referred in these terms to the role he himself had played: 'I was sent to Kiev. The Trotskyists were very active there and we did a lot to eliminate them ... The Industrial Academy was a nest of Rights and Trotskyists. We crushed them in order that the Party line might triumph.' (Minutes of the June 1957 Plenum, *Istoricheskii Arkhiv* 2-6 (1993); 1 (1994.).

26. Khrushchev had in 1920 voted for a Trotskyist revolution and while Stalin was alive he went in fear lest this offence be brought against him. In 1935 he set about purging the Moscow Party organisation, for which he was responsible. In 1938 he insisted that even low-ranking officials be arrested. After the war he raged against the 'nationalists' in the Ukraine. Back in Moscow, in 1949, he was involved in the 'Leningrad affair'.

27. This was A. I. Uspensky, head of the Ukraine NKVD under Khrushchev and Yezhov. Guessing what was awaiting him, on 14 November 1938 Uspensky went into hiding. Stalin accused Yezhov of warning him. Beria's men did not manage to catch him until April 1939. Of the repressions in the Ukraine, Khrushchev writes, imperturbably: 'We were still conducting arrests. It was our view that these arrests served to strengthen the Soviet state and clear the road for the building of socialism on Marxist-Leninist principles.' Khrushchev, op. cit. 97-146.

28. This happened to Stepan Bandera, assassinated in the West in 1959.

29. Leonid Khrushchev became a pilot. He was reported missing in March 1943.

30. Khrushchev liquidated the hierarchy of the Uniate Church in the Ukraine. On 21 February 1948 he issued an order for 'deportation from the Ukraine of parasitic and anti-social elements.' On 7 May 1948 a commission made up of Malenkov, Zhdanov, Rodionov, Khrushchev, Suslov and Kruglov was given the task of generalising the measures taken in Ukraine and issuing an order for 'deportation of anti-social elements' from other parts of the USSR as well. This was done on 2 June. GARF, *Osobaya papka Stalina*, f. 9401, op.2, d.200. It was the beginning of fresh mass repressions.

31. Djilas is less categorical: 'Rather short and stocky, but brisk and agile, he was strongly hewn out of one piece ... Khrushchev is not a gourmand, though he eats no less than Stalin and drinks even more.' Djilas, op. cit. 97.

32. That was not everyone's opinion. Djilas says that Beria 'was somewhat plump, greenish and pale, and with soft, damp hands. With his square-cut mouth and bulging eyes behind his pince-nez, he suddenly reminded me of Vujkoviæ, one of the chiefs of the Belgrade Royal Police who specialised in torturing Communists ... The similarity extended even to his expression – a certain self-satisfaction and irony mingled with a clerk's obsequiousness and solicitude. Beria was a Georgian, like Stalin, but one could not tell this at all from the looks of him ... Even in this respect he was nondescript.' Djilas, op. cit. 86. The American ambassador Bedell-Smith gave a more indulgent picture of Beria, comparing him to a professor or a scholar, with a big forehead, a frank expression, firm lips and a calm, reserved air. Bedell-Smith, op. cit. 70.

33. Bedell-Smith disliked Molotov for his dullness, despite the Soviet leader's correct and courteous manner. Bedell-Smith, op. cit. 64.

34. Zhemchuzhina's case was discussed in the Politburo on 10 August 1939. At that time she was People's Commissar of Fisheries. The NKVD had exposed a network of 'German spies' and 'wreckers' in this commissariat. Zhemchuzhina was merely warned about her 'lack of discernment in choosing the people around her.' On 24 October, however, Stalin returned to the attack and had her dismissed. In November she was put in charge of the textile industry.

35. Mikhoels once compared her to Esther and described her as 'a worthy daughter of the Jewish people.' Kostychenko, op. cit. 105.

36. She was expelled from the Central Committee.

37. Stalin made him divorce her at the end of 1948. Many years later Molotov said to Chuev: 'To me befell the happiness to have had her as my wife. Beautiful, intelligent and, the main thing, a genuine Bolshevik.' Chuev, *Molotov Remembers* 323.

38. Saburov fell into disgrace in June 1957: 'He did us much harm with his liberal weaknesses,' said Khrushchev at the Plenum which condemned the anti-Party group.

39. The Union Republics differed from the autonomous republics in the RSFSR in having a frontier with a foreign country. Beria seems to have recalled B. Mdivani's proposals regarding the Russian Federation.

Chapter 8: The Bomb

1. Frédéric Joliot-Curie had offered the Soviet Ambassador all the information possessed by himself and his friends. 'French scientists ... will always be at your disposal without asking for any information in return,' he assured one of Molotov's deputies. Zubok, V. & Pleshakov, C. *Inside the Kremlin's Cold War* (Harvard, 1996)15.

2. This was the commission on the uranium problem which was set up on 30 July 1940, at the instigation of scientists who warned their government about the implications of nuclear fission. On the Soviet nuclear programme, see Holloway, D. *Stalin and the Bomb* (Yale, 1994); Zaloga *op. cit.*; and the publications of the *Cold War International History Project Bulletin* issued by the Wilson Center.

3. In November 1941 the NKVD received from its agents a report on work being done in Great Britain on the uranium bomb. Beria passed this to Stalin, who saw in it merely British propaganda.

4. On 10 March 1942 Beria prepared for Stalin a synthesis of the reports from his networks on the development of the nuclear project in the United States and Great Britain. He proposed the creation of a special commission for a Soviet atomic programme. Stalin agreed. Molotov and Pervukhin (who was then People's Commissar of the Chemical Industry) were put in charge of it. In May 1942 Stalin let himself be convinced that it was possible to make an atomic bomb.

5. On 11 February 1943 Stalin set up a special committee for producing atomic energy for military purposes. It was headed by Molotov, with Beria as his deputy. Sudoplatov, op. cit. 182.

6. It was on Ioffe's recommendation that the project was entrusted to Kurchatov in March 1943.

7. In June 1945 'Kurchatov appealed to Stalin to appoint Beria as head of the atomic project.' Sudoplatov, op. cit. 200. The physicist Yuli Khariton wrote later: 'Many atomic industry veterans believe that if the project had remained under Molotov's leadership such quick success in carrying out our work would not have been possible.' Zubok, op. cit. 149.

8. On 20 August 1945 the State Defence Committee formed the special commission charged with work on the bomb, made up of Malenkov, Voznesensky, Zavenyagin, Kurchatov, Kapitsa, Makhnev and Pervukhin, with Beria as chairman. It was given priority power to requisition resources in every sector of the economy. At the same time there were set up, under the commission, a technical council and a first principal directorate within the Council of Ministers, both to be chaired by B. Vannikov. Beria was to centralise and check on all the services entrusted with collecting intelligence about nuclear research abroad. *Cold War International History Project*, Woodrow Wilson Center for Scholars, Washington DC (1996) 269.

9. This well-known Soviet physicist soon left the special commission and fell into disgrace. *Istoricheskii Arkhiv* 6 (1994) 112-13.

10. This was department S, in charge of atomic spying. It was formed in the NKVD in February 1944.

11. Sudoplatov had been so closely associated with Beria that he managed to survive 26 June 1953 only by pretending to be mad. He was, however, imprisoned until 1968. Sudoplatov, op. cit., Chapters 12 and 13.

12. In April 1945 two emissaries of Beria, A. Zavenyagin and V. Makhnev, went to Berlin and set about recruiting German scientists and digging them out from the concentration camps into which other branches of the NKVD had thrown them.

13. This was the case, for example, with Engineer Grotrupp.

14. Kurchatov, too, tried to make Stalin see reason when he spurred the scientists to get the bomb ready quicker. He pointed out that the country was in ruins, so many people had been killed and there were all-round shortages. Zaloga, op. cit. 27.

15. This was true of all the sectors administered by Beria: arrests were less frequent there than elsewhere. 'As soon as we were put under the NKVD, arrests of employees practically ceased, at every level ... After the war our ministry was taken away from Beria and arrests resumed, faster than ever,' testified V.I. Novikov, who was in charge of artillery production during the war. 'Everything that depended on Beria had to function with the precision and exactness of a watch.' Nekrasov, op. cit. 229-37.

16. Sharia was dismissed on 3 June 1948, on the pretext that he had written in 1943 a 'religious and mystical' poem, at a time when he was grieving for his son's death. Arrested in 1951, he was freed by Beria in March 1953.

17. 'The two things he could not bear were wordiness and vagueness of expression on the part of his subordinates.' Romanov, *op. cit.* 179.

18. The Georgian First Secretary, Mirtskhulava, told the Plenum of 1-7 July 1953: 'Take the case of Kiknadze. He's a former Menshevik. Beria said to me that he was a good administrator. I agreed that he was a good administrator, but he was not a Party member. "True," said Beria, "and he'll never join the Party, but he is a good organiser, and that's all that matters." '

19. Yet, in his memoirs, Khrushchev gives a positive judgement of Serov: 'He was an honest, incorruptible, reliable comrade despite his mistakes ... He was among those mobilised when we started drafting military men into the service of the NKVD.' Khrushchev, op. cit. 115.

20. After Beria's fall, Zavenyagin gave free rein to his rancour against his former boss. He declared at the Plenum of 2-7 July 1953: 'I worked with Beria over a long period and observed him. His chief feature was obvious – he despised people. He despised the entire Soviet people, he despised the Party, he despised the Party's leaders. And it was this contempt of his that blinded him. He looked on the members of the Presidium as idiots who could at any moment be taken by the throat and isolated.'

21. By organising the famous *sharashki* described by Solzhenitsyn in *The First Circle*. These were research units administered by the Fourth Special Section of the NKVD. The scientist prisoners enjoyed in them living conditions that were infinitely better than those of ordinary *zeks*. The first research unit of this type was formed in Butyrka prison, in Moscow, in 1929, and employed 'bourgeois experts' who had been accused of sabotage. Beria generalised the system from spring 1940 onwards. Golovanov, op. cit.

22. Tupolev was arrested in October 1937. He soon confessed to being a French spy (since 1924) and being responsible for many acts of sabotage. In 1938 he was given the task of constructing a bomber in a *sharashka* specially created for the purpose – Research Unit No. 29 of the NKVD, where 800 engineers worked. This unit built a fighter which was tested in April 1940. On Stalin's order this fighter was transformed into a bomber – the Pe2, which emerged in June 1940.

23. Korolev and Petlyakov were arrested in 1938, charged with leading 'a Russian Fascist organisation' and 'sabotaging' the construction of new weapons. Korolev was found guilty by the Military Collegium on 27 September 1938. Their verdict was annulled on 13 June 1939. In February 1939 he had been brought back from Siberia and installed in a *sharashka*. On 26 May 1940, Korolev was nevertheless sentenced to eight years' forced labour, for sabotage. In September 1940 he was assigned to Research Unit No. 29, where Petlyakov and Myasishchev's groups also worked. They were freed in the summer of 1940 and Korolev in July 1944. Golovanov, op. cit.

24. Korolev's biographer, Ya. Golovanov, gives this version of the conversation, provided by Tupolev. Beria: 'As soon as your aircraft flies you will all be set free.' Tupolev: 'Don't you think that we would make aircraft even if we were at liberty?' Beria: 'Certainly. But it would be risky. The traffic in the streets is crazy and you might get run over.' Golovanov, op. cit. 282.

25. Beria tried, for example, to persuade Stalin to abolish the NKVD's special Collegium in October 1945. *Istoricheskii Arkhiv* 4 (1996) 135.

26. Khrushchev notes that 'Stalin hardly ever bothered to consult with members of the Politburo.' Khrushchev, op. cit. 177.

27. Introduced in 1932, during the collectivisation campaign, the passport system tied the peasant to his *kolkhoz* and prevented him from 'voting with his feet.' After Stalin's death, on 20 May 1953 Beria secured his colleagues' approval for abolition of the restrictions connected with the passport regime. On 16 June 1953, a few days before his fall, he set about attacking this Communist variant of serfdom. The MVD's Order No. 00357 provided that, henceforth, peasants would be able to obtain a temporary passport if they took a job in a different region. The frontier zones would no longer be closed to them. These measures were, of course, cancelled after Beria's fall, although, later Khrushchev emancipated the peasants. *Istochnik* 4 (1994) 11.

28. For everything concerning the struggle for power in the USSR between 1945 and 1952, see Zhukov, Y.K. 'Borba za vlast v rukovodstve SSSR v 1945-52 godakh', *Voprosy Istorii* 1 (1995), and this writer's contribution to the colloquium on Khrushchev the proceedings of which were published in 1994 by the Gorbachev Foundation.

29. The reference is to the arrests of Minister of Aviation Shakhurin and Air Marshal Novikov in April 1946. As we have seen, Novikov's testimony was also used against Zhukov.

30. On 4 May 1946 Malenkov lost his job in the Central Committee's secretariat. The Politburo resolution noted that 'Comrade Malenkov bears responsibility for the shortcomings in the industry entrusted to his charge, and when he was aware of the situation he failed to inform the Central Committee.' This affair gave Stalin confidence that Abakumov could attack the powerful Beria-Malenkov tandem who controlled military industry and had emerged stronger from the war. Stalin carried out his operation with his usual deliberation and care:

the first pieces of evidence used (a letter of denunciation from the vice-minister of aviation, A.S.Yakovlev) dated from autumn 1945. Kostyrchenko, op. cit. 70.

31. He managed it in August 1946. Malenkov became deputy chairman of the Council of Ministers and was given charge of communications and electronics. Shortly afterwards, Stalin asked him to build the Tu-4 bomber, modelled on the American B29.

32. Was it through this policy of Beria's that the order to shoot the Polish officers was signed by the Politburo on 5 March 1940? How are we to explain this curious phrase of Molotov's, referring to the lists of persons sentenced to death which were signed by the Politburo members. 'I would sign for Beria whatever was signed by Stalin, and forwarded to me.' Chuev, op. cit. 296.

33. Stalin got rid of Merkulov because, in his own words, 'the man was too soft.' Kutuzov, op. cit. 86.

34. Merkulov was accused by Malenkov of seeking 'to put the Central Committee under the control of the NKGB.' Malenkov, op. cit. 52. Abakumov was rewarded for successfully setting up the Shakhurin-Novikov case.

35. This Information Committee was killed off in November 1951 and replaced by something more modest, attached to the Foreign Affairs Ministry. After Stalin's death, Beria criticised its analyses, which were always perfectly in tune with Leninist orthodoxy. They always endorsed Stalin's mistaken policies and thereby worsened the harmful consequences of those policies, Beria declared to a group of MVD officers in May 1953. Zubok, V. 'Soviet Intelligence and the Cold War ...', *Cold War International History Project* December (1992); VIP9/1995, op. cit.

Chapter 9: Disillusionment

1. In October 1942 Churchill had written in a note to the Foreign Office that it would be a disaster if Russian barbarism were to overwhelm the culture and independence of Europe's venerable states. He hoped to see a United States of Europe in which barriers between states were reduced to the minimum. Gilbert, M. *Churchill*, (London, 1991) 731.After the war he was an eloquent advocate of European federalism.

2. It was created on 6 May 1940. *Komintern* op. cit. 61.

3. They meant the ephemeral governments headed by Sanatescu and Radescu. In March 1945 the Soviets imposed the Communist P. Groza on Romania.

4. Was Beria influenced by the projects for a Danubian Confederation, dear to Churchill, who, at the time of the Teheran conference, dreamt of 'recreating the Austro-Hungarian Empire in modern form'?

5. A member of the Hungarian Communist Party since 1918, Imre Nagy emigrated to the USSR in 1929 and became an NKVD agent in 1933. The archives have revealed that at least 15 persons, including E. Varga, were arrested on the basis of a report by Nagy. Despite this zeal, which the NKVD appreciated, Nagy was expelled from the Communist Party in 1936. Back in the Party in 1939 he wrote that the Hungarian proletariat was not loyal to the cause of Socialism, which contributed to him getting the reputation of being a dubious political element. Musatov, V.L. 'Tragedia Imre Nagy', *Novaya i noveishaya istoria* 1 (1991). The documents incriminating Nagy were published in *Rodina* 2, 1993, pp. 55-57. He headed the Hungarian revolt in 1956 and was executed in 1957.

6. He had been taken prisoner by the Soviets in September 1939 and then freed after recruitment by the NKVD.

7. Gomulka led the Polish Communists' resistance to the Germans from the autumn of 1943. Beria seems to have had a predilection for the 'national' Communists, those who fought against the occupiers and who soon came into conflict with the ones who had 'taken cover' in Moscow and returned to their countries in the baggage-wagons of the Red Army. Contrary to what Sergo Beria implies, these 'national' Communists were often Bolsheviks of a more fanatical and extremist type than the 'Moscow men.' That, however, was not the case with Gomulka. On 15 May 1944 he wrote a letter to Stalin in which he set out his views on the new Poland. He declared himself against the Communist Party's monopoly, against interference in the affairs of the Peasant Party and against application of the Soviet model to Poland. He made clear that the Polish Communist Party was firmly opposed to collectivisation. *SSSR-Polska. Mekhanizmy podchinenia, 1944-49* (Moscow, 1995).

8. Meaning those who held the conception of a federal Czechoslovakia included in a Central European Confederation. Beneš had advocated, from the end of 1938, expulsion of the Sudeten Germans.

9. This is also the diagnosis of someone close to Beneš. 'For years on end Beneš had disarmed the democrats by making them believe that he had Gottwald in his pocket. He wanted to put Stalin in his pocket likewise.' (Fejtö, op. cit., p. 204). Talking of Beneš, on his return from Moscow in December 1943, Cadogan, the permanent head of the Foreign Office, expressed regret that the Czech leader was 'cosy in an exaggerated sense of his own importance and political wisdom.' Brandes, op. cit. 503.

10. However, Masaryk was much more aware than Beneš of the Soviet danger. He agreed with Sikorski when the latter proposed that they form the Central-European Confederation without delay and face the Great Powers with a fait accompli. But he proved unable to resist Beneš. Brandes, op. cit. 443.

11. Head of the Czechoslovakian Communist Party, Prime Minister in June 1945. He replaced Beneš in 1948.

12. In 1948 Zapotocky headed the trade unions which had been brought under Communist influence and played a decisive role in the Communist coup d'état of February 1948.

13. Svoboda had been sent by Beneš to Istanbul in January 1941 in order to make contact with the NKVD. Brandes, op. cit. 140.

14. General Svoboda commanded the Czechoslovak units on the Soviet front. On Gottwald's orders he had refrained from joining the Party. He was a sentimental Russophile. As Minister of Defence in June 1945 he brought the Army over to the Communist side at the time of the Prague coup. Fejtö, op. cit.

15. A leader of the Czech Social-Democrats, in reality a Communist mole used by Moscow to destroy the Social-Democratic Party. Ambassador to Moscow from July 1941. Head of the government in 1945-46.

16. Khrushchev confirms the increase in Beria's power in the war period. 'During the war Beria had become more brazen than ever. As Stalin lost control and even lost his will during the period of our retreat from the Germans, Beria became the terror of the Party. His growing influence was obvious to me from the composition of Stalin's entourage ... In my view it was during the war that Stalin started to be not quite right in the head. After the war Beria became a member of the Politburo and Stalin started to worry about Beria's increasing influence. More than that, Stalin started to fear Beria ... Stalin feared that he would be the first person Beria might choose [to eliminate].' Khrushchev, op. cit. 310-11.

17. Khrushchev writes that at this time Stalin thought nothing was beyond his power. In October 1945 the Soviets had 477 divisions. They had, altogether, 12,700,000 men under arms and 35,000 combat aircraft. The American military estimated that Stalin would be able to conquer Europe in 45 days. In 1947 the USSR had 173 divisions, the USA only nine. Down to 1948 the Americans considered that, in the event of a Soviet attack, the only option for the West was to abandon the continent and organise resistance in Great Britain and the Middle

East. After 1948 they began to doubt whether it would be possible to defend Great Britain. Ross, M.T. *American War Plans 1945-50* (London, 1996) 5.

18. Khrushchev says that Stalin treated the policy to be pursued in the peoples' democracies as his exclusive domain. 'He jealously guarded foreign policy in general and our policy towards other socialist countries in particular as his own special province.' Khrushchev, op. cit. 316.

19. However, Khrushchev on several occasions accuses Beria of being chiefly responsible for the worsening of relations between the USSR and Turkey.

20. On 20 March 1945, Moscow denounced the 1925 treaty of friendship with Turkey and demanded the return of Kars and Ardahan, together with a revision of the Montreux Convention which gave Turkey control of the Straits. In August-September 1946 the USSR demanded that defence of the Straits be made a joint responsibility of Turkey and the USSR. Backed by the United States, Turkey refused to yield to Stalin's demands. Soviet pressure on Turkey did not cease until May 1953, when the USSR formally renounced its demands.

21. Starting in December 1945 some Georgian historians began publishing a series of articles justifying the USSR's territorial demands for the Turkish provinces on the Black Sea.

22. Between 1945 and 1948 nearly 100,000 Armenians returned to Soviet Armenia. A movement for repatriation was started among other *émigrés*, including the Russians, but the Armenians were the only ones to respond on a large scale, in the hope of recovering the territories lost to Turkey.

23. The USSR began to take an interest in the Kurds in 1942. At the end of 1945 it sought to integrate Kurdish separatism into its own expansionist policy. A Kurdish democratic republic was proclaimed at Mahabad, in northern Iran, in December 1945. Stalin decided to provide military training to Barzani's Kurds, who had taken refuge in Azerbaijan (17 May 1947). Abakumov ordered that Bagirov be kept in the dark about this, which may indirectly confirm that Beria was opposed to this policy. Bagirov would not have failed to tell him everything. Sudoplatov, op. cit. 259-60.

24. On 11 August 1944 Beria sent Stalin and Molotov an analytical report on the world's oil resources. In this he mentioned the solidarity of the British and Americans against any third country. 'The British, and perhaps the Americans as well, are trying to prevent Iran from granting concessions to the USSR for exploitation of oil in northern Iran.' In September 1944 Kavtaradze asked Iran for an oil concession covering Iran's five northern provinces. On October 11 the Iranian government rejected all requests for concessions. The Tudeh (Communist) Party organised mass demonstrations. Tension was extreme. On 2 December the Mejlis adopted a law forbidding the Prime Minister to grant concessions or even to conduct negotiations concerning them. Egorova, N.I. 'Iranskii krisis, 1945-46', *Novaya i noveishaya istoria* 3 (1994) 24-42.

25. In May 1945 the British withdrew their troops from Iran but the Soviets refused to withdraw theirs. This enabled Pishevari to establish a Communist regime in (Iranian) Azerbaijan. In August the Communist Party organised an insurrection.

26. A member of the Comintern and leader of the Democratic Party of (Iranian) Azerbaijan, created on 6 September 1945.

27. Soviet forces left Iran in May 1946 and the republic of (Iranian) Azerbaijan was liquidated by Iranian troops in December.

28. An Iranian nationalist leader. A strong advocate of nationalisation of Iran's oil industry, he was appointed Prime Minister in April 1951 but was dismissed by the Shah in August 1953. His period in power was marked by the collapse of the nationalised oil industry and extreme socialistic demagogy.

29. However, in his confidences to Chuev, Molotov allows a critical attitude to Stalin to show through. 'Stalin said: "Go ahead! Press them for joint possession!" Me: "They [the Western powers] won't allow it." Stalin: "Demand it!" ' And he comments. 'This was our mistake.' Chuev, op. cit. 73. Stalin's aggression is largely corroborated in Volkogonov's study of him.

30. Minister of Foreign Affairs in Russia's Provisional Government of February-May 1917.

31. This forced merger of Communists and Socialists in the Soviet occupation zone brought the division of Germany nearer. 'Our first objective, organising the Soviet occupation zone under effective Soviet control, has been more or less achieved. The time has now come to extend into the Western zones. The instrument for this expansion will be the Socialist Unity Party,' Stalin told the German Communists at the beginning of April 1946. Loth, W. *Stalins ungeliebtes Kind* (Rowohlt, 1994) 59. Mergers like this were imposed by Stalin in all the peoples' democracies. In Hungary Imre Nagy, 'Beria's man,' opposed such a merger. Musatov, V.L. 'Tragedia Imre Nadzha,' *Novaya i Noveishaya Istoria* 1 (1994).

32. Between December 1945 and April 1946 20,000 German Social-Democrats were imprisoned or reported missing.

33. By 2 March 1945, 4,389 enterprises were dismantled and transferred to the USSR: 2,885 in Germany, 1,137 in Poland, 206 in Austria, 11 in Hungary, 54 in Czechoslovakia, and 96 in Manchuria. In March 1946 the Soviet leadership came to realise that this policy was absurd, and thereafter the USSR took reparations from Germany's current production. Knyshevsky, P.N. *Dobycha* (Moscow, 1994).

34. Malenkov headed the committee for restoring the economy of the liberated territories, entrusted with the dismantling of East German industry, and was opposed to Zhdanov, who favoured making deductions from Germany's current production, because he acted as patron to the German Communists. Voznesensky began by favouring the policy of dismantling but at the end of the summer of 1945 he went over to Zhdanov's side. Knight, op. cit. 143; Sulyanov, A. *Arestovat v Kremle* (Minsk, 1991) 224; Loth, op. cit. 67.

35. In the 1960s the Soviets returned some of the works of art they had confiscated to the GDR. However, this question continues to poison German-Russian relations.

36. The Marshall Plan's offer of American economic aid to Europe was extended to the USSR and the states of Central Europe. At first Stalin was tempted to accept the American credits, but he reversed his position when he learnt that 'Marshall aid' was also to be given to the three western occupation zones in Germany. Zubok, *Inside the Kremlin's Cold War* 104-5.

37. By his blockade of Berlin between June 1948 and May 1949 Stalin sought to prevent the Western powers from creating a West-German State. The West replied by supplying the Berliners by means of an airlift. Narinsky, M.M. 'Berlinsky krisis 1948-49', *Novaya i noveishaya istoria* 3 (1995) 16-29.

38. The situation was certainly tempting. At this time the United States had two divisions in Europe, Britain had three and France had two, while the USSR had 65, perfectly equipped, of which 25 were in Germany.

39. This happened: NATO was formed on 4 April 1949.

40. Wilhelm Pieck, the GDR's first president, was nicknamed 'the East German Hindenburg'.

41. Stalin always argued in terms of historical precedents. Many allusions in talks with various interviewers show that he foresaw a German power reconstituted within ten or fifteen years which would start a new war to get Germany's own back.

42. In April 1946 Dekanozov and Vyshinsky suggested in a memorandum to

Stalin that the Soviets should publicly declare approval of the creation of a Jewish state in Palestine. Sudoplatov, op. cit. 292.

43. On 30 April 1948 Gromyko said at the UN: 'The hard sacrifices imposed on the Jewish people in Europe by the Hitlerite tyranny emphasise the need for the Jews to have a state of their own and justify their demand for the creation of an independent Jewish state in Palestine.' Kostyrchenko, op. cit. 11. The state of Israel was proclaimed in May 1948.

44. In July 1947 he appointed one of his best agents, G. M. Heifetz, formerly Soviet vice-consul in San Francisco, to be deputy to Fefer in the leadership of the Jewish Anti-Fascist Committee. Heifetz recorded the requests of numerous Soviet Jews who wanted to fight for the state of Israel. He was arrested soon afterward. (Kostyrchenko, op. cit., p. 42.) The Israelis won their first war with the Arabs thanks to arms sent by Czechoslovakia.

45. The Jewish emissaries received permission to buy arms in Czechoslovakia in December 1947. Raanan, op. cit. 81.

46. On 21 September 1948 Ehrenburg wrote in *Pravda*: 'All free Jews see the Soviet Union as their fatherland ...' This signalled the turn in Soviet policy on Israel after Stalin had realised that the new state would not be a Soviet pawn in the Middle East.

47. In October 1948 Henry Morgenthau, who was the chairman of 'Joint,' said of Israel that it would be 'the only state in the region on which we should be able to count as a solid base in our defence against Communism.' Kostyrchenko, op. cit. 114.

48. The Comintern warned the Yugoslav Communist Party in September 1940 against a tendency to 'overestimate its strength.' Tito was elected General Secretary of the Party in October 1940 *Komintern* op. cit. 430. Relations between Tito and Stalin seemed excellent in May 1946, when Stalin even urged Tito to take good care of himself, since 'I shan't live much longer ... and you will still be there for Europe.' 'Molotov and I are both Serbs,' *he added, more affable than ever. Istoricheskii Arkhiv 2* (1993) 16-35.

49. The British made contact with Tito's partisans in September 1941. They sent two military missions to Tito in the spring of 1943, at the time when Churchill was thinking of landing troops in the Balkans in order to support Allied operations in Italy. British aid to the partisans became regular in June 1943. On Eden's initiative the Soviets sent a military mission to Tito in February 1944. At Teheran, 'the role of Yugoslavia in the war was dismissed by Stalin as of minor importance.' Churchill, op. cit. Vol. V 413. See Wolff, R.L. *The Balkans in Our Time* (NY, 1978) 223; Brandes, op. cit. 207-62.

50. For a long time the only help given by the Soviets to Tito's partisans was broadcasts from the Free Yugoslav radio station in Georgia.

51. The matter of the monarchy had already for a long time been an apple of discord between Tito and Stalin. In October 1947 Tito told Stalin that there could be no question of allowing King Peter to return to Yugoslavia. This unilateral decision angered Stalin. In September 1944 he returned to the charge, explaining to Tito: 'You need not restore him forever. Take him back temporarily, and then you can slip a knife into his back at a suitable moment.' The Yugoslav monarchy was abolished in November 1945. Wolff, op. cit. 232.

52. In August 1944 Churchill had warned Tito similarly: 'I hope that you, Marshal, will think twice before you join such a battle with your sturdy Serbian peasantry.' Wolff, op. cit.. 230.

53. The Yugoslav agrarian reform of August 1945 was not, in fact, aimed at collectivisation. In other spheres, however, the Yugoslav Communists showed themselves to be fanatical Marxists. At the end of the war 82 per cent of their industry had already been nationalised. Yugoslavia was the first of the peoples' democracies to adopt, in April 1947, a five-year plan.

54. Tito dreamt of a federation embracing Bulgaria, Romania and Greece and linked with a northern federation that would unite Poland, Czechoslovakia and Hungary. Raanan, op. cit. 45, 135, 148.

55. Tito seemed an unlikely participant in such a project. At the beginning of 1948 the Communists had urged their Austrian comrades to set up a state under their own control in the Soviet occupation zone, and had also incited the Italian Communists to take power in Northern Italy. On the question of the Balkan Federation and Stalin's break with Tito, see Gibyanskii, L.Ya. 'Kominform v deistvii, 1947-48. Po arkhivnym dokumentam', *Novaya i noveishaya istoria* 1 and 2, 1996.

56. When Bulgaria and Yugoslavia signed a treaty of peace and co-operation in August 1947 without consulting Moscow, Stalin was greatly offended. When, however, the Prime Minister of Romania, P. Groza, offered Hungary a customs union, the prudent Rákosi consulted Suslov, on 19 February 1948, about the line he should take. Suslov replied that such projects were artificial. At the beginning of 1948 Molotov gave his approval to a customs union between Bulgaria and Romania, but Stalin had not been kept informed, and Molotov was obliged to go back on this.

57. The Yugoslav Communist Party had supervised the Albania Communists and considered that relations between Albania and Moscow should be conducted through Belgrade. In the summer of 1947 the Soviet leadership was concerned about this situation and began to establish direct links between Moscow and Tirana. On 19 January 1948, without consulting Moscow, Tito asked the Albanian leaders for permission to install a military base in the south of Albania. They agreed. The Kremlin reacted sharply.

58. The Cominform resolution of 28 June 1948 denouncing Tito called also for collectivisation and the liquidation of small-scale trade and handicraft businesses. It was drafted by Malenkov, Suslov and Zhdanov.

59. The Cominform was set up in September 1947, replacing the Comintern. It was drafted by Malenkov, Suslov and Zhdanov.

60. Khrushchev put the quarrel with Tito down to Stalin's senility.

61. The denunciation of Tito in June 1948 gave the starting signal for the great trials in the people's democracies in which all the victims were accused of having favoured the federation project proposed by Tito.

62. On 23 January 1948, *Pravda* published a statement by Dimitrov advocating an East-European federation. This brought down a furious telegram from Stalin which blamed him for 'facilitating the struggle of the Anglo-Saxon powers' against the peoples' democracies. On 10 February the Bulgarian and Yugoslav leaders were summoned by Stalin and given strong reprimands. In late February, Tito went one stage further by calling for union between Albania and Yugoslavia.

63. Actually, Dimitrov, like Gomulka, at first showed a certain reticence regarding the witch-hunt.

64. Djilas writes of Dimitrov that 'he struck me as being a sick man ... The colour of his skin was either unhealthily red or pale ... This prematurely old, almost crushed man still radiated a powerful conscious energy and vigour.' Djilas, op. cit. 29.

65. Stalin condemned co-operation between Bulgaria and Yugoslavia after having briefly considered a federation between the two countries, in the hope that the Bulgarian Communists, much more obedient to Moscow, would bring the Yugoslavs into line.

66. The archives show that the real reason for the break with Tito was 'his claim to play a leading role in the Balkan and Danubian countries,' to employ the formula that appears in a note from the foreign policy department of the Central Committee, dated 18 March 1948. Gibyanskii, op. cit.

67. She was a minister in the Romanian Communist government from 1947, but was accused of a 'Right deviation' in 1952. Her father and brother lived in Israel.

68. During the entire period of the 'struggle against cosmopolitanism' the Caucasian press, which was controlled by Beria, published no anti-Semitic articles. Raanan, op. cit. 79.

69. On 12 October 1946 Abakumov wrote to Stalin to warn him against Jewish nationalism and the leaders of the Jewish Anti-Fascist Committee. The Committee was accused of echoing the complaints of Jews who returned to liberated Ukraine and Byelorussia to find that they had been despoiled. Sudoplatov, op. cit. 294.

70. Opinions differ on this question. For Khrushchev, 'anti-semitism grew like a tumour inside Stalin's own brain' *Khrushchev Remembers* 269. 'I remember Stalin saying: "The good workers at the factory should be given clubs so they can beat the hell out of those Jews at the end of the working day." ' *The Glasnost Tapes* 263. In 1946, Mikhoels met Zhemchuzhina and spoke about persecution being suffered by Jews at the hands of the local authorities. He asked her advice: should he write to Zhdanov or to Malenkov? Zhemchuzhina replied: 'Stalin concentrates all power in himself and nobody has any influence on him. I don't advise you to write to him. He doesn't like the Jews and he won't help us.' Kostyrchenko, op. cit. 56.

71. Kaganovich told Chuev: 'Stalin was not anti-semitic. He simply found that most of his opponents were Jewish. Stalin took account of my national feelings and was most tactful on this point. One day he even asked me: "Why do you look so sad and gloomy when we laugh at jokes about the Jews, whereas Mikoyan doubles up with mirth when he hears jokes about the Armenians?" ' I replied: "You are well aware of national feelings, Comrade Stalin. The Jews have been thrashed so many times that they have become like a sensitive plant, they clench themselves when they are touched." Stalin said: 'What a good comparison!' He understood me. "Like a sensitive plant," he repeated. That pleased him.'(Chuev, *Tak govoril Kaganovich*, 175.

72. Sudoplatov tells how Khrushchev complained in 1947 about the Jews' return to Kiev: 'They are flying to the Ukraine like crows from Tashkent and Samarkand.' Sudoplatov, op. cit. 294. In 1956 Khrushchev said to Canadian Communists that 'the Jewish problem in the USSR has been artificially manufactured by all sorts of Abramoviches. It's not a problem. It's like a fly on a bull's horn.' *Istochnik* 3 (1994) 96.

73. In 1949, however, in the midst of the campaign against cosmopolitanism, Mekhlis had a heart attack, from which he was to die in February 1953. Supporters of the thesis that Stalin was anti-Semitic, such as A.Vaksberg, consider that Stalin kept a few Jews in his immediate circle so as to camouflage his Judeophobia.

74. Stalin opened the sluice-gates of anti-Semitism in 1948, when he realised that the Jewish Anti-Fascist Committee, far from serving merely as a tool of propaganda abroad, was transforming itself into a veritable representative institution of the Jews in the USSR. In January 1948 he had Mikhoels assassinated. Kostyrchenko, G.V. 'Kampania po borbe s kosmopolitizmom v SSSR', *Voprosy istorii* 8 (1994) 47-60.

75. According to Vaksberg, in March 1948 Stalin's plan was to blame the death of Mikhoels on the Zionists, on the grounds that they resented his refusal to join their conspiracy and his determination to stay an honest Soviet patriot. Vaksberg, op. cit. 177.

76. On 20 November 1948 the Jewish Anti-Fascist Committee was dissolved by Malenkov.

77. Beria's role in creating the Jewish Anti-Fascist Committee must have been known to Soviet Jews and led them to see him as their protector. In May 1944 the

Committee passed to Beria letters from Jews who came from the western regions of the USSR and had fled from the German occupation. On returning to their homes they encountered arbitrary behaviour by the local authorities and the anti-Semitism successfully implanted by the Germans. Beria ordered an inquiry which came to nothing. Kostyrchenko, 'Kampania ...,' op. cit. 51.

78. On 6 November 1946 Zhdanov gave the main speech on the anniversary of the Bolshevik Revolution. He spoke of the atomic threat which the imperialists were hanging over 'the fraternal Slav countries,' and stigmatised calumnies directed against 'the national character of the Russians.' Raanan, op. cit. 40.

79. Vavilov was accused of having a father who had lived in Germany. He was horribly tortured over a period of eleven months, suffering 400 'interrogations'. Albats, E. *La bombe à retardement* (Paris, 1959) 82.

80. Beria offered Vavilov a 'safe job' in an institute supervised by the NKVD. However, Vavilov declined Beria's protection and fell victim to the intrigues of Lysenko and Co. Nevertheless, while Lysenkoism raged, Beria did manage to preserve an oasis of genetic biology camouflaged by the atomic project. Kononovich, A. 'Rezhim sekretnosti kak sposob zashchity ot durakov', *Nezavisimaya Gazeta* 29 July (1997)

81. However, Molotov says that 'Beria was fearful of Voznesensky and very much against him.' Chuev, *Molotov Remembers* 292. At the Plenum in June 1957 Zhukov said: 'The Gosplan affair was to Beria's advantage as he did not want Voznesensky as Deputy Minister, a post he himself coveted. And not only did Malenkov not criticise the way the Gosplan affair was investigated, he gave Andreyev the task of finding further incriminating evidence.' *Istoricheskii Arkhiv* 3 (1993) 22-6; 4 (1993) 74. Also Rudenko's speech, ibid., 1 (1994) 58.

82. Malenkov took umbrage at Kuznetsov's influence with Stalin. He owed his temporary disgrace in May 1946 to intrigues by Zhdanov and Kuznetsov. *Istoricheskii Arkhiv* 1 (1994) 34; Aksyutin, Y. Pyatyi premier', *Rodina* 5 (1994) 82. In July 1948, however, Malenkov recovered his job in the Central Committee's Secretariat and his previous positions, including control of cadres. He also inherited control of ideology after Zhdanov's death in August 1948.

83. Leningrad organised a trade fair in December 1948. Malenkov alleged that the decision to do this had been taken by the RSFSR's Council of Ministers behind the backs of the USSR's Council of Ministers. On 15 February 1949 the Leningrad leaders Kuznetsov, Popkov and Rodionov were dismissed. This was the beginning of the 'Leningrad affair'. On 5 March Voznesensky, who came from Leningrad, was removed from his post of chairman of Gosplan.

84. Malenkov accused them, *inter alia*, of seeking to create a Communist Party for Russia.

85. Khrushchev emphasises the role played by Beria in the 'Leningrad affair'. Voznesensky, he says, in his capacity as head of Gosplan, had resisted Beria's demands and tried to distribute the country's resources more equitably, which meant cutting the budgets of some ministries in Beria's domain. According to Khrushchev, Beria's intimacy with Stalin at this time gave him immense power. Khrushchev, op. cit. 251.

86. Archives and testimonies recently made accessible confirm that the visible instigator of the 'Leningrad affair' was Malenkov, even if Beria cannot have been unhappy at the disappearance of possible rivals. But the truth about this affair may never be known, as Malenkov destroyed the relevant documents after the defeat of the 'anti-Party group' in June 1957. Medvedev, op. cit. 148; *Izvestia TsK KPPS* 2 (1989).

87. Here again, Khrushchev emphasises the role played by Beria. He alleges that Beria used Malenkov to undermine Stalin's confidence in the Leningraders.

Malenkov, being a member of the Central Committee's Secretariat, saw all information that was destined for Stalin and was in a position to manipulate it so as to provoke his anger and suspicion.

88. According to Khrushchev, Stalin wanted to make Voznesensky chairman of the State Bank. *Khrushchev Remembers*, 251.

89. Khrushchev claims that Abakumov was 'Beria's man,' saying that 'he never reported to anyone, not even to Stalin, without checking first with Beria.' Khrushchev, op. cit. 256.

90. In this letter Ryumin told Stalin that Abakumov had covered up a big Zionist plot and murdered a witness, Dr Etinger, at the beginning of 1951. According to Ryumin, this Etinger had hastened the death of Shcherbakov in 1945.

91. Khrushchev and the other members of the Politburo thought that the conflicts between Beria and Stalin were 'lovers' tiffs,' being convinced that Georgians always ended by coming to terms with each other, and so they judged it more prudent to keep good relations with Beria despite his apparent disgrace.

92. A nationalist party formed in 1912. In 1922 the Comintern imposed an alliance between the Chinese Communists and nationalists.

93. This refers to the defeat of the Communist revolt in Canton and the Comintern's break with Chiang Kai-shek in 1927.This defeat was because of Stalin's policy: he was beginning to carry out his turn directed against the 'Rights,' imposing on the Comintern the line of 'class against class.'

94. In 1923.

95. In 1945-46 Chiang was on two occasions invited to Moscow. The Soviets offered to support him if he would turn away from the United States. In July 1946 Moscow gave up the idea of a coalition with the nationalists after the successes won by the Communist forces in May and June. In January 1947 Moscow broke off negotiations with Chiang. On 21 September 1949 the People's Republic of China was proclaimed. For a Soviet point of view on relations with China, see the memoirs of A.M. Ledovsky in *Novaya i Noveishaya istoria* 5 (1990).

96. This view of Mao was shared by numerous American experts, such as Kennan and Acheson, who saw in him a new Tito and never believed in a lasting alliance between Communist China and the USSR. Leffler, op. cit. 250.

97. No Soviet leader appears to have considered Mao a genuine Marxist. Was this due to reports from the Soviet advisers attached to the Chinese Communists? One of them, I. Kovalev, even alleged that Mao would prove unable to resist pressure from 'the right wing of the Chinese bourgeoisie, which has pro-American tendencies.' Zubok, 'To Hell With Yalta', *Cold War International History Project* 6 and 7 December (1992) 25. In 1956 Mao complained that when the Chinese revolution took place Stalin said that it was a false revolution – but 'we did not protest.' ibid. 173.

98. In February 1950 he gave China a meagre loan of only 300,000 dollars.

99. This is confirmed by statements made later by Mao. In 1956 he told a Yugoslav delegation that Stalin had obstructed the Chinese revolution and treated him as a sort of Tito. Stalin, according to Mao, liked to think he was above everyone else and could not stand criticism. ibid. 149-51. In 1958 Mao complained to the Soviet ambassador that he had been 'personally attacked by Stalin, Molotov and Beria during his first visit to Moscow.' ibid. 156.

Chapter 10: Stalin's Grand Design

1. In December 1949 Stalin told Mao: 'Japan has not yet recovered. The United States talk a lot about war, but they fear it. Europe is frightened of war ...' Volkogonov, D. *Sem Vozhdei* (Moscow, 1995) 250. Stalin's remarks, together with

Sergo Beria's account which follows, show that he never believed in a 'threat' from NATO, despite what has long been claimed by historians in the West who want to put the blame for the Cold War on the United States. The prudence that he recommended to his vassals, when he enjoined them not to act openly and to advance slowly, was in line with his usual tactics and did not mean he had abandoned his maximalist objective.

2. Head of the North Korean Communist Party and of the government of North Korea until his death. Some Soviet archives regarding the Korean War were published in the *Cold War International History Project Bulletin*. 5 (1995) and 6-7 (1996). See also, in 6-7, the article by Bazhanov, E. 'Assessing the Politics of the Korean War.'

3. In conformity with Communist etiquette Stalin gave no explicit order, but made his thinking clear in March 1949 in this dialogue with Kim. 'Stalin asks how many American troops there are in South Korea. Kim answers that there are up to 20,000 men ... Stalin asks if there is a national Korean army in the South. Kim answers that there is, the number is around 60,000 men ... Stalin (joking) asks, and are you afraid of them? Kim: No, we are not afraid, but we should like to have naval units. Stalin asks which army is stronger – North or South? Pak Hok-yong answers that the Northern army is stronger ... Stalin says ... that Korea needs to have military planes.' *CWIHPB*, 5 (1995) 5. An agreement for military aid was made in June 1949 between the USSR and North Korea.

4. Down to the autumn of 1949 Stalin restrained Kim's ardour, advising him only to try to organise a rebellion in the South. He thought it possible to proceed to military action from January 1950: the USSR had exploded its bomb in August 1949, the American forces had left South Korea in September, and the Chinese Communists had triumphed without any reaction coming from the USA.

5. Stalin was sure that the United States would not go to war for Korea. He based his confidence on a declaration made by Secretary of State Dean Acheson on 12 January 1950 which did not include Korea in the Americans' defence perimeter in the Pacific. China undertook to send troops if the South Koreans appealed to the Japanese.

6. North Korea attacked on 25 June 1950. On 27 June Truman authorised American forces to go to the aid of South Korea. Seoul fell on 28 June.

7. The Americans counter-attacked after the landing at Inchon on 15 September 1950.

8. On 7 October 1950 General McArthur ordered the United Nations forces to cross the 38th Parallel, which marked the frontier between North and South Korea. As the North Koreans found themselves in a desperate situation, China intervened on 16 October, under pressure from Stalin, who had decided to abandon Kim if the Chinese would not pull his chestnuts out of the fire. The Chinese forces launched a powerful counter-offensive on 25 October. On 1 November Soviet aircraft began to take part in the fighting. On 26 December the Chinese reached the 38th Parallel.

9. A letter from Stalin to Mao at the beginning of October 1950 shows how ready he was to start a third world war: 'The United States may get drawn into a big war for reasons of prestige. China will then be drawn into a war, and the USSR, having a pact of mutual assistance with China, will also enter the conflict. Should we be afraid of this? I think not, because, together, we shall be stronger than the United States and Britain. The other countries of Europe do not constitute any serious military power, in the absence of Germany, which cannot now come to the aid of the United States. If war is inevitable it would be better for it to begin now and not in several years' time, when Japanese militarism has been re-established and is allied to the USA.' Volkogonov, op. cit. 296.

10. On 30 November, Truman indicated that he might consider using nuclear weapons against China. In April 1951 he decided to deploy nuclear weapons in the Pacific theatre of operations. Leffler, op. cit. 406.

11. Negotiations for an armistice in Korea did not get under way till after Stalin's death. Stalin thought it was in his interest to prolong hostilities because, as he told Mao, the war was shaking Truman's regime and damaging the prestige of the Anglo-American forces. *CWIHPB* 6-7 (1996) 34.

12. On 20 August 1952 Stalin said to Chou En-lai that the Korean war had exposed America's weakness. All the Americans had were aircraft and the atomic bomb. The Germans had conquered France in twenty days, but the Americans had still not got the better of little Korea in two years already. *CWIHPB*, op. cit. 13.

13. In November 1950 the American General Staff adopted the Reaper Plan, which foresaw war breaking out on 1 July 1954. For the first time, the American strategists accepted the possibility of a conflict in the near future with the USSR, begun by several simultaneous Soviet offensives in Europe and the Middle East. The Plan assumed active participation by the Federal German Republic in Europe's defence. Even in 1951, however, the Anglo-Saxon strategists continued to think that it would not be possible to defend the Rhine for any length of time and that the West would have to fall back to the Pyrenees and a bridgehead in the south of Italy. Ross, op. cit. 146-7.

14. This is confirmed by a self-justifying note sent by Shtemenko to Khrushchev on 21 July 1953, after Beria's fall. 'Towards the end of May 1952 Beria telephoned me and asked about the situation in the Defence Ministry ... I replied that there were a number of unsolved problems, particularly in the Armaments Bureau ... Beria told me to send a report on these questions to Comrade Stalin and emphasise particularly that the matters which depend on the Armaments Bureau have not been settled. That day, perhaps even the previous day, Comrade Vasilevsky and I had decided to send a report on these problems to comrade Stalin ...' *Voenno-istoricheskii Zhurnal* 1 (1995). In his diaries Admiral Kuznetsov records: 'On 31 July 1952 I drew up a report on the shortcomings in our Navy which were costing us billions. This report was buried in Bulganin's corridors ...' ibid. 2 (1993).

15. Thus, Sudoplatov knew of only one aspect of the negotiations with Germany in July 1941. (Author's note.)

16. It combined enriched uranium and plutonium.

17. At the July 1953 Plenum several speakers accused Beria of trying to get personal control of the arms programme. Malyshev said: 'We have begun to search in the archives and have discovered that Beria signed a number of important decisions without informing the Central Committee or the government, in particular concerning the research plan for 1953, which was linked to a very important centre working on the atomic bomb.'

18. In January 1951 the defence ministers of the peoples' democracies were summoned to Moscow, to be told by Stalin of his intention to occupy all Europe, the Korean war having shown the weakness of the United States. Kaplan, K. *Dans les archives du Comité Central* (Paris, 1978) 165.

19. Twenty thousand German engineers were working in the USSR. Many of them had not gone there voluntarily, having been deported by the Soviets on 22 October 1946. There were among them 300 German specialists in missile technology. Golovanov, op. cit. 372; Zaloga, op. cit. 121. A Soviet defector, Colonel G.A. Tokaev, has left an interesting description of the way in which the NKVD carried off the German scientists. Tokaev, G.A. *Stalin Means War* (London, 1951).

20. The United States had secured the services of 492 German specialists in missile technology. Golovanov, op. cit. 340.

21. One of the most distinguished German 'defectors' to the Soviet camp,

Lieutenant von Einsiedel, Bismarck's great-grandson, explained thus the thinking of the Germans who worked for the USSR: 'They saw in joining the Soviet bloc the only way for Germany to recover a role as Great Power, for its technological superiority would soon ensure for Germany a preponderant position in a union of Soviet states.' Schumann, F. *Der rote Graf* (Frankfurt-am-Oder, 1994)120. Beria was well aware of the attitudes of the Germans in the USSR, as the NKVD produced regular detailed reports on them.

22. The German engineer, Eugen Sanger, proposed in August 1944 to construct a long-range bomber to be operated by jet engines in the upper atmosphere. In 1947, Stalin was still persisting with this project despite the contrary advice of his experts. He even wanted to kidnap Sanger from France. Zaloga, op. cit. 124; Tokaev, op. cit. 93.

23. The Soviets set up the technical commission on rockets in Berlin in May 1945. On 13 May 1946, after the return from Germany of Ustinov's deputy, V.M. Ryabikov, the Soviet government created research centres for studying the technology of long-range missiles. The construction of missiles had become a priority for Stalin. In June 1947 a base for testing the missiles was built at Kapustin Yar. Golovanov, op. cit. 364-77.

24. The first Soviet missile was launched on 29 January 1939. It weighed 210 kilos and had a range of 50 kilometres. The first Soviet missile put into mass production was tested in September 1947. Its range was 280 kilometres. Golovanov, op. cit. 195-403.

25. In 1950 the Soviets began to develop, in parallel, a short-range missile, the R11, having the same characteristics as the R1 but easier to handle; the R5, with a range of 1,200 kilometres; and the R3, with a range of 3,000 kilometres. Zaloga, op. cit. 129.

26. It was in February 1952 that the motor-car works at Dnepropetrovsk was, on Ustinov's order, transformed into a factory for building missiles.

27. In 1949-50 Stalin also wanted to take up the German project for a nuclear super-torpedo to be launched from a submarine. He abandoned it only as a result of Admiral Kuznetsov's stubborn opposition. (Zaloga, op. cit. 173.

28. It made its first flight in 1936. It was the equivalent of America's B-17.

29. At the beginning of 1944 Stalin ordered Tupolev to develop a plane with a range of 3,000 kilometres and capable of carrying five tonnes of bombs. In July 1944 the Soviets got possession of an American B-29 and Stalin told Tupolev to copy it. The first Tu-4 was tested in July 1947. The first bomber regiment began to be operational in 1949. Zaloga, op. cit. 71-2.

30. Nevertheless it greatly alarmed the Americans because it would enable the Soviets to bomb the cities in North America. In 1948 Stalin set up two new programmes intended to give a longer range of action to the Tu-4. Refuelling in flight was successfully tested in June 1949. Zaloga, op. cit. 76-7.

31. The Americans estimated at 20 or 30 the number of atomic bombs possessed by the USSR at the beginning of the 1950s.

32. This was doubtless the Tu-16, which had a range in excess of 5,000 kilometres and could carry three tonnes of bombs.

33. In December 1945 Stalin decided to develop jet-aircraft. In 1946 the LA-120R was given auxiliary rocket engines and reached the speed of 805 kilometres per hour, and the prototypes of the MiG-9 were tested successfully. In March 1948 Stalin asked Korolev to write a memorandum on the respective advantages of jet bombers and missiles. Golovanov, op. cit. 364sqq.

34. And lessons from the Korean War. The MiG-15s shot down a good few American B-29s. If the latter had not been escorted by fighters the American losses would have been still greater.

35. The Soviets began in 1949 to build an anti-aircraft missile, the R-101, which reproduced the Germans' *Wasserfall*. Zaloga, op. cit. 130. The R-113 succeeded this. Moscow's defences against attack from the air were considered operational by the West in 1954. Isby, DC. *Weapons and Tactics of the Soviet Army* (Jane's, 1988) 365.

36. This bomber, the M-4, was ordered by Stalin in March 1951. The prototype was completed and tested in January 1953. The plane's performances were considered disappointing. It was not able to make the trip to and from the USA without in-flight refuelling. Nevertheless, it was shown off at the military parade of 1 May 1954 and gave the Americans a shock. Zaloga, op. cit. 83.

37. The R-5, which began to be mass-produced at the beginning of 1953 had a range of 1,200 kilometres.

38. In August 1952 the American strategists estimated that the forces of NATO were now capable of resisting a Soviet assault on Europe. Leffler, op. cit. 463. This was without taking account of America's superiority in nuclear weapons. In 1953 the United States already possessed 2,350 atomic bombs, whereas the USSR had only a few dozen – a hundred according to some estimates. True, the Soviets had a thousand bombers while the Americans had no more than 750, of which the 85 B-365 were able, flying from the USA, to reach any place in the USSR. Zaloga, op. cit. 79.

39. The Americans began a programme of anti-aircraft defence in 1949, when the Soviets had exploded their atomic bomb. The system did not take shape until the summer of 1954. Zaloga, op. cit. 78.

40. In November 1951 the United States and Yugoslavia signed a pact of mutual assistance. Tito made an informal agreement with Montgomery whereby he was to deploy a corps of the Yugoslav Army to defend the Ljubljana Gap in the event of a Soviet attack. The NATO strategists hoped that the West would manage to hold on to southern Italy with the help of the thirty Yugoslav divisions. Ross, op. cit. 147; Leffler, op. cit. 418-9.

41. In the spring of 1952 Stalin ordered that a hundred divisions of jet bombers be created. A Soviet officer relates that 'we wondered what motivated this decision and concluded that our country was actively preparing for war.' Ostroumov, N.N. 'Armada, kotoraya ne vzletela', *Voenno-istoricheskii Zhurnal* 10 (1992) 39-40. At the same time Stalin ordered the development of a new inter-continental turbo-jet bomber, the Tu-95. It was tested in November 1952 and its performance found disappointing. Zaloga, op. cit., 85-6.

42. Khrushchev thought otherwise. 'In the days leading up to Stalin's death we believed that America would invade the Soviet Union and we would go to war. Stalin trembled at this prospect. How he quivered! ... He knew that we were weaker than the United States.' Khrushchev, *The Glasnost Tapes* 100. However, when he wrote to Mao on 27 December 1952 about the possibility of an American offensive in Korea, Stalin added: 'It is perfectly possible that these plans may be modified by the Eisenhower administration in the direction of reducing tensions on the Korean front.' *CWIHPB* 6-7 (1996) 80. Stalin would seem not to have taken seriously Eisenhower's tough talk. In a speech in Warsaw on 20 March 1956, at the Sixth Plenum of the Polish United Workers' Party, Khrushchev said of Stalin that if he had lived a little longer he might have started another war. *CWIHB* 10 (1998) 46.

43. Starting with the Korean War, the Americans had made a powerful effort at re-armament, which was to bear fruit in 1954, especially in Europe. American military expenditure had increased fivefold in two years. The Americans had begun making plans to defend the east bank of the Rhine. In January 1953 America's war production was seven times as great as in June 1950. Leffler, op. cit. 386-490.

44. Numerous converging testimonies describe the ambience of this period between the 19th Party Congress and Stalin's death. Vaksberg says that it was 'pervaded by a terrifying atmosphere in which new catastrophes were anticipated on a far more nightmarish scale than anything that had gone before.' Lieutenant N.N. Ostroumov, deputy director of the operational department of the Air Force, writes: 'Public consciousness was gradually being prepared ... for war.' (Holloway, op. cit. 292.

45. No American plan ever provided for a preventive strike, even when the USSR possessed a nuclear arsenal. America's plans provided only for massive-scale use of atomic bombs in the event of a Soviet attack, so as to compensate for NATO's inferiority in conventional weaponry. Ross, op. cit.

46. This was a constant feature in Stalin's behaviour. In January 1950 he advised Kim Il-sung to await an attack by South Korea and organise a counter-offensive that would lead to conquest of the South. *CWIHPB*, 5, (1995) 8. These instructions explain why Communist propaganda did its utmost to show that the Korean War, regardless of the facts, had been begun by the South.

47. This refers to the famous note of 10 March 1952, in which Stalin called for a Germany neutral and reunited.

48. In his speech Malenkov recalled Stalin's phrase at the 18th Party Congress; 'We are not afraid of threats from the aggressors and we are ready to return twice over any blows that the warmongers may inflict on us ...' But he also declared: 'Peaceful coexistence between capitalism and communism is perfectly possible, and even co-operation between them if they wish it.'

49. In April 1952 the East German leaders received Stalin's order to form an army without delay. In July Stalin called on them to hasten the building of Socialism in the GDR.

50. This prospect was taken very seriously by the American strategists. General Bradley warned in 1950 that if Russia were to control the whole continental mass of Eurasia, Soviet imperialism would have a base from which to rule the whole world. Leffler, op. cit. 370.

51. On 21 March 1953, a few days after Stalin's death, Beria proposed that the 'great construction works of Socialism' be wound up. He won his point on 27 May, when the Council of Ministers decided to abandon 'the construction of irrigation systems and canals which are not required in the immediate interests of agriculture.'

52. This was a project aimed at 'proletarianising' what was left of the peasantry by making the muzhiks quit their huts and plots of land in order to enter 'agro-towns.'

53. A Russian satirical writer who excelled in mocking the Tsarist bureaucracy. According to Mirtskhulava, Malenkov and Molotov tried to use the fiasco of the 'agro-towns' to get Khrushchev dismissed, but Beria intervened and dissuaded Stalin from punishing him.

54. The campaign for regrouping the collective farms began at the beginning of 1950.

55. Marr was Lysenko's equivalent in linguistics. He prophesied that with the coming to power of the proletariat and its 'dialectical materialist thinking' spoken languages would disappear, being replaced by a 'single language' of pure 'classless thought,' 'freed from natural matter.' Thom, *La Langue de bois* (Paris, 1987) 108-13.

56. According to Molotov, 'Beria himself was much afraid of Stalin.' Chuev, op. cit. 339.

57. 'How could so intelligent a man do all those dreadful things?' Khrushchev asks himself in his memoirs. Khrushchev's reflections frequently echo remarks by Beria which have been recorded here. It is clear that the men close to Stalin must have spent much time analysing the tyrant. Khrushchev's de-Stalinisation resulted from the de-Stalinisation that took place while Stalin was still alive, in the narrow circle of those around him, for which Beria was doubtless the driving force.

58. 'After the defeat of Hitler, Stalin believed that he was in the same position as Alexander I after the defeat of Napoleon – that he could dictate the rules for all Europe. Stalin even started believing that he could dictate new rules to the whole world ... Stalin no longer had the capacity for restraint.' Khrushchev, *The Glasnost Tapes* 144.

59. 'Those last years with Stalin were hard times. The government virtually ceased to function. Stalin selected a small group which he kept close to him at all times, and then there was another group of people whom he didn't invite for an indefinite period in order to punish them. Any one of us could find himself in one group one day and in the other the next.' *Khrushchev Remembers* op. cit. 296-7.

60. One of the young wolves promoted by Stalin at this time, the First Secretary in Byelorussia, P.K. Ponomarenko, recalled that 'Stalin could do nothing against the quartet made up of Beria, Malenkov, Bulganin and Khrushchev. They were inseparable and dominated the Politburo. Even Stalin could do nothing against them.' *Sovershenno sekretno* 3 (1990) 13.

61. This speech is a real masterpiece of its kind. Beria quotes Stalin, but each of his quotations bears a double meaning. 'No state, the Soviet Union included, says Comrade Stalin, can ... embark on great construction works which cost tens of billions, reduce the prices of consumer goods ... and at the same time increase its armed forces and develop its military industry. It is easy to understand that so foolish a policy would bring any state to bankruptcy ... Whereas the imperialist cannibals are engaged in inventing various means of exterminating the flower of mankind ..., in our country, as Comrade Stalin says, man is the most precious capital and the happiness and well-being of the people are the chief concern of the state.'

62. This resolution, prepared by Stalin in deepest secrecy, revealed the existence of a 'Mingrelian nationalist organisation' whose aim was 'to liquidate the Soviet regime in Georgia with the help of the imperialist powers.' By launching this affair, Stalin sought to destroy the base of the pyramid of Beria's power through extirpating his supporters in his fief, Georgia. Fairbanks, C.H. 'Clientelism and Higher Politics in Georgia, 1949-53', *Transcaucasia* (Ann Arbor, 1983).

63. 'After the 19th Party Congress, Stalin created among the new Presidium members some wide-ranging commissions to look into various matters. In practice these commissions turned out to be completely ineffectual because everyone was left to his own devices ... Everyone in the orchestra was playing on his own instrument any time he felt like it and there was no direction from the conductor.' Khrushchev, op. cit. 197.

64. Rukhadze was given the task of looking into the connections between the Mingrelians in Georgia, Turkey and Paris. He accused Beria of organising a conspiracy against Stalin in Georgia and of concealing the fact that he was Jewish. Sergo Beria says that the Russian anti-Semites spread a rumour that this father was a Jew, a rumour which still circulates. Sudoplatov, op. cit. 321sqq.

65. Beria's men in Georgia were dismissed, having been accused of maintaining connections with the Georgian *émigrés* in Paris. The Mingrelians were alleged to have wished to secede from the USSR in order to join with Turkey against it.

66. In Stalin's dossier on the Mingrelians, Gegechkori appeared as an 'American spy' who maintained a network of agents in the USSR.

67. 'Beria turned the whole thing round in his favour ... Beria assigned himself to go to Georgia and administer the punishment of the Mingrels, the imaginary enemies.' Khrushchev, op. cit. 312.

68. The head of the Georgian Government, Bakradze, a longtime supporter of

Beria, tried to make his listeners forget that fact when he spoke at the Plenum of 2-7 July 1953, giving the version favoured by Khrushchev: 'We can judge how much a careerist Beria was by his ignoble conduct in connection with the so-called affair of the Mingrelian nationalists. He knew from the start that it was a provocation, he knew that he had composed dossiers compromising honest men, it was he who had protected the provocateurs Mgeladze and Rukhadze, he knew that they were torturing honest officials and yet, down to the last moment ... he did nothing. On the contrary, he poured oil on the flames, as can be seen if you read his speech to the April 1952 Plenum of the Georgian Communist Party.'

69. After the Congress, Stalin unloosed a violent diatribe against the men around him. He accused Molotov of having, when drunk, promised the British ambassador to publish the British press in Russian, and also of having proposed to create a Jewish autonomous republic in the Crimea, etc. He accused Mikoyan of engaging in subversive activity, treated Voroshilov as an idiot who had sold himself to the British, and attacked Beria on account of Tito's treason. For some time already Stalin had been calling his lieutenants 'British spies.' *Den* 8 (1993); *Istoricheskii Arkhiv* 4 (1993) 40. The advice he gave to Chou En-lai on 19 September 1952 reflects his paranoid state of mind: he warned him of British and American agents in China's state apparatus who might even resort to poisoning the country's leaders. *CWIHPB* 6-7 (1996) 19.

70. In his 'secret' report to the 20th Party Congress Khrushchev gave the same interpretation. 'He had a Presidium of 25 members elected so as to eliminate the old members of the Politburo and bring in less experienced persons who would flatter him even more. We may even suppose that he did this intending to get rid of the former members of the Politburo, wiping out the traces of those reprehensible acts of his which we are talking about today.'

71. Slansky was accused, *inter alia*, of having tried to shorten the life of Comrade Gottwald 'with the help of doctors with a shady past'.

72. In June the head of the Georgian MGB, N. Rukhadze, was dismissed. He had led the attack on the Mingrelians but Stalin blamed him for not getting satisfactory results.

73. On 11 July a secret instruction from the Central Committee ordered the MGB to 'unmask the group of doctors who are trying to make attempts on the lives of the leaders of Party and State.' Kostyrchenko, op. cit. 305.

74. This was the case with Professor L.B. Berlin, old Professor M.I. Pevsner, who died under torture, and B.S. Levin, who were all arrested in January 1952 as 'British spies.' For the 'Doctors' Plot' see Kostyrchenko, op. cit. 289-365.

75. Egorov was arrested in October 1952 and accused of having 'incapacitated Maurice Thorez,' assassinated Dimitrov (who died of cirrhosis of the liver in 1949), Zhdanov and Shcherbakov, and sabotaged the detoxification cure of Vasili Stalin.

76. He examined Stalin at the beginning of 1952 and advised him to retire. Stalin saw this as a plot to put him out of power. Furious, he resolved to do without doctors in future. He summoned Ignatiev in January 1952 and told him that unless he unmasked the American terrorists among the doctors he would join Abakumov in prison. Vinogradov, who was 70 years old, was arrested in November 1952.

77. Professor Vinogradov did indeed resist for a long rime before confessing, when half-dead, that he had been recruited by the British agent M. Kogan, a Kremlin doctor who had died of cancer in 1951, and had then worked for the agent Pevsner, who had died in 1952.

78. A. Vaksberg alleges that huts had been under construction in Siberia since February 1953. Naturally, the deportation had to be requested by the Jews themselves. A number of prominent Jews, such as Vannikov, had agreed to sign a letter to this effect, which was to have appeared in *Pravda*. Vaksberg, op. cit. 259-70.

79. Nina Beria had also a nephew, Teimuraz Shadia, who, having been taken prisoner by the Germans, became a commander in the Georgian national legion which fought alongside the Wehrmacht. Later he joined the SS and combated the resistance in France. After the Liberation he was helped by Gegechkori and discreetly picked up in Paris in 1945 by Sharia, on Beria's orders. Stalin learnt of this from Rukhadze in December 1951 and had him arrested. He was accused of serving as liaison agent between the Mingrelian nationalists protected by Beria and Gegechkori. (Stolyarov, *Palachi t zherty*, pp. 230-231.)

80. 'All of us around Stalin were under a death sentence,' wrote Khrushchev, recalling the twilight of Stalin's regime. (Khrushchev, op. cit., p. 307.) 'Beria used to express his disrespect for Stalin more and more boldly. He used to talk more candidly with Malenkov than with me, but he often spoke disrespectfully and even insultingly about Stalin in my presence.' Khrushchev, op. cit. 314. And Kaganovich told the July 1953 Plenum that 'he said to us: "Stalin doesn't realise that if he tried to arrest me the Chekists would organise an insurrection." '

81. [Stalin] 'knew Beria would stop at nothing to save himself ... He saw that Beria was thorough but not completely sincere.' Chuev, op. cit. 234-6.

82. A rumour soon ran than Beria had poisoned Stalin. Molotov said that he boasted of this to him. 'While on the rostrum of the Mausoleum ... on 1 May 1953 ... he said "I did him in." ' Chuev, op. cit. 237.

83. According to a witness 'Malenkov ... motioned with his finger (signalling that the delegates should not accept Stalin's resignation). Mikoyan was very calm. Molotov said: "Comrade Stalin, you are our teacher." Stalin, cupping his hand behind his ear, as he did not hear well in his last years, barked: "All of us here are the pupils of Lenin. Of Lenin! Lenin!" ' Zubok, op. cit. 73.

84. He was exiled in July 1952 and arrested in December. In May 1952 Malenkov had given Stalin a report showing that the Ninth Directorate of the KGB, headed by Vlasik and responsible for protecting members of the government, devoured enormous quantities of caviare, which they recorded as having been consumed by members of the government. Stalin, furious, at once dismissed Vlasik. Aksyutin, Yu. 'Pyatyi premier', *Rodina* 5 (1994) 83.

85. Volkogonov gives this version of the facts. Stalin dismissed those who were with him on 1 March at 4 a.m. He had a heart attack the same day, at about 8 p.m. His guards found him lying on the ground at 11 p.m. They summoned Beria, who said to them: 'You can see that Comrade Stalin is sleeping deeply. Leave, and don't disturb him.' Only on 2 March did the members of the Presidium call on Stalin, accompanied by doctors. Volkogonov, op. cit. 315-28.

86. 'No sooner had Stalin fallen ill than Beria started going round spewing hatred against him and mocking him.' Khrushchev, op. cit. 318.

87. 'As soon as Stalin died, Beria was radiant. He was regenerated. To put it crudely, he had a housewarming over Stalin's corpse before it was even put in its coffin.' Khrushchev, op. cit. 322.

88. He died at 9.50 p.m. An hour earlier the leading circle of the Presidium had already assembled and decided to appoint Malenkov head of the government. Stalin was thus dismissed while still alive. *Istochnik* 1, 106-11.

89. There were many casualties.

90. Beria said: 'Workers in industry and agriculture and our intelligentsia can work confidently in peace, certain that the Soviet government will take care to defend scrupulously the rights provided by the Stalin Constitution.' Mikoyan told the July 1953 Plenum: ' I said to him after his speech: "You mentioned the rights enjoyed by every citizen which are guaranteed by the Constitution. From anyone else's lips that would be a political declaration: from the lips of the Minister of Internal Affairs it is a programme for action." And he replied: "I will carry it out." '

Chapter 11: The First de-Stalinisation

1. Malenkov took the chair at the presidium of the Council of Ministers, assisted by four deputy chairmen: Beria, Molotov, Bulganin and Kaganovich. The presidium was reduced to ten members: Malenkov, Beria, Molotov, Voroshilov, Khrushchev, Bulganin, Kaganovich, Mikoyan, Saburov and Pervukhin.

2. 'I remember Stalin ... sitting at the table ... and expounding on who would succeed him ... He dismissed Beria. Beria could not be chairman of the Council of Ministers because he was not a Russian. He was Georgian. The position needed a Russian.' Khrushchev, *The Glasnost Tapes* 38-9.

3. The alliance between Beria and Malenkov did not deceive Khrushchev: 'I could see Beria neither liked nor respected Malenkov ... Beria once said to me something like the following: "Listen, about this spineless fellow Malenkov. He's nothing but a billy goat. He'll bolt if you don't hold him on a leash. But he's a Russian and very proper. He may come in handy." ' Khrushchev, op. cit. 313. Molotov had the same opinion. 'Malenkov and Beria were supposedly great friends, but I never believed this.' Chuev, op. cit. 335.

4. This version differs fundamentally from that given by Khrushchev. *Khrushchev Remembers*, 319. He claims that he said to Bulganin, while they were watching by Stalin's death-bed, that they must prevent Beria from taking over the MVD.

5. At the July 1953 Plenum Khrushchev said: 'I am profoundly convinced that Beria is not a Communist and never has been ... I have often heard his ideas about the Party and the building of Socialism. The last occasion was when we were discussing the situation in the GDR and in Hungary. We considered that they should avoid having the same leader as head of the Party and chairman of the Council of Ministers. During the discussion Comrade Rákosi said: "I need advice. What questions should fall within the competence of the Council of Ministers and what questions should be dealt with by the Central Committee?" ... To which Beria replied, with contempt: "What are you saying about the Central Committee? It is for the Council of Ministers to decide everything, and the Central Committee can busy itself with cadres and propaganda." This statement left me flabbergasted. It meant that Beria rejected the leading role of the Party ...'

6. 'That scoundrel Beria liked to say that the Central Committee should busy itself solely with propaganda and to some extent with cadres. That was what the reduced the Central Committee's role to' said Kaganovich at the same Plenum.

7. At the July 1953 Plenum, Beria's colleagues strove to show that all the reforms proposed by Beria were motivated by his desire to take power. In the same breath they accused him of having sought to liquidate the Communist regime and destroy the Soviet state, thereby admitting that he had a political plan. Molotov: 'Beria had secretly formed a plan aimed at preventing the building of communism in our country, that's obvious.' Kaganovich: 'He wanted to undermine the doctrine of Marx-Engels-Lenin-Stalin. It was not just that he underestimated it, he was completely ignorant of it ... This was not a deviation from the Party line, it was a dangerous counter-revolutionary plot against the Party and the government.' Khrushchev: 'He wanted to strengthen his authority and then completely destroy the Party.' Andreev: 'He had a plan to liquidate the Soviet regime in our country, down to the smallest details.'

8. Mikoyan reported to the July 1953 Plenum what Beria had said to him about reforming the MVD. 'We must restore the rule of law, the situation in the country is intolerable. We have a large number of prisoners, we must release them and stop sending people to the camps. We must reduce the numbers of the MVD; we are not protecting people but spying on them. We must change that, send these guardians to Kolyma and keep only two or three for the members of the government.' Even Khrushchev admits the initiative taken by Beria in the rehabilitations. 'Some people had been freed right after Stalin's death. Beria had raised the matter.' Khrushchev, *The Glasnost Tapes* 40.

9. In a report by Kruglov and Serov, dated 22 August 1953, sent to Khrushchev and Malenkov, concerning the state of the MVD after Beria, we read: 'Our intelligence network abroad suffered considerable damage as a result of Beria's criminal order given in April of this year to recall to Moscow, simultaneously, all the residents in foreign countries, which paralysed our intelligence activity.' *TsKhSD*, f.89, 18-28.

10. Beria's activity in this sphere can be seen especially in the disappearance of mentions of Stalin in the media. The Stalinist official film-maker Chiaureli had painful experience of this. When he reported triumphantly that he had finished a scenario about the great Stalin he was subjected to this tirade: 'Forget that filth! Stalin was a swine, a scoundrel, a tyrant! He made us live in fear! He terrorised the entire people! His power was based solely on fear! Thank God that we are free of him!' Krotkov, Y. in Nekrasov, op. cit. 257.

11. Beria was accused of having wanted to rewrite history so as to make his own role more prominent while knocking Stalin off his pedestal. At Beria's trial Sharia testified that Beria had called for revision, not only of the history of the Second World War but also of events preceding the war. He ridiculed the war with Finland, adding that 'if Stalin had listened to him we would have avoided that mistaken war.' *Istoricheskii Zhurnal* 10 (1991) 57.

12. Pospelov wrote the secret report read by Khrushchev at the 20th Congress.

13. Actually, the Presidium had approved this measure on 3 April 1953. But Beria acted on his own in announcing it in *Pravda* of 4 April in the form of a communiqué from the MVD. 'He had his reasons for freeing people. He impressed them with the notion that it was Beria who had restored them to liberty – not the Party, not the Government, but Beria,' Khrushchev observed acidly, at the July Plenum.

14. Ryumin wanted to present Abakumov as the head of a Zionist organisation within the MGB and tortured him at length in hope of getting a confession. However, Abakumov held out and confessed nothing. Stolyarov, op. cit. 53.

15. This was how, at the July Plenum, Kaganovich described this activity of Beria's: 'Hardly had Stalin died when Beria started to discredit him ... The first stage in his attack on the Party was an attack on Stalin. On the morning of Stalin's death, when he had not yet been buried, Beria began preparing for his coup d'état. He set himself to spread horrible stories about Stalin, telling each of us things that Stalin had allegedly said about us, and claiming that Stalin had waged war against him, Beria ... He depicted Stalin in the most offensive terms. All this on the pretext that we must now begin a new life ... Beria made a sensation out of the freeing of the doctors.'

16. On 10 April a resolution of the Presidium put an end to the Mingrelian Conspiracy. Beria at once sent Dekanozov to Georgia to release the Mingrelians.

17. On 24 March, Beria submitted to his colleagues a report showing that there were 2,526,402 prisoners in the Gulag, of whom 221,435 were 'state criminals.' He proposed that one million be set free, advocating an amnesty for all those whose sentences were for less than five years and all who had been sentenced for economic crimes and for certain war crimes. On 27 March the 'Voroshilov' amnesty was announced, prepared by Beria: 1,178,422 prisoners were released. GARF, f. 9414, op. 1, 507.

18. Resolution of 28 March 1953. The transfer of the Gulag to the Ministry of Justice was annulled after Beria's fall, and it was not till 1997 that this measure was adopted in Russia.

19. 'After Stalin's death, the struggle between Beria and Malenkov became a fight to the death, even though the impression was given, outwardly, that the Beria-Malenkov tandem was as friendly as ever and that the two were preparing to govern the country together.' Krotkov in Nekrasov, op. cit. 255.

20. Ignatiev was dismissed from the Central Committee on 28 April 1953. Beria proposed that the Party's Central Commission investigate his past activities. After Beria's fall, on 7 July Ignatiev recovered his post with the Central Committee. He had been made head of State Security in July 1951, on Malenkov's recommendation. An inquiry into Ignatiev's doings would be aimed directly at Malenkov, who had been involved in the affair of the Jewish Anti-Fascist Committee and in the persecution of the Jewish doctors.

21. A fraudulent trial held in 1930, the intention of which was to intimidate the technical intelligentsia. Khrushchev admits, in the *Glasnost Tapes* 40, that 'we were afraid to lift the curtain and look backstage.'

22. After Beria had been eliminated, Khrushchev would in 1954 continue to pose as the defender of Communist orthodoxy against Malenkov. On 26 July, for instance, he said: 'Those who expect a change in the Party's orientation, abandonment of Stalin's policy, are cherishing unfounded hopes.' Aksyutin, Yu. 'Pyatyi premier', *Rodina* 5 (1994) 87.

23. 'Beria showed particular determination in this sphere,' Molotov noted at the July 1953 Plenum.

24. 'This was the first time in the history of our multi-national state that experienced cadres devoted to our Party were dismissed for no other reason than that they were Russian,' lamented the First Secretary of the Byelorussian Communist Party, Patolichev, at the July 1953 Plenum.

25. The head of the Ukrainian Communist Party, Kirichenko, speaking at the July Plenum, reported with indignation that Beria's men 'advised that we bring back some White Guards from Paris, that we recall from emigration some people who had fled from western Ukraine.' Beria had appointed to head the MVD in the Ukraine one Meshik, a person 'with a dubious past and whose father, mother, brother and aunt live in New York.'

26. In January 1944 the Union Republics had been authorised to create territorial army formations. *Istoricheskii Arkhiv* 1 (1992) 63.

27. At the July Plenum Sneckus, the head of the Lithuanian Communist Party, testified: 'Last year we made it clear that we could not put Lithuanian Communists in the MGB because of all those uncles and aunts living abroad who could not be overlooked (Lithuania has 800,000 *émigrés* out of a population of 2,700,000). Ignatiev decided not to do it. But then along came Beria, who put on a generous air and announced a new approach.'

28. 'It was without the Central Committee's knowledge that he took the decision to explode the hydrogen bomb,' said Malenkov at the July Plenum.

29. It does seem, though, that none of the members of the Presidium was aware of the decision to test the H-bomb in July 1953. Malenkov was taken by surprise when, after Beria's fall, Kurchatov and Malyshev asked him for authority to go ahead with the test that had been arranged. Golovanov, op. cit. 457-8.

30. At the July Plenum this pro-Western attitude of Beria's was regarded as particularly suspect: 'We have, so far, no proof that Beria was a spy in foreign pay, but that is not what is essential. It is clear that he was in the service of the bourgeoisie, that he tried to corrupt the leadership of the Bolshevik Party by inculcating alien habits and methods ... He wanted to replace Marxism with Americanism ... His anti-Soviet plans assumed support from the imperialist camp ... because he could count only on support from enemies of the Soviet Union in order to seize power.' (Molotov.)

31. Molotov was to explain later his similarity of view with Khrushchev on the German question: 'Khrushchev had a streak of Russian patriotism about him which Beria lacked.' Chuev, op. cit. 337.

32. Khrushchev said at the July 1953 Plenum: 'It was the discussion of the German question that best unmasked Beria as a provocateur and imperialist agent. He proposed that construction of socialism be given up in the GDR and that concessions be made to the West ... He said: "We must create a democratic and neutral Germany" ...'

33. Khrushchev at the July Plenum: 'Beria went so far as openly to propose abandonment of the building of Socialism in East Germany and tried in a thousand ways to get our Party to agree to giving up its German policy. He used all his eloquence to convince us that the USSR should be satisfied with seeing Germany unite in a bourgeois state, that a bourgeois Germany need not be closely linked with the other imperialist states, that today a bourgeois Germany could exist that was neither aggressive nor imperialist. It became clear that Beria was not a Communist.'

34. 'When we discussed these problems Beria denounced Comrade Ulbricht and the other German comrades in terms that made us blush,' said Khrushchev at the July Plenum.

35. Policy to be followed in the GDR was the theme of the famous session of the Presidium held on 27 May 1953. It resulted in a resolution of the Council of ministers, adopted on 2 June, entitled 'Measures for improving the political situation in the GDR.'

36. Hence Molotov's embarrassed explanations at the July Plenum 'This letter showed that Beria wanted to establish close relations with "Com. Tito" and "Com. Rankoviæ," in other words to come to an understanding with Tito and Rankoviæ, who were acting as enemies of the Soviet Union. Is it not clear that this letter, written without the Government's knowledge, was another shameless attempt to stab the Soviet state in the back and openly serve the imperialist camp?' The letter was said to have been seized from Beria when he was arrested.

37. This meeting took place on 13 June 1953. Actually, Malenkov made a vehement criticism of Rákosi's policy but Beria was more precise in his demands. 'The Red Army will not stay in Hungary forever,' he told Rákosi. Consequently it was necessary to 'stop beating prisoners ... change policy regarding the middle peasants,' abandon the policy of all-out armament and leave the economy to the Government. *CWIHPB*, 10 (1998) 85.

38. Malenkov reported to the July Plenum the words of A.Z. Kobulov to a colleague in the MVD: 'You can't imagine the power that Beria has. He is boldly smashing the entire old order, not only in our country but also in the democratic countries.'

39. Caused by Ulbricht's decision to increase work-norms without increasing wages.

40. When Mossadegh came to power, the Americans proposed to reply with a coup d'état that would put the Shah back on the throne. My father warned the Presidium. He did not have time to do anything. One month after his fall, Mossadegh was overthrown by the Americans and imprisoned and the Shah returned to the throne. The leaders of the USSR, delighted at having got rid of my father, paid no attention to what was happening in Iran. (Author's note.)

41. Bakradze, the head of the Georgian Government, told the July Plenum that 'Beria did considerable damage in our country. He protected a large number of bourgeois, anti-Soviet, nationalist intellectuals who thought they were free to do as they liked.'

42. Lyudvigov was a coward and testified against my father at his trial, reporting all his diatribes against Stalin – which did not save him from getting a

15-year sentence, whereas others, braver than he, got only ten years. (Author's note.)

43. This is still an open question. According to some sources Beria was bringing MVD troops to Moscow when he was overthrown. Kaganovich said at the July Plenum: 'We have to recognise frankly that if the Presidium had delayed only a little the elimination of Beria, even if by no more than a few days, we should have had a very different situation here today.' In October 1957, when Zhukov was removed, Khrushchev said: 'Beria, too, had elite forces. He had brought these assassins to Moscow before his arrest and we may wonder whose heads would have been cut off, had he not been unmasked.' Khotimskii, N. 'Poslednaya opala marshala Zhukova', *Vechernaya Moskva*, 23 February 1995.

44. Malenkov exclaimed at the July Plenum: 'Fortunately we needed only three months in order to discern the true face of this adventurer ... and to crush this viper, to finish with this tumour, this rottenness which was poisoning the healthy atmosphere of the monolithic Leninist-Stalinist collective.'

45. Molotov's analysis at the July Plenum is interesting: 'He wanted to exploit Comrade Stalin's death for his subversive purposes. Like our enemies abroad, he counted on the Party being weakened at that time, on disarray in our ranks, so that he could profit by that situation ... He thought that the period following Stalin's death would be the best moment to strike at the Party.'

Chapter 12: Fall

1. On the eve of his arrest, 25 June, Beria submitted a proposal to the Central Committee that Ignatiev's responsibilities in the 'Leningrad affair' be investigated. Pikhoia, 'XX s'ezd,' 9th broadcast, *Radio Svoboda*, 1996.

2. Was Sergo Beria deceived? Khrushchev made a point of spreading the rumour that Beria was dead so as to prevent any attempt at a coup by his supporters. A recent testimony does confirm the version according to which Beria was assassinated at his home on the morning of 26 June. The witness was A. Vedenin, who claims to have been one of the group sent to liquidate Beria. Gorzhainov, S. 'Operatsia Osobnyak,' *Nedelya* 22 (1997) 26-7). As we shall see, versions of Beria's death are numerous and quite contradictory.

3. Here is one, contributed by Khrushchev soon after the event, at the July Plenum. 'When we realised that we were dealing with a provocateur there were no more differences among us, and the division that he had tried to sow in our minds ceased at once ... We organised a session of the Council of Ministers to which were invited those members of the Central Committee's Presidium who were not already members of the Presidium or the Council of Ministers. Then we opened the session of the Central Committee's Presidium – and came out with it there and then, telling Beria to his face, "you are a provocateur, you are not a Communist and the cup is full." You should have seen that hero: he at once shrank himself, perhaps worse (laughter) ...'

4. When Zhukov fell into disgrace, Khrushchev ceased to mention his role in the arrest of Beria.

5. However, according to an account given by the journalist F. Burlatsky, Zhukov said, when asked by Khrushchev to take a hand in the arrest of Beria: 'I've never been a gendarme, but this task I'll perform with pleasure. What do I have to do?' The writer claims that 'Zhukov hated Beria.' Burlatskii, 'Posle Stalina,' *Novy Mir* 10 (1988). In his account given to Chuev, Molotov mentions Zhukov's presence at the head of the military men who came to arrest Beria.

6. A. Mirtskhulava, the First Secretary of the Georgian Communist Party from April 1953, gives valuable evidence which throws light on the background to the

July Plenum: 'Molotov objected to the way Khrushchev wanted to arrest Beria. He proposed that his case be discussed in his presence at a session of the Politburo. Khrushchev refused this, saying: "If we raise the matter in his presence he will kill us. No, we must lock him up first and talk about his case afterward." Molotov was faced with an accomplished fact.'

7. Recalling Zhukov's disgrace in his memoirs, Khrushchev uses an enigmatic phase which could well refer to the 'designs' mentioned here. 'He didn't correctly understand his role as Minister of Defence and we were compelled to take action against him in order to prevent him from going through with certain schemes which he had concocted.' Khrushchev, op. cit. 162. The minutes of the sessions of the Presidium on 19 and 26 October 1957, when Zhukov was condemned, have now been declassified, so that we know that Zhukov was accused by Khrushchev and Suslov of seeking 'to deprive the Party of control over the Army and aiming to establish a dictatorship of one man in the armed forces.' *CWIHP* 10 (1998) 19.

8. Zhukov was found guilty at the October 1967 Plenum of having 'violated the Leninist principles governing leadership of the armed forces and following a policy of eliminating the Party's organs and the Military Councils.' *Istochnik* 3 (1995) 80. He was censured for having formed an elite force of 2,500 men without the Party's knowledge. Only Shtemenko knew about it. Khotimskii, N. 'Poslednaya opala marshala Zhukova', *Vechernaya Moskva* 23 February 1995.

9. This version does not square with most accounts, even if we, rightly, distrust Khrushchev's. Kaganovich and Molotov told Chuev how Beria had been arrested at an emergency session of the Politburo (Kaganovich's expression) on 26 June. The Politburo members set out their complaints. Beria tried to defend himself but was arrested. Kaganovich also tells how Khrushchev informed him of his intentions: 'He did not say anything about Beria being a spy, but he did say that he was intriguing to overthrow the Politburo and take power ... We were not shown, neither me nor Molotov, any documents proving that Beria was linked with the imperialist states.' Chuev, *Tak govoril Kaganovich* 45-66. It is clear that Beria could not have been arrested without Malenkov's agreement. The only question is: why and when did Malenkov line up with Khrushchev?

10. According to Mirtskhulava, 'Molotov was indignant because Beria was being blamed for having so many mistresses. "Stick to political charges. We've no need of those stories," he said. Molotov was also reserved concerning the charges of espionage. "I regard Beria as an agent of imperialism. Agent does not mean spy." ' Chuev, *Molotov Remembers* 341.

11. On the eve of the Plenum Mirtskhulava was summoned to the Kremlin. 'I found Bagirov there but I was not allowed to talk to him alone. Khrushchev said to me: "We have arrested Beria." I almost fainted. I thought Beria must have done something wrong, that he'd killed someone, in short, that he had deserved this arrest. Then Khrushchev said: "We were friends and all that, but then he wanted to take all power." He added: "Tomorrow Malenkov will speak at the Plenum: You, too, must make a speech." I said: "Nikita Sergeevich, I can see that I shall not be allowed to say anything good about him, but I don't know anything bad." "Pull yourself together, a Georgian must speak." I had to embroider the theme "Beria as agent of imperialism," when they had no proof and didn't even dare say which state Beria was supposed to be an agent of.'

12. Khrushchev writes: 'After Beria's trial we had found ourselves trapped by the version which we'd created in the interests of protecting Stalin's reputation.' Khrushchev, op. cit. 351. Beria's trial was also the first stage in an offensive aimed against Malenkov and the beginning of the Party organs' campaign to get their own back on the Government apparatus.

13. The investigation stage of the trial was entrusted to Procurator General

Rudenko, one of Khrushchev's men. According to witnesses, Beria behaved provocatively, confessing only to what the Public Prosecutor's office had succeeded in proving and showing emotion only when his family was mentioned. The dossier filled 19 volumes. The trial took place on 18-22 December. The interrogations were transmitted directly to the Kremlin. Six of Beria's confederates were tried with him and executed: V. Dekanozov, V. Merkulov, L. Vlodzimirsky, P. Meshik, S. Goglidze and B. Kobulov.

14. General Moskalenko was given the task of arresting Beria by Khrushchev.

15. According to Mirtskhulava, 'it was a double that they tried in place of Beria, who himself had died long before. They were obliged to fabricate a trial owing to reactions abroad. Khrushchev couldn't hold his tongue in any company. He admitted that the trial was a complete fake. I heard him say: "Had we kept him alive he could have been able to recruit everybody, to escape and to have us all shot. That's why we executed him soon after arresting him." ' The trial was needed because it gave Khrushchev weapons to use against his rivals in the struggle for power. But the Beria affair is still on many respects a taboo subject and the mystery which still surrounds it remains to be cleared up.

16. Beria had indeed kept contact with the *émigré* Menshevik government in Paris. He reported to Stalin on the meetings between his emissaries and the Georgian emigration. His report on Sharia's visit to Paris in the spring of 1945 has been declassified. GARF, *Osobaya papka Stalina*, f. 9401, op. 2, d. 93.)

17. On 17 January 1954, doubtless following this episode, Nina Beria wrote a letter to Khrushchev: ' ... I was Beria's wife for more than 30 years, I bore his name, and it is a terrible accusation that is now brought against me. Especially as, until this arrest, I was devoted to him ... I did not guess that he was an enemy of the Soviet regime, as I was told during the investigation. It must be said that I was not the only one to be deceived in him, since the Soviet people likewise put their trust in him ... During the whole period of our life together I saw him only at meals and at night, and when in 1942 I learnt that he was unfaithful to me I refused to be his wife any more. In 1943 I went to live in the country, then I lived with my son's family. I several times proposed that we divorce, so that he might marry a woman who, perhaps, would love him ... He refused, saying that without me he would go off the rails. Believing in the power of habit, I stayed: I wanted him to have a family in which he could find rest ... I knew nothing at all about this immoral conduct, which was revealed to me only during the investigation. I had thought that his infidelity was episodic and I partly blamed myself for it as, at that time, I was often absent, visiting my son, who was studying in another town ... I am already old and I have only one request, to be allowed to busy myself with my son's family, my three grandchildren, who need a grandmother ... If the Procurator finds me guilty of a crime against the Soviet Union, I ask only that the verdict be prompt. I have not strength left to withstand the physical and moral suffering that I am enduring. Only a quick death will deliver me from these woes, and that is what I expect from your humanity and your compassion.' *Istochnik* 2 (1994) 76.

18. Allusion to the letters written by Beria in captivity: see n. 19.

19. In the first days of his imprisonment Beria wrote several letters to the Presidium in which he recalled the bonds between him and the others and the services he had rendered to the Soviet Union. He asked to be assigned to some obscure job in which he could still be useful. He pleaded with Malenkov to look after his mother, his wife and his son, Sergo. According to the latter, these letters are forgeries, fabricated by Khrushchev in order to compromise his rivals through their relations with Beria. However, the letters give the impression of being authentic documents. The last of them is dated 1 July. It contains an urgent call for help: 'Comrades, they are going to murder me without trial or judgement, after five days in prison. Please intervene at once.' It is probable that Beria was executed soon after this. *Istochnik* 4 (1994) 3-14.

20. He did not change his opinion on this point. In his memoirs he declares that Beria's triumph would have meant the end of the Communist regime. 'In the late 1940s I was already convinced that when Stalin died we would have to do everything possible to prevent Beria from occupying a leading position in the Party. I even thought that Beria's success might mean the failure of the revolution. It might mean losing the gains of the revolution. It was already my opinion that Beria might divert the progress of the country from a Socialist to a capitalist course ... I'd known for a long time that he was no Communist.' Khrushchev, op. cit. 314-35.

21. After the war and until Khrushchev's reign most Soviet ambassadors were trained at the Higher School of Diplomacy which had been established in 1939. Khrushchev, and Brezhnev after him, preferred to give diplomatic posts to Party functionaries, often men who were in disgrace. Karyakin, op. cit. 131.

Chapter 13: Who Was My Father?

1. In one of her few interviews with the press, given when she was 86, Nina Beria showed herself a perfectly orthodox Stalinist. 'The Soviet regime had to win. Stalin wrote that there were enemies of socialism. These enemies really existed ... Stalin wanted to build a great and powerful state. And he succeeded. To be sure, there were victims'. The fate of her husband inspired these thoughts: 'One should think only of one's homeland. I have before me the example of Stalin, Ordzhonikidze, Beria and others. They thought they were fighting for the happiness of all the peoples. And what was the result? They gave nothing to their homeland and their own people. The other peoples rejected them. It can be said that these Georgians died without a homeland'. (*Sovershenno sekretno*, no. 9. 1990.) Nina Beria's remark reported here by her son is revealing: for her, politics was totally blocked out by the national element.

2. It was in 1939 that the Soviet archives were entrusted to the NKVD.

3. Beria's interest in Flavius Josephus is revealing, in the same way as his interest in Saakadze and Mazeppa. Flavius Josephus, a Jewish historian born in AD 37, author of *The Jewish War*, visited Rome under Nero and became convinced that Roman power was irresistible. He tried to dissuade his compatriots from revolting against it, and became a Roman citizen after the fall of Jerusalem in AD 70. Beria's historical preoccupations seem to have constantly revolved around the problem of relations between natives and empires, of the sincerity of a native's rallying to an empire which has enslaved his homeland, of the definition of treason.

4. Flavius Josephus wrote in the introduction to his work: "If you find something wrong in what I say ... when I lament over my country, be so good, disregarding the rules of historiography, as to excuse this sorrow of mine. For, of all the cities that fell to the Roman power, it was our own that, after attaining the highest degree of happiness, fell into the greatest misery ..." (I-11.)

5. Grand Prince of Moscow, died 1341. He was entrusted with collecting the tribute on behalf of the Khan of the Golden Horde, and used the money he made to buy land. He doubled the area of the Moscow principality.

6. Mongol conqueror, d. 1227. He invaded northern China, Central Asia and South Russia.

7. Genghis Khan's grandson. He led the Mongol conquerors into Europe, 1240-1242.

8. Shah Abbas came to the throne of Persia in 1587. Aware of the danger of a Russian thrust towards the Caucasus, he followed a policy of enslaving Georgia.

9. Saakadze took refuge among the Turks and fought for their Sultan, but fell victim to palace intrigues and was beheaded by order of the Sultan in 1629.

10. Hetman (chief) of the Ukrainian Cossacks. He organised the anti-Polish insurrection of 1648. Thanks to an alliance with the Crimean Tatars, he won victories over the Poles. Betrayed by the Tatars, he sought support from the Sultan in 1651, then in 1654 signed a treaty of union with Russia which made him a vassal of the Tsar.

11. Mazeppa was appointed Hetman of the Ukraine in 1687 with the Tsar's support. Fabulously rich, he favoured the arts, opened schools, established printing presses and built many churches. He tried to reconcile the interests of the Ukraine, his own interests and those of Moscow. He helped Peter the Great in his expedition against the Turks in 1696 and became a valued adviser to the Tsar. He took advantage of the Swedish King Charles XII's expedition against Poland in 1703 to obtain from the Tsar authority to unify the Ukraine. In 1708, however, Mazeppa went over to the side of Charles XII, Peter's sworn enemy. In exchange for this alliance the Swedes undertook to deliver the Ukraine from Russian domination. After the Swedes' defeat at Poltava in June 1709 Mazeppa took refuge in Moldavia (which then belonged to the Ottoman Empire) and died there in September 1709.

12. By this treaty, which was sought by King Irakli II, Russia established a protectorate over Georgia – promising, at the same time, not to interfere in that country's internal affairs. The Russians did not greatly trouble themselves to defend Georgia. In 1785 King Irakli II was obliged to pay tribute to the Muslims and in 1795 Tbilisi was sacked by Aga Mehmed Khan. In 1801 the entire royal family of Georgia was deported to Russia, and Georgia was annexed to the Tsar's empire.

13. The Cossacks did indeed soon perceive the inconvenience of the alliance with Russia. The Tsar's officials started to interfere in their affairs. In 1656 Russia let her Ukrainian allies down by signing the Treaty of Vilna with Poland. Comparing his Swedish with his Russian allies, Khmelnitsky observed that only the Swedes were men of honour. He died in 1657 (Subtelny, *Ukraina istoria*, p. 178.)

14. Russian and Ukrainian historians still argue today over the content of the 1654 treaty of Pereyaslav. For Russians it signified the attachment of the Ukraine to the Russian Empire: for the Ukrainians it meant only alliance against Poland, or a protectorate.

15. In the summer of 1918.

16. Kaganovich made the same observation at the July 1953 Plenum: "Beria showed the greatest contempt for the trade unions. Every comrade remembers how he described the trade unions as a rabble of good-for-nothings and incompetents ... He had no use for the working class."

17. He was president of the ephemeral Constituent Assembly which was dissolved by the Bolsheviks in January 1918, two days after it met. The SR (Socialist Revolutionary) Party was formed in 1902. It advocated a direct transition from feudalism to socialism and the use of terrorism.

18. Head of the SR's fighting organisation. In 1908 his links with the Okhrana were exposed.

19. Stolypin was assassinated on 14 September 1911 by a police provocateur who was anxious to rehabilitate himself in the eyes of his revolutionary comrades. Stolypin had already been in disgrace for some time, particularly because he had warned the Tsar against Rasputin.

20. An admirer of Garibaldi, Chavchavadze was the leader of Georgia's literary and national movement at the end of the 19th century. He was murdered in 1907, apparently by bandits.

21. An agent of the Okhrana from 1910. Malinovsky was the spokesman of the Bolshevik group in the 4th Duma. Lenin thought highly of him for his extremism and refused to listen to those in his circle who warned him against the eloquent Malinovsky. He did not yield to the evidence until 1918, when the Tsarist police archives were opened. Malinovsky was executed in November 1918. (Volkogonov, *Sem' vozhdei* pp. 36-37.)

22. In March 1915 the Germans began to finance the revolutionary movements in Russia. The ex-socialist Parvus was a supplier to the German Army and their contact with the Bolsheviks. On 8 January 1918 von Schanz, director of the Reichsbank in Berlin, wrote to Trotsky that "50,000,000 gold roubles have been put at the disposal of the People's Commissars". In June 1918 an additional payment of 40,000,000 Reichsmarks was made to the Bolsheviks. (Volkogonov, *Lenin*, pp. 202-232.)

23. Yet such an assault took place in 1922-1923 in Georgia as in the rest of the USSR. In the spring of 1924 Patriarch Ambrose was sent to prison for having sought help for Georgia from the Western powers at the Genoa Conference in April 1922. (Duguet, *Moscou et la Géorgie martyre*.)

24. Opposed to the reform of Orthodox texts and rituals introduced by Patriarch Nikon in 1652, Archpriest Avvakum launched the schism of the "Old Believers" and was burnt alive in 1682.

25. Stolypin's reform, introduced in autumn of 1906, attacked the village commune with a view to creating a class of peasant small property-owners.

26. Molotov said of Beria that he "was a man who, so to speak, was not so much a man of the past as a man of the future ... Among the reactionary elements he was the activist. That's why he strove to clear the way for a return of private property. Anything else lay outside his field of vision. He did not avow socialism." (Chuev, ed., *Molotov Remembers*, op. cit., p. 232.)

Bibliography and Sources Used
for the Notes

Sources

Afanasyan, S., *L'Arménie, l'Azerbaïdjan et la Géorgie, de l'indépendance à l'instauration du pouvoir soviétique* (Paris, 1981).

Albats, E., *La bombe à retardement* (Paris, 1959).

Albert, Andrzej, *Najnowsza historia Polski* (London, 1994).

Aleksandrov-Agentov, A.M., *Ot Kollontai do Gorbacheva* (Moscow, 1994).

Allen, W.E.D., *Caucasian Battlefields* (Cambridge, UK, 1953).

Allilueva, S., *Twenty letters to a Friend* (London, 1967).

Anders, W. *Mémoires* (Paris, 1948).

Badstübner, R., and Loth, W., *Aufzeichnungen zu Deutschlandpolitik* (Berlin 1994).

Baring, A., *Der 17. Juni 1953* (Stuttgart, 1983).

Bedell-Smith, W., *Trois années à Moscou* (Paris, 1950).

Berezhkov, V., *Kak ya stal perevodchikom Stalina* (Moscow, 1993).

Bohlen, C., *Witness to History* (New York, 1973).

Boldin, V., *Krushenie pedestala* (Moscow, 1995).

Bordyugov, T.A., and Matveev, T.F., *SSSR Polsha, Mekhanizm podchineniya 1944-1949* (Moscow, 1995).

Borshchagovsky, A., *Obvinyaetsa krov* (Moscow, 1994).

Brandes, D., *Grossbritannien und seine osteuropäischen Allierten 1939-1943* (Munich, 1988).

Bryant, Arthur, *The Turn of the Tide 1939-1943* (London, 1958).

Bugay, N.F., *Iosif Vissarionovich Lavrentyu Berii: ikh nado deportirovat,* (Moscow, 1992).

Bungert, H., *Das Nationalkomittee und der Westen* (Stuttgart, 1997).

Chebrikov, V.M., *Istoriya sovetskikh organov gosudarstvennoi bezopasnosti,* Vysshaya krasnoznamennaya shkola (KGB, Moscow, 1977).

Chuev, F.I., *Molotov Remembers* (Chicago,1993).

Chuev, F.I., *Tak govoril Kaganovich* (Moscow, 1992).

Churchill, W., *Memoirs*, vol. V (London, 1959).

Courtois, S., *Le Livre noir du communisime* (Paris, 1997).

De Gaulle, C., *Mémoires de Guerre* (Paris, 1959).

De Lastours, S., *Toukhatchevski* (Paris, 1996).

Djilas, M., *Conversations with Stalin* (London, 1963).

Duguet, R., *Moscou et la Geórgie martyre* (Paris, 1927).

Duplan, C., and Giret, V., *La vie en rouge* (Paris 1994).

Erkin, F.C., *Les Relations turco-soviétiques et la question des Détroits* (Ankara, 1968).

Fejtö, F., *Le coup de Prague* (Paris, 1976).

Fest, J., *Plotting Hitler's Death* (New York, 1996).

Gilbert, M., *Churchill* (London, 1991).

Gnedin, E., *Vykhod iz labirinta* (Moscow 1995).

Golovanov, Ya., *Korolev. Fakty i mify* (Moscow 1994).

Gorodetsky, G., *Soviet Foreign Policy* (London, 1994).

Grose, P., *Gentleman Spy* (London, 1995).
Hayter, W., *The Kremlin and the Embassy* (London, 1966).
Hilger, G., and Meyer, A., *The Incompatible Allies* (New York, 1953).
Hixson, W.L., *George F. Kennan* (Columbia U.P., 1984).
Holloway, D., *Stalin and the Bomb* (Yale U.P., 1994).
Isby, D.C., *Weapons and Tactics of the Soviet Army* (Jane's, 1988).
Kaplan, K., *Procés politiques à Prague* (Paris, 1980), and *Dans les archives du Comité Central* (Paris, 1978).
Karski, J., *The Great Powers and Poland* (University Press of America, 1995).
Karyagin,V.V., *Diplomaticheskaya zhizn za kulisami i na stsene* (Moscow, 1994), and Kavkazskie *Orly* (Moscow, 1993).
Khlevnyuk, O., *Stalin i Ordzhonikidze* (Moscow,1993), and *Le Cercle du Kremlin* (Paris, 1995).
Khrushchev, N., *Khrushchev Remembers* (1971), and *The Glasnost Tapes* (1990).
Kirilina, A., *L'Assassinat de Kirov* (Paris, 1995).
Knight, A., *Beria* (Princeton U.P., 1993).
Knyshevsky, P.N., *Dobycha* (Moscow, 1994).
Komintern i vtoraya mirovaya voina (Moscow, 1994).
Komplektov, V.G., *Polpredy soobshchayut* (Moscow, 1990).
Kostyrchenko, G., *V plenu krasnogo faraona* (Moscow, 1994).
Kvashonkin, A.V., *Bolshevistkoe rukovodstvo, Perepiska 1912-1927* (Moscow, 1996).
Lebedeva, N.S., *Katyn* (Moscow, 1994).
Leffler, M.P., *A Preponderance of Power* (Stanford, 1992).
Leonhard, W., *The Kremlin since Stalin* (Oxford U.P., 1962).
Lobanov, M., *Stalin* (Moscow, 1995).
Loth, Wilfried: *Stalins ungeliebter Kind* (Rowohlt, 1994).
Malcolm, N., *Bosnia: A Short History* (Papermac, 1996).
Malenkov, A.G., *O moiom otse Georgii Malenkove* (Moscow, 1992).
Manvelishvili, A., *Histoire de la Géorgie* (Paris, 1951).
Medvedev, R.A., *All Stalin's Men* (Blackwell, 1983).
Mix-Yacoub: *Le Problème du Caucase* (Paris, 1933).
Mouradian, C., *L'Arménie* (Ramsay, 1990).
Mühler, P.von zur: *Zwischen Hakenkreuz und Sowjetstern* (Düsseldorf, 1971).
Nekrasov, V.F., *Beria: Konets karery* (Moscow, 1991).
Nekrich, A., *L'Armée rouge assassinée* (Paris, 1968).
Raack, R.C., *Stalin's Drive to the West, 1938-1945* (Stanford, 1995).
Raanan. G., *International Policy Formation in the USSR* (Archon, 1983).
Romanov, A.I., *Nights Are Longest There* (Boston, 1972).
Ross, S.T., *American War Plans 1945-1950*, (London, 1996).
Rzheshevsky, O.A., *Vtoraya Mirovaya Voina* (Moscow, 1995).
Schoenhals, K.P., *The Free Germany Movement* (Greenwood Press, 1989).
Schumann, F., *Der rote Graf* (Frankfurt-am-Oder, 1994).
Semiryaga, M., *The Winter War* (Moscow, 1990).
Sherwood, R., *Roosevelt and Hopkins* (New York, 1948).
Shreider, M., *NKVD iznutri* (Moscow, 1995).
Simonov, K., *Glazami cheloveka moego pokoleniya* (Moscow, 1990).
Sinitsyi, Yelisei T., *Rezident svidetelsvuet* (Moscow 1996).
Sudoplatov, P. and A., *Special Tasks* (London, 1994).
Stalin's Letters to Molotov 1925-1936 (1995).
Stolyarov, K., *Palachi i zhertvy* (Moscow, 1997).
Sturua, N.I., *Voprosy novoi i noveishei istorii Gruzii* (Tbilisi, 1987).
Subtelny, O., *Ukraina Istoria* (Kiev, 1994).
Sulyanov, A., *Arestovat v Kremle* (Minsk, 1991).

376 *Beria, My Father*

Thom, Françoise: *La Langue de bois* (Paris, 1987).
Tokaev, G.A., *Stalin Means War* (London, 1951).
Tomarkine, A., *Les Lazes en Turquie* (Istanbul, 1995).
Vaksberg, A., *Stalin against the Jews* (New York, 1994).
Volkogonov, D., *Lenin* (Moscow, 1994), and *Sem Vozhdei* (Moscow, 1995).
Wittlin, T., *Beria* (London, 1973).
Wolfe, B.D., *Lénine, Trotski, Staline* (Paris, 1951).
Wolff, R.L., *The Balkans In Our Time* (New York, 1978).
Wolton, T., *La France sous influence* (Paris, 1997).
Yakovlev, A.N., Pikhoya R., and Geishtor, A., *Katyn* (Moscow, 1997).
Yakovlev, A.N., and Pikhoya, R., *Lubyanka* (Moscow 1997), and 1941 god (Moscow, 1998).
Yakovlev, A.S., *Tsel zhizni* (Moscow 1987).
Zaloga, S.J., *Target America* (Presidio, 1993).
Zhukov, G.K., *Vospominaniya i Razmyshleniya* (Moscow 1995).
Zubok, V., and Pleshakov, C., *Inside the Kremlin's Cold War* (Harvard U.P.,1996).

Archives

GARF, *Osobaya papka Stalina f.r.* – 9401, op. 2, d. 64-235.
GARF, F 9414 c., op. 1, 136, 137, 138, 143, 144, 152, 507, c662, 663, c664 UC.
GARF, *Prikazy MVD*, 9401c., 1a, 515, 1g 521.
RTsKhIDNI, f.85, o.413, d.29, f.85, o.29, d.414.
TsKhSD, f. 89, 18-9, 18-28
Archives of the Georgian emigration (on microfilm at BDIC).

Articles and monographs

Aksyutin, Yu., 'Poslevoennye nadezhdy', *Rodina* 12 (1993).
Aksyutin, Yu., 'Pyatyi premier', ibid. 5 (1994).
Bazhanov, E., 'Assessing the politics of the Korean War', in Cold War International History Project, Woodrow Wilson Center for Scholars, Washington D.C., 6 and 7 (1996).
Beichman, A., 'In A Smoke-Filled Room … Stalin's Defeat in 1944', Working Papers in International Studies, Hoover Institution, August 1994.
Blagoveshchensky, F., 'V gostyakh u P.A. Sharii', *Minuvshee*, 7 (1989).
Bobylev, P.N., 'K kakoi voine gotovilsa generalny shtab RKKA v 1941 godu?', *Novaya i Noveishaya Istoria* 6 (1995).
Bugay, N.F., 'Pogruzheny v eshelony ….', *Istoria SSSR* 1 (1991).
Burlatsky, F., 'Posle Stalina', *Novy Mir* 10 (1988).
Cold War International History Project, op. cit., 5 (1995); 6 and 7 (1996); 10 (1998).
'Communist Takeover and Occupation of Georgia', Special Report No. 6 of the Select Committee on Communist Aggression, House of Representatives, 31 December 1954.
Egorova, N.I., 'Iranskii krisis 1945-1946', *Novaya i noveishaya istoria* 3 (1994).
Fairbanks, C.H., 'Clientilism and Higher politics in Georgia, 1949-1953', *Transcaucasia* (Ann Arbor, 1983).
Fenton, B., 'The Secret Strategy to Launch Attack on the Red Army. Churchill's Plan for Third World War against Stalin', *Daily Telegraph* 1 October (1998).
Fis, R., 'Ot Voroshilova do Gracheva', *Moskovskie Novosti* 17 (1995).
Gibyanskii, L. Ya., 'Kominform v deistvii 1947-1948, Po arkhivnym dokumentam', *Novaya i Noveishaya istoria* 1 and 2 (1996).

Gorzhainov, S., 'Operatsia 'Osobnyak'', *Nedelya* 22 (1997).

Khotimskii, N., 'Poslednaya opala marshala Zhukova', *Vechernaya Moskva* 23 February (1995).

Konstantinov, A., 'Zakhar – rezident Lavrentia', *Sovershenno sekretno* 10 (1993).

Kononov, A., 'Rezhim sekretnosti kak sposob zashchity ot durakov', *Nezavisimaya Gazeta* 29 July (1997).

Korobochkin, M., 'Opozdavshie'', *Rodina* 12 (1995).

Kostyrchenko, G.V., 'Kampania po borbe s kosmopolitizmom v SSSR', *Voprosy Istorii* 8 (1994).

Koval, K.I., 'Zapiski upolnomochennogo GKO na territorii Germanii', *Novaya i noveishaya istorii* 3 (1994); 2 (1995).

Kutuzov, V., 'Mertvaya petlya Abakumova', *Rodina* 3 (1998).

Labonne, R., 'Les pays turcs et la politique orientale des Soviets', *Revue de Paris* 15 August (1922).

Ledovsky, A.M., 'Memoirs', *Novaya i noveishaya istoria* 5 (1990).

Lunin, E., 'Palachi', *Leningradskaya Pravda* 5 August (1989).

Matrosov, V., 'Na pervom rubezhe voini', *Krasnaya Zvezda* 5 June (1991).

Musatov, V.L., 'Tragedia Imre Nadzha', *Novaya i noveishaya istoria* 3 (1995).

Narinsky, M.M., 'Berlinskii krisis 1948-1948', *Novaya i noveishaya istoria* 3 (1995). 'I.V. Stalin i M. Torez', ibid. 1 (1996).

Nicolaysen, Helena: 'SD Networks in Transcaucasia and Stalin: the Rise of a Regional Party Functionary (1887-1902)' (Hoover Institution, 1991).

Ostroumov, N.N., 'Armada, kotoraya ne vzletsela', *Voenno-istoricheskii Zhurnal* 10 (1992).

Parsadanova, V.S., 'Armia Andersa na territorii SSSR', *Novaya i noveishaya istoria* 5 (1998).

Parsadanova, V.S., 'K istorii Katynskogo dela', ibid. 4 (1990).

Parsadanova, V.S., 'Vladislav Sikorski', *Voprosy Istorii* 9 (1994).

Pechenkin, A.A., 'Gosudarstvenny Komitet Oborony v 1941 godu', *Otechestvennaya Istoria* 4 and 5 (1994).

Sarnov, B., 'My sideli u Lili Brik', *Literaturnaya Gazeta* 26 February (1997).

Sepilov, D.T., 'Vospominaniya', *Voprosy Istorii* 3, 4 and 5 (1998).

Sheinis, Z., 'M.M. Litvinov', *Sovershenno sekretno* 4 (1992).

Sipols, V. Ya., 'Tainye dokumenty strannoi voiny', *Novaya i noveishaya istoria* 3 (1993).

Soskov, E., 'Ne v svoikh sanjakh', *Rodina* 5 (1997).

Swietochowski, T., 'Russkii Azerbaidzhan', *Khazar* 3 (1990).

Vitkovski, A., 'Chechevitsa', *SB* 1 and 2 (1996).

Wehner, M., 'Le soulèvement géorgién', *Communisme* 42, 43 and 44 (1995).

Zhukov, Yu.,'Borba za vlast v rukovodste SSSR v 1945-1952 godakh', *Voprosy istorii* 1 (1995).

Zubok, V., 'Soviet Intelligence and the Cold War: the 'Small' Committee of Information, 1952-1953', in Cold War International History Project, op. cit. (1992).

Zubok, V., 'To Hell with Yalta', ibid. 6 and 7 (1996).

Journals

Den, no. 8, February 1993.

Duel, no.25, 1997.

Istochnik, nos. 1. 2, 3 and 4, 1994; nos. 1,2 and 3, 1995; no.6, 1996.

Istoricheskii Arkhiv, no. 1, 1992; nos. 2,3,4,5 and 6, 1993; nos. 1 and 6, 1994, no.2; 1995; no.4, 1996.

Izvestia TsK KPSS, nos 2 and 7, 1989; No. 9, 1990; no. 1/2, 1991; nos. 3 and 4, 1991.
Novaya i Noveishaya Istoria, no. 2, 1993.
Obshchaya Gazeta, 22-28 July 1994.
Otechestvennaya Istoria, no. 2, 1995.
Otechestvennye Arkhivy, no. 3, 1994.
Rodina, no. 5, 1992; no. 2, 1993, nos. 3 and 4, 1994.
Sovershenno Sekretno, nos. 3, 8 and 9, 1990; no.4, 1992.
Vechernii Klub, 22 December 1992.
VIP, no. 9, 1995.
Voenno-istoricheskii Zhurnal, no. 7, 1959; nos. 1, 3, 5, 6 and 7, 1990; no. 10, 1991; no. 12, 1992; nos. 1, 2, 3, 4, 5 and 6, 1993; nos. 4, 6 and 8, 1994; nos. 1 and 2, 1995.
Voennyi Arkhiv, 1993,
Voprosy Istorii, no. 1, 1993.

Biographical Notes

(covering the period dealt with in the book)

Abakumov, V.S., Head of special section of State Security in 1941, head of Smersh in April 1943, Minister of State Security in May 1946, dismissed 4 July 1951, shot December 1954.

Aleksandrov, G.F., Head of Agitprop September 1940 to September 1947, candidate member of Central Committee in 1946 Stalin Prizewinner in 1943, Academy member in 1946. He fell into disgrace in 1955.

Andreyev, A.A., Politburo member 1932 to October 1952. Chairman of Central Control Commission in 1930. Secretary of Central Committee, 1935. Vice-Chairman of Council of Ministers 1946-1953. Chairman of Party Control Commission 1939-1952. Chairman of Committee on Collective Farm Affairs under the Council of Ministers, September 1946 to February 1947. Member of the Presidium of Supreme Soviet from March 1953.

Aryutyunov, G.A., First Secretary, Communist Party of Armenia, 1937 to 1953.

Bagirov, D.A., Head of Cheka in Azerbaijan. First Secretary of Azerbaijan Communist Party in 1937. Member of Central Committee in March 1939, Expelled from Presidium 17 July 1953. Expelled from CPSU, March 1954. Shot May 1956.

Bakradze, V.M., Second Secretary of Georgia Party in 1936-1937. Candidate member of Central Committee, head of Georgian Government in 1953.

Budenny, S.M., Soviet Marshal (1935), Vice-Commissar of Defence in August 1940, Commander-in-Chief of the Army of the Caucasus in April-May 1942, commander of Cavalry in 1943.

Bulganin, N.I., Cheka functionary 1918-1922, Director of State Bank 1938-1941, Politburo member 1945-1958, Vice-Minister of Defence November 1944, Minister of Defence March 1947 to 1949 and 1953 to 1955, Chairman of the Council of Ministers 1955, resigned 1958.

Dekanozov, V.G., Member of Azerbaijan Cheka 1921, head of Foreign Department of State Security in 1939, vice-Minister of Foreign Affairs in May 1939, Ambassador to Berlin December 1940 to June 1941, member of Central Committee in February 1941, ambassador to Bulgaria 1943-1945, Vice-President of the Radio Committee, Minister of Internal Affairs in Georgia April-June 1953, arrested 30 June 1953, shot in December 1953.

Ehrenburg, I: Soviet writer, Vice-President of World Peace Council 1950.

Fadeyev, A., Soviet writer, chairman of Stalin Prize Committee, President of Writers' Union, suicide 1956.

Galler, L.M., Vice-Minister of the Navy 1940, arrested 1948, died in prison 1950.

Goglidze, S.A., head of NKVD in Transcaucasia November 1934, head of Leningrad NKVD in 1939, Vice-Minister of MGB in 1951, head of Uzbekistan

MGB, head of 3rd chief Directorate and Vice-Minister of MGB February 1952, head of 3rd Directorate of MVD March-June 1953, shot December 1953.

Golikov, F.I., Deputy Chief of General Staff and head of Military Intelligence June 1940.

Ignatiev, S.D., Cheka officer 1920, Party Secretary in Bashkiria 1943-1946, 2nd Secretary of Byelorussian Communist Party 1947-1949, Minister of State Security July 1951 to 1953, dismissed April 1953, reintegrated in Central Committee after Beria's fall, Party Secretary in Bashkiria 1953-1954, and in Tataria 1957-1966.

Kaftanov, S.V., Minister of Higher Education 1937-1946.

Kaganovich, L.M., Politburo member 1930, First Secretary in Ukraine 1925-28, First Secretary of Moscow Party 1930-1935, Commissar of Heavy Industry in 1937, Commissar of Oil Industry in 1939, First Secretary in Ukraine 1947, the Party's Number Two in the first half of the 1930s, Commissar of Transport 1935-1937, 1938-1942, 1943-1944, member of the Presidium of Central Committee in 1952, Vice-Chairman of USSR Council of Ministers, expelled from Central Committee 1957.

Kaganovich, M.M., Lazar Kaganovich's brother, Minister of Armaments 1937-1939, Minister of Aeronautical Construction 1939-1940, suicide February 1941.

Kapitsa, P.L., Director of Physics Institute 1935-1946 and from 1955, author of works on elementary particles, magnetic phenomena and hydrodynamics.

Kapler, A., Soviet script-writer and film-director, wrote script for films *Lenin in October* and *Lenin in 1918*. Arrested 1944, released March 1953.

Karakhan, L.M., Member of Petrograd Soviet, Vice-Commissar of Foreign Affairs 1927-1934, Ambassador to Poland 1921, to China 1923-1926, to Turkey 1934. Executed 1937.

Kavtaradze, S., Deputy Procurator of USSR Supreme Count 1924-1927, expelled from Party and imprisoned for Trotskyism, freed 1941, director of Middle-East department and Vice-Commissar of Foreign Affairs 1943-1945, Ambassador to Iran, then to Romania 1945-1954.

Keldysh, M.V., well-known Soviet mathematician.

Khariton, Y.B., Soviet Physicist, specialist in applied nuclear physics, member of USSR Academy of Sciences 1953.

Khrushchev, N.S., First Secretary, Moscow Communist Party 1935-1938, First Secretary Ukraine Communist Party 1938-1946, December 1947 to December 1949, First Secretary, Moscow Communist Party December 1949 to 1953, Politburo member March 1939, First Secretary of CPSU 1953, dismissed 1964.

Kikoin, I.K., Soviet Physicist, researcher from 1943 at Institute of Atomic Energy.

Kirichenko, A.I., First Secretary, Ukrainian Communist Party, June 1953, candidate member of Presidium of Central Committee.

Kirov, S.M., head of Eleventh Army, fighting Whites in Caucasia, member of Central Committee of Azerbaijan Communist Party, member of Central Committee 1923, First Secretary of Leningrad Communist Party 1926, Politburo member 1930, assassinated December 1934.

Kobulov, A.Z., Head of NKVD in Ukraine 1939, resident in Berlin 1940, 1951-1953 deputy director of Gulag, head of Directorate of Prisoners of War, April-June 1953 deputy of Control Inspectorate MVD.

Kobulov, B.Z., Cheka officer in Georgia, removed from MVD under Stalin, Candidate member of Central Committee March 1939, Vice-Minister of Internal Affairs, March 1953, arrested June 1953, shot December 1953.

Konev, I.S., Marshal 1944, commander in Austria 1945-1946, commander of Warsaw Pact forces 1955-1960.

Kulik, G.I., Vice-Minister of Defence 1939, Marshal 1940, blamed for Kerch disaster November 1941, removed from Central Committee 1944, dismissed in 1946, arrested in 1947, executed in 1950.

Kurchatov, I.V., Physicist, founder 1943 of Institute of Atomic Energy, member of special commission for making atomic bomb August 1945, creator of first atomic reactor 1946.

Kuznetsov, A.A., Member of Central Committee 1939, First Secretary of Leningrad Communist Party 1945-1946, Secretary of Central Committee responsible for supervising security organs 1946, head of cadres department of Central Committee, Politburo member September 1947, shot 30 September 1950.

Kuznetsov, N.G.G., Admiral 1941, Minister of Navy April 1939, dismissed 1946, again Minister of Navy July 1951-March 1953, then Vice-Minister of Defence until 1956.

Kruglov, S.N., NKVD officer 1939, Vice-Commissar of NKVD 1943, Minister of Internal Affairs January 1946-March 1953, 1953-March 1956.

Litvinov, M.M., Commissar of Foreign Affairs 1935-1939, ambassador to USA December 1941-April 1943, Vice-Minister of Foreign Affairs until July 1946.

Lozovsky, S.A., Head of Profintern 1920-1937, member of Comintern E.C. 1927-1935, Vice Commissar of Foreign Affairs 1939-1946, member of leading committee of Jewish Antifascist Committee in 1942, director of Sovinformburo 1945-June 1947, arrested January 1949, shot August 1952.

Lyudvigov, B., head of Beria's secretariat.

Maisky, I.M., Diplomat, ambassador to London 1932-1943, Vice-Minister of Foreign Affairs 1939-1946, arrested February 1953, tried in 1957, amnestied in 1970.

Makhnev, V.A., Vice-Minister of Munitions 1941-1945, member of the special commission for making the atomic bomb, August 1945.

Malenkov, G.M., head of section of leading Party organisations in 1934, member of Central Committee responsible for cadres policy March 1939, deputy member of Politburo February 1941, Politburo member March 1946, secretary of Central Committee 1939-1946, 1948-1953, deputy chairman of Council of Ministers August 1946, Chairman of Council of ministers March 1953 to 1955, deputy chairman of Council of Ministers 1955-1957, dismissed and exiled 1957.

Malyshev, V.A., Member of Central Committee, Minister of Medium Mechanical Construction.

Mamulov, S., Head of cadres department, Georgian Communist Party, head of Beria's secretariat.

Maslennikov, I.P., General 1944, commander of frontier guards 1941, Vice-Minister of Internal Affairs 1939-1941, 1948-1953, suicide 1953.

Mekhlis, L.Z., Member of Orgburo 1938-1952, editor-in-chief of *Pravda*, head of Political Administration of Red Army January 1938, Minister of State Control and deputy chairman of Sovnarkom, September 1940, Vice-Minister of Defence 1941-1942, succeeded Merkulov at head of Reparations Administration October 1950.

Merkulov, V.N., Cheka officer in Georgia, member of Central Committee of Georgian Communist Party 1937, Beria's deputy as head of NKVD and of State Security February 1941-July 1941, April 1943-May 1946, member of Central Committee in March 1939 head of Reparations Administration 1946-1950, shot in December 1953.

Meshik, P.A., Head of NKVD's economic administration March 1941, deputy to Abakumov as head of Smersh April 1943 to August 1945, deputy chairman of first chief directorate of Council of Ministers, Minister of Internal Affairs in Ukraine April 1953, arrested June 1953, shot December 1953.

Mgeladze, A.I., First Secretary of Abkhazia regional Party committee 1953-1952, First secretary of Georgian Communist Party April 1952-April 1953. Removed from Central Committee in May 1953.

Mikhoels, S.M., Actor, Director of Moscow Yiddish Theatre, Chairman of Jewish Antifascist Committee formed in 1942, assassinated 13 January 1948 by order of Stalin.

Mikoyan, A.I., Central Committee member 1923, Politburo 1935-1966. Commissar of Foreign Trade 1938 – March 1949, Commissar of Agroalimentary Industry1934, member of Presidium of Central Committee, Deputy Chairman of Council of Ministers 1937-1955.

Milshtein, S., Head of section of Central Committee of Georgian Communist Party, deputy director of GRU 1940, Vice-Minister of Ukrainian MVD April 1953.

Mirtskhulava, A.I., Secretary of Georgian Komsomol, head of government of Abkhazia, First Secretary of Georgian Communist Party April to September 1953.

Molotov, V.M., Central Committee member 1921-1957, Politburo 1926-1957, Chairman of Sovnarkom 1930 – May 1941, Commissar of Foreign Affairs May 1939 – March 1949, Vice-Prime-Minister 1941-1957, Minister of Foreign Affairs 1953-1956, expelled from Central Committee and Politburo 1957, Ambassador to Mongolia 1957-1960.

Novikov, A.A., Marshal 1944, commander of air force, Vice-Minister of Aviation 1942-1943, accused of sabotage and arrested 1946, rehabilitated May 1953.

Ordzhonikidze, S., Secretary of Kavburo 1920, Secretary of Transcaucasian Communist Party, Politburo member 1930, chairman of Party's Central Control Commission 1926-1930, commissar of heavy industry 1932, suicide 1937.

Pervukhin, M.G., Member of Presidium of Central Committee 1952-1957, Deputy Chairman of Council of Ministers 1940-1946, head of Extraordinary Commission for the atomic programme 1942, Commissar of Chemical Industry 1942-1950, member of Special Commission for making the atomic bomb August 1945, Minister of Electrical Power Industry 1939-1940, 1940-1944 and from March 1953 to April 1954, Deputy Chairman of the Council of Ministers December 1953 to 1957, 1958-1962, Ambassador to the GDR, 1962-1969, head of Gosplan.

Popov, G.M., First Secretary, Moscow Communist Party, 1946-1949.

Poskrebyshev, A.N., Head of Secret Department of Central Committee 1930-1952, Stalin's secretary.

Pospelov, P.N., Editor-in-chief of *Pravda* 1940, dismissed in June 1949, then director of the Institute of Marxism-Leninism. He was to be one of the authors of Khrushchev's 'secret' report to the 20th Congress.

Rapava, A.N., Minister of Security in Georgia 1938-1948, Minister of Justice 1948, dismissed 1951, arrested 1953, shot September 1955.

Rokossovsky, K., Marshal, arrested 1937, released March 1940, Poland's Minister of Defence October 1949, Vice-Minister of Defence, USSR, 1956-1962.

Rudenko, R.A., Principal USSR representative on Nuremberg Tribunal 1945-1946, USSR Procurator July 1953, member of Central Committee 1961.

Rukhadze, M.M., Head of Smersh in Caucasia, Security Minister in Georgia 1947-1952, arrested July 1952, shot September 1955.

Ryumin, M.D., Abakumov's deputy in the Special Section of State Security 1941, head of investigations department of MGB July – November 1952, arrested April 1953, condemned to death July 1954.

Saburov, M.Z., Head of Gosplan 1941-1942, Deputy chairman of Sovnarkom 1941-1942, Deputy Chairman of Sovnarkom 1941-1944, member of Presidium of Central Committee 1952-1957, Minister of Mechanical Construction March-June 1953, head of Gosplan June 1953-May 1955, Deputy Chairman of Council of Ministers 1941-1944, 1947-1953, December 1953 to 1955.

Serov, I., Head of NKVD in Ukraine September 1939, in 1941-1954 First Vice-Minister of State Security, deputy to Zhukov in military government in Berlin, May 1945, vice-minister of Internal Affairs March 1947, chairman of KGB 1954-1958, head of GRU in 1958.

Shakurin, A.I., Minister of Aeronautics, dismissed December 1945, accused of sabotage 1946, rehabilitated May 1953, vice-minister of Aviation 1953-1959.

Sharia, P.A., Member of Central Committee of Georgian Communist Party, in charge of ideological questions until 1948, arrested 1952 and 1953.

Shcherbakov, A.S., Secretary of Moscow Party Committee from 1938 till his death in 1945, candidate member of Politburo 1941, member of Orgburo 1939, in charge of propaganda January 1940, head of Agitprop May 1941, head of Soviformburo 1941, head of Army's Political Directorate June 1942.

Shtemenko, S.M., Head of Operational Directorate of General Staff May 1943, Chief of General Staff 1948, dismissed June 1952.

Shvernik, N.M., Candidate member of Politburo 1939-1952, member of Orgburo 1930-1946, from 1946 to 1953 chairman of Presidium of Supreme Soviet, from 1930 to 1944 in charge of trade unions, chairman of Party Control Commission 1956-1966.

Sudoplatov, P.A., Head of NKVD Special Missions in 1941, head of 4th Directorate of NKVD/NKGB 1942-1946, deputy head of Directorate of Foreign Intelligence, from 1951 to 1953 director of No. 1 Desk, MGB, from March to May 1953 deputy director of First Chief Directorate of MVD, from May to August 1953 director of section of MVD, arrested in August 1953, condemned to 15 years imprisonment in 1958.

Suslov, M.A., First Secretary of Stavropol region in 1939, chairman of Central Committee's bureau for Lithuania, 1944, head of department of foreign policy March 1946, head of Agitprop September 1947, Secretary of Central Committee 1947-1982, editor-in-chief of *Pravda* 1949-1950, member of Presidium October

1952, Politburo member from 1955 to his death in 1982.

Timoshenko, S.K., Marshal (1940), commander of Kiev Military Region, Commissar of Defence May 1940-July 1941.

Tolbukhin, F.I., Marshal (1944), head of Allied Control Commission in Bulgaria September 1944.

Tukhachevsky, M.N., Red Army officer, Chief of General Staff 1925, Vice-Commissar of War 1931, Marshal 1935, shot June 1937.

Tupolev, A.N., Aircraft designer, arrested 1937, freed 1941, member of Academy of Sciences 1953, rehabilitated 1955.

Tyulenev, I.V., General, commander of Caucasian Front, May 1942 to July 1945.

Ustinov, D.F., Minister of Armaments June 1941 to 1953, Marshal, Minister of Defence 1976-1984.

Vannikov, B.L., Member of Central Committee, Minister of Military Industry 1937, Minister of Armaments 1939, arrested June 1941, Vice-Minister of Armaments July 1946, Minister of Munitions in February 1942, head of First Chief Directorate of Council of Ministers 1945-1953.

Varga, E.S., Hungarian economist, author of *Changes in Capitalist Economy at the End of the Second World War* (1946), Director of the Institute of World Politics and Economics 1927-1947.

Vasilevsky, A.M., Marshal (1943), chief of general staff 1942-1945, commander-in-chief Far East forces June 1945, Minister of Armed Forces 1949-1953, First Vice-Minister of Defence 1953-1957.

Vavilov, N.I., Geneticist, arrested August 1940, died January 1943.

Vlasik, N.S., Chief of Stalin's bodyguard 1931, exiled May 1952, arrested December 1952, sentenced 1955 to five years' exile.

Vlasov, A.A., General, captured by Germans 1942, head of Nazi-controlled Committee for Liberation of the Peoples of Russia, hanged 1946.

Voroshilov, K.E., Red Army officer, Marshal 1935, member of Central Committee 1921-1961, then 1966 to his death in 1969, Politburo member 1926-1960, Commissar of War 1934 to May 1940, Vice-Commissar of Defence 1941-1944, Deputy Chairman of Council of Ministers 1940-1953, Chairman of Presidium of Supreme Soviet March 1953 to 1960.

Voznesensky, N.A., Member of Central Committee 1939-1949, Politburo member 1947, head of Gosplan 1942-1949, shot September 1950.

Vyshinsky, A.Zh., Procurator-General USSR 1935-1939, member of Central Committee, March 1939, deputy chairman of Sovnarkom June 1939, Vice-Minister of Foreign Affairs September 1940, Minister of Foreign Affairs March 1949 to 1953.

Wasilewska, W., Polish writer from Western Ukraine, colonel in Red Army, President of Union of Polish Patriots, played active role in sovietisation of intelligentsia of W. Ukraine, Vice-Prime Minister of Ukraine.

Yakovlev, A.S., Aeronautical engineer, Vice-Minister of Aviation 1940-1946.

Yakovlev, N.D., Marshal of Artillery, arrested February 1952, for 'sabotage', released 1953.

Yezhov, N.I., secretary of Central Committee and member of Orgburo 1934, Chairman of Party Control Commission, head of Economic Department and Department of Administrative Organs 1935, head of NKVD September 1936 – November 1938, executed 1940.

Zavenyagin, A.P., NKVD colonel, director of Magnitogorsk metallurgical combine, deputy to Ordzhonikidze in commissariat of heavy industry, member of special commission for making atomic bomb, August 1945, Vice-Minister of NKVD 1941 to August 1951, candidate member of Central Committee, Deputy Chairman of First Chief Directorate of Council of Ministers.

Zhdanov, A.A., Party secretary in Gorky, member of Central Committee 1930, member of Orgburo 1934-1938, secretary of Central Committee 1934, Politburo member March 1939, head of Agitprop August 1939 – September 1940 and May 1945, first secretary of Leningrad Communist Party 1934-1944, died August 1948.

Zhemchuzhina, P., Married Molotov 1921, head of administration of cosmetic industry, Vice-Minister, then Minister of Agroalimentary Industry November 1937, Minister of Fishing Industry January 1939, of Textile Industry November 1939, dismissed June 1948, candidate member of Central Committee March 1939 to February 1941, arrested January 1945, freed March 1953.

Zhukov, G.K., Commander of Kiev Military Region 1940-1946, Vice-Chairman of defence and Chef of General Staff, February – July 1941 and 1942-1945, Marshal, head of military government of Berlin May 1945 – March 1946, head of Odessa Military District, then of Ural Military Region, 1946-1953, first Vice-Minister of Defence, March 1953, member of Central Committee June 1953, Minister of Defence 1955 to October 1957.

Index of Names

Index of Places